ORGANIZATIONS

Behavior — **Structure** — **Processes**

ORGANIZATIONS

Behavior ▬ **Structure** ▬ **Processes**

▬

JAMES L. GIBSON

Kincaid Professor
College of Business and Economics
University of Kentucky

JOHN M. IVANCEVICH

Hugh Roy and Lillie Cranz Cullen Chair and
Professor of Organizational Behavior and Management
University of Houston

JAMES H. DONNELLY, JR.

Turner Professor
College of Business and Economics
University of Kentucky

▬

Seventh Edition

IRWIN

Homewood, IL 60430   Boston, MA 02116

Associate publisher: Martin F. Hanifin
Developmental editor: Kama Brockmann
Project editor: Jean Roberts
Production manager: Bette K. Ittersagen
Designer: Maureen McCutcheon
Artist: Rolin Graphics
Part and chapter photographer: Lindfors Photography
Compositor: Carlisle Communications, Ltd.
Typeface: 10/12 Bembo
Printer: Von Hoffmann Press, Inc.

Library of Congress Cataloging-in-Publication Data

Gibson, James L.
    Organizations: behavior, structure, processes / James L. Gibson,
John M. Ivancevich, James H. Donnelly, Jr. — 7th ed.
      p.   cm.
    Includes bibliographical references and index.
    ISBN 0-256-08046-1
    ISBN 0-256-09878-6 (International Student Edition)
    1. Organization.   2. Organizational behavior.   3. Leadership.
   4. Organizational effectiveness.   I. Ivancevich, John M.
II. Donnelly, James H.   III. Title.
    HD58.7.G54   1991
    658.4 — dc20   90 − 36445
                                     CIP

Printed in the United States of America

1 2 3 4 5 6 7 8 9 0 VH 7 6 5 4 3 2 1 0

OBJECTIVES OF THIS EDITION

The changes sweeping the world in Europe, the Pacific Rim, Latin America, and North America have been astounding: the Berlin Wall has crumbled, dictators have been removed from office, calls for the restructuring of entire economic and management systems are heard daily, and citizens have been given opportunities to vote for their leaders. Properly managing these rapid changes, shifting economies, and the production enterprises in society is now the major challenge facing the world. Politicians can make declarations about freedom, autonomy, and restructuring, but it is managers who must implement the changes.

The objective of the seventh edition of *Organizations: Behavior, Structure, Processes* is to present a realistic, relevant, and complete view of people working in organizations around the world. Instead of focusing on the United States, we have expanded our approach to include worldwide issues, problems, and considerations. The U.S. manager must work, negotiate, conduct business, and compete for customers with managers from around the world.

The text provides theories, research results, and applications that apply to people in worldwide organizations. Realism, relevance, and thoroughness have been our targets in developing the chapters, cases, and exercises for this and previous editions. Over the history of *Organizations: Behavior, Structure, Processes,* student and instructor feedback has indicated that our objective has been achieved.

A theme introduced early and carried throughout the book is that effective management of organizational behavior requires an understanding of theory, research, and practice. Given this theme, our task is to present and interpret organizational behavior theory and research so that students can comprehend the three characteristics common to all organizations—behavior, structure, processes—as affected by actions of managers. Accordingly, we illustrate how organizational behavior theory leads to research and how both theory and research provide the basic foundation for practical applications in business firms, hospitals, educational institutions, and governmental agencies.

We have attempted to move our readers from the role of bystanders or rote readers to the role of active participants. When students become more involved in weighing and evaluating the decisions a manager must make, the dynamics and vitality of managing people become more real, relevant, and complete.

NEW MATERIAL IN THIS EDITION

The seventh edition includes important new subject matter as well as additional learning approaches. Explained at the end of this preface is one of those learning approaches: our new "integrated color coding" system for the figures that appear in this text. This system will help readers better understand the figures throughout the book. The new subject matter is elaborated below.

First, we have integrated international material into the entire book. At one time, the international aspects of managing organizational behavior mattered only to a few American enterprises. International management was in the domain of large, multinational firms, not the average manufacturer or service firm. Today, discussing any concept of managing organizational behavior for any size firm requires an appreciation of the international scene. What happens in a Toyota plant in Osaka, Japan, influences what happens in a Ford plant in Chicago.

Second, we have made a conscious effort to use examples of managing organizational behavior in firms of all sizes. This is not a book on managing Fortune 500 organizational behavior. The millions of new jobs being created in the United States occur in medium and small firms. Thus, the examples we use of medium and small firms highlight their importance.

Third, we have expanded our coverage of leadership. Leadership is such a major factor in the world that we decided to establish two leadership chapters rather than the single one included in the previous edition. Chapter 11 focuses on trait and behavioral leadership issues, while Chapter 12 addresses situational, charismatic, and transformational leadership theory, research, and practice. Throughout the leadership discussion we maintain a balance of theory, research, and application.

Fourth, reviewers of the text encouraged us to combine the reward and evaluation material, topics covered in separate chapters in previous editions. Concluding that the reviewers were correct, we have created a combined reward and evaluation chapter (Chapter 6).

Fifth, as our first rule for any revision, the material in existing chapters was updated. Material on expectancy theory, negotiating, conflict resolution, creativity and innovation, mentoring, company turnarounds, punishment, social support, Type A, not-for-profit organizations, flexible manufacturing, groupthink, social support networks, transformational and charismatic leadership, quality of work life, career counseling, and other topics was added or expanded in appropriate chapters. In all cases, the new material complements existing material. A listing of additional references at the end of each chapter provides current sources for readers who desire more in-depth discussions of these and other topics.

Sixth, positive reactions to the experiential exercises in the last four editions have encouraged us to change and modify some of the exercises in this edition. We have also retained the most requested and popular end-of-chapter cases included in the previous edition and have added several new ones. Each case has been written to emphasize a particular issue or managerial technique. The cases cover a variety of different types and sizes of organizations and include problems of all levels of management.

Seventh, the "Organizations: Close-Ups" have been enthusiastically received by students and instructors. The Close-Ups report actual applications of the concepts and theories presented in the chapter. They appear at the point where the concept or theory is discussed in the text. Most of the chapters in this edition contain at least three Close-Ups. Presenting actual managerial applications of text materials narrows the gap between classroom and real world.

Eighth, discussions of social responsibility and ethical issues from industry to industry, company to company, and country to country appear throughout the text. Americans do not have the only viewpoint about social responsibility, and managers must resolve specific ethical questions. Students are introduced to some of the more pressing issues.

Ninth, hard work, planning, and consideration for teaching the course went into preparing the supplements for the text. We believe they are among the best ever prepared. Special care was devoted to developing supplements of the highest quality. Both students and instructors were considered, which adds to the students' understanding and the instructor's ability to teach an exciting course. The Instructor's Manual, Lecture Resource Manual, color transparencies, Test Bank, and Computerized Test Service are excellent for both in-class and out-of-class assignments.

In addition to the practical relevance of the experiential exercises, cases, Close-Ups, and self-report questionnaires, the text discussion itself carries out our intention to interpret the practical significance of theory and research. Of course, many issues in organizational behavior are unresolved, and alternative theories compete. In these instances, issues are presented, and readers are encouraged to consider the relative strengths of each theory. Where appropriate, we acknowledge the tenuousness of both contemporary theory and practice.

To focus reader interest and to highlight the contingent nature of much of the subject matter, each chapter again begins by introducing an appropriate "Organizational Issue for Debate." The debates are short presentations of arguments both for and against a popular principle, theory, or application. Some issues are new; others have been retained and expanded from the previous edition.

FRAMEWORK OF THIS EDITION: SEVEN MAJOR PARTS

The content of the book is organized in a sequence based on the three previously cited characteristics common to all organizations: behavior, structure, and processes. This order has been followed in response to the requests of numerous adopters, who found it easier to discuss the material on human behavior first, followed by the material on structure and processes. In this edition, each major part has been written as a self-contained unit and can be presented in whatever sequence the instructor prefers.

Part One—Introduction—consists of two introductory chapters. Chapter 1 discusses the significance of organizations as a means by which societies produce and distribute goods and services and introduces readers to the format and rationale for the book. Chapter 2 develops important ideas concerning the roles of management in achieving effective individual, group, and organizational performance.

Part Two—Behavior within Organizations: The Individual—includes five chapters that focus on *individual behavior* in organizations. Separate chapters are devoted to individual characteristics and differences (Chapter 3); content and process motivation theories and applications(Chapters 4 and 5); evaluating, rewarding, and punishing behavior (Chapter 6); and individual stress (Chapter 7).

Part Three—Behavior within Organizations: Groups and Interpersonal Influence—focuses on *group behavior and interpersonal influence* in organizations. Its five chapters focus on group behavior (Chapter 8), intergroup behavior and conflict management (Chapter 9), power and politics (Chapter 10), and leadership (Chapters 11 and 12).

Part Four—The Structure and Design of Organizations—includes three chapters. Separate chapters are devoted to the anatomy of organizations (Chapter 12), job design (Chapter 13), and organizational design (Chapter 14). The latter two follow a micro (job design)–macro (organizational design) sequence.

Part Five—The Processes of Organizations—includes three chapters. Chapters 16 and 17 deal with communication and decision making. Chapter 18 addresses socialization and career processes.

Part Six—Developing Organizational Effectiveness—is a two-chapter sequence that presents the theory of organizational development in the context of an integrated model (Chapter 19) and then describes and evaluates the more widely used OD techniques (Chapter 20).

The book concludes with two appendixes. Appendix A covers procedures and techniques for studying *Organizations: Behavior, Structure, Processes*. Referring directly to Appendix A, readers can examine research procedures and quantitative and qualitative techniques used in studying organizational behavior. Appendix B contains three comprehensive cases that are intended to encourage users to integrate materials, concepts, and models found in the text.

CONTRIBUTORS TO THIS EDITION

Authors do not just happen to end up one day with seventh edition books. Arriving at this juncture takes teamwork, the work of the publisher, a dedicated sales force, satisfied students, adopters, and outstanding reviewers. Many friends, colleagues, and scholars also have made this a successful book. We always attempt to recognize each person who has helped us; if we have omitted someone, please accept our apologies. In addition, thousands of students whom we personally have taught have helped us improve, update, and revise our work.

The authors wish to acknowledge the contributions of reviewers of all editions. Their suggestions are reflected in this text. The numerous comments, recommendations, and detailed suggestions of colleagues over the history of the book have been incorporated throughout these chapters.

Reviewers of the Present Edition

Patrick R. Vann
University of Colorado

Leon L. Smith
University of North Alabama

Loren Falkenberg
University of Calgary

Richard A. Feinberg
Purdue University

Allen J. Schuh
California State University—Hayward

Ariel S. Levi
Wayne State University

Charles W. Luckenbill
Indiana University

David A. Tansik
University of Arizona

Steven L. McShane
Simon Fraser University

Erik Larson
Oregon State University

Reviewers of Previous Editions

John L. Berton
Louisiana State University at Shreveport

Gerald Biberman
University of Scranton

Richard S. Blackburn
University of North Carolina, Chapel Hill

Carmen Caruana
St. John's University

Dick Daft
Vanderbilt University

Sara M. Freedman
University of Houston

Cynthia V. Fukami
University of Denver

Arthur G. Jago
University of Houston

Richard E. Kopelman
Baruch College—The City University of New York

Mitchell McCorcle
Case Western Reserve University

Marilyn A. Morgan
University of Virginia

Larry K. Michaelson
University of Oklahoma

Samuel Rabinowitz
New York University

Arnon E. Reichers
The Ohio State University

Robert Zawacki
University of Colorado at Colorado Springs

A special thank you is due Margaret Fenn of the University of Washington, who permitted us to use her case. We also wish to thank Victor Vroom of Yale University and Arthur Jago for permitting us to use their creative ideas and cases to develop a part of our leadership presentation.

Finally, Richard Furst, dean of the College of Business and Economics, University of Kentucky, provided much support for our efforts. Ginger Roberts and Jacque Franco were invaluable in making numerous changes, preparing many drafts, and making sure that everything was done right. Of course, they are not responsible for any errors which the authors failed to remove. This revision was truly a team effort of many dedicated, intelligent, and motivated people.

James L. Gibson
John M. Ivancevich
James H. Donnelly, Jr.

Each edition of *Organizations* has contained many figures, diagrams, and models. They were used to highlight, illustrate, summarize, and integrate. Over the years of teaching organizational behavior and management, we have heard a common lament from students: "What do these boxes and arrows in the figures and exhibits mean?" The student views a figure, which authors use to tie things together or to summarize, and is puzzled by the diagram.

In this edition, we employ a color coding technique that we hope will lessen students' confusion. In any diagram, figure, or model that involves presumed independent, dependent, moderator, or feedback variables/factors, a color code will be used. For example, Figure 2–5 is presented on page 40 and it appears below.

The color rust designates independent variables, presumed to be those that are influencing other variables or are manipulated or controlled in an experiment, and the color plum designates a dependent variable, presumed to be the consequent of the independent variable(s). Dark green specifies moderator variables or presumed factors that influence the degree and kind of relationship between other variables. Dark gray specifies what is considered to be a feedback linkage in the illustration.

Emphasis here is on the word *presumed*. In most cases, the literature, research, and evidence only suggest that these are independent, dependent, moderator, and/or feedback variables. We do not claim that these are always scientifically derived, perfectly valid designations. The color code, when it is used, is only a guideline to help the learning process. We are attempting to bring some order and continuity to the numerous figures used in the text.

When a figure, illustration, or model does not contain the colors rust, plum, dark green, or dark gray, the evidence does not suggest that these are independent, dependent, moderator, or feedback variables. The authors or other individuals have simply illustrated the variables presented.

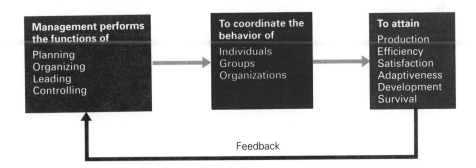

BRIEF CONTENTS

DETAILED CONTENTS

ORGANIZATIONS

Behavior — **Structure** — **Processes**

INTRODUCTION

1

The Study of Organizations

LEARNING OBJECTIVES

After completing Chapter 1, you should be able to:

DEFINE
what is meant by the term *organizational behavior.*

DESCRIBE
the role of organizations in our society.

DISCUSS
why the manager is considered an essential force in improving productivity.

COMPARE
the scientific and nonscientific ways of learning about management.

IDENTIFY
the reasons why managing workplace behavior in the United States is likely to be different from managing workplace behavior in another country, such as Germany.

As we prepare this edition of *Organizations: Behavior, Structure, Processes,* the world is in a state of change. The new thinking in East Germany, Czechoslovakia, Hungary, Poland, the Soviet Union, Latin America, Mexico, the Middle East, and Africa has raised many questions about the adequacy of management practices. Will traditional frameworks, models, and applications fit the changes in economies, government thinking, and powerful individual desires and drives to achieve freedom and technological advancements?[1]

We enter the 1990s faced with tremendous opportunities. The United States finds itself in a world of increasingly shared power and leadership. Managers from West Germany, Canada, Japan, the Netherlands, France, Italy, and Great Britain, along with American managers, are in extremely important positions.[2] In each country, the long-run pursuit of well-being is largely dependent on the work force's ability to achieve higher productivity growth. Citizens in Africa, Peru, Mexico, the United States, and the Soviet Union want more goods, services, and leisure time. Higher productivity permits a nation to make more choices, to satisfy human needs, and to accomplish more in terms of medical care, education, and agricultural gains.

There is no mystery to improving productivity. A large factor in productivity increases is the proper management of human resources. Americans are no smarter than Germans, nor are they better workers than Brazilians. The fact that the United States became such a productive nation in the 1950s and 60s is largely the result of sound management practices and techniques. Americans planned efficiently, organized systematically, and led workers effectively. Also, Americans came up with new techniques, new methods, and new styles of management that fit the time, the work force, and the mission. In the United States in the 1950s and 60s, productivity improvement was a state of mind.

As we enter the 1990s, managers are going to have to recapture the feel, the state of mind, the passion, and the desire to be effective, to produce high-quality products, and to provide the best service possible. The importance of managing human resources has not been questioned. However, attention to the details of managing people has slipped badly in the past two decades. Managing people effectively in organizations is the most essential ingredient for retaining a comfortable standard of living, remaining one of the world's economic leaders, and improving the quality of life for all citizens.[3] The quality of life is connected to the quality of work. As the Close-Up about quality and management points out, quality of work is a new state of mind that managers must instill throughout organizations.

Whether we are talking about a pizza parlor in East Orange, New Jersey, a steelcase manufacturing plant in Monterrey, Mexico, or a cooperative produce shop in Vilnius, Lithuania, management within an organizational setting is important. The clerk in the produce shop in Lithuania wants to earn a fair day's

---

[1]Christopher A. Bartlett and Sumantra Ghoshal, *Managing across Borders* (Boston: Harvard Business School Press, 1989).

[2]Louis S. Richman, "How American Can Triumph," *Fortune,* December 18, 1989, pp. 52–66.

[3]Joseph A. Maciarello, Jeffrey W. Burke, and Donald Tilley, "Improving American Competitiveness: A Management Systems Perspective," *Academy of Management Executive,* November 1989, pp. 294–303.

QUALITY AND MANAGEMENT AN INSEPARABLE PAIR

Professional baseball has the Cy Young Award for the best pitcher. In Hollywood, the Academy Awards ceremony is held to issue Oscars for outstanding performance. In American business, there is the Malcolm Baldridge National Quality Award. A gold-plated corncob embedded in an obelisk of crystal and named after the late secretary of commerce is a cherished award. Achievements in quality are becoming the backbone of international competitiveness. A firm survives only through having high-quality products and/or service.

Each year, the Baldridge competition becomes more fierce. In 1989, 40 companies filed applications, paid fees, and spent hundreds of employee hours answering quality-related questions. Firms want to win because a Baldridge award has tremendous promotional value. In the past, Xerox, Milliken & Co., and Motorola have captured the award and have used it to proclaim their dedication to quality.

Quality is likely to remain a top priority of firms engaged in international competition. Achieving top quality means that an organization's work force is going to have to work long and hard hours. Employees are also going to have to pay attention to customer needs, expectations, and preferences. A manager, no matter how good he or she is at performing management tasks, is viewed as a failure if a firm's products or services are of poor quality. The manager and the product or service are considered inseparable; and they really are, if we sit back and think about quality and what it means.

Source: Amanda Bennett and Jolie Solomon, "Is Quality Award Becoming Job 1 for U.S. Companies?" *The Wall Street Journal*, November 3, 1989, pp. B1, B9.

pay for his work, the company president in Mexico has to purchase the best equipment to compete internationally, and the pizza owner has to have personnel to work. The work behaviors of these individuals occur within organizations. In order to better understand these behaviors, we believe that one must formally study **organizations,** people, processes, and structure. This is what this book is about—organizations, large and small, domestic and international, successful and unsuccessful. We believe that we can learn by studying, dissecting, analyzing, and observing organizations.

ORGANIZATIONS
Entities that enable society to pursue accomplishments that cannot be achieved by individuals acting alone.

THE IMPORTANCE OF STUDYING ORGANIZATIONAL BEHAVIOR

Why does Ric Nunzio always seem to hire older employees for his pizza parlor? Why is Javier Diaz–Maybiez the best decision maker in deciding what piece of equipment to purchase? Why does Val Kupolus always complain that he is not paid enough to sell produce at the Vilnius produce stand? These are the types of questions that are studied, analyzed, and debated in the field called **organizational behavior.** The formal study of organizational behavior began to develop around 1948 to 1952. This still emerging field attempts to help

ORGANIZATIONAL BEHAVIOR
Study of individuals and groups within organizational settings.

managers understand people better so that productivity improvements can be achieved through better management practices.

The behavioral sciences—especially psychology, sociology, and cultural anthropology—have provided the basic framework and principles for the field of organizational behavior. Each behavioral science discipline provides a slightly different focus, analytical framework, and theme for helping managers answer questions about themselves, nonmanagers, and environmental forces (e.g., competition, legal requirements, and social-political changes).

Since organizational behavior (OB) has evolved from multiple disciplines, we will use the following definition of OB throughout this book:

> The study of human behavior, attitudes, and performance within an organizational setting; drawing on theory, methods, and principles from such disciplines as psychology, sociology, and cultural anthropology to learn about *individual* perceptions, values, learning capacities, and actions while working in *groups* and within the total *organization;* analyzing the external environment's effect on the organization and its human resources, missions, objectives, and strategies.

This multidisciplinary view of organizational behavior illustrates a number of points. First, OB is a *way of thinking.* Behavior is viewed as operating at individual, group, and organizational levels. This approach suggests that when studying OB we must identify clearly the level of analysis—individual, group, and/or organizational—being used. Second, OB is *multidisciplinary:* it utilizes principles, models, theories, and methods from other disciplines. The study of OB is not a discipline or a generally accepted science with an established theoretical foundation. It is a field that only now is beginning to grow and develop in stature and impact. Third, there is a distinctly *humanistic orientation* within organizational behavior. People and their attitudes, perceptions, learning capacities, feelings, and goals are of major importance to the organization. Fourth, the field of OB is *performance oriented.* Why is performance low or high? How can performance be improved? Can training enhance on-the-job performance? These are important issues facing practicing managers. Fifth, the *external environment* is seen as having significant impact on organizational behavior. Sixth, since the field of OB relies heavily on recognized disciplines, the role of the *scientific method* is important in studying variables and relationships. As the scientific method has been applied to research on organizational behavior, a set of principles and guidelines on what constitutes good research has emerged.[4] Finally, the field has a distinctive *applications orientation;* it is concerned with providing useful answers to questions that arise in the context of managing operations.

To help you learn how to manage individuals and groups as resources of organizations, this book focuses on the behavior of *individuals and groups, organizational structure and job design, and processes.* Developing the model presented in this book required the use of several assumptions. These assumptions are explained briefly in the following paragraphs, which precede the model.[5]

---

[4]Edward E. Lawler III, Alan M. Mohrman, Jr., Susan A. Mohrman, Gerald E. Ledford, Jr., Thomas G. Cummings, and associates, *Doing Research that Is Useful for Theory and Practice* (San Francisco: Jossey-Bass, 1985).

[5]John B. Miner, "The Validity and Usefulness of Theories in an Emerging Organizational Science," *Academy of Management Review,* April 1984, pp. 296–306.

Organizational Behavior Follows Principles of Human Behavior

The effectiveness of any organization is influenced greatly by human behavior. People are a resource common to all organizations. The pizza parlor, the manufacturing plant, and the produce stand employ and interact with people.

One important principle of psychology is that each person is different. Each has unique perceptions, personalities, and life experiences; different capabilities for learning and for handling stress; and different attitudes, beliefs, and aspiration levels. To be effective, managers of organizations must view each employee or member as a unique embodiment of all these behavioral factors.

Organizations Are Social Systems

The relationships among individuals and groups in organizations create expectations for the behavior of individuals. These expectations result in certain roles that must be performed. Some people must perform leadership roles, while others must play the roles of followers. Middle managers, because they have both superiors and subordinates, must perform both roles. Organizations have systems of authority, status, and power, and people in organizations have varying needs from each system. Groups in organizations also have a powerful impact on individual behavior and on organizational performance.

Multiple Factors Shape Organizational Behavior

A person's behavior in any situation involves the interaction of his or her personal characteristics and the characteristics of the situation. Thus, identifying all of the factors is time-consuming and difficult; frequently, the task is impossible.

To help us identify the important managerial factors in organizational behavior, however, we use the **contingency** (or *situational*) **approach.** The basic idea of the contingency approach is that there is no one best way to manage: a method that is very effective in one situation may not work at all in others. The contingency approach has grown in popularity because research has shown that, given certain characteristics of a job and certain characteristics of the people doing the job, some management practices work better than others. Thus, the Mexican manufacturing plant's manager of operations who is faced with a poorly performing group does not assume that a particular approach will work. In applying the contingency approach, he or she diagnoses the characteristics of the individuals and groups involved, the organizational structure, and his or her own leadership style before deciding on a solution.

Structure and Processes Affect Organizational Behavior and the Emergent Culture

An organization's **structure** is the formal pattern of how its people and jobs are grouped. Structure often is illustrated by an organization chart. **Processes** are activities that give life to the organization chart. Communication, decision

CONTINGENCY APPROACH
Approach to management that believes there is no one best way to manage in every situation and managers must find different ways that fit different situations.

STRUCTURE
Blueprint that indicates how people and jobs are grouped together in organization. Structure is illustrated by organization chart.

PROCESSES
Activities that breathe life into organization structure. Common processes are communication, decision making, socialization, and career development.

making, and organization development are examples of processes in organizations. Sometimes, understanding process problems such as breakdowns in communication and decision making will result in a more accurate understanding of organizational behavior than will simply examining structural arrangements.

The pattern of basic assumptions used by individuals and groups to deal with the organization and its environment is called its culture. In straightforward terms, the organization's culture is the personality, the atmosphere, or the "feel" of the enterprise. A firm's culture results in shared thoughts, feelings, and talk about the organization. IBMers share norms about dress code, business practices, and promotion systems. Wal-Mart associates share emotions about working for the chain and coming to work on time with a positive attitude. It is the sharing that bonds employees together, that can create a feeling of togetherness.[6]

Cultures of organizations can be positive or negative. An enterprise culture is positive if it contributes to the improvement of productivity. A negative culture can hinder behavior, disrupt group effectiveness, and hamper the impact of a well-designed organization.

Effective managers know what to look for in terms of structure, process, and culture and how to understand what they find. Therefore, managers must develop diagnostic skills; they must be trained to identify conditions symptomatic of a problem requiring further attention. Problem indicators include declining profits, declining quantity or quality of work, increases in absenteeism or tardiness, and negative employee attitudes. Each of these problems is an issue of organizational behavior.

A MODEL FOR MANAGING ORGANIZATIONS: BEHAVIOR, STRUCTURE, PROCESSES

A model for understanding organizational behavior is presented in Figure 1–1. It shows how the many topics covered in this book can be combined into a meaningful study of organizational behavior.

The Organization's Environment

Figure 1–1 draws attention to the relationships between organizations and the society that creates and sustains them. Within a society, many factors influence an organization, and management must be responsive to them. Every organization must respond to the needs of its customers or clients, to legal and political constraints, and to economic and technological changes and developments. The model reflects environmental forces interacting within the organization. Throughout our discussion of each aspect of the model, we identify and examine the relevant environmental factors.

---

[6]Fred E. Fiedler and Joseph E. Garcia, *New Approaches in Effective Leadership: Cognitive Resources and Organizational Performance* (New York. John Wiley & Sons, 1988).

FIGURE 1—1

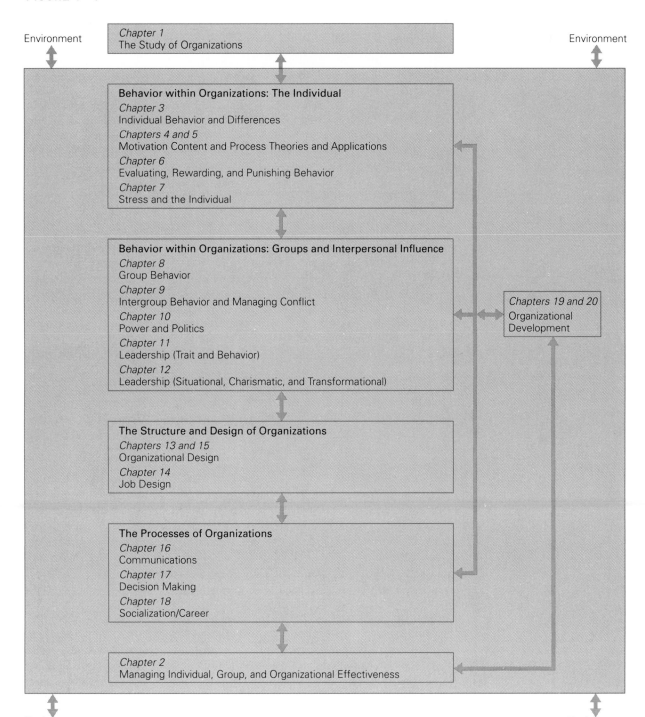

Behavior within Organizations: The Individual

Individual performance is the foundation of organizational performance. Understanding individual behavior is, therefore, critical for effective management, as illustrated in this account:

> Ted Johnson has been a field representative for a major drug manufacturer since he graduated from college seven years ago. He makes daily calls on physicians, hospitals, clinics, and pharmacies. During his time in the field, prescription rates have decreased. Despite this, Ted's sales of his firm's major drugs have increased, and he has won three national sales awards given by the firm. Yesterday, Ted was promoted to sales manager for a seven-state region. He will no longer be selling but instead will be managing 15 other representatives. Ted accepted the promotion because he believes he knows how to motivate and lead salespeople. He commented, "I know the personality of the salesperson. They are special people. I know their values and attitudes and what it takes to motivate them. I know I can motivate a sales force."

In his new job, Ted Johnson will be trying to maximize the individual performances of 15 sales representatives. In doing so, he will be dealing with several facets of individual behavior. Our model includes four important influences on individual behavior and motivation in organizations: individual characteristics, individual motivation, rewards and appraisal, and stress.

Individual characteristics.   Because organizational performance depends on individual performance, managers such as Ted Johnson must have more than a passing knowledge of the determinants of individual performance. Psychology and social psychology contribute a great deal of relevant knowledge about the relationships among attitudes, perceptions, personality, values, and individual performance. Individual capacity for learning and for coping with stress has become more and more important in recent years. Managers cannot ignore the necessity for acquiring and acting on knowledge of the individual characteristics of both their subordinates and themselves.

Individual motivation.   Motivation and ability to work interact to determine performance. Motivation theory attempts to explain and predict how the behavior of individuals is aroused, started, sustained, and stopped. Unlike Ted Johnson, not all managers and behavioral scientists agree on what is the "best" theory of motivation. In fact, the complexity of motivation may make an all-encompassing theory of how it occurs impossible. However, managers must still try to understand it. They must be concerned with motivation because they must be concerned with performance.

Rewards and appraisal.   One of the most powerful influences on individual performance is an organization's reward system. Management can use rewards (or punishment) to increase performance by present employees. It can also use rewards to attract skilled employees to the organization. Performance appraisals, paychecks, raises, and bonuses are important aspects of the reward system, but they are not the only aspects. Ted Johnson makes this point very clear in the above account when he states, "I know what it takes to get them to perform." Performance of the work itself can provide employees with rewards, particularly if job performance leads to a sense of personal responsibility, autonomy, and meaningfulness. These intrinsic rewards are also

---

SEMCO'S UNIQUE REWARD PRACTICES

ORGANIZATIONS:
CLOSE-UP

Semco is one of Brazil's fastest-growing firms. Its five factories produce marine pumps, digital scanners, commercial dishwashers, truck filters, and mixing equipment. Semco's customer list includes Alcon, Saab, Nestle, AMI, Mitsubishi, and Carrier. The company does little employment advertising, because people want to work for Semco. Word-of-mouth news about vacancies generates up to 300 applications for every position available.

An example of the Semco style of management involves the compensation system. The company did away with the Frederick Taylor–inspired hourly pay system. Everyone receives a monthly salary. So what's new? A lot of firms have done this.

Semco, however, does it in a unique way. Once or twice a year, it conducts a salary market survey. Each employee is told to figure out where he or she stands, or where he or she should be in the survey. The survey opens up communication and initiates thinking. The employees tell Semco what they will be paid.

A Semco employee who asks for too little receives it—ask and you shall receive. An employee who asks for too much receives it for at least the first year. After the year, a manager will say the employee is not worth the money. Either the pay is lowered, a new job is found for the employee, or the job is eliminated. With few exceptions (according to Semco), a compromise is worked out.

The same open procedure is used with titles: individuals can make up their own titles. Their job title means a lot to many people. If a person wants to have the title "Chief Sultan of Production Operations," so be it.

The Semco reward system is fun for the employees, and it is also attracting potential workers in large numbers. Semco believes that its philosophy and practices of organizational behavior work for the company. Whether these practices can or will work elsewhere is a question that others will have to answer.

Source: Ricardo Semler, "Managing without Managers," *Harvard Business Review,* September–October 1989, pp. 76–84.

---

supplemented with extrinsic rewards, or what an organization, a manager, or a group can provide a person in terms of monetary and nonmonetary factors.

Organizations use some unique types of reward systems. One of the more unique ones is described in the Semco Close-Up, which illustrates how a firm in Brazil uses compensation rewards.

Stress. Stress is an important result of the interaction between the job and the individual. In this context, as a state of imbalance within an individual, stress often manifests itself in such symptoms as insomnia, excessive perspiration, nervousness, and irritability. Whether stress is positive or negative depends on the individual's tolerance level. People react differently to situations that outwardly seem to induce the same physical and psychological demands. Some individuals respond positively through increased motivation and commitment to finish the job. Other individuals respond less desirably by turning to such outlets as alcoholism and drug abuse. Hopefully, Ted Johnson will respond positively to the stresses of his new job.

Behavior within Organizations: Groups and Interpersonal Influence

Group behavior and interpersonal influence are also powerful forces affecting organizational performance, as illustrated in the following account:

> Kelly McCaul spent two and one-half years as a teller in a small-town bank in Ft. Smith, Arkansas. During that time, she developed close personal friendships with her co-workers. These friendships extended off the job as well. Kelly and her friends formed a wine-and-cheese club, as well as the top team in the bankwide bowling league. In addition, several of them took ski trips together each winter.
>
> Two months ago Kelly was promoted to branch manager. She was excited about the new challenge but was a little surprised that she got the promotion, since some other candidates in the branch had been with the bank longer. She began the job with a great deal of optimism and believed her friends would be genuinely happy for her and supportive of her efforts. However, since she became branch manager, things haven't been quite the same. Kelly can't spend nearly as much time with her friends, because she is often away from the branch attending management meetings at the main office. Because of a training course that she must attend two evenings a week, she has missed the last two wine-and-cheese club meetings. And she senses that some of her friends have been acting a little differently toward her lately.
>
> Recently, Kelly said, "I didn't know that being a part of the management team could make that much difference. Frankly, I never really thought about it. I guess I was naive. I'm seeing a totally different perspective of the business and have to deal with problems I never knew about."

Kelly McCaul's promotion has made her a member of more than one group. In addition to being part of her old group of friends at the branch, she is also a member of the management team. She is finding out that group behavior and expectations have a strong impact on individual behavior and interpersonal influence. Our model includes four important aspects of group and interpersonal influence on organizational behavior: group behavior, intergroup behavior and conflict, power and politics, and leadership.

Group behavior.   Groups form because of managerial action and because of individual efforts. Managers create work groups to carry out assigned jobs and tasks. Such groups, created by managerial decisions, are termed *formal groups.* The group that Kelly McCaul manages at her branch is a group of this kind.

Groups also form as a consequence of employees' actions. Such groups, termed *informal groups,* develop around common interests and friendships. The wine-and-cheese club at Kelly McCaul's branch is an informal group. Though not sanctioned by management, groups of this kind can affect organizational and individual performance. The effect can be positive or negative, depending on the intention of the group's members. If the group at Kelly's branch decided informally to slow the work pace, this norm would exert pressure on individuals who wanted to remain a part of the group. Effective managers recognize the consequences of individuals' needs for affiliation.

Intergroup behavior and conflict.   As groups function and interact with other groups, each develops a unique set of characteristics, including structure, cohesiveness, roles, norms, and processes. The group in essence creates its own culture. As a result, groups may cooperate or compete with other groups, and intergroup competition can lead to conflict. If the management of Kelly's bank instituted an incentive program with cash bonuses to the branch bringing in the most new customers, this might lead to competition and conflict among the branches. While conflict among groups can have beneficial results for an organization, too much or the wrong kinds of intergroup conflict can have very negative results. Thus, managing intergroup conflict is an important aspect of managing organizational behavior.

Power and politics.   Power is the ability to get someone to do something you want done or to make things happen in the way you want them to happen. Many people in our society are very uncomfortable with the concept of power. Some are deeply offended by it. This is because the essence of power is control over others. To many Americans, and also a growing number of people around the world, this is an offensive thought.

   However, power does exist in organizations. Managers derive power from both organizational and individual sources. Kelly McCaul has power by virtue of her position in the formal hierarchy of the bank. She controls performance evaluations and salary increases. However, she may also have power because her co-workers respect and admire the abilities and expertise she possesses. Managers must therefore become comfortable with the concept of power as a reality in organizations and managerial roles.

Leadership.   Leaders exist within all organizations. They may be found in formal groups, like the bank's Kelly McCaul, or in informal groups. They may be managers or nonmanagers. The importance of effective leadership for obtaining individual, group, and organizational performance is so critical that it has stimulated a great deal of effort to determine the causes of such leadership. Some people believe that effective leadership depends on traits and certain behaviors, separately and in combination; other people believe that one leadership style is effective in all situations; still others believe that each situation requires a specific leadership style.

The Structure and Design of Organizations

To work effectively in organizations, managers must have a clear understanding of the organizational structure. Viewing an organization chart on a piece of paper or framed on a wall, one sees only a configuration of positions, job duties, and lines of authority among the parts of an organization. However, organizational structures can be far more complex, as illustrated in the following account:

   Dr. John Rice was recently appointed dean of the business school at a major university. Prior to arriving on campus, Rice spent several weeks studying the funding, programs, faculty, students, and organizational structure of the business school. He was trying to develop a list of priorities for things that he believed would require immediate attention during his first year as dean. The president of the university had requested that he have such a list of priorities available when he arrived on campus.

During his first official meeting with the president, Rice was asked the question he fully expected to be asked: "What will be your number one priority?" Rice replied: "Although money is always a problem, I believe the most urgent need is to recognize the business school. At present, students can only major in either accounting or business administration. The accounting department has 20 faculty members. The business administration department has 43 faculty members, including 25 in marketing, 16 in management, and 12 in finance. I foresee a college with four departments—accounting, management, marketing, and finance—each with its own chairperson. I believe such a structure will enable us to better meet the needs of our students. Specifically, it will facilitate the development of programs of majors in each of the four areas. Students must be able to major in one of the four functional areas if they are going to be prepared adequately for the job market. Finally, I believe such an organizational structure will enable us to more easily recruit faculty, since they will be joining a group with interests similar to their own."

As this account indicates, an organization's structure is the formal pattern of activities and interrelationships among the various subunits of the organization. Our model includes two important aspects of organizational structure: job design and organizational design. It also includes the concept referred to as culture.

Job design.   Job design refers to the process by which managers specify the contents, methods, and relationships of jobs to satisfy both organizational and individual requirements. Dr. Rice will have to define the content and duties of the newly created chairperson position and the relationship of that position to the dean's office and to the individual faculty members in each department.

Organizational design.   Organizational design refers to the overall organizational structure. Dr. Rice plans to alter the basic structure of the business school. The result of this effort will be a new *structure* of tasks and authority relationships that he believes will channel the behavior of individuals and groups toward higher levels of performance in the business school.

Organization culture.   Each organization has a culture or what is referred to as a pattern of assumptions that are developed by the employees as they learn to cope with the work and the environment. As the dean of the college, Dr. Rice will establish research, teaching, and service expectations that will become the cultural norms. For example, a faculty member will have to conduct research, teach effectively, and provide service to earn tenure. The cultural norms will set the tone of the college.

The Processes of Organizations

Certain behavioral processes give life to an organizational structure. When these processes do not function well, unfortunate problems can arise, as illustrated in this account:

When she began to major in marketing as a junior in college, Sandy Sherman knew that someday she would work in that field. Once she completed her M.B.A., she was more positive than ever that marketing would be her life's work. Because of her excellent academic record, she received several outstanding job offers. She decided to accept the offer from one of the nation's largest consulting firms, believing that this job would allow her to gain experience in several areas of marketing and to engage in a variety of exciting work. Her last day on campus, she told her favorite professor, "This has got to be one of the happiest days of my life, getting such a great career opportunity."

Recently, while visiting the college placement office, the professor was surprised to hear that Sandy had told the placement director that she was looking for another job. Since she had been with the consulting company less than a year, the professor was somewhat surprised. He decided to call Sandy and find out why she wanted to change jobs. This is what she told him: "I guess you can say my first experience with the real world was a 'reality shock.' Since joining this company, I have done nothing but gather data on phone surveys. All day long, I sit and talk on the phone, asking questions and checking off the answers. In graduate school, I was trained to be a manager, but here I am doing what any high school graduate can do. I talked to my boss, and he said that all employees have to pay their dues. Well, why didn't they tell me this while they were recruiting me? To say there was a conflict between the recruiting information and the real world would be a gross understatement. I'm an adult. Why didn't they provide me with realistic job information and then let me decide if I wanted it? A little bit of accurate communication would have gone a long way."

Our model includes three behavioral processes that contribute to effective organizational performance: communication, decision making, and socialization and career development.

Communication.   Organizational survival is related to the ability of management to receive, transmit, and act on information. The communication process links the organization to its environment as well as to its parts. Information flows to and from the organization and within the organization. Information integrates the activities within the organization. Sandy Sherman's problem arose because the information that flowed *from* the organization was different from the information that flowed *within* the organization.

Decision making.   The quality of decision making in an organization depends on selecting proper goals and identifying means for achieving them. With good integration of *behavioral* and *structural* factors, management can increase the probability that high-quality decisions are made. Sandy Sherman's experience illustrates inconsistent decision making by different organizational units (personnel and marketing) in the hiring of new employees. Organizations rely on individual decisions as well as group decisions, and effective management requires knowledge about both types of decisions.

Since managerial decisions affect people's lives and well-being, ethics play a major role.[7] Was Sandy provided with realistic and truthful information about the job? If not, was there a breach of ethics on the part of the recruiter? Since managers have power by virtue of their positions, the potential for unethical decision making is present. With all of the newspaper and television accounts of scandals in business, government, medicine, politics, and the law, there is evidence that ethics in terms of decision making need to be given serious attention.

---

[7]F. Neil Brady, *Ethical Managing: Rules and Results* (New York: Macmillan, 1990).

Socialization and career.   Individuals enter organizations to work and to pursue personal career goals: Sandy Sherman joined the consulting firm because she believed that it was presenting her with a great career opportunity. Organizations employ individuals to perform certain tasks—the jobs of the organization structure. Thus, individual and organizational interests and goals must be brought into congruence if both are to be effective. Sandy Sherman's goals are, at this time, incongruent with those of her organization. Individuals move through time and jobs along career paths more or less prescribed by the organization. The extent to which they are successful in a career depends, in part at least, on the extent to which they adapt to the organization's demands.

SOCIALIZATION

Refers to the processes by which members learn the cultural values, norms, beliefs, and required behavior that permit them to be effective contributors to the organization.

The process by which the individual is made aware of the organization's expectations is termed **socialization.** Socialization may be formal, as when orientation programs are established for new employees, or informal, as when the manager and co-workers tell the new employee relevant details about the organization's expectations. Sandy Sherman's socialization consisted of an abrupt statement from her boss that all employees had to "pay their dues." Career development and socialization are interrelated activities that affect the performance of both the organization and the individual.

Performance Outcomes: Individual, Group, and Organizational

Individual performance contributes to group performance, which in turn contributes to organizational performance. In truly effective organizations, however, management helps create a positive synergy—that is, a whole that is greater than the sum of its parts.

No one measure, or criterion, adequately reflects performance at any level. The next chapter introduces the idea that organizational performance must be considered in multiple measures within a time frame. Ineffective performance at any level is a signal to management to take corrective action. All of management's corrective actions focus on elements of organizational behavior, structure, or processes.

Organizational Development and Change

Sometimes, proper performance can be achieved only by making significant changes in the total organization. Organizational change is the planned attempt by management to improve the overall performance of individuals, groups, and the organization by altering structure, behavior, and processes. If the change is correctly implemented, individuals and groups should move toward more effective performance. Concerted, planned, and evaluated efforts to improve performance have great potential for success.

CONCLUSION

The focus of this book is on the developing field of management known as organizational behavior. Organizational behavior studies the behavior of individuals and groups in organizational settings. The framework within which the contents of this book are presented is based on three characteristics common to *all* organizations: the *behavior* of individuals and groups, the *structure* of organizations (that is, the design of the fixed relationships that exist among the jobs in an organization), and the *processes* (e.g., communication and decision making) that make organizations "tick" and give them life. The model presented in Figure 1–1 has evolved from our concept of what all organizations are.

Thus, our purpose in this book is to review theory and research on what we describe as the behavior, structure, and processes of organizations. A major interest is the behavioral sciences that have produced theory and research concerning human behavior in organizations. However, no attempt has been made here to write a book that teaches the reader "behavioral science." The continuous theme throughout the book is *the management of organizational*

behavior. Given this theme, our task is to *interpret* behavioral science materials so that students of management can comprehend the behavior, structure, and process phenomena as these are affected by actions of managers. It is our intention to provide readers with a basis for applying the relevant contributions of behavioral science to the management of organizations.

Since our goal is to help you become a more effective manager, the next chapter deals with managing organizations effectively. It serves as the foundation for studying the remainder of the book.

DISCUSSION AND REVIEW QUESTIONS

1. Thinking of an organization (e.g., bank, grocery store, school) you most recently visited, describe the types of indicators you noted that would help you determine the firm's culture.

2. Why is it believed that managers play an essential role in improving an organization's productivity?

3. Why do you think we have organized our book about organizational behavior around individual performance, group performance, and organizational performance?

4. Do you believe that organizations pervade your life? List each organization to which you belong. Do these organizations have any impact on your life? List and discuss each impact.

5. In dealing with many organizations today, one often encounters red tape and inefficiency in a generally unresponsive and ineffective organization. One of the goals of management is to achieve the opposite: an efficient and effective organization. What management skills are needed to help an organization become effective?

6. What role can the field of organizational behavior play in a country that is undergoing massive restructuring and reform, such as the Soviet Union?

7. Think of a particularly frustrating experience that you have had recently with an organization. It may have occurred at school, at work, or when you were dealing with an organization as a customer, patient, or citizen. Describe the experience and try to outline some possible causes.

8. "The kinds of problems faced by America today are such that they can only be solved by organizations." Comment.

9. Would a manager of a small firm (say, 25 employees) really have to be concerned about establishing an organization structure? Explain.

10. Describe how a manager who had worked for 15 years in Los Angeles would apply a contingency management approach when he is transferred to a similar managerial position within the same firm but in an office located in Barcelona, Spain.

ADDITIONAL REFERENCES

Bennis, W. *Why Leaders Can't Lead: The Unconscious Conspiracy Continues.* San Francisco: Jossey-Bass, 1989.

d'Amboise, G., and M. Muldowney. "Management Theory for Small Business: Attempts and Requirements." *Academy of Management Review,* April 1988, pp. 226–40.

Krant, A. I.; P. R. Pedigo; D. D. McKenna; and M. D. Dunnette. "The Role of the Manager: What's Really Important in Different Management Jobs." *Academy of Management Executive,* November 1989, pp. 286–93.

Porter, M. E. *The Competitive Advantage of Nations.* New York: Free Press, 1990.

Powell, G. N. *Women and Men in Management.* Newbury Park, Calif.: Sage, 1988.

Tichy, N., and R. Charan. "Speed, Simplicity, Self-Confidence: An Interview with Jack Welsh." *Harvard Business Review,* September–October 1989, pp. 112–20.

Vaill, P. B. *Managing as a Performing Art: New Ideas for a World of Chaotic Change.* San Francisco: Jossey-Bass, 1989.

Zeithaml, V. A.; A. Parasuraman; and L. L. Berry. *Delivering Quality Service.* New York: Free Press, 1990.

2

Managing Individual, Group, and Organizational Effectiveness

AN ORGANIZATIONAL
ISSUE FOR DEBATE   MANAGEMENT MAKES A DIFFERENCE

ARGUMENT FOR*

Thomas J. Peters, Robert H. Waterman, Jr., and Nancy Austin believe that management is the difference between successful and unsuccessful business organizations. Their books *In Search of Excellence* (Peters and Waterman), *A Passion for Excellence* (Peters and Austin), *Thriving on Chaos* (Peters), and *The Renewal Factor* (Waterman) present their evidence and conclusions. In view of the books' popularity and commercial success (they can be found on the desks of most practitioners and teachers of management), they must have struck responsive chords in management as well as nonmanagement groups. The optimistic theme of the books has great appeal at a time when America suffers economic instability and erosion of commercial dominance in the face of dramatic changes in international competition.

The appeal of the "management makes a difference" theme is that business has the power to reverse the trend of economic decay. All that needs to be done is to adopt the managerial practices of those firms that have achieved high levels of success. Presumably, relatively successful firms are managed differently than relatively unsuccessful ones. Thus, Peters and Waterman set out to demonstrate those differences in managerial practice that make a difference in organization performance.

They first identified a group of firms that had achieved uncommon success, as measured by six criteria: (1) asset growth, (2) equity growth, (3) ratio of market price to book value, (4) return on total capital, (5) return on equity, and (6) return on sales. The firms that scored highest on these six criteria included IBM, Texas Instruments, Dana Corporation, and Procter & Gamble. The authors identified 36 firms that achieved the highest levels of performance on the six criteria during the period 1961–1980.

What managerial practices were unique to these 36 firms? According to Peters and Waterman, there were eight unique practices. Corporate excellence is achieved by managers who

1. Have a bias for action.
2. Stay in close contact with the needs and problems of their customers.
3. Encourage a spirit of autonomy and entrepreneurship among employees.
4. Believe in and act on the attitude that people are the keys to productivity.
5. Create simple organizations.
6. Engender and develop a corporate culture that gives meaning to the work of employees.
7. Encourage the existence of both loose and tight controls.
8. Stick to the basic mission of the organization.

The lesson is clear. Less successful organizations can be transformed into successful ones by managers who can implement all eight practices.

Thus, to the question of whether management makes a difference, Peters, Waterman, and Austin come down on the positive side. Managers do make a difference; indeed, they are *the* difference.

ARGUMENT AGAINST†

Not everyone accepts the idea that management is the most critical factor in organizational performance. In fact, some individuals believe that management is relatively unimportant compared to the effects of economic, social, political, and cultural factors. Even if management does make a difference, Peters, Austin, and Waterman haven't demonstrated it. According to critics, they fail to make the case for their position because of inadequacies in evidence and logic. The evidence that supports the case is both narrow and anecdotal.

The narrowness is due to their criteria of "success," all six of which measure financial success. Other measures of success (e.g., effectiveness) could yield a different sample of firms. Moreover, if one used a different time frame, for example 1951–1970, would the sample be different? Or if a follow-up is done for the period 1981–2000, will the sample be different? If firms drop out of the list of "excellently managed," does this mean that they are no longer managed according to the eight practices?

Peters, Austin, and Waterman's thesis that management makes the difference is the only logical explanation because they examined *only* management differences. They failed to include any consideration of technology, market dominance, control of critical raw materials, national policy, and/or culture. When they gathered information about the firms, Peters, Austin, and Waterman ignored these potential causes of business success. Consequently, they could not logically conclude that these causes had an effect on business success. Their critics point out that any firm will be unable to achieve success against IBM, for example, without some protected technological edge; or that an oil company can successfully compete without access to low-cost crude oil supplies, no matter how consistently its management applies the eight practices. But because these potential causes of corporate success are not analyzed, Peters and Waterman can only infer that management is the cause—that being the *only* cause they analyzed.

But what about the analysis itself? Is the evidence conclusive? According to critics, the analysis relies on secondary and anecdotal evidence. The secondary evidence includes articles appearing in *The New York Times, Fortune,* and *Harvard Business Review*. While the ideas expressed in these articles may reflect truth or at least informed opinion, they cannot be accepted as preferable to evidence gathered from the firms themselves. Perhaps even more damaging to Peters and Waterman's case is that many points are supported with anecdotes. For example, they support their conclusion about McDonald's concern for product quality with the recollections of a young business executive who worked for the fast-food chain as a 17-year-old high school student. The case for Hewlett-Packard's customer orientation is based on remarks Peters overheard in a Palo Alto bar.

The point is not whether McDonald's is concerned for product quality or whether Hewlett-Packard is customer oriented. The point is that the evidence *cited* does not make the case. The fact that readers have generally accepted Peters and Waterman's evidence as valid lends greater support to the effectiveness of public relations and advertising in selling their book than to the effectiveness of management in the firms studied.

Thus, even though managers may make a difference, the case is yet to be made. Peters, Austin, and Waterman have not made it. But then, who is willing to say that managers make *no* difference?

*Based on Thomas J. Peters and Robert H. Waterman, Jr., *In Search of Excellence* (New York: Harper & Row, 1982); Thomas J. Peters and Nancy Austin, *A Passion for Excellence* (New York: Harper & Row, 1985); Thomas J. Peters, *Thriving on Chaos* (New York: Alfred A. Knopf, 1987); Robert H. Waterman, Jr., *The Renewal Factor* (New York: Bantam Books, 1987).

†Based on Daniel T. Carroll, "A Disappointing Search for Excellence," *Harvard Business Review,* November–December 1983, pp. 78–79, 83–84, 88; Michael A. Hitt and R. Duane Ireland, "Peters and Waterman Revisited: The Unended Quest for Excellence," *Academy of Management Executive,* May 1987, pp. 91–98; Alan B. Thomas, "Does Leadership Make a Difference to Organizational Performance?" *Administrative Science Quarterly,* September 1988, pp. 388–400.

EFFECTIVENESS

In the context of organizational behavior, the optimal relationship among five components: production, efficiency, satisfaction, adaptiveness, and development.

This chapter discusses how managers can influence individual, group, and organizational effectiveness. Since a major purpose of this text is to contribute to the academic preparation of future managers, this issue must be analyzed thoroughly. Many writers on management and organizational behavior have attempted to develop a general theory of management. But, as the Organizational Issue for Debate suggests, whether managers do (or can) influence **effectiveness** is difficult to determine. Even though each of us can cite instances of corporate excellence achieved through management excellence, we are reluctant to infer general principles from these instances.

Although no general theory of management presently exists, that does not mean we are totally ignorant about management and its role in organizations. This textbook is based on the belief that valuable insights about management are to be found in the literature of organizational behavior.

In the wake of the political and commercial turmoil that marked the end of the 1980s, managers of organizations face great personal and professional challenge. Many of the foundations for business practice must be revised as managers cope with competition from countries once thought to be archenemies and with technology once thought to be possible only in Buck Rogers comic strips. That the environments in which organizations exist are changing is no startling revelation. However, the importance of management as a force to deal with those changing environments can be challenged, as emphasized in the opening debate.

As we noted in the previous chapter, the field of organizational behavior identifies three *levels of analysis:* (1) individual, (2) group, and (3) organizational. Theorists and researchers have accumulated a vast amount of information about each of the three. These levels of analysis coincide with the three levels of managerial responsibility. That is, managers are responsible for the effectiveness of individuals, groups of individuals, and organizations themselves.

For example, Lee Iacocca, the widely respected president of Chrysler Corp., took on the task of improving Chrysler's effectiveness (the organizational level of responsibility). By all accounts, Iacocca met that responsibility. But how did he do it? And by what criteria do we assess the degree to which Chrysler is more effective? Iacocca might respond that Chrysler is more effective because individuals on the assembly lines produced a higher-quality product (the individual level of responsibility), the engineering divisions designed more reliable automobiles (the group level of responsibility), and the federal government guaranteed loans that forestalled bankruptcy (the organizational level of responsibility).

This chapter presents important ideas about effectiveness, management, and organizational culture. We begin with a discussion of the three different perspectives referred to in the above paragraphs. Next, we discuss three influential approaches to evaluating effectiveness: the goal, systems, and multiple-constituency models of effectiveness. Our own effort to integrate these three models is developed in the discussion of the time dimension model of effectiveness. The time dimension model enables us to suggest specific criteria for judging effectiveness. We describe the functions and roles that managers can perform to attain and maintain acceptable levels of individual, group, and organizational effectiveness in the context of a specific organizational culture.

PERSPECTIVES ON EFFECTIVENESS

Three perspectives on effectiveness can be identified. At the most basic level is *individual* effectiveness, which emphasizes the task performance of specific employees or members of the organization. The tasks to be performed are parts of jobs or positions in the organization. Managers routinely assess individual effectiveness through performance evaluation processes that are the bases for salary increases, promotions, and other rewards available in the organization.

Individuals seldom work alone, in isolation from others in the organization. Usually, employees work in groups, necessitating yet another perspective on effectiveness: *group* effectiveness. In some instances, group effectiveness is simply the sum of the contributions of all its members. For example, a group of scientists working on unrelated projects would be effective to the extent that each individual is effective. In other instances, group effectiveness is more than the sum of the individual contributions—for example, an assembly line that produces a finished product as a result of the contributions of each individual.

The third perspective is that of *organizational* effectiveness. Organizations consist of individuals and groups; therefore, organizational effectiveness consists of individual and group effectiveness. However, organizational effectiveness is more than the sum of individual and group effectiveness. Through synergistic effects, organizations are able to obtain higher levels of performance than the sum of their parts. In fact, the rationale for organizations as means for doing the work of society is that they can do more work than is possible through individual effort.

The effectiveness of business organizations is critically important for society. From time to time, publications that report business and economic events conduct opinion surveys about business performance. The Close-Up reports on *Fortune*'s survey.

The relationship among the three perspectives on effectiveness is shown in Figure 2–1 (p. 28). The connecting arrows imply that group effectiveness depends on individual effectiveness and that organizational effectiveness depends on group effectiveness. The exact relationships among the three perspectives vary depending on such factors as the type of organization, the work it does, and the technology used in doing that work. The figure also recognizes the *synergistic* effects of the three perspectives. Thus, group effectiveness is larger than the sum of individual effectiveness because of the synergies realized through joint efforts.

The job of management is to identify the *causes* of organizational, group, and individual effectiveness. The distinction between the causes of effectiveness and the indicators of effectiveness can be difficult for both managers and researchers.[1] However, the term *effectiveness* derives from the term *effect,* and we use the term in the context of cause-effect relationships. As noted in Figure 2–2 (p. 28), each level of effectiveness can be considered a variable that is caused by other variables—namely, the causes of effectiveness.

---

[1]Arie Y. Lewin and John W. Minton, "Determining Organizational Effectiveness: Another Look and an Agenda for Research," *Management Science,* May 1986, p. 514.

FORTUNE'S SURVEY OF THE MOST ADMIRED CORPORATIONS

In 1989, *Fortune* magazine polled more than 8,000 senior executives, outside directors, and financial analysts to determine which corporations they held in highest esteem. The survey, which covered 305 companies in 32 industry groups, asked those polled to rate the 10 largest companies in their own industry "on eight attributes of reputation":

1. Quality of management.
2. Quality of products or services.
3. Innovativeness.
4. Long-term investment value.
5. Financial soundness.
6. Ability to attract, develop, and keep talented people.
7. Community and environmental responsibility.
8. Use of corporate assets.

Respondents to the survey rated each company from 0 (poor) to 10 (excellent) on each of the eight attributes.

According to *Fortune*, Merck & Company was rated the most admired company for the fourth consecutive year. The respondents, all from other companies in the pharmaceuticals industry, gave Merck an average of 8.90 on the eight attributes. Other corporations that ranked in the top 10 included Philip Morris (8.78), Rubbermaid (8.42), Procter & Gamble (8.37), 3M (8.21), PepsiCo (8.16), Wal-Mart Stores (8.16), Coca-Cola (8.15), Anheuser-Busch (7.96), and Du Pont (7.93).

Respondents rated Merck highest on four of the eight attributes. Philip Morris was rated first in long-term investment value and in quality of management. Johnson & Johnson was noted for its community and environmental responsibility, and Berkshire Hathaway was given top honors for its wide use of corporate assets. Key aspects of Merck's continued dominance include the ability to consistently increase profits (earnings per share have risen at least 25 percent for 14 consecutive quarters), to constantly introduce successful new drugs (since 1981, Merck has introduced 10 major drugs, each accounting for over $100 million in annual sales), and to retain a

Management and organizational behavior literature has reported various theories and research purporting to provide insight into the causes of effectiveness at each of the three levels of analysis. For example, causes of individual effectiveness include ability, skill, knowledge, attitude, motivation, and stress. "Individual differences" in these areas account for differences in effectiveness in individual performance. Some of the more usual causes of differences in group and organizational effectiveness are also noted in Figure 2–2.[2] These

---

[2]One of the more ambitious attempts to determine causes of organizational effectiveness is reported in John Child, "Managerial and Organizational Factors Associated with Company Performance—Part I," *Journal of Management Studies,* October 1974, pp. 175–89; John Child, "Managerial and Organizational Factors Associated with Company Performance—Part II:

high emphasis on R&D spending ($755 million, or 11 percent of sales, in 1989). Merck's most significant new drugs include Mevacor, which cuts cholesterol levels by as much as 40 percent, and Primaxin, a powerful antibiotic.

Reasons for the leaders' success vary. Philip Morris has risen from number seven to number two in two years, largely by giving shareholders outstanding returns year after year; during the 1980s, the company produced annual increases of approximately 20 percent in earnings per share. Rubbermaid was rewarded for a sustained growth record and the ability to churn out new quality products. Close attention to details, such as adding antistatic chemicals to plastic so products won't attract dust, and to customer comments has allowed Rubbermaid to rank among the top seven companies for the past five years. 3M, by fostering an environment conducive to innovation, has introduced new products at a rate of about 200 a year; approximately 25 percent of each division's sales are generated from products introduced within the last five years. Anheuser-Busch has boosted its brand's share of the $15 billion U.S. beer market from 28 percent in 1980 to 43 percent in 1989.

Just as diverse were the reasons that led to placing companies at the bottom of the rankings. Three computer companies—Wang Laboratories, Control Data, and Unisys—were rated low for their inability to generate stockholder returns. Gibralter Financial, rated the least admired company in all eight categories surveyed, has had its two operating subsidiaries seized by federal thrift operators for holding a bundle of money-losing real estate loans. Texas Air, engaged in much publicized fights with employees over pay and benefit issues, continued to receive low ratings.

To see that fame can be fleeting, consider the case of IBM. Rated the most admired company for the first four years of the survey, IBM now ranks 45th. Even in its own industry, IBM placed second, behind Hewlett-Packard. IBM's inability to devise a convincing strategy for coping with a shift in market demand from mainframe computers to powerful desktop machines has contributed greatly to its woes. IBM recently announced a $2.3 billion cost-cutting drive to try to regain its former dominance in the computer industry.

Source: Sarah Smith, "America's Most Admired Corporations" and "Leaders of the Most Admired," *Fortune*, January 29, 1990, pp. 40–92.

potential causes of effectiveness are discussed at length in subsequent chapters. Other causes are also presented. However, the reality of organizational life is that few unambiguous cause-effect relationships exist. In most instances, evaluation judgments must take into account multiple causes and circumstances.[3] The Close-Up on effectiveness describes how managers of a small bank acted on the causes of low bank effectiveness.

A Contingency Analysis," *Journal of Management Studies*, February 1975, pp. 12–27. This study did not reach definitive conclusions, due no doubt to the inherent complexity of the concept of organizational effectiveness.

[3]Jeffrey D. Ford and Deborah A. Schnellenberg, "Conceptual Issues of Linkage in the Assessment of Organizational Performance," *Academy of Management Review*, January 1982, pp. 49–58.

FIGURE 2—1

Three Perspectives on
Effectiveness

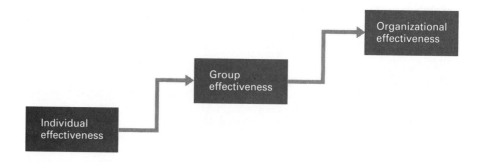

FIGURE 2—2

Causes of Effectiveness

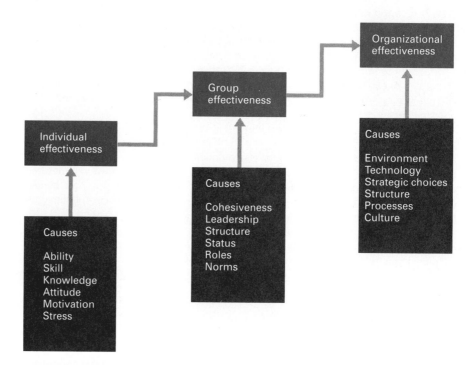

THREE INFLUENTIAL APPROACHES TO EVALUATING EFFECTIVENESS

Thus far, we have assumed a definition of effectiveness. We have used the term as though we all share a common understanding of the term. In fact, there is no universal agreement as to what effectiveness means, in either a theoretical or practical sense. Differences in defining effectiveness reflect adherence to one of three general approaches: the goal approach, the systems theory approach, and the multiple constituency approach. These approaches are discussed in both the literature and practice of organizational behavior.[4]

___

[4]Stephen Strasser, J. D. Eveland, Gaylord Cummins, O. Lynn Deniston, and John H. Romani, "Conceptualizing the Goal and System Models of Organizational Effectiveness," *Journal of Management Studies,* July 1981, p. 323. Kim Cameron, "Critical Questions in Assessing Organi-

ORGANIZATIONS:
CLOSE-UP

EFFECTIVENESS IN SMALL BANKS

Banks, large and small, have felt the effects of competition in recent years. Old ways of banking and managing banks are no longer effective in an environment that rewards an effective provider of financial services. One small bank competing in a regional market discovered the importance of individual effectiveness for overall organizational effectiveness when it began to make the transition from a bank to a financial service organization.

The bank began the transition by doing a survey of customer service satisfaction, which showed it to be last of 20 surveyed banks. Management immediately analyzed the causes of this low ranking. The important causes were people-oriented factors—jobs, working conditions, and salaries. Employees were unable to satisfy customers because their jobs rewarded for narrow ranges of activity; elimination of "teller errors," for example, was the primary goal of tellers, not serving customer needs. The bank's management responded by redesigning jobs so that employees could provide complete services for a small number of clients. Workstations were redesigned to accommodate the latest microcomputer technology. And employee status was upgraded from clerical to professional.

The bank now recruits people who show interest and aptitude for service and then makes major investments in their career development. Because the bank has fostered the reputation for effective and sincere human resource management, it is able to attract and keep personnel even in the face of efforts of other banks to recruit them. The bank's management strongly believes that overall organization performance can be traced directly to individual effectiveness.

Goal Approach

The goal approach to defining and evaluating effectiveness is the oldest and most widely used evaluation approach.[5] According to the **goal approach to effectiveness,** an organization exists to accomplish goals. An early and influential practitioner and writer in management and organizational behavior stated: "What we mean by effectiveness . . . is the accomplishment of recognized objectives of cooperative effort. The degree of accomplishment indicates the degree of effectiveness."[6] The idea that organizations, as well as individuals and groups, should be evaluated in terms of goal accomplishment has widespread commonsense and practical appeal. The goal approach reflects purposefulness, rationality, and achievement—the fundamental tenets of contemporary Western societies.

GOAL APPROACH TO
EFFECTIVENESS
Perspective on effectiveness
that emphasizes central role of
goal achievement as criterion for
assessing effectiveness.

zational Effectiveness," *Organizational Dynamics,* Autumn 1980, pp. 66–80, identifies two other approaches: the internal process approach and the strategic constituencies approach. The former can be subsumed under the systems theory approach, and the latter is a special case of the multiple-goal approach.

[5]Michael Keeley, "Impartiality and Participant-Interest Theories of Organizational Effectiveness," *Administrative Science Quarterly,* March 1984, p. 1.

[6]Chester I. Barnard, *The Functions of the Executive* (Cambridge, Mass.: Harvard University Press, 1938), p. 55.

ORGANIZATIONS:
CLOSE-UP

IMPROVING EFFECTIVENESS OF KNOWLEDGE WORKERS

Despite widespread concern for controlling cost, improving productivity, and attaining higher levels of quality, the jobs of knowledge workers remain largely unexamined. The challenge is to identify and to quantify exactly what a knowledge worker produces. Unlike line workers, who perform tasks on tangible objects, the knowledge worker produces ideas and concepts. Clerical, professional, and even managerial personnel have typically been exempt from analyses that document their contributions to the "bottom line." In the absence of acceptable procedures for determining appropriate output, the knowledge workers do their jobs according to very personal bases and personalized preferences: they often come and go as they please; they set their own priorities. They tend to be undermanaged and underutilized.

But this condition must change, and much managerial effort is now allocated to finding and implementing measures of what knowledge workers produce—the goals of their jobs. Management by objectives has not been effective in this effort because of the difficulty of attributing specific outcomes to the efforts of specific individuals.

Sources: Thomas C. Tuttle and John J. Romanowski, "Assessing Performance and Productivity in White-Collar Organizations," *National Productivity Review,* Summer 1985, pp. 211–24; E. James Coates, "Three Models for White Collar Productivity Improvement," *Industrial Management,* March–April 1986, pp. 7–13.

Many management practices are based on the goal approach. One widely used practice is management by objectives, where managers specify in advance the goals that they expect their subordinates to accomplish and then evaluate periodically the degree to which these goals are accomplished. The actual specifics of management by objectives vary from case to case: the manager and subordinate may discuss the objectives and attempt to reach mutual agreement, or the manager may simply assign the goals. The idea is to specify in advance the goals that are to be sought. Management by objectives can be useful whenever there is a strong relationship between job behavior and a measurable outcome, the objective.

Some individuals perform jobs that are difficult to relate to measurable outcomes. For example, knowledge workers present a particularly difficult challenge to managers who must improve performance, as noted in the Close-Up on that subject.

Other widespread management practices reflecting the goal approach include program budgeting and zero-based budgeting, cost-benefit analysis, linear programming, and incentive pay systems. Each of these practices begins with the assumption that the individual, group, or organization has an overriding goal that managers can identify and measure.

Yet, for all its appeal and apparent simplicity, the goal approach has problems.[7] Some of the more widely recognized difficulties include:

---

[7] E. Frank Harrison, *Management and Organization* (Boston: Houghton Mifflin, 1978), pp. 404–14, is an excellent survey of limitations of the goal approach.

1. Goal achievement is not readily measurable for organizations that do not produce tangible outputs. For example, the goal of a college is to provide a liberal education at a fair price. But how would one know whether the college reaches that goal? What is a liberal education? What is a fair price? For that matter, what is education?

2. Organizations attempt to achieve more than one goal, and the achievement of one goal often precludes or diminishes their ability to achieve other goals. A business firm states that its goal is to attain a maximum profit and to provide absolutely safe working conditions. These two goals are in conflict because the achievement of one is at the expense of the other.

3. The very existence of a common set of "official" goals to which all members are committed is questionable. Various researchers have noted the difficulty of obtaining consensus among managers as to the specific goals of their organization.[8]

One of the narrowest views of effectiveness defines it as "the financial viability of an organization."[9] An organization that is financially viable can pay its bills as they are due, and the more effective organization will have funds in reserve. Proponents of this view state that, though narrow, it is very useful because it overcomes the limitations of the wider idea of the goal approach. For example, the measurement of financial viability is relatively easy, compared with the measurement of managements' "real" goals. Return on assets and return on equity are straightforward, readily available measures of financial viability for business firms. Nonbusiness organizations have similar measures: educational institutions can measure financial viability as revenue per student; government agencies can measure it as revenue per employee.[10] The idea that organizational effectiveness can be simply defined and easily measured has considerable appeal.

The goal approach exerts a powerful influence on the development of management and organizational behavior theory and practice. To say that managers should achieve the goals of the organization is easy. However, to know *how* to do this is much more difficult.

Systems Theory Approach

The alternative to the goal approach is the systems theory approach. Through systems theory, the concept of effectiveness can be defined in broader terms that enable managers to understand the causes of individual, group, and organizational effectiveness.

Systems theory enables us to describe the behavior of organizations both internally and externally. Internally, we can see how and why people inside organizations perform their individual and group tasks. Externally, we can relate the transactions of organizations with other organizations and institutions. All organizations acquire resources from the larger environment of which each is a part and, in turn, provide goods and services demanded by that

SYSTEMS THEORY
Approach to analysis of organizational behavior that emphasizes necessity for maintaining basic elements of input-process-output and for adapting to larger environment that sustains organization.

---

[8]Terry Connolly, Edward J. Conlon, and Stuart Jay Deutsch, "Organizational Effectiveness: A Multiple-Constituency Approach," *Academy of Management Review,* April 1980, p. 212.

[9]James L. Price and Charles W. Mueller, *Handbook of Organizational Measurement* (Marshfield, Mass.: Pitman Publishing, 1986), pp. 128–30.

[10]Ibid., pp. 132–34.

FIGURE 2—3
The Basic Elements of a
System

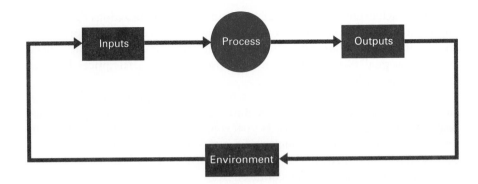

larger environment. Managers must deal simultaneously with the internal and external aspects of organizational behavior. This essentially complex process can be simplified, for analytical purposes, by employing the basic concepts of systems theory.

In the context of systems theory, the organization is one of a number of elements that interact interdependently. The flow of inputs and outputs is the starting point in the description of the organization. In the simplest terms, the organization takes resources (inputs) from the larger system (environment), processes these resources, and returns them in changed form (output). Figure 2–3 displays the fundamental elements of the organization as a system.

Systems theory can also describe the behavior of individuals and groups. The "inputs" of individual behavior are "causes" that arise from the workplace. For example, the cause could be a manager's directives to perform a certain task. The input (cause) is then acted on by the individual's mental and psychological processes to produce a particular outcome. The outcome the manager prefers is, of course, compliance with the directive; but depending on the states of the individual's processes, it could be noncompliance. We could similarly describe the behavior of a group in systems theory terms. For example, the behavior of a group of employees to unionize (outcome) could be explained in terms of perceived managerial unfairness in the assignment of work (input) and the state of the group's cohesiveness (process). We use the terms of system theory throughout this text to describe and explain the behavior of individuals and groups in organizations.

Systems theory and feedback.   The concept of the organization as a system that is related to a larger system introduces the importance of feedback. As noted above, the organization is dependent on the environment not only for its inputs but also for the acceptance of its outputs. It is critical, therefore, that the organization develops means for adjusting to environmental demands. The means for adjustment are information channels that enable the organization to recognize these demands. In business organizations, for example, market research is an important feedback mechanism.

In simplest terms, feedback is information that reflects the outcomes of an act or a series of acts by an individual, group, or organization. Throughout this text, we will see how important feedback is for reinforcing learning and for developing personality, group behavior, and leadership. Systems theory emphasizes the importance of responding to the feedback information.

Examples of the input-output cycle.   The business firm has two major categories of inputs: human resources and natural resources. Human inputs consist of the people who work in the firm—operating, staff, and managerial personnel—contributing their time and energy to the organization in exchange for wages and other rewards, tangible and intangible. Natural resources are the nonhuman inputs processed or used in combination with the human element to provide other resources. A steel mill uses people and blast furnaces (along with other tools and machinery) to process iron ore into steel and steel products. An auto manufacturer takes steel, rubber, plastics, fabrics, and—in combination with people, tools, and equipment—makes automobiles. A business firm survives as long as its output is purchased in the market in quantities and at prices that enable it to replenish its depleted stock of inputs. In some instances, conditions in the marketplace may threaten **the** very survival of an organization, which must change or dissolve.

A university uses resources to teach students, for research, and to provide technical information to society. Survival depends on its ability to attract students' tuition and taxpayers' dollars in sufficient amounts to pay faculty and staff salaries and the other costs of resources. If a university's output is rejected by the larger environment, so that students enroll elsewhere and taxpayers support other public endeavors, or if a university expends too many resources in relation to its output, it will cease to exist. Like a business firm, a university must provide the right output at the right price if it is to survive.[11]

As a final example of systems theory, a hospital's inputs are its professional and administrative staff, equipment, supplies, and patients. The patients are processed through the application of medical knowledge and treatment. To the extent that its patients are restored to the level of health consistent with the severity of disease or injury suffered, the hospital is effective.

Systems theory emphasizes two important considerations: (1) The ultimate survival of the organization depends on its ability to adapt to the demands of its environment. (2) In meeting these demands, the total cycle of input-process-output must be the focus of managerial attention. Therefore, criteria of effectiveness must reflect each of these two considerations, and effectiveness must be defined accordingly. The systems approach explains why resources have to be devoted to activities that have little to do with achieving the organization's goal.[12] In other words, adapting to the environment and maintaining the input-process-output flow require that resources be allocated to activities only indirectly related to the organization's primary goal.

Multiple-Constituency Theory of Organizational Effectiveness

The application of systems theory concepts to the discussion of organizational effectiveness shows the importance of the external environment. Systems theory also identifies the importance of achieving a balance among the various parts of the system, of which an organization is but one part. In practical and

[11]James L. Perry and Hal G. Rainey, "The Public-Private Distinction in Organization Theory: A Critique and Research Strategy," *Academy of Management Review,* April 1988, pp. 182–201.

[12]Amitai Etzioni, "Two Approaches to Organizational Analysis: A Critique and a Suggestion," in *Assessment of Organizational Effectiveness,* ed. Jaisingh Ghorpade (Santa Monica, Calif.: Goodyear Publishing, 1971), p. 36.

MULTIPLE CONSTITUENCY
APPROACH TO
EFFECTIVENESS
Perspective that emphasizes the
relative importance of different
groups' and individuals' interests
in an organization.

concrete terms, in the **multiple constituency approach to effectiveness,** the phrase "achieving balance among the various parts of the system" means satisfying the interests of all those individuals and groups of individuals who have a stake in the organization, the organization's constituency.[13] (In contrast, the goal approach emphasizes that organizations are chartered to accomplish goals.)

Individuals and groups of individuals having stakes in an organization include its employees (nonmanagers and managers), shareholders, directors, suppliers, creditors, officials at all levels of government, managers of competitive and cooperative organizations, and the general public. Each of these individuals and groups of individuals expects the organization to behave in ways that benefit them, but these expectations may or may not be compatible with those of other individuals and groups. Given that an organization can be judged effective or ineffective depending on who is making the judgment, how can managers ever achieve effectiveness in the sense of satisfying all the claims of the organization's constituency?

One approach would be to state that there is no way to determine the relative importance of the constituent claims and that there are as many evaluations of effectiveness as there are individuals making judgments. This relativistic view assumes that all claims on the organization are valid, no basis exists for ordering their importance, and thus no basis exists for making an overall judgment of organizational effectiveness.[14]

How then is management to act? One answer is provided by the idea that each constituent controls resources of value to the organization. At any point in time, these resources are more or less important, and the organization is effective to the extent that it satisfies the interest of the group controlling the most important resource.[15] Thus, the interests of stockholders supersede the interests of employees when the organization must acquire equity funds in order to survive. Or the interests of the government regulatory official supersede the interests of stockholders when conformity to safety regulations requires investment in safe working conditions. This view can be extended to a concept of the organization as an arena in which the different groups negotiate their claims through the development of coalitions capable of combining the power of members of the coalition. Managers of the organization achieve effectiveness by identifying the most powerful coalitions and satisfying the demands of the most influential members of those coalitions.

Whether the organization is effective when satisfying the most powerful group involves value judgment. All judgments of effectiveness involve value judgment. To state that one should satisfy the most powerful group at the expense of the least powerful group is to make a personal statement of what is ultimately important. Since many different sources of value judgments exist, there can be no final, "right" answer to the question: Is the organization effective? Nor will there be such an answer when the focus is individual and group effectiveness. Values reflect human judgments about what is important, and those judgments shift with individuals, place, and time.

---

[13]Raymond F. Zammuto, "A Comparison of Multiple Constituency Models of Organizational Effectiveness," *Academy of Management Review,* October 1984, pp. 600–616.

[14]Connolly et al., "Organizational Effectiveness."

[15]Jeffrey Pfeffer and Gerald R. Salancik, *The External Control of Organizations* (New York: Harper & Row, 1978).

Management's values are especially important for understanding organizational effectiveness. One emerging point of view identifies a set of competing values that vie for management's attention.[16] The *competing values model* states that managers must choose between values that stress (1) control or flexibility and (2) an internal or external focus. Four combinations of these choices can be defined:

— A manager who values control and an internal focus would strive for stability and continuity of the organization.

— A manager who values control and an external focus would strive for production and efficiency.

— A manager who values flexibility and an internal focus would strive for employee satisfaction and cohesion.

— A manager who values flexibility and an external focus would strive for adaptability and growth.

Managers choose from among these four possibilities in a relative way. Thus, their organizations will reflect degrees of acceptance of these basic values. The paradox, according to the competing values model, is that managers must choose from among what appear to be mutually exclusive values. How, it is asked, can an organization be both flexible and controlled? How can it be both internally and externally focused? These questions will doubtlessly persist as the environments of organizations continue to include larger groups of constituents that make different, and often competing, demands on organizations.[17]

One recent study of the applicability of multiple-constituency theory suggests that it may in fact integrate both the systems and goal approaches to effectiveness.[18] The study documents that some constituencies favor outcomes related to means (the process element in systems) while others favor outcomes related to ends (the outcome element in systems). Thus, it is possible to use the multiple-constituency theory to combine the goal and systems approaches to obtain a more appropriate approach to organizational effectiveness. However, even if differences are resolved between the goal and systems approaches with respect to what different constituencies desire from organizational performance, these desires can shift with time.

THE TIME DIMENSION MODEL OF ORGANIZATIONAL EFFECTIVENESS

The concept of organizational effectiveness in this book relies on our previous discussion of systems theory, plus one additional point: the dimension of time. Recall that two main conclusions of systems theory are that effectiveness criteria must reflect (1) the entire input-process-output cycle, not simply

---

[16]Robert E. Quinn, *Beyond Rational Management* (San Francisco: Jossey-Bass, 1988), pp. 46–50.

[17]Robert E. Quinn and Kim S. Cameron, eds., *Paradox and Transformation* (Cambridge, Mass.: Ballinger, 1988).

[18]Anne S. Tsui, "An Empirical Examination of the Multiple Constituency Model of Organizational Effectiveness," *Academy of Management Proceedings,* 1989, pp. 188–92.

output, and (2) the interrelationships between the organization and its larger environment. Thus:

1. Organizational effectiveness is an all-encompassing concept that includes a number of component concepts.
2. The managerial task is to maintain the optimal balance among these components and constituencies.

Presently, we are proposing a tentative set of ideas. Much additional research is needed to develop knowledge about the components of effectiveness. Little consensus has been reached about these relevant components, their interrelationships, and the effects of managerial action on them.[19] We are attempting to provide the basis for asking the right questions about what constitutes effectiveness and how those qualities that characterize it interact.

The dimension of time enters into the model when an organization is conceptualized as an element of a larger system (the environment) that through *time* takes, processes, and returns resources to the environment. The ultimate criterion of organizational effectiveness is whether it sustains itself in the environment. *Survival* of the organization, then, is the long-run measure of organizational effectiveness. Survival requires adaptation, and adaptation often involves predictable sequences. As the organization ages, it is likely to pass through different phases. Some writers suggest that an organization has a life cycle: it forms, develops, matures, and declines in relation to environmental circumstances. We are all aware of the rise and fall of organizations, even entire industries; today, the personal computer industry is on the rise, and the steel industry is declining. Marketing experts acknowledge the existence of product market life cycles. It seems reasonable to conclude that organizations also have life cycles. Consequently, the appropriate criteria of effectiveness must reflect the stage of the organization's life cycle.[20]

CRITERIA OF EFFECTIVENESS

Management and others with interests in the organization must have indicators to assess its probability of survival. In actual practice, managers use a number of short-run indicators of long-run survival, such as productivity, efficiency, accidents, turnover, absenteeism, quality, rate of return, morale, and employee satisfaction.[21] Any of these can be relevant for particular purposes. For simplicity, we will use three criteria of short-run effectiveness as representative

---

[19]J. Barton Cunningham, "Approaches to the Evaluation of Organizational Effectiveness," *Academy of Management Review,* July 1977, pp. 463–74; Richard M. Steers, "Problems in Measurement of Organizational Effectiveness," *Administrative Science Quarterly,* December 1975, pp. 546–58.

[20]Kim S. Cameron and David A. Whetten, "Perceptions of Organizational Effectiveness over Organizational Life Cycles," *Administrative Science Quarterly,* December 1981, pp. 525–44; Robert E. Quinn and Kim Cameron, "Organizational Life Cycles and Shifting Criteria of Effectiveness: Some Preliminary Evidence," *Management Science,* January 1983, pp. 33–51.

[21]John P. Campbell, "On the Nature of Organizational Effectiveness," in *New Perspectives on Organizational Effectiveness,* ed. Paul S. Goodman and Johannes M. Pennings (San Francisco: Jossey-Bass, 1979), pp. 36–39.

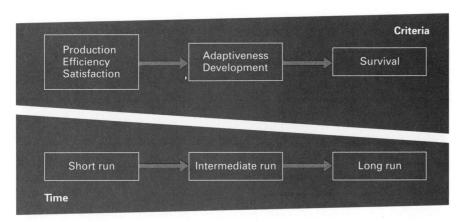

FIGURE 2—4

Time Dimension Model of
Effectiveness

of all such criteria. They are *production, efficiency,* and *satisfaction.* Two other criteria, which reflect effectiveness in the intermediate time period, complete the time dimension model: *adaptiveness* and *development.* Their relationship to the time dimension is shown in Figure 2–4, and they are defined as follows:

Production

As used here, production reflects the ability of the organization to produce the quantity and quality of output the environment demands. The concept excludes any consideration of efficiency, which is defined below. Measures of production can be profit, sales, market share, students graduated, patients released, documents processed, clients served, and the like. These measures relate directly to the output consumed by the organization's customers and clients.

Efficiency

Efficiency is the ratio of outputs to inputs. This short-run criterion focuses attention on the entire input-process-output cycle, yet it emphasizes the input and process elements. Measures of efficiency include rate of return on capital or assets; unit cost; scrappage and waste; downtime; cost per patient, student, or client; occupancy rates; and the like. Measures of efficiency must inevitably be in ratio terms; the ratios of benefit to cost, output, or time are the general forms of these measures.

Satisfaction

The idea of the organization as a social system requires that some consideration be given to the benefits received by its participants as well as by its customers and clients. Satisfaction and morale are similar terms that refer to the extent to which the organization satisfies the needs of employees. We will use the term *satisfaction* to refer to this criterion. Measures of satisfaction include employee attitudes, turnover, absenteeism, tardiness, and grievances.

Adaptiveness

Adaptiveness is the extent to which the organization *can and does* respond to internal and external changes. Contrary to its use elsewhere, adaptiveness is viewed here as an intermediate criterion, being more abstract than production, efficiency, or satisfaction. It refers to management's ability to sense changes in the environment as well as within the organization itself. Ineffectiveness in achieving productivity, efficiency, and satisfaction can signal the need to adapt managerial practices and policies, or the environment may demand different outputs or provide different inputs, thus necessitating change. To the extent that the organization cannot or does not adapt, its survival is in jeopardy.

Three aspects of adaptability affect organizational effectiveness. First is the ability to respond to changes in the external environment. Systems theory stresses the importance of adaptation to external stimuli. Second is the ability to respond to changes in the internal environment. Individuals and groups within the organization must be responsive to changes in other individuals and groups within the same organization. Third, the organization must be able to adapt its planning, organizing, leading, and controlling practices and policies in response to those changes.[22]

The usual measures of adaptiveness for research purposes are provided by responses to questionnaires. But how can one really know whether the organization is effectively adaptive? Unlike the short-run measures of effectiveness, there are no specific and concrete measures of adaptiveness. The management can implement policies that encourage a sense of readiness for change; and certain managerial practices, if implemented, facilitate adaptiveness. Yet, when the time comes for an adaptive response, the organization either adapts or does not—and that is the ultimate measure.

Development

Another way organizations ensure their effectiveness over time is by investing resources in ways that enable them to meet future environmental demands. Even though such use of resources generally reduces production and efficiency in the short run, properly managed development efforts are often keys to survival. For example, an organization with a single product line has little chance of survival if a competitor makes a technological breakthrough. Consequently, most organizations willingly invest resources to expand their product line as protection against competitive disadvantages associated with a single product. From the standpoint of human resources, development efforts frequently take the form of training programs for managerial and nonmanagerial personnel.[23] Costly in the short run, these programs provide long-run payoffs by developing the capability of the organization's most important resource.

[22]Daniel R. Denison and Aneil K. Mishra, "Organizational Culture and Organizational Effectiveness: A Theory and Some Preliminary Empirical Evidence," *Academy of Management Proceedings,* 1989, p. 169.

[23]Raymond A. Katzell and Richard A. Guzzo, "Psychological Approaches to Productivity Improvement," *American Psychologist,* April 1983, pp. 468–72.

Development and adaptiveness have to do with the organization's responsiveness to environmental change. Development refers to proactive strategies that build capacity to respond to changes, should they occur. Adaptiveness, on the other hand, refers to the organization's ability to react to change in the environment. Organizations can increase their effectiveness in the long run by developing contingency plans and by selecting the correct plan when environmental changes create the need to adapt.

The time dimension enables us to evaluate effectiveness in the short, intermediate, and long run. For example, we could evaluate a particular organization as effective in terms of production, satisfaction, and efficiency criteria but ineffective in terms of adaptiveness and development. A manufacturer of buggy whips may be optimally effective in the short run but have little chance of survival. Thus, maintaining optimal balance means, in part, balancing the organization's performance over time.

The time dimension model of effectiveness enables us to understand the work of managers in organizations. They are there to identify and influence the causes of individual, group, and organizational effectiveness in the short, intermediate, and long run. Let us examine the nature of managerial work in that light.

THE NATURE OF MANAGERIAL WORK

Theories describing managerial work are many and varied.[24] The first attempts were undertaken in the early 1900s by writers of the Classical School of Management.[25] They proposed that managerial work consists of distinct yet interrelated *functions* that constitute the *managerial process*. The view that management should be defined, described, and analyzed in terms of what managers do has prevailed, but whether the functions as identified by the Classical School are appropriate is a matter of continuing debate.

No doubt, management can be defined as a *process,* that is, as a series of actions, activities, or operations that lead to some end. The definition of management should also include that the process is undertaken by more than one person in most organizations. This definition should be broad enough to describe management wherever it is practiced, yet specific enough to identify differences in the relative importance of the functions associated with a particular manager's job. Such a definition has not been fully developed.

---

[24]Discussions of the history of management thought can be found in Daniel A. Wren, *The Evolution of Management Thought* (New York: Ronald Press, 1972); Claude S. George, Jr., *The History of Management Thought* (Englewood Cliffs, N.J.: Prentice Hall, 1968); W. Jack Duncan, *Great Ideas in Management: Lessons from the Founders and Foundations of Management Practice* (San Francisco: Jossey-Bass, 1988).

[25]The term *Classical School of Management* refers to the ideas developed by a group of practitioners who wrote of their experiences in management. Notable contributions to these ideas include Frederick W. Taylor, *Principles of Management* (New York: Harper & Row, 1911); Henri Fayol, *General and Industrial Management,* trans. J. A. Conbrough (Geneva: International Management Institute, 1929); James D. Mooney, *The Principles of Organization* (New York: Harper & Row, 1947); James D. Mooney, *The Elements of Administration* (New York: Harper & Row, 1944).

FIGURE 2–5

Management's Contribution
to Effectiveness

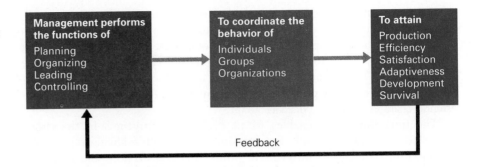

Other concepts of management emphasize the roles that managers play in organizations. Henry Mintzberg's influential study of the roles of top management identified three primary managerial roles: (1) interpersonal, (2) decisional, and (3) informational.[26] Each of these roles has several related activities that distinguish it from the others. But interpersonal role activities clearly involve the manager with other people both inside and outside the organization. Decisional role activities involve the manager in making decisions about operational matters, resource allocation, and negotiations with the organization's constituencies. The informational role involves the manager as a receiver and sender of information from and to a variety of individuals and institutions.

The concept of management developed here is based on the assumption that the necessity for managing arises whenever work is specialized and undertaken by two or more persons. Under such circumstances, the work must be *coordinated,* which creates the necessity for managerial work. The nature of managerial work, then, is to coordinate the work of *individuals, groups,* and *organizations* by performing four management functions: *planning, organizing, leading,* and *controlling.* The contribution of management to effectiveness is depicted in Figure 2–5.

Expanding the list to include other functions is certainly possible, but these four can be defined with sufficient precision to differentiate them and, at the same time, to include all others that management writers have proposed. All managers at all levels of the organization perform these functions. The relative importance of one function vis-à-vis another depends on where the manager is in the organization and the problems and issues to be faced. But the ability to discern the relative importance of each may very well distinguish excellent from so-so managers.[27]

Planning Effective Performance

The planning function includes defining the ends to be achieved and determining *appropriate means to achieve the defined ends.* The purposive (i.e., end-seeking) nature of organizations necessitates this function. Planning

[26]Henry Mintzberg, *The Nature of Managerial Work* (Englewood Cliffs, N.J.: Prentice Hall, 1980).

[27]Allen I. Kraut, Patricia R. Pedigo, D. Douglas McKenna, and Marvin D. Dunnette, "The Role of the Manager: What's Really Important in Different Management Jobs," *Academy of Management Executive,* November 1989, pp. 286–93.

activities can be complex or simple, implicit or explicit, impersonal or personal. For example, a sales manager forecasting the demand for the firm's major product may rely on complex econometric models or on casual conversations with sales representatives in the field. The intended outcomes of planning activities are the organization members' mutual understandings about what they should be attempting to achieve. These understandings may be reflected in complicated plans specifying the intended results or in a general agreement among the members.

Discussions of the planning function are often confused by the absence of definitions of such terms as *mission, goal,* and *objective.* Managers and authors will use the terms differently, depending on their backgrounds and purposes. In some instances, the terms, particularly *goal* and *objective,* are interchangeable. In other instances, the terms are specifically defined, but there is no general agreement as to these definitions. However, the pivotal position of planning as a management function requires us to make the meanings of these key concepts very explicit.

Mission. Society expects organizations to serve specific purposes. These purposes are the missions of organizations. Effective managers will state the mission of their organization in terms of those conditions that, if realized, will ensure the organization's survival. Therefore, missions are criteria for assessing the long-run effectiveness of an organization.

Statements of mission are to be found in laws, articles of incorporation, and other extraorganizational sources. Mission statements are broad, abstract, and value laden and, as such, are subject to various interpretations. For example, the mission of a state public health department as expressed in the law that created it mandates the agency to "protect and promote the health and welfare of the citizens of the Commonwealth." From its mission, the organization will create its specific programs.

Statements of organizational missions can be powerful motivators. Managers are rediscovering the power of ideas and ideals as ways to mobilize the commitment of individuals and groups to accomplish high levels of performance. Studies of charismatic leadership have established the importance of mission statements as key elements of effective management.[28]

Goals. Future states or conditions that contribute to the fulfillment of the mission are goals. More concrete and specific than a mission, goals express relatively intermediate criteria of effectiveness. But they can also be stated in terms of production, efficiency, and satisfaction. For example, one goal of a public health agency could be stated as "the eradication of tuberculosis as a health hazard by the end of 1995." In a business setting, a goal might be "to have viable sales outlets established in every major population center of the country by the end of 1992."

It is entirely possible for an organization to have multiple goals contributing to its mission. For example, a hospital may pursue patient care, research, and

---

[28]Jay A. Conger, Rabindra N. Kanungo, and associates, *Charismatic Leadership: The Elusive Factor in Organizational Effectiveness* (San Francisco: Jossey-Bass, 1988).

training. Universities typically state three significant goals: teaching, research, and community service. The existence of multiple goals places great pressure on managers to coordinate not only the routine operations of the units striving for these goals but also to plan and allocate scarce resources to the goals.

Objectives. Derived from goals and relatively specific and measurable, objectives are short run. The public health agency's objective can be stated as "to reduce the incidence of tuberculosis from 6 per 10,000 to 4 per 10,000 by the end of the current year." The firm seeking to have sales outlets in all major population centers could state its current year's objective as "to open and begin operations in Chicago, Los Angeles, Louisville, and New York." Thus, just as goals are derived from the organization's mission, so are objectives derived from the goals.

Thus, mission statements reflect managements' attempts to state the long-term criteria for assessing organizational performance. Goals derive from the organization's mission and provide criteria for assessing organizational performance in the intermediate (one- to five-year) period. And each goal can be the basis for specific objectives that are the bases for determining the effectiveness of the organization in the short run.

Planning involves specifying not only where the organization is going but how it intends to get there. The development of a coherent set of mission, goals, and objectives defines the scope and direction of the organization's activities. In fact, the development of a set of activities (or means) follows from the prior determination of ends. Alternatives must be analyzed and evaluated in terms of criteria that follow from the mission, goals, and objectives. Thus, managers by their own decisions can affect how they and their organizations will be evaluated. They decide what ends are legitimate and, therefore, what criteria are relevant.[29] Then, having determined the appropriate means, they must undertake the next managerial function: organizing.

Organizing Effective Performance

The organizing function includes all managerial activities required to translate planned activities into a structure of tasks and authority. In a practical sense, the organizing function involves five specific activities.

1. *Defining the nature and content of each job in the organization.* This activity has tangible results: job specifications, position descriptions, or task definitions. These documents indicate what is expected of persons holding the job in the way of responsibilities, outcomes, and objectives. In turn, the skills, abilities, and training required to meet the defined expectations are also specified.

2. *Determining the bases for grouping the jobs together.* The essence of defining jobs is specialization, that is, dividing the work. But once the overall task has been subdivided into jobs, those jobs must be combined into groups, or departments. The managerial decision involves the selection of appropriate bases for grouping. For example, all jobs requiring similar machinery may be

---

[29]Quinn, *Beyond Rational Management.*

grouped together, or the manager may decide to group jobs according to the product or service they produce.

3. *Delegating authority to the assigned manager.* The preceding activities create groups of jobs with defined tasks. It then becomes necessary to determine to what extent managers of the groups should be able to make decisions and use the resources of the group without higher approval. This right is termed *authority*.

4. *Deciding the size of the group.* Jobs are grouped to facilitate supervision of the activities. Obviously, there is a limit on the number of jobs that one person can supervise; but the precise number varies, depending on the situation. For example, it is possible to supervise a greater number of similar, simple jobs than of dissimilar, complex jobs. The appropriate *span of control* is also affected by other factors, such as the competence of the supervisor, the routineness of the group's overall task, the extent of geographic dispersion, and the availability of standardized procedures.

5. *Devising integrative methods and procedures.* An organization's structure comprises many different parts doing different things. These differences must be integrated into a coordinated whole, and it is management's responsibility to devise integrating methods and processes. If the differences among jobs and departments are not too great, then the simple exercise of authority is sufficient to integrate the differences. For example, the manager of a small yogurt shop can easily integrate the work of the order takers by issuing directives. But the manager of a multiproduct, multidivisional organization will have to rely on more complex cross-functional teams, product and customer service managers, and electronic communications.[30]

Once the structure of tasks and authority is in place, it must be given life. Management must recruit and select appropriate individuals to perform the jobs. The process of finding and placing people in jobs is termed *staffing*. In some large organizations, specialized units (e.g., personnel departments) perform staffing activities. Individual effectiveness requires a good fit between job requirements and individual abilities. Thus, even when staffing is done in a specialized unit, the activity remains an important management responsibility.

The interrelationships between planning and organizing are apparent. The planning function determines organizational ends and means; that is, it defines the "whats" and "hows." The organizing function decides the "whos": who will do what with whom to achieve the desired end results. The structure of tasks and authority should facilitate the fulfillment of planned results if the next management function, leading, is performed properly.

Leading Effective Performance

The leading function involves the manager in close, day-to-day contact with individuals and groups. Thus, this function is uniquely personal and interpersonal. Even though planning and organizing provide guidelines and directives in the form of plans, job descriptions, organization charts, and policies, people

---

[30]Henry Mintzberg, "Organization Design: Fashion or Fit?" *Harvard Business Review,* January–February 1981, pp. 103–16.

do the work. And people vary. Because they have unique needs, ambitions, personalities, and attitudes, they perceive the workplace and their jobs differently. Managers must take these unique perceptions and behaviors into account, and somehow direct them toward common purposes. One thoughtful and sensitive observer of leadership behavior has encouraged managers to become even more knowledgeable about human psychology as a means to more effective performance.[31]

Leading places the manager squarely in the arena of individual and group behavior, where functioning requires knowledge of individual differences and motivation, group behavior, power, and politics. In short, the leading function requires knowledge of ways to influence individuals and groups to accept and pursue organizational objectives, often at the expense of personal objectives.

Leading involves the day-to-day interactions between managers and their subordinates. The full panorama of human behavior is evident: Individuals work, play, communicate, compete, accept and reject others, join groups, leave groups, receive rewards, and cope with stress. Of all the management functions, leading is the most human oriented. Therefore, it is not surprising that the overwhelming bulk of organizational behavior theory and research relates to this function. And while much of the literature and conventional wisdom affirms the importance of leadership, some evidence suggests that the importance of leadership is overrated.[32]

Leaders in executive positions represent the organization to its external constituencies, using words and symbols to express the abstract ideals of the organization and what it stands for. The organization's mission statement provides a starting point for performing this leadership role; but without the ability to use powerful language and metaphors, the executive leader—even one with effective interpersonal skills—will fail.[33]

Controlling Effective Performance

The controlling function includes activities managers undertake to ensure that actual outcomes are consistent with planned outcomes. The exercise of control requires three basic conditions.

1. *Standards.* Norms of acceptable outcomes, or *standards,* must be articulated. These standards, which reflect goals and objectives, are found in accounting, production, marketing, financial, and budgeting documents. In more specific ways, they are reflected in procedures, performance criteria, rules of conduct, professional ethics, and work rules. Standards, therefore, reflect desirable levels of achievement defined by criteria of effectiveness.

2. *Information.* Actual and planned outcomes must be compared, using appropriate and reliable information. Many organizations have developed

[31]Harry Levinson, "You Won't Recognize Me: Predictions about Changes in Top-Management Characteristics," *Academy of Management Executive,* May 1988, pp. 119–25.

[32]Alan B. Thomas, "Does Leadership Make a Difference to Organizational Performance?" *Administrative Science Quarterly,* September 1988, pp. 388–400.

[33]James M. Kouzes and Barry Z. Posner, *The Leadership Challenge: How to Get Extraordinary Things Done in Organizations* (San Francisco: Jossey-Bass, 1988); Perry Pascarella and Mark A. Frohman, *The Purpose-Driven Organization: Unleashing the Power of Direction and Commitment* (San Francisco: Jossey-Bass, 1989).

sophisticated information systems that provide managers with control data. Prime examples are the standard cost accounting and quality control systems that modern manufacturing firms use extensively. In other instances, the sources of information may consist only of supervisors' observations of the behavior of people assigned to their departments.

3. *Corrective action.* If actual outcomes are ineffective, managers must take corrective action. Without the ability to take corrective action, the controlling function has no point or purpose: it becomes an exercise without substance. Corrective action is possible if, during the organizing function, managers have been assigned the authority to take action. Simply stated, managers undertake control to determine *whether* intended results are achieved and if not, *why* not. Based on their controlling activities, they conclude that the planning function is faulty or that the organizing function is faulty, or both. Corrective action, then, is the completion of a logical controlling sequence. The activities that make up controlling include employee selection and placement, materials inspection, performance evaluation, financial statement analysis, and other well-recognized managerial techniques.

The concept of management as the four functions of planning, organizing, leading, and controlling is certainly not complete. Nothing in this conceptualization indicates the specific behaviors or activities associated with each function, nor is there any recognition of the relative importance of these functions for overall organizational effectiveness. However, these four functions conveniently and adequately define management.

Management functions require the application of technical and administrative skills. They also require the application of human relations skills, the ability to deal with and relate to *people.* The literature of organizational behavior stresses the importance of people, and many observers and practitioners of management believe that managing people effectively is the key to improving production and efficiency in contemporary corporations.

Managerial Work and the Behavior, Structure, and Processes of Organizations

The concept of managerial work developed in the preceding pages can now be brought into perspective and summarized in Figure 2–6. The focus of this text is the *behavior of individuals and groups in organizations.* The purpose of managers is to achieve coordinated behavior so that an organization is judged effective by those who evaluate its record. Those who evaluate organizations can be concerned with any number of specific or general criteria and with either output, process, or input measures.[34] To achieve coordinated behavior and to satisfy evaluators, managers engage in activities intended to *plan, organize, lead,* and *control* behavior. Because task and authority relationships are major determinants of individual and group behavior,[35] managers must design organizational *structures* and *processes* to facilitate communication among employees.

---

[34]Frank Hoy and Don Hellriegel, "The Kilmann and Herden Model of Organizational Effectiveness for Small Business Managers," *Academy of Management Journal,* June 1982, pp. 308–22.

[35]Gregory H. Gaertner and S. Ramnarayan, "Organizational Effectiveness: An Alternate Perspective," *Academy of Management Review,* January 1983, pp. 97–107.

FIGURE 2–6

Relationships among the
Management Functions and
Individual, Group, and
Organizational Effectiveness

Management Functions	Sources of Effectiveness		
	Individuals	Groups	Organizations
Planning	Objectives	Goals	Missions
Organizing	Job designs Delegated authority	Department bases Department size	Integrative methods and processes
Leading	Person-centered influence	Group-centered influence	Entity-centered influence
Controlling	Individual standards of performance	Group standards of performance	Organization standards of performance

Thus, the relationships between management, organizations, and effectiveness seem straightforward: effective individual, group, and organizational performance should be the result of effective planning, organizing, leading, and controlling. The Close-Up describes one CEO's efforts to make management simple by reducing it to a "checklist." But management is not that simple. Management writers, such as Peters and Waterman[36] (whose ideas are the subject of this chapter's Organizational Issue for Debate), have brought the importance of organizational culture to our attention. We next discuss briefly some of the implications of organizational culture for organizational effectiveness.

ORGANIZATIONAL CULTURE

Organizations possess what is referred to as a culture. When referring to an organizational culture, we mean something similar to the culture in a society. An organization's culture consists of shared values, beliefs, assumptions, perceptions, norms, artifacts, and patterns of behavior. According to culture experts, culture is to the organization what personality is to the individual—a hidden, yet unifying theme that provides meaning, direction, and mobilization.[37]

Second, organizational culture is a way of looking at and thinking about behavior of and in organizations, a perspective to take for understanding what is occurring. In this manner, organizational culture refers to a collection of themes that attempt to explain and predict how organizations and people in them behave in different circumstances.[38]

---

[36]Thomas J. Peters and Robert H. Waterman, Jr., *In Search of Excellence* (New York: Harper & Row, 1982).

[37]Ralph H. Kilmann, Mary J. Saxton, and Roy Serpa and associates, *Gaining Control of the Corporate Culture* (San Francisco: Jossey-Bass, 1985), p. 1x.

[38]J. Steven Ott, *The Organizational Culture Perspective* (Monterey, Calif.: Brooks/Cole Publishing, 1989), p. 1.

BOB DANIELL'S CHECKLIST FOR MANAGING IN THE 1990s

Robert F. Daniell became CEO of United Technologies Corporation in 1986, when the company was in deep trouble. Customers were shopping elsewhere for the firm's mainline products. For example, demand for Pratt & Whitney jet engines, Otis elevators, and Carrier air conditioners was evaporating.

From that dismal beginning, United Technologies came back on track, and Daniell believes that much of the success is due to his commitment to and implementation of four principles of management:

1. *Flatten the hierarchy.* Daniell reduced the number of management levels throughout the far-flung company. For example, he reduced the management layers at Pratt & Whitney from eight to four.

2. *Empower the worker.* Decentralize decision making to the lowest possible level. Pratt & Whitney field representatives now make multimillion dollar decisions about warranty claims, whereas they used to have to get top management approval for such decisions.

3. *Get close to the customer.* Get out with the customers. Find out what they want. Bring them on board for product design. Pratt & Whitney lends some of its top engineers to customers for a year and pays their salaries to boot.

4. *Train, train, train.* Training is the name of the game at United Technologies. More than 5,000 senior and middle managers are getting 40 hours of classroom instruction on the new management. Customers participate in some sessions to identify problems that the managers must then analyze and propose solutions for.

Compare these four principles of management with those Peters, Waterman, and Austin propose. What are the underlying currents and themes? How do these principles enable managers to achieve high levels of individual, group, and organizational performance? Which concepts and models of effectiveness underlie them? And where do the management functions fit in?

Source: "Where 1990's-Style Management Is Already Hard at Work," *Business Week*, October 23, 1989, pp. 92–93, 96, 98.

Organizational culture, in simple terms, is considered to be the "personality" or "feel" of the organization.[39] Culture influences the way people act within organizations: How they perform, view their job, work with colleagues, and look at the future are largely determined by cultural norms, values, and beliefs. These ingredients constitute the culture. The culture at Chrysler, for example, has been influenced by market conditions, competition, Lee Iacocca's personality, and the union's demands. The culture at Walt Disney Corporation was influenced by the ideas, feelings, and creativity of the founder, Walt Disney.

Despite being an important concept, organizational culture as a perspective from which to observe and understand behavior within organizations has its limitations. First, it is not the only way to view organizations. We have already

[39]Ibid.

discussed the goal and systems view without so much as mentioning culture. Second, as with so many concepts, organizational culture is not defined the same way by any two popular theorists or researchers. Some of the definitions of culture follow:

— Symbols, language, ideologies, rituals, and myths.[40]
— Organizational scripts derived from the personal scripts of the organization's founder(s) or dominant leader(s).
— Is a product; is historical; is based on symbols; and is an abstraction from behavior and the products of behavior.[41]
— "A pattern of basic assumptions invented, discovered, or developed by a group as it learns to cope with its problems of external adaptation and internal integration—that has worked well enough to be considered valid and therefore to be taught to new members as the correct way to perceive, think, and feel in relation to those problems."[42]

These definitions suggest that organizational culture consists of a number of elements, such as assumptions, beliefs, values, rituals, myths, scripts, and languages. These elements have been captured in the work of Edgar Schein, who contends that culture involves three layers. Layer I includes artifacts and creations which are visible but often not interpretable. An annual report, a newsletter, wall dividers between workers, and furnishings are examples of artifacts and creations. At layer II are values, or the ideas that are important to people. Values are conscious, affective desires or wants. In layer III are the basic assumptions people make that guide their behavior. Included in this layer are assumptions that tell individuals how to perceive, think about, and feel about work, performance goals, human relationships, and the performance of colleagues. Figure 2–7 presents the Schein three-layer model of organizational culture.

Negative cultures are counterproductive to management efforts to bring about performance improvements. Consider what can happen in the banking industry. Although exceptions exist, the cultures of contemporary banks on the whole emphasize values and beliefs that discourage the behavior required to compete in the recently deregulated banking industry. Bank cultures that value conservative, status quo behavior are incompatible with the need to be aggressive and competitive in the marketplace. Some banks have attempted major overhauls in their corporate cultures in an effort to make them more dynamic. First Chicago and Bank of America are among the major banks that have exerted considerable efforts to redirect their cultures.[43]

The realization that organizational culture is an important cause of organizational effectiveness is widespread in management practice.[44] Not so widespread, however, is understanding of how management can change an organizational culture that inhibits organizational effectiveness. Many man-

[40]A. M. Pettegrew, "On Studying Cultures," *Administrative Science Quarterly,* 1979, pp. 579–81.

[41]D. Jongeward, *Everybody Wins: Transactional Analysis Applied to Organizations* (Reading, Mass.: Addison-Wesley Publishing, 1973).

[42]Edgar H. Schein, *Organizational Culture and Leadership* (San Francisco: Jossey-Bass, 1985), p. 9.

[43]Bro Uttal, "The Corporate Culture Vultures," *Fortune,* October 17, 1983, p. 71.

[44]See "Corporate Culture: The Hard-to-Change Values that Spell Success or Failure," *Business Week,* October 27, 1980, pp. 148–60.

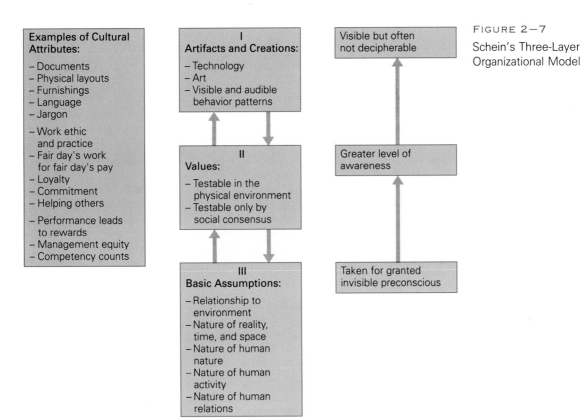

Examples of Cultural Attributes:

– Documents
– Physical layouts
– Furnishings
– Language
– Jargon

– Work ethic and practice
– Fair day's work for fair day's pay
– Loyalty
– Commitment
– Helping others

– Performance leads to rewards
– Management equity
– Competency counts

**I
Artifacts and Creations:**

– Technology
– Art
– Visible and audible behavior patterns

**II
Values:**

– Testable in the physical environment
– Testable only by social consensus

**III
Basic Assumptions:**

– Relationship to environment
– Nature of reality, time, and space
– Nature of human nature
– Nature of human activity
– Nature of human relations

Visible but often not decipherable

Greater level of awareness

Taken for granted invisible preconscious

FIGURE 2—7

Schein's Three-Layer Organizational Model

Source: E. H. Schein, "Does Japanese Management Style Have a Message for American Managers?" *Sloan Management Review,* Fall 1981, p. 64.

agement practitioners and consultants in the field are experimenting with alternative change approaches.[45] Much more will be learned as managers move into the 1990s. At this point, however, we can suggest some tentative guidelines for changing culture.[46]

First, you must understand that organizational culture—the system of shared values, beliefs, and norms—is the product of the interaction among the selection process; the managerial functions; the organization's behavior, structure, and process; the larger environment in which the organization exists; and the removal process shown in Figure 2–8. Organizational culture encompasses both the managerial functions and organizational characteristics. Management is both a cause of and a part of organizational characteristics. The existing culture of any organization reflects past and present managerial planning, organizing, leading, and controlling activities. For example, a manufacturing plant culture that values operations efficiency (quality of output, efficient use of resources) does so because manufacturing managers have stated missions, goals, and objectives in those terms. These managers evaluate employees in terms of accuracy—for example, minimum number of quality errors—and

---

[45]Uttal, "The Corporate Culture Vultures."

[46]Vijay Sathe, "Some Action Implications of Corporate Culture: Manager's Guide to Action," *Organizational Dynamics,* August 1983, pp. 4–23.

FIGURE 2—8

Organizational Culture and Effectiveness

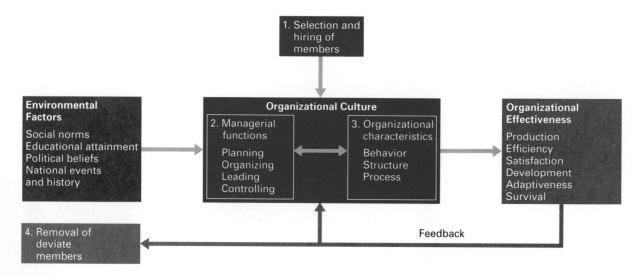

they publicly proclaim the importance of doing things right. Manufacturing executives have created the culture by virtue of their own managerial actions, and they hire and socialize employees to adopt and accept the important beliefs and values of that culture.

Employees who are not well matched with or suited to the organizational culture will exit, voluntarily or involuntarily. Deviants are often isolated or ostracized; they are cut off from communications, are not involved in rituals, and may be simply ignored. In some cases, deviants may be asked to leave or to resign. The deviant can be identified by examining effectiveness measures.

At each of the four points identified in Figure 2–8 (1, 2, 3, or 4), management can intervene to alter the organizational culture. While it is correct to state that organizational culture is difficult to change, an understanding of where to begin the cultural change process appears to be important for managing organizational behavior. Studies comparing the performance of American firms with that of European, Japanese, and other Asian competitors have introduced concepts of culture and changing culture as possible explanations of differences in competitive effectiveness. This line of study suggests that discussing organizational behavior without including culture as a specific organizational variable is incomplete analysis.[47]

If management can create organizational culture, management should be able to use the same means to change it. But it is not that simple or easy a task. Cultures are self-reinforcing. Once in place, cultures provide stability and certainty for their members. Individuals know what is expected, what is important, and what to do. They quite naturally resist any threatened

---

[47]R. Lucas, "Political-Cultural Analysis of Organizations," *Academy of Management Review,* 1987, pp. 144–56; William G. Ouchi and Allan L. Wilkins, "Organizational Culture," *Annual Review of Sociology,* 1985, pp. 457–83.

SPEED SAVES JOBS

John Young, Hewlett-Packard's (H-P) CEO, is pushing the idea that "speed" is what is needed to compete, to respond to changes, and to earn reasonable profits. Young believes that international competitors have turned new technologies into new products and processes more rapidly than H-P. Consequently, they've reaped the benefits of taking technology to the market and earning more market share. In an attempt to make speed a part of H-P's culture, Young introduced a program called BET, for break-even time. He challenged employees to cut by half the interval between having a new idea or product on the drawing board and marketing it profitably. Young is hoping that BET will instill in managers a desire to be fast moving, aggressive, and unafraid of speed.

Honda is also building speed into its culture. Shorchero Irumagiri, a managing director at Honda, emphasizes the need to find speedy answers to problems. Finding solutions now is what results in profits, growth, and jobs tomorrow. Sitting by while problems mount up is not competitive in the highly competitive automobile market.

Domino's Pizza put speed into the culture of making and delivering pizzas. Customers receive a $3 discount on any pizza that takes longer than 30 minutes from the time of ordering to arrive at their home. Domino's pizza makers watch films of fast pizza makers. Making and delivery of a hot pizza is built on speed. Domino's is now the second-largest pizza chain after Pizza Hut. It is closing fast on the size leader. Competitive advantage in many businesses in the future will have to think about H-P, Honda, and Domino's drive to introduce speed into the organizational culture. Failure to grasp the importance of speed will mean many lost jobs, bankruptcies, and lost customers.

Source: Brian Dumaine, "How Managers Can Succeed through Speed," *Fortune*, February 13, 1989, pp. 54–59.

disruption of the existing culture. An interesting notion of introducing speed into the culture of a firm is presented in the Close-Up "Speed Saves Jobs."

Managers must practice planning, organizing, leading, and controlling that are consistent with the beliefs and values of the desired culture. All four functions can contribute to changing the culture, but it is generally agreed that leading is the most important. By personal example and behavior, managers can demonstrate how things should be done. But they must be capable managers and respected leaders.

The intended effect of organizational structure and process is to predetermine what people will do, with whom they will do it, what decisions they will make, what information they will receive, and when, how, and how often they will perform certain actions and make certain decisions. Managers interact with other managers and with nonmanagers in individual and group settings to establish plans, policies, procedures, rules, job descriptions, reporting channels, and lines of authority and communication. All of these actions and interactions create an organizational culture that will have a significant impact, both positive and negative, on individual, group, and organizational effectiveness.

SUMMARY OF KEY POINTS

— The concepts of effectiveness and management have been developed in this chapter. Based on organizational behavior theory and research, these concepts underlie the practice of management, which is the focus of this book.

— An overriding consideration documented in many studies of managerial work is that the managerial process is inherently a human process—people relating to people. Recognition of this fact establishes the importance of understanding human behavior in the workplace. The behavior of individuals and groups is principally important for achieving effective organizational performance, but the behavior of managers themselves also needs to be understood.

— Managerial techniques are all directed toward improving effectiveness. To understand their impact, it is necessary to develop an understanding of the concept of effectiveness. Although the term is widely used, its meaning is not widely understood.

— Two competing concepts of effectiveness derive from two competing theories of organizations. According to goal theory, organizations are rational, purposive entities that pursue specific missions, goals, and objectives. Accordingly, how well they function (i.e, how effective they are) is seen in terms of how successful they are in achieving their purposes. Systems theory assumes organizations are social entities that exist as parts of larger environments and, in order to survive, function to satisfy the demands of that environment.

— The multiple-constituency perspective on organizational effectiveness recognizes that organizations exist to satisfy the demands of many different individuals and institutions (constituencies), each with expectations the organization must satisfy through its performance.

— The time dimension model of effectiveness integrates goal, systems, and multiple-constituency perspectives, stressing the effects of the organization moving through time. As the organization does so, it needs short- and intermediate-run indicators of its progress toward long-run survival. These indicators are the criteria of effectiveness and are applicable in the evaluation of individual, group, and organizational effectiveness.

— The nature of managerial work derives from the necessity to coordinate work in organizations. By their nature, organizations exploit the benefits of specialization, which by its nature requires coordination. Managers coordinate specialized work through the application of planning, organizing, leading, and controlling functions. These functions require that managers determine and influence the causes of individual, group, and organizational effectiveness.

— Management work focuses on the behavior of individuals and groups and the process and structure of organizations. The considerable interdependence of behavior, process, and structure complicates the efforts of management.

— Organizational culture refers to the personality or the feel of an organization.

— How a person performs on the job is determined by cultural norms, values, and beliefs.

DISCUSSION AND REVIEW QUESTIONS

1. Assess the relative importance of management to the performance of an organization that you know something about. For example, interview the professors in the college you attend and ask them whether they think chairpersons, deans, and presidents make a significant difference in the performance of the college, including individual professors and academic departments.

2. How would you respond to the statement that the primary and perhaps only reason for the existence of a business firm is to make a profit for the owners of the firm?

3. In your judgment, which are the most effective organizations in contemporary American society? Why are they the most effective, and what evidence do you have to support that opinion?

4. Can the effectiveness of an organization ever be evaluated in absolute terms? Or must effectiveness criteria always be stated in relative terms? Explain and give examples to support your argument.

5. Is the distinction between short-run, intermediate, and long-run criteria meaningful for evaluating the effectiveness of a college course? Explain.

6. What contribution does the "multiple-constituency" concept make to our understanding of organizational effectiveness? In particular, does the concept make it easier or harder for a manager to know when he or she has accomplished effective performance for the group or organization? Explain.

7. If you were a training director responsible for instructing first-line supervisors in the techniques of supervision, how would you evaluate the effectiveness of your training program? Is the goal model of effectiveness useful? Is the systems model useful?

8. "Effectiveness criteria are relevant only in terms of the evaluator. For example, the state legislators look for some things, the federal people look for other things. I give each group whatever it wants." Comment on this statement, which was made by the administrator of a state governmental agency.

9. How would you evaluate the effectiveness of contemporary American society in terms of production, efficiency, satisfaction, adaptiveness, and development? Rate each criterion on a five-point scale and compare your evaluation with that of other classmates.

10. What are the cultural components that exist in a firm such as McDonald's?

ADDITIONAL REFERENCES

Angle, H. L., and J. L. Perry. "An Empirical Assessment of Organizational Commitment and Organizational Effectiveness." *Administrative Science Quarterly,* 1981, pp. 1–14.

Bluedorn, A. C. "Cutting the Gordian Knot: A Critique of the Effectiveness Tradition in Organizational Research." *Sociology and Social Research,* 1980, pp. 477–96.

Bryant, J. "Assessing Company Strength Using Added Value to Gauge Effectiveness of Corporate Strategies." *Long Range Planning,* 1989, pp. 34–44.

Cameron, K. S. "Effectiveness as Paradox: Consensus and Conflict in Conceptions of Organizational Effectiveness." *Management Science,* 1986, pp. 539–53.

Cameron, K. S., and D. A. Whetton, eds. *Organizational Effectiveness: A Comparison of Multiple Models.* New York: Academic Press, 1983.

David, F. R. "How Companies Define Their Mission." *Long Range Planning,* 1989, pp. 90–97.

Frost, P. J.; L. F. Moore; M. R. Louis; C. C. Lundberg; and J. Martin. *Organizational Culture.* Beverly Hills, Calif.: Sage Publications, 1985.

Mangham, I. *Power and Performance in Organizations.* New York: Basil Blackwell, 1988.

Mendelow, A. L. "Setting Corporate Goals and Measuring Organizational Effectiveness: A Practical Approach." *Long Range Planning,* 1983, pp. 70–76.

Meyer, M. W., and L. G. Zucker. *Permanently Failing Organizations.* Newbury Park, Calif.: Sage Publications, 1989.

Price, J. L. "The Study of Organizational Effectiveness." *Sociological Quarterly,* 1972, pp. 3–15.

Quinn, R. E., and J. Rohrbaugh. "A Spatial Model of Effectiveness Criteria." *Management Science,* 1983, pp. 363–77.

Robinson, R. B., Jr. "Measures of Small Firm Effectiveness for Strategic Planning Research." *Journal of Small Business Management,* 1983, pp. 22–29.

Salancik, G. R. "A Single Value Function for Evaluating Organizations with Multiple Constituencies." *Academy of Management Review,* 1984, pp. 617–25.

Shipper, F., and C. S. White. "Linking Organizational Effectiveness and Environmental Change." *Long Range Planning,* 1983, pp. 99–106.

Snow, C. C., and L. G. Hrebiniak. "Strategy, Distinctive Competence, and Organizational Performance." *Administrative Science Quarterly,* 1980, pp. 317–36.

Staw, B. M.; P. I. McKechnie; and S. M. Puffer. "The Justification of Organizational Performance." *Administrative Science Quarterly,* 1983, pp. 582–600.

Stupack, R. J. "Back to the Future: Organizational Effectiveness." *Bureaucrat,* 1988, pp. 30–32.

Webb, R. J. "Organizational Effectiveness and the Voluntary Organization." *Academy of Management Journal,* 1974, pp. 663–77.

Wiener, Y. "Forms of Value Systems: A Focus on Organizational Effectiveness and Cultural Change and Maintenance." *Academy of Management Review,* 1988, pp. 534–45.

Yuchtman, E., and S. E. Seashore. "A Systems Resource Approach to Organizational Effectiveness." *American Sociological Review,* 1967, pp. 891–903.

BEHAVIOR WITHIN ORGANIZATIONS
The Individual

3

Individual Behavior
and Differences

LEARNING OBJECTIVES

*After completing Chapter 3,
you should be able to:*

DEFINE
perception and explain its
role in understanding
and coping with
organizational life.

DESCRIBE
how personality can influence an individual's behavior
within an organization.

DISCUSS
why it is important for managers to work hard at matching people with jobs.

COMPARE
the meanings of ability
and skill.

IDENTIFY
why it is very difficult to
change a person's attitude.

AN ORGANIZATIONAL
ISSUE FOR DEBATE   INDIVIDUAL-PERSONALITY THEORIES

ARGUMENT FOR

One group of personality theorists proposes that personalities contain individual differences that are not just transient but enduring—consistent over time and across situations. Thus, a person who respected and obeyed his or her father would probably continue to do so in any situation and would probably display the same attitude toward other fatherlike figures. That is, the person would submit to the wishes or orders of authority figures.

For example, individual-personality theorists would explain the behavior of employees named Jim, Mary, and Paul in terms of early childhood development, general patterns of thinking and behaving, or development of self-actualization. Jim's needs, patterns of behavior, and self-development made him a unique individual. Jim's uniqueness, like Mary's or Paul's is important for a manager to recognize. By understanding the role of individual differences in shaping behavior, a manager is able to explain an employee's behavior as well as help the individual match his or her unique strengths to a work situation.

Theorists and researchers use the term *individual differences* to refer to three related assumptions: (1) individuals differ from one another in significant ways; (2) any particular individual's difference from others holds true in many situations; and (3) individuals maintain their characteristic differences over a considerable period of time.

Although managers may be unable to administer and interpret a personality test to measure individual differences, they need to look closely at behavior patterns, similarities and differences, and behavioral consistency over time. Managers' observations and understanding of individual differences permit them to work effectively with employees. Ignoring the existence of individual differences tends to encourage the practice of "robot management" (managing every subordinate in the same manner).

ARGUMENT AGAINST

The individual-personality theories are assumed to be too narrow. Researchers have stated that, after years of research, little has been produced by those advocating an individual-difference explanation of behavior. World-famous behaviorist B. F. Skinner's approach to explaining behavior differs significantly from other social psychology approaches, but they share a common set of assumptions that are contrary to the individual-difference assumptions. The more recently developed social personality theories assume that (1) the major influences on human behavior come from the environment and (2) situational rather than individual differences should therefore be the primary focus of attention.

Skinner and others believe that the individual is open to his or her environment and significantly influenced by it. The major vocabulary used in these theories include such terms as *stimulus, interaction, reinforcement,* and *imitation;* only some of the environmental or social personality theorists describe the individual as having drives, cognitions, and needs. The theories of Skinner and others are often referred to as "social theories of personality" because of the importance these theories attach to social interactions in an individual's environment.

According to Skinner's view, it makes no sense to talk about the needs, drives, and attitudes of Jim, Mary, and Paul. The causes of their behavior lie outside them, in the environment. Thus, individual differences are a moot point or issue. External rewards and punishments shape the way Jim, Mary, and Paul behave on the job.

Some claim that, with an emphasis on the environment and situational differences instead of on individual differences, reinforcement theory and social learning theory can answer the question of why people behave as they do. The person is interacting with the "real world," not operating in isolation in some kind of "vacuum tube" insulated from events, other people, and situations.

Any attempt to learn why people behave as they do in organizations requires some understanding of individual differences. Managers spend considerable time making judgments about the fit between individuals, job tasks, and effectiveness. Both the manager's and the subordinate's characteristics typically influence such judgments. Without some understanding of behavior, decisions about who performs what tasks in a particular manner can lead to irreversible long-run problems.

Each employee is different in many respects. A manager needs to ask how such differences influence the behavior and performance of subordinates. This chapter highlights some of the individual differences and dispositions that can make one person a significantly better performer than another person. The chapter also pays close attention to several of the more crucial individual differences that managers should consider.

Rather than taking sides on the opposing contentions in the opening Organizational Issue for Debate—that, on the one hand, individual differences need to be studied and understood and, on the other hand, the environment is the key to understanding behavior—we feel that both viewpoints have merit. In this chapter, we help answer the question "Why do individual differences exist?" We also talk about how the environment affects individual differences. It is incorrect to assume that individual differences have no connection at all with the environment—work, family, community, and society. They are inextricably intertwined.

THE BASIS FOR UNDERSTANDING BEHAVIOR

The manager's observation and analysis of individual behavior and performance require consideration of three sets of variables that directly influence individual behavior, or what an employee does (e.g., produces output, sells automobiles, services machines). The three sets of variables are classified as individual, psychological, and organizational. Within each set are a number of subsets. For example, the individual variables include abilities and skills, background, and demographic variables. Figure 3–1 illustrates that an employee's behavior is complex because it is affected by diverse environmental variables and many different individual factors, experiences, and events. Such individual variables as abilities/skills, perceptions, personality, and experiences affect behavior.

FIGURE 3–1

Individual-Behavior Framework

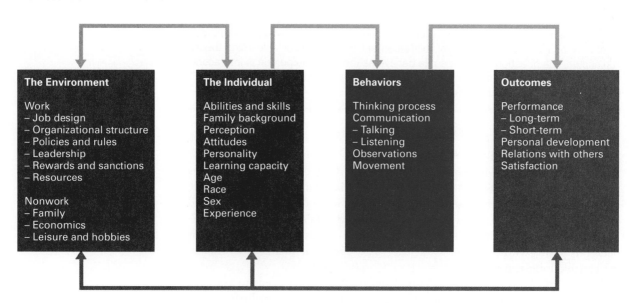

The Environment	The Individual	Behaviors	Outcomes
Work – Job design – Organizational structure – Policies and rules – Leadership – Rewards and sanctions – Resources Nonwork – Family – Economics – Leisure and hobbies	Abilities and skills Family background Perception Attitudes Personality Learning capacity Age Race Sex Experience	Thinking process Communication – Talking – Listening Observations Movement	Performance – Long-term – Short-term Personal development Relations with others Satisfaction

Whether any manager can modify, mold, or reconstruct behaviors is a much-debated issue among behavioral scientists and managerial practitioners. Although they usually agree that changing any individual psychological factor requires thorough diagnosis, skill, patience, and understanding on the part of a manager, there is no universally agreed-upon method managers can use to change personalities, attitudes, perceptions, or learning patterns. (The behavior patterns of people are always changing, albeit slightly.) Any manager would certainly like to bring about behavior changes that result in improved performance.

Managers today are faced with sweeping demographic changes in the workplace. There are more unskilled workers, women, and black, Hispanic, and Asian applicants and employees. In the 1990s, there will also be fewer people in the human resource pool, which means that more attention must be paid to improving the performance of the available people.[1]

Because many workers may lack needed skills, managers will probably have to devote more time to educating, training, and creating a positive motivational atmosphere for employees. Managers are going to have to determine how to make work better, more rewarding and challenging. Unless they can accomplish this agenda, the outcomes associated with work—such as quality, quantity, and service—will suffer.

Employees' behaviors lead to outcomes. They can result in positive long-term performance and personal growth or the opposite, poor long-term performance and a lack of growth. As Figure 3–1 also illustrates, behaviors and outcomes serve as feedback to the person and the environment.

---

[1]Liz Roman Gallese, "Wooing the New Worker," *Business Month,* July 1989, pp. 48–53.

Human behavior is too complex to be explained by one sweeping generalization. Only a sampling of the relevant variables that influence human behavior is presented in Figure 3–1. Since coverage of each of the variables presented in this figure is beyond the scope of this book, most of our attention is given to three major psychological variables: perception, attitudes, and personality. These three form the foundation for our discussion of motivation, group behavior, and leadership. Learning and motivation variables are discussed in Chapters 4 and 5, and a presentation of the organizational variables is found in other chapters of the book.

Figure 3–1 suggests that effective management requires that individual behavior differences be recognized and, when feasible, taken into consideration while managing organizational behavior. To understand **individual differences,** managers must (1) observe and recognize the differences, (2) study variables that influence individual behavior, and (3) discover relationships among the variables. For example, managers are in a better position to make optimal decisions if they know the attitudes, perceptions, and mental abilities of employees, as well as how these and other variables are related. It is also important to know how each variable influences performance. Being able to observe differences, understand relationships, and predict linkages facilitates managerial attempts to improve performance.

Behavior, as outlined in Figure 3–1, is anything that a person does. *Talking* to a manager, *listening* to a co-worker, *filing* a report, *typing* a memo, and *placing* a completed unit in inventory are behaviors. So are *daydreaming, reading* this book, and *learning* how to use a firm's accounting system. The general framework indicates that behavior depends on the types of variables shown in Figure 3–1. Thus, it can be stated that B = f(I, E): an employee's behavior (B) is a function of individual (I), and environmental (E) variables. The behavior that results on the job is unique to each individual, but the underlying process is basic to all people.

After years of theory building and research, it is generally agreed that:

1. Behavior is caused.
2. Behavior is goal directed.
3. Behavior that can be observed is measurable.
4. Behavior that is not directly observable (for example, thinking and perceiving) is also important in accomplishing goals.
5. Behavior is motivated.

To emphasize these points of agreement, consider the case of Jim (mentioned in the Organizational Issue for Debate), who usually has been an average performer but who recently became a high performer. A manager's analysis (which may be totally incorrect) of this behavior change might be as follows: Jim recently increased his efforts to perform. He has shown more interest in his work and has expressed interest in a vacancy in another department. This suggests that the improved performance occurred because Jim became motivated to work harder to gain a possible promotion.

Another explanation of Jim's behavior change might be that personnel cutbacks have him worried. He doesn't want to lose his job, and the fear of job loss motivates him to do more work.

INDIVIDUAL DIFFERENCES
Study of individual differences in individuals' attitudes, perceptions, and abilities. Because individuals are unique as well as similar, such study helps managers explain differences in performance levels.

BEHAVIOR
Anything a person does, such as talking, walking, thinking, or daydreaming.

The desired result of any employee's behavior is effective performance. In organizations, therefore, individual and environmental variables affect not only behavior but also performance. An important part of a manager's job is to define performance in advance—that is, to state what results are desired. Performance-related behaviors are directly associated with job tasks that need to be accomplished to achieve a job's objectives. For a manager, performance-related behavior would include such actions as identifying performance problems; planning, organizing, and controlling the work of employees; and creating a motivational climate for subordinates.[2]

Focusing their attention on performance-related behaviors, managers search for ways to achieve optimal performance. If employees are not performing well or consistently, managers must investigate the problem. These six questions can help managers focus on performance problems:

1. Does the employee have the skills and abilities to perform the job?
2. Does the employee have the necessary resources to perform the job?
3. Is the employee aware of the performance problem?
4. When did the performance problem surface?
5. What is the reaction of the employee's co-workers to the performance problem?
6. What can I do as a manager to alleviate the performance problem?

These questions and their answers again call attention to the complexity of individual behavior and performance differences. They also indicate that when performance problems are identified, some form of managerial action is required.

INDIVIDUAL VARIABLES

The individual variables presented in Figure 3–1 may be classified as abilities and skills, background, and demographic. Each of these classes of variables helps explain individual differences in behavior and performance. However, only abilities and skills are discussed in this chapter. Background and demographic variables are discussed throughout the book.

Abilities and Skills

Some employees, although highly motivated, simply do not have the abilities or skills to perform well. Abilities and skills play a major role in individual behavior and performance. An **ability** is a trait (innate or learned) that permits a person to do something mental or physical. **Skills** are task-related competencies, such as the skill to operate a lathe or a computer. In this book, the terms are used interchangeably in most cases. Remember that B = f(I, E). Table 3–1 identifies a set of 10 mental abilities that make up what is commonly referred to as intelligence.[3] Managers must decide which mental abilities are

ABILITY

Trait, biological or learned, that permits person to do something mental or physical.

SKILLS

Task-related competencies.

[2]Robert Albanese and David D. Van Fleet, *Organizational Behavior: A Managerial Viewpoint* (Hinsdale, Ill.: Dryden Press, 1983), p. 52.

[3]Marvin D. Dunnette, "Aptitudes, Abilities, Skills," in *Handbook of Industrial and Organizational Psychology,* ed. Marvin D. Dunnette (Skokie, Ill.: Rand McNally, 1976), pp. 481–82.

TABLE 3–1

Mental Abilities =
Intelligence

Mental Ability	Description
1. Flexibility and speed of closure	The ability to "hold in mind" a particular visual configuration.
2. Fluency	The ability to produce words, ideas, and verbal expressions.
3. Inductive reasoning	The ability to form and test hypotheses directed at finding relationships.
4. Associative memory	The ability to remember bits of unrelated material and to recall.
5. Span memory	The ability to recall perfectly for immediate reproduction a series of items after only one presentation of the series.
6. Number facility	The ability to rapidly manipulate numbers in arithmetic operations.
7. Perceptual speed	Speed in finding figures, making comparisons, and carrying out simple tasks involving visual perceptions.
8. Deductive reasoning	The ability to reason from stated premises to their necessary conclusion.
9. Spatial orientation and visualization	The ability to perceive spatial patterns and to manipulate or transform the image of spatial patterns.
10. Verbal comprehension	Knowledge of words and their meaning as well as the application of this knowledge.

Source: Adapted from Marvin D. Dunnette, "Aptitudes, Abilities, and Skills," in *Handbook of Industrial and Organizational Psychology*, ed. Marvin D. Dunnette (Skokie, Ill.: Rand McNally, 1976), pp. 481–83.

required to successfully perform each job. For example, a language interpreter who is helping a manager put together a business deal with a Soviet enterprise would especially need to have language fluency, ability, number facility, and verbal comprehension. These abilities would have to exist in both English and Russian. The astute manager would search for the interpreter who had these abilities.

A secretary's job may especially require span memory, perceptual speed, and verbal comprehension as well as various physical skills (see Table 3–2) to operate word-processing equipment. Managers attempt to match each person's abilities and skills with the job requirements. The matching process is important because no amount of leadership, motivation, or organizational resources can make up for deficiencies in abilities or skills. **Job analysis,** used to take some of the guesswork out of matching, is the process of defining and studying a job in terms of tasks or behaviors and specifying the responsibilities, education, and training needed to perform the job successfully.[4]

Every job is made up of two things: people and job tasks. Matching people with jobs suited for their abilities and skills is often a problem.[5] Why do people

JOB ANALYSIS

Process of defining and studying a job in terms of behavior and specifying education and training needed to perform the job.

---

[4]For a complete discussion of job analysis, see John M. Ivancevich and William F. Glueck, *Foundations of Personnel/Human Resource Management*, 3rd ed. (Plano, Tex.: Business Publications, 1989), pp. 140–64.

[5]C. Thomas Dortch, "Job-Person Match," *Personnel*, June 1989, pp. 48–57.

TABLE 3–2
Sample of Physical Skills

Physical Skill	Description
1. Dynamic strength	Muscular endurance in exerting force continuously or repeatedly.
2. Extent flexibility	The ability to flex or stretch trunk and back muscles.
3. Gross body coordination	The ability to coordinate the action of several parts of the body while the body is in motion.
4. Gross body equilibrium	The ability to maintain balance with nonvisual cues.
5. Stamina	The capacity to sustain maximum effort requiring cardiovascular exertion.

Source: Adapted from Edwin A. Fleishman, "On the Relation between Abilities, Learning, and Human Performance," *American Psychologist*, November 1972, pp. 1017–32.

end up in jobs in which they are not productive, satisfied, or fulfilled? The effort to match jobs involves the following activities: employee selection, training and development, career planning, and counseling. To be successful in matching a person's abilities and skills to the content of the job, a manager must examine content, required behaviors, and preferred behaviors. Content is the "what" of the job—the job description, responsibilities, goals and objectives, and specific tasks. Required behaviors are the "how" of the job—how it must be done in terms of quantity, quality, cost, and timing.

Preferred behaviors are often ignored in matching people and jobs. In order to be selected, some applicants do not honestly explain their preferences. Because they want the job so badly, they hold back, keep silent, or even mislead interviewers. Managers must attempt to determine a person's preference in terms of goals, style, career values, and achievement motives. An "ideal job" is one in which a person's skills and abilities can be applied to produce work that is satisfactory, fulfilling, and challenging. This is the goal of matching a person with the job.

INDIVIDUAL PSYCHOLOGICAL VARIABLES

Unraveling the complexity of psychological variables such as perception, attitudes, and personality is an immense task. Even psychologists have a difficult time agreeing on the meaning and importance of these variables, so our goal is to provide meaningful information about them that managers can use in solving on-the-job behavior and performance problems. The manager must continually observe individuals because what goes on inside a person can be easily hidden.

Perception

PERCEPTION
Process by which individual gives meaning to the environment. It involves organizing and interpreting various stimuli into a psychological experience.

Perception, as depicted in Figure 3–2, is the cognitive process by which an individual gives meaning to the environment. Perception is the process individuals use to select, organize, store, and interpret stimuli into a meaningful and coherent picture of the world. Because each person gives his or her

FIGURE 3—2

The Perceptual Process

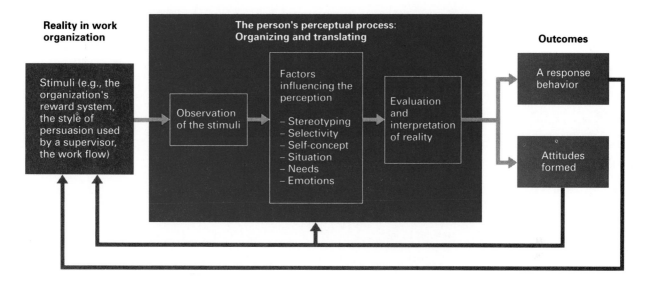

own meaning to stimuli, different individuals "see" the same thing in different ways.[6] The way an employee sees a situation often has much greater meaning for understanding behavior than does the situation itself. Stated more thoroughly:

> The cognitive map of the individual is not, then, a photographic representation of the physical world: it is, rather, a partial, personal construction in which certain objects, selected out by the individual for a major role, are perceived in an individual manner. Every perceiver is to some degree a nonrepresentational artist, as it were, painting a picture of the world that expresses his or her individual view of reality.[7]

Because perception involves acquiring specific knowledge about objects or events at any particular moment, it occurs whenever stimuli activate the senses. Because perception involves cognition (knowledge), it includes the interpretation of objects, symbols, and people in the light of pertinent experiences. In other words, perception involves receiving stimuli, organizing them, and translating or interpreting the organized stimuli to influence behavior and form attitudes.

Each person selects various cues that influence his or her perceptions of people, objects, and symbols. Because of these factors and their potential imbalance, people often misperceive another person, group, or object. To a considerable extent, people interpret the behavior of others in the context of the setting in which they find themselves.

---

[6]Walter R. Nord, ed., *Concepts and Controversy in Organizational Behavior* (Santa Monica, Calif.: Goodyear Publishing, 1976), p. 22.

[7]David Krech, Richard S. Crutchfield, and E. L. Ballachey, *Individual and Society* (New York: McGraw-Hill, 1962), p. 20.

FIGURE 3—3

Perceptual Differences and Behavior

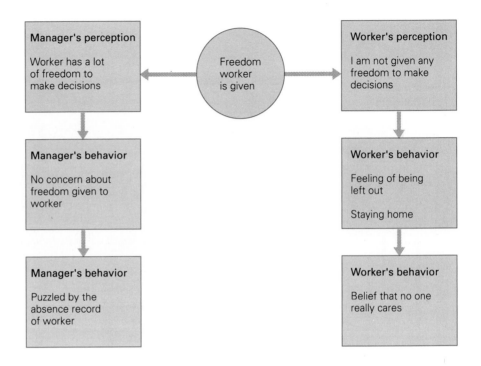

The following organizational examples point out how perception influences behavior:

1. A manager believes that an employee is given opportunities to use his judgment about how to do the job, while the employee feels that he has absolutely no freedom to make judgments.

2. A subordinate's response to a supervisor's request is based on what she thought she heard the supervisor say, not on what was actually requested.

3. The manager considers the product sold to be of high quality, but the customer making a complaint feels that it is poorly made.

4. An employee is viewed by one colleague as a hard worker who gives good effort and by another colleague as a poor worker who expends no effort.

5. The salesperson regards her pay increase as totally inequitable, while the sales manager considers it a very fair raise.

6. One line operator views the working conditions as miserable; a co-worker right across the line regards the working conditions as pleasant.

These are a few of numerous daily examples of how perceptions can differ. Managers must recognize that perceptual differences exist. Figure 3–3 illustrates how perception works. Suppose the worker in this example has been told that he has the freedom to make decisions about how the job is to be designed. Note that the manager and the employee perceive the job design freedom in different ways; they have different perceptions of the employee's amount of freedom.

Type of Recognition	Supervisors' Perceptions of Frequency	Subordinates' Perceptions of Frequency
Privileges	52%	14%
More responsibility	48	10
A pat on the back	82	13
Sincere and thorough praise	80	14
Training for better jobs	64	9
More interesting work	51	5

TABLE 3—3

The Perceptual Gap between Supervisors and Subordinates

Source: Adapted from Rensis Likert, *New Patterns in Management* (New York: McGraw-Hill, 1961), p. 91.

Rensis Likert's research clearly showed that managers and subordinates often have different perceptions. He examined the perceptions of superiors and subordinates to determine the amounts and types of recognition that subordinates received for good performance. Both supervisors and subordinates were asked how often superiors provided rewards for good work. The results, presented in Table 3–3, show significant differences in what the two groups perceived. Each group viewed the type of recognition being given at a different level. In most cases, the subordinates reported that very little recognition was provided by their supervisors and that rewards were infrequent. The supervisors saw themselves as giving a wide variety of rewards for good performance. Likert's study illustrates how marked differences may exist between superiors' and subordinates' perceptions of the same events.

Perceptual organization. Organization is an important aspect of perception.[8] One of the most elemental organizing principles of perception is the tendency to pattern stimuli in terms of *figure-ground* relationships. Not all stimuli reach one's awareness with equal clarity. The factor focused on is called the *figure.* That which is experienced and is out of focus is called the *ground.* (Figure 3–4 shows how, in certain situations, the figure-ground relationship is ambiguous. Do you see faces or a wine glass?) As you read this text, your perceptions are organized in terms of figure and ground. In every perceptual act, the figure-ground principle is operating.[9] For example, a figure-ground workplace situation would be a union organizer who stands out more than other workers. As the union pushes to organize the work force, the organizer stands out more and more to management.

The organizing nature of perception is also apparent when similar stimuli are grouped together and when stimuli in close proximity are grouped. Another grouping principle that shapes perceptual organization is called *closure,* which is the tendency to want to close something with missing parts. Some individuals have a strong need to complete a configuration, a job, or a project. This has significance in the workplace because, for example, prevent-

---

[8]Michael W. Levine and Jeremy M. Shefner, *Fundamentals of Sensation and Perception* (Reading, Mass.: Addison-Wesley Publishing, 1981), p. 17.

[9]B. Von Haller Gilmer, *Applied Psychology* (New York: McGraw-Hill, 1975), p. 229.

FIGURE 3—4

Figure-Ground Relationship

FIGURE 3—5

Perceptual Closure

ing a person with a high need for closure from finishing a job or task could lead to frustration or a more drastic behavior, such as quitting. Figure 3–5 is an example of closure. Do you feel the need to complete the drawing of the tiger?

Stereotyping.   The manner in which managers categorize others often reflects a perceptual bias. The term **stereotype** has been used to describe judgments made about people on the basis of their ethnic group membership. Other stereotypes also need to be guarded against. For example, most Americans stereotype used-car salespeople, men stereotype women executives, managers stereotype union stewards, and female workers stereotype male managers. Most people engage in stereotyping.

STEREOTYPE

Set of beliefs that one has about a group of other individuals.

Age has been the basis for stereotyping employees. Researchers have found that managerial actions against older workers are influenced by stereotyping.[10] For example, suppose that a new job opening involves travel, long hours, and attending a lot of meetings. The company might decide that the job requires someone with a lot of energy and good health. A manager with a negative bias against older candidates, assuming that older workers lack energy and are usually not in good health, does not even consider them. Thus, a perceptual bias excludes from consideration any worker past whatever age the manager considers as being old. Stereotyping can result in improper programs for promotion, motivation, job design, or performance evaluation. It can also

---

[10]Benson Rosen and Thomas H. Jerdee, "The Influence of Age Stereotypes on Managerial Decisions," *Journal of Applied Psychology,* August 1976, pp. 428–32.

result in not selecting the best person for a position. The organization suffers from stereotyping that results in the rejection of talented people.

Selective perception.   The concept of selective perception is important to managers, who often receive large amounts of information and data and may tend to select information that supports their viewpoints. People ignore information or cues that might make them feel discomfort. For example, a skilled manager may be concerned primarily with an employee's final results or output. Since the employee is often cynical and negative when interacting with the manager, other managers may assume that the employee will receive a poor performance rating. However, this manager weeds out the negative features or cues and rates the subordinate on the basis of results. This is a form of selective perception.

The manager's characteristics.   People frequently use themselves as benchmarks in perceiving others. Research indicates that (1) knowing oneself makes it easier to see others accurately,[11] (2) one's own characteristics affect the characteristics identified in others,[12] and (3) persons who accept themselves are more likely to see favorable aspects of other people.[13] Basically, these conclusions suggest that managers perceiving the behavior and individual differences of employees are influenced by their own traits. If they understand that their own traits and values influence perception, they can probably perform a more accurate evaluation of their subordinates. A manager who is a perfectionist tends to look for perfection in subordinates, just as a manager who is quick in responding to technical requirements looks for this ability in subordinates.

Situational factors.   The press of time, the attitudes of the people a manager is working with, and other situational factors all influence perceptual accuracy. If a manager is pressed for time and has to fill an order immediately, his or her perceptions are influenced by time constraints. The press of time literally forces the manager to overlook some details, rush certain activities, and ignore certain stimuli, such as requests from other managers or from superiors.

Needs.   Perceptions are significantly influenced by needs and desires. In other words, the employee, the manager, the vice president, and the director see what they want to see. Like the mirrors in the fun house at the amusement park, needs and desires can distort the world the manager sees.
   The influence of needs in shaping perceptions has been studied in laboratory settings. Subjects in various stages of hunger were asked to report what they saw in ambiguous drawings flashed before them. Researchers found that as

---

[11]R. D. Norman, "The Interrelationships among Acceptance-Rejection, Self-Other Identity, Insight into Self, and Realistic Perception of Others," *Journal of Social Psychology,* May 1953, pp. 205–35.
[12]J. Bossom and Abraham H. Maslow, "Security of Judges as a Factor in Impressions of Warmth in Others," *Journal of Abnormal and Social Psychology,* July 1957, pp. 147–48.
[13]K. T. Omivake, "The Relation between Acceptance of Self and Acceptance of Others Shown by Three Personality Inventories," *Journal of Consulting Psychology,* December 1954, pp. 443–46.

hunger increased, up to a certain point, the subjects saw more and more of the ambiguous drawings as articles of food. Hungry subjects saw steaks, salads, and sandwiches, while subjects who had recently eaten saw nonfood images in the same drawings.[14]

Emotions.   A person's emotional state has a lot to do with perception. A strong emotion, such as total distaste for an organizational policy, can make a person perceive negative characteristics in most company policies and rules. Determining a person's emotional state is difficult. Because strong emotions often distort perceptions, managers need to discern which issues or practices trigger strong emotions within subordinates.

Attitudes

ATTITUDES
Mental states of readiness for need arousal.

Attitudes are determinants of behavior because they are linked with perception, personality, and motivation. An **attitude** is a positive or negative feeling or mental state of readiness, learned and organized through experience, that exerts specific influence on a person's response to people, objects, and situations. Each of us has attitudes on numerous topics—about unions, exercise, dieting, career goals, friends, and government tax laws, for example. This definition of attitude has certain implications for managers. First, attitudes are learned. Second, attitudes define one's predispositions toward given aspects of the world. Third, attitudes provide the emotional basis of one's interpersonal relations and identification with others. And fourth, attitudes are organized and are close to the core of personality. Some attitudes are persistent and enduring; yet, like each of the psychological variables, attitudes are subject to change.[15]

Attitudes are intrinsic parts of a person's personality. Several theories attempt to account for the formation and change of attitudes. One such theory proposes that people "seek a congruence between their beliefs and feelings toward objects" and suggests that the modification of attitudes depends on changing either the feelings or the beliefs.[16] The theory further assumes that people have structured attitudes composed of various affective and cognitive components. The interrelatedness of these components means that a change in one precipitates a change in the others. When these components are inconsistent or exceed the person's tolerance level, instability results. Instability can be corrected by (1) disavowal of a message designed to influence attitudes, (2) "fragmentation" of the attitudes, or (3) acceptance of the inconsistency so that a new attitude is formed. The theory proposes that affect, cognition, and behavior determine attitudes and that attitudes, in turn, determine affect, cognition, and behavior.

---

[14]J. Anthony Deutsch, W. G. Young, and T. J. Kalogeris, "The Stomach Signals Satiety," *Science,* April 1978, pp. 23–33.

[15]Martin Fishbein and Isek Ajzen, *Belief, Attitude, Intention, and Behavior: An Introduction to Theory and Research* (Reading, Mass.: Addison-Wesley Publishing, 1975).

[16]M. J. Rosenberg, "A Structural Theory of Attitudes," *Public Opinion Quarterly,* Summer 1960, pp. 319–40.

Affect—the emotional, or "feeling," component of an attitude—is learned from parents, teachers, and peer group members. One study illustrates how the affective component can be measured. A questionnaire was used to survey the attitudes of a group of students toward the church. The students then listened to tape recordings that either praised or disparaged the church. As the tapes played, the emotional responses of the students were measured with a galvanic skin response (GSR) device. Both prochurch and antichurch students responded with greater emotion (displayed by GSR changes) to statements that contradicted their attitudes than to those that reflected their attitudes.[17]

AFFECT
The emotional segment of an attitude.

Cognition—the cognitive component of an attitude consists of the person's perceptions, opinions, and beliefs. It refers to the thought processes, with special emphasis on rationality and logic. An important element of cognition is the evaluative beliefs held by a person. Evaluative beliefs are manifested as the favorable or unfavorable impressions someone holds toward an object or person.

COGNITION
The perception, opinion, or belief segment of an attitude.

Behavior—the behavioral component of an attitude refers to the tendency of a person to act toward someone or something in a certain way: friendly, warm, aggressive, hostile, apathetic, or any of many other ways. Such actions could be measured or assessed to examine the behavioral component of attitudes.

BEHAVIOR
The action that results from an attitude.

Figure 3–6 presents the three components of attitudes in terms of work factors such as job design, company policies, and fringe benefits. These stimuli trigger affective (emotional), cognitive (thought), and behavioral responses. In essence, the stimuli result in the formation of attitudes, which then lead to one or more responses—affective, cognitive, or behavioral.

The theory of affective, cognitive, and behavioral components as determinants of attitudes and attitude change has a significant implication for managers. They must be able to demonstrate that the positive aspects of contributing to the organization outweigh the negative aspects. Many managers achieve effectiveness by developing generally favorable attitudes in their employees toward the organization and the job.

Attitudes have many sources: family, peer groups, society, and previous job experiences. Early *family* experiences help shape the attitudes of individuals; the attitudes of young children usually correspond to those of their parents. As children reach their teen years, they begin to be more strongly influenced by *peers*. Peer groups are able to influence attitudes because individuals want to be accepted by others. Teenagers seek approval by sharing similar attitudes or by modifying attitudes to comply with those of a group.

Culture, mores, and language influence attitudes. The attitudes of French Canadians toward France, of Americans toward people in the Soviet Union, and of Cubans toward capitalism are learned in *society*. Within the United States are subcultures—ethnic communities, ghetto communities, and religious groups—that help shape the attitudes of people.

Through *job experiences,* employees develop attitudes about pay equity, performance review, managerial capabilities, job design, and work group

[17]H. W. Dickson and Elliot McGinnies, "Affectivity and Arousal of Attitudes as Measured by Galvanic Skin Responses," *American Journal of Psychology,* October 1966, pp. 584–89.

FIGURE 3—6

The Three Components of
Attitudes

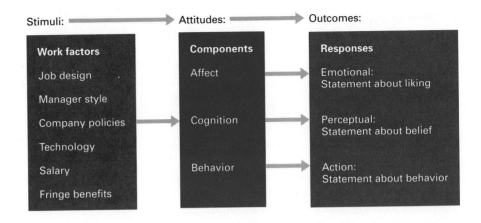

affiliation. Previous experiences can account for some of the individual differences in attitudes toward performance, loyalty, and commitment.

Individuals strive to maintain consistency among the components of attitudes. However, contradictions and inconsistency often occur, resulting in a state of disequilibrium. The tension stemming from such a state is reduced only when some form of consistency is achieved.

COGNITIVE DISSONANCE
Mental state of anxiety that occurs when there is conflict among individual's various cognitions (e.g., attitudes and beliefs) after decision has been made.

The term **cognitive dissonance** describes a situation where there is a discrepancy between the cognitive and behavioral components of an attitude.[18] Any form of inconsistency is uncomfortable; therefore, individuals attempt to reduce dissonance. *Dissonance,* then, is viewed as a state within a person that, when aroused, elicits actions designed to return the person to a state of equilibrium. For example, the chief executive officer (CEO) of a cigarette company may experience cognitive dissonance if he believes that he is honest and hardworking but that cigarettes contribute to lung cancer. He may think, "I am a good human being, but I am in charge of a firm producing a cancer-contributing product." These thoughts create inconsistency. Instead of quitting and giving up his successful career, he is more likely to modify his thoughts or cognitions. He could state, "Our firm has manufactured a cigarette that is now very safe and free of cancer-producing products." Or he may think that cigarette smoking actually improves the mental well-being of smokers, that it helps them reduce or cope with stress. When inconsistency in attitudes arises, the person can attempt to work the problem out cognitively or behaviorally. The CEO in the example used a cognitive process to reduce his dissonance.

Cognitive dissonance has important organizational implications. First, it helps explain the choices made by an individual with attitude inconsistency. Second, it can help predict a person's propensity to change attitudes. If individuals are required, for example, by the design of their jobs or occupations to say or do things that contradict their personal attitudes, they may change those attitudes to make them more compatible with what they have said or done.

---

[18]Leon Festinger, *A Theory of Cognitive Dissonance* (Evanston, Ill.: Row, Peterson, 1957).

Changing attitudes. Managers are often faced with the task of changing employees' attitudes because existing attitudes hinder job performance. Although many variables affect attitude change, they can all be described in terms of three general factors: trust in the sender, the message itself, and the situation.[19] Employees who do not trust the manager will not accept the manager's message or change an attitude. Similarly, if the message is not convincing, there is no pressure to change.

The greater the prestige of the communicator, the greater the attitude change.[20] A recent example of how the communicator's prestige influences attitude is Mikhail Gorbachev's achievements with his *glasnost* and *perestroika* programs. He has convinced many people that the Soviet Union should no longer be referred to as the "evil empire." Gorbachev's style, message, and charisma have produced significant changes in many people's attitude toward the Soviet Union.[21] A manager who has little prestige and is not shown respect by peers and superiors is in a difficult position if the job requires changing the attitudes of subordinates so that they work more effectively. Thus, managers need to be aware of their prestige rating among employees. If they have prestige, they should use it to change attitudes. If they do not have prestige, attitude change may be virtually impossible.

Liking the communicator produces attitude change because people try to identify with a liked communicator and tend to adopt attitudes and behaviors of the liked person.[22] Not all managers, however, are fortunate enough to be liked by each of their subordinates. Therefore, liking the manager is a condition for trusting the manager.

Even if a manager is trusted, presents a convincing message, and is liked, the problems of changing people's attitudes are not solved. The strength of the employee's commitment to an attitude is important. A worker who has decided not to accept a promotion is committed to the belief that it is better to remain in his or her present position than to accept the promotion. Attitudes that have been expressed publicly are more difficult to change because the person has shown commitment, and changing is admitting a mistake.

How much people are affected by attempts to change their attitude depends in part on the situation. While listening to or reading a persuasive message, people are sometimes distracted by other thoughts, sounds, or activities. And studies indicate that people distracted while they listen to a message show more attitude change because the distraction interferes with silent counterarguing.[23]

Distraction is just one of many situational factors that can increase persuasion. Another factor that makes people more susceptible to attempts to

---

[19]Jonathan L. Freedman, J. Merrill Carlsmith, and David O. Sears, *Social Psychology* (Englewood Cliffs, N.J.: Prentice Hall, 1974), p. 271. Also see Dennis Coon, *Introduction to Psychology* (St. Paul, Minn.: West Publishing, 1977), pp. 626–29.

[20]Ibid., p. 272.

[21]Charles R. Morris, "The Coming Global Boom," *Atlantic Monthly,* October 1989, pp. 51–64; Stanley Hoffman, "What Should We Do in the World?" *Atlantic Monthly,* October 1989, pp. 84–96.

[22]H. C. Kelman, "Process of Opinion Change," *Public Opinion Quarterly,* Spring 1961, pp. 57–78.

[23]R. A. Osterhouse and T. C. Brock, "Distraction Increases Yielding to Propaganda by Inhibiting Counterarguing," *Journal of Personality and Social Psychology,* March 1977, pp. 344–58.

change attitudes is pleasant surroundings. The pleasant surroundings may be associated with the attempt to change the attitude.

Attitudes and values.   Values are linked to attitudes in that a value serves as a way of organizing attitudes. **Values** are defined "as the constellation of likes, dislikes, viewpoints, shoulds, inner inclinations, rational and irrational judgments, prejudices, and association patterns that determine a person's view of the world."[24] Certainly, the work a person does is an important aspect of his or her world. Moreover, the importance of a value constellation is that once internalized it becomes, consciously or subconsciously, a standard or criterion for guiding one's actions. The study of values, therefore, is fundamental to the study of managing. Some evidence exists that values are also extremely important for understanding effective managerial behavior.[25]

Values affect the perceptions not only of appropriate ends but also of appropriate means to those ends. From the design and development of organizational structures and processes to the utilization of particular leadership styles and the evaluation of the performance of subordinates, value systems are persuasive. An influential theory of leadership is based on the argument that managers cannot be expected to adopt a leadership style that is contrary to their "need structures," or value orientations.[26] Moreover, when managers evaluate the performance of subordinates, the effects of the managers' values are noticeable. For example, one researcher reports that managers can be expected to evaluate subordinates with values similar to their own as more effective than subordinates with dissimilar values.[27] The impact of values is more pronounced in decisions involving little objective information and, consequently, a greater degree of subjectivity.

Another aspect of the importance of values occurs when the interpersonal activities of managers bring them into a confrontation with different, and potentially contradictory, values. Studies have shown that assembly-line workers, scientists, and persons in various professional occupations are characterized by particular, if not unique, value orientations.[28] Day-to-day activities create numerous situations in which managers must relate to others with different views of what is right or wrong. Conflicts between managers and workers, administrators and teachers, and line and staff personnel have been documented and discussed in the literature of management. The manner

---

VALUES

Guidelines and beliefs that person uses when confronted with situation in which choice must be made.

---

[24]E. Spranger, *Types of Men* (Halle, Germany: Max Niemeyer Verlag, 1928). Quoted in V. S. Flowers et al., *Managerial Values for Working* (New York: American Management Associations, 1975), p. 11.

[25]Flowers and associates undertook a questionnaire study of members of the American Management Associations. Questionnaires were mailed to 4,998 members, and the researchers were able to use 1,707 replies. Based on these results and other studies, the authors state that the impact of values on managerial and nonmanagerial behavior is sufficiently important to account for some variation in the relative effectiveness of managers.

[26]Fred E. Fiedler, *A Theory of Leadership Effectiveness* (New York: McGraw-Hill, 1967).

[27]J. Senger, "Managers' Perceptions of Subordinates' Competence as a Function of Personal Value Orientations," *Academy of Management Journal,* December 1971, pp. 415–24.

[28]For example, see Flowers et al., *Managerial Values;* Renato Tagiuri, "Value Orientations and Relationships of Managers and Scientists," *Administrative Science Quarterly,* June 1965, pp. 39–51.

in which these conflicts are resolved is particularly crucial to the effectiveness of the organization.[29]

IBM is often mentioned as a values model firm.[30] This label is based on the fact that IBM managers practice management rooted in three tenets: commitment to excellence, respect for the individual, and service for the customer. At IBM, the motto is to establish priorities and then attack them in an orderly fashion.

Attitudes and job satisfaction.   **Job satisfaction** is an attitude that individuals have about their jobs. It results from their perception of their jobs, based on factors of the work environment, such as the supervisor's style, policies and procedures, work group affiliation, working conditions, and fringe benefits. While numerous dimensions have been associated with job satisfaction, five in particular have crucial characteristics:[31]

> *Pay*—the amount received and the perceived equity of pay.
>
> *Job*—the extent to which job tasks are considered interesting and provide opportunities for learning and for accepting responsibility.
>
> *Promotion opportunities*—the availability of opportunities for advancement.
>
> *Supervisor*—the abilities of the supervisor to demonstrate interest in and concern about employees.
>
> *Co-workers*—the extent to which co-workers are friendly, competent, and supportive.

In some studies, these five job satisfaction dimensions have been measured by the Job Descriptive Index (JDI). Employees are asked to respond yes, no, or ? (can't decide) as to whether a word or phrase describes their attitudes about their jobs. The JDI attempts to measure a person's satisfaction with specific facets of the job. Other measures of job satisfaction, such as the Brayfield-Rothe measures, are more general. Figure 3–7 presents sample items from four scales measuring job satisfaction.

A major reason for studying job satisfaction is to provide managers with ideas about how to improve employee attitudes. Many organizations use attitude surveys to determine levels of employee job satisfaction. National surveys have indicated that, in general, 75 to 80 percent of workers are satisfied with their jobs.[32] Of course, though they are interesting, national surveys may not reflect the degree of job satisfaction in a specific department or organization. Also, simply asking people how satisfied they are creates a problem; there

JOB SATISFACTION
Attitude that workers have about their jobs, which results from their perceptions of the jobs.

---

[29]American firms have increasingly tended to use foreign nationals to manage overseas offices. This has created a concern for understanding the impact of culture on managers' values. See W. T. Whitely and George W. England, "A Comparison of Value Systems of Managers in the U.S.A., Japan, Korea, India, and Australia," in *Proceedings of the Thirty-Fourth Annual Meeting of the Academy of Management,* 1974, p. 11; R. B. Peterson, "A Cross-Cultural Perspective of Supervisory Values," *Academy of Management Journal,* March 1972, pp. 105–17.

[30]T. L. Brown, "When Values Collide," *Industry Week,* July 21, 1986, pp. 29–32.

[31]P. C. Smith, L. M. Kendall, and Charles L. Hulin, *The Measurement of Satisfaction in Work and Retirement* (Skokie, Ill.: Rand McNally, 1969).

[32]K. E. DeBats, "The Continuing Personnel Challenge," *Personnel,* May 1982, pp. 332–44.

FIGURE 3—7

Sample Items from Four
Widely Used Job Satisfaction
Scales

Brayfield-Rothe Satisfaction Scale (General Measure)

My job is like a hobby to me.

| Strongly agree | Agree | Undecided | Disagree | Strongly disagree |

I enjoy my work more than my leisure time.

| Strongly agree | Agree | Undecided | Disagree | Strongly disagree |

Job Descriptive Index (Facet Measure)

How well does each word describe your pay? Circle Y if it does describe your pay, N if it does not describe your pay, or ? if you cannot decide.

Less than I deserve   Y   N   ?   Insecure   Y   N   ?   Highly paid   Y   N   ?

GM Faces Scale (General Measure)

Consider all aspects of your job. Circle the face which best describes your feelings about your job in general.

      7   6   5   4   3   2   1

Minnesota Satisfaction Questionnaire (Facet Measure)

On my present job, this is how I feel about...

1. Being able to keep busy all the time.

| Very dissatisfied | Dissatisfied | Neutral | Satisfied | Very satisfied |

2. The praise I get for doing a good job.

| Very dissatisfied | Dissatisfied | Neutral | Satisfied | Very satisfied |

---

is a bias toward giving a positive answer, since anything less indicates that the person is electing to stay in a dissatisfying job.

Satisfaction and job performance.   One of the most debated and controversial issues in the study of job satisfaction is its relationship to job performance. In the 1950s, many managers believed that a satisfied worker was a high-performing employee. However, most research studies find no clear link between satisfaction and performance. Some workers are satisfied with work and are poor performers. Of course, there are employees who are not satisfied but are excellent performers.

Because determining which variable is affecting the other is difficult when performance and satisfaction are positively related, three views have been advanced: (1) satisfaction causes performance; (2) performance causes satisfaction; and (3) rewards intervene, and there is no inherent relationship.[33] (Figure

---

[33]Charles N. Greene, "The Satisfaction-Performance Controversy," *Business Horizons,* October 1972, pp. 31–41.

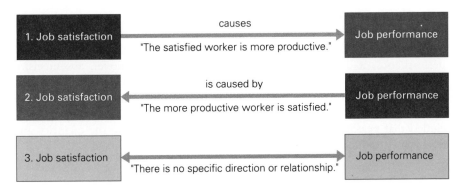

FIGURE 3—8

Satisfaction-Performance
Relationships: Three Views

3–8 shows these three viewpoints.) The first two views are supported weakly by research. A review of 20 studies dealing with performance-satisfaction relationships found a low association between performance and satisfaction.[34] Thus, evidence is rather convincing that a satisfied worker is not necessarily a high performer: managerial attempts to satisfy everyone do not yield high levels of production. Likewise, the assumption that a high-performing employee is likely to be satisfied is not supported. The third view, that factors such as rewards mediate the performance-satisfaction relationship, *is* supported by research findings. This means that performance is not a consequence of satisfaction, or vice versa.

From a practical standpoint, however, most managers would like to have satisfied and productive workers (a goal requiring a lot of effort and sound decision making on the manager's part). So managers continue to be interested in job satisfaction despite evidence that satisfaction does not determine, in any significant way, the level of performance. As suggested by some theorists and researchers, however, performance has a broader meaning than simply units or quality of production.[35] Performance also covers a variety of citizenship behaviors, including showing untrained colleagues how to complete a job, helping a fellow worker complete a job when he or she is not feeling well, making positive comments in the community about the organization, working extra hard to deliver promised goods or services, and not complaining when management does not provide resources as promised. These behaviors are more prevalent among satisfied workers.[36]

Another reason for continued management interest is that research has found a moderate correlation between satisfaction and turnover. Evidence also exists of a moderate relationship between satisfaction and absenteeism. Dysfunctional turnover and absenteeism are expensive in terms of costs, lost opportunities, and overall morale. Some evidence shows a relationship between satisfaction and union activity. Dissatisfaction stemming from perceptions of pay inequities, poor supervisor-subordinate relationships, and

[34]Victor H. Vroom, *Work and Motivation* (New York: John Wiley & Sons, 1964).

[35]Dennis W. Organ, "A Reappraisal and Reinterpretation of the Satisfaction-Causes-Performance Hypothesis," *Academy of Management Review,* January 1977, pp. 46–53.

[36]Dennis W. Organ and Mary Konovsky, "Cognitive versus Affective Determinants of Organizational Citizenship Behavior," *Journal of Applied Psychology,* February 1989, pp. 157–64.

inadequate working conditions initiate and sustain activities such as voting for union representation.[37]

Although job satisfaction does not influence quantity and quality of performance, it does influence citizenship behaviors, turnover, absenteeism, and preferences and opinions about unions. Because of these influences, managers continue to search for techniques and programs that improve employee job satisfaction. Many practicing managers have apparently concluded that performance means more than simply counting the quantity and quality of production.

Personality

PERSONALITY
Stable set of characteristics and tendencies that determine commonalities and differences in behavior of people.

The relationship between behavior and personality is perhaps one of the most complex matters that managers have to understand. **Personality** is significantly influenced by cultural and social factors. Regardless of how it is defined, however, psychologists generally accept certain principles:

1. Personality is an organized whole; otherwise, the individual would have no meaning.
2. Personality appears to be organized into patterns that are to some degree observable and measurable.
3. Although personality has a biological basis, its specific development is a product of social and cultural environments.
4. Personality has superficial aspects, such as attitudes toward being a team leader, and a deeper core, such as sentiments about authority or the Protestant work ethic.
5. Personality involves both common and unique characteristics. Every person is different from every other person in some respects, while being similar to other persons in other respects.

These five ideas are included in this definition of personality:

An individual's personality is a relatively stable set of characteristics, tendencies, and temperaments that have been significantly formed by inheritance and by social, cultural, and environmental factors. This set of variables determines the commonalities and differences in the behavior of the individual.[38]

A review of the determinants shaping personality (Figure 3–9) indicates that managers have little control over them. However, no manager should conclude that personality is an unimportant factor in workplace behavior simply because it is formed outside the organization. The behavior of an employee cannot be understood without considering the concept of personality. In fact, personality is so interrelated with perception, attitudes, learning, and motivation that any attempt to understand behavior is grossly incomplete unless personality is considered.

---

[37]Mark Fichman, "Motivational Consequences of Absence and Attendance: Proportional Hazard Estimation of a Dynamic Motivation Model," *Journal of Applied Psychology,* February 1988, pp. 119–34.

[38]This definition is based on Salvatore R. Maddi, *Personality Theories: A Comparative Analysis* (Homewood, Ill.: Dorsey Press, 1989), p. 63.

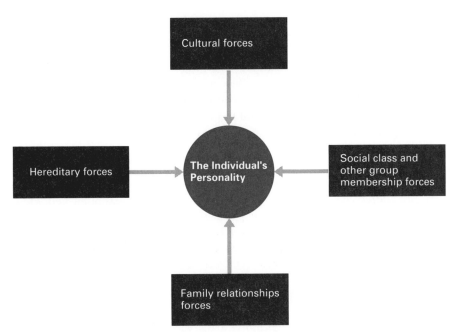

FIGURE 3—9

Some Major Forces
Influencing Personality

Theories of personality. Three theoretical approaches to understanding personality are the trait approach, the psychodynamic approach, and the humanistic approach.

Trait personality theories. Just as the young child always seems to be searching for labels by which to classify the world, adults also label and classify people by their psychological or physical characteristics. Classification helps to organize diversity and reduce the many to a few.

Gordon Allport was the most influential of the trait theorists. In his view, traits are the building blocks of personality, the guideposts for action, the source of the individual's uniqueness. Traits are inferred predispositions that direct the behavior of an individual in consistent and characteristic ways. Furthermore, traits produce consistencies in behavior because they are enduring attributes, and they are general or broad in scope.[39]

For decades, psychologist Raymond B. Cattell has studied personality traits, gathering many measures of traits through behavioral observation, records of people's life histories, questionnaires, and objective tests.[40] On the basis of his research, Cattell has concluded that 16 basic traits underlie individual differences in behavior. The research resulted in the development of Cattell's 16PF (16 personality factors) questionnaire, which measures the degree to which people have these traits. Among the traits he identified are reserved-outgoing, practical-imaginative, relaxed-tense, and humble-

TRAIT PERSONALITY
THEORIES
Based on the premise that predispositions direct the behavior of an individual in a consistent pattern.

[39]Raymond B. Cattell, *Personality and Mood by Questionnaire* (San Francisco: Jossey-Bass, 1973); Raymond B. Cattell, *The Scientific Analysis of Personality* (Chicago: Aldine Publishing, 1966).
[40]Ibid.

assertive. All 16 of Cattell's traits are bipolar; that is, each trait has two extremes (e.g., relaxed–tense).

Trait theories have been criticized as not being real theories because they do not explain how behavior is caused. The mere identification of such traits as tough-minded, conservative, expedient, reserved, or outgoing does not offer insight into the development and dynamics of personality. Furthermore, trait approaches have not been successful in predicting behavior across a spectrum of situations, due to the fact that situations (the job, the work activities) are largely ignored in trait theories.

PSYCHODYNAMIC PERSONALITY THEORIES
Freudian approach which discusses the id, superego, and ego. Special emphasis is placed on unconscious determinants of behavior.

Psychodynamic personality theories. The dynamic nature of personality was not addressed seriously until Sigmund Freud's work was published. Freud accounted for individual differences in personality by suggesting that people deal with their fundamental drives differently. To highlight these differences, he pictured a continuing battle between two parts of personality, the id and the superego, moderated by the ego.[41]

The *id* is the primitive, unconscious part of the personality, the storehouse of fundamental drives. It operates irrationally and impulsively, without considering whether what is desired is possible or morally acceptable. The *superego* is the storehouse of an individual's values, including moral attitudes shaped by society. The superego, which corresponds roughly to conscience, is often in conflict with the id: the id wants to do what feels good, while the superego insists on doing what is "right." The *ego* acts as the arbitrator of the conflict. It represents the person's picture of physical and social reality, of what leads to what and of which things are possible in the perceived world. Part of the ego's job is to choose actions that gratify id impulses without having undesirable consequences. Often, the ego has to compromise, to try and satisfy both id and superego. This sometimes involves using ego defense mechanisms—mental processes that resolve conflict among psychological states and external realities. Table 3–4 presents some of the ego defense mechanisms used by individuals.

Even Freud's critics admit that he made contributions to the modern understanding of behavior. His emphasis on unconscious determinants of behavior is important. The significance he attributed to early-life origins of adult behavior gave impetus to the study of child development. In addition, his method of treating neurosis through psychoanalysis has added to our understanding of how to get people back on the right track toward effective functioning.[42]

HUMANISTIC PERSONALITY THEORIES
Place emphasis on growth and self-actualization of people.

Humanistic personality theories. Humanistic approaches to understanding personality emphasize the growth and self-actualization of the individual and the importance of how people perceive their world and all of the forces influencing them. Carl Rogers' approach to understanding personality is

[41]Sigmund Freud, "Psychopathology of Everyday Life," in *The Complete Psychological Works of Sigmund Freud (Standard Edition)*, ed. J. Strachey (London: Hogarth Press, 1960).
[42]Philip G. Zimbardo, *Psychology and Life* (Glenview, Ill.: Scott, Foresman, 1985), p. 382.

TABLE 3—4

Some Ego Defense
Mechanisms

Mechanism	How It Is Applied in an Organization
Rationalization	Attempting to justify one's behavior as being rational and justifiable. (I had to violate company policies to get the job finished.)
Identification	Increasing feelings of worth by identifying self with person or institution of illustrious standing. (I am working for Jim, who is really the best manager in the country.)
Compensation	Covering up weakness by emphasizing desirable traits or making up for frustration in one area by overgratification in another. (I may be a harsh manager, but I play no favorites.)
Denial of reality	Protecting self from unpleasant reality by refusing to perceive it. (There is no chance that this company will have to let people go because of the economy.)

humanistic, or people centered.[43] His advice is to listen to what people say about themselves and to attend to those views and their significance in the person's experiences. Rogers believes that the most basic drive of the human organism is toward *self-actualization*—the constant striving to realize one's inherent potential.

It is difficult to criticize theories that are so people centered. Some critics complain, however, that the humanists never explain clearly the origin of the mechanism for attaining self-actualization. Other critics point out that people must operate in an environment largely ignored by the humanists; an overemphasis on self neglects the reality of having to function in a complex environment.

Each of the major theoretical approaches improves our understanding of personality. Trait theories provide a catalog that *describes* the individual. Psychodynamic theories integrate the characteristics of people and *explain* the dynamic nature of personality development. Humanist theories emphasize the *person* and the importance of self-actualization to personality. Each approach attempts to highlight the unique qualities of an individual that influence his or her behavior patterns.

Measuring personality characteristics.   **Personality tests** measure emotional, motivational, interpersonal, and attitudinal characteristics. Hundreds of such tests are available to organizations. One of the most widely used is the **Minnesota Multiphasic Personality Inventory (MMPI).** It consists of statements to which a person responds: true, false, or cannot say. MMPI items cover such areas as health, psychosomatic symptoms, neurological disorders, and social attitudes, as well as many well-known neurotic or psychotic manifestations such as phobias, delusions, and sadistic tendencies.[44]

Managers in organizations are not enthusiastic about using the MMPI. It is too psychologically oriented, is associated with "shrinks" (psychologists and

PERSONALITY TEST

Test used to measure emotional, motivational, interpersonal, and attitude characteristics that make up person's personality.

MINNESOTA MULTIPHASIC PERSONALITY INVENTORY (MMPI)

Widely used inventory for assessing personality.

---

[43]Carl Rogers, *On Personal Power: Inner Strength and Its Revolutionary Impact* (New York: Delacorte, 1977).

[44]Anne Anastasi, *Psychological Testing* (New York: Macmillan, 1976), chaps. 17–19.

THE MYERS-BRIGGS TYPE INDICATOR (MBTI) IS PREFERRED BY MANAGERS

Apple, Exxon, and General Electric, as well as Murray Manufacturing and Douglas Electronics (small firms with about 800 employees each), are using the Myers-Briggs Type Indicator (MBTI) scale to learn about personality. In the 1920s, noted Swiss psychoanalyst Carl Jung developed a cognitive style theory of personality, which the American mother-daughter team of Katherine Briggs and Isabel Briggs Myers later converted into a scale that organizations like to use. The scale is called the Myers-Briggs Type Indicator.

Jung had proposed that two dimensions, sensation and intuition, influence a person's perception. Also, two dimensions, thinking and feeling, affect individual judgment. He believed that an individual's cognitive style is determined by the pairing of a person's perception and judgment tendencies. Myers and Briggs developed a test (Samples: Which word appeals to you more, build/invent? In a large group, you more often introduce others or are introduced?) so that respondents can discover their personality or cognitive style type. The test identifies people as extroverted or introverted (E or I), sensing or intuitive (S or N), thinking or feeling (T or F), and perceiving or judging (P or J). A person's answers are divided and classified into 16 different personality types.

Four of the combinations and some typical occupations are cited on page 83.

Can the MBTI be so good that over 2 million people a year use it to diagnose personality? Jim Talman, vice president of Bayson, a small firm that sells electrical parts in the Southwest and Mexico, believes that it is. Bayson uses it to identify sales personnel who can do the best job selling in Mexico. It is one of a number of techniques the firm uses to find the best sales personnel for that job, in which language proficiency, cultural sensitivity, and openness in working with customers in

MYERS-BRIGGS TYPE INDICATOR (MBTI)

Scale that assesses personality or cognitive style. Based on scores, respondents are classified as extroverted or introverted, sensory or intuitive, thinking or feeling, and perceiving or judging. Sixteen different personality combinations are classified by interpretation of the MBTI scores.

psychiatrists), and has a reputation of being used to help people with problems. A tool managers find more comfortable is the **Myers-Briggs Type Indicator (MBTI)**, briefly described in a Close-Up.

Projective tests, also used to assess personality, have people respond to a picture, an inkblot, or a story. To encourage free responses, only brief, general instructions are given; for the same reason, the test pictures or stories are vague. The underlying reason for this is that each individual perceives and interprets the test material in a manner that displays his or her personality. That is, the individual projects his or her attitudes, needs, anxieties, and conflicts.

A *behavioral measure* of personality involves observing the person in a particular situation. For example, an individual may be given a specific work situation problem to solve. The problem-solving ability of the person is studied in terms of the steps taken, time required to reach a solution, and quality of the final decision.

Each of these measures of personality has drawbacks: Self-report tests have an accuracy problem. Projective tests require a subjective interpretation by a trained person. Behavioral measures rely on a small sample of a person's behavior.

Sensation-Thinking: Thorough, logical, practical, and application oriented.	Sensation-Feeling: Committed, responsible, conscientious.
Auditor of CPA firm, quality control supervisor, or safety engineer.	Union negotiator, social worker, drug supervisor.
Intuitive-Thinking: Creative, independent, critical.	Intuitive-Feeling: Charismatic, people oriented, and sociable.
Lawyer, systems analyst, college professor.	Politician, public relations specialist, human resource director.

Mexico are important. In addition, Bayson has found that the high-scoring sensation-feeling and extroverted salespeople have the best sales records in Mexico.

Bayson hasn't validated the MBTI, but management still believes that it helps them make better selections. Citicorp, 3M, and the U.S. Armed Forces, as well as thousands of other firms, also apparently find some value in the MBTI. Whether it is essentially sound, valid, and reliable, we really are not sure. But it seems to have appeal in the corporate community.

Source: Discussions with corporate executives in El Paso, Texas; Juarez, Mexico; Houston; and San Antonio in summer and fall 1989. See Don Hellriegal, John W. Slocum, Sr., and Richard W. Woodman, *Organizational Behavior* (St. Paul, Minn.: West, 1989); Thomas More, ''Personality Tests Are Back,'' *Fortune*, March 30, 1987, pp. 74–82. If you are interested in the MBTI content, contact Consulting Psychologists Press, Inc., Palo Alto, CA 94306.

Personality and behavior.   An issue of interest to behavioral scientists and researchers is whether the personality factors measured by such inventories as the MBTI, the MMPI, or the 16PF questionnaire or by projective tests or by behavioral measures collected in controlled settings can predict behavior or performance in organizations. Using a total inventory to examine whether personality is a factor in explaining behavior is rarely done in organizational behavior research. Typically, a few select personality factors such as locus of control, creativity, or Machiavellianism are used to examine behavior and performance.

Locus of control.   The **locus of control** of individuals determines the degree to which they believe that their behaviors influence what happens to them. Some people believe that they are autonomous—that they are masters of their own fate and bear personal responsibility for what happens to them. They see the control of their lives as coming from inside themselves. Rotter calls these people *internals*.[45] Rotter also holds that many people view

LOCUS OF CONTROL
Personality characteristic that describes people who see control of their lives coming from inside themselves as *internalizers*. People who believe their lives are controlled by external factors are *externalizers*.

---

[45]Julian B. Rotter, "Generalized Expectancies for Internal versus External Control of Reinforcement," *Psychological Monographs* 1, no. 609 (1966), p. 80.

themselves as helpless pawns of fate, controlled by outside forces over which they have little, if any, influence. Such people believe that the locus of control is external rather than internal. Rotter calls them *externals.*

Rotter devised a scale containing 29 items to identify whether people are internalizers or externalizers.[46] The statements are concerned with success, failure, misfortune, and political events. In each item, one statement reflects a belief in internal control, the other in external control. (The exercise at the end of the chapter will provide you with information on your internal-external tendencies.)

A study of 900 employees in a public utility found that internally controlled employees were more content with their jobs, more likely to be in managerial positions, and more satisfied with a participative management style than were employees who perceived themselves to be externally controlled.[47]

An interesting study of 90 entrepreneurs examined locus of control, perceived stress, coping behaviors, and performance.[48] The study was done in a business district over a three and one-half year period following flooding by Hurricane Agnes. Internalizers were found to perceive less stress than did externalizers and to employ more task-centered coping behaviors and fewer emotion-centered coping behaviors. In addition, the task-oriented coping behaviors of internalizers were associated with better performance.

Creativity. Creativity may be viewed in many ways. First, you may consider the creative person as mad. The madness of creative artists such as Van Gogh and Nijinsky is often cited as proof of this view. Research evidence, however, offers no support for it. Instead, creative people have been found to have superior ego strength and handle problems constructively. Second, you can see the creative person as being disconnected from the art of creativity. Creativity, in this view is a mystical act. Third, you can conclude that to be creative, a person must be intelligent. However, research shows that some intelligent people are creative and that others are not.[49] Finally, you can view creativity as a possibility open to every person, as an expression of personality that can be developed.[50] This view and an increasing amount of research indicate that creativity can be taught. That is, individuals can learn to be creative.[51]

Many studies have examined creativity. Life histories, personality characteristics, and tests are often scrutinized to determine a person's degree of creativity. In a typical test, subjects might be asked to examine a group of

[46]Julian B. Rotter, "External Control and Internal Control," *Psychology Today,* June 1971, p. 37.

[47]T. R. Mitchell, C. M. Smyser, and S. E. Weed, "Locus of Control: Supervision and Work Satisfaction," *Academy of Management Journal,* September 1975, pp. 623–31.

[48]Carl R. Anderson, "Locus of Control, Coping Behaviors, and Performance in a Stress Setting: A Longitudinal Study," *Journal of Applied Psychology,* August 1977, pp. 446–51.

[49]Lewis M. Terman and Melita Oden, *The Gifted Child at Midlife* (Stanford, Calif.: Stanford University Press, 1959).

[50]Stanley S. Gryskiewicz, "Restructuring for Innovation," *Issues and Observations,* November 1981, p. 1; Isaac Asimov, "Creativity Will Dominate Our Time after the Concepts of Work and Fun Have Been Blurred by Technology," *Personnel Administrator,* December 1983, p. 42.

[51]E. T. Smith, "Are You Creative?" *Business Week,* September 30, 1985, pp. 80–84.

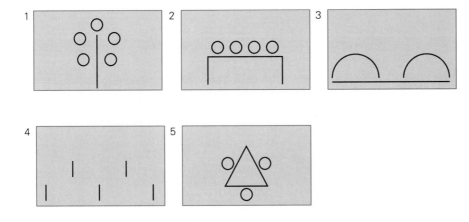

FIGURE 3—10

Testing Creativity

drawings and then answer what the drawings represent. Figure 3–10 presents a sample of a line drawing test that is used to determine the creativity of young children.[52] Novel and unusual answers are rated as being creative.

Managers who adopt either of the first two views of creativity might attempt to keep creative people out of the organization. Adoption of the third view might result in the hiring of only highly intelligent people. However, if management views creativity as a personality factor that can be developed, then it would move ahead to initiate development procedures. The Close-Up on creativity illustrates what organizations and training can do to encourage that trait. In most cases, unfortunately, creativity is not encouraged in organizations.[53]

Organizations can help develop creativity by:[54]

1. *Buffering.* Managers can look for ways to absorb the risks of creative decisions.

2. *Organizational time-outs.* Give people time off to work on a problem and allow them to think things through.

3. *Intuition.* Give half-baked ideas a chance.

4. *Innovative attitudes.* Encourage everyone to think of ways to solve problems.

5. *Innovative organizational structures.* Let employees see and interact with many managers and mentors.

Managerial interest in developing creativity seems worthwhile. A review of research findings indicates that creative individuals share important characteristics. They are self-confident and motivated to succeed, they approach life enthusiastically, and they push on even when they must overcome obstacles.[55] These characteristics are important and valuable in any organization.

---

[52]Michael A. Wallach and Nathan Kogan, *Modes of Thinking in Young Children* (New York: Holt, Rinehart & Winston, 1965).

[53]Roger Von Oech, *A Kick in the Seat of the Pants* (New York: Harper & Row, 1986).

[54]Gryskiewicz, "Restructuring," p. 3.

[55]F. H. Barron, *Creativity and Personal Freedom* (New York: Van Nostrand Reinhold, 1968); Donald W. MacKinnon, "Personality and the Realization of the Creative Potential," *American Psychologist,* March 1963, pp. 273–81.

NOODLING AND TRAINING MAY SPUR CREATIVITY

Do you know who Jack Kilby is? A second baseman for the Los Angeles Dodgers? No. A senator from Georgia? No. An astronaut in training? No. Jack Kilby, in 1957, invented the integrated circuit while working at Texas Instruments. He invented the microchip—the microchip that has allowed the computer industry to become an industry.

Jack believes creativity must be encouraged in organizations. He believes all technical people should be allowed to spend 10 percent of their time on personal ideas, off-the-wall experiments, or what can be called "noodling around." Let people just wonder and experiment. 3M is one firm that permits 15 percent of a person's time to be spent on noodling.

Another idea for encouraging creativity is to conduct training programs. Organized efforts to teach people to be more creative go back to at least 1937, when General Electric began a two-year program. However, some people feel creativity can no more be taught or instilled by training than can ambidexterity, perfect pitch, or a taste for cod-liver oil. They believe creativity is a kind of neurochemical quality that you either have at birth or never possess.

Roger Von Oech (rhymes with heck) disagrees with the "you are born with it" theory. His position is that (1) we are all born with a creativity quality, but society and its institutions regulate and socialize us into noncreative thought patterns, and (2) these patterns can be broken by the use of certain techniques, exercises, and training. Von Oech is known in the business world as a creative-thinking consultant. His corporate clients include Apple, Du Pont, IBM, ITT, Kaiser, NASA, Sears, Wells Fargo, and Xerox. His creative training seminars run about two days, involve about 15 people each, and address high-tech engineering and marketing problems. The usual

Machiavellianism.   Imagine yourself in the following situation with two other people: Thirty new $1 bills are on the table to be distributed in any way the group decides. The game is over as soon as two of you agree to how it will be divided. Obviously, the fairest distribution would be $10 each. However, a selfish party could cut out the third person, and the remaining two would each end up with $15. Suppose that one person suggests this alternative to you and that, before you can decide, the left-out person offers to give you $16, taking $14 as his or her share and cutting out the other person. What would you do?

Machiavellianism, a concept derived from the writings of Niccolo Machiavelli, an Italian philosopher and statesman (1469–1527), helps answer the question.[56] Machiavelli was concerned with the manipulation of people and with the orientations and tactics used by manipulators versus nonmanipulators.[57] The term *Machiavellianism* is associated with being a political maneuverer and power manipulator. It is a term that has a negative connotation.

MACHIAVELLIANISM
Term used to describe political maneuvers in an organization. Used to designate person as a manipulator and power abuser.

[56]Richard Christie and Florence L. Geis, eds., *Studies in Machiavellianism* (New York: Academic Press, 1970).
[57]Ibid.

seminar begins with a film, followed by a lecture and creativity exercises. Von Oech believes that people learn creative thinking, not by being talked to but by doing.

The Von Oech method of training attempts to unlock a number of attitudes that stifle creativity in organizations. The "mental locks" discussed in the seminar were first treated in his now best-selling book *A Whack on the Side of the Head*. Some of these locks are:

1. *The right answer.* This is a fallacy. Thinking there is only one correct answer halts the search for other ideas.
2. *Be practical.* In other words, stifle your imagination. This is another idea killer.
3. *To err is wrong.* Not to err is not to experiment.
4. *Play is frivolous.* This is nonsense. People with playful attitudes come up with many good ideas.
5. *Don't be foolish.* This is bad advice. If we never tried anything that might make us look ridiculous, we would still be in caves.
6. *I'm not creative.* This is the worst mental lock. Self-condemnation stifles everything.

Whether the approach is noodling or training, the emphasis is on permitting and encouraging creativity. Managers who fail to nurture and support creativity are likely to be on the short end of the competitive world.

Source: "Creative Management," *Business Month,* July 1989, p. 18; Jack Gordon and Ron Zemke, "Making Them More Creative," *Training,* May 1986, pp. 30–45.

From anecdotal descriptions of power tactics and the nature of influential people, various scales have been constructed to measure Machiavellianism. In one scale, the questions are organized around a cluster of beliefs about tactics, people, and morality. The Close-Up presents the short form of this MACH scale. (Remember, this is only a brief scale, so interpretation of scores should be done with caution.)

This particular MACH scale differentiates between high and low Machiavellians on the basis of how closely people endorse Machiavelli's rules of conduct.[58] In the money allocation game, the individuals who get the lion's share are those who score high on this scale; the LOW MACH scorers get only slightly less than would be expected by a fair, one-third split. In a job situation, HIGH MACH scorers would probably be suited for activities such as selling, negotiating, and acquiring limited resources. LOW MACH scorers would seem to be better suited for structured, routine, and nonemotional situations. Planning, conceptualizing, and working out details would probably be activities best suited for LOW MACH scorers in organizations.

---

[58]Florence L. Geis and T. H. Moon, "Machiavellianism and Deception," *Journal of Personality and Social Psychology,* October 1981, pp. 766–75.

MEASURING YOUR MACHIAVELLIAN TENDENCIES

Organizations are interested in the Machiavellian tendencies of their managers. A number of scales can provide a general idea of these tendencies. This 10-item scale will provide you with your own Machiavellianism score. Take a few minutes and answer the 10 items. Indicate your reactions by circling one number for each statement, according to the following scale:

1 = Disagree a lot.   4 = Agree a little.
2 = Disagree a little.   5 = Agree a lot.
3 = Neutral.

1. The best way to handle people is to tell them what they want to hear.	1	2	3	4	5
2. When you ask someone to do something for you, it is best to give the real reason for wanting it rather than giving reasons that might carry more weight.	1	2	3	4	5
3. Anyone who completely trusts anyone else is asking for trouble.	1	2	3	4	5
4. It is hard to get ahead without cutting corners here and there.	1	2	3	4	5
5. It is safest to assume that all people have a vicious streak and it will come out when given a chance.	1	2	3	4	5
6. One should take action only when sure it is morally right.	1	2	3	4	5
7. Most people are basically good and kind.	1	2	3	4	5
8. There is no excuse for lying to someone else.	1	2	3	4	5
9. Most people forget the death of a parent more easily than the loss of their property.	1	2	3	4	5
10. Generally speaking, individuals will not work hard unless they're forced to do so.	1	2	3	4	5

The scale is scored as follows: First, for responses to items 2, 6, 7, and 8, reverse the score so that 5 becomes 1, 4 becomes 2, and so on. Second, add up scores on all 10 items (as adjusted). This is your total MACH score. An average score on this form is about 25. If you scored much higher than this, say 38, you would be classified as a HIGH MACH. If you scored much lower than 25, you would be classified as a LOW MACH.

Remember, this test cannot provide the final answer about your Machiavellian tendencies. Accurately assessing personality is much more difficult.

Source: Richard Christie and Florence L. Geis, eds. Studies in Machiavellianism (New York: Academic Press, 1970). Reprinted by permission.

The Organizational Issue for Debate that opened this chapter presented two views about personality. The content of the chapter indicates that both views make reasonable points. First, you must understand individual differences before you worry about how the person interacts with the work environment (a point made by advocates of the individual-difference approach). Second, as shown by the framework used to review influences on behavior (Figure 3–1), environmental (organizational) variables directly influence behavior. No individual operates in a vacuum. The "real world" consists of people, environmental forces, and situational events. Thus, instead of choosing sides in the debate, it is more reasonable to consider the merits of both sides.

SUMMARY OF KEY POINTS

— Employees joining an organization must adjust to a new environment, new people, and new tasks. The manner in which people adjust to situations and other people depends largely on their psychological makeup and their personal backgrounds.

— Individual perceptual processes help people face the realities of the world. People are influenced by other people and by situations, needs, and past experiences. While a manager is perceiving employees, they are also perceiving the manager.

— Attitudes are linked with behavioral patterns in a complex manner. They are organized, and they provide the emotional basis for most of a person's interpersonal relations. Changing attitudes is extremely difficult and requires, at the very least, trust in the communicator and strength of message.

— Job satisfaction is the attitude workers have about their jobs. Research findings suggest that a satisfied worker is not necessarily a higher performer.

— Personality, developed long before a person joins an organization, is influenced by hereditary, cultural, and social determinants. To assume that personality can be modified easily can result in managerial frustration and ethical problems. Managers should try to cope with personality differences among people and not try to change personalities to fit their model of the ideal person.

— Personality variables, such as locus of control, creativity, and Machiavellianism, are associated with behavior and performance. Although difficult to measure, these variables appear to be important in explaining and predicting individual behavior.

DISCUSSION AND REVIEW QUESTIONS

1. Suppose that an employee, Joan Shirer, is opposed to the introduction of a new financial control system. Joan has worked for 15 years with the old, manual system. Now the firm is introducing a new, computer-based system. How would you go about attempting to change Joan's attitude about the new system?

2. Some people believe that perception is a more important explanation of behavior than is "reality." Why is this assumption about perception made?

3. Explain why managers who are not treated favorably by their superiors have problems in changing their subordinates' negative attitudes toward the organization?

4. Matching a person with a job suited for his or her abilities, skills, and preferences is difficult. Why must managers work at attempting to make the best match possible?

5. Provide some examples of selective perception that could be used in purchasing a new automobile and in accepting a new position with an organization.

6. Some people state that being too concerned about dealing with individual differences can cause chaos in an organization. Do you agree? Why?

7. How would you attempt to determine the job satisfaction of a group of employees?

8. Why would a manager act differently in leading a subordinate who is an internal than in leading another subordinate who is an external?

9. It is generally agreed that value systems are largely developed before people begin to work for an organization. What are the managerial implications of this fact?

10. How could a manager encourage individual creativity among subordinates? Outline a reasonable plan of action.

ADDITIONAL REFERENCES

Arable, K.; J. Child; and T. Kagono. *Innovation and Management: International Comparisons.* New York: de Gruyter, 1988.

Bernstein, A. J., and S. C. Rozen. *Dinosaur Brains: Dealing with All Those Impossible People at Work.* New York: John Wiley & Sons, 1989.

Buss, D. M., and N. Canton. *Personality Psychology.* New York: Springer-Verlag, 1989.

Carlisle, K. E. *Analyzing Jobs and Tasks.* Englewood Cliffs, N.J.: Educational Technology Publications, 1986.

Carlson, J. G. "Affirmative: In Support of Researching The Myers-Briggs Type Indicator." *Journal of Counseling and Development,* April 1989, pp. 484–86.

Farley, F. "The Big I in Personality." *Psychology Today,* 1986, pp. 44–52.

Gordon, M. T., and S. Riger. *The Female Fear.* New York: Free Press, 1989.

Henry, R., and C. L. Hulin. "Changing Validities, Ability-Performance Relations and Utilities." *Journal of Applied Psychology,* April 1989, pp. 365–67.

Hirshhorn, L. *The Workplace Within: The Psychodynamics of Organizational Life.* Cambridge, Mass.: MIT Press, 1988.

Ijiri, Y., and R. L. Kuhn, eds. *New Directions in Creative and Innovative Management: Bridging Theory and Practice.* Cambridge, Mass.: Ballinger, 1988.

Kanfer, R.; P. L. Ackerman; and R. Cudeck. *Abilities, Motivation and Methodology.* Hillsdale, N.J.: Erlbaum, 1989.

Klivington, K. *The Science of Mind.* Cambridge, Mass.: MIT Press, 1989.

Lee, A. S. "Case Studies as Natural Experiments." *Human Relations,* February 1989, pp. 117–37.

Weiss, A. *Managing in Peak Performance.* Cambridge, Mass.: Ballinger, 1989.

Wriston, W. B. "The State of American Management." *Harvard Business Review,* January–February 1990, pp. 78–83.

VIOLENCE IN THE WORKPLACE

Murder in the workplace is fortunately a rare tragedy. However, it has happened often enough in the past few years that managers (and future managers) may want to take note. The FBI estimates that 30 fatal workplace assaults took place in 1988, more than twice as many incidents as in 1982.

In the summer of 1989, two tragic incidents occurred:

September 14: Joseph Wesbacker, 47, a former employee, shot 20 people with an AK-47 assault rifle in a Louisville, Kentucky, printing plant. Eight died. He also killed himself.

August 10: John Merlin Taylor, 52, an Escondido, California, post office employee, shot his wife, then went to the Orange Glen post office and killed two co-workers and wounded a third before killing himself.

Are these personality flaws? Why do these tragedies occur? Can they be prevented? The answers are neither clear nor obvious.

Perhaps the most fatal spree in modern times was that of Pat Sherrill in Oklahoma. Sherrill's home revealed the dark side of his personality, a hidden side: rifles, shotguns, pistols, stacks of soft-tipped bullets — an arsenal of hate. He had expressed a hate for dogs, women, his boss, and his job. He seemed to hate every job he held after leaving the U.S. Marine Corps. At daybreak, Wednesday, August 20, 1986, in Edmond, Oklahoma, the pent-up hate exploded. Within 20 minutes, Pat Sherrill and 14 of his co-workers were dead.

On this fatal day, 44-year-old Pat Sherrill loaded three semiautomatic pistols, put them inside a letter carrier's bag, shouldered it, and stormed into the post office. Ninety people were inside when the shooting rampage began. The first shot was intended for Sherrill's boss, Bill Beard, who had threatened to fire him.

Police said most of those killed were found near their workstations. Bodies, spent cartridges, and empty bullet clips were scattered throughout the building. Using the post office as a shooting gallery, Sherrill roamed around shooting at anything he could see.

The first news reports of the mass killings said that Sherrill was distraught about the possibility of losing his job. One television news reporter asked a question about Pat Sherrill's supervisor: "Should a boss be able to tell when his employee is about to break down?" The implication was that an astute manager could have prevented Sherrill's rampage.

There were a lot of indications that Pat Sherrill was an emotionally and psychologically disturbed person. He was a loner, an oddball who would not speak to people, not even to co-workers who spoke to him. He never smiled or laughed. He was always angry at something. Some of his neighbors referred to him as "Crazy Pat."

Pat Sherrill's job was extremely important to him. He thought that no one appreciated his contributions to the post office. He argued with his boss on several occasions about his job, co-workers, and job performance. Sherrill had a history of arguing, being absent, and disrupting work. During his 18-month tenure as a letter carrier, he received a number of suspensions.

Thankfully, murder in the workplace is rare. However, a growing number of shootings, physical attacks, and provocative actions are occurring in the workplace. In most cases, employees are aggressively lashing out at the company or their bosses.

Source: Martha T. Moore, "Isolation, Frustration Are Often Causes," *USA Today*, September 22, 1989, pp. B1–B2.

The rash of workplace tragedies raises some questions, such as:

— Can managers be trained to spot stressed-out employees and help guide them to professional counselors?
— Should managers be held partially responsible for any tragedy?
— Can hiring and firing programs be improved? Any disgruntled person who loses a job or doesn't receive what he or she believes is owed is a potential problem.
— Can management really determine what is going on inside a person's mind and do something about it before a tragedy occurs?

These kinds of questions are asked after each shooting spree occurs.

What accounts for a person's murderous trek through the workplace? A simple answer would be a lot of things—inherited traits, learned tendencies, a frustrated childhood, and failures in adult life. There is, however, no simple answer to how any of the fatal tragedies might have been avoided.

Questions for Consideration

1. Some people act out their frustration through angry aggression, while others withdraw and become passive. Can managers be trained to better predict how frustrated individuals will react?
2. Can preselection testing programs identify potentially dangerous people? Why or why not?
3. Should a company be held accountable for the deaths of employees or a murderer? Why or why not?
4. What events in American society may be contributing to the increasing number of workplace murderers?

SELF-PERCEPTION: ARE YOU ON TARGET?

Objectives

1. To learn how you perceive yourself.
2. To determine the perceptions that others have of you.
3. To find areas in which your self-perception and the perceptions that others have of you do not match.

Related Topics

The perceptions we have of others, our jobs, and our families are all projected onto other people or things. We also have self-perceptions, our own internal picture of what we are. Sometimes, we are surprised that others do not perceive us as we think they do.

Starting the Exercise

Individually complete the list by writing on a separate sheet of paper the statements that best describe you. Some of the statements may not apply to you. If so, do not place them on your sheet.

Have a classmate do the same thing—write down the statements that describe you on a separate sheet of paper. Also have a close friend or a family member prepare a list of statements that describe you.

Collect the lists from the classmate and the friend or family member. Analyze the results. What differences did you find between your self-perception and others' perceptions of you?

Completing the Exercise

1. Form groups of three members to discuss what you each found. Did the others find discrepancies in their perceptions versus others'?
2. Discuss why these discrepancies were found. What common error do we make in perceiving both ourselves and the way others perceive us? Are you someone who:
   a. Listens carefully to what others say?
   b. Tends to make snap judgments?
   c. Is rushed by time?
   d. Prefers to work alone?
   e. Daydreams a lot?
   f. Is competitive?
   g. Is argumentative?
   h. Has a good sense of humor?
   i. Is satisfied with life?
   j. Is defensive?
   k. Has trouble relaxing?
   l. Is emotional?
   m. Is warm and friendly?
   n. Wants to finish the job on time?
   o. Is independent?
   p. Becomes upset easily?
   q. Can't keep a secret?
   r. Always asks for help?
   s. Is friendly?
   t. Gets nervous under pressure?

EXPERIENTIAL EXERCISE

WHO CONTROLS YOUR LIFE? THE ROTTER INTERNAL-
EXTERNAL SCALE

Objectives

1. To determine whether you believe you control your destiny or you believe that what happens in life is due to luck or chance.
2. To relate your internal/external attributes to other segments of your life — home, school, family, community.

Related Topics

Being self-aware helps a person understand his or her behavior better.

Starting the Exercise

Read the following statements and indicate whether you agree more with choice A or choice B.

Choice A	Choice B
1. Making a lot of money is largely a matter of getting the right breaks.	1. Promotions are earned through hard work and persistence.
2. I have noticed that there is usually a direct connection between how hard I study and the grades I get.	2. Many times, the reactions of teachers seem haphazard to me.
3. The number of divorces indicates that more and more people are not trying to make their marriages work.	3. Marriage is largely a gamble.
4. It is silly to think that one can really change another person's basic attitudes.	4. When I am right, I can convince others.
5. Getting promoted is really a matter of being a little luckier than the next person.	5. In our society, a person's future earning power depends on his or her ability.
6. If one knows how to deal with people, they are really quite easily led.	6. I have little influence over the way other people behave.
7. The grades I make are the result of my own efforts; luck has little or nothing to do with it.	7. Sometimes, I feel that I have little to do with the grades I get.
8. People like me can change the course of world affairs if we make ourselves heard.	8. It is only wishful thinking to believe that one can readily influence what happens in our society at large.
9. Much of what happens to me is probably a matter of chance.	9. I am the master of my fate.
10. Getting along with people is a skill that must be practiced.	10. It is almost impossible to figure out how to please some people.

Source: Julian B. Rotter, "External Control and Internal Control," *Psychology Today,* June 1971, p. 42. Copyright 1971 by the American Psychological Association. Adapted with permission.

4

Motivation
Content Theories and Applications

LEARNING OBJECTIVES

After completing Chapter 4,
you should be able to:

DEFINE
motivation in terms
that would be meaningful to
managers.

DESCRIBE
the difference between
Maslow's need hierarchy and
Alderfer's ERG theory of
motivation.

DISCUSS
McClelland's explanation
of learned needs in terms of
the economic achievement
of a society (e.g., United
States, USSR, and Japan).

IDENTIFY
the reasons why an
individual's needs change
over the course of a
work career.

COMPARE
four content theories and
how they explain motivation.

CAN SELF-ACTUALIZATION BE ACHIEVED?

ARGUMENT FOR

You will read in this chapter that Abraham Maslow proposed a five-level need hierarchy. He suggested that once the first four levels of needs have been satisfied, an individual's behavior would be motivated by the self-actualization need. This is the need to fulfill oneself by maximizing the full use of one's abilities, skills, and potential. Maslow gives a very positive picture of the self-actualized person: no longer motivated by deficiencies, the self-actualized person is motivated to grow and become all that he or she is capable of becoming.

Maslow spent considerable effort attempting to define and clarify the major characteristics of the self-actualized person. He based his conclusions on the informal study of personal acquaintances, friends, and public and historic figures such as Abraham Lincoln and Thomas Jefferson. Some of the individual characteristics he identified in self-actualized persons were:

1. The ability to perceive people and events accurately.
2. The ability to remove themselves from the normal turmoil of life.
3. A problem and task orientation. They seemed to have a mission in life to do something that was worthwhile.
4. The ability to derive personal satisfaction from their own personal development in doing something worthwhile.
5. The capacity to love and experience life in a very intense manner.
6. An interest in the goals toward which they were working. But in many instances, the way in which the goals were pursued was itself a goal.
7. A high degree of creativity in their work.

Maslow's self-actualized person has mastered the lower needs and is motivated by what Maslow called growth motivation. It was Maslow's belief that many people do not reach the stage of self-actualization, because of poor environmental conditions. There is also the need to take risks, which Maslow believed was a difficult step to take. He believed that self-actualization could be achieved with the proper environmental conditions and willingness to take risks to grow.

ARGUMENT AGAINST

Unquestionably, Maslow's need hierarchy theory is widely accepted. But with little research evidence to support it, his attempt is not even partially acceptable. Maslow was subjective and biased in every procedure that he used. In fact, many of the living individuals whom he studied preferred to remain anonymous, making it impossible for other researchers to check the accuracy of his conclusions.

A strong elitist orientation shows in Maslow's view of self-actualization. His claim that everyone from Abraham Lincoln to the least skilled manufacturing line worker has the potential to self-actualize is an exaggeration. He is simply not realistic and shows little understanding of life for a working man or woman. People confined by a meager education, blue-collar jobs, or societal expectations are very unlikely to approach a state of self-actualization. Can 27 million illiterate Americans reach a state of self-actualization? How about the millions of blue-collar workers and many managers who never will be able to self-actualize?

Thus, Maslow's claim that a motivation to self-actualize exists in the general population is overstated. Some individuals certainly have the drive to self-actualize, but many others possess no such drive. In fact, in the blue-collar world of the 1990s, self-actualization may not even be feasible. Workers are concerned about job security, self-esteem, and working conditions.

The issue of the perfect state of self-actualization must also be raised. In reading Maslow's list of characteristics, one is impressed with the view that being self-actualized is a perfect state. There undoubtedly have been and are self-actualized individuals who are tyrannical, unethical, ruthless, boring, and irritating. For the most part, these self-actualized misfits are neither described nor mentioned in Maslow's writings.

In summary, Maslow's view that most people have an intense drive and the potential to self-actualize (1) has not been supported by research, (2) is elitist in tone, and (3) is not of any value to managers attempting to create a positively charged atmosphere of motivation.

Motivation, although an important determinant of individual performance, is not the only factor. Other variables such as effort, ability, and previous experience also influence performance. This chapter, however, concentrates on the motivation process as it affects behavior and individual performance.

Why some employees perform better than others is a continual and perplexing problem facing managers. To explain such differences, several interesting and important variables have been used—for example, ability, instinct, and aspiration levels, as well as personal factors such as age, education, and family background. The pursuit of the happy/productive worker is still considered a worthwhile though difficult endeavor.[1]

Despite its obvious importance, motivation is difficult to define and to analyze. By one definition, motivation has to do with (1) the direction of behavior, (2) the strength of the response (i.e., effort) once an employee chooses to follow a course of action, and (3) the persistence of the behavior, or how long the person continues to behave in a particular manner.[2] Another view suggests that the analysis of motivation should concentrate on the factors that incite and direct a person's activities.[3] One theorist emphasizes the goal-directedness aspect of motivation.[4] Another states that motivation is "concerned with how behavior gets started, is energized, is sustained, is directed, and is stopped, and what kind of subjective reaction is present in the organism while all this is going on."[5]

A careful examination of each of these views leads to several conclusions about motivation:

[1]Barry M. Staw, "Organizational Psychology and the Pursuit of the Happy/Productive Worker," *California Management Review*, Summer 1986, p. 40.

[2]John P. Campbell, Marvin D. Dunnette, Edward E. Lawler III, and Karl E. Weick, *Managerial Behavior, Performance and Effectiveness* (New York: McGraw-Hill, 1970), p. 340.

[3]John W. Atkinson, *An Introduction to Motivation* (New York: Van Nostrand Reinhold, 1964).

[4]Dalbir Bindra, *Motivation: A Systematic Reinterpretation* (New York: Ronald Press, 1959).

[5]Marshall R. Jones, ed., *Nebraska Symposium on Motivation* (Lincoln: University of Nebraska Press, 1955), p. 14.

1. Theorists present slightly different interpretations and place emphasis on different factors.
2. It is related to behavior and performance.
3. Goal directedness is involved.
4. It results from events and processes that are internal or external to the individual.

Motivating employees was an important topic as far back as 1789. Samuel Slater, a pioneer who introduced textile manufacturing to America, was very concerned about creating a work setting that was comfortable for workers to do their jobs. Other efforts to create a positive motivational work climate ranged from George M. Pullman's company town to Henry Ford's profit-sharing plan. The Edison Electric Illuminating Company of Boston provided tennis courts and bowling alleys. Other firms planted gardens for workers or constructed libraries and athletic facilities.

One reason for corporate generosity was fear of the trade union movement, but there were other motivators. One was greed, the desire to get employees to work harder for less money. Another was humanitarianism, the willingness to treat employees well. And some corporate leaders believed it was simply good business to satisfy workers' needs for good working conditions, a fair day's pay, and social interaction.

Perhaps one of the most radical experiments in creating a work environment that had the potential to motivate workers occurred in the late 1800s at the Pullman Company. George Pullman built a company town with houses to rent, stores, schools, a church, and a company plant.[6] He wanted to provide his employees with a feeling of community, a place of employment, and opportunities to practice religion and to educate their children. When the national economy slid into a depression, however, events in Pullman, Illinois, turned sour. Pullman cut his workers' wages without lowering rents or prices in the town. What started as an experiment to help workers satisfy various needs eventually spurred workers into attempting to organize a union. Pullman's workers went out on strike, riots occurred, and federal troops were called in to restore order.

Since that time, researchers have learned much about motivation. Managers need to consider these insights when attempting to create positive motivational atmospheres for their employees.

WHAT IS MOTIVATION?

Imagine that you are driving past a McDonald's fast-food restaurant and notice your best friend's car parked outside. Glancing at your watch, you see that it is 12:45 P.M. You assume that your friend was hungry and stopped to eat lunch. Your assumptions concern your friend's motivation for going into McDonald's. You stop, enter the restaurant to visit your friend, and find him talking to the store manager. Based on this observation, you are not sure that your assumption about your friend's motivation is correct.

---

[6]"Great Moments in Workstyle," *Inc.*, January 1986, pp. 52–53.

When you saw your friend's car parked outside the restaurant, you assumed that it was there for a specific purpose, that hunger motivated his presence there. **Motivation** is the concept we use when we describe the forces acting on or within an individual to initiate and direct behavior. We use the concept to explain differences in the intensity of behavior, regarding more intense behaviors as the result of higher levels of motivation, and also to indicate the direction of behavior (e.g., when you are tired or sleepy, you direct your behavior toward getting some sleep).

MOTIVATION
Concept that describes forces acting on employee that initiate and direct behavior.

Motivation is an explanatory concept that we use to make sense out of the behaviors we observe. In other words, motivation is inferred. Instead of measuring it directly, we must manipulate certain conditions and observe how behavior changes.[7] From the changes we observe, we improve our understanding of the underlying motivation. You assumed that your best friend had made a quick stop to eat lunch when you saw the car parked outside the fast-food restaurant. But your inference was not correct, because your friend was actually talking to the manager about a weekend job. The lesson is clear: we must always be cautious in making motivational inferences. As more and more information is accumulated, however, our inferences become more accurate because we can eliminate alternative explanations.

Managers prefer positively motivated employees because they strive to find the best way to perform their jobs. Motivated employees are interested in producing high-quality products or services; they are more likely to be productive than are nonmotivated or apathetic workers. They want to come to work, to be a part of the team, and they are interested in helping, supporting, and encouraging co-workers. Finding a universal set of principles to motivate employees is not likely to occur. There is simply no one approach for managers to learn and apply. The Close-Up about motivation describes why a universal approach is out of the question.

THE STARTING POINT: THE INDIVIDUAL

Most managers are faced with the task of motivating a diverse and in many respects unpredictable group of people. The diversity results in different behavioral patterns that in some manner are related to needs and goals.

Needs are deficiencies that an individual experiences at a particular point in time. The deficiencies may be physiological (e.g., a need for food), psychological (e.g., a need for self-esteem), or sociological (e.g., a need for social interaction). Needs are energizers or triggers of behavioral responses. The implication is that when needs (deficiencies) are present, the individual is more susceptible to managers' motivational efforts.

NEEDS
Deficiencies that individual experiences at particular point in time.

In any discussion of motivation, the importance of goals is apparent. The motivational process, as interpreted by most theorists, is goal directed. The goals, or outcomes, an employee seeks are viewed as forces that attract the person. Accomplishing desired goals can result in a significant reduction in need deficiencies.

As illustrated in Figure 4–1, people seek to reduce need deficiencies, which trigger a search process for ways to reduce the tension they cause. A course of

---

[7]Herbert Petri, *Motivation: Theory and Research* (Belmont, Calif.: Wadsworth, 1979), p. 4.

MOTIVATION IS NOT AND WILL NOT BE A SCIENCE

Efforts to create a science of motivating employees have, for the most part, failed. The most serious blow to a grand theory of motivation has come from a changing business climate. The nature of employment is changing. Service industries are replacing manufacturing ones. Blue-collar workers are becoming almost extinct. Today's white-collar workers are better educated, question authority, and are turned off by bureaucratic rules and procedures.

The changing nature of work and the work force has compelled companies to experiment more with a whole host of motivators, including:

— Methods of performance-related pay; stock options and employee share ownership deals.
— More and better communication. Surveys show that employers want more open communication and workers want management to tell them more frequently how the company is doing and where it is going.
— Meet-the-president meetings and open-door policies. Such meetings, used at firms like American General Life Insurance Company, permit employees to discuss work and strategy matters with the top person.

The old "carrot and stick" approach to motivation is considered too simplistic. What is emerging is a more open, flexible type of motivation prescription. Management is using experiments to find out what works best to satisfy employees' needs in their company. Being paid well is important, but it is also crucial to feel good about the firm you work for, to know what is going on, and to share in all the benefits of being successful. A grand theory of motivation is not likely to even be considered in the 1990s.

Source: "All about People," *Economist*, July 29, 1989, pp. 59–60.

action is selected, and goal-directed behavior occurs. After a period of time, managers assess that behavior. Performance evaluation will result in rewards or punishments being delivered. Such outcomes are weighed by the person, and need deficiencies are reassessed. This, in turn, triggers the process, and the circular pattern begins again.

MOTIVATION THEORIES: A CLASSIFICATION SYSTEM

Each person is attracted to some set of goals. To predict behavior with any accuracy, a manager must know something about an employee's goals and about the actions that the employee has to take to achieve them. Numerous motivation theories and research findings attempt to provide explanations of the behavior-outcome relationship.

Theories of motivation fall into two categories: content and process theories.[8] **Content theories** focus on the factors within the person that

CONTENT MOTIVATION
THEORIES
Theories that focus on factors within person that energize, direct, sustain, and stop behavior.

[8]Campbell et al., *Managerial Behavior*, pp. 340–56.

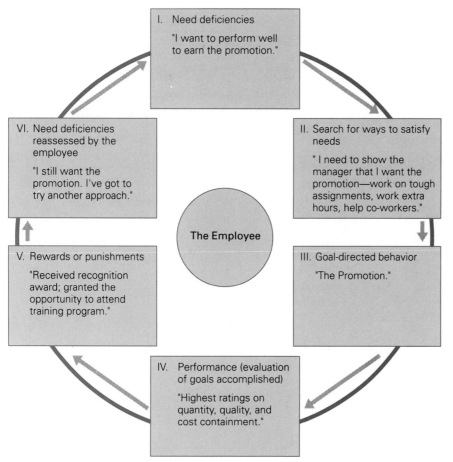

FIGURE 4-1

The Motivational Process:
An Initial Model

energize, direct, sustain, and stop behavior. They attempt to determine the specific needs that motivate people. **Process theories** provide a description and analysis of how behavior is energized, directed, sustained, and stopped. Both categories have important implications for managers, who are by nature of their jobs involved with the motivational process. Table 4-1 concisely summarizes the basic characteristics of content and process theories of motivation from a managerial perspective.

PROCESS MOTIVATION
THEORIES

Theories that describe and analyze how behavior is energized,
directed, sustained, and stopped.

This chapter covers some of the most publicized content theories, while the next chapter discusses some process theories of motivation. The content theories focus on individual needs in explaining job satisfaction, worker behavior, and reward systems. The theories suggest that individual need deficiencies activate tensions within a person that trigger a behavioral response. For managers to be effective, the content theories suggest that they must:

1. Determine what needs trigger desired performance, group, and personal behaviors.

2. Be able to offer meaningful rewards that help the employee satisfy needs.

TABLE 4–1

Managerial Perspective of Content and Process Theories of Motivation

Theoretical Base	Theoretical Explanation	Founders of the Theories	Managerial Application
Content	Focuses on factors within the person that energize, direct, sustain, and stop behavior. These factors can only be inferred.	**Maslow**—five-level need hierarchy. **Alderfer**—three-level hierarchy (ERG). **Herzberg**—two major factors called hygiene-motivators. **McClelland**—three learned needs acquired from the culture: achievement, affiliation, and power.	Managers need to be aware of differences in needs, desires, and goals because each individual is unique in many ways.
Process	Describes, explains, and analyzes how behavior is energized, directed, sustained, and stopped.	**Vroom**—an expectancy theory of choices. **Skinner**—reinforcement theory concerned with the learning that occurs as a consequence of behavior. **Adams**—equity theory based on comparisons that individuals make. **Locke**—goal-setting theory that conscious goals and intentions are the determinants of behavior.	Managers need to understand the *process* of motivation and how individuals make choices based on preferences, rewards, and accomplishments.

3. Know when to offer appropriate rewards to optimize performance behavior.

4. Not assume that a person's need deficiencies will repeat themselves in a regular pattern. People change because of experiences, life events, aging, cultural and environmental changes, and other factors.

Maslow's need hierarchy, Alderfer's ERG theory, Herzberg's two-factor theory, and McClelland's learned needs theory are four important content theories of motivation. Each has an impact on managerial practices.

MASLOW'S NEED HIERARCHY

NEED HIERARCHY MODEL

Maslow's theory that assumes that person's needs depend on what he or she already has. In a sense, then, a satisfied need is not a motivator. Human needs, organized in hierarchy of importance, are physiological, safety, belongingness, esteem, and self-actualization.

One of the most widely cited and discussed motivation theories is the **need hierarchy model** proposed by Abraham Maslow.[9] The lowest-level needs are the physiological needs, and the highest-level needs are for self-actualization. Maslow defined human needs as:

---

[9]Abraham H. Maslow, "A Theory of Human Motivation," *Psychological Review*, July 1943, pp. 370–96. Also see Abraham H. Maslow, *Motivation and Personality* (New York: Harper & Row, 1954).

1. *Physiological*—the need for food, drink, shelter, and relief from pain.
2. *Safety and security*—the need for freedom from threat; that is, the security from threatening events or surroundings.
3. *Belongingness, social, and love*—the need for friendship, affiliation, interaction, and love.
4. *Esteem*—the need for self-esteem and for esteem from others.
5. *Self-actualization*—the need to fulfill oneself by maximizing the use of abilities, skills, and potential.

Maslow's theory assumes that a person attempts to satisfy the more basic needs (physiological) before directing behavior toward satisfying upper-level needs (self-actualization). The importance of the self-actualization need in motivation was highlighted in this chapter's Organizational Issue for Debate. Are you satisfying or can you satisfy the self-actualization need on the job, at school, or at home? The lower-order needs must be satisfied before a higher-order need such as self-actualization begins to control the behavior of a person. According to Maslow, a satisfied need ceases to motivate. When a person decides that he or she is earning enough pay for contributing to the organization, money loses its power to motivate.

Maslow proposed that the typical adult in society had satisfied about 85 percent of the physiological need; 70 percent of the safety and security needs; 50 percent of the belongingness, social, and love needs; 40 percent of the esteem need; and 10 percent of the self-actualization need. As stated in the Organizational Issue for debate, critics believe that the estimate of 10 percent satisfaction of the self-actualization need is absurd when applied to blue-collar workers. Many of these workers are simply trying to survive. Maslow's assertions about relative need satisfaction are shown graphically in Figure 4–2.

Because of the great need deficiencies in the self-actualization and esteem categories, managers should try to implement strategies to correct these deficiencies. Such attempts have a higher probability of succeeding than does directing attention to the already satisfactorily fulfilled lower-order needs.

In addition to dealing with individual differences in needs, managers also face the issue that needs, work style, and work ethics may differ across cultures. Some Americans perceive foreigners as lazy and not motivated, seeing them as poor workers with "no work ethic."[10] In the United States, competition is now the name of the game, as international markets fill with numerous competitors; everyone wants to be a winner. Money is also a driving force. A satisfactory wage is essential, or American workers are likely to be discontented.

On the other hand, when Japanese, West German, Swiss, or Dutch companies take over American firms or invest in the United States, they are concerned with getting the American labor force to produce. The problem boils down not to laziness but to conflict between culturally different patterns of job behavior, management styles, and the role that work plays in employees' lives.[11] For example, Americans are job oriented rather than company

---

[10]Lennie Copeland and Lewis Griggs, "Getting the Best from Foreign Employees," *Management Review,* June 1986, p. 22.

[11]A. Bennett, "American Culture Is Often a Puzzle for Foreign Managers in the U.S.," *The Wall Street Journal,* February 12, 1986, p. 29.

FIGURE 4–2

The Typical Person's Need
Deficiency and Satisfaction

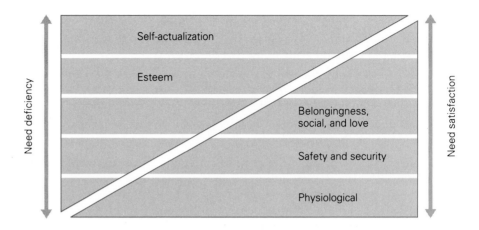

oriented. Latin Americans work not for the job or company but for themselves. Australians say they are motivated to do a good job to earn a vacation.
In China or Yugoslavia, a monetary bonus for outstanding performance could
cause an employee embarrassment or even humiliation.[12]

Selected Need Hierarchy Research

A number of research studies have tested the need hierarchy theory. The first
reported field research that tested a modified version of Maslow's need
hierarchy was performed by Lyman W. Porter.[13] Initially, he assumed that
physiological needs were being adequately satisfied for managers, so he
substituted a higher-order need called autonomy, defined as the person's
satisfaction with opportunities to make independent decisions, set goals, and
work without close supervision. The Close-Up about assessing the relative
importance of needs provides a portion of the needs assessment scale that
Porter developed.

Since the early Porter studies, other studies have reported:

1. Managers high in the organization chain of command place greater
   emphasis on self-actualization and autonomy.[14]
2. Managers at lower organizational levels in small firms with less than 500
   employees are more satisfied than their counterparts in large firms with
   more than 5,000 employees. Managers at upper levels in large companies, however, are more satisfied than their counterparts in small
   companies.[15]

---

[12]Lennie Copeland and Lewis Griggs, *Going International* (New York: Random House, 1985).

[13]Lyman W. Porter, "A Study of Perceived Need Satisfaction in Bottom and Middle Management
Jobs," *Journal of Applied Psychology,* February 1961, pp. 1–10.

[14]Lyman W. Porter, *Organizational Patterns of Managerial Job Attitudes* (New York: American
Foundation for Management Research, 1964).

[15]Lyman W. Porter, "Job Attitudes in Management: Perceived Deficiencies in Need Fulfillment as
a Function of Size of the Company," *Journal of Applied Psychology,* December 1963, pp. 386–97.

3. American managers overseas are more satisfied with autonomy opportunities than are their counterparts working in the United States.[16]

In general, Maslow's theory has not been supported by field research studies.[17] Therefore, we do not recommend using the theory to predict behavior. The hierarchy, seemingly a simplified attempt to explain human needs, does explain aspects of human behavior in our society. But it is not accurate enough to explain individual-level behavior.

ALDERFER'S ERG THEORY

Alderfer agrees with Maslow that individuals' needs are arranged in a hierarchy.[18] However, his proposed need hierarchy involves only three sets of needs:[19]

1. *Existence*—needs satisfied by such factors as food, air, water, pay, and working conditions.
2. *Relatedness*—needs satisfied by meaningful social and interpersonal relationships.
3. *Growth*—needs satisfied by an individual making creative or productive contributions.

Alderfer's three needs—existence (E), relatedness (R), and growth (G), or ERG—correspond to Maslow's in that the existence needs are similar to Maslow's physiological and safety categories; the relatedness needs are similar to the belongingness, social, and love category; and the growth needs are similar to the esteem and self-actualization categories.

In addition to a difference in the number of categories, Alderfer's **ERG theory of motivation** and Maslow's need hierarchy differ on how people move through the different sets of needs. Maslow proposed that unfulfilled needs are predominant and that the next higher level of needs is not activated or triggered until the predominant need is adequately satisfied. Thus, a person only progresses up the need hierarchy once adequate satisfaction of the lower-level need occurs for that particular person. In contrast, Alderfer's ERG theory suggests that, in addition to the satisfaction-progression process that Maslow proposed, a frustration-regression process is also at work. That is, if a person is continually frustrated in attempts to satisfy growth needs, relatedness needs reemerge as a major motivating force, causing the individual

ERG THEORY OF MOTIVATION
Theory developed and tested by Alderfer that categorizes needs as existence, relatedness, and growth.

[16]John M. Ivancevich, "Perceived Need Satisfactions of Domestic versus Overseas Managers," *Journal of Applied Psychology,* August 1969, pp. 274–78.

[17]Edward E. Lawler III and J. L. Suttle, "A Causal Correlation Test of the Need Hierarchy Concept," *Organizational Behavior and Human Performance,* April 1972, pp. 265–87; Douglas T. Hall and K. E. Nougaim, "An Examination of Maslow's Need Hierarchy in an Organizational Setting," *Organizational Behavior and Human Performance,* February 1968, pp. 12–35.

[18]Clayton P. Alderfer, "An Empirical Test of a Need Theory of Human Needs," *Organizational Behavior and Human Performance,* April 1969, pp. 142–75.

[19]Clayton P. Alderfer, *Existence, Relatedness, and Growth: Human Needs in Organizational Settings* (New York: Free Press, 1972).

ASSESSING THE IMPORTANCE OF NEEDS

Questionnaires have been developed for use in research studies, training programs, and discussion groups to provide insight into needs and motivation, based on Maslow's need hierarchy. One of the most widely used of these questionnaires was prepared by Lyman W. Porter. Although you may not be working in an organization at present, it might be interesting to see how important various need characteristics are to you.

Answer according to your feelings about the most recent job you had or about the job you currently hold. Circle the number on the scale that represents your feeling: 1 (very unimportant) to 7 (very important).

	1	2	3	4	5	6	7
1. The feeling of self-esteem you get from being in that job.	1	2	3	4	5	6	7
2. The opportunity for personal growth and development in that job.	1	2	3	4	5	6	7
3. The prestige of the job inside the company (that is, regard received from others in the company).	1	2	3	4	5	6	7
4. The opportunity for independent thought and action in that job.	1	2	3	4	5	6	7
5. The feeling of security in that job.	1	2	3	4	5	6	7
6. The feeling of self-fulfillment you get from being in that position (that is, the feeling of being able to use your own unique capabilities, realizing your potential.	1	2	3	4	5	6	7
7. The prestige of the job outside the company (that is, the regard received from others not in the company).	1	2	3	4	5	6	7
8. The feeling of worthwhile accomplishment in that job.	1	2	3	4	5	6	7

to redirect efforts toward satisfying a lower-order need category. Figure 4–3 presents the ERG theory as proposed by Alderfer.

Consider the case of Mary Higgins, a registered nurse in the pediatric unit in Methodist Hospital in Tampa, Florida. Mary is a single parent who is very concerned with job security, pay, and co-worker interaction and friendship. She must work to support her family and also enjoys the social aspect of work. Her performance is outstanding, and she has satisfied these existence and relatedness needs. A head nurse position becomes available in intensive care. However, two other candidates are identified with more experience and outstanding performance records in intensive care. Mary is dropped from further consideration for the higher-paying job and becomes frustrated, disappointed, and concerned about her future.

Tina Mayes, her supervisor, explains to Mary why she is not being considered, assuring her that other opportunities will occur and that her value to other pediatric nurses is immeasurable. In fact, Tina and three co-workers take Mary to dinner to talk with her. This seems to help, and Mary, after a few

9. The opportunity in that job to give help to other people.	1	2	3	4	5	6	7
10. The opportunity in that job for participation in the setting of goals.	1	2	3	4	5	6	7
11. The opportunity in that job for participation in the determination of methods and procedures.	1	2	3	4	5	6	7
12. The authority connected with the job.	1	2	3	4	5	6	7
13. The opportunity to develop close friendships in the job.	1	2	3	4	5	6	7

Now that you have completed the questionnaire, score it as follows:

Rating for question 5 = _____, divided by 1 = _____ security.

Rating for questions 9 and 13 = _____, divided by 2 = _____ social.

Rating for questions 1, 3, and 7 = _____, divided by 3 = _____ esteem.

Rating for questions 4, 10, 11, and 12 = _____, divided by 4 = _____ autonomy.

Rating for questions 2, 6, and 8 = _____, divided by 3 = _____ self-actualization.

The instructor has national norm scores for presidents, vice presidents, and upper middle-level, lower middle-level, and lower-level managers, with which you can compare your mean importance scores. How do your scores compare with the scores of managers working in organizations?

Source: Lyman W. Porter, *Organizational Patterns of Managerial Job Attitudes* (New York: American Foundation for Management Research, 1964), pp. 17, 19.

days of feeling frustrated, comes to work and seems to begin enjoying her work colleagues. Mary has redirected her need for the promotion to the relatedness category.

Alderfer's ERG explanation of motivation provides an interesting suggestion to managers about behavior. If a subordinate's higher-order needs (e.g., growth) are being blocked, perhaps because of a company policy or the lack of resources, then it is in the manager's best interest to attempt to redirect the subordinate's efforts toward relatedness or existence needs. The ERG theory implies that individuals are motivated to engage in behavior to satisfy one of the three sets of needs.

ERG: Limited Research to Date

The ERG theory has not stimulated many research studies. Thus, empirical verification cannot be claimed for the ERG explanation. Salancik and Pfeffer proposed that need models such as Maslow's and Alderfer's have become

FIGURE 4—3

ERG Theory Relationships among Frustration, Importance, and Satisfaction of Needs

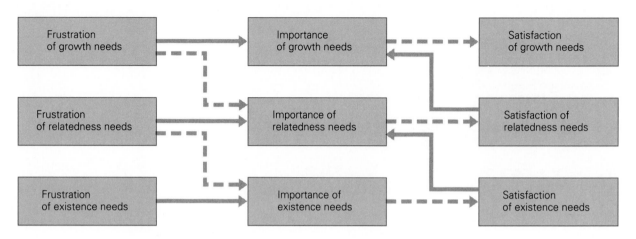

Source: F. J. Landy and D. A. Trumbo, *Psychology of Work Behavior,* rev. ed. (Homewood, Ill.: Dorsey Press, 1980).

popular because they are consistent with other theories of rational choice and because they attribute freedom to individuals.[20] The idea that individuals shape their actions to satisfy unfulfilled needs gives purpose and direction to individual activity. Furthermore, Salancik and Pfeffer claimed, need explanations are also popular, despite little research verification, because they are simple, easily expressed views of human behavior. Must need theories be verifiable to be of value to a manager?[21] Or are managers and practitioners less impressed by research-verified explanations than by simple, commonsense explanations?

Alderfer certainly didn't accept the Salancik and Pfeffer critique of need explanations of motivation.[22] He proposed that available research evidence supported at least the conceptualization of the ERG theory. Other evidence to support portions of the ERG theory has been added to the literature since his debate with Salancik and Pfeffer.

One study examined the ERG theory of motivation with regard to the human life cycle,[23] using Levinson's theory of life-cycle development, which includes seven stages (e.g., early adult transition, 18–22 years old; midlife transition, 40–45 years old). Results indicated that (1) individuals whose parents achieved higher educational levels had significantly higher scores for

---

[20]Gerald R. Salancik and Jeffrey Pfeffer, "An Examination of Need-Satisfaction Models of Job Attitudes," *Administrative Science Quarterly,* September 1977, pp. 427–56.

[21]Barry M. Staw, N. E. Bell, and J. A. Clausen, "The Dispositional Approach to Job Attitudes," *Administrative Science Quarterly,* March 1986, p. 56.

[22]Clayton P. Alderfer, "A Critique of Salancik and Pfeffer's Examination of Need-Satisfaction Theories," *Administrative Science Quarterly,* December 1977, pp. 658–69.

[23]Clayton P. Alderfer and Richard A. Guzzo, "Live Expectancies and Adults' Enduring Strength of Desires in Organizations," *Administrative Science Quarterly,* September 1979, pp. 347–61.

strength of desire for growth, (2) men had higher scores for strength of existence needs and lower scores for strength of relatedness than did women, and (3) black participants showed significantly higher existence needs than did white participants.

In another study of ERG theory, researchers collected data from 208 employees working in 13 different jobs in a telephone company.[24] In general, the ERG categories were supported. However, researchers discovered a more rigid need hierarchy than that proposed by Alderfer. For example, relatively few individuals (17 out of 208) reported high growth-need satisfaction when satisfaction of relatedness and existence needs were either moderate or low. Alderfer placed much less emphasis on the hierarchy notion than had Maslow.

HERZBERG'S TWO–FACTOR THEORY

Psychologist and management consultant Frederick Herzberg developed the **two-factor content theory of motivation.**[25] The two factors are the dissatisfiers-satisfiers, or the hygiene-motivators, or the extrinsic-intrinsic factors, depending on who is discussing the theory. The original research testing this theory included a group of 200 accountants and engineers. Herzberg used interview responses to questions such as, "Can you describe, in detail, when you felt exceptionally good about your job?" and "Can you describe, in detail, when you felt exceptionally bad about your job?" Rarely were the same kinds of experiences categorized as both good and bad. This systematic procedure resulted in the development of two distinct kinds of experiences—satisfiers and dissatisfiers.

Herzberg's initial study resulted in two specific conclusions. First, there is a set of *extrinsic* conditions, the job context. They include:

Salary (pay).

Job security.

Working conditions.

Status.

Company procedures.

Quality of supervision.

Quality of interpersonal relations among peers, with superiors, and with subordinates.

The presence of these conditions to the satisfaction of the employee does not necessarily motivate him or her. But their absence results in dissatisfaction among employees. Because they are needed to maintain at least a level of "no dissatisfaction," the extrinsic conditions are called the *dissatisfiers,* or *hygiene,* factors.

HERZBERG'S TWO-FACTOR THEORY OF MOTIVATION View that job satisfaction results from the presence of intrinsic motivators and that job dissatisfaction stems from not having extrinsic factors.

---

[24]J. P. Wanous and A. Zwany, "A Cross-Sectional Test of Need Hierarchy Theory," *Organizational Behavior and Human Performance,* February 1977, pp. 78–97.

[25]Frederick Herzberg, B. Mausner, and B. Synderman, *The Motivation to Work* (New York: John Wiley & Sons, 1959).

Second, a set of *intrinsic* conditions, the job content, is also present. These conditions include:

Achievement.	Advancement.
Recognition.	The work itself.
Responsibility.	The possibility of growth.

The absence of these conditions does not prove highly dissatisfying. But when present in the job, they build strong levels of motivation that result in good job performance. Therefore, they are called the *satisfiers,* or *motivators.*

Prior to Herzberg's work, those studying motivation viewed job satisfaction as a unidimensional concept. That is, they placed job satisfaction at one end of a continuum and job dissatisfaction at the other end of the same continuum: if a job condition caused job satisfaction, removing it would cause dissatisfaction; similarly, if a job condition caused job dissatisfaction, removing it would cause job satisfaction. Herzberg's model basically assumes that job satisfaction is not a unidimensional concept. His research leads to the conclusion that two continua are needed to interpret job satisfaction correctly. Figure 4–4 illustrates the two different views of job satisfaction.

Today, as we move toward a world economy, managers need to understand the motivation of workers from different cultures. American firms are building plants, offices, and distribution centers around the world. Compaq Computer (U.S.) located a plant in Scotland and had to hire Scottish employees. Toyota (Japan) built a plant in Kentucky and hired American employees. Herzberg believes that, despite major cultural differences across countries, more commonalities exist than was previously assumed. The Close-Up "Workers' Needs around the World" reports on findings based on the Herzberg theory. It shows that for U.S. workers, about 80 percent of the factors in job satisfaction originate from motivators. In the case of Finnish supervisors, about 90 percent of job satisfaction factors stem from motivators. The Japanese profile indicates that, like U.S. workers, they are made more happy by motivators.

Critique of Herzberg's Theory

Of all the available content theories, we believe the most criticized is Herzberg's. Several reasons account for this. First, the theory was originally based on a sample of accountants and engineers. Critics ask whether this limited sample can justify generalizing to other occupational groups. The technology, environment, and background of the two occupational groups are distinctly different from those of other groups, such as nurses, medical technologists, salespeople, computer programmers, clerks, and police officers.[26]

Second, some researchers believe that Herzberg's work oversimplifies the nature of job satisfaction, leading to the assumption that a manager can easily

---

[26]R. J. House and L. Wigdor, "Herzberg's Dual-Factor Theory of Job Satisfaction and Motivation: A Review of the Empirical Evidence and a Criticism," *Personnel Psychology,* Winter 1967, pp. 369–80; J. Schneider and Edwin Locke, "A Critique of Herzberg's Classification System and a Suggested Revision," *Organizational Behavior and Human Performance,* July 1971, pp. 441–58.

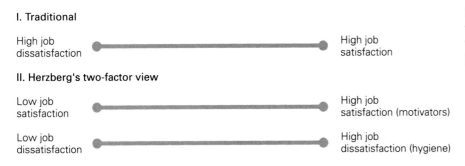

I. Traditional

High job
dissatisfaction ●━━━━━━━━━━━━━━━━━━━● High job
satisfaction

II. Herzberg's two-factor view

Low job
satisfaction ●━━━━━━━━━━━━━━━━━━━● High job
satisfaction (motivators)

Low job
dissatisfaction ●━━━━━━━━━━━━━━━━━━━● High job
dissatisfaction (hygiene)

FIGURE 4—4

Traditional and Herzberg
View of Satisfaction-
Dissatisfaction

help produce job satisfaction. This, of course, is not an accurate view of how complex and difficult job satisfaction is in terms of workplace manipulation.

Other critics focus on Herzberg's methodology because it requires people to look at themselves retrospectively. Can people be aware of all that motivated or dissatisfied them? These critics believe subconscious factors are not identified in Herzberg's analysis. Also, the "recency of events" bias of being able to recall one's most recent job conditions and feelings is embedded in the methodology.[27]

Another criticism of Herzberg's work is that little attention has been directed toward testing the motivational and performance implications of the theory.[28] In the original study, only self-reports of performance were used, and in most cases, the respondents were reporting on job activities that had occurred over a long time. Herzberg has offered no explanation as to why various extrinsic and intrinsic job factors should affect performance. The two-factor theory also fails to explain why various job factors are important.

When the available evidence is reviewed, it is surprising that Herzberg's theory has withstood the test of time. The two-factor theory, not even mentioned by many academic researchers, remains popular with managers, who continue to discuss the theory and attempt to increase motivation by using Herzberg's identified motivators. It is his motivation theory that spells out specific job factors that managers can work with to create a motivational atmosphere. (The job factors are discussed in more detail in Chapter 14, on job design.) Herzberg's theory brings out clearly the differences in perspectives held by practicing managers and academics. Instead of taking sides, we believe that Herzberg's explanation will continue to be cited and used by managers in the United States and around the world in the 1990s and that it warrants discussion and consideration of a potential applied approach to motivation.[29]

[27]Abraham K. Korman, *Industrial and Organizational Psychology* (Englewood Cliffs, N.J.: Prentice Hall, 1971), pp. 148–50.

[28]Edward E. Lawler III, *Motivation in Work Organizations* (Monterey, Calif.: Brooks/Cole Publishing, 1973), p. 72.

[29]In discussing motivation applications with numerous managers in Europe, the Pacific Rim, and Latin America, more references and questions are referred to the Herzberg explanation and approach than any other theory. Herzberg's writings and explanations have found their way into many countries.

WORKERS' NEEDS AROUND THE WORLD:
MORE SIMILARITIES THAN DIFFERENCES

Herzberg suggests that his theory is not just for Americans. He reports data that indicate that his hygiene-motivator theory applies to different worker populations. Shown here are profiles comparing U.S., European, and Japanese samples.

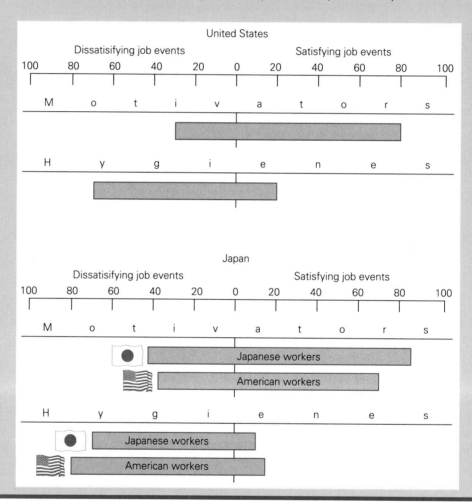

McCLELLAND'S LEARNED NEEDS THEORY

LEARNED NEEDS THEORY
Theory which proposes that a person with a strong need will be motivated to use appropriate behaviors to satisfy the need. A person's needs are learned from the culture of a society.

David C. McClelland has proposed a **learned needs theory** of motivation closely associated with learning concepts. He believes that many needs are acquired from the culture of a society.[30] Three of these *learned needs* are the

[30]David C. McClelland, "Business Drive and National Achievement," *Harvard Business Review*, July–August 1962, pp. 99–112.

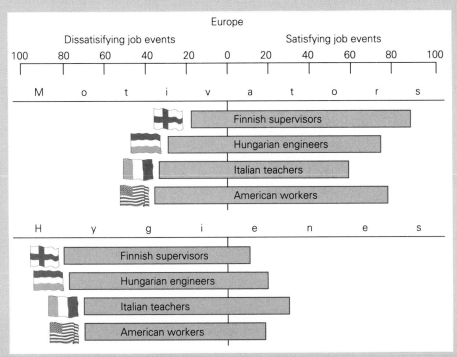

Note: Motivators are defined as the intrinsic elements of the job (e.g., achievement, the work itself). Hygienes are the job's extrinsic elements (e.g., company policy, working conditions).

Other researchers disagree with the Herzberg view of similarities across cultures. A study of American, Japanese, and Canadian negotiators found significant differences in general satisfaction, ability to adapt, and interpersonal interaction patterns.* More research is certainly needed to determine where similarities and differences exist. It is important to identify these areas to give management motivational practices a higher probability of success.

*Nancy J. Adler and John L. Graham, "Cross-Cultural Interaction: The International Comparison Fallacy," *Journal of International Business Studies,* Fall 1989, pp. 515–37.

Source: Presented in detail in Frederick Herzberg, "Worker's Needs: The Same around the World," *Industry Week,* September 21, 1987, pp. 29–32.

need for achievement (n Ach), the need for affiliation (n Aff), and the need for power (n Pow). McClelland proposes that when a need is strong in a person, its effect is to motivate that person to use behavior leading to its satisfaction. For example, a worker with a high n Ach would set challenging goals, work hard to achieve the goals, and use skills and abilities to achieve them.

How is, for example, the need for achievement (n Ach) measured? It is not enough to assume that those who work hard and long have a need for achievement, while those who work slowly or in spurts do not. To assess

THEMATIC APPERCEPTION
TEST (TAT)

Projective test that uses person's analysis of pictures to evaluate such individual differences
as need for achievement, need
for power, and need for affiliation.

individual differences in the three proposed needs, the **Thematic Apperception Test (TAT)** is used.[31] A person is shown pictures and asked to write a
story about what he or she sees portrayed in them.

For example, the picture in Figure 4–5 would be presented to a person.
What story does the picture illustrate? People tend to write stories that reflect
their dominant needs. For example, individuals with a high or dominant
achievement need typically write a story about Figure 4–5 that contains
achievement factors. McClelland or the evaluators, in reviewing a response to
a picture, would search the written stories for recurring themes of hard work,
extra effort, gratification received from success, and the setting of challenging
goals as indications of a high need for achievement. McClelland believes that
achievement, affiliation, and power needs can be inferred from the stories a
person writes about a number of such pictures. He states:

> If you want to understand motives behind . . . actions, find out what's on a
> person's mind. If you want to find out what's on a person's mind, don't ask him,
> because he can't always tell you accurately. Study his fantasies and dreams. If you do
> this over a period of time, you will discover the themes to which his mind returns
> again and again. And these themes can be used to explain his actions.[32]

McClelland proposes that a society's economic growth is based on the level
of need achievement inherent in its population[33] and that entire economically
backward cultures (nations) can be dramatically improved by stimulating the
need for achievement in the populace. If McClelland is correct, and some
research supports his theory, his approach could have a significant impact on
motivation in general. He also contends that motivation could be taught in
organizational and nonorganizational settings.[34]

Research on n Ach

Most research evidence offered in support of McClelland's learned needs
theory has been provided by McClelland or his associates. In most cases, the
research on the need for achievement has received the majority of attention
from organizational behavior theorists and researchers. The research has
provided a profile of the high achievers in society.[35]

— High n Ach persons prefer to avoid easy and difficult performance goals.
 They actually prefer moderate goals that they think they can achieve.

— High n Ach persons prefer immediate and reliable feedback on how they
 are performing.

— The high n Ach person likes to be responsible for solving problems.

[31]R. Murray, *Thematic Apperception Test Pictures and Manual* (Cambridge, Mass.: Harvard
University Press, 1943).

[32]David C. McClelland, *Motivational Trends in Society* (Morristown, N.J.: General Learning Press,
1971).

[33]McClelland, "Business Drive." McClelland proposes that a society's economic growth is based
on the level of need achievement inherent in its population.

[34]David C. McClelland, "Toward a Theory of Motive Acquisition," *American Psychologist,* May
1965, pp. 321–33.

[35]David C. McClelland and D. Burnham, "Power Is the Great Motivator," *Harvard Business
Review,* March–April 1976, pp. 100–111.

FIGURE 4—5

Sample of Thematic
Apperception Test (TAT)
Picture

Source: Adapted with permission of the Tests and Scoring Division, McBer and Company, 137 Newbury Street, Boston, Massachusetts 02116.

In one ambitious project, researchers tried to raise the achievement motivation of businessmen in an entire village in India. This program, the Kakinada project, consisted of encouraging the businessmen to have high-achievement fantasies, to make plans that would help them realize the goals of a successful entrepreneur, and to communicate with one another about their goals and their methods of reaching them. The businessmen became more productive as entrepreneurs, started several large industries, enlarged their businesses, and hired more than 5,000 of their neighbors. In a 10-year reassessment of the program, achievement motivation levels and results were still exceptional.[36]

Research has both provided the basis for developing a profile of those with high n Ach and pointed out the complexity of the achievement motive. High–n Ach individuals who focus on attaining success and those who focus on avoiding failure differ.[37] Those who focus on attaining success tend to set more realistic goals and to choose moderately difficult tasks.

In most of the research on n Ach, the subjects have been men. One study, however, compared the achievement needs of college men and women.[38] This study determined that women appeared to fear success more than men did.

---

[36]David C. McClelland, "Managing Motivation to Expand Human Freedom," *American Psychologist,* March 1978, pp. 201–10.

[37]W. V. Meyer, "Achievement Motive Research," in *Nebraska Symposium on Motivation,* ed. William J. Arnold (Lincoln: University of Nebraska Press, 1968).

[38]M. S. Horner, "Fail: Bright Women," *Psychology Today,* November 1969, pp. 36–38.

Students were asked to complete a story that began: "At the end of first-term finals, Anne finds herself at the top of her class." For male subjects, John was the name used. When the male and female stories prepared by the students were analyzed, 62 percent of the women expressed conflict over Anne's success, while only 9 percent of the men expressed conflict over John's success. Researchers concluded that women had a greater negative imagery about success, because their stories contained significantly more references to social rejection, anxiety, or a negative self-image.

The "fear of success hypothesis" was sensationalized by the popular press as an example of a personality type created by sexist ideology. Since then, over 200 studies have followed up on various aspects of women's fear of success.[39] The conclusion was that fear of success (achievement) is not a personality attribute of women. Rather, it is better conceived as a strong avoidance reaction in both women and men, triggered by certain social-economic-historic conditions. Instead of measuring a fear of success, the researcher in the original study may have actually been measuring a person's assessment of the negative consequences associated with deviation from traditional sex roles. A fear that the woman who deviates from sex role standards will be rejected by men may be particularly strong among women. One study found that some men do indeed fear being "outdone" by women and so prefer to work alone on achievement tasks rather than with a woman.[40]

Based on theory and research, McClelland has made specific suggestions about developing a positive high need for achievement (that is, a high n Ach where there is no fear of success). Using McClelland's prescriptions, a manager would be encouraged to:

1. Arrange job tasks so that employees receive periodic feedback on performance, providing information that enables them to make modifications or corrections.
2. Point out to employees models of achievement. Identify and publicize the accomplishments of achievement heroes, the successful people, the winners, and use them as models.
3. Work with employees to improve their self-image. High n Ach people like themselves and seek moderate challenges and responsibilities.
4. Introduce realism into all work-related topics: promotion, rewards, transfer, development opportunities, and team membership opportunities. Employees should think in realistic terms and think positively about how they can accomplish goals.

There are a number of criticisms of McClelland's work. First, the use of the projective TAT to determine the three needs has been questioned. While projective techniques have some advantages over self-report questionnaires, the interpretation and weighing of a story are at best an art. Validation of such analysis is extremely important and often neglected. A critical-incident technique has been used to examine motivation in a developing country,[41] but more research is

---

[39]David Tresemer, ed., "Current Trends in Research on Fear of Success," *Sex Roles,* Spring 1976, entire issue.

[40]J. Condry and S. Dyer, "Fear of Success: Attribution of Cause to the Victim," *Journal of Social Issues,* Summer 1976, pp. 63–83.

[41]P. D. Machungiva and N. Schmitt, "Work Motivation in a Developing Country," *Journal of Applied Psychology,* February 1983, pp. 31–42.

FIGURE 4—6

A Graphic Comparison of Four Content Theories of Motivation

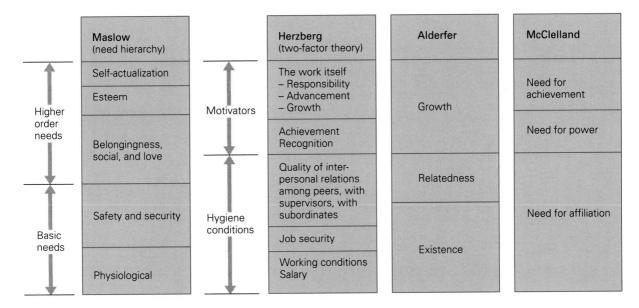

needed to determine whether critical incidents or other methods can be used as a measurement method for assessing the McClelland-type needs.

Second, McClelland's claim that n Ach can be learned is in conflict with a large body of literature stating that the acquisition of motives normally occurs in childhood and is very difficult to alter in adulthood. McClelland acknowledges this problem but points to evidence in politics and religion to indicate that adult behaviors can be changed.[42]

Third, McClelland's notion of learned needs is questioned on the grounds of whether the needs are permanently acquired. Research is needed to determine whether acquired needs last over a period of time. Can something learned in a training and development program be sustained on the job? This is the issue that McClelland and others have not been able to clarify.

A SYNOPSIS OF THE FOUR CONTENT THEORIES

Each of the four content theories explains behavior from a slightly different perspective. None of the theories can or should be used by managers as the sole basis for explaining or inferring motivation. Although some critics are skeptical, it appears that people have innate and learned needs and that various job factors result in a degree of satisfaction. Thus, each of the theories provides managers with some understanding of behavior and performance.

The four theories are graphically compared in Figure 4–6. McClelland proposed no lower-order needs. However, his needs for achievement and power are not identical with Herzberg's motivators, Maslow's higher-order

---

[42]McClelland, "Business Drive."

TABLE 4—2

Comparison of Four Content Theories of Motivation

Content Motivation Theories	Assumptions Made	How Motivation Is Measured	Practical Application Value	Problems and Limitations
Maslow's need hierarchy	Individuals attempt to satisfy basic needs before directing behavior toward higher-order needs.	Maslow, as a clinical psychologist, used his patients in asking questions and listening to answers; Organizational researchers have relied on self-report scales.	Makes sense to managers and gives many a feeling of knowing how motivation works for their employees.	Does not address the issue of individual differences; has received limited research support; and fails to caution about the dynamic nature of needs—needs change.
Alderfer's ERG theory	Individuals who fail to satisfy growth needs become frustrated, regress, and refocus attention on lower-order needs.	Self-report scales are used to assess three need categories.	Calls attention to what happens when and if need satisfaction does not occur; frustrations can be a major reason why performance levels are not attained or sustained.	Not enough research has been conducted; available research is self-report in nature, which raises the issue of how good the measurement is. Another issue is whether individuals really have only three need areas.
Herzberg's two-factor theory	Only some job features and characteristics can result in motivation. Some of the characteristics that managers have focused on may result in a comfortable work setting, but do not motivate employees.	Ask employees in interviews to describe critical job incidents.	Talks in terms that managers understand. Identifies motivators that managers can develop, fine-tune, and use.	Assumes that every worker is similar in needs and preferences; fails to meet scientific measurement standards; has not been updated to reflect changes in society with regard to job security and pay needs.
McClelland's learned needs	The needs of a person are learned from the culture (society); therefore, training and education can enhance and influence a person's need strength.	Thematic Apperception Test (TAT), a projective technique that encourages respondents to reveal their needs.	If a person's needs can be assessed, then management can intervene through training to develop needs that are compatible with organizational goals.	Interpreting the TAT is difficult; the effect that training has on changing needs has not been sufficiently tested.

needs, or Alderfer's growth needs, although there are some similarities. A major difference between the four content theories is McClelland's emphasis on socially acquired needs. Also, the Maslow theory offers a static need hierarchy system; Alderfer presents a flexible, three-need classification approach; and Herzberg discusses intrinsic and extrinsic job factors.

Each theory has strengths and limitations that practicing managers need to consider and be cautious about. Table 4–2 briefly highlights the main characteristics of each model. As is typically the case when competing theories exist, no one theory has clear-cut superiority over another. Among practicing managers, Maslow and Herzberg are more well known and are used frequently to explain worker motivation.

Clearly, each of the theories presented—Maslow's need hierarchy, Alderfer's ERG theory, Herzberg's two-factor theory, and McClelland's achieve-

ORGANIZATIONS:
CLOSE-UP

THE QUALITY FACTOR

A crucial concept for businesspeople around the world is quality improvement. As the quality of goods gets better in West Germany, Japan, France, and Canada, it must also get better in the United States. To not get better will mean to drop out of the race, to not compete. In today's race for global leadership, victory belongs to neither the speedsters—who shortcut quality—nor the plodders—who arrive behind the competition. It belongs to competitors who combine the best qualities of both: the speed to be out front and the consistency to stay ahead.

The role that a motivated work force plays in staying ahead of competition in terms of quality needs to become a top priority. Any motivation program must emphasize quality again and again. In Gallup polls in 1987 and 1989, American executives in large and small manufacturing and service companies indicated the importance of motivation. When executives were asked to rate the importance of eight different ways of improving quality in general throughout American business, motivation was at the top of the list. Employee education showed the greatest increase in ratings: 39 percent of executives rated employee education very important (10 on a 10-point scale), up from 30 percent in 1987. Improving quality by means of a "change in corporate culture" received more ratings of 10 than any other method—46 percent, up from 43 percent.

The table shows the proportion of respondents rating each method an 8, 9, or 10:

Method	1989	1987
Employee motivation	86%	85%
Change in corporate culture	85	82
Employee education	84	74
Process control	59	53
Expenditure on capital equipment	44	45
More control over suppliers	41	36
Improved administrative support	34	28
More inspections	29	29

Source: "The Race to Quality Improvement," *Fortune*, September 25, 1989, p. 515 (special section).

ment, affiliation, and power needs—can be criticized because of the methods used to test the theory and the conclusions reached (think back to the Organizational Issue for Debate about self-actualization). Whether we are discussing self-actualization, growth needs, recognition, or the need for achievement, there are problems of empirical support, bias in interpretation, and the creation of workplace conditions that aid in the satisfaction of the particular need. But despite these and other problems, managers must understand what motivation involves.

Each of the content theories purports to present the clearest, most meaningful, and most accurate explanation of motivation. One concept that none of the content theories addresses, however, is the quality of the work being done by the employee. Do employees have a need to perform so that a high quality of product or service is the outcome? When Motorola is identified as a winner of the Malcolm Baldrige national Quality Award, it is because management stressed quality improvement. Clarity, meaningfulness, and accuracy are important; but as the Close-Up on the quality factor illustrates (see p. 119), motivation on the job today must include a discussion of quality. Is quality an intrinsic or extrinsic factor? Is it a part of the need for achievement? Is it related to the self-actualization need? Any theory of motivation that fails to address quality improvement is incomplete because of the importance of such a factor in an increasingly competitive world.

SUMMARY OF KEY POINTS

— Any management attempt to improve the job performance of individuals must utilize motivation theories. This results from the fact that motivation is concerned with behavior or, more specifically, goal-directed behavior.

— A major reason why behaviors of employees differ is that the needs and goals of people vary. Social, cultural, hereditary, and job factors influence behaviors. To understand the circular nature of motivation, managers must learn about the needs of subordinates.

— The theories of motivation can be classified as being either content theories or process theories. This chapter reviews four of the more widely cited content theories. These theories focus on factors within the person (e.g., needs, goals, motives) that energize, direct, sustain, and stop behavior.

— The Maslow theory assumes that people have a need to grow and develop. The implication is that motivational programs have a higher probability of success if the upper-level need deficiencies are reduced. Although Maslow's need hierarchy has not met rigorous standards of scientific testing, it appears that an ade-

quately fulfilled need does not provide a good target for managers in building motivators that can influence performance.

— Alderfer offers a three-level need hierarchy of existence, relatedness, and growth needs. In addition to the satisfaction-progression process proposed by Maslow, Alderfer states that there is also a frustration-regression process at work that plays a major role in motivating people.

— Herzberg's two-factor theory of motivation identifies two types of factors in the workplace, satisfiers and dissatisfiers. One apparent weakness of the theory is that its findings have not been replicated by other researchers. Despite this and other shortcomings, it does focus on job-related factors in managerial terminology.

— McClelland has proposed a theory of learned needs. The behavior associated with the needs for achievement, affiliation, and power is instrumental in the job performance of an individual. Managers should attempt to acquire an understanding of these needs.

DISCUSSION AND REVIEW QUESTIONS

1. Which content theory of motivation would have the most promise for explaining motivation and helping in the economic growth of developing Third World countries? Explain.

2. What motivational lessons could be learned from the Pullman Company's attempts to take care of workers' needs from "cradle to grave"?

3. Describe the major differences between Maslow's need hierarchy and Alderfer's ERG explanation of motivation.

4. As suggested, many academics ignore Herzberg's theory of motivation, while managers believe that it has practical value. Can the theory be embraced by academics as having any value? How?

5. Why would it be interesting to examine and compare the needs, discussed by McClelland, in young, middle-aged, and older people in the United States, Japan, East Germany, Poland, Egypt, Argentina, and Sweden?

6. It is generally accepted that people are likely to be

motivated by different things at different ages and points in their lives. What must managers do so that the dynamic nature of motivation becomes part of managerial practice?

7. Explain motivation in terms that a manager could apply on the job.

8. In your opinion, how common is it for a manager to be faced with subordinates who have different pre-

dominant needs? In this situation, what should a manager do?

9. Why is it important to understand that a manager must infer the motivation level of subordinates?

10. Why is the Thematic Apperception Test (TAT) so difficult to use for interpreting motivation?

ADDITIONAL REFERENCES

Bartlett, C. A., and S. Ghoshal. *Managing across Borders.* Boston: Harvard Business School Press, 1989.

Brown, C., and M. Reich. "When Does Union-Management Cooperation Work? A Look at NUMMI and GM–Van Nuys." *California Management Review,* Summer 1989, pp. 26–37.

Day, D., and S. B. Silverman. "Personality and Job Performance: Evidence of Incremental Validity." *Personnel Psychology,* Spring 1989, pp. 25–36.

Harris, P. R., and R. T. Moran. *Managing Cultural Differences.* Houston: Gulf Publishing, 1987.

Hughes, T. P. *American Genesis: A Century of Invention and Technological Enthusiasm.* New York: Viking, 1989.

Kanter, R. M. "The New Managerial Work." *Harvard Business Review,* November–December 1989, pp. 85–92.

Putti, J. M.; S. Aryee; and T. K. Liang. "Work Values and Organizational Commitment: A Study in the Asian Context." *Human Relations,* March 1989, pp. 275–88.

Thomas, R. R., Jr. "From Affirmative Action to Affirming Diversity." *Harvard Business Review,* March–April 1990, pp. 107–17.

CASE FOR
ANALYSIS

—

Thinking about starting or buying a business? If so, you have probably heard many times that most new business ventures fail within five years and that the two most common causes of failure are lack of financing and poor management. If you think this assessment sounds unduly pessimistic, we have good news for you. Most of what you have heard about the chances of succeeding in small business is more myth than reality, painting a far more dismal picture than actually exists.

Reflecting back on American business history, you should not be surprised by this. Alfred P. Sloan, the guiding genius behind General Motors, graduated at the top of his class from Massachusetts Institute of Technology. On the other hand, Ray Kroc, the founder of McDonald's, did not graduate from high school. We have similar difficulties predicting success using such other descriptive characteristics as age, sex, and prior work experience.

At a time when the Fortune 500 firms are aggressively downsizing to become more "entrepreneurial," newly formed companies have become the principal creators of jobs in the American economy. And the trend is growing. In 1965, there were 204,000 business start-ups in the country; by 1988, that annual figure had grown to nearly 700,000.

But how realistic is the entrepreneurial dream? Does the potential to create a successful business lie within each of us? Is it the predominant need that drives us, or does it take some special combination of traits? Research into these questions is beginning to yield answers, but as yet there is nearly unanimous agreement on only one fact: the need for money is not the driving force. Rather, says psychologist and management consultant Harry Levinson, president of the Levinson Institute in Belmont, Massachusetts, entrepreneurs work with such single-minded intensity because they are psychologically compelled to.

Other researchers argue that, regardless of gender, enterprise often proceeds from deep psychic disruption. As author George Gilder remarks, "It's really hard to be an entrepreneur. You have to commit yourself obsessively to a project that might well fail, and you have to forgo all kinds of gratifications and do all kinds of jobs that other people don't want to do."

John J. Kao, an associate professor of business administration at the Harvard Business School, highlights the importance of self-actualization. "This model posits entrepreneurship as a desire for personal growth and development," and "above all else the desire to create something, whether a new product or process, a new organization or new way of doing business." When Sandra Kurtzig describes creating ASK Computer Systems, for example, she speaks fondly of "nurturing an idea, taking a seed and growing it into a baby." She also recalls the pleasure she took in hiring "good people and feeling responsible for them."

Other researchers also emphasize the entrepreneur's creative drive. David McClelland, the author of the learned needs theory discussed in Chapter 4, found that entrepreneurs, like artists, tend to be strongly invested in their work. They are motivated by the need for achievement, challenge, and the opportunity to be innovative.

Entrepreneurs have also been likened to juvenile delinquents. "It's not that they break the law or are dishonest," says psychoanalyst Abraham Zaleznik, a professor at

Source: Henry H. Beam and Thomas A. Carey, "Could You Succeed in Small Business?" *Business Horizons*, September–October 1989, pp. 65–69; Diane Cole, "The Entrepreneurial Self," *Psychology Today*, June 1989, pp. 60–63.

Harvard Business School. "But they do have one thing in common: they don't have the normal fear or anxiety mechanisms." Often, in fact, they seem to act on impulse, to be reckless.

Fred Smith's story of tide bucking is among the best known. He researched and wrote the basic plan for Federal Express as a paper in college. His professor derided the very idea of a next-day air express company and flunked him on the paper. But Smith went ahead anyway and—after some very lean years—proved his vision to be spectacularly right.

Entrepreneurs have often been members of a religious or racial minority who have had to build their own innovative paths to achievement and recognition. And it is no accident that Liz Claiborne, the first female Fortune 500 CEO who didn't inherit her position through family connections, took what *Working Woman* magazine dubbed "the outside route to the top" by starting her own firm.

In our time, the greatest source of entrepreneurial material has been politics, war, and the resulting international caravan of refugees. Gilder writes:

> In nearly every nation, many of the most notable entrepreneurs are immigrants. Immigration usually entails violation of ancestral ties and parental obligations. Dealing in their youths with convulsive change, thrown back on their own devices to create a productive existence . . . immigrants everywhere suffer the guilt of disconnection from their home and families and ally easily with the forces of the future against the claims of the past.

Perhaps the prototypical immigrant success story is Jack Tramiel, chairman of Atari, Inc. (the computer company), who came to America after surviving the horrors of Auschwitz in World War II. The Polish-born Tramiel turned a former typewriter repair shop into the Commodore International computer corporation. He frankly regards the practice of business as a battle for survival, the equivalent of war. Characterized by *Forbes* magazine as "abrasive and autocratic" when he was forced out of Commodore in 1984, Tramiel rebuilt Atari into a force in the personal computer industry after it had been given up for dead by its previous owner.

Nonetheless, for every immigrant like Tramiel, schooled in the harshest adversity, there is a comfortable, middle-class American—Steve Jobs (Apple and NEXT computers) or Sandra Kurtzig—who simply felt compelled to realize a vision or an ambition. So is there, after all, a distinct entrepreneurial personality? Many experts have looked at the available evidence and are not convinced the species is distinct.

But the lives entrepreneurs lead are observably different, and so are their achievements. As Joseph Schumpeter, one of the earliest economists to recognize and extol the place of the entrepreneur within capitalist society, once wrote, "To act with confidence beyond the range of familiar beacons and to overcome . . . resistance requires aptitudes that are present in only a small fraction of the population." And it is a simple fact that most of us choose lives that are less intense, less perilous, and not so filled with grand ambition.

Entrepreneurship is as varied as human ingenuity and enterprise, and so are the needs, goals, and motives that drive it. Its prevalence among those uprooted by political upheaval, victimized by discrimination, or oppressed by the daily grind suggest that the entrepreneur, like the artist or the intellectual, is simply looking for freedom—of expression and of the spirit.

Just as there is no one explanation of an entrepreneur's motivation (that internal drive), no specific set of principles found in motivational theories will help us understand entrepreneurship. But it is safe to predict that, whatever the next decade holds for the economies of the Soviet Union, East Germany, Poland, Hungary, Bulgaria, and Czechoslovakia, the self-motivation of citizens will be important. After years of being controlled and not being able to express themselves freely, the people of the Eastern bloc are about to unleash a tremendous wave of self-motivation. Are there entrepreneurs lurking in these countries? We think there are, and the content motivation theories will help us understand their behavior.

Questions for Consideration

1. How can content theories be used to understand entire nations that are attempting to unleash entrepreneurial practices?
2. What role does self-actualization play in entrepreneurship?
3. Can a person be trained or educated to become an entrepreneur? Explain.

APPLYING MOTIVATION THEORY

1. To evaluate the merits of different motivation theories.
2. To emphasize the decisions that must be made by managers in motivating people.
3. To apply motivation principles.

Related Topics

The manager's need to make decisions to succeed. The difficulty of diagnosing situations.

Starting the Exercise

Set up groups of five to eight students to read the facts and the situation facing Margo Williams.

The Facts

In the chapter, several popular content theories were discussed. Some of the major points raised were the following:

Maslow: Motivation involves satisfying needs in a hierarchical order.

Herzberg: Some job factors are intrinsically satisfying and motivate individuals.

McClelland: Motives are acquired from a person's culture.

Alderfer: In addition to the satisfaction-progression process proposed by Maslow, a frustration-regression process is at work.

With these four theories in mind, review the work situation currently facing Margo Williams.

Margo Williams is a project engineer director in a large construction company. She is responsible for scheduling projects, meeting customers, reporting progress on projects, controlling costs, and developing subordinates. A total of 20 men and eight women report to Margo. All of them are college graduates with at least eight years of job experience. Margo has an engineering Ph.D. but only four years of project engineering experience.

The biggest problems facing Margo involve the lack of respect and response that she receives from her subordinates. Margo's supervisor has considered these problems and assumes that her moderate record of success could be improved if she could correct the situation. Margo is now considering a course of action that could motivate her subordinates to show more respect and respond more favorably to her requests.

Completing the Exercise

1. Set up small discussion groups of five to eight students to develop a motivation plan for Margo. The group should work on developing a plan that uses the content motivation principles discussed in this chapter.
2. After the group has worked together for about 30 minutes, a group leader should present the plan to the class.
3. Discuss each group's plan for the remainder of the class period.

5

Motivation
Process Theories and Applications

LEARNING OBJECTIVES

After completing Chapter 5, you should be able to:

DEFINE
three types of learning useful to managers.

DESCRIBE
why goal setting has become a popular motivation application in organizations.

DISCUSS
how self-regulation can be useful in developing a motivation program in an organization setting.

COMPARE
the predictive power of equity, expectancy, and reinforcement theory in terms of productivity, absenteeism, and job satisfaction.

IDENTIFY
the three dimensions of self-efficacy.

PARTICIPATIVE MANAGEMENT IS AN ETHICAL IMPERATIVE

ARGUMENT FOR*

Participation has become an integral feature of quality of work life, quality circles, employee stock option plans, and new plant designs. Some empirical evidence suggests that a number of organizational and personal benefits can result from participation. When properly applied, it is effective in improving performance, productivity, and job satisfaction. Employees—individually, as members of a manager-employee team, or as part of a group of co-workers—may participate in decision making, goal setting, salary decision making, and changing the organization's structural arrangements.

Marshall Sashkin is convinced that participative management is an ethical imperative. He believes that evidence from 50 years of research has clearly, consistently, and strongly demonstrated its effectiveness in terms of motivational and specific outcomes. Sashkin suggests specific steps managers can take to implement what he calls "ethical participative management": giving subordinates more control and responsibility; setting goals with subordinates; and soliciting employees' ideas for making changes, making subordinates' job assignments, and forming work groups in which co-workers participate as equals.

Alfred Marrow, a social psychologist and president of the Harwood Company, expressed his view of research conducted in his firm:

> The results provided convincing evidence that open communication, greater self-direction, and broadly based participative approaches were a considerably more practical and profitable way to use human talent than the traditional approach, in which management decides what employees should do and then orders them to do it. . . . Productivity is high, costs are competitive, and the employees are gratifyingly satisfied.

Although Sashkin's value-based argument is forceful, he clearly states that participative management is not practical in every situation. Also, he states that not every worker wants to participate. But if Sashkin is even partially correct with his enthusiastic claim that participative management is an ethical imperative, then some workers can become more motivated by participating.

Sashkin's position is that more managers should implement participative management techniques now. The participative management revolution is based on a moral imperative, research evidence, and experience. What more support is needed for managers to address motivation and productivity problems?

ARGUMENT AGAINST†

Like most management techniques, participation has become somewhat controversial (especially when individuals such as Marshall Sashkin claim an ethical imperative for its use by management). Some negative consequences are associated with it. Peer pressure against those not enthusiastic about participating may be damaging. There is also the difficulty of readjustment if participation is suddenly cut off because of a new program or a new manager's style. But advocates of participation never clearly portray the potential negative consequences.

Edwin Locke, David Schweiger, and Gary Latham believe that Sashkin has exaggerated the value and use of participative management. In reviewing the same literature that Sashkin uses to support his position, these scholars claim that the research evidence indicates that a variety of interventions—participation being only one of them—could have been responsible for improvements in productivity. Their review indicates that in 26 percent of the studies, participation in decision making is superior to authoritative or top-down management; in 26 percent, authoritative methods are superior; and in 49 percent, neither method is superior. Results collected from studies of participative goal setting versus superior-set goal setting were similar.

Locke and his colleagues also raise the issue of participation's contribution to employee morale and satisfaction. Sashkin suggests that a happy worker is more committed and more productive. However, no such claim can be supported from over 30 years of research. Managers are cautioned not to follow Sashkin's incorrect interpretation and assume that high productivity automatically follows when job satisfaction increases.

Sashkin's assertion that participation is an ethical imperative receives particular attention from his critics. The Sashkin thesis follows this logic: (1) it is ethically wrong for managers to actively harm subordinates; (2) managers who do not use participation harm people by frustrating their basic needs; (3) to be ethical, therefore, a manager must use participation. Locke and his colleagues reject Sashkin's view that job satisfaction is the employee's right and that an organization is duty-bound to provide it. Physically harming employees is not acceptable: however, psychological harm is another issue. If management could not engage in psychological harm, how could employees be reprimanded, fired for dishonest behavior, or required to undergo training to meet quality standards?

Sashkin's critics believe that pronouncements like his are too definitive to be taken seriously. Participative management is not a panacea. Sometimes it works well, sometimes it fails. It should not be elevated to such a state of importance because logic, research, and experience fail to support such stature.

*The "ethical imperative" debate was initiated by Marshall Sashkin, "Participative Management Is an Ethical Imperative," *Organizational Dynamics,* Spring 1984, pp. 5–22. Dr. Sashkin then responded to a paper that criticized this view. His response is found in Marshall Sashkin, "Participative Management Remains an Ethical Imperative," *Organizational Dynamics,* Spring 1986, pp. 62–75.
†Edwin A. Locke, David M. Schweiger, and Gary P. Latham, "Participation in Decision Making: When Should It Be Used?" *Organizational Dynamics,* Winter 1986, pp. 65–79. Also see Bill Saporito, "The Revolt against Working Smarter," *Fortune,* July 21, 1986, pp. 58–65.

Chapter 4 examined four *content* theories of motivation, which are concerned about what specific things motivate people. In this chapter, we examine four **process motivation theories,** which attempt to explain and describe how behavior is energized, directed, sustained, and stopped. The four major process theories of motivation presented in this chapter are (1) reinforcement, (2) expectancy, (3) equity, and (4) goal setting. In discussing each, we show how the motivation process works in organizational settings.

The Organizational Issue for Debate examines the argument concerning **participative management** as an ethical imperative. Both views are well argued. They illustrate that differences in interpretation and perception play a significant role in designing motivational programs. This chapter discusses the four persuasive views of process motivation supported by various parties. Examine each view and decide which one or more of them contribute to our

PROCESS MOTIVATION THEORIES
Theories that provide description and analysis of process by which behavior is energized, directed, sustained, and stopped.

PARTICIPATIVE MANAGEMENT
Concept of managing that encourages employees' participation in decision making and matters that affect their jobs.

understanding of motivation. Because learning is such an important concept in motivation, it is discussed before the four theories are presented.

LEARNING

Learning is one of the fundamental processes underlying behavior. Most behavior within organizations is learned behavior. Perceptions, attitudes, goals, and emotional reactions are learned. Skills—for example, programming a computer or counseling a troubled employee—can be learned. The meanings and uses of language are learned.

Learning is the process by which a relatively enduring change in behavior occurs as a result of practice. The words *relatively enduring* signify that the change in behavior is more or less permanent. The term *practice* is intended to cover both formal training and uncontrolled experiences. The changes in behavior that characterize learning may be adaptive and promote effectiveness, or they may be nonadaptive and ineffective.

Three types of learning are important in developing and altering behavior. These are classical conditioning, operant conditioning, and social learning.

In understanding each of these types of learning, four basic concepts need to be clearly understood. First, a person's **drives** must be considered. A drive is an aroused condition resulting from deprivation or some specific stimulation. Primary drives (e.g., hunger) are inherent. By contrast, secondary drives (e.g., being anxious about attending a performance review feedback session) are learned. Once a drive has been learned, it triggers behavior.

A second basic concept is stimulus. A **stimulus** is a cue that is the occasion for a response. A supervisor's request is a stimulus to complete a job. The time on the clock is a stimulus to get up and go to a committee meeting. Stimuli, then, set the stage for a response or a series of responses. In some cases, the stimulus that calls forth a response is obvious. In other cases, the stimulus for a particular response is obscure.

The third basic concept is response. A **response** is the behavioral result of stimulation. It is any activity of the person, whether or not the stimulus is identifiable or the activity is observable. Responses are linked to stimuli in that when a stimulus occurs, a response is likely to follow. Responses in work organizations may be oral, written, manual, or attitudinal.

The final basic concept is the reinforcer. A **reinforcer** is any object or event that increases or sustains the strength of a response. Common reinforcers used in organizations are praise from a supervisor, a merit increase in pay, and transfer to a desirable job.

Classical Conditioning

The study of classical conditioning began with the work of the Russian physiologist Ivan Pavlov around the beginning of the 20th century. While studying the automatic reflexes associated with digestion, Pavlov noticed that his laboratory dog salivated not only in the presence of food but also at the presentation of other stimuli before food was placed in its mouth. He reasoned that food automatically produced salivation. The phenomenon was an inherent

---

LEARNING
Process by which relatively enduring change in behavior occurs as result of practice.

DRIVE
When person is aroused because he or she is deprived or stimulated.

STIMULUS
Cue that encourages some type of response.

RESPONSE
Person's behavioral activity that has resulted from a stimulus.

REINFORCER
Any object or event that increases or sustains the response given by a person.

association; Pavlov therefore labeled food an *unconditioned stimulus* and salivation an *unconditioned response.* Since he believed that the response of salivating to other, seemingly unrelated stimuli had to be learned, he labeled it a *conditioned response,* initiated by a *conditioned stimulus.*

As part of his experiments, Pavlov rang a bell (conditioned stimulus) and then placed food in the dog's mouth (unconditioned stimulus). Soon the bell alone evoked salivation. Thus, salivation produced by food is an unconditioned response, whereas salivation produced by the bell alone is a conditioned (or learned) response.[1]

Operant Conditioning

The name most closely associated with operant conditioning is that of B. F. Skinner, the world-famous behaviorist. This form of conditioning is concerned with learning that occurs as a *consequence of* behavior. (In classical conditioning, the sequence of events is *independent of* the subject's behavior.) Behaviors that can be controlled by altering the consequences (reinforcers and punishments) that follow them are referred to as **operants.** An operant is strengthened (increased) or weakened (decreased) as a function of the events that follow it. Most workplace behaviors are operants. Examples of operant behaviors include performing job-related tasks, reading a budget report, pulling a defective part off a production line, listening to a customer's complaint about poor service, or coming to work on time. Operants are distinguished by virtue of being controlled by their consequences.

> OPERANTS
>
> Behaviors that can be controlled by altering reinforcers and punishments that follow them.

In classical conditioning, the response to be learned is already present in the animal and may be triggered by the presentation of the appropriate unconditioned stimulus. In operant conditioning, however, the desired response may not be present in the subject. For example, teaching a subordinate to prepare an accurate weekly budget report is an example of operant conditioning. No identifiable stimulus automatically evokes the response of preparing the budget. The manager works with the subordinate and reinforces him or her for preparing an accurate budget. Figure 5–1 illustrates the operant conditioning process.

The relationships of $S_1 \rightarrow R_1 \rightarrow S_2 \rightarrow R_2$ are referred to as the contingencies of reinforcement.[2] This sequence is also described as the A—B—C operant mode. A designates the antecedent or stimulus that precedes the behavior, B. And C is the consequence, or what results from the behavior. Skinner believes that such consequences will be acted out in the future.[3] This notion lends itself particularly well to the study of various learning principles such as reinforcement and knowledge of results.

---

[1]An excellent presentation of the conditioning process is given in Bernard M. Bass and J. A. Vaughn, *Training in Industry: The Management of Learning* (Monterey, Calif.: Brooks/Cole Publishing, 1966). Also see Alan E. Kazdin, *Behavior Modification in Applied Settings* (Homewood, Ill.: Richard D. Irwin, 1980).

[2]W. Clay Hamner, "Reinforcement Theory and Contingency Management in Organizational Settings," in *Organizational Behavior and Management: A Contingency Approach,* ed. Henry L. Tosi and W. Clay Hamner (Chicago: St. Clair Press, 1974), pp. 86–112.

[3]B. F. Skinner, "Whatever Happened to Psychology and The Science of Behavior," *American Psychologist,* August 1987, pp. 780–86.

FIGURE 5—1

An Example of Operant
Conditioning

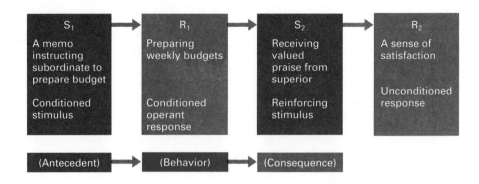

SOCIAL LEARNING

Extension of Skinner's work initiated by noted psychologist Albert Bandura. Bandura's view is
that behavior is function of continuous interaction between cognitive (person), behavioral, and
environmental determinants.
Contrary to Skinner, Bandura believes cognitive functioning must
not be ignored in explaining and
modifying behavior.

Social Learning

Albert Bandura of Stanford University extended and expanded on the work of
Skinner, illustrating how people acquire new behavior by imitating role
models (learning vicariously). **Social learning** refers to the fact that we
acquire much of our behavior (e.g., hitting a golf ball, giving a speech, using
a computer program) by observation and imitation of others in a social
context. Bandura stresses the point that cognitive functioning must not be
ignored in explaining, understanding, and modifying individual behavior.[4]

The Bandura-inspired view of behavior is that it is a function of both
personal characteristics and environmental conditions. According to Bandura,
social learning theory explains behavior in terms of a continuous interaction
between cognitive, behavioral, and environmental determinants.[5] Figure 5–2
illustrates the reciprocal relationships between cognition, behavior, and the
environment.[6]

Social learning theory introduces vicarious learning (modeling), symbolism, and self-control. Parents, friends, heroes, and respected leaders are
imitated because we identify with them. Each of us also uses symbolism as
guides for our behavior. (We know not to pull the exit release handle on the
airplane because of the mental picture we have of the consequences of a sudden
loss in cabin pressure; we set personal goals to motivate ourselves; we use
mental reminders to remember a customer's name.) We also attempt to
exercise self-control by not smoking, not drinking excessively, and not
physically throwing out of the office the person who makes a personally
disparaging remark about our family or ethnic background.

A central part of social learning theory is the concept of **self-efficacy**,[7]
defined as the belief that one can perform adequately in a particular situation.
Self-efficacy has three dimensions: *magnitude,* the level of task difficulty a
person believes he can attain; *strength,* referring to the conviction regarding

SELF-EFFICACY

Belief that one can perform
adequately in a situation. Has
three dimensions: magnitude,
strength, and generality.

---

[4]Robert Wood and Albert Bandura, "Social Cognitive Theory of Organizational Management,"
Academy of Management Review, July 1989, pp. 361–84.

[5]Albert Bandura, *Social Learning Theory* (Englewood Cliffs, N.J.: Prentice Hall, 1977), p. vii.

[6]For an excellent and concise discussion of social learning theory as applied to organizations, see
Robert Kreitner and Fred Luthans, "A Social Learning Approach to Behavioral Management:
Radical Behaviorists 'Mellowing Out'," *Organizational Dynamics,* Autumn 1984, pp. 47–65.

[7]Albert Bandura, "Self-Efficacy. Toward a Unifying Theory of Behavioral Change," *Psychological
Review,* 1977, pp. 191–215.

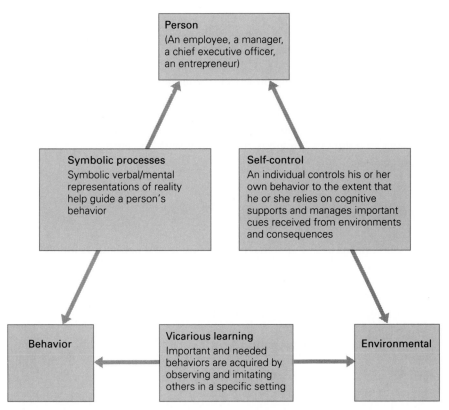

FIGURE 5—2

A Social Learning Theory
Model

Source: Adapted from Robert Kreitner and Fred Luthans, "A Social Learning Approach to Behavioral Management: Radical Behaviorists 'Mellowing Out,'" *Organizational Dynamics,* Autumn 1984, p. 55. © American Management Association, New York. All rights reserved.

magnitude as strong or weak; and *generality,* the degree to which the expectation is generalized across situations. An employee's sense of capability (Can I do the job?) influences her or his perception, motivation, and performance. We don't ever try to do a job or task when we expect to be ineffective. How would you like to try to stop Michael Jordan from scoring in a basketball game? How would you like to write a speech as emotion packed as Abraham Lincoln's Gettysburg Address? We avoid people, settings, and situations when we don't feel up to the level of performance that is required.

Self-efficacy judgments influence our choices of tasks, situations, and companions, how much effort we will expend, and how long we will try. How hard and long a student pursues a course or an area of study depends more on his or her sense of self-efficacy than on actual ability.

Self-efficacy has been related to other motivation concepts. Edwin Locke and associates suggested that self-efficacy provides an integrating mechanism between sound learning theory and goal-setting approaches.[8] Feedback is important in formulating efficacy perceptions that interact with goal setting to

[8]Edwin A. Locke, E. Frederick, Cynthia Lee, and Philip Bobko, "The Effect of Self-Efficacy, Goals, and Task Strategies on Task Performance," *Journal of Applied Psychology,* 1984, pp. 241–51.

enhance performance motivation. Self-efficacy is related to effort-performance relationships in expectancy motivation theory.

The Pygmalion effect refers to enhanced learning or performance resulting from the positive expectations of others. Some believe that self-efficacy may be involved in the Pygmalion effect through the persuasive influence of others holding positive expectations.[9] A leader's expectations about job performance might be viewed as an important input to the employee's efficacy perception. The strength of the persuasion would be influenced by the leader's credibility, previous relationship with the employee, influence in the organization, and so on.

REINFORCEMENT THEORY

The basic assumption of operant conditioning is that behavior is influenced by its consequences. B. F. Skinner's work with animals led to the use of the term *operant conditioning*. The term more often used to describe operant conditioning principles applied to individuals is behavior modification (also called B-mod and behavior mod). Thus, **behavior modification** is individual learning by reinforcement.

Organizational behavior modification, or "OB Mod," (also indicated as OBM) is a more general term coined to designate "the systematic reinforcement of desirable organizational behavior and the nonreinforcement or punishment of unwanted organizational behavior."[10] Thus, OB Mod is an operant approach to organizational behavior. "Organizational" has been added to indicate that the operant approach is being used in work settings. In this discussion, the terms *behavior modification* and *organizational behavior modification* are used interchangeably.

Principles of Operant Conditioning

Several principles of operant conditioning can aid managers attempting to influence behavior. *Reinforcement* is an extremely important principle of learning. In a general sense, motivation is an internal cause of behavior, while reinforcement is an external cause. Thus, **positive reinforcement** is anything that both increases the strength of response and induces repetitions of the behavior that preceded the reinforcement.[11] Without reinforcement, no measurable modification of behavior takes place.

Managers often use *positive reinforcers* to modify behavior. In some cases, reinforcers work as predicted; however, in other cases, they do not modify behavior in the desired direction because of competing reinforcement contin-

BEHAVIOR MODIFICATION
Approach to motivation that uses principles of operant conditioning. In this text, used interchangeably with term *organizational behavior modification*.

ORGANIZATIONAL BEHAVIOR MODIFICATION (OBM)
Operant approach to organizational behavior. In this text, used interchangeably with term *behavior modification*.

POSITIVE REINFORCEMENT
Action that increases the likelihood of a particular behavior.

[9]Marilyn E. Gist, "Self-Efficacy: Implications in Organizational Behavior and Human Resource Management," *Academy of Management Review,* July 1987, pp. 472–85.
[10]Fred Luthans and Robert Kreitner, *Organizational Behavior Modification and Beyond* (Glenview, Ill.: Scott, Foresman, 1985). Also Fred Luthans, *Organizational Behavior* (New York: McGraw-Hill, 1985), p. 303.
[11]Luthans, *Organizational Behavior,* p. 250.

gencies. When reinforcers are not made contingent on the behavior desired by the manager, desired behaviors do not occur. Also, giving reinforcers long after the occurrence of the desired behaviors decreases the probability of their recurrence.

Negative reinforcement refers to an increase in the frequency of a response following removal of a negative reinforcer immediately after the response. An event is a *negative reinforcer* only if its removal after a response increases the performance of that response. A familiar example of negative reinforcement in the summer months in Phoenix and Houston is turning on the automobile air conditioner on a stiflingly hot day. Turning on the air conditioner (the behavior) usually minimizes or terminates an aversive condition, namely being hot (negative reinforcer). This increases the probability of having an operating air conditioning system in the summer months. Similarly, exerting a high degree of effort to complete a job may be negatively reinforced by not having to listen to a nagging boss. By working hard, the employee is able to keep the boss away. The unpleasant boss is removed because the employee works hard.

Punishment is an uncomfortable consequence of a particular behavioral response.[12] A professor who takes off 10 points for each day a paper is late is using punishment. A mechanic who doesn't hand in his report and is suspended for one day with a loss of pay is being punished. Punishment, when applied, is sending the message to not do something. It is certainly a controversial method of behavior modification. Some people believe that punishment is the opposite of reward and is just as effective in changing behavior. Others consider punishment a poor approach to learning because:

1. The results of punishment are not as predictable as those of reward.
2. The effects of punishment are less permanent than those of reward.
3. Punishment is frequently accompanied by negative attitudes toward the administrator of the punishment, as well as toward the activity that led to the punishment.

Despite the potential costs of using punishment, it has been and will continue to be used as a method of altering behavior. In situations where the costs of not punishing outweigh the advantages, punishment may be an appropriate method. For example, punishing a worker who deliberately and overtly slows down the flow of work may be an economically necessary way of altering behavior. (However, there might be ways of dealing with the problem other than punishment.) The point is that punishment and its use depend on the situation and on the manager's style of altering behavior. Punishment is discussed in more detail in the next chapter.

Extinction reduces undesired behavior. When positive reinforcement for a learned response is withheld, individuals continue to practice that behavior for some period of time. If this nonreinforcement continues, the behavior decreases and eventually disappears. The decline in the response rate because of nonreinforcement is defined as extinction.

NEGATIVE REINFORCEMENT
Reinforcement that strengthens a response because the response removes some painful or unpleasant stimulus or enables the organism to avoid it.

PUNISHMENT
Consequence that results in the suppression (decrease in frequency) of the behavior that brought it about.

EXTINCTION
Decline in response rate because of nonreinforcement.

---

[12]W. Edward Craighead, Alan E. Kazdin, and Michael J. Mahoney, *Behavior Modification* (Boston: Houghton Mifflin, 1976), pp. 112–20.

An important base for these four important principles is Thorndike's classic *law of effect:*

> Of several responses to the same situation, those that are accompanied or closely followed by satisfaction (reinforcement) . . . will be more likely to recur; those which are accompanied or closely followed by discomfort (punishment) . . . will be less likely to occur.[13]

The idea that the consequences of behavior—reward or punishment—are critical in determining future behavior remains an important foundation for the use of operant conditioning in organizational settings.

Recall that positive reinforcement occurs when a positively valued consequence (e.g., a promotion) follows a response to a stimulus. Negative reinforcement occurs when a behavior causes an undesirable factor to be taken away (e.g., the nagging boss). Punishment occurs when an undesired behavior is followed by an unbearable consequence (e.g., loss of pay). In punishment, the behavior is weakened by withdrawing something positive.

Reinforcement Schedules

Properly timing the rewards or punishments used in an organization is extremely important. The timing of these outcomes is called *reinforcement scheduling.* In the simplest schedule, **continuous reinforcement,** the response is reinforced each time it occurs. If reinforcement occurs only after some instances of a response and not after each response, an **intermittent reinforcement** schedule is being used. In both cases, the behavior is *strengthened* because of the reinforcement.

Continuous and intermittent reinforcement schedules, however, produce important differences in performance. First, during the initial development of a response (e.g., learning and applying a new job skill), continuous reinforcement is preferred because it accelerates early performance. Second, when the goal is to sustain a response (e.g., good performance), intermittent schedules are more effective.

Examples of relatively continuous reinforcement might be receiving praise after every unit is produced or being greeted warmly every day by the supervisor. Intermittent reinforcement may occur, for example, in connection with preparing a report for the boss (who only occasionally will compliment you) or running for an elective union position (only occasionally do you win these elections).

Types of intermittent schedules.   Intermittent reinforcement can be scheduled in several ways. Reinforcers can be delivered by a manager on the basis of a time interval. This is referred to as an *interval schedule,* meaning that the response is reinforced after a specified time interval. Reinforcers can also be delivered after a certain number of responses. This is referred to as a *ratio schedule* because the schedule specifies the responses required for each reinforcement.

---

[13]Edward L. Thorndike, *Animal Intelligence* (New York: Macmillan, 1911), p. 244.

CONTINUOUS REINFORCEMENT
Schedule designed to reinforce behavior every time behavior exhibited is correct.

INTERMITTENT REINFORCEMENT
Schedule that results in reinforcing behavior only after some responses and not after each response.

FIGURE 5–3

Intermittent Schedules of Reinforcement Used by Managers

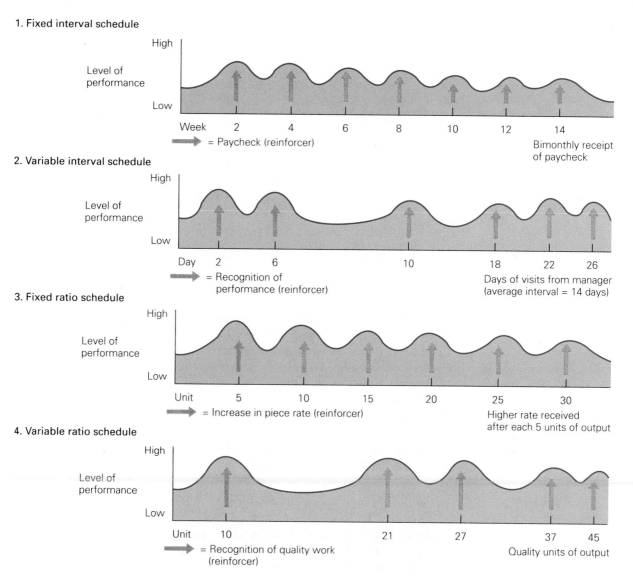

Source: Based on Dennis W. Organ and W. Clay Hamner, *Organizational Behavior* (Plano, Tex.: Business Publications, 1982), p. 76.

Interval schedules can be either *fixed* or *variable.* A fixed interval schedule requires that an unvarying time interval must pass before the reinforcer is available. Figure 5–3 highlights the intermittent schedules that managers can use. The *fixed interval schedule* is illustrated by an employee receiving a bimonthly paycheck: every two weeks, the individual is paid (reinforced). A *variable interval schedule* uses an interval that varies around an average. For example, reinforcers become available after 2, 6, 10, 18, 22, and 26 days. This averages to a reinforcer every 14 days.

A *fixed ratio reinforcement schedule* involves issuing a reinforcer after a fixed number of responses have occurred. For example, every fifth response or unit of output, if it is of acceptable quality, is reinforced. A *variable ratio schedule* also requires that a certain number of responses occur before the manager delivers a reinforcer. However, the number varies around an average. The example in Figure 5–3 shows that over the course of producing 140 units the average reinforcement occurs every 28 units: 10, 21, 27, 37, and 45, or 140, divided by five reinforcements. The manager would examine the 10th unit, 21st unit, and so forth, and call attention to the excellent quality of work.

Research has shown that higher rates of response are usually achieved with ratio than with interval schedules.[14] This finding is understandable since high response rates do not necessarily speed up the delivery of a reinforcer in an interval schedule, as they do with ratio schedules. Table 5–1 summarizes the effects various reinforcement schedules have on behavior.

Behavior Modification: A Managerial Perspective

Behavior modification is based on the assumption that behavior is more important than its "psychological causes," such as the needs, motives, and values held by individuals.[15] Thus, a behaviorist such as B. F. Skinner focuses on specific behaviors and not on such intangibles as esteem needs or personality structure. For example, a behaviorist, told that an employee is not performing well, would probably ask, "What specific behaviors led to this conclusion?" Discrete and distinguishable behaviors are the most important bases in developing any behavior modification plan to correct a performance problem.

In addition to the attention devoted to discrete and distinguishable behaviors, there is an emphasis on the consequences of behavior. For example, suppose that all new management trainees are given a two-day training program on preparing budget reports. Shortly after the training sessions, managers notice that few reports are prepared correctly. One explanation may be that the training program was ineffective. This may be the problem. However, behaviorists might approach the problem from a different direction. First, they could determine whether the trainees understand the importance of correct reports. They might then find out which trainees are turning in correct reports and what consequences, if any, are being received by these trainees. It could be that turning in correct reports results in nothing, that there are no observable consequences. In the same manner, submitting an incorrect report may also result in no consequences, positive or negative. The behaviorists' findings might result in developing a program of positive and negative consequences (e.g., recognition, praise, a meeting with the boss to go over mistakes). Behaviorists believe people tend to repeat behaviors that lead to positive consequences. This principle could serve as a cornerstone in improving the report accuracy of trainees.

---

[14]T. C. Mawhinney and T. A. Mawhinney, "Operant Terms and Concepts Applied to Industry," in *Industrial Behavior Modification,* ed. Richard M. O'Brien, Alyce M. Dickinson, and Michael P. Rosow (New York: Pergamon Press, 1982).

[15]Ron Zemke, "So Long, Skinner . . . Hello Cog Sci?" *Training,* February 1983, p. 40.

TABLE 5—1

Reinforcement Schedules and Their Effects on Behavior

Schedule	Description	When Applied to Individual	When Removed by Manager	Organizational Example
Continuous	Reinforcer follows every response.	Faster method for establishing new behavior.	Faster method to cause extinction of new behavior.	Praise after every response; immediate recognition of every response.
Fixed interval	Response after specific time period is reinforced.	Some inconsistency in response frequencies.	Faster extinction of motivated behavior than variable schedules.	Weekly, bimonthly, monthly paycheck.
Variable interval	Response after varying period of time (an average) is reinforced.	Produces high rate of steady responses.	Slower extinction of motivated behavior than fixed schedules.	Transfers; promotions; recognition.
Fixed ratio	A fixed number of responses must occur before reinforcement.	Some inconsistency in response frequencies.	Faster extinction of motivated behavior than variable schedules.	Piece rate; commission on units sold.
Variable ratio	A varying number (average) of responses must occur before reinforcement.	Can produce high rate of response that is steady and resists extinction.	Slower extinction of motivated behavior than fixed schedules.	Bonus; award; time off.

Source: Adapted from O. Behling, Charles Schriesheim, and James Tolliver, "Present Theories and New Directions in Theories of Work Effort," *Journal of Supplement Abstract Service of the American Psychological Association,* 1974, p. 57.

The proposed application of behavior modification in organizations follows a five-step problem-solving process similar to that displayed in Figure 5–4:[16]

1. Managers must identify and define the specific behavior. A behavior is pinpointed when it can be accurately observed and reliably recorded. To be pinpointed as an important behavior, there must be positive answers to these questions: (1) Can it be seen? (2) Can it be measured?[17]

2. Managers must measure or count the occurrences of the pinpointed behavior. This count provides managers with a clear perspective of the strength of the behavior under the present, or before-change, situation. The count serves as the means of evaluating any later changes in behavior. Managers can graph these data to determine whether the behavior is increasing, decreasing, or remaining the same.

3. Managers conduct an analysis of the ABCs of the behavior,[18] also called functionally analyzing the behavior.[19] In **ABC analysis,** the A designates analyzing the antecedents of the actual behavior, B; the B designates the pinpointed critical behaviors; and the C indicates the contingent consequence.

ABC ANALYSIS

Analysis of antecedents, behavior, and consequences when investigating work- or job-related issues.

---

[16]Two excellent and very similar behavior modification problem-solving processes are found in L. M. Miller, *Behavior Management* (New York: John Wiley & Sons, 1978), pp. 64–66; Luthans, *Organizational Behavior,* pp. 270–89.

[17]Fred Luthans and J. Schweizer, "How Behavior Modification Techniques Can Improve Total Organizational Performance," *Management Review,* September 1979, pp. 43–50.

[18]Thomas K. Connellan, *How to Improve Human Performance: Behaviorism in Business and Industry* (New York: Harper & Row, 1978), pp. 48–75.

[19]Luthans, *Organizational Behavior,* p. 276.

FIGURE 5−4

Applied Behavior
Modification: A Manager's
Step-by-Step Procedure

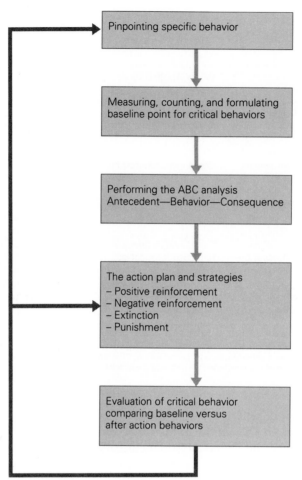

Feedback to make changes

Specific analyses of the ABCs attempt to determine where the problems lie. Thomas Connellan has developed a set of performance analysis questions to get at the problem source.[20] These are presented in Table 5−2. The ABC analysis permits managers to consider performance analysis questions important in formulating any specific program. In analyzing absenteeism, for example, managers using a question format and the type of framework displayed in Table 5−3 are systematically viewing the problem of absenteeism in terms of antecedents, behaviors, and consequences.

4. The first three steps in an applied behavior modification program set the stage for the actual step. The goal of operant conditioning is to strengthen desirable and observable critical performance behaviors and to weaken undesirable behaviors. The strategies for accomplishing these goals, discussed earlier in this section, are positive reinforcers, negative reinforcers, punish-

[20]Connellan, *How to Improve Human Performance*, p. 51.

Antecedent
Does the employee know what is expected?
Are the standards clear?
Have they been communicated?
Are they realistic?

Behavior
Can the behavior be performed?
Could the employee do it if his or her life depended on it?
Does something prevent its occurrence?

Consequence
Are the consequences weighted in favor of performance?
Are improvements being reinforced?
Do we note improvement even though the improvement may still leave the employee below company standards?
Is reinforcement specific?

TABLE 5—2

Performance Analysis Questions

Source: Thomas K. Connellan, *How to Improve Human Performance: Behaviorism in Business* (New York: Harper & Row, 1978), p. 51.

A Antecedents	B Behavior(s)	C Consequence(s)
Family problems: spouse, children	Staying home	Public reprimand
Personal health	Shopping	Private reprimand
Illness	Oversleeping	Written record and reprimand
Jury duty	Getting up late	Reduction in pay
No transportation	Attending sporting event	Suspension
Company policies	Working at home	Firing
Group norm	Visiting	Social isolation from group
Friends visiting	Serving on jury	
Injured on way to work	In emergency room at hospital	
Hangover	At doctor's office	
No child care facilities		
Do not have proper tools or clothing		

TABLE 5—3

Using the ABC Analysis on an Absenteeism Problem

Source: Adapted from Fred Luthans and Mark Martinko, "An Organizational Behavior Modification Analysis of Absenteeism," *Human Resource Management,* Fall 1976.

ment, and extinction. The application of these four strategies is presented in terms of the ABCs in Figure 5–5. Managers prefer to use positive reinforcement in most applied behavior modification programs. However, identifying positive reinforcers is not always easy. The most obvious approach for managers to take is to ask subordinates what is rewarding. Another identification method is to use attitude surveys asking about job reward preferences.

5. The fifth step involves evaluation. A major weakness in many applied motivational programs is that formal evaluations are not conducted. The evaluation of an applied program permits the manager to trace and review changes in behavior before and after the implementation of an action program. The use of evaluation permits managers to measure performance on an

FIGURE 5—5

Reinforcement Strategies Applied to ABC Analysis

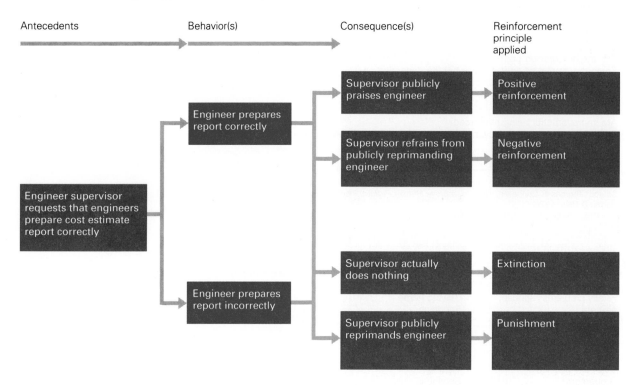

ongoing basis.[21] Furthermore, evaluation can provide feedback to managers on the behaviors exhibited. This feedback enables managers to make necessary and timely corrections in the program.

Research on Reinforcement Theory

Research on reinforcement theory applications is often limited to small samples, single organizations, and brief periods of time. Furthermore, on some occasions, it has resulted in unexpected findings. For example, one study compared the effects of continuous and variable ratio by using piece-rate bonus pay plans. Contrary to predictions, the continuous schedule yielded the highest level of performance. One reason cited for the less than expected effectiveness of the variable ratio schedules was that some employees working on these schedules were opposed to the pay plan. They perceived the plan as a form of gambling, and this was not acceptable to them.[22]

---

[21]Fred Luthans, R. Paul, and L. Taylor, "The Impact of Contingent Reinforcement on Retail Salespersons' Performance Behaviors: A Replicated Field Experiment," *Journal of Organizational and Behavior Management,* Spring–Summer 1985, pp. 25–35.

[22]Gary A. Yukl, Kenneth N. Wexley, and J. E. Seymore, "Effectiveness of Pay Incentives under Variable Ratio and Continuous Reinforcement Schedules," *Journal of Applied Psychology,* February 1977, pp. 19–23.

One characteristic of behavior modification research is its emphasis on the scientific approach. Researchers clearly define concepts, carefully classify variables, and present results so that the data trends and changes can be easily distinguished.

The list of organizational behavior modification users includes Michigan Bell Telephone, Ford Motor Co., American Can Company, United Air Lines, Warner-Lambert Company, Chase Manhattan Bank, Procter & Gamble, and Standard Oil of Ohio. The results of some applications of behavior modification principles are summarized in Table 5–4.

A survey of empirical research on organizational behavior modification (OBM) examined research involving quantity of performance, quality of performance, absenteeism, employee safety, employee energy conservation and theft, and customer service.[23] The researchers found generally strong evidence that OBM is making and can make a positive contribution to organizational behavior. Absenteeism rates, quality of production, and employee safety behaviors appear to improve more often than not when using OBM.

An interesting study was conducted to determine what leaders should do to orchestrate optimal team performance, using an operant model.[24] The model highlighted three categories of supervisory behavior: *consequences,* recognizing work well done; *monitors,* sampling the work; and *team coordination,* identifying when, where, and how team members' action should be coordinated. A sailboat regatta was arranged, including a fleet of 10 J-24 sailboats, 19 skippers, 36 crew members, 11 observers, and 4 members of the varsity coaching staff. Racing success was more prevalent for leaders who collected performance information or gave feedback during the race. The skippers who let their crews know when they were doing things right or wrong were more likely to be successful in leading teams to victory. The hypothesis concerning team coordination was not supported. The affirmation of the importance of consequences and monitors in the operant approach suggests that managers need to carefully gather information about how well employees are performing and feed that information back in a timely fashion.

Criticisms of Behavior Modification

Critics have attacked behavior modification on a number of grounds. A frequent concern with the use of reinforcers is that there is no "real" change in behavior: the person is just being "bribed" to perform. Bribery refers to the illicit use of rewards to corrupt someone's conduct. In reinforcement, however, outcomes are delivered for behaviors designed to benefit the person and the organization. Thus, this criticism, although logical, really does not apply to the reinforcers usually used in organizations.

[23]Kirk O'Hara, C. Merle Johnson, and Terry A. Beehr, "Organizational Behavior Management in the Private Sector: A Review of Empirical Research and Recommendations for Further Investigation," *Academy of Management Review,* October 1985, pp. 848–64.
[24]Judith L. Komaki, Mitzi L. Desselles, and Eve D. Bowman, "Definitely Not a Breeze: Extending an Operant Model of Effective Supervision to Teams," *Journal of Applied Psychology,* June 1989, pp. 522–29.

TABLE 5—4

Results of Applying Behavior Modification Programs in Organizations: A Summary

Organization	Types of Employees	Goals of Program	Frequency of Feedback	Positive Reinforcers Applied	Results
Michigan Bell Telephone	Operating level (e.g., mechanics, maintenance workers)	Decrease turnover and absenteeism Increase productivity Improve union-management relations	Lower level—daily and weekly Higher level—monthly and quarterly	Praise and recognition Opportunity to see oneself improve	Attendance performance has improved by 50 percent Productivity and efficiency have continued to be above standard where positive reinforcement is being used
Connecticut General Life Insurance Company	Clerical and first-line supervisors	Decrease absenteeism Decrease lateness	Immediate	Self-feedback System feedback Earned time off	Chronic absenteeism and lateness have been drastically reduced Some divisions refused to use positive reinforcement because it was "outdated"
General Electric Company	Employees at all levels	Meet EEO objectives Decrease absenteeism and turnover Improve training Increase productivity	Immediate—uses modeling and role play as training tools to teach users	Praise Rewards Constructive feedback	Cost savings Increased productivity Increased self-esteem in minority groups Decreased direct labor cost
B. F. Goodrich Company	Manufacturing employees at all levels	Improve meeting of schedules Increase productivity	Weekly	Praise Recognition Freedom to choose one's own activity	Productivity increases of over 300 percent

Source: Adapted from W. Clay Hamner and Ellen P. Hamner, "Behavior Modification on the Bottom Line," *Organizational Dynamics,* Spring 1976, pp. 12–14.

Locke believes that to view reinforcements as modifying responses automatically, independent of a person's beliefs, values, or mental processes, is simply a wrong way to view human behavior. He says that this theory is simple and appealing but that the facts do not support it. He claims that people can learn by seeing others get reinforcement and by imitating those who are not reinforced. There is also self-reinforcement, which operant conditioning theorists ignore.[25]

[25]Edwin A. Locke, "The Myths of Behavior Mod in Organizations," *Academy of Management Review,* October 1977, pp. 543–53. In addition to Locke's critique of operant conditioning, also see Jerry L. Gray, "The Myths of the Myths about Behavior Mod in Organizations: A Reply to Locke's Criticisms of Behavior Modification," *Academy of Management Review,* January 1979, pp. 121–29; M. Parmerlee and C. Schwenk, "Radical Behaviorism: Misconceptions in the Locke-Gray Debate," *Academy of Management Review,* October 1979, pp. 601–7.

Another criticism focuses on the point that individuals can become too dependent on extrinsic reinforcers (e.g., pay). Thus, behavior may become dependent on the reinforcer and never performed without the promise of the reinforcer. The point is also made that when reinforcement is no longer provided, the behavior eventually becomes extinct. However, some studies show that extinction does not always occur when reinforcers are terminated.[26] Unfortunately, these studies involve mostly children and mental patients. Whether the same results can be expected of normal adults has not been adequately tested.

BEHAVIORAL SELF-MANAGEMENT

Smoking cessation, dieting, personal growth and development, and an exercise regimen each involve the notion of self-control. The motivation of oneself has received some attention in the organizational literature in the past decade.[27] The concepts of self-motivation have evolved primarily from the social learning theory literature and related work in self-control. In the organization literature, this process has been referred to as **behavioral self-management (BSM).**

> Self-management, which is often called self-control, is defined as follows: "A person displays self-control when, in the relative absence of immediate external constraints, he engages in behavior whose previous probability has been less than that of alternatively available behaviors."[28]

Several features of self-management need to be noted. Self-management is a process whereby a person is faced with immediate response alternatives (e.g., work moderately hard; work very hard to complete the job) involving different consequences. Self-management behavior may include personal performance goals, self-instructions on how to achieve goals, self-administered consequences, a plan to behave in a particular manner, or a strategy for personally developing a set of skills.

In BSM, a person is assumed to have some control over his or her behavior, cognitive processes, and contingent consequences. Everyone practices it to some degree.[29] Usually we set certain behavior standards and reward or punish ourselves according to personal judgments we make about how our behavior relates to these standards.

BEHAVIORAL SELF-MANAGEMENT (BSM) Process whereby person is faced with immediate response alternatives involving different consequences and selects or modifies behavior by managing cognitive processes, causes, or consequences.

---

[26]Gordon L. Paul and Robert J. Lentz, *Psychosocial Treatment of Chronic Mental Patients: Milieu versus Social Learning Programs* (Cambridge, Mass.: Harvard University Press, 1977). Also Dennis C. Russo and Robert L. Koegel, "A Method for Integrating an Autistic Child into a Normal Public School Classroom," *Journal of Applied Behavior Analysis,* October 1977, pp. 579–90.

[27]Albert Bandura, *Social Learning Theory* (Englewood Cliffs, N.J.: Prentice Hall, 1977).

[28]C. E. Thoreson and Michael J. Mahoney, *Behavioral Self-Control* (New York: Holt, Rinehart & Winston, 1974), p. 12.

[29]Charles C. Manz, "Self-Leadership: Toward an Expanded Theory of Self-Influence Processes in Organizations," *Academy of Management Review,* July 1986, pp. 585–600.

A Self-Regulation Model

Since effective self-management appears to offer potential benefits to employees and organizations, a general framework could prove useful. Frederick Kanfer has proposed a three-stage model that has managerial application value. The Kanfer model of self-regulation as applied to a work situation is presented in Figure 5–6. According to the model, when a nonroutine event (e.g., new boss, unexpected equipment breakdown) disrupts the normal work pattern, a person begins to practice self-examination, or what Kanfer designates as self-regulation.

A new boss taking over is a nonroutine occurrence. The event would initiate such thoughts as "How am I performing?" and "How will I need to perform to project a good impression to the new boss?" This is stage 1, self-monitoring. Self-evaluation (stage 2) would involve comparing the previous boss with the new boss and deciding whether previous performance will be sufficient to impress the new boss. In stage 3, self-reinforcement, the person would exercise his or her own reinforcement for performing at an acceptable level. Kanfer proposes that self-regulation occurs quickly and without much awareness by a person.[30]

BSM may appear to be simply another variant of organizational behavior modification. However, there is a distinct difference in terms of the importance of cognitive processes in BSM. Bandura eloquently combined the principles of learning with an emphasis on human interactions in a social setting. In contrast to OBM, the behavioral self-management approach stresses the uniquely human cognitive processes involved in acquiring and maintaining patterns of behavior.

Research on Behavior Self-Management

Research that examines BSM in well-controlled organizational settings is limited. Until a more significant number of studies are conducted and reported, the practical value of BSM will be questioned.

One well-done study examined skills in self-management and how they impact on attendance at work.[31] An experimental group of employees was trained in self-management procedures. The principles of self-management, the identification of problem attendance behaviors, goal setting, self-monitoring, and the self-administration of reinforcers and punishers were presented, discussed, and demonstrated to the trainees. A control group did not receive any formal training in self-management skills. Employee attendance was significantly higher in the training group. The study illustrated that employees in organizational settings could benefit from self-management training. Until this study was conducted, training in self-management had been restricted to people in clinical or educational settings.

---

[30]Frederick H. Kanfer, "Self-Management Methods," in *Helping People Change: A Textbook of Methods,* ed. Frederick H. Kanfer and Arnold P. Goldstein (New York: Pergamon Press, 1980), p. 339.

[31]Colette A. Frayne and Gary P. Latham, "Application of Social Learning Theory to Employee Self-Management of Attendance," *Journal of Applied Psychology,* August 1987, pp. 387–92.

FIGURE 5—6

Kanfer's Self-Regulation Methods

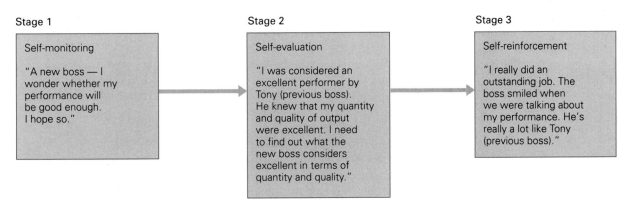

Stage 1

Self-monitoring

"A new boss — I wonder whether my performance will be good enough. I hope so."

Stage 2

Self-evaluation

"I was considered an excellent performer by Tony (previous boss). He knew that my quantity and quality of output were excellent. I need to find out what the new boss considers excellent in terms of quantity and quality."

Stage 3

Self-reinforcement

"I really did an outstanding job. The boss smiled when we were talking about my performance. He's really a lot like Tony (previous boss)."

EXPECTANCY THEORY

One of the more popular expectancy explanations of motivation was developed by Victor Vroom.[32] The majority of studies conducted (about 50) have been done to test the accuracy of expectancy theory in predicting employee behavior. They were done prior to 1980.[33] Since the early studies, about 20 additional studies have been conducted to test the theory.

Vroom defines *motivation* as a process governing choices among alternative forms of voluntary activity. In his view, most behaviors are under the voluntary control of the person and are consequently motivated.

Terminology

In order to understand the **expectancy theory of motivation,** it is necessary to define the terms in the theory and explain how they operate. The most important terms are discussed in this section.

First- and second-level outcomes. The first-level outcomes resulting from behavior are associated with doing the job itself. These outcomes include productivity, absenteeism, turnover, and quality of productivity. The second-level outcomes are those events (rewards or punishments) that the first-level outcomes are likely to produce, such as merit pay increase, group acceptance or rejection, and promotion.

Instrumentality. This is the perception by an individual that first-level outcomes are associated with second-level outcomes. Vroom suggests that

EXPECTANCY THEORY OF MOTIVATION

Theory in which employee is faced with set of first-level outcomes and selects outcome based on how choice is related to second-level outcomes. Preferences of individual are based on strength (valence) of desire to achieve second-level state, and perception of relationship between first- and second-level outcomes.   .

---

[32]Victor H. Vroom, *Work and Motivation* (New York: John Wiley & Sons, 1964).

[33]David A. Nadler and Edward E. Lawler III, "Motivation: A Diagnostic Approach," in *Perspectives on Behavior in Organizations,* ed. J. Richard Hackman, Edward E. Lawler III, and Lyman W. Porter (New York: McGraw-Hill, 1977), pp. 26–38. Also see Edwin A. Locke, "Personnel Attitudes and Motivation," *Annual Review of Psychology,* 1973, pp. 457–80.

INSTRUMENTALITY
Concept in expectancy theory of motivation in which person's perception of association of first- and second-level outcomes is determined.

VALENCE
Strength of person's preference for particular outcome.

EXPECTANCY
Perceived likelihood that particular act will be followed by particular outcome.

instrumentality can take values ranging from -1, indicating a perception that attainment of the second level is certain without the first outcome and impossible with it, to $+1$, indicating that the first outcome is necessary and sufficient for the second outcome to occur. Since this reflects an association, it can be thought of in terms of correlation.

Valence. The preference for outcomes, as seen by the individual, is termed **valence.** For example, a person may prefer a 9 percent merit increase over a transfer to a new department, or the transfer over relocation to a new facility. An outcome is *positively* valent when it is preferred and *negatively* valent when it is not preferred or is avoided. An outcome has a valence of zero when the individual is indifferent to attaining or not attaining it. The valence concept applies to first- and second-level outcomes. For example, a person may prefer to be a high-performing (first-level outcome) employee because he or she believes that this will lead to a merit increase in pay (second-level outcome).

Expectancy. This term refers to the individual's belief concerning the likelihood or subjective probability that a particular behavior will be followed by a particular outcome. That is, **expectancy** is the assigned chance of something occurring because of a behavior. Expectancy has a value ranging from 0, indicating no chance that an outcome will occur after the behavior or act, to $+1$, indicating certainty that a particular outcome will follow an act or a behavior. Expectancy is considered in terms of probability.

In the work setting, individuals hold an *effort-performance expectancy.* This expectancy represents the individual's perception of how hard it is to achieve a particular behavior (say, completing the budget on time) and the probability of achieving that behavior. For example, Joan, who is preparing a budget, may have a high expectancy that if she works around the clock she can complete the budget on time; on the other hand, she may perceive that her chances of finishing on time are about 40 percent if she works only during the day. Given a number of alternative levels of behavior to finish the budget (working 8 hours, 10 hours, or around the clock), she will choose the level of performance that has the greatest motivational force associated with it. In other words, when faced with *choices* about behavior, the person performing the task goes through a process of questioning: Can I perform at that level if I give it a try? If I perform at that level, what will happen? Do I prefer the things that will happen?

The term *force* is equated with motivation. The intent of expectancy theory is to assess the magnitude and direction of all the forces acting on the individual. The act with the greatest force is the one most likely to occur.

The term *ability* designates a person's potential for doing the job or work; it refers to the person's physical and mental abilities to do the job and not to what the person will do. That potential may or may not be utilized.

Principles of Expectancy Theory

Integration of the important expectancy theory concepts generates three major principles:[34]

---

[34]Dennis W. Organ and Thomas S. Bateman, *Organizational Behavior: An Applied Psychological Approach* (Plano, Tex.: Business Publications, 1986).

1. $P = f(M \times A)$. Performance is considered to be a multiplicative function of motivation (the force) and ability.
2. $M = f(V_1 \times E)$. Motivation is a multiplicative function of the valence for each first-level outcome (V_1) and the perceived expectancy that a given behavior will be followed by a particular first-level outcome. If expectancy is low, there will be little motivation. Similarly, if the valence of an outcome is zero, neither the absolute value nor variations in the strength of the expectancies of accomplishing it will have any effect.
3. $V_1 = V_2 \times I$. The valence associated with various first-level outcomes is a multiplicative function of the sum of the valences attached to all second-level outcomes and the instrumentalities that attainment of the first-level outcome has for achieving each second-level outcome.

Figure 5–7 uses numerical values to illustrate how expectancy theory works conceptually. The situation portrayed involves Joan, a budget specialist, who is faced with various performance (first- and second-level) outcomes. Starting at the second-level outcome point (the right side), the valence associated with finishing the budget on time is calculated by $V_1 = V_2 \times I$, or $V_1 = (6 \times 0.6) + (3 \times 1.0) + (1 \times 0.3)$, or 6.9.

We are assuming that Joan has indicated her preferences for these three outcomes. She indicates a strength of preference of 6 for a day off, a 3 for recognition and compliments from the boss, and a 1 for a mention of performance in her personnel file. Her preference ratings indicate Joan values the day off much more than the two other outcomes. Her valences are multiplied by the instrumentalities, her perceptions of the association of performance outcomes, and each of the second-level outcomes. Thus, for the "finishing budget on time" performance, this would be $6(.6) + 3(1.0) + 1(.3) = 6.9$.

The motivational force for the condition of finishing the budget on time is calculated by $M = f(V_1 \times E)$, or $M = 6.9 \times 0.4$, or 2.76. The motivational force for finishing the budget on the required day but after the deadline is 2.24, while finishing the budget the day after the deadline has a force of 0.20. Thus, the strongest force or motivation would be directed toward finishing the budget on time.

Management Implications of Expectancy Theory

Managers can certainly use expectancy theory in developing their own motivation programs.[35] However, some managerial actions must be taken to improve the theory's value. First, managers must determine which second-level outcomes are important to employees. In our example, Joan valued a day off. Simply providing a notation in her personnel file commenting on her performance was not as valued as the day off. Managers who know what subordinates prefer can attempt to provide the highly valued outcomes. Because (as this kind of outcome preference information points out) individuals prefer different outcomes, motivation programs should be designed with enough flexibility to address such differences in individual preference.

---

[35]U. R. Larson, "Supervisor's Performance Feedback to Subordinates: The Effect of Performance Valence and Outcome Dependence," *Organizational Behavior and Human Decision Processes* 37 (1986), pp. 391–409.

FIGURE 5−7

Application of Expectancy Theory: Joan's Situation

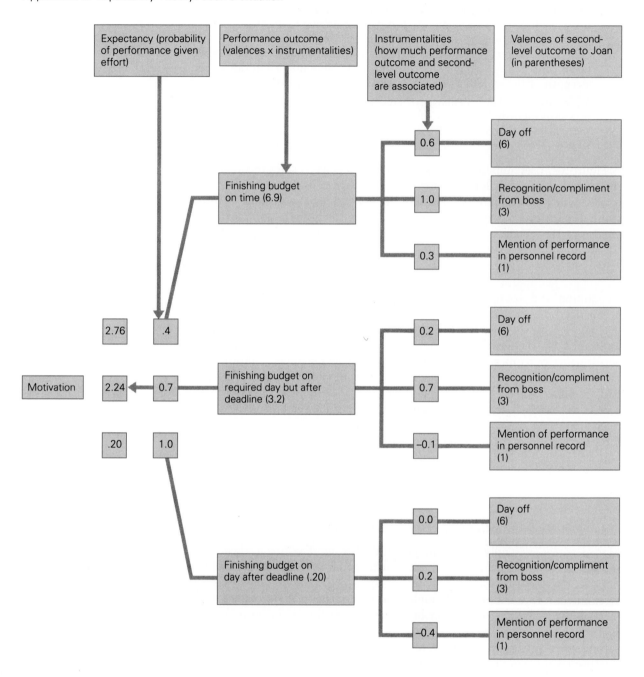

Second, managers should link desired second-level outcomes to the performance goals of the organization. Showing through example that there is an association between performance goals and desired second-level outcomes increases the employees' belief that hard work and good performance result in outcomes they prefer.

Expectancy theory assumes employees allocate their behavior according to anticipated consequences of actions. Workers weigh the information available to them and make decisions according to the value of the consequences and their own probabilities of achieving what they prefer. Expectancy theory views behavior as the product of what employees believe will happen in the future.

Research on Expectancy

Each year brings more empirical research on expectancy theory. A few studies have used students in laboratory experiments. However, most research has been conducted in field settings. One interesting study, for example, examined performance-outcome instrumentality in a temporary organization.[36] The experiment used either an hourly rate of pay (low instrumentality) or a piece rate (high instrumentality). After individuals worked for three four-hour days under one pay system, they were shifted to the other system and worked three more days. Immediately following the shift in pay systems and for all three subsequent days, the performance of the subjects shifted to the high-instrumentality system was higher than their own performance under the low-instrumentality system and higher than the performance of the subjects who were shifted to the low-instrumentality system.

Another research area focused on the valence and behavior portion of the model. The results have been mixed.[37] However, three conditions apparently must hold for the valence of outcomes to be related to effort. Performance-outcome instrumentalities must be greater than zero; effort-performance expectancies must be greater than zero; and there must be some variability in the valence of outcomes.[38]

Criticisms of Expectancy Theory

Theorists, researchers, and practitioners (to a lesser extent) continue to work on defining, measuring, and applying expectancy concepts. Many difficulties are encountered when testing the model.[39] One problem involves the issue of effort, or motivation itself. The theory attempts to predict choice or effort. However, without a clear specification of the meaning of effort, the variable

[36]Robert D. Pritchard and P. J. DeLeo, "Experimental Test of the Valence-Instrumentality Relationships in Job Performance," *Journal of Applied Psychology,* April 1973, pp. 264–79.

[37]H. Garland, "Relation of Effort-Performance Expectancy to Performance in Goal Setting Experiences," *Journal of Applied Psychology* 68 (1984), pp. 79–84.

[38]John P. Campbell and Robert D. Pritchard, "Motivation Theory in Industrial and Organizational Psychology," in *Handbook of Industrial and Organizational Psychology,* ed. Marvin D. Dunnette (Skokie, Ill.: Rand McNally, 1976), pp. 84–95.

[39]John Miner, *Theories of Organizational Behavior* (Hinsdale, Ill.: Dryden Press, 1980), pp. 133–67.

cannot be adequately measured. Typically, self, peer, or supervisor ratings of effort are used. Unfortunately, each study seems to have its own definition, measurement, and research design.

The issue of first-level performance outcomes presents another difficulty. Expectancy theory, as a process theory, does not specify which outcomes are relevant to a particular individual in a situation. Each researcher addresses this issue in a unique way. Consequently, no systematic approach is being used across investigations.

Furthermore, the expectancy approach contains an implicit assumption that all motivation is conscious. Individuals are assumed to consciously calculate the pleasure or pain they expect to attain or avoid; then a choice is made. Although it is generally accepted that individuals are not always conscious of their motives, expectancies, and perceptual processes, expectancy theory says nothing about subconscious motivation. For the most part, this point has been neglected in the theory.

Most of the available field studies testing the model have relied on employees from a single organization who were doing the same or similar jobs. These studies seriously limit and restrict the range of expectancies and instrumentalities. This type of research also raises the issue of whether results from these studies can be generalized to other samples. Is it valid to make generalizations?

Thus, although the research results have been promising, there are some major problems with the theory, research, and application of expectancy motivation. Over the years, additions to the original model have made the expectancy theory a complex model to understand and apply.

EQUITY THEORY

EQUITY THEORY OF MOTIVATION

Theory that examines discrepancies within Person after Person has compared his or her input/outcome ratio to that of reference person.

Adams, while working as a research psychologist with the General Electric Co. in Crotonville, New York, developed and tested an **equity theory of motivation.** The essence of equity theory is that employees compare their efforts and rewards with those of others in similar work situations. This theory of motivation is based on the assumption that individuals, who work in exchange for rewards from the organization, are motivated by a desire to be equitably treated at work. Four important terms in this theory are:

1. *Person*—the individual for whom equity or inequity is perceived.
2. *Comparison other*—any individual(s) or group used by Person as a referent regarding the ratio of inputs and outcomes.
3. *Inputs*—the individual characteristics brought by Person to the job. These may be achieved (e.g., skills, experience, learning) or ascribed (e.g., age, sex, race).
4. *Outcomes*—what Person received from the job (e.g., recognition, fringe benefits, pay).

Equity exists when employees perceive that the ratios of their inputs (efforts) to their outcomes (rewards) are equivalent to the ratios of other employees. Inequity exists when these ratios are not equivalent: an individual's

FIGURE 5—8

The Equity Theory of Motivation

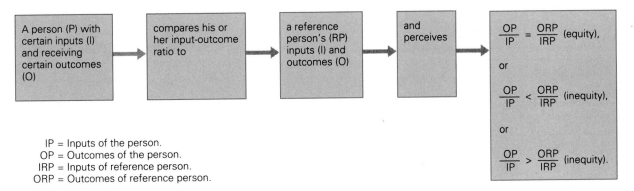

IP = Inputs of the person.
OP = Outcomes of the person.
IRP = Inputs of reference person.
ORP = Outcomes of reference person.

own ratio of inputs to outcomes could be greater or less than that of others.[40] Figure 5–8 illustrates the equity theory of motivation in general, and Table 5–5 gives an example. Note that Jeff has considered five points of comparison and has assigned hypothetical values, or weights, to the importance of each point. Jeff is assessing his outcomes as 5 and inputs as 4, for a 1.25 index, while Jeff assesses Bob's situation as 6 inputs and 2 outcomes, or 3.0. (The two major differences in this case are Jeff's being paid $4,000 less than Bob and his 18 months more experience than Bob's.) Thus, Jeff concludes that he gets less out of the job than does Bob. In essence, he believes that he is being underpaid relative to Bob, and he feels distressed or troubled by this unexplainable inequity.[41]

Change Procedures to Restore Equity

Equity theory suggests alternative ways to restore a feeling or sense of equity. Some examples of restoring equity would be:

1. *Changing inputs.* Jeff may decide to put less time or effort into the job. Other inputs that could be changed are reliability, cooperation with others, initiative, and acceptance of responsibility.

2. *Changing outcomes.* Jeff may decide to confront his boss and ask for a raise, more time off, or better assignments.

3. *Changing attitudes.* Instead of changing inputs or outcomes, Jeff may simply change his attitude. Instead of actually putting in more time at work, Jeff may decide that "I put in enough time" to make a good contribution.

---

[40]J. Stacey Adams, "Toward an Understanding of Equity," *Journal of Abnormal and Social Psychology,* November 1963, pp. 422–36.

[41]Richard C. Husemann, John D. Hatfield, and Edward W. Miles, "A New Perspective on Equity Theory: The Equity Sensitivity Construct," *Academy of Management Review,* April 1987, pp. 222–34.

TABLE 5—5

Jeff's Concept of Equity Theory: An Application

Outcomes and Inputs	Weighted Value of Outcomes and Inputs	Jeff	Bob	Weighted Value of Outcomes and Inputs
College degree (input)	1	Yes	Yes	1
CPA (input)	1	Yes	Yes	1
Experience on job (input)	2	18 months	None	0
Executive dining room privileges (outcome)	1	Yes	Yes	1
Annual salary (outcome)	4	$27,000	$31,000	5

$$\frac{\text{Outcomes } (1 + 4)}{\text{Inputs } (1 + 1 + 2)} \qquad \frac{\text{Outcomes } (1 + 5)}{\text{Inputs } (1 + 1)}$$

$$\frac{5}{4} < \frac{6}{2}$$

(Jeff) $1.25 < 3.00$ (Bob)

4. *Changing the reference person.* The reference person (Bob) can be changed by making comparisons with the input-outcome ratios of some other person. This change can restore equity.

5. *Changing the inputs or outcomes of the reference person.* If the reference person is a co-worker, it might be possible to attempt to change his or her inputs. Asking Jeff to slow down or to take more responsibility on projects are examples of such an attempt.

6. *Changing the situation.* Jeff might quit the job to alter feelings in inequity. He could also transfer to get away from an inequitable situation.

Each of these methods is designed to reduce or change the feelings of discomfort and tension created by inequity. Equity theory proposes that when inequity exists a person is motivated to take one or more of these six steps.

Research on Equity

Most of the research on equity theory has focused on pay as the basic outcome.[42] One study incorporated workplace elements into an equity theory framework.[43] Employees reassigned to offices of workers two levels above them in the management hierarchy were expected to perform at a higher level than employees reassigned to offices of more modestly overpaid workers one level above them. Similarly, employees reassigned to offices of workers two levels below them would be expected to perform at a lower level than employees reassigned to offices of more modestly underpaid workers one level

---

[42]P. S. Goodman and A. Friedman, "An Examination of Adam's Theory of Inequity," *Administrative Science Quarterly,* December 1971, pp. 271–88.

[43]Jerald Greenberg, "Equity and Workplace Status: A Field Experiment," *Journal of Applied Psychology,* November 1988, pp. 606–13.

below them. The findings indicated that employees assigned to higher-status offices increased their performance (a response to overpayment inequity) and those reassigned to lower-status offices lowered their performance (a response to underpayment inequity). The study supported equity theory's predictions that the reaction to an inequity will be proportioned to the magnitude of the inequity experienced. It is also important to note that the workplace environment—not pay inequity—was the forced point in the study.

A review of the research reveals that the comparison other is not always clarified. A typical research procedure is to ask a person to compare his or her inputs and outcomes with those of a specific person. Two issues to consider are whether comparison others are within the organization and whether they change during a person's work career.

Several individuals have questioned the extent to which inequity that results from overpayment (rewards) leads to perceived inequity. Locke argues that employees are seldom told they are overpaid. He believes that individuals are likely to adjust their idea of what constitutes an equitable payment to justify their pay.[44] Because employer-employee exchange relationships are highly impersonal when compared to exchanges between friends, perceived overpayment inequity may be more likely when friends are involved. Thus, individuals probably react to overpayment inequity only when they believe that their actions have led to a friend's being treated unfairly. The individual receives few signals from the organization that it is being treated unfairly.

Most equity research focuses on short-term comparisons.[45] What is needed is longitudinal studies that examine inequity over a period of time. What happens over time as the inequity remains, or is increased, or is decreased? These questions and research to answer them could provide insight into the dynamic character of equity theory and individual responses.[46]

Another interesting criticism of equity theory is that it ignores reactions to inequities in terms of decision making. Is it not likely that two people will react somewhat differently to the same magnitude of inequity if they believe different things caused the inequity? Folger has introduced the notion of *referent cognitions theory* to explore the role that decision-making procedures play in shaping perceptions of inequity.[47] In a work situation, suppose a manager allocates merit raises on the basis of a performance appraisal review. One employee, Mark, may resent the manager, believing that another approach based on critical incidents and work on difficult assignments *should* have been used to allocate the merit raises.

---

[44]Edwin A. Locke, "The Nature and Causes of Job Satisfaction," in *Handbook of Industrial and Organizational Psychology,* ed. Marvin D. Dunnette (Skokie, Ill.: Rand McNally, 1976), pp. 1297–1349.

[45]Robert Vecchio, "Predicting Worker Performance in Inequitable Settings," *Academy of Management Review,* January 1982, pp. 103–10.

[46]Richard A. Cosier and Daniel R. Dalton, "Equity Theory and Time: A Reformulation," *Academy of Management Review,* April 1983, pp. 311–19.

[47]Robert Folger, "Reformulating the Preconditions of Resentment: A Referent Cognitions Model," in *Social Comparison, Justice, and Relative Deprivation: Theoretical, Empirical, and Policy Perspectives,* ed. John C. Masters and William P. Smith (Hillsdale, N.J.: Erlbaum & Associates, 1987), pp. 153–215.

Referent cognitions theory predicts resentment of unfair treatment when procedures yield poor outcomes for a person.[48] A study of manufacturing plant employees found that individuals care a great deal about the justice of decision-making procedures in pay raise allocations; moreover, the issues of commitment and trust in the organization are impacted by procedural decision making. The researchers concluded that, in the allocation of pay raises, concerns other than the distributive issues need to be seriously considered. They thus implied that an equity theory explanation of motivation is too restricted and incomplete.[49]

GOAL-SETTING THEORY

GOAL SETTING

Process of establishing goals. In many cases, involves superior and subordinate working together to set subordinate's goals for specified period of time.

Since 1968, when E. A. Locke presented his what must now be considered classic paper,[50] there has been considerable and growing interest in applying goal setting to organizational problems and issues. Locke proposed that **goal setting** was a cognitive process of some practical utility. His view is that an individual's **conscious goals** and intentions are the primary determinants of behavior. That is, "one of the commonly observed characteristics of intentional behavior is that it tends to keep going until it reaches completion."[51] Once a person starts something (e.g., a job, a new project), he or she pushes on until a goal is achieved. Intent plays a prominent role in goal-setting theory. Also, the theory places specific emphasis on the importance of conscious goals in explaining motivated behavior. Locke has used the notion of intentions and conscious goals to propose and provide research support for the thesis that harder conscious goals result in higher levels of performance if these goals are accepted by the individual.

CONSCIOUS GOALS

Main goals that person is striving for and is aware of when directing behavior.

The Goal-Setting Process

GOAL

Specific target that individual is trying to achieve; the target (object) of an action.

A **goal** is the object of an action; it is what a person attempts to accomplish. For example, the attempt to produce four units on a production line, or to cut direct costs by $3,000, or to decrease absenteeism in a department by 12 percent is a goal. Frederick W. Taylor has had a direct influence on the current thinking about goals and goal-setting practices.

Locke states that Taylor used assigned goals as one of his key techniques of scientific management. Each employee was assigned a challenging but attainable goal based on the results of time and motion study. The methods by which the individual achieved the assigned goal (e.g., the tools used, the work procedures followed, the pacing needed to do the job) were spelled out in detail.[52]

---

[48]Russell Cropanzano and Robert Folger, "Referent Cognitions and Task Division Autonomy: Beyond Equity Theory," *Journal of Applied Psychology,* April 1989, pp. 293–99.

[49]Robert Folger and Mary A. Konovsky, "Efforts of Procedural and Distributive Justice on Reactions to Pay Raise Decisions," *Academy of Management Journal,* March 1989, pp. 115–30.

[50]Edwin A. Locke, "Toward a Theory of Task Motivation and Incentives," *Organizational Behavior and Human Performance,* May 1968, pp. 157–89.

[51]Thomas A. Ryan, *Intentional Behavior* (New York: Ronald Press, 1970), p. 95.

[52]Frederick W. Taylor, *The Principles of Scientific Management* (New York: W. W. Norton, 1947).

Thus, Locke points out the significant influence of Taylor in his formulation of goal setting. Locke also carefully describes the attributes of the mental (cognitive) processes of goal setting. The attributes he highlights are goal specificity, goal difficulty, and goal intensity.

Goal specificity is the degree of quantitative precision (clarity) of the goal. **Goal difficulty** is the degree of proficiency or the level of performance sought. *Goal intensity* pertains to the process of setting the goal or of determining how to reach it.[53] To date, goal intensity has not been widely studied, although a related concept, **goal commitment,** has been considered in some studies. Goal commitment is the amount of effort used to achieve a goal.

Figure 5–9 portrays applied goal setting from a managerial perspective, showing the sequence of events for such a goal-setting program. The key steps in goal setting are (1) *diagnosis* of whether the people, the organization, and the technology are suited for goal setting; (2) *preparing* employees via increased interpersonal interaction, communication, training, and action plans for goal setting; (3) *emphasizing* the attributes of goals that should be understood by a manager and subordinates; (4) *conducting* intermediate reviews to make necessary adjustments in established goals; and (5) *performing* a final review to check the goals set, modified, and accomplished. Each of these steps needs to be carefully planned and implemented if goal setting is to be an effective motivational technique. In too many applications of goal setting, steps outlined in or issues suggested by Figure 5–9 are ignored.

Goal-Setting Research

Locke's 1968 paper contributed to a considerable increase in laboratory and field research on goal setting. Another force behind the increase in interest and research was the demand of managers for practical and specific techniques that they could apply in their organizations. Goal setting offered such a technique for some managers.[54] The degree of support for goal setting as a viable motivational technique is captured best by the authors of a meta-analytic study of the effects of goal setting on task performance. They stated:

> If there is ever to be a viable candidate from the organizational sciences for elevation to the lofty status of a scientific law of nature, then the relationships between goal difficulty, specificity, commitment, and task performance are most worthy of serious consideration.[55]

Research has shown that specific goals lead to higher output than do vague goals such as "Do your best."[56] Field experiments using clerical workers, maintenance technicians, marketing personnel, truckers, engineers, typists,

GOAL SPECIFICITY
Degree of quantitative precision of goal.

GOAL DIFFICULTY
Degree of proficiency or level of goal performance being sought.

GOAL COMMITMENT
Amount of effort actually used to achieve goal.

[53]Edwin A. Locke, K. N. Shaw, L. M. Saari, and Gary P. Latham, "Goal Setting and Task Performance: 1969–1980," *Psychological Bulletin,* July 1981, p. 129.

[54]Edwin A. Locke, "The Ubiquity of the Technique of Goal Setting in Theories of and Approaches to Employee Motivation," *Academy of Management Review,* July 1978, p. 600.

[55]Anthony J. Mento, Robert P. Steel, and Ronald J. Karren, "A Meta-Analytic Study of the Effects of Goal Setting on Task Performance: 1966–1984," *Organizational Behavior and Human Decision Processes,* February 1987, p. 53.

[56]Locke, "Toward a Theory."

FIGURE 5—9

Goal Setting as Applied in Organizations

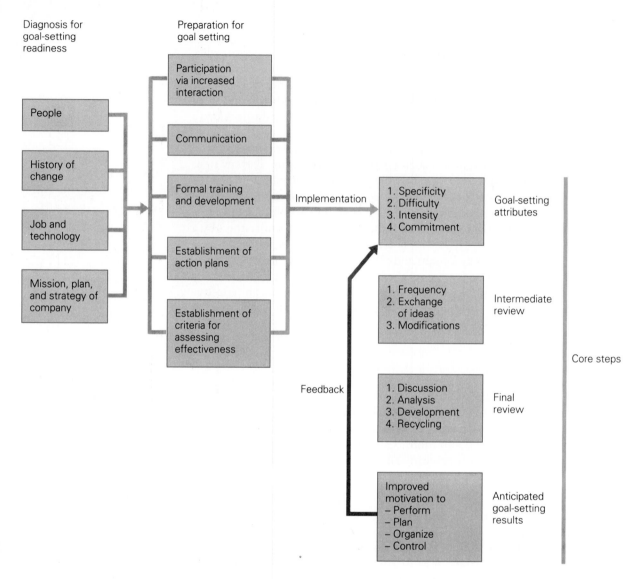

and manufacturing employees have compared specific versus do-your-best goal-setting conditions.[57] The vast majority of these studies support, partly or in total, the hypothesis that specific goals lead to better performance than do vague goals. In fact, in 99 out of 100 studies reviewed by Locke and his associates, specific goals produced better results.[58]

[57]For a complete analysis, see Locke et al., "Goal Setting."
[58]Ibid.

One study in particular highlights the practical significance of setting specific goals.[59] As part of a logging operation, truck drivers had to load logs and drive them to a mill for processing. An analysis of the performance of each trucker showed that the truckers were often not filling their trucks to the maximum allowable weight. For the three months in which underloading was being studied, the trucks were seldom loaded in excess of 58 to 63 percent of capacity.

Researchers believed that underloading resulted from management's practice of simply instructing the truckers to do their best in loading the trucks. Researchers concluded that setting a specific goal could be the operational impetus needed to improve the situation. They assigned a specific goal of 94 percent of capacity to the drivers. No driver, however, was disciplined for failing to reach the assigned goal. No monetary rewards or fringe benefits other than praise from the supervisor were given for improvements in performance. No specific training or instruction was given to the managers or the drivers.

Within the first month after the goal was assigned, performance increased to 80 percent of the truck's limit. After the second month, however, performance decreased to 70 percent. Interviews with the drivers indicated that they were testing management's promise not to take disciplinary action if goals were not met. After the third month, performance exceeded 90 percent of capacity. This performance was being maintained seven years after the original research.

The results of this field experiment are impressive. They suggest that setting specific goals can be a powerful force. The value of goal setting is reflected in a statement of the researchers:

> The setting of a goal that is both specific and challenging leads to an increase in performance because it makes it clearer to the individual what he is supposed to do. This in turn may provide the worker with a sense of achievement, recognition, and commitment, in that he can compare how well he is doing now versus how well he has done in the past and in some instances, how well he is doing in comparison to others.[60]

At NutriSystem, specific and challenging goals are used to help clients lose weight. The Close-Up spells out how goal setting is used at 1,400 NutriSystem weight-loss centers.

The difficulty factor.   Generally, the more difficult the goal, the higher the level of performance. But a point of diminishing returns appears to be a real issue in goal difficulty. Although laboratory and field studies find that people with high (difficult) goals consistently perform better, there is a critical point.[61] If and when a goal is perceived as so difficult that it is virtually impossible to attain, the result is often frustration rather than achievement.

The difficulty of the United Fund's fund-raising goals points up the issue of frustration.[62] The more difficult the goal, the more money that was raised.

---

[59]Gary P. Latham and J. J. Baldes, "The Practical Significance of Locke's Theory of Goal Setting," *Journal of Applied Psychology,* February 1975, pp. 122–24.

[60]Ibid., p. 124.

[61]Locke et al., "Goal Setting."

[62]A. Zander and T. T. Newcomb, "Goal Levels of Aspirations in United Fund Campaigns," *Journal of Personality and Social Psychology,* June 1967, pp. 157–62.

ORGANIZATIONS: CLOSE-UP

NUTRISYSTEM FRANCHISES USE GOAL SETTING

NutriSystem, founded in 1971, has a lot of motivation principles embedded in its philosophy. The company franchises weight-loss centers that look like medical offices (symbolic), charges customers a hefty join-up fee ("it must be good"), offers weekly therapy sessions, and uses goal setting to help clients lose weight. Also, NutriSystem clients are required to buy prepackaged, calorie-controlled entrees.

The diet business is booming. Nearly one in every five Americans is overweight. As most people know, there is no long-term cure for the truly overweight. Studies show that, within five years, most dieters are likely to gain back any weight they lose.

About 750,000 people a year sign up for NutriSystem's program. Here's how it works: The client is welcomed by a professional-looking weight-loss consultant in a white lab coat. After a weigh-in by the consultant, the client's measurements, age, and so forth are plugged into a computer called the weight monitor. The monitor determines an ideal weight. A polaroid picture is taken and placed in a personal file. The client fills out a psychological questionnaire, then pays in advance according to the weight he or she wants to lose. Successful clients can recoup up to half of their up-front fee by maintaining their target weight for a year. The target weight is the goal set by the client with the help of the consultant.

Goals, targets, self-control, incentives, and a professional atmosphere are all part of NutriSystem's approach. Although the consultants probably have little knowledge of all the motivation concepts you have been reading about, they are applying them to the diet business. The application of motivation theories to this business has made some clients very happy (they lose weight), some clients very sad (they don't lose weight or they gain lost weight back), and the owners of NutriSystem franchises a profit.

Source: Matthew Schifrin, "Living Off the Fat of the Land," *Forbes*, November 13, 1989, pp. 186–96.

This was true, however, only when the goals were seen as attainable. When they were viewed as unattainable, the morale of fund-raisers suffered.

Goal acceptance is extremely important to any discussion of the effectiveness of goal setting. One method used to enhance goal acceptance is to permit individuals to participate in goal setting. Researchers suggest that when an individual faces a difficult goal, participative goal setting enhances goal acceptance more than assigned goal setting. In a two-part study, researchers found that participative and representative goal setting (group-elected members represented others in negotiating goals) significantly increased individual goal acceptance; consequently, individual goal acceptance significantly contributed to performance.[63]

---

[63]Miriam Erez, P. Christopher Earley, and Charles L. Hulin, "The Impact of Participation on Goal Acceptance and Performance: A Two-Step Model," *Academy of Management Journal*, March 1985, pp. 50–66. Also Miriam Erez and Frederick H. Kanfer, "The Role of Goal Acceptance in Goal Setting and Task Performance," *Academy of Management Review*, 1983, pp. 454–63.

FIGURE 5–10

The Goal Difficulty–Performance Relationship: Three Motivation Views

Locke has contrasted goal setting with the expectancy and need-for-achievement explanations of motivation.[64] Figure 5–10 highlights the differences in the explanations of the goal difficulty–performance relationship proposed by these three theories. Expectancy theory predicts increased performance will result from easier goals, since the probability of success (and also the probability of being rewarded) increases. The need-for-achievement prediction is that difficult goals improve performance up to a point but that when goals are too difficult, performance suffers.

One explanation of the goal difficulty–performance relationship is presented as graph III in Figure 5–10. Locke predicts that a person's performance will increase as goal difficulty increases, assuming that the person is committed and has the ability to perform. A ceiling of performance (B) is reached. Individuals who lack commitment to difficult goals have decreasing or poor performance (C).

---

[64]Edwin A. Locke and Gary P. Latham, *Goal Setting: A Motivational Technique that Works* (Englewood Cliffs, N.J.: Prentice Hall, 1984), p. 22.

The difficulty of goal setting has been linked to cardiovascular responses. Results in one study showed that subjects expecting to perform a moderately difficult task showed significant increases in their blood pressure.[65] Subjects performing easy tasks showed little physiological reactivity. The issue of physiological response among goal setters needs to be examined further because of the potential legal consequences that may be introduced by employees who do not meet goals and are subsequently fired, transferred, or demoted.

Adding the participation factor. In one of the more interesting studies of goal setting, a joint design of a series of experiments was conducted to study the effect of participation on goal commitment and performance.[66] Locke served as a third-party mediator of the two views held by Latham and Erez. Latham proposed that when goal difficulty is held constant, there are virtually no differences in goal commitment or performance, regardless of whether the goal was assigned or set participatively. Erez believed that participation in goal setting is crucial to goal commitment; that is, if a person does not participate, there is little commitment to accomplish the goal.

A series of four experiments was conducted at the University of Maryland and the University of Washington to test the two viewpoints of goal setting. There was no effect of value for participation on goal commitment or performance in any of the four experiments. The mediator aptly explained that a number of differences in design and procedures occurred even when two excellent researchers were allegedly studying the same phenomenon. The way the researchers gave instructions and exactly what they said seemed to have an influence on the participants. Giving self-efficacy instructions to a participative group seems also to have biased the results. The same self-efficacy instructions were not given to what are called test participants (they were told what was expected in terms of output in the actual experiment, based on how they performed in the trial run).

The study is commendable for its completeness, the participation of researchers who disagreed with each other's previous findings, and the use of a third-party mediator. Each of these features contributes to improved public confidence in organizational research. However, despite Locke's comments that the results of laboratory studies generalize well to the field, the laboratory setting is a weakness of the study.[67] Organizational practitioners would pay more attention to the results of such an innovative study if employees and work settings were used.

Can these results be replicated in organizations in the United States and around the world? As Eastern bloc countries attempt to improve the perfor-

---

[65]B. Wright, R. J. Contrada, and M. J. Patane, "Task Difficulty, Cardiovascular Response and the Magnitude of Goal Valence," *Journal of Personality and Social Psychology,* 1986, pp. 837–43.

[66]Gary P. Latham, Miriam Erez, and Edwin A. Locke, "Resolving Scientific Disputes by the Joint Design of Crucial Experiments by the Antagonists: Application to the Erez-Latham Dispute regarding Participation in Goal Setting," *Journal of Applied Psychology,* November 1988, pp. 753–72.

[67]Edwin A. Locke, ed., *Generalizing from Laboratory to Field Settings* (Lexington, Mass.: Lexington Books, 1986).

mance of their economies and enterprises, will goal setting be effective? The collectivist and centralized economies of Hungary, Poland, the Soviet Union, and East Germany may not be suited for participative goal setting. The cultures of these and other countries may significantly moderate the effects, if any, of goal-setting programs. After years of having decisions handed down from top-level administrators and bureaucrats, many individuals are not used to participating. They were told what to do, and they complied. Researchers have found that a country's culture does moderate the effects of both decision-making and goal-setting strategies on performance when different goals are used.[68]

Individual differences.   Scattered throughout the goal-setting literature are studies that examine the effects of individual differences on goal setting. Most of these studies have dealt with the effects of education, race, and job tenure on the goal-setting process. A study involving electronics technicians found that goal difficulty (challenge) was significantly related to performance only for those technicians with 12 or more years of education. For technicians with less education, goal clarity (i.e., having a clear understanding of the goal) and goal feedback (i.e., receiving feedback on how results matched the goal) were significantly related to performance.[69]

In a field experiment, loggers working under assigned, participative, and do-your-best conditions were compared. Researchers found that participative goal setting affected the performance of the less educated loggers but not of the more educated loggers.[70]

One study examined three explanations of why participation in goal setting may lead to increased job performance: the social factor of group discussion, the motivational factor of being involved in the goal-setting process, and the cognitive factor of information sharing.[71] Results of this study of white-collar employees indicated that the social and motivational factors increased performance quantity, learning the task, goal acceptance, group commitment, and satisfaction.

Another study examined race as a goal-setting variable. It determined that goal clarity and goal feedback were related to performance for blacks only.[72] In contrast, goal difficulty (challenge) was found to be related to performance for whites only. The researchers proposed that clarity and feedback may have affected the black goal setters because they had a higher need for security. Goal clarity and accurate feedback are ways of increasing security.

---

[68]Miriam Erez, "The Congruence of Goal Setting Strategies with Sociocultural Values and Its Effect on Performance," *Journal of Management,* 1986, pp. 83–90; Miriam Erez and P. Christopher Earley, "Comparative Analysis of Goal Setting Strategies across Cultures," *Journal of Applied Psychology,* November 1987, pp. 658–65.

[69]John M. Ivancevich and J. Timothy McMahon, "Education as a Moderator of Goal-Setting Effectiveness," *Journal of Vocational Behavior,* August 1977, pp. 83–94.

[70]Gary P. Latham and Gary A. Yukl, "Assigned versus Participative Goal Setting with Educated and Uneducated Wood Workers," *Journal of Applied Psychology,* June 1975, pp. 299–302.

[71]Miriam Erez and R. Arad, "Participative Goal Setting: Social, Motivational, and Cognitive Factors," *Journal of Applied Psychology,* 1986, pp. 591–97.

[72]John M. Ivancevich and J. Timothy McMahon, "Black-White Differences in a Goal Setting Program," *Organizational Behavior and Human Performance,* December 1977, pp. 287–300.

Goal Setting: An Application at Tenneco, Inc.[73]

Tenneco is a large, diversified company operating in eight major industries. The Tenneco companies include J. I. Case, manufacturer and marketer of farm and construction equipment, and Packaging Corporation of America, a vertically integrated supplier of paperboard, folding cartons, and corrugated containers. Unlike most users of goal setting, Tenneco decided to emphasize not only performance goals but also personal development goals in its program.

The chairman of the board at Tenneco issued statements, memos, and guidelines on the goal-setting effort. The emphasis on personal development was to be accomplished through a program whose goals focused on performance and development criteria of success for managers. The program was designed by a task force representing each of Tenneco's companies.

One phase specifically stressed at Tenneco was formally training the goal-setting participants (managers) in "how to do it." A corporate-level training package was prepared, which each company altered, added to, or subtracted from as needed. The training package explained what goal setting was, how it was to be used, and the skills needed for effective goal setting.

Reexamine Figure 5–9, since this is basically the sequence of events and the framework of Tenneco's goal-setting program. Management systematically diagnosed, prepared for goal setting, and implemented each of the core steps—goal setting, intermediate reviews, and a final review. Evaluations of the Tenneco goal-setting program found that:

1. Morale improved after the program was implemented.

2. The work environment was more relaxed (less job tension) for users of the goal-setting program.

3. The program was more successful in those Tenneco units in which management (supervisors) actively participated in and supported goal setting.

4. Time must be spent in diagnosis, training, and evaluation so proper alterations in procedures and goal setting could be made.

5. Many individuals had difficulty establishing personal development goals. This difficulty may have been caused by a climate that for years overemphasized performance. Many individuals had not had to think in terms of their own personal development.

6. Patience is needed before deciding whether an applied goal-setting program such as Tenneco's is a success or failure. Those using goal setting should allow six months, a year, or even longer before reaching any conclusions. At Tenneco, numerous improvements and some negative results (irritation with paperwork, feelings of not being trained properly or long enough to do the goal setting) did not show up until one or two years after the program had been initiated.

---

[73]Based on the detailed study as presented in unpublished reports and executive summaries and in John M. Ivancevich, J. Timothy McMahon, J. William Streidl, and Andrew D. Szilagyi, Jr., "Goal Setting: The Tenneco Approach to Personnel Development and Management Effectiveness," *Organizational Dynamics,* Winter 1978, pp. 58–80.

ORGANIZATIONS:
CLOSE-UP

SELF-SET GOALS: SOME HELPFUL POINTERS

Setting goals is popular in every occupation. Lee Iacocca is known to be a daily goal setter. Most professional athletes, such as Michael Jordan in basketball and A. J. Foyt in auto racing, are goal setters. So are world-renowned heart surgeon Denton Cooley and millions of others who write down goals and continually take stock of how they are doing. You, too, can benefit from self-set goals. Ask yourself these questions, which can be converted into specific goals:

— Is my knowledge of my job progressing?

— How developed are my people skills?

— Have I improved and increased my network of contacts?

— What other skills should I be working on (problem solving, managing time more efficiently, negotiating)?

— Do other people respect me? What can I do to improve the respect others have for me?

— How does this week's/month's/year's performance match up with similar periods of past performance?

— Out of everything I have done at work in the past three months, of which three things am I most proud? Least proud?

Personal goal setting developed along these lines can help everyone stay motivated. Chances are, these and similar questions can help you take a close look at your strengths, weaknesses, and potential. Thus, goal setting does not have to be the formal type established within your company; it can come totally from you on a regular basis.

Tenneco is not presented as either a success or a failure of applied goal setting. Instead, it provides a view of the complexities, details, and hard work associated with such programs. There is no easy or ideal way to apply goal setting. Advance preparation for successes, failures, and changes along the way seems to be the best way to approach goal setting in work organizations.

Although Tenneco, Inc., is a large firm with a goal-setting program, much is to be gained by developing an individual program. The Close-Up on self-set goals introduces some pointers for setting up a personal goal-setting program.

Criticisms of Goal Setting

Unfortunately, there are some arguments against using goal setting or becoming too enthusiastic about it. Some managers and researchers have found that:

Goal setting is rather complex and difficult to sustain. At Tenneco, for example, difficulties across divisions became somewhat disruptive when corporate guidelines were implemented.

Goal setting works well for simple jobs—clerks, typists, loggers, and technicians—but not for complex jobs. Goal setting with jobs in which goals are not easily measured (e.g., teaching, nursing, engineering, accounting) has posed some problems.

Goal setting encourages game playing. Setting low goals to look good later is one game played by subordinates who do not want to be caught short. Managers play the game of setting an initial goal that is generally not achievable and then finding out how subordinates react.

Goal setting is used as another check on employees. It is a control device to monitor performance.

Goal accomplishment can become an obsession. In some situations, goal setters have become so obsessed with achieving their goals that they neglect other important areas of their jobs.

Under the right conditions, goal setting can be a very powerful technique for motivating employees. When used correctly, carefully monitored, and actively supported by managers, it can improve performance. (Goal difficulty and goal acceptance are two attributes that need to be considered by management.) The clear implication for managers is that getting employees to set and strive to attain specific, relatively hard goals can generate a strong motivational force.

REVIEWING MOTIVATION

In Chapters 4 and 5, a number of popular, empirically tested, and practical theories of motivation were portrayed. That the theories are typically pitted against one another in the literature is unfortunate, since each theory can help managers better understand workplace motivation. Each theory attempts to organize, in a meaningful manner, major variables associated with explaining motivation in work settings.

The *content* theories concentrate on individuals, placing primary emphasis on the characteristics of people. Each of the *process* theories has a specific orientation. Reinforcement theory focuses on the work environment, virtually ignoring the notion of individual needs and attitudes. Expectancy theory emphasizes individual, job, and environmental variables; it recognizes differences in needs, perceptions, and beliefs. Equity theory primarily addresses the relationship between attitudes toward inputs and outcomes and toward reward practices. Goal-setting theory emphasizes the cognitive processes and the role of intentional behavior in motivation.

Each of the theories we have presented has something to offer managers, and various parts of the theories are complementary in many respects. The Close-Up questioning whether managers have to be psychologists points out that each of the motivation theories discussed to this point has value if used correctly.

The psychologists and social psychologists who formulated these theories were experts in explaining needs, motives, and values. They were not, however, so astute at explaining what managers could do to motivate employees. And, despite the abundance of theories, research, and complementarity, many managers still choose to ignore the academically generated theories of motivation.

SHOULD MANAGERS BE PSYCHOLOGISTS? NO!

Do you have to be a psychologist to understand and use the motivation theories presented in this chapter? We hope not. The theories point out that managers cannot know with certainty what goes on inside an employee's head. Motivation is merely an abstract concept invented from evidence taken from observed behavior and designed to explain the behavior from which it is taken. Yes, motivation is something that comes from within, but managers still do not know exactly what goes on inside.

Some believe that it's up to the manager and the company to set the stage, to create the atmosphere that allows the employee's internal motivation to appear. To do so, managers need to tailor rewards to individual motivation. The manager has to search and find out what makes an individual tick, what triggers the internal state that is eventually observed by managers as higher performance or less absenteeism. The details, complexities, and problems associated with needs, motives, values, and physical responses to work are not really in the domain of managers. The manager is an amateur in this arena, which is really better suited for the professional psychologist. Likewise, the psychologist is an amateur when it comes to the day-to-day operations of managing people and creating stimulating work environments.

Thus, the psychologist is the expert best prepared to discuss, analyze, and interpret needs, drives, and values. On the other hand, the manager is the expert when it comes to creating the atmosphere in which an employee's internal motivation can grow and be sustained. Experts in one area can look rather foolish and even be dangerous in another area. Managers need to beware and use their expertise where they are experts.

But, if anything, Chapters 4 and 5 indicate that instead of ignoring motivation, managers must take an active role in motivating their employees. Nine specific conclusions are reached:

1. Managers can influence the motivation of employees. If performance needs to be improved, then managers need to intervene and help create an atmosphere that encourages, supports, and sustains improvement. Motivation can be managed.

2. Managers must remember that ability, competence, and opportunity play a role in motivation. A person with little ability or few skills will have a difficult time being productive. An organization with no opportunities available and with obstacles such as poor equipment, inadequate working conditions, and ill-mannered managers will be hard pressed to help create an atmosphere that encourages general motivation and self-motivation.

3. Managers need to be sensitive to variations in employees' needs, abilities, and goals. They must also consider differences in preferences (valences) for rewards. Individual differences mean that tailoring motivational efforts should be a part of managers' attempts to motivate.

4. Continual monitoring of needs, abilities, goals, and preferences of employees is each individual manager's responsibility and is not the singular domain of personnel/human resource managers.

TABLE 5—6

The Predictive Power of Selected Motivation Theories*

	Theories					
	Need-Based†	Reinforcement	Behavioral Self-Management	Expectancy	Equity‡	Goal-Setting
Productivity	6§	6	6	7	7	9
Absenteeism		8	8‖	8	8	
Job satisfaction	6				6	6#

*Ratings are based on a scale of 1 to 10. 10 being the highest.
†Includes theories of Maslow, Herzberg, Aldefer, and McClelland.
‡Based primarily on studies of pay issues.
§Primarily found for employees with a high need for achievement.
‖Limited number of studies.
#Satisfaction levels are higher if goal program is considered fair, meaningful, and more than a control mechanism.

5. Some individuals practice a high degree of self-regulation and personal motivation. Managers must attempt to channel self-motivated behavior into productive results.

6. Managers as role models can be very influential in motivating employees. Social learning occurs on a regular basis, and managers must be aware that their style, techniques, and work behavior are being observed and can be easily imitated.

7. When employees note that valued outcomes can be achieved through performance, a major part of the motivation strategy has succeeded.

8. Establishing goals to direct behavior is an important part of any motivational program.

9. Managers should try to provide employees with jobs that offer equity, task challenge, diversity, and a variety of opportunities for need satisfaction.

In simple terms, the theme of our discussion of motivation is that the *manager needs to be actively involved*. If motivation is to be energized, sustained, and directed, managers have to understand needs, intentions, preferences, goals, reinforcement, and comparison. Failure to learn about these concepts results in many missed opportunities to motivate employees in a positive manner.

Table 5–6 briefly summarizes how well the various themes and approaches predict productivity, absenteeism, and job satisfaction. The ratings are based on available empirical research conducted in organizations primarily in the United States and Canada. The ratings also use the judgments of researchers, anecdotal information, and managerial opinions.[74] While the data presented are not scientifically validated in every instance, they are based on multiple sources of information.

---

[74]Frank J. Landy and W. S. Becker, "Motivation Theory Reconsidered," in *Research in Organizational Behavior*, ed. Larry L. Cummings and B. M. Stewart (Greenwich, Conn.: JAI Press, 1987), p. 33.

SUMMARY OF KEY POINTS

— A central part of Bandura's social learning theory is the concept of self-efficacy; that is, the belief that a person knows that he or she can perform adequately in a particular situation.

— Reinforcement theory relies on applying the principles of operant conditioning to motivate people. A major assumption of operant conditioning is that behavior is influenced by its consequences.

— The nature of reinforcements and punishments and how they are employed influences behavior. Thus, reinforcement scheduling, or the timing of consequences, is an important feature of motivation.

— A concept that has evolved from social learning theory is called self-motivation. The concept of self-control is at the core of what is now called behavioral self-management in the organization literature.

— The expectancy theory of motivation is concerned with the expectations of a person and how they influence behavior. One value of this theory is that it can provide managers with a means for pinpointing

desirable and undesirable outcomes associated with task performance.

— Equity theory focuses on comparisons, tension, and tension reduction. To date, most of the research work on equity theory has involved pay. Equity theory is a more straightforward and understandable explanation of employee attitudes about pay than is expectancy theory. The manager should be aware that people compare their rewards, punishments, tasks, and other job-related dimensions to those of others.

— Goal-setting theory proposes that an individual's goals and intentions are the primary determinants of behavior. Perhaps the most empirically supported approach to motivation, goal setting continues to be refined and studied in laboratory and field settings.

— Despite impressive supportive studies, goal setting has been criticized as working primarily for easy jobs, encouraging game playing, and operating as another control check on employees.

DISCUSSION AND REVIEW QUESTIONS

1. What are some similarities and differences between the reinforcement and expectancy explanations of motivation?

2. Could a manager who understands equity theory utilize this knowledge in developing pay programs? How?

3. How does self-control play a role in motivation?

4. Apply Kanfer's model of self-regulation to a personal family, work, or school situation in which you are currently involved. Discuss each of the stages and the questions you should be asking.

5. What ethical considerations should be considered before using a behavior modification program in a work setting?

6. The authors stressed that the Table 5–6 data were not scientifically validated; that is, the data are subject to

different interpretations. Why, after all the years of research, are the authors cautious in their statements about the data?

7. Why would it be difficult to use a "change the situation" approach to restore equity during hard economic times?

8. Compare the research results on behavior modification and goal setting. Are there differences in the research being conducted on these two approaches?

9. Explain the three dimensions of self-efficacy. To illustrate the dimensions, use a particular task that you are attempting to master.

10. What is the major difference between a Skinner and a Bandura analysis of motivation?

ADDITIONAL REFERENCES

Anderson, S., and J. Rodin. "Is Bad News Always Bad? Cue and Feedback Effects on Intrinsic Motivation." *Journal of Applied Social Psychology,* May 1989, pp. 449–67.

Andrasik, F. "Organizational Behavior Modification in Business Settings: A Methodological and Content Review." *Journal of Organizational Behavior Management,* Spring 1989, pp. 59–77.

Dornstein, M. "Pay Equity Evaluations of Occupations and Their Bases." *Journal of Applied Social Psychology,* September 1988, pp. 905–24.

Hollenberk, J. R.; C. R. Williams; and H. J. Klein. "An Empirical Examination of the Antecedents of Commitment to Difficult Goals." *Journal of Applied Psychology,* February 1989, pp. 18–23.

Locke, E. A.; D. Chah; S. Harrison; and N. Lustgarten. "Separating the Effects of Goal Specificity from Goal Level." *Organizational Behavior and Human Decision Processes,* April 1989, pp. 270–87.

Martinko, M. J.; D. J., White; and B. Hassell. "An Operant Analysis of Prompting in a Sales Environment." *Journal of Organizational Behavior Management,* Spring 1989, pp. 93–107.

Pritchard, R. D.; S. D. Jones; P. L. Roth; K. K. Stuebing; and S. E. Ekeberg. "Effects of Group Feedback, Goal Setting, and Incentives on Organizational Productivity." *Journal of Applied Psychology,* May 1988, pp. 337–58.

—
CASE FOR
ANALYSIS
—

JACK WELCH OF GENERAL ELECTRIC: A NEUTRON BOMB OR A MOTIVATOR?

Jack Welch, chairman of General Electric Co. (GE), has been referred to as "Neutron Jack" (when he enters a GE facility, the building remains standing but the workers are wiped out). Welch picked up the nickname by cutting more than 100,000 workers from GE's payroll in five years. He eliminated the jobs through layoffs, attrition, and the sale of businesses. He bought companies worth $16 billion. He sold companies worth $9 billion. When Welch took over at age 45, he was GE's youngest chairman. Then, GE was referred to as a "GNP company," one whose growth and prosperity never exceeded that of the overall economy.

Welch set out to create a company that could outpace the economy and thrive even in the toughest times. He utterly transformed GE, reshaping the corporate culture to reflect his relentless energy and informal but rigorous style. Welch sorted operations according to a simple criterion: to keep from being sold or shuttered, each had to be number 1 or number 2 in its market. He grouped businesses that he said met the test into three circles: services, such as GE Credit Corp. and a unit that maintains nuclear power plants; technology products in high-growth markets, such as jet engines and plastics; and what Welch calls the core businesses. These are the classic big players in such mature industries as light bulbs and electric motors. Exhibit 1 tells how a dozen GE businesses rank in the United States and in the world.

Welch is a sensitive, no-nonsense man who views the world as competitively tough. He sees global markets coming to be dominated by a few powerful steamrollers like Philips, Siemens, and Toshiba. To compete, a firm like GE must be bold, free of bureaucratic red tape, and staffed by self-motivated, proud, and quick-moving managers and employees. People who don't personally know Welch may fear his blunt, somewhat abrasive style. However, those who spend time around him tend to like his intelligence, humor, and openness.

GE can be enormously exciting for those in the right places or attuned to the Welch mentality. By all accounts, the degree to which Welch has transformed the company's bureaucratic culture is astonishing. From the start, he made plain the GE managers have to achieve unsurpassed quality at Scroogelike cost and capture the required market share. If they fail, they go.

In eliminating managerial layers, Welch moved authority for most decisions down to 20 operating divisions. He promotes a feeling of what he calls ownership, urging managers to act like entrepreneurs instead of hired help. Welch says he also promotes free communication: "We are out to get a feeling and a spirit of total openness. That's alien to a manager of 25 or 30 years who got ahead by knowing a little bit more than the employee who works for him." Welch says he wants to instill in managers "the confidence to lead and the confidence to share."

Welch's emphasis on communication and camaraderie sometimes becomes extreme. GE's 112 corporate officers devoted long hours to commenting on drafts of a statement of corporate values that Welch titled, "What We Want to Be."

And he is not shy about expressing his opinions on how to manage and motivate people. Here are a few of his thoughts:

> *On being a tough manager:* "I got a raw deal with all those things about tough-guy Jack—fear, intimidation, guns and sticks and whips and chains. If you're mean, you don't

Source: Stratford P. Sherman, "The Mind of Jack Welch," *Fortune,* March 27, 1989, pp. 38–50; "General Electric's Hungarian Deal," *New York Times,* November 19, 1989, p. 14F; Peter Petre, "What Welch Has Wrought at GE," *Fortune,* July 7, 1986, pp. 42–47.

171

EXHIBIT 1

How a Dozen GE Businesses
Rank

	In the United States	In the World
Aircraft engines	First	First
Broadcasting (NBC)	First	Not applicable
Circuit breakers	First, tied with Square D and Westinghouse	First, tied with Merlin Gerin, Siemens, and Westinghouse
Defense electronics	Second behind GM's Hughes Electronics	Second, behind GM's Hughes Electronics
Electric motors	First	First
Engineering plastics	First	First
Factory automation	Second, behind Allen-Bradley	Third, behind Siemens and Allen-Bradley
Industrial and power systems: turbines, meters, drive systems, power transmission controls	First	First
Lighting	First	Second, behind Philips
Locomotives	First	First, tied with GM's Electro-Motive
Major appliances	First	Second, behind Whirlpool and tied with Electrolux
Medical diagnostic imaging	First	First

Note: Rankings are based on information from, respectively: Avmark and Forecast Int'l; companies' reported data; National Electrical Manufacturers Association (NEMA) and companies' reported data; *Defense Electronics;* companies' reported data; Society of the Plastics Industry; NEMA and companies' reported data; NEMA and companies' reported data; NEMA and companies' reported data; *Fortune* estimate based on units sold reported by *Trains* and *Extra Twenty-Two Hundred South;* First Boston and companies' reported data; *Fortune* estimate based on units sold reported by *Diagnostic Imaging.*
Source: *Fortune,* March 27, 1989.

belong at General Electric. Let me tell you why the name Neutron Jack is wrong. Competitiveness means taking action. Nuking somebody means you kill him. We start a renewal process. When people leave our company, we provide a soft landing. People who have been removed for not performing may be angry, but not one will say he wasn't treated with dignity. I don't think anyone would say he was treated unfairly, other than that bad management might have messed up the strategy. We can look ourselves in the mirror every morning and say we did what we could."

On anxiety among employees left at GE: "If you're a middle manager who's not going anywhere, not trained in tomorrow's technology, it's a tough issue, tough all across America. If you look at what we did as a nation and what companies like GE did over the last 25 years, a lot of people didn't stay current as we went from electromechanical to electronic technology. A lot of methods changed, and a lot of people didn't change with them. If you're a middle manager in General Electric who is pretty well plateaued out, do you like what's happening to you? Probably you're concerned."

On the role of GE's top management: "[Vice Chairman] Larry Bossidy knows GE Credit. He built it. I know the plastics business. [Vice Chairman] Ed Hood knows jet engines. After that, we start to get into very shallow water. But we know people. We know how to spot good ones more often than we spot bad ones — we don't bat 1.000 — and we know how to allocate resources."

On freedom in the American system: Welch believes that the U.S. system of free enterprise is an advantage that Americans have over the Japanese. "It allows people like me to become chairman of GE in one generation; it allows the talented young employees in our company to move up fast. . . . The idea of liberation and improvement for our work force is not enlightenment—it's a competitive necessity.

The need for leaders: "Call people managers and they are going to start managing things, getting in the way. The job of a leader is to take the available resources—human and financial—and allocate them rigorously. Not to spread them out evenly, like butter on bread. That's what bureaucrats do."

The quality Welch seems to value in people is self-confidence, and he works hard to inspire it in others. He is a believer that people must control their own destinies or someone else will.

Questions for Consideration

1. Welch practices a hard-nosed management style. How can such a no-nonsense approach create a motivational atmosphere? Does Jack Welch use negative reinforcement, goal setting, or behavioral self-management? Or does he use a combination of techniques?

2. Jack Welch has set goals to be number one in various markets. Assume that it is both a difficult and an assigned goal. What does goal-setting research say about the impact of such goals on performance?

3. Welch believes that the American concept of freedom gives U.S. firms a competitive advantage in the global marketplace. What does he mean?

4. Do you believe that Jack Welch is an advocate of Skinner's operant conditioning approach? Why?

EXPERIENTIAL EXERCISE

Objectives

1. To show what is meant by the term *goal*.
2. To illustrate guidelines for preparing goals.
3. To involve readers with some ideas about evaluating the quality of a goal.

Related Topics

Goals are statements of measurable results that a person is attempting to accomplish. They help a person develop a plan to turn expectations and wishes into reality. Goals are found in most motivation applications in organizations. In behavior modification programs, for example, goals are the targets of behavior changes.

Starting the Exercise

Each person is to work alone for at least 30 minutes with this exercise. After sufficient time has elapsed for each person to work through the exercise, the instructor will go over each goal and ask for comments from the class or group. The discussion should display each participant's understanding of goals and what will be needed to improve his or her goal-writing skills.

The Facts

Writing and evaluating goals seem simple, but they are often not done well in organizations. The press of time, previous habits, and little concern about the attributes of a goal statement are reasons why goals are often poorly constructed.* Actually, a number of guidelines should be followed in preparing goals. Remember these points:

1. A well-presented goal statement contains four elements:
   a. An action or accomplishment verb.
   b. A single and measurable result.
   c. A date of completion.
   d. A cost in terms of effort, resources, money, or some combination of these factors.

2. A well-presented goal statement is short; it is not a paragraph. It should be presented in a sentence.

3. A well-presented goal statement specifies only what and when and doesn't get into how or why.

4. A well-presented goal statement is challenging and attainable. It should cause the person to stretch his or her skills, abilities, and efforts.

5. A well-presented goal statement is meaningful and important. It should be a priority item.

6. A well-presented goal statement must be acceptable to you, so that you will try hard to accomplish the goal.

The goal statement model should be:

---

*For a discussion of how to set goals, see George Morrisey, *Getting Your Act Together* (New York: John Wiley & Sons, 1980), especially chap. 7.

To (action or accomplishment verb) (single result) by (a date — keep it realistic) at (effort, use of what resources, cost).

An example for a production operation:

To reduce the production cost per unit of Mint toothpaste by at least 3 percent by March 1, at a changeover-of-equipment expense not to exceed $45,000.

Examine the four statements that are presented as goal statements. Below each, write a critique of the statement. Is it a good goal statement? Why? Discuss your viewpoints in the class discussion.

1. To reduce my blood pressure to an acceptable level.

_____

_____

_____

2. To make financial investments with a guaranteed minimum return of at least 16 percent.

_____

_____

_____

3. To spend a minimum of 45 minutes a day on a doctor-approved exercise plan, starting Monday, lasting for six months, at no expense.

_____

_____

_____

4. To spend more time reading non-work-related novels and books during the next year.

_____

_____

_____

6

Evaluating, Rewarding, and Punishing Behavior

LEARNING OBJECTIVES

After completing Chapter 6, you should be able to:

DEFINE
the primary objectives of performance evaluation.

DESCRIBE
the content and the strengths and weaknesses of five innovative reward systems.

DISCUSS
the advantages and disadvantages of peer and self-appraisals.

COMPARE
the effectiveness of salary and bonus pay plans.

IDENTIFY
the strengths and shortcomings of behaviorally anchored rating scales (BARS), ranking methods, and graphic rating scales as performance evaluation methods.

AN ORGANIZATIONAL ISSUE FOR DEBATE

IS PAY FOR PERFORMANCE EFFECTIVE?

ARGUMENT FOR

A growing number of companies are implementing gainsharing, piece-rate, and other incentive reward programs for good reason: linking an employee's pay tightly to performance produces dividends for both employee and company.

An effective pay-for-performance program motivates employees because most people highly value money. Employees resent everyone receiving the same raises, automatically provided regardless of performance. Pay based on performance gives people the chance to earn more for doing more. An effective program also provides employees with clear performance objectives toward which to strive. It enables an employee to monitor his or her performance over time, relative to the objectives. According to psychological research, the simple act of monitoring one's own performance encourages individuals to compete against themselves and better their previous performance levels.

A good pay-for-performance program also improves the performance appraisal process, for three reasons. First, the program gives performance appraisal more meaning because both supervisor and subordinate take the process more seriously, given that the outcome can significantly affect the employee's paycheck. Thus, managers are more deliberate in conducting the appraisal and in giving the clear performance feedback that employees want. Second, the appraisal process is less subjective, because the pay-for-performance program provides clear, objective targets by which an employee is evaluated. Third, the appraisal process provides fewer surprises for the employee, because the performance standards have been established and discussed long before the appraisal occurs. Management expectations have been clearly communicated.

Beyond these payoffs, a good pay-for-performance program can provide employees with a greater sense of ownership and involvement in the company, because employees participate in setting performance standards, developing accountability statements, and establishing career performance goals. And organizations get more mileage from their compensation dollars because the better employees receive higher pay, which motivates them to maintain or improve their performance, while poorly performing employees are paid less and in this regard are encouraged to leave the company. In sum, there is no motivational substitute for linking employee compensation to performance as tightly as possible.

ARGUMENT AGAINST

In theory, pay for performance looks like the ideal reward system. However, in practice, several realities cripple the strategy's effectiveness.

First, many people *are* motivated by money but not, however, if the amount of the award is based on a flawed system. Pay for performance is flawed by the pressures of giving differential appraisal ratings. Many managers end up giving about the same rating and pay increase to everyone. If they don't, some employees will resent the ratings, because most people (according to research) rate themselves as above-average performers. Those who are rated average or below will resent, even oppose the system. Employees would be more satisfied with automatic, tenure-based increases in pay, because such increases provide the valued security of consistent improvement in pay, which is better than a system with no guarantees at all.

Pay-for-performance programs also run into trouble when supervisors have difficulties making reliable differentiations in performance across employees who perform a given job, which is a frequent problem. Pay-for-performance programs are also costly to implement, because performance standards and measures must be established and maintained for every job. These time-consuming demands raise the question: Are the pay-for-performance benefits worth the implementation costs?

Pay-for-performance advocates assert that such programs are motivational; but even with clear performance objectives and measurements and a fair appraisal process, pay increases lose motivational power because rewards are provided only once a year (following the annual review). According to reinforcement theory, rewards should be quickly provided after desired performance is exhibited. However, this isn't done in most pay-for-performance programs.

Because they reward individual performance, pay-for-performance programs hinder teamwork; employees are essentially competing against each other for raises. And pay-for-performance programs are ill-suited to the current trend of downsizing and cost cutting, when more companies are allocating less for merit-based increases. Tiny, performance-based raises render pay-for-performance programs ineffective.

Source: Thomas Rollins, "Pay for Performance: Is It Worth the Trouble?" *Personnel Administrator*, May 1988, pp. 42–46.

As the previous two chapters indicate, rewards are a critical element of any organizational strategy for motivating employees. To motivate, rewards must be valued by employees, and their distribution must be equitable. All other factors being equal, the organization's better-performing employees should receive more rewards than lesser-performing employees. Whether this occurs in a given organization depends largely on the performance evaluation system—the systematic process by which each employee's performance and potential for future development are evaluated. The process essentially determines how much each employee receives. Thus, it must be valid, accurate, reliable, and legally correct; and it should provide useful information concerning an employee's strengths and weaknesses.

Developing effective reward and performance evaluation systems constitutes two critical and challenging management tasks. Concerning rewards, management must deal with individual differences—as noted in the Organizational Issue for Debate. For example, some employees desire a strong pay-for-performance system, while others prefer a system that provides more secure, tenure-based rewards. Management must also consider that employee preferences differ concerning the content of rewards. Cafeteria fringe benefits, discussed in this chapter, are one innovative reward system expressly developed in response to differing preferences.

In developing a performance evaluation system, management must evaluate the strengths, weaknesses, and costs of each prospective appraisal technique. And management must keep in mind that performance evaluation is an inherently subjective, often emotional process, one that is vulnerable to human biases by those who evaluate.

To enhance your understanding of performance evaluation, this chapter focuses on various systems (their uses, types, and applications), reward approaches, and the use of punishment techniques. We present a model of individual rewards and discuss the different reward types, the relationship between rewards and some key organizational variables, and five notable innovative reward systems. We also briefly discuss two less pleasant potential outcomes of performance evaluation—discipline and punishment.

PERFORMANCE EVALUATION

PERFORMANCE EVALUATION
Systematic, formal evaluation of an employee's job performance and potential for future development.

Many varieties of **performance evaluation** systems are used in organizations. In most, the evaluation system is designed to provide both the ratee and the rater (manager) with information about job performance.[1] However, before any performance evaluation system is selected, there should be a clear understanding among raters and ratees about the objectives of the system. Two broadly stated purposes of performance evaluation are to reach an *evaluative,* or *judgmental,* conclusion about job performance and to *develop* employees through the system.[2] These purposes are compared in Table 6–1.

As the table demonstrates, the objectives, time orientation, and roles of the rater and ratee substantially differ between judgmental and developmental evaluations. For this reason, most experts recommend that supervisor-subordinate sessions addressing salary or promotion (the outcomes of judgmental evaluation) be kept separate from those dealing with personal and career development.[3]

Beyond these two broad purposes, a well-designed and efficiently implemented performance evaluation system can serve other, more specific functions. The system's chief objectives are to review past performance; to serve as the primary basis for making decisions concerning salary, promotion, retention, and termination; and to provide employees with performance feedback.[4] Performance evaluation can also be motivational if it provides ratees with some understanding of what is expected of them.

Performance evaluation can improve managerial understanding. A formal program encourages managers to observe the behavior of subordinates. Through increased and more thorough observations, improved mutual understanding between supervisors and subordinates can result. Information gathered through observation also provides a basis for determining the organization's personnel and training needs, although organizations typically view

---

[1]Gary P. Latham and Kenneth N. Wexley, *Increasing Productivity through Performance Appraisal* (Reading, Mass.: Addison-Wesley Publishing, 1981).

[2]Larry L. Cummings and Donald P. Schwab, *Performance in Organizations* (Glenview, Ill.: Scott, Foresman, 1973), p. 5.

[3]W. Schiemann, *Managing Human Resources/1983 and Beyond* (Chestnut Hill, Mass.: Opinion Research, 1983).

[4]J. N. Cleveland, Kevin R. Murphy, and Robert E. Williams, "Multiple Uses of Performance Appraisal: Prevalence and Correlates," *Journal of Applied Psychology,* February 1989, p. 132.

TABLE 6—1

Two Major Purposes of
Performance Evaluation:
A Comparison

Points of Comparison	Major Purposes	
	Judgmental	Developmental
Time orientation	Past performance.	Future performance.
Objective	Improving performance by changing behavior through reward system.	Improving performance through self-learning and personal growth.
Method	Use of rating scales, comparisons, and frequency distributions.	Counseling, mutual trust, goal setting, and career planning.
Supervisor's role (rater)	A judge who appraises.	A supportive counseling and encouraging person who listens, helps, and guides.
Subordinate's role (ratee)	Listens, reacts, and attempts to defend past performance.	Actively involved in charting future job performance plans.

Source: Adapted from Larry L. Cummings and Donald P. Schwab, *Performance in Organizations* (Glenview, Ill.: Scott, Foresman, 1973), p. 5.

these functions as less important outcomes of the appraisal process.[5] Information from evaluations can also be used to test the effectiveness of selection and placement techniques and decision making, by comparing evaluations with test scores, interviewers' ratings, and other selection devices.

One other important purpose of performance evaluation is to reduce favoritism in making important reward-related decisions. Perceived favoritism can strain supervisor-subordinate relationships and create low employee morale and dissatisfaction with company policies.[6] In this regard, rater training in the *process* of conducting effective performance appraisals is important; however, many organizations fail to provide such training.[7]

Performance Criteria

The performance evaluation program at any level within the organizational hierarchy must at some point focus on the criterion issue. **A criterion** is a standard or test by which performance is judged. For example, in golf, a criterion of a golfer's competence is the score. The lower the score, the better the golfer's performance.[8] In organizations, the criterion should reflect the employee's contribution to the job. In performance evaluation, the criterion is the dependent or predicted measure (i.e., standard) for appraising the effectiveness of an individual employee.

CRITERION

Standard, measure, or benchmark by which performance is judged.

[5]Ibid.; Jay L. Hall, Barry Z. Posner, and J. W. Harder, "Performance Appraisal Systems: Matching Practice with Theory," *Group and Organization Studies*, March 1989, p. 55.

[6]M. Perry, J. More, and N. Parkinson, "Does Your Appraisal System Stretch Up?" *Personnel Journal*, May 1987, pp. 82–87.

[7]J. Laumeyer and T. Beebe, "Employees and Their Appraisal," *Personnel Administrator*, December 1988, p. 78.

[8]Robert M. Guion, *Personnel Testing* (New York: McGraw-Hill, 1965), p. 90.

Requirements of a performance criterion.   Several requirements should be met before a variable qualifies as a performance criterion. First, a criterion should be *relevant* to the individual and the organization. Determining what is relevant is itself controversial; some person or group must make a judgment about what constitutes relevance. Once the relevant criterion has been selected, an effort must be made to develop a sound and valid measure of the variable.

Second, the criterion must be reliable. This involves agreement between evaluations made at different points in time. If the results from the two evaluations show little agreement, there would be some uncertainty about whether the criterion was stable.

Third, a performance criterion may be relevant and reliable and still be useless in evaluating employees. It is useful only if it can *discriminate* between good performers and poor performers. If all employees are good performers, then there is no need to discriminate. If, however, there are good, average and poor performers, then the evaluation criterion must discriminate.

Finally, the criterion must be *practical*. It must mean something to the rater and ratee. If the criterion serves no practical function, then it becomes something that is evaluated but offers no meaning.

Selecting appropriate criteria for performance evaluation is further complicated by the fact that criteria are often dynamic. That is, criteria that are valid, reliable, and practical at one point in an employee's career may become inappropriate over a period of time. For example, during the first year or so on the job, producing 15 units a week may be acceptable for an employee. However, as the employee acquires experience, confidence, and career goals, this level of production may become inappropriate. An experienced employee might be expected to average about 25 units a week.

Performance criteria and the law.   The Equal Employment Opportunity Commission (EEOC), the federal agency responsible for administering and enforcing the Civil Rights Act of 1964, issued the Uniform Guidelines on Employment Selection Procedures in 1978. These guidelines have an impact on performance evaluation because they view evaluations as a selection procedure.[9] The guidelines state that a procedure such as a performance evaluation must not have an adverse impact on any person or group protected by the Civil Rights Act.

Most performance evaluation procedures utilize paper-and-pencil methods to identify specific work behavior. As previously mentioned, management uses the outcomes of evaluations to make promotion, pay, transfer, and other human resource decisions. The potential for bias and poor judgment exists in many parts of the process. For example, managers serving as raters could use criteria that are not important in performing a job or could allow racial or gender-based prejudices to influence their evaluations of subordinates.

Since employers have been losing many race, sex, and age discrimination cases, understanding the law seems to be a major concern. Court rulings provide managers with guidelines on the issues of criteria, validity, and

---

[9]Richard I. Henderson, *Performance Appraisal* (Reston, Va.: Reston Publishing, 1984), p. 337.

reliability, three extremely important concepts if a case reaches the courts. In an empirical study, Feild and Holly identified five specific appraisal system characteristics that play a major role in how courts have ruled: type of organization, type of evaluation instrument used, the reliance on job analysis, the presence of written instructions to raters, and the method of feeding evaluation results back to subordinates.[10]

The U.S. circuit court in *Brito* v. *Zia Company* (1973) found that Zia Company was in violation of Title VII of the Civil Rights Act of 1964 when a disproportionate number of a protected group were laid off on the basis of low performance scores.[11] Zia also failed in accordance with the law to "introduce evidence of validity . . . consistency of empirical data. . . . The court found that the evaluations were based on best judgments and opinions . . . but not on any specific performances that were supported by some kind of record."[12]

In the *Jackson* v. *Kreps* (1979) case, performance evaluation was ruled to be discriminatory.[13] The court found that four white applicants for a promotion were classified "highly qualified," while no blacks received more than a "qualified" rating. The court awarded the employee (Jackson) back pay and promotion to the next vacancy that occurred.

These and other court cases and rulings emphasize the importance of validity in any performance evaluation system.[14] The principal kinds of validity that are relevant for making performance evaluations are briefly presented in Table 6–2. As shown, numerous types of validity exist.[15] The important point to note is that validity is inferred and not directly measured. Managers have to make a judgment about the validity of the criteria they are using. The federal courts are now insisting that proper consideration be given to the validity and reliability of performance evaluation instruments.

To comply with federal laws regarding performance evaluation, the criteria, validity, and reliability issues must be carefully considered. Managers also need to review previous court rulings. They must be sure that:

— The overall performance evaluation process is standardized, balances results and behavior, and is as objective as possible.[16]

— Performance standards are based on job-related criteria developed through a thorough, formal job analysis.[17]

---

[10]Hubert S. Feild and William H. Holley, "The Relationship of Performance Appraisal System Characteristics to Verdicts in Selected Employment Discrimination Cases," *Academy of Management Journal,* June 1982, pp. 392–406.

[11]*Brito* v. *Zia Company,* 478 F.2d 1200 (1973).

[12]Ibid.

[13]*Jackson* v. *Kreps,* 20 FEP 1532 (1979).

[14]L. S. Kleiman and R. L. Durham, "Performance Appraisal, Promotion, and the Courts: A Critical Review," *Personnel Psychology,* Spring 1981, pp. 103–21.

[15]Richard I. Henderson, *Compensation Management* (Reston, Va.: Reston Publishing, 1982), pp. 378–400.

[16]R. W. Goddard, "Is Your Appraisal System Headed for Court?" *Personnel Journal,* January 1989, p. 118.

[17]Ibid.

TABLE 6—2

Types of Validity Used in
Determining Acceptability of
Performance Evaluation
Criteria

Type of Validity	Brief Description
Concurrent	Statistical correlation between a predictor (an item on the evaluation form) and actual job performance.
Content	The degree to which scores or ratings on the evaluation are a representative sample of all the job behaviors required to perform the job.
Criterion-related	Whenever individual-difference measures are used, criterion-related validity should be examined. Scores or ratings on the evaluation are related to some criterion (e.g., expert judgment). If the criterion is available at the same time that the predictor is measured, concurrent validity is being assessed.
Predictive	In contrast to concurrent validity, if criterion data are not available until after predictor scores are obtained, then predictive validity is being measured. Thus, predictive validity is oriented toward the future, while concurrent validity is oriented toward the present.
Construct	The degree to which scores may be interpreted as measuring a property such as potential, motivation, or commitment. It is important to obtain a degree of objectivity in assessing construct validity.
Convergent	The correlation between the same properties or traits as rated by different raters is significantly different from zero.
Discriminant	The correlation between the same traits as rated by different raters should be higher than the correlation between different traits as rated by the same rater. Also, the correlation between the same traits as rated by different raters should be higher than the correlation between different traits as rated by different raters.

— Employees are aware of the performance criteria/standards well before any evaluation occurs.[18]

— Subjective ratings are considered as only one input in the evaluation decisions.

— Raters are trained in the use of the performance evaluation forms and process.

— Raters have daily contact with and are able to frequently observe ratees.

— The evaluation is conducted independently by more than one rater for each ratee.[19]

— Evaluations by individual raters are reviewed by the next level of management.[20]

— The evaluation system is validated and regularly audited to determine to what degree the system is working.[21]

— A mechanism for employee appeal is provided.[22]

---

[18]P. S. Eyres, "Legally Defensible Performance Appraisal Systems," *Personnel Journal*, July 1989, p. 61.

[19]D. E. Thompson, C. R. Klasson, and G. L. Lubben, "Performance Appraisal and the Law: Policy and Research Implications of Court Cases," paper presented at the Academy of Management Meeting, Atlanta, Georgia, August 1979, pp. 5–6.

[20]Goddard, "Is Your Appraisal System Headed for Court?" p. 118.

[21]Ibid.

[22]Wayne F. Cascio and H. John Bernardin, "Implications of Performance Appraisal Litigation for Personnel Decisions," *Personnel Psychology*, Summer 1981, pp. 211–26.

FIGURE 6–1

The Four Main Phases of Performance Evaluation

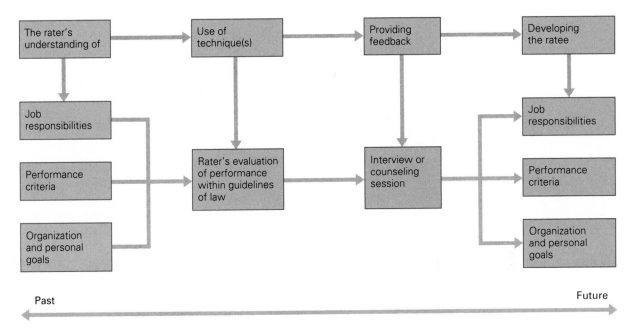

The law and the need for a formal performance evaluation system have greatly affected what organizations now use. In essence, no matter what process is used, managers or raters must make judgments about ratees, and these judgments must be based on scientifically derived criteria. Figure 6–1 illustrates the central importance of criteria in the performance evaluation process. Furthermore, the chart indicates the importance of the law to the process, the role of the rater in providing feedback to and developing ratees, and the part played by the ratee in understanding responsibilities, criteria, and goals.

Beyond establishing valid performance criteria, designing an effective performance evaluation system involves determining (1) who will evaluate performance, (2) when and how often performance will be appraised, and (3) what evaluation technique(s) will be used in the appraisal. Each of these issues is discussed in the following sections.

Selecting Raters and Timing/Frequency of Evaluations

Raters.   One or more of four parties inside an organization can evaluate an employee's performance:

Employee's supervisor(s).   At the lower and middle levels of an organization, about 95 percent of all evaluations are conducted by the employee's immediate supervisor. This occurs in part because the management hierarchy reinforces the right and duty of supervisors to make evaluative and developmental decisions concerning subordinates, especially since the supervisor administers the rewards or punishments that are outcomes of the evaluation process.[23] However, many supervisors dislike their evaluation tasks; they resent "playing God" with another person's career. Some feel uncertain about their evaluations because they are unskilled (and often untrained) in conducting appraisals. Moreover, supervisors must live with their decisions; the subordinate they rate poorly today, they must work with tomorrow. These factors can cause supervisors to give higher than deserved ratings.[24] Some of these problems can be alleviated—and appraisals with more validity can be obtained—by having more than one rater and utilizing supervisors who are on an organizational level the same as or higher than the ratee's immediate supervisor.[25]

Employee's peers.   Appraisal by one's working peers is often a very effective evaluation method. According to research, ratings by peers are more stable over time and often have more predictive validity than do ratings by supervisors, and peer ratings more often focus on the ratee's performance and output.[26] However, peer evaluations are infrequently used in organizations, partly because of management's concerns that peers will be too lenient or too biased in their appraisals (giving friends higher ratings) and lack sufficient understanding of the ratee's job to provide a fair and accurate appraisal. Some managers also believe that peer evaluation undermines their authority.

At the Logan plant of Schreiber Foods, peer appraisal has been in effect since 1985. There, hourly employees rate one or more peers on six performance dimensions (e.g., attendance, attitude, cooperation, safety habits) and on dimensions specific to a respective employee's job. For each ratee, five peer appraisers who regularly observe the ratee provide evaluations on written forms. These are submitted to the ratee's supervisor, who eliminates the highest and lowest ratings on each dimension and averages the remaining ratings. The supervisor later meets with the ratee to review the averaged ratings.

About 80 percent of the employees report they are satisfied with the system, primarily because of the frequent performance feedback sessions, the feedback's focus on areas for improvement, and the input from several raters.[27] However, effective peer appraisal requires that employees want to motivate their peers (some may resist), that they can observe behaviors relevant to the dimensions being evaluated, and that they are not overtaxed in rating too many peers.[28]

Employee.   Having employees evaluate their own performance is beneficial in four respects. Self-appraisal facilitates employee development, because it requires that the employees focus on job behavior and performance and identify and examine strengths and weaknesses. Because employees tend to

---

[23]Latham and Wexley, *Increasing Productivity,* p. 80.

[24]M. Cayer, D. J. DiMattia, and J. Wingrove, "Conquering Evaluation Fear," *Personnel Administrator,* June 1988, p. 53.

[25]Cummings and Schwab, *Performance,* p. 104.

[26]Latham and Wexley, *Increasing Productivity,* pp. 84–85.

[27]Glenn McEvoy, P. F. Buller, and S. R. Roghaar, "A Jury of One's Peers," *Personnel Administrator,* May 1988, 94ff.

[28]Latham and Wexley, *Increasing Productivity,* p. 88.

accept the findings of self-appraisal, they are more proactive in building on their identified strengths and alleviating shortcomings.[29] Self-appraisals also clarify differences in supervisor and subordinate opinion concerning the employee's job demands and performance.[30] They also tend to boost the employee's participation and reduce defensiveness in the appraisal feedback interview.

However, self-appraisals are hindered by inflated and self-serving ratings that occur when employees feel threatened by the process and need to protect a positive self-image. Also, agreement between employee and supervisor ratings is usually low.[31] For these reasons, self-appraisal is typically used for developmental rather than evaluative purposes.

Employee's subordinates.   A small but growing number of organizations are implementing subordinate evaluations of managers, in part because subordinates are a rich source of information and perspective concerning their manager's behavior.[32] In frequent contact with their supervisors, subordinates observe numerous performance-related behaviors, often including those not seen by the manager's boss. Subordinate insights are especially useful in assessing the supervisor's people management skills.[33]

However, subordinate appraisals can be problematic. Subordinates often question assurances that their identity and ratings will remain anonymous, and they consequently provide lackluster, though generally positive, ratings of their boss. Sometimes, subordinates can conspire as a group to "massacre" a deeply disliked superior. Also, when subordinate appraisals are used to make pay raise and promotion decisions, managers may make hiring decisions based on their idea of who would provide them with favorable ratings.[34]

For these reasons, subordinate appraisals to date have been used primarily for manager development purposes. Experts recommend that both manager and subordinates participate in developing the appraisal questionnaire, which boosts employee commitment and reduces the manager's defensiveness about the appraisal. The questionnaire should focus only on job behaviors that subordinates observe; and no fewer than four subordinates should evaluate a manager, so that rater anonymity is not compromised.[35]

Evaluation timing and frequency.   According to research, most organizations conduct evaluations annually on or near an employee's anniversary date (the date of hire).[36] Some organizations maintain a single-day approach, in which all employee appraisals are conducted at the same time. While administratively convenient, this approach tends to overtax raters and reduces rating accuracy.

---

[29]J. W. Lawrie, "Your Performance: Appraise It Yourself," *Personnel,* January 1989, p. 22.

[30]Latham and Wexley, *Increasing Productivity,* p. 82.

[31]Donald J. Campbell and Cynthia Lee, "Self-Appraisal in Performance Evaluation: Developmental versus Evaluation," *Academy of Management Review,* April 1988, p. 303.

[32]Walter Kiechel, "When Subordinates Evaluate the Boss," *Fortune,* June 19, 1989, p. 201.

[33]Glenn M. McEvoy, "Evaluating the Boss," *Personnel Administrator,* September 1988, p. 116.

[34]L. Reibstein, "Firms Ask Workers to Rate Their Bosses," *The Wall Street Journal,* June 13, 1988, p. 13.

[35]Kiechel, "When Subordinates Evaluate," p. 202.

[36]D. B. Fedor and M. R. Buckley, "Issues Surrounding the Need for More Frequent Monitoring of Individual Performance in Organizations," *Public Personnel Management,* Winter 1988, pp. 435–36.

TABLE 6—3

Categories of Performance
Evaluation Methods

	Traits	Behaviors
Type of information collected to determine performance	What the employee is.	How the employee is performing the job.
Methods used	Graphic rating scales, ranking methods, weighted checklists, descriptive essays.	Behaviorally anchored rating scales.

Given research findings that frequent feedback is more useful to employees, more frequent evaluations and feedback sessions are recommended. However, organizations have not adopted this practice, largely because the process is time-consuming and places stress on raters. One way to reconcile the ideal with reality is for managers to give frequent informal feedback and then formally summarize performance at evaluation time.

ALTERNATIVE EVALUATION METHODS

If pressed for an answer, most managers could offer a general description of the job performance of subordinates. However, a more formal and systematic procedure than asking for the opinions of managers is generally used. Managers usually select a performance evaluation procedure that minimizes conflict with ratees, provides relevant feedback to ratees, and contributes to the achievement of organizational goals. The manager attempts to find, develop, and implement a performance evaluation program that can benefit the employee, other managers, the work group, and the organization.

Managers typically select one or a combination of the methods presented in this section. The methods can be placed in two categories, which are shown in Table 6–3.

Graphic Rating Scales

As the oldest and most widely used performance evaluation procedure, the scaling technique appears in many forms. Generally, the rater is supplied with a printed form for each subordinate to be rated. The form contains job performance qualities and characteristics that are to be rated. The rating scales are distinguished by (1) how exactly the categories are defined, (2) the degree to which the person interpreting the ratings can tell which response was intended by the rater, and (3) how carefully the performance dimension is defined for the rater.

GRAPHIC RATING SCALE

Rater is given a form on which he or she rates an employee's qualities and characteristics.

Figure 6–2 presents samples of some of the common **graphic rating scales.** The first distinguishing feature among rating scales, the meaning of the possible response categories, is usually handled by the use of anchor statements or words placed at points along a scale. Rating scales (a), (b), (c), (d), and (h) use anchors. The second distinguishing feature among rating scales is the degree to which the person interpreting the ratings can tell which response was

FIGURE 6—2

Some Samples of Rating Scale Formats

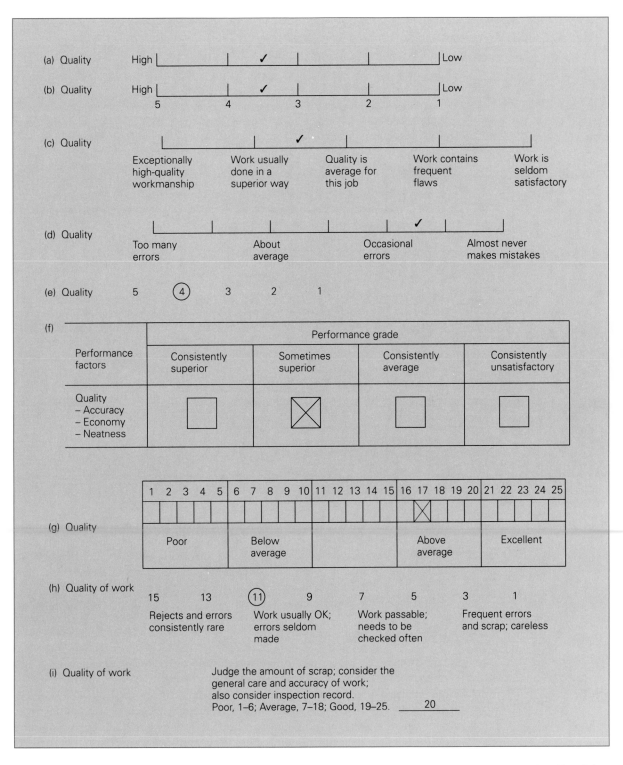

Variations on a graphic rating scale; each line represents one way in which a judgment of the quality of a person's work may be given. From Robert M. Guion, *Personnel Testing* (New York: McGraw-Hill, 1965), p. 98. Copyright 1965, McGraw-Hill Book Company.

ORGANIZATIONS:
CLOSE-UP   PROCEED WITH CAUTION

In the early 1970s, the U.S. Air Force realized that the appraisal form used to evaluate its officers was seriously flawed. The form's overgeneralized job descriptions communicated little about expectations concerning the job performed by the appraised officer. Also, several rating factors were largely irrelevant to the jobs that many officers performed. Above all, the form, consisting largely of graphic rating scales, provided no control over inflated ratings. By 1973, over 90 percent of the officer corps received scores of 10 (on a 1–10 scale) in performance and promotion potential. Thus, the appraisal form was virtually useless as a tool for making decisions concerning promotion, transfer, retention, and training, even though the form served as the principal basis for such decisions.

In 1974, the Air Force implemented a major change. Forced distribution was introduced in the section that required evaluation of the officer's overall potential, relative to his or her peers, for assuming greater responsibilities. Of the peer officers evaluated by a rater, 22 percent could receive top scores of 6, and 28 percent could receive scores of 5, with the remaining 50 percent distributed over scores 1–4. The initial raters (first- or second-level supervisors) were encouraged to use the forced distribution; use was mandatory for the officer who was the final reviewing authority.

The change produced differentiated evaluations; it also created far-reaching problems that the Air Force had never anticipated. First, many officers intensely disliked the forms, especially those who, after years of "outstanding" ratings, were suddenly inferior to half of the officer corps. The ratings generated strain and conflict between the lesser-ranked officers and the supervisors directly or indirectly responsible for their ratings. The "have-nots" questioned their supervisors' abilities and fairness. By decree, half of the supervisors themselves were ranked as average or worse, and their own ratings, when communicated to subordinates through the grapevine, did little to improve supervisor-subordinate relationships.

intended. The clarity of response intention is exemplified in scales (e), (f), and (g). Quality of work, the third feature, can be interpreted differently by various raters. Therefore, a performance dimension needs to be defined for each rater. Scales (a), (b), (e), and (g) give the rater little performance dimension definition. Scales (c) and (h) provide the rater with a fairly good definition of the performance dimension.

Ranking Methods

Some managers use a rank-order procedure to evaluate all subordinates. The ratees are ranked according to their relative worth to the company or unit on one or more performance dimensions. The procedure usually involves identifying the best performer and the worst performer, who are ranked in the first and last positions on the ranking list. The next best and next poorest performers are then filled in on the list. This rank-ordering continues until all subordinates are placed on the list. The rank ordering performance evaluation method forces the rater to discriminate.

RANKING METHODS

Ranking of ratees on the basis of relevant performance.

The **ranking method** has some problems. For one, ratees in the central portion of the list may not be much different from each other on the

Second, given that the forced distributions were ultimately made or approved by the final reviewing officer, subordinate officers sought increased visibility with top-level officers, exaggerating the urgency of particular issues they handled to escalate them upward in the chain of command. This tactic wasted top management's time spent on decisions that could have been made by lower-level officers. Supervisors also sought greater visibility by claiming undeserved credit for their subordinate officers' successes.

The forced distribution system also discouraged teamwork among peer officers, because each realized that one officer's gain in the forced distribution system was another one's loss. The have-not officers also recognized a catch-22 situation: To improve their ratings, they had to demonstrate higher potential, which was only possible by obtaining more demanding and responsible jobs. However, those were reserved for the "have" officers, producing a highly dysmotivating two-level caste system. Also, given that the forced distribution rated an officer's potential relative to his peers, many top-rated, "have" officers realized that if they accepted an even more challenging assignment, they would place themselves in competition with higher-performing peers, thus increasing the chance that they would themselves be have-nots in the next rating cycle. Thus, to maintain their top ratings, many of the force's best officers sought assignments with a lower-priority unit with many "have nots." All this did little to effectively utilize the force's top talent.

The lesson from the Air Force's experience: approach any change in performance appraisal systems with great care, realizing the potentially dramatic and negative repercussions that change may produce.

Source: Mark A. McBriarty, "Performance Appraisal: Some Unintended Consequences," *Public Personnel Management*, Winter 1988, pp. 421–34.

performance rankings. Another problem involves the size of the group being evaluated. It becomes more difficult to rank large groups of subordinates.

Other ranking methods are also used. For example, in the *paired comparison* method, every subordinate is compared with every other. The supervisor is asked to identify the best performer from each pair. A supervisor with eight subordinates would have:

$$\text{Pairs} = \frac{N(N-1)}{2}$$

or

$$\text{Pairs} = \frac{8(8-1)}{2} = 28$$

In another ranking method, *forced distribution*, raters evaluate employees in some fixed distribution of categories, such as 10 percent in low, 20 percent in low average, 40 percent in average, 20 percent in high average, and 10 percent in high. The method alleviates inflated ratings, but it can produce some unintended effects, which are discussed in the Close-Up that urges caution.

Weighted Checklists

The **weighted-checklist** rating consists of statements that describe various types and levels of behavior for a particular job or group of jobs. Each statement has a weight, or value, attached to it. The rater evaluates each subordinate by checking those statements that describe the behavior of the individual. The check marks and corresponding weights are summated for each subordinate.

The weighted checklist makes the rater think in terms of specific job behaviors. Separate checklists are usually established for each different job or group of jobs. However, this procedure is difficult to develop and very costly.

Descriptive Essays

The **descriptive essay** method of performance evaluation requires the rater to describe each ratee's strong and weak points. Some organizations require every rater to discuss specific points in the evaluation, while others allow raters to discuss whatever they believe is appropriate. One limitation of the descriptive essay evaluation is that it provides little opportunity to compare ratees on specific performance dimensions. Another limitation is the inadequate writing skills of raters.

Behaviorally Anchored Rating Scales

Smith and Kendall developed **behaviorally anchored rating scales (BARS),** or behavior expectation scales (BES).[37] The BARS approach relies on the use of critical incidents to construct the rating scale. A critical incident is "any observable human activity that is sufficiently complete in itself to permit inferences and predictions to be made about the person performing the work."[38] Once the important areas of performance have been identified and defined by employees who know the job, critical-incident statements are used as anchors to discriminate between high, moderate, and low performance. The BARS rating form usually covers 6 to 10 specifically defined performance dimensions, each with various descriptive anchors. Each dimension is based on observable behaviors and is meaningful to the employees being evaluated.

Figure 6–3 shows a BARS for engineering competence. The dimension is defined for the rater; the anchors define the particular response categories for the rater; and the response made by the rater is specific and easy to interpret. If the ratee is given a 7 on this dimension, he or she is provided with the specific performance incident that the rater used to make such a rating.

Thorough reviews of the literature have concluded that BARS are (1) costly to construct, (2) require significant time to put into use, and (3) are not much better in improving rating errors than graphic rating scales or weighted

---

[37]P. C. Smith and L. M. Kendall, "Retranslation of Expectations: An Approach to the Construction of Unambiguous Anchors for Rating Scales," *Journal of Applied Psychology,* April 1963, pp. 149–55.

[38]J. C. Flanagan, "The Critical Incident Technique," *Psychological Bulletin,* April 1954, p. 329.

Engineering Competence
(the technical ability and skill utilization as applied to any assigned job)

Place a single X on the appropriate point on the vertical scale.

_____ [Ratee Name]

FIGURE 6—3

A BARS Performance
Dimension for an Engineer

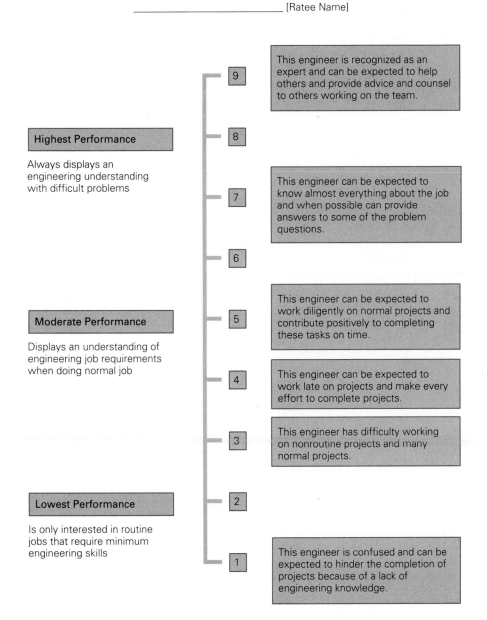

Highest Performance

Always displays an engineering understanding with difficult problems

Moderate Performance

Displays an understanding of engineering job requirements when doing normal job

Lowest Performance

Is only interested in routine jobs that require minimum engineering skills

9 | This engineer is recognized as an expert and can be expected to help others and provide advice and counsel to others working on the team.

8

7 | This engineer can be expected to know almost everything about the job and when possible can provide answers to some of the problem questions.

6

5 | This engineer can be expected to work diligently on normal projects and contribute positively to completing these tasks on time.

4 | This engineer can be expected to work late on projects and make every effort to complete projects.

3 | This engineer has difficulty working on nonroutine projects and many normal projects.

2

1 | This engineer is confused and can be expected to hinder the completion of projects because of a lack of engineering knowledge.

checklists.[39] Despite some discouraging research findings and constructive criticisms, BARS are still being used by numerous organizations. Their continued popularity is based on various proposed advantages. Since job-knowledgeable employees participate in the actual development steps, the final form should be reliable, valid, and meaningful. It should also cover the full domain of the job. A common problem of traditional performance evaluation programs is that they do not tap all aspects of the job.[40]

The use of BARS is also valuable for providing insights when developing training programs. The skills to be developed are specified in actual behavioral incidents rather than abstract or general skills. Trainees in a BARS-based program could learn what behaviors are expected and how job performance is evaluated.[41]

The literature also implies that rater errors are reduced through the use of a behaviorally anchored system. Presumably, they are minimized because of the independence between the dimensions rated and the reliability of BARS.[42] However, some critics of BARS present results indicating that this approach is not always the most reliable, valid, and practical. They also suggest the need for more research comparing BARS with other traditional evaluation methods.[43]

Research suggests that a BARS program can minimize subordinate, or ratee, defensiveness toward evaluation. By being involved in the development of a BARS, subordinates can have input, and their ideas can be incorporated into the final BARS. Development of the scale should involve both superiors and subordinates so that all parties can contribute to the creation of the evaluation criteria and the behavioral incidents used as anchors.

A REVIEW OF PERFORMANCE EVALUATION METHODS

Table 6–4 compares the main points of the various evaluation approaches discussed. The usefulness of each method is debatable. From one organization to another, systems will vary in usefulness because of the individuals doing the rating or because of the criteria being used. Every method discussed thus far has both costs and benefits. Since performance evaluation is such an integral part of managing within organizations, recognizing the strengths, weaknesses, and best uses for a particular method is an important job for managers.

---

[39]R. Jacobs, D. Kafry, and Sheldon Zedeck, "Expectations of Behaviorally Anchored Rating Scales," *Personnel Psychology,* Autumn 1980, pp. 595–640.

[40]J. P. Campbell, Marvin D. Dunnette, Richard D. Arvey, and L. W. Hellervik, "The Development and Evaluation of Behaviorally Based Rating Scales," *Journal of Applied Psychology,* February 1973, pp. 15–22.

[41]M. R. Blood, "Spin-Offs from Behavioral Expectations Scale Procedures," *Journal of Applied Psychology,* August 1974, pp. 513–15.

[42]Sheldon Zedeck and H. T. Baker, "Nursing Performance as Measured by Behavioral Expectation Scales: A Multitrait-Multirater Analysis," *Organizational Behavior and Human Performance,* June 1972, pp. 457–66; K. R. Murphy and V. A. Pardaffy, "Bias in Behaviorally Anchored Rating Scales: Global or Scale-Specific?" *Journal of Applied Psychology,* April 1989, pp. 343–46.

[43]Donald P. Schwab, Herbert G. Heneman III, and T. A. DeCotiis, "Behaviorally Anchored Rating Scales: A Review of the Literature," *Personnel Psychology,* Winter 1975, pp. 549–62.

TABLE 6—4

Performance Evaluation Methods: Characteristics Important to Managers

	Method				
Characteristic	Graphic Rating Scales	Ranking	Weighted Checklists	Essays	BARS
Acceptability to subordinates	Fair	Fair/poor	Fair	Poor	Good
Acceptability to management	Fair	Fair/poor	Fair	Poor	Good
Useful in reward allocations	Poor	Poor	Fair	Fair	Good
Useful in counseling and developing subordinates	Poor	Poor	Poor	Fair	Good
Meaningful dimensions	Rarely	Rarely	Sometimes	Rarely	Often
Ease of developing actual program	High	High	High	Low	Low
Development costs	Low	Low	Low	Moderately high	High

DEVELOPING EMPLOYEES THROUGH PERFORMANCE EVALUATION FEEDBACK

Regardless of how individual job performance information is collected—BARS, rating scale, or combination of two or more methods—the rater must provide formal feedback to the ratee. Providing accurate feedback in a formal feedback interview is essential for the employee to build upon strengths and improve performance.

Conducting such an interview is a difficult task. Supervisors are often uncomfortable about discussing ratees' weaknesses or problems, and ratees often become defensive when personal weaknesses or failures are pointed out by a rater.[44] However, providing feedback effectively is a critical management skill because effective feedback can be motivational and can encourage the development of ratees as they pursue valued goals.

James Goodale offers some helpful guidelines for managers to follow when conducting feedback interviews:[45]

1. Clearly state the purpose of the interview.
2. Encourage and permit the employee to talk about past performance.
3. Focus initially on positive feedback points.
4. Shift to areas that need improvement.
5. Set specific goals with the employee.
6. Specify a follow-up session to review progress.

---

[44]Cayer et al., "Conquering Evaluation Fear," p. 98; S. D. Truskie, "Get Better Results from Performance Reviews," *The Wall Street Journal,* October 4, 1982, p. 28.

[45]James G. Goodale, *The Fine Art of Interviewing* (Englewood Cliffs, N.J.: Prentice Hall, 1982), pp. 68–96, 169–85.

Too often, performance evaluation interviews focus on the past year or on plans for the short run. Rarely do a manager and a subordinate discuss careers.[46] Recall that in our presentation of the performance evaluation process (Figure 6–1) the future development of the ratee is considered extremely important. The creation of challenging tasks helps prepare subordinates for future jobs that require the use of more skills and abilities. Managers need to have knowledge about the various career tracks available within the organization and their requirements. It seems worthwhile for them to consider and be prepared to discuss the lifelong sequence of job experiences and jobs of subordinates, as part of the evaluation interview. Only through managerial consideration of career goals can the evaluation process become a development experience as well as a judgmental analysis of job performance.

Organizations use a variety of rewards to attract and retain people and to motivate them to achieve their personal and organizational goals. As we've noted, the manner and timing of reward distribution are important issues that managers must address almost daily. If managers develop and distribute rewards effectively, the reward system creates a climate that results in more challenging and satisfying jobs. The rewards also have significant effects on behavior and performance.

Unfortunately, managers are also frequently faced with the task of eliminating undesirable behavior and performance via the use of punishment. Although a controversial topic, punishment is an everyday reality of organizational life. Thus, determining ways to use punishment effectively — minimizing the negative and maximizing its positive consequences — is an important management issue. Developing and using rewards and punishment — two essential management tasks — are discussed in the following sections.

ORGANIZATIONAL REWARD SYSTEMS

A Model of Individual Rewards

The main objectives of reward programs are (1) to attract qualified people to *join* the organization, (2) to *keep* employees coming to work, and (3) to *motivate* employees to achieve high levels of performance. A model illustrating how rewards fit into the overall policies and programs of an organization is useful to managers. Figure 6–4 presents a model that integrates satisfaction, motivation, performance, and rewards. It suggests that the motivation to exert effort is not enough to cause acceptable performance. Performance results from a combination of the effort of an individual and that person's ability, skill, and experience. Management evaluates each individual's performance either formally or informally. As a result of the evaluation, it distributes two types of rewards: intrinsic or extrinsic. The rewards are evaluated by the individual. To the extent that the rewards are adequate and equitable, the individual achieves a level of satisfaction.

---

[46]Gene W. Dalton, Paul H. Thompson, and R. L. Price, "A New Look at Performance by Professionals," *Organizational Dynamics,* Summer 1977, pp. 19–42.

FIGURE 6—4

The Reward Process

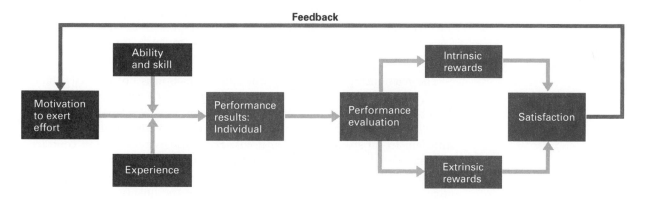

A significant amount of research has been done on what determines whether individuals are satisfied with rewards. Edward Lawler has summarized five conclusions based on the behavioral science research literature:[47]

1. *Satisfaction with a reward is a function both of how much is received and of how much the individual feels should be received.* This conclusion is based on the comparisons that people make. When individuals receive less than they feel they should, they are dissatisfied.

2. *An individual's feelings of satisfaction are influenced by comparisons with what happens to others.* People tend to compare their efforts, skills, seniority, and job performance with those of others. They then attempt to compare rewards; that is, they compare their own inputs with the inputs of others relative to the rewards received. This input-outcome comparison was discussed when the equity theory of motivation was introduced in Chapter 5.

3. *Satisfaction is influenced by how satisfied employees are with both intrinsic and extrinsic rewards. Intrinsic rewards* are valued in and of themselves; they are related to performing the job. Examples would be feelings of accomplishment and achievement. *Extrinsic rewards* are external to the work itself; they are administered externally. Examples would be salary and wages, fringe benefits, and promotions. There is some debate among researchers as to whether intrinsic or extrinsic rewards are more important in determining job satisfaction. The debate has not been settled, because most studies suggest that both rewards are important.[48] One clear message from the research is that extrinsic and intrinsic rewards satisfy different needs.

4. *People differ in the rewards they desire and in the relative importance different rewards have for them.* Individuals differ on what rewards they prefer. In

[47]Edward E. Lawler III, "Reward Systems," in *Improving Life at Work,* ed. J. Richard Hackman and J. L. Suttle (Santa Monica, Calif.: Goodyear Publishing, 1977), pp. 163–226.

[48]Terence R. Mitchell, "Motivation: New Directions for Theory, Research, and Practice," *Academy of Management Review,* January 1982, pp. 80–88.

fact, preferred rewards vary at different points in a person's career, at different ages, and in various situations.

5. *Some extrinsic rewards are satisfying because they lead to other rewards.* For example, a large office or an office that has carpeting or drapes is often considered a reward because it indicates the individual's status and power. Money is a reward that leads to such things as prestige, autonomy and independence, security, and shelter.

The relationship between rewards and satisfaction is not perfectly understood, nor is it static. It changes because people and the environment change. There are, however, some important considerations that managers could use to develop and distribute rewards. First, the rewards available must be sufficient to satisfy basic human needs. Federal legislation, union contracts, and managerial fairness have provided at least minimal rewards in most work settings. Second, individuals tend to compare their rewards with those of others. People make comparisons regardless of the quantity of the rewards they receive. If inequities are perceived, dissatisfaction occurs. Finally, the managers distributing rewards must recognize individual differences. Unless individual differences are considered, the reward process invariably is less effective than desired. Any reward package should (1) be sufficient to satisfy basic needs (e.g., food, shelter, clothing), (2) be considered equitable, and (3) be individually oriented.[49]

INTRINSIC AND EXTRINSIC REWARDS

In Figure 6–4, rewards are classified into two broad categories: extrinsic and intrinsic. In either category, the first consideration is how the rewards are *valued* by employees. Individuals put forth little effort unless the reward has *value*. Both extrinsic and intrinsic rewards can have value.[50]

Extrinsic Rewards

EXTRINSIC REWARDS
Rewards external to job, such as pay, promotion, or fringe benefits.

Financial rewards: salary and wages.   Money is a major **extrinsic reward.** It has been said that "although it is generally agreed that money is the major mechanism for rewarding and modifying behavior in industry . . . very little is known about how it works."[51] To really understand how money modifies behavior, the perceptions and preferences of the person being rewarded must be understood, which of course is a challenging task for managers. Success requires careful attention and observation of employees. In addition, managers must be trusted, so that workers freely communicate their feelings about financial rewards.

Unless employees see a connection between performance and merit increases, money is not a powerful motivator. In some cases, a well-designed

---

[49]Lawler, "Reward Systems," p. 168.

[50]Richard A. Guzzo, "Types of Rewards, Cognitions and Work Motivation," *Academy of Management Review,* January 1979, pp. 75–86.

[51]R. L. Opsahl and Marvin D. Dunnette, "The Role of Financial Compensation in Industrial Motivation," *Psychological Bulletin,* August 1966, p. 114.

IS A CEO WORTH $1 BILLION?

Steven J. Ross, co-CEO of the newly merged Time Warner Inc., received options in 1989 to purchase 1.8 million shares of the company's stock at $150 a share (an award from Time Warner's board that is ultimately valued at over $1 billion), in addition to his annual $1.2 million salary. Ross's prize, along with spiraling CEO pay levels, has fueled the controversy over whether large-company CEOs are worth what they are paid. Each year, CEOs of Fortune 500–sized companies earn, on average, $1 million in salary and over $2 million in stock options, five times more than their counterparts in Great Britain. Also, CEO pay has been growing at a much faster rate than that of U.S. workers.

Contributing to the controversy are the findings of a recent study by Graef S. Crystal, the acknowledged dean of U.S. compensation consultants. Utilizing multiple regression analysis, Crystal analyzed the relationship between company performance and the pay of CEOs of 214 Fortune companies. Company performance was shown in terms of a sophisticated "Performance IQ" score combining several 1988 performance measures, including net income, and growth in sales and shareholders' equity over the past five years.

Crystal found a faint relationship between CEO pay and company performance: the average Performance IQ score for the lowest-paying companies was 100; the average for the highest-paying companies was 103. Other factors related to CEO pay: company size (a 10 percent increase in size produces a 2 percent increase in pay), CEO tenure (a CEO earns 8 percent less pay for every 10 years of service), industry type (retailing and transportation companies pay low), location (working in New York brings a 25 percent increase in pay), business risk, and compensation risk. Altogether, these factors explained only 39 percent of the variance in CEO pay.

Many of the 214 CEOs later surveyed by *Fortune* justified their pay, pointing to the impact their jobs have on employees and society. However, 48 percent believe that the link between their pay and company performance should be strengthened. Many shareholders agree; a growing number are filing excessive-compensation suits against their companies. However, to date, signs of a strengthened CEO pay–company performance relationship have yet to appear on the horizon of the Fortune 500 companies.

Source: Graef S. Crystal, "Seeking the Sense in CEO Pay," *Fortune,* June 5, 1989, pp. 90ff; Carrie Gottlieb, "So What *Is* the Best Way to Pay?" *Fortune,* June 5, 1989, pp. 109ff.

appraisal system can make the pay-performance connection clear in the minds of employees. This clarity does not just happen; managers must work hard at communicating the performance–financial reward connection.[52] Increasingly, critics charge that the pay-performance relationship should be strengthened for the job of chief executive in large corporations and that Fortune 500 chief executive officers (CEOs) are grossly overpaid. This controversy is discussed in the Close-Up on CEOs.

---

[52]Hugh J. Arnold, "Task Performance, Perceived Competence, and Attributed Cause of Performance as Determinants of Intrinsic Motivation," *Organizational Behavior and Human Decision Processes,* December 1985, pp. 876–86.

TABLE 6−5

Evaluation of Pay Incentive Plans in Organizations

Type of Pay Plan	Performance Criteria	Perceived Pay-Performance Linkage	Minimization of Negative Consequences	Perceived Relationship between Other Rewards and Performance
Salary plan				
For individuals	Productivity	Good	Neutral	Neutral
	Cost effectiveness	Fair	Neutral	Neutral
	Superiors' rating	Fair	Neutral	Fair
For group	Productivity	Fair	Neutral	Fair
	Cost effectiveness	Fair	Neutral	Fair
	Superiors' rating	Fair	Neutral	Fair
For total organization	Productivity	Fair	Neutral	Fair
	Cost effectiveness	Fair	Neutral	Fair
	Profits	Neutral	Neutral	Fair
Bonus plan				
For individuals	Productivity	Excellent	Poor	Neutral
	Cost effectiveness	Good	Poor	Neutral
	Superiors' rating	Good	Poor	Fair
For group	Productivity	Good	Neutral	Fair
	Cost effectiveness	Good	Neutral	Fair
	Superiors' rating	Good	Neutral	Fair
For total organization	Productivity	Good	Neutral	Fair
	Cost effectiveness	Good	Neutral	Fair
	Profits	Fair	Neutral	Fair

Source: Adapted from Edward E. Lawler III, *Pay and Organizational Effectiveness* (New York: McGraw-Hill, 1971), p. 165, table 9–3.

Many organizations utilize an incentive pay plan to motivate employees. Lawler presents the most comprehensive summary of the various pay plans and their effectiveness as motivators (see Table 6–5).[53] Each plan is evaluated on the basis of the following questions:

1. How effective is it in creating the perception that pay is related to performance?
2. How well does it minimize the perceived negative consequences of good performance?
3. How well does it contribute to the perception that important rewards other than pay (e.g., praise and interest shown in the employee by a respected superior) result in good performance?

When each criterion is looked at separately, some interesting patterns evolve. Individual salary and bonus plans seem to be effective if management is attempting to link pay and performance.[54] The least effective way of accom-

---

[53]Edward E. Lawler III, *Pay and Organizational Effectiveness* (New York: McGraw-Hill, 1971), pp. 164–70.

[54]J. F. Bache, "Merit Increase Programs—Do We Really Pay for Performance?" *Supervision*, May 1986, pp. 14–17.

plishing this is to implement a total organizational salary plan. This makes sense because individuals may not perceive their impact on organizational outcomes such as productivity, cost effectiveness, and profits.

Bonus plans are generally more effective than the salary plans, especially for the first objective of linking pay and performance. Bonus plans are typically related to the current performance of employees; salary plans are often related to past performance. Neither minimizes the potential negative consequences of linking pay and performance.

If management is attempting to relate nonpay rewards to performance, group and total organization plans are more suitable than individual plans. In essence, if people believe that other rewards stem from performance, they encourage improved performance among peers throughout the organization.

Perhaps it is futile to think about developing a perfect pay plan. This discussion should clearly illustrate that no one plan can accomplish every desirable objective. The evidence indicates that bonus plans, where they can be used, are generally the best salary or wage plan. Also, individually based plans are superior to group and organizational plans. To be effective in motivating employees, incentives should (1) be related to specific behavioral patterns (for example, better performance), (2) be received immediately after the behavior is displayed, and (3) reward the employee for consistently displaying the desired behavior.

A widely publicized incentive plan has existed at Lincoln Electric Company since 1907. The Close-Up gives some background on the "Best Compensation Plan in America."

Financial rewards: fringe benefits. In the United States, organizations spend approximately $610 billion annually on employee benefits.[55] In most cases, fringe benefits are primarily financial. Some, however, such as IBM's recreation program for employees and General Mills' picnic grounds, are not entirely financial. The major financial fringe benefit in many organizations is the pension plan. For most employees, the opportunity to participate in the pension plan is a valued reward. Fringe benefits, such as pension plans, health insurance, and vacations, are not usually contingent on the performance of employees; in most cases, they are based on seniority or attendance.

Interpersonal rewards. The manager has some power to distribute such **interpersonal rewards** as status and recognition. Managers and co-workers both play a role in granting job status. By assigning individuals to prestigious jobs, the manager can attempt to improve or remove the status a person has. However, if co-workers do not believe that an employee merits a particular job, status is not likely to be enhanced. In some situations, by reviewing performance, managers can grant what they consider to be job changes that improve status.

Much of what was just stated about status also applies to recognition. In a reward context, **recognition** refers to managerial acknowledgment of employee achievement that could result in improved status. Recognition from a manager could include public praise, expressions of a job well done, or special

INTERPERSONAL REWARDS
Extrinsic rewards, such as receiving recognition or being able to interact socially on the job.

RECOGNITION
Management acknowledgment of work well done.

---

[55]M. E. Grossman, "Benefits: Costs and Coverage," *Personnel Journal,* May 1986, pp. 74–79.

THE BEST COMPENSATION PLAN IN AMERICA

Outside Cleveland, Ohio, Lincoln Electric Company and its 1,800 production workers quietly meet 40 percent of the world's demand for arc-welding equipment. Employees achieve this staggering amount of output by working at a pace equal to two to three times the productivity of their competitors, including the Japanese. While Lincoln's employees produce the most, they also make the best: Lincoln's product quality tops the industry, and Lincoln often sells its products at the lowest prices because the company is the industry's low cost leader. Their unbeatable strategy has provided increasing profits every year for several decades (except the recession years of 1982–83, when the construction industry tumbled).

Making the most and the best at the lowest cost requires intensely motivated employees. The key source of motivation is Lincoln's unique 56-year-old compensation plan that contains the following elements:

— *Piece-rate pay:* Production employees are paid totally by piece rate (no hourly wage or salary). The more you make, the more you earn. However, if the quality of your output falls below Lincoln's high standards, you correct the problems on your own time.

— *Bonus system:* The size of an employee's bonus for the year is determined by the total points received on four factors: output quantity, quality, dependability, and cooperation (this factor includes consideration of the ideas the employee provides management for working smarter and better). If 100 points are earned (25 points per factor), the bonus equals the employee's total piece-rate

attention.[56] The extent to which recognition is motivating depends, as do most rewards, on its perceived value and on the connection that the individual sees between it and behavior.

Promotions.   For many employees, promotions do not happen often; some never experience even one in their careers. Managers making promotion reward decisions attempt to match the right persons with the jobs. Criteria often used to reach promotion decisions are performance and seniority. Performance, if it can be accurately assessed, is often given significant weight in promotion reward allocations.

INTRINSIC REWARDS

Rewards that are part of the job itself. Responsibility, challenge, and feedback characteristics of the job are intrinsic rewards.

Intrinsic Rewards

Completion.   The ability to start and finish a project or job is important to some individuals. These people value *task completion*. The effect that completing a task has on a person is a form of self-reward. Some people have a need to complete tasks. Opportunities that allow such people to complete tasks can have a powerful motivating effect.

---

[56]Phillip M. Podsakoff, W. D. Tudor, and R. Skov, "Effects of Leader Contingent and Noncontingent Reward and Punishment Behaviors on Subordinate Performance and Satisfaction," *Academy of Management Journal*, December 1982, pp. 810–21.

pay for the year. Scores over 100 earn an even larger bonus. Many employees double their annual pay, with some earning over $50,000 a year (not bad, given that most employees have only a high school education).

— *Job security:* Work for Lincoln two years and you are guaranteed 30 hours of work each week thereafter. Lincoln guarantees employment to protect employees from economic downturns and to assure them that their productivity ideas won't someday cost them their jobs. Lincoln has not had a layoff since World War II.

Although Lincoln's pay is good and performance is exceptional, life at Lincoln is not for everyone. The facilities, though well equipped, are spare, windowless, and not air-conditioned. (A recent proposal to air-condition the plant was rejected by employees, who wanted to keep costs down and their bonus pool untouched.) There are no paid holidays, sick days, or dental insurance. The pressure to perform is intense; employees work through breaks to boost output (and their bonuses) and on weekends during busy periods. On average, 25 percent of all new employees leave during the first three months; but virtually all who survive the initiation remain for at least 30 years.

Source: Stanley J. Modic, "Fine-Tuning a Classic," *Industry Week,* March 6, 1989, pp. 15–16, 18; Bruce G. Posner, "Right from the Start," *Inc.,* August 1988, pp. 95–96.

Achievement.   Achievement is a self-administered reward that is derived from reaching a challenging goal. David C. McClelland has described individual differences in those striving for achievement.[57] Some seek challenging goals, while others seek moderate or low goals. In goal-setting programs, difficult goals may result in a higher level of individual performance than do moderate goals. Even in such programs, however, individual differences must be considered before reaching conclusions about the importance of achievement rewards.

Autonomy.   Some people want jobs that provide them with the right and privilege to make decisions; they want to operate without being closely supervised. A feeling of autonomy could result from the freedom to do what the employee considers best in a particular situation. In jobs that are highly structured and controlled by management, it is difficult to create tasks that lead to a feeling of autonomy.

Personal growth.   The personal growth of any individual is unique. Individuals experiencing such growth can sense their development and see how their capabilities are being expanded. By expanding their capabilities, employees can maximize or at least satisfy skill potential. Some become

[57]David C. McClelland, *The Achieving Society* (New York: Van Nostrand Reinhold, 1961).

TABLE 6–6

Types and Sources of Selected Extrinsic and Intrinsic Rewards

Type	Source		
	Manager	Group	Individual
Extrinsic			
Financial			
Salary and wages	D		
Fringe benefits	D		
Interpersonal	D	D	
Promotion	D		
Intrinsic			
Completion	I		D
Achievement	I		D
Autonomy	I		D
Personal growth	I		D

Note: D = Direct source of the reward.
       I = Indirect source of the reward.

dissatisfied with their jobs and organizations if not allowed or encouraged to develop their skills.

The rewards included in this section are distributed or created by managers, work groups, or individuals. Table 6–6 summarizes the rewards we have discussed. As the table indicates, managers can play either a direct or an indirect role in developing and administering the rewards.

The Interaction of Intrinsic and Extrinsic Rewards

The general assumption has been that intrinsic and extrinsic rewards have an independent and additive influence on motivation. That is, motivation is determined by the sum of the person's intrinsic and extrinsic sources of motivation.[58] This straightforward assumption has been questioned by several researchers. Some have suggested that in situations in which individuals are experiencing a high level of intrinsic rewards, the addition of extrinsic rewards for good performance may cause a decrease in motivation.[59] Basically, the person receiving self-administered feelings of satisfaction is performing because of intrinsic rewards. Once extrinsic rewards are added, feelings of satisfaction change because performance is now thought to be due to the extrinsic rewards. The addition of extrinsic rewards tends to reduce the extent to which the individual experiences self-administered intrinsic rewards.[60]

---

[58]Daniel C. Feldman and Hugh J. Arnold, *Managing Individual and Group Behavior in Organizations* (New York: McGraw-Hill, 1983), p. 164.

[59]Edward L. Deci, "The Effects of Externally Mediated Rewards on Intrinsic Motivation," *Journal of Personality and Social Psychology*, 1971, pp. 105–15. Also Edward L. Deci, *Intrinsic Motivation* (New York: Plenum Press, 1975).

[60]Barry M. Staw, *Intrinsic and Extrinsic Motivation* (Morristown, N.J.: General Learning Press, 1975).

The argument concerning the potential negative effects of extrinsic rewards has stimulated a number of research studies. Unfortunately, these studies report contradictory results. Some researchers report a reduction in intrinsic rewards following the addition of extrinsic rewards for an activity;[61] others have failed to observe such an effect.[62] A review of the literature found that 14 of 24 studies supported the theory that extrinsic rewards reduce intrinsic motivation;[63] 10 did not support it. Of the 24 studies reviewed, only two used actual employees as subjects. All of the other studies used college students or grade school students. In studies of telephone operators and clerical employees, the theory was not supported.[64] Managers need to be aware that no scientifically based and reported study substantiates that extrinsic rewards have a negative effect on intrinsic motivation.

Rewards, Turnover, and Absenteeism

Managers may assume that low turnover is a mark of an effective organization. However, some organizations would benefit if disruptive and low performers quit.[65] Thus, the issue of turnover needs to focus on *who* is leaving as well as on frequency.

Ideally, if managers could develop reward systems that retained the best performers and caused poor performers to leave, the overall effectiveness of an organization would improve.[66] To approach this ideal state, an equitable and favorably compared reward system must exist. The feelings of *equity* and *favorable comparison* have an external orientation. That is, the equity of rewards and favorableness involve comparisons with external parties. This orientation is used because quitting most often means that a person leaves one organization for an alternative elsewhere.

No perfect means exist for retaining high performers. A reward system based on **merit ratings** should encourage most better performers to remain with the organization. Also, the reward system needs some differential that discriminates between high and low performers. High performers must

MERIT RATING
Formal rating system applied to hourly paid employees.

---

[61]Barry M. Staw, "The Attitudinal and Behavior Consequences of Changing a Major Organizational Reward," *Journal of Personality and Social Psychology,* June 1974, pp. 742–51.

[62]Cynthia D. Fisher, "The Effects of Personal Control, Competence, and Extrinsic Reward Systems on Intrinsic Motivation," *Organizational Behavior and Human Performance,* June 1978, pp. 273–87. Also James S. Phillips and Robert G. Lord, "Determinants of Intrinsic Motivation: Locus of Control and Competence Information as Components of Deci's Cognitive Evaluation Theory," *Journal of Applied Psychology,* April 1980, pp. 211–18.

[63]K. B. Boone and Larry L. Cummings, "Cognitive Evaluation Theory: An Experimental Test of Processes and Outcomes," *Organizational Behavior and Human Performance,* December 1981, pp. 289–310.

[64]E. M. Lopez, "A Test of Deci's Cognitive Evaluation Theory in an Organizational Setting," paper presented at the 39th annual convention of the Academy of Management, Atlanta, Georgia, August 1979.

[65]Dan R. Dalton, Daniel M. Krackhardt, and Lyman W. Porter, "Functional Turnover: An Empirical Assessment," *Journal of Applied Psychology,* December 1981, pp. 716–21.

[66]Dan R. Dalton and W. D. Tudor, "Turnover: A Lucrative Hard Dollar Phenomenon," *Academy of Management Review,* April 1982, p. 212.

receive significantly more extrinsic and intrinsic rewards than the low performers.[67]

Absenteeism, no matter for what reason, is a costly and disruptive problem facing managers.[68] It is costly because it reduces output and disruptive because it requires that schedules and programs be modified. Absenteeism in the United States is estimated to result in the loss of over 400 million workdays per year, or about 5.1 days per employee.[69] Employees go to work because they are motivated to do so; the level of motivation remains high if an individual feels that attendance leads to more valued rewards and fewer negative consequences than alternative behaviors.

Managers appear to have some influence over attendance behavior. They have the ability to punish, establish bonus systems, and allow employee participation in developing plans. Whether these or other approaches reduce absenteeism is determined by the value of the rewards perceived by employees, the amount of the rewards, and whether employees perceive a relationship between attendance and rewards. These same characteristics appear every time we analyze the effects of rewards on organizational behavior.

Rewards and Job Performance

Behaviorists and managers agree that extrinsic and intrinsic rewards can be used to motivate job performance. It is also clear that certain conditions must exist if rewards are to actually motivate: the rewards must be *valued* by the person, and they must be related to a specific level of job performance.[70]

In Chapter 5, expectancy motivation theory was presented. According to that theory, people associate every behavior with certain outcomes or rewards or punishments. In other words, an assembly-line worker may believe that by behaving in a certain way he or she will get certain things. This is a description of the *performance-outcome expectancy*. On one hand, a worker may expect that a steady performance of 10 units a day will eventually result in a transfer to a more challenging job. On the other hand, a worker may expect that a steady performance of 10 units a day will result in being considered a rate buster by co-workers.

Each outcome has a *valence*, or value, to the person. Because each person has different needs and perceptions, outcomes such as pay, promotion, a reprimand, or a better job have different values for different people. Thus, in considering which rewards to use, a manager has to be astute in considering individual differences. If valued rewards are used to motivate, they can result in the exertion of effort to achieve high levels of performance.

---

[67]E. J. Brennan, "Merit Pay: Balance the Old Rich and the New Poor," *Personnel Journal*, May 1985, pp. 82–84.

[68]Gary Johns and N. Nicholson, "The Meanings of Absence: New Strategies for Theory and Research," in *Research in Organizational Behavior*, ed. Barry M. Staw and Larry L. Cummings (Greenwich, Conn.: JAI Press, 1982), pp. 127–72.

[69]Richard M. Steers and Susan R. Rhodes, "A New Look at Absenteeism," *Personnel*, November–December 1980, pp. 60–65.

[70]Porter et al., *Behavior*, p. 352.

Rewards and Organizational Commitment

There is little research on the relationship between rewards and organizational commitment.[71] **Commitment** to an organization involves three attitudes: (1) a sense of identification with the organization's goals, (2) a feeling of involvement in organizational duties, and (3) a feeling of loyalty for the organization.[72] Research evidence indicates that the absence of commitment can reduce organizational effectiveness.[73] Committed people are less likely to quit and accept other jobs. Thus, the costs of high turnover are not incurred. In addition, committed and highly skilled employees require less supervision. Close supervision and a rigid monitoring control process are time-consuming and costly. Furthermore, a committed employee perceives the value and importance of integrating individual and organizational goals. The employee thinks of his or her goals and the organization's goals in personal terms.

Intrinsic rewards are important for the development of organizational commitment. Organizations able to meet employees' needs by providing achievement opportunities and by recognizing achievement when it occurs have a significant impact on commitment.[74] Thus, managers need to develop intrinsic reward systems that focus on personal importance or self-esteem, to integrate individual and organizational goals, and to design challenging jobs.

COMMITMENT

A sense of identification, loyalty, and involvement expressed by an employee toward the organization or unit.

INNOVATIVE REWARD SYSTEMS

The typical list of rewards that managers can and do distribute in organizations has been discussed. We all know that pay, fringe benefits, and opportunities to achieve challenging goals are considered rewards by most people. It is also generally accepted that rewards are administered by managers through such processes as reinforcement, modeling, and expectancies. What are some of the newer and innovative, yet largely untested, reward programs that some managers are experimenting with? Five different reward approaches that are not widely tested are cafeteria-style fringe benefits, banking time off, paying all employees a salary, skill-based pay, and gainsharing. The strengths and weaknesses of these five approaches are summarized in Table 6–7.

Cafeteria-Style Fringe Benefits

In a cafeteria-style plan, management places an upper limit on how much the organization is willing to spend on fringe benefits. Employees then decide how

[71]Fred Luthans, H. S. McCaul, and N. G. Dowd, "Organizational Commitment: A Comparison of American, Japanese, and Korean Employees," *Academy of Management Journal,* March 1985, pp. 213–19.

[72]B. Buchanan, "To Walk an Extra Mile: The Whats, Whens, and Whys of Organizational Commitment," *Organizational Dynamics,* Spring 1975, pp. 67–80.

[73]Richard T. Mowday, Lyman W. Porter, and Richard M. Steers, *Employee-Organization Linkages* (New York: Academic Press, 1982).

[74]J. P. Curry, D. S. Wakefield, James L. Price, and Charles W. Mueller, "On the Causal Ordering of Job Satisfaction and Organizational Commitment," *Academy of Management Journal,* December 1986, pp. 847–58.

TABLE 6—7

Five Innovative Reward Approaches: A Summary and Comparison

Reward Approach	Major Strengths	Major Weaknesses	Research Support
Cafeteria-style fringe benefits	Since employees have different desires and needs, programs can be tailored to fit individuals.	Administration can become complex and costly. The more employees involved, the more difficult it is to efficiently operate the approach.	Limited, since only a few programs have been scientifically examined.
Banking time off	Can be integrated with performance in that time-off credits can be made contingent on performance achievements.	Requires that an organization have a valid, reliable, and equitable performance appraisal program.	Extremely limited.
All-salaried teams	Eliminates treating some employees as insiders and some as outsiders. Everyone is paid a salary and is a member of the team.	Assumes that everyone wants to be a team member and paid a salary. Some individuals value being nonmanagers and nonsalaried.	None available.
Skill-based pay	Employees must clearly demonstrate skill before receiving any pay increases.	Training costs to upgrade employee skills are higher than under conventional pay systems. Labor costs increase if employees learn many skills. Employees may "top out."	Very limited, with no direct skill-based versus conventional pay compensation studies available.
Gainsharing	Can enhance teamwork. Employees focus on objectives, learn more about the organization, and may be more productive.	If plans focus only on productivity, employees may ignore other important objectives.	Very limited.

they would like to receive the total fringe benefit amount. Employees develop individualized, personally attractive fringe benefit packages. Some employees take all of the fringes in cash; others purchase special medical protection plans. **Cafeteria-style fringe benefits** provide individuals with the benefits they prefer rather than the benefits that someone else establishes for them.

Using a cafeteria-style plan offers some distinct advantages. First, it allows employees to play an active rather than a passive role in making decisions about the allocation of fringe benefits. Second, employees receive the benefits of greatest personal value to them. This provides many people with a psychologically uplifting feeling. Third, the cafeteria-style plan makes the economic value of fringe benefits obvious to each employee; it highlights the value of fringes. In many situations, employees grossly underestimate the value of the fringe benefits their employers provide.

Some administrative problems are associated with cafeteria plans.[75] Because of the different preferences of employees, records become more complicated. For a large organization with a cafeteria plan, a computer system is almost essential to do the record-keeping. Another problem involves group insurance

CAFETERIA-STYLE FRINGE BENEFITS

Benefit plan in which an employee is allowed to develop and allocate a personally attractive fringe benefit package. Employee is informed of total fringe benefits allowed and then distributes benefits according to his or her preferences.

[75]J. H. Shea, "Cautions about Cafeteria-Style Benefit Plans," *Personnel Journal*, January 1981, p. 37.

premium rates. Most life and medical insurance premiums are based on the number of employees participating. It is difficult to predict the participation level under a cafeteria plan.

TRW Corporation placed approximately 12,000 employees on a cafeteria plan. It allows employees to rearrange and redistribute their fringe benefit packages every year. Over 80 percent of the TRW participants have changed their benefit packages since the plan was initiated.[76]

Banking Time Off

Time off from work is attractive to most people. In essence, most companies have a time-off system built into their vacation programs. Employees receive different amounts of time off, based on the years they have worked for the organization. An extension of such a time-off reward could be granted for certain levels of performance. That is, a bank of time-off credits could be built up contingent on performance achievements.

Today, some organizations are selecting their best performers to attend educational and training programs. One company in Houston selects the best performers and provides them with an opportunity to attend an executive educational program. Being eligible is largely contingent on the performance record of the individual. Those finally selected are given two Fridays off a month to attend classes.

The All-Salaried Team

In most organizations, managers are paid salaries and nonmanagers receive hourly wages. The practice of paying all employees a salary is supposed to improve loyalty, commitment, and self-esteem. The notion of being a part of a team is projected by the salary-for-everyone practice. One benefit of the all-salary practice considered important by nonmanagers is that it eliminates punching a time clock. To date, rigorous investigations of the influence, if any, of the all-salary practice are not available. It does seem to have promise when applied to some employees.

Skill-Based Pay

In traditional compensation systems, characteristics of the job performed (e.g., its difficulty and complexity) determine an employee's pay rate and range. However, in **skill-based pay** programs, the employee's pay depends not on the job but on the level and number of job-related skills the employee possesses.

In many skill-based programs, employees work as members of semiautonomous teams. When hired, an employee is paid a starting rate and receives pay increases as he or she learns new skills that are required by the team. Once an employee learns all of the team skills, opportunities are provided to learn skills outside the unit and throughout the organization. Pay increases accom-

SKILL-BASED PAY
Wages paid at rate calculated and based on skills employees possess and display in performing jobs.

---

[76]Lawler, "Reward Systems," p. 182.

pany each new set of skills the employee masters. In skill-based programs that do not utilize teams, an employee moves up one pay grade for each job learned, and jobs can be learned in any sequence. Often, the size of pay raises is the same regardless of the content of jobs learned.[77]

Skill-based pay programs afford several benefits. The key advantage is a more highly skilled and flexible work force. Productivity can increase, and supervisory costs are often reduced. Employees are more motivated to gain and use their skills; they often perceive their pay as being more equitable; and they have a better understanding of how their jobs fit into the organization.[78]

Pay levels and training costs, however, often increase. Employees can be frustrated when no openings are available in job areas for which they are newly trained. And a long-term problem may arise if employees have "topped out"—they've learned all the skills needed by the organization and have nowhere to go. Dissatisfaction and turnover may result.[79] Overall, a careful cost-benefit analysis should be conducted before implementing a skill-based pay program.

Gainsharing

GAINSHARING

Employees share in the financial rewards of achieving set objectives.

In a **gainsharing** program, performance objectives (e.g., productivity, quality, customer service) are established for an organizational unit (a plant or division) and sometimes for the overall organization. If the objectives are met or surpassed, all employees share in the benefits, typically receiving bonuses. Gainsharing is currently the fastest-growing incentive program in the United States, partly because of a widespread belief that gainsharing spurs motivation and teamwork. About 26 percent of U.S. companies utilize the program, with 75 percent of the plans installed since 1980.[80]

Carrier, the heating and air-conditioning equipment manufacturer and a subsidiary of United Technologies, provides an example of how gainsharing works. Carrier set as a benchmark the 1.8 hours that production employees take to make a finished product (the average time for 1986). When employees beat this benchmark with acceptable-quality products, the labor savings are split 50–50 between the subsidiary and every employee in the plant, from machinists to secretaries to managers. To keep employees informed, plant productivity information is posted daily on the plant bulletin boards, and employees are encouraged to provide timesaving ideas. In 1988, Carrier's 2,500 employees received over $3 million in bonus pay for being over 25 percent more productive than the 1986 benchmark.[81]

Although many observers believe that an effective gainsharing program can boost productivity, cut absenteeism and turnover, and improve product quality, some critics assert that these effects are not long lasting and that research on results is very limited. However, most agree that gainsharing is

[77]Fred Luthans and M. L. Fox, "Update on Skill-Based Pay," *Personnel,* March 1989, pp. 26, 28.

[78]R. L. Bunning, "Skill-Based Pay," *Personnel Administrator,* June 1989, pp. 65–70.

[79]Luthans and Fox, "Update," p. 28.

[80]Nancy J. Perry, "Here Come Richer, Riskier Pay Plans," *Fortune,* December 19, 1988, pp. 52, 54.

[81]Ibid., p. 54.

most effective in business units with fewer than 500 employees and when rewards are based on results that employees can directly affect.[82]

The link between the performance evaluation system and reward distribution was shown in Figure 6–4. The discussion of this and other linkages in the reward process suggests the complexity of using rewards to motivate better performance. Managers need to use judgment, diagnosis, and the resources available to reward their subordinates. Administering rewards is perhaps one of the most challenging and frustrating tasks that managers must perform.

PUNISHMENT AND DISCIPLINE

Analysis and discussion of job motivation in organizational management focus primarily on eliciting desired behavior and performance. However, managers occasionally are faced with undesired behavior and inadequate performance.[83] Despite their unpleasant connotations, punishment and disciplinary measures are used to eliminate undesired behavior and poor performance.[84] Some managers and researchers argue that there is no justification for the use of punishment in organizational settings. Others believe that at times punishment is the most efficient and effective way to change behavior. Examples of behaviors that are typically punished in organizations include stealing, violating safety regulations, using illegal drugs on the job, absenteeism, fighting, work slowdowns, and falsifying expense accounts.

Punishment is the presentation of an aversive event or the removal of a positive event following a response, that decreases the frequency of the response.[85] A relationship, or contingency, exists between some defined response and some aversive consequence or stimulus (e.g., a pay reduction for being absent, a publicized memo informing an employee of poor performance). Some managers resist the use of punishment on the moral grounds that pain is bad and should always be avoided. **Discipline** is the use of some form of punishment or sanction when employees deviate from the rules. Not all disciplinary measures turn out to be punishment.[86] For example, suppose that frequent absence results in a three-day suspension from work. If the disciplined person doesn't like the job and prefers to stay home, he or she has not been punished.

Managers prefer to acknowledge that their firms have discipline programs as opposed to admitting that punishment is used. But instead of focusing on discipline programs, we prefer to discuss punishment. The punishment literature contains the theoretical framework and basis for organizational progressive discipline programs (whereby a sequence of penalties for violations is administered, each one slightly more severe than the previous one).

PUNISHMENT
Presenting an uncomfortable consequence for a particular behavior response or removing a desirable reinforcer because of a particular behavior response. Managers can punish by application or by removal.

DISCIPLINE
The use of some form of punishment or sanction when employees deviate from rules or procedures.

---

[82]T. L. Ross, L. Hatcher, and R. A. Ross, "From Piecework to Companywide Gainsharing," *Management Review*, May 1989, pp. 22–26; Perry, "Here Come Richer," p. 54.

[83]D. L. Kanter, "Managing Jaundiced," *New Management*, Spring 1986, pp. 50–56.

[84]Richard D. Arvey and John M. Ivancevich, "Punishment in Organizations: A Review, Propositions, and Research Suggestions," *Academy of Management Journal*, January 1980, pp. 123–32.

[85]Alan E. Kazdin, *Behavior Modification in Applied Settings* (Homewood, Ill.: Dorsey Press, 1984), p. 33.

[86]I. G. Asherman, "The Corrective Discipline Process," *Personnel Journal*, July 1982, p. 528.

Punishment and Behavior

The earliest theoretical explanation of punishment was advanced by Edward Thorndike.[87] He proposed that punishment exerted its effect on behavior by weakening the connection between a stimulus and a response. According to this theory, if the proverbial child caught with a hand in the cookie jar were immediately punished, it would on subsequent occasions no longer be under the influence of the cookie jar or the cookies in it. The jar and the cookies would have lost their power to control the behavior of reaching into the jar. Later, Thorndike decided that punishment really had no weakening effect on behavior,[88] arriving at his reevaluation of punishment by questioning his original position. He argued that wherever punishment appears to weaken a response, it is an indirect effect. Punishment may or may not weaken a response, but it clearly cannot be the mirror image of the action of reward. For example, if an employee's response is rewarded, it is apparent that repetition of this response may also be rewarding; but if an employee's response is punished, it is not clear to the person which of the other available responses will be rewarded. In effect, Thorndike suggested that punishment does an exemplary job of telling a person what not to do but by itself carries no information that tells an individual which particular alternative course of behavior should be followed.

Arguments against Using Punishment

Reasons other than moral have been advanced against the use of punishment. First, the purpose of punishment presumably is to reduce the occurrence of the specific behavior being punished. However, if severe enough and applied over sufficient time, it may also suppress the occurrence of socially desirable behaviors.

Second, some assume that the use of punishment results in undesirable side effects (e.g., anxiety, aggressiveness). In addition, those being punished may attempt to escape or avoid (e.g., absenteeism, turnover) or show hostility toward (e.g., sabotage) management. Research support for the presence of undesirable emotional side effects of punishment is not particularly strong. A review of the literature indicates that only one of numerous studies supported this assumption.[89] The review indicated that, rather than undesirable emotional side effects, improvement in subject behavior occurred as a result of punishment. Perhaps negative side effects are more likely to occur if managers are indiscriminately and unfairly punitive.[90]

---

[87]Edward L. Thorndike, *Educational Psychology, vol. 2H: The Psychology of Learning* (New York: Columbia University Teachers College Bureau of Publications, 1913).

[88]Edward L. Thorndike, *Reward and Punishment in Animal Learning,* Contemporary Psychological Monograph 8, no. 39 (1983).

[89]J. M. Johnson, "Punishment of Human Behavior," *American Psychologist,* November 1972, pp. 1033–54.

[90]Phillip M. Podsakoff, "Determinants of a Supervisor's Use of Rewards and Punishments: A Literature Review and Suggestions for Further Research," *Organizational Behavior and Human Performance,* February 1982, pp. 58–83.

Third, punishment effects are only temporary; once the threat of punishment is removed, the undesirable response returns full force. Thus, the threat of punishment must always be there or be used. Punishment does work; this may produce positive reinforcement for the managers to continue its use.

Fourth, through observational learning, punishment may result in negative responses from peers of the punished person. For example, individuals observing a manager punishing a colleague may imitate this behavior among themselves or toward management. In effect, the manager is teaching employees aggressive, impersonal behavior, which is exactly what punishment is designed to eliminate.

Conditions of Punishment

Despite logical arguments against the use of punishment in organizations, certain conditions can make its use feasible and more effective.

Timing. The time at which punishment is administered is important.[91] Research suggests that the effectiveness of punishment is enhanced when the aversive event is delivered soon after the punished response.

Intensity. Punishment achieves greater effectiveness when the aversive stimulus is relatively intense. The implication of this condition is that to be effective, punishment should get the immediate attention of the person being punished.[92]

Scheduling. The effects of punishment depend partly on the punishment schedule. Punishment can be meted out after every poor response or after a certain number of poor responses occur. Punishment after every response (continuous schedule), a variable or fixed period of time after the undesired behavior occurred (variable or fixed interval schedules), or after a variable or fixed number of responses have occurred (variable or fixed ratio schedules) is delivered on the basis of schedules. Some research indicates that punishment is most effective if administered on a continuous schedule. Consistency is also important. A manager should punish a respective behavior in the same way across all individuals who exhibit the undesired behavior.

Clarification. Cognition plays an important role in punishment.[93] Providing clear, unambiguous reasons for the punishment and notice of future consequences if the response recurs is particularly effective. Providing reasons emphasizes to the person which specific response is responsible for the manager's action. It essentially informs the person exactly what not to do.

---

[91]A. Trenholme and A. Baron, "Immediate and Delayed Punishment of Human Behavior by Loss of Reinforcement," *Learning and Motivation,* February 1975, pp. 62–79.

[92]Johnson, "Punishment."

[93]Dennis W. Organ and W. Clay Hamner, *Organizational Behavior* (Plano, Tex.: Business Publications, 1982), pp. 97–98.

Impersonality.   Punishment should focus on a specific response, not on the person or general patterns of behavior.[94] The more impersonal the punishment, the less likely the person punished is to experience undesirable emotional side effects and permanent strains in the relationship with the manager.

This section is intended to clarify the issue of punishment in organizations. Certainly, we prefer the predominant use of positive reinforcement. However, when managers are faced with stopping a persistently undesirable response, positive reinforcement, negative reinforcement, or extinction alone may not be enough. These and other suggested alternatives may all be ineffective or costly. In such cases, punishment is used and will undoubtedly continue to be used. Although punishment is a complex and controversial process, ignoring its use is not likely to enhance management's understanding of its application.

---

[94]Michael Domjan and Barbara Burkhard, *The Principles of Learning and Behavior* (Monterey, Calif.: Brooks/Cole Publishing, 1982), p. 264.

SUMMARY OF KEY POINTS

— Performance evaluation is a formal process wherein a subordinate's job performance and potential for future development are evaluated. As the basis for reward-related decisions and for developing subordinates, performance evaluation also has motivational, knowledge, improvement, research, and organizational planning, training, and development purposes.

— Establishing criteria is one important part of developing an evaluation system. A criterion is a dependent or predicted measure for appraising the effectiveness of employees. A good criterion must be relevant, stable, practical, and able to discriminate between ratees.

— A few of the widely used performance evaluation techniques are graphic rating scales, ranking procedures, weighted checklists, descriptive essays, and BARS.

— The behaviorally anchored rating scale (BARS) is an evaluation technique that uses critical incidents or examples of specific job behaviors to determine the various levels of performance. Developing a BARS is time-consuming and costly; but if both raters and ratees are involved, greater acceptance of the program by ratees can result.

— Reward systems seek to attract people to join the organization, to keep them coming to work, and to motivate them to perform at high levels.

— Organizations typically provide two types of rewards. *Extrinsic* rewards are those external to the job, such as promotions, fringe benefits, and pay. *Intrinsic* rewards are associated with doing the job. They include responsibility, challenge, and meaningful work.

— If effectively used, rewards can affect such individual behaviors as turnover, absenteeism, performance, and commitment. Research evidence showing how rewards influence these behaviors is still rather limited.

— Innovative reward strategies used by managers include cafeteria-style fringe benefits, banking time off, skill-based pay, an all-salaried work force, and gainsharing. These strategies have not been thoroughly studied by researchers.

— Punishment in organizations involves presenting an aversive event or removing a positive event following an undesired response in order to decrease the frequency of the response. Though punishment is controversial and several arguments exist opposing its use, punishment can be effective if management duly considers timing, intensity, scheduling, clarification of reasons, and impersonality.

DISCUSSION AND REVIEW QUESTIONS

1. Since no one evaluation method is superior to another, which combination of methods would be potentially informative, accurate, and equitable?

2. Why is it exceptionally difficult to distribute rewards based on merit?

3. Consider a job that you have held or presently hold. Identify the criteria used to evaluate your performance. Assess the criteria's quality in terms of validity and reliability. Could other, more valid and reliable criteria be used? Explain.

4. If equity and favorable comparisons are so important in reward systems, how can an organization develop a program generally viewed as equitable and favorable?

5. Given its cost, under what conditions do you believe a BARS evaluation system is a justified approach to appraising employees? Explain.

6. In a free society, is punishment justified as a managerial strategy for correcting behaviors? Why?

7. Of the five innovative reward systems described in the chapter, which system in your opinion would be the most challenging to successfully implement and maintain? Explain.

8. According to recent research, managers at the upper levels of the organization are the least likely to have their performance regularly evaluated. Why is this the case? What is the potential impact of this neglect?

9. How important is it for a rater to actually observe critical behaviors of a ratee before providing an evaluation?

10. What type(s) of research is needed to determine whether the different innovative reward systems can be organizationally successful? Explain.

ADDITIONAL REFERENCES

Bernardi, H. J. "Increasing the Accuracy of Performance Measurement: A Proposed Solution to Erroneous Attributions." *Human Resource Planning,* 1989, pp. 239–50.

Blasi, J. R. *Employee Ownership: Revolution or Ripoff?* Cambridge, Mass.: Ballinger, 1988.

Cleveland, J. N.; K. R. Murphy; and R. E. Williams. "Multiple Uses of Performance Appraisal: Prevalence and Correlates." *Journal of Applied Psychology,* February 1989, pp. 130–35.

Fisher, C. D. "Current and Recurrent Challenges in HRM." *Journal of Management,* June 1989, pp. 157–80.

Gaugler, B. B., and G. C. Thornton III. "Number of Assessment Center Dimensions as a Determinant of Assessor Accuracy." *Journal of Applied Psychology,* August 1989, pp. 611–18.

Gellerman, S. W., and W. G. Hodgson. "Cyanimid's New Take on Performance Appraisal." *Harvard Business Review,* May–June 1988, pp. 36–37, 40–41.

Giffin, M. E. "Personnel Research on Testing, Selection, and Performance Appraisal, 1963–1988." *Public Personnel Management,* Summer 1989, pp. 127–37.

Howard, A. "Who Reaches for the Golden Handshake?" *Academy of Management Executive,* May 1988, pp. 133–44.

Kanungo, R. N., and M. Mendonca. "Evaluating Employee Compensation." *California Management Review,* Fall 1988, pp. 23–39.

Kerr, J., and J. W. Slocum, Jr. "Managing Corporate Culture through Reward Systems." *Academy of Management Executive,* May 1987, pp. 99–108.

Levy, M. "Almost-Perfect Performance Appraisals." *Personnel Journal,* April 1989, pp. 76, 78, 80, 83.

Mohrman, A. M., Jr.; S. M. Resnick-West; and E. E. Lawler III. *Designing Performance Appraisal Systems.* San Francisco: Jossey-Bass, 1989.

Riccucci, N. M., and G. R. Wheeler. "Positive Employee Performance: An Innovative Approach to Employee Discipline." *Review of Public Personnel Administration,* February 1987, pp. 49–63.

Schneier, C. E. "Capitalizing on Performance, Management, Recognition, and Rewards Systems." *Compensation and Benefits Review,* March–April 1989, pp. 20–30.

Swabe, A. I. R. "Performance-Related Pay: A Case Study." *Employee Relations,* 1989, pp. 17–23.

THE POLITICS OF PERFORMANCE APPRAISAL

Every Friday, Max Steadman, Jim Cobun, Lynne Sims, and Tom Hamilton meet at Charley's after work for drinks. The four friends work as managers at Eckel Industries, a manufacturer of arc-welding equipment in Minneapolis. The one-plant company employs about 2,000 people. The four managers work in the manufacturing division. Max, 35, manages the company's 25 quality control inspectors. Lynne, 33, works as a supervisor in inventory management. Jim, 34, is a first-line supervisor in the metal coating department. Tom, 28, supervises a team of assemblers. The four managers' tenure at Eckel Industries ranges from one year (Tom) to 12 years (Max).

The group is close-knit; Lynne, Jim, and Max's friendship stems from their years as undergraduate business students at the University of Minnesota. Tom, the newcomer, joined the group after meeting the three at an Eckel management seminar last year. Weekly get-togethers at Charley's have become a comfortable habit for the group and provide an opportunity to relax, exchange the latest gossip heard around the plant, and give and receive advice about problems encountered on the job.

This week's topic of discussion: performance appraisal, specifically the company's annual review process, which the plant's management conducted in the last week. Each of the four managers completed evaluation forms (graphic rating scales) on all of his or her subordinates and met with each subordinate to discuss the appraisal.

Tom: This was the first time I've appraised my people, and I dreaded it. For me, it's been the worst week of the year. Evaluating is difficult; it's highly subjective and inexact. Your emotions creep into the process. I got angry at one of my assembly workers last week, and I still felt the anger when I was filling out the evaluation forms. Don't tell me that my frustration with the guy didn't bias my appraisal. I think it did. And I think the technique is flawed. Tell me—what's the difference between a five and a six on "cooperation"?

Jim: The scales are a problem. So is memory. Remember our course in personnel in college? Philips said that according to research, when we sit down to evaluate someone's performance in the past year, we will only be able to actively recall and use 15 percent of the performance we actually observed.

Lynne: I think political considerations are always a part of the process. I know I consider many other factors besides a person's actual performance when I appraise him.

Tom: Like what?

Lynne: Like the appraisal will become part of his permanent written record that affects his career. Like the person I evaluate today, I have to work with tomorrow. Given that, the difference between a five and a six on cooperation isn't that relevant, because frankly, if a five makes him mad and he's happy with a six . . .

Max: Then you give him the six. Accuracy is important, but I'll admit it—accuracy isn't my primary objective when I evaluate my workers. My objective is to motivate and reward them so they'll perform better. I use the review process to do what's best for my people and my department. If that means fine-tuning the evaluations to do that, I will.

Source: Kim A. Stewart, University of Denver. Several perspectives were drawn from an insightful study reported in Clinton O. Longenecker, Henry P. Sims, Jr., and Dennis A. Gioia, "Behind the Mask: The Politics of Employee Appraisal," *Academy of Management Executive*, August 1987, pp. 183–91.

Tom: What's an example of fine-tuning?

Max: Jim, do you remember three years ago when the company lowered the ceiling on merit raises? The top merit increase that any employee could get was 4 percent. I boosted the ratings of my folks to get the best merit increases for them. The year before that, the ceiling was 8 percent. The best they could get was less than what most of them received the year before. I felt they deserved the 4 percent, so I gave the marks that got them what I felt they deserved.

Lynne: I've inflated ratings to encourage someone who is having personal problems but is normally a good employee. A couple of years ago, one of my better people was going through a painful divorce, and it was showing in her work. I don't think it's fair to kick someone when they're down, even if their work is poor. I felt a good rating would speed her recovery.

Tom: Or make her complacent.

Lynne: No, I don't think so. I felt she realized her work was suffering. I wanted to give her encouragement; it was my way of telling her she had some support and that she wasn't in danger of losing her job.

Jim: There's another situation where I think fine-tuning is merited—when someone's work has been mediocre or even poor for most of the year, but it improves substantially in the last two, three months or so. If I think the guy is really trying and is doing much better, I'd give him a rating that's higher than his work over the whole year deserves. It encourages him to keep improving. If I give him a mediocre rating, what does that tell him?

Tom: What if he's really working hard, but not doing so great?

Jim: If I think he has what it takes, I'd boost the rating to motivate him to keep trying until he gets there.

Max: I know of one or two managers who've inflated ratings to get rid of a pain in the neck, some young guy who's transferred in and thinks he'll be there a short time. He's not good, but thinks he is and creates all sorts of problems. Or his performance is OK, but he just doesn't fit in with the rest of the department. A year or two of good ratings is a sure trick for getting rid of him.

Tom: Yes, but you're passing the problem on to someone else.

Max: True, but it's no longer my problem.

Tom: All the examples you've talked about involve inflating evaluations. What about deflating them, giving someone less than you really think he deserves? Is that justified?

Lynne: I'd hesitate to do that, because it can create problems. It can backfire.

Max: But it does happen. You can lower a guy's ratings to shock him, to jolt him into performing better. Sometimes, you can work with someone, coach them, try to help them improve, and it just doesn't work. A basement-level rating can tell him you mean business. You can say that isn't fair, and for the time being, it isn't. But what if you feel that if the guy doesn't shape up he faces being fired in a year or two, and putting him in the cellar, ratingswise, will solve his problem? It's fair in the long run if the effect is that he improves his work and keeps his job.

Jim: Sometimes, you get someone who's a real rebel, who always questions you, sometimes even oversteps his bounds. I think deflating his evaluation is merited just to remind him who's the boss.

Lynne: I'd consider lowering someone's true rating if they've had a long record of rather questionable performance, and I think the best alternative for the person is to consider another job with another company. A low appraisal sends him a message to consider quitting and start looking for another job.

Max: What if you believe the situation is hopeless, and you've made up your mind that you're going to fire the guy as soon as you've found a suitable replacement. The courts have chipped away at management's right to fire. Today, when you fire someone, you'd better have a strong case. I think once a manager decides to fire, appraisals become very negative. Anything good that you say about the subordinate can be used later against you. Deflating the ratings protects yourself from being sued and sometimes speeds up the termination process.

Tom: I understand your points, but I still believe that accuracy is the top priority in performance appraisal. Let me play devil's advocate for a minute. First, Jim, you complained about our memory limitations introducing a bias into appraisal. Doesn't introducing politics into the process further distort the truth by introducing yet another bias? Even more important, most would agree that one key to motivating people is providing true feedback—the facts about how they're doing so they know where they stand. Then you talk with them about how to improve their performance. When you distort an evaluation—however slightly—are you providing this kind of feedback?

Max: I think you're overstating the degree of fine-tuning.

Tom: Distortion, you mean.

Max: No, fine-tuning. I'm not talking about giving a guy a seven when he deserves a two or vice versa. It's not that extreme. I'm talking about making slight changes in the ratings when you think that the change can make a big difference in terms of achieving what you think is best for the person and for your department.

Tom: But when you fine-tune, you're manipulating your people. Why not give them the most accurate evaluation and let the chips fall where they may? Give them the facts and let them decide.

Max: Because most of good managing is psychology. Understanding people, their strengths and shortcomings. Knowing how to motivate, reward, and act to do what's in their and your department's best interest. And sometimes, total accuracy is not the best path. Sometimes, it's not in anybody's best interest.

Jim: All this discussion raises a question. What's the difference between fine-tuning and significant distortion? Where do you draw the line?

Lynne: That's about as easy a question as what's the difference between a five and a six. On the form, I mean.

Questions for Consideration

1. Based on your view of the objectives of performance evaluation, evaluate the perspectives about performance appraisal presented by the managers.

2. In your opinion, at what point does "fine-tuning" evaluations become unacceptable distortion?

3. Assume you are the vice president of personnel at Eckel Industries and that you are aware that fine-tuning evaluations is a prevalent practice among Eckel managers. If you disagree with this perspective, what steps would you take to reduce the practice?

MAKING CHOICES ABOUT REWARDS

Objectives

1. To illustrate individual differences in reward preferences.
2. To emphasize that both extrinsic and intrinsic rewards are considered important.
3. To enable people to explore the reasons for the reward preferences of others.

Related Topics

Since rewards are so pervasive in organizational settings, they tend to be linked to merit, seniority, and attendance. In fact, they are so related to organizational behavior that few issues of work life can be discussed without mentioning rewards.

Starting the Exercise

After reviewing Exhibit 1, individuals should work alone to establish their own lists of reward preferences. The instructor should set up groups of four to six students to examine individual preferences and complete the exercise.

The Facts

It is possible to develop an endless list of on-the-job rewards. Presented in a random fashion in Exhibit 1 are some of the rewards that could be available to employees.

Completing the Exercise

Phase I: 25 minutes.

1. Using Exhibit 1, each individual should make a list of extrinsic rewards and a list of intrinsic rewards.
2. Each person should then rank the items on his or her lists from the most important to least important.
3. From the two lists, rank the *eight* most important rewards. How many are extrinsic, and how many are intrinsic?

Phase II: 30 minutes.

1. The instructor sets up groups of four to six individuals.
2. The individual lists in which the extrinsic and intrinsic categories were developed should be discussed within the groups.
3. The final rank orders of the eight most important rewards decided on within the groups should be placed on a board or chart at the front of the room.
4. The rankings should be discussed within the groups. Which major differences between individual-generated and group-generated lists were found?

EXHIBIT 1

Some Possible Rewards for
Employees

Company picnics	Smile from manager	Participation in decisions
Watches	Feedback on performance	Stock options
Trophies	Feedback on career progress	Vacation trips for excellent performance
Piped-in music	Larger office	Manager asking for advice
Job challenge	More prestigious job	Informal leader asking for advice
Achievement opportunity	More job involvement	Office with a window
Vacation	Use of company recreational facilities	The privilege of completing a job from start to finish
Autonomy		Paid sabbatical
Pay increase		Health club membership
Recognition		Day care services
Company car		Financial counseling
		College tuition grants
		Entertainment expense account

7

Stress and the Individual

AN ORGANIZATIONAL
ISSUE FOR DEBATE

FIRMS SHOULD REDUCE STRESS THROUGH
HEALTH PROMOTION

ARGUMENT FOR

Organizations should become involved in health promotion in a major way to help reduce stress. One of the most sophisticated programs available is Control Data Corporation's "Stay Well" program. Advocates claim this program has been so successful that it is now available to other companies through a Control Data subsidiary, the Life Extension Institute. "Stay Well" is designed to help employees reduce out-of-pocket health care costs and find out how to be healthier, feel better, and live longer. All full-time employees and their spouses are eligible to participate at no cost.

The program's health screening and confidential health risk profile provide the basis for a detailed report to employees revealing their greatest health risks. As part of the program, three categories of courses and classes are offered: (1) Wellness education courses are designed to provide basic information about health and lifestyle. Employees learn about fitness, weight control, hypertension, coronary heart disease, alcohol, tobacco, cancer, and fundamentals of self-health management. (2) Lifestyle change courses, longer and more comprehensive than the wellness courses, are designed to facilitate significant lifestyle changes that can affect health. Employees learn about stress control, nutrition, diet, and smoking cessation. (3) Patient education courses provide information and skills for coping with chronic illnesses experienced by an employee or family member. Employees learn about measuring blood pressure, living with diabetes, and recovering from heart attacks.

ARGUMENT AGAINST

No matter how simple or sophisticated the health promotion program, there is little available evidence that it is worth the expense. Control Data's "Stay Well" program is very expensive; most firms lack the financial resources to adopt such a broad-based program. Firms have not been able to justify building million-dollar exercise facilities, because they have not adequately evaluated their programs over time.

Critics charge that health promotion is really a bribe designed to take employees' minds off poor working conditions, organizational structure, or inadequate monetary compensation and rewards. This argument is based on the premise that initiating a health promotion program is really less costly for management than treating major inadequacies.

Health promotion programs have not been scientifically validated or supported. If they were as good as advocates claim, more firms would adopt them. In reality, they have been pushed by special-interest groups that benefit economically. It would be better for an organization to address the real problems in its organization structure, job design, and reward systems than to spend dollars on exercise equipment, aerobics videotapes, and weight control lectures. Each person's health, appearance, and well-being are his or her responsibility; employers should not become involved. For instance, who is responsible if, while doing aerobics in the company health center, an employee suffers or dies from a sudden heart attack? Legally and in terms of other benefits, an organization does better to encourage its employees to seek health promotion activities outside the organization.

Interest in occupational stress has become widespread in recent years. How-ever, the existence of stress is not new; our cave-dwelling ancestors experi-enced it every time they left their caves and encountered their enemy, the saber-toothed tiger. The tigers of yesteryear are gone, but they have been replaced by other predators: work overload, a nagging boss, time deadlines, the threat of job loss, poorly designed jobs, marital disharmony, the drive to keep up with the Joneses. These work and nonwork predators interact and create stress for individuals on and off the job.

This chapter focuses primarily on individuals at work in organizations and on the stress created in this setting. Much of the stress experienced by people in our industrialized society originates in organizations; even the stress that originates elsewhere affects behavior and performance in these same organi-zations.

WHAT IS STRESS?

Ask five people what stress is, and you are likely to hear at least five definitions. The businessperson views stress as frustration or emotional tension; the air-traffic controller sees it as a problem of alertness and concentration; the biochemist thinks of it as a purely chemical event. In an uncomplicated way, stress is best considered as something that involves the interaction of the individual with the environment.[1] Most definitions of stress recognize the individual and the environment in terms of a stimulus interac-tion, a response interaction, or a stimulus-response interaction.

A *stimulus definition of stress* would be: Stress occurs when a force or stimulus acting on the individual results in a response of strain, where strain is pressure or, in a physical sense, deformation. One problem with this definition is that it fails to recognize that two people subjected to the same stress may show far different levels of strain.

A *response definition of stress* would be: Stress is the physiological or psychological response of an individual to an environmental stressor, which is a potentially harmful external event or situation. In the stimulus definition, stress is an external event; here, it is an internal response. This definition fails to enable anyone to predict the nature of the stress response or even whether there will be such a response.

An example of a *stimulus-response definition* is that stress is the consequence of the interaction between an environmental stimulus and the response of the individual. Stress is viewed as more than either a stimulus or a response; it is the result of a unique interaction between stimulus conditions in the environ-ment and the individual's predisposition to respond in a certain way.

A Working Definition

Each of the above three definitions offers important insights into what constitutes stress. Therefore, each is used to develop a working definition for this chapter. We define **stress** as

STRESS
Adaptive response, mediated by individual differences and/or psy-chological processes, resulting from an environmental action, situation, or event that places excessive psychological and/or physical demands on a person.

---

[1]Michael T. Matteson and John M. Ivancevich, *Controlling Stress in the Workplace: An Organiza-tional Guide* (San Francisco: Jossey-Bass, 1987).

an adaptive response, mediated by individual differences and/or psychological processes, that is a consequence of any external (environmental) action, situation, or event that places excessive psychological and/or physical demands on a person.

This working definition portrays stress in a more negative light than do most definitions. We have, however, included the term *excessive* in our definition because, certainly, not all stress is negative. The stress that Dr. Hans Selye, the pioneer of stress research, referred to as eustress (from the Greek *eu,* meaning good, as in euphoria) is stimulating in a positive sense. Eustress is necessary in our lives.

Our working definition allows us to focus attention on specific environmental conditions as potential sources of stress. Such conditions are called stressors. Whether stress is felt or experienced by a particular individual depends on that individual's unique characteristics. Furthermore, the definition emphasizes an adaptive response. The vast majority of a person's responses to stimuli in the work environment do not require adaptation; thus, they are not really potential sources of stress.

Keep in mind that a variety of dissimilar situations—work effort, fatigue, uncertainty, fear, emotional arousal—are capable of producing stress. Therefore, to isolate a single factor as the sole cause is extremely difficult.[2]

THE PSYCHOPHYSIOLOGY OF STRESS

If for some reason you happened to place your hand on a hot stove, a number of predictable events would occur. You would experience pain. There would also be tissue damage as successive layers of skin were exposed to the stove. Depending on your reaction time, the hand would be pulled away from the stove. You might even utter a few choice words.

This event displays an interaction between you and the environment. It is an event that results in physical and psychological consequences. It is also an event that magnifies what stress is and how we respond to it—physically and psychologically.

The General Adaptation Syndrome

GENERAL ADAPTATION SYNDROME (GAS)

Description of three-phase defense reaction that a person establishes when stressed. Phases are called alarm, resistance, and exhaustion.

Selye conceptualized the psychophysiological responses to stress.[3] He considered stress a nonspecific response to any demand made on an organism and labeled the three-phase defense reaction that a person establishes when stressed as the **general adaptation syndrome (GAS).** Selye called the defense reaction general because stressors had effects on several areas of the body; adaptation refers to a stimulation of defenses designed to help the body adjust to or deal with the stressors; and syndrome indicates that individual pieces of the reaction occur more or less together. The three distinct phases are called alarm, resistance, and exhaustion.

[2]Rita E. Numerof, *Managing Stress* (Rockville, Md.: Aspen, 1983), p. 7.
[3]Hans Selye, *The Stress of Life* (New York: McGraw-Hill, 1976). Also Hans Selye, *Stress without Distress* (Philadelphia: J. B. Lippincott, 1974).

FIGURE 7-1

Selye's General Adaptation Syndrome (GAS)

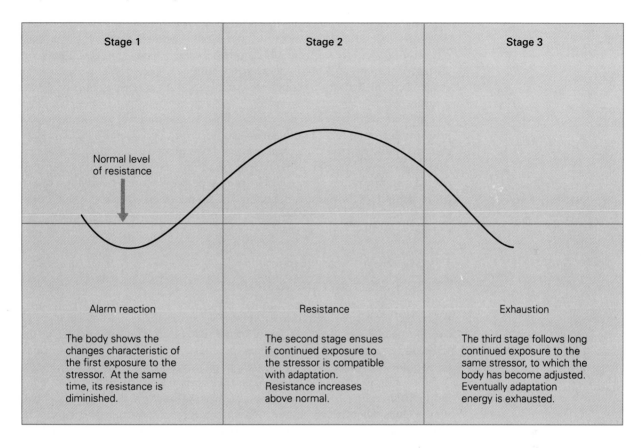

Stage 1	Stage 2	Stage 3
Alarm reaction	Resistance	Exhaustion
The body shows the changes characteristic of the first exposure to the stressor. At the same time, its resistance is diminished.	The second stage ensues if continued exposure to the stressor is compatible with adaptation. Resistance increases above normal.	The third stage follows long continued exposure to the same stressor, to which the body has become adjusted. Eventually adaptation energy is exhausted.

The *alarm* stage is the initial mobilization by which the body meets the challenge posed by the stressor. When a stressor is recognized, the brain sends a biochemical message to all of the body's systems. Respiration increases, blood pressure rises, pupils dilate, muscles tense up, and so forth.

If the stressor continues, the GAS proceeds to the *resistance* stage. Signs of being in the resistance stage include fatigue, anxiety, and tension. The person is now fighting the stressor. While resistance to a particular stressor may be high during this stage, resistance to other stressors may be low; a person has only finite sources of energy, concentration, and ability to resist stressors. Individuals are often more illness prone during periods of stress than at other times.[4]

The final GAS stage is *exhaustion*. Prolonged and continued exposure to the same stressor may eventually use up the adaptive energy available, and the systems fighting the stressor become exhausted. The three stages of the GAS are presented in Figure 7-1.

---

[4]Seyle, *Stress without Distress,* p. 5.

Research points out that major and minor stressors may lead to changes in immune system functioning.[5] It is suggested that declines in immune function are frequently related to the heightened distress associated with the duration and intensity of the stressor, the prior health of the individual, and recent exposure to pathogen. For example, significant declines in natural killer (NK) cell activity were found in blood samples obtained from 75 medical students during final examinations, in contrast to samples collected at nonexamination times.[6] NK cell activity is thought to be an important defense against colds and viruses.

The examination period is a time of high stress for a medical student (also probably for students in law, business, engineering, and liberal arts). The sleep patterns, poor nutrition, disturbances, and heightened anxiety that interact at examination time could contribute to poorer immune function. Distress-related immunosuppression could be prevalent in the stage 3 exhaustion phase. More research on immune functioning and on major and minor work stressors in work populations could be important in attempting to bring work-related stress costs under better control.[7]

STRESS AND WORK: A MODEL

For most employed individuals, work is more than a 40 hour a week commitment. Even if the actual work time is 40 hours, most individuals spend 10 or more hours a day on work-related activities when hours for travel time, preparation for work, lunchtime, and so on, are added in.

Not only is a lot of time spent on work-related activities but many individuals find a substantial portion of their satisfaction and identity in their work. Consequently, work and nonwork activities are interdependent. The distinction between stress at work and stress at home is an artificial one at best. For example, sources of stress at work spill over into a person's nonwork activities. As a consequence of stressors experienced at work, the individual may come home irritable, short tempered, and fatigued and argue with the spouse. The resulting marital conflict may be a source of subsequent stress that in turn negatively affects job performance. Thus, stress at work and stress away from work are often interrelated.

This chapter's main concern, however, is with stressors at work. To better understand the link between stressors, stress, and consequences, we have developed an integrative model of stress and work. A managerial perspective is used to develop the parts of the model shown in Figure 7–2. The model divides stressors at work into four categories: physical evironmental, individual, group, and organizational. The model also presents five potential catego-

---

[5]Janice Kiecolt-Glaser and Ronald Glaser, "Psychosocial Moderators of Immune Function," *Annals of Behavior Medicine,* Summer 1987, pp. 16–20.

[6]T. K. Kiecolt-Glaser, W. Garner, Carl Speicher, Gerald M. Penn, J. E. Holliday, and Ronald Glaser, "Psychosocial Modifiers in Immunocompetence in Medical Students," *Psychosomatic Medicine,* 1984, pp. 7–14.

[7]William McKinnon, Carol S. Weisse, C. Patrick Reynolds, Charles A. Bowles, and Andrew Baum, "Chronic Stress Leukocyte Subpoputative, and Humoral Response to Latent Viruses," *Health Psychology,* Winter 1989, pp. 389–402.

FIGURE 7–2

Stress and Work: A Working Model

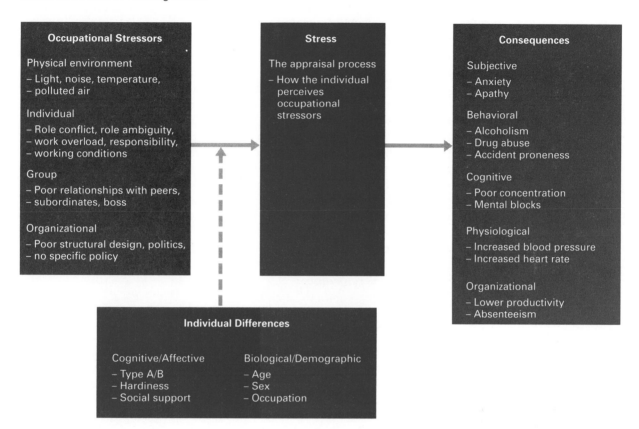

ries of the effects of stress. In this book, we are concerned primarily with the effects that influence job performance.

The model introduces "individual differences" that can affect reactions to stress.[8] Individual differences investigated by occupational stress researchers have included age, sex, work addition, self-esteem, and community involvement. We will discuss the three that have received the most research attention: Type A, life change events, and social support.

Physical Environmental Stressors

Physical environmental stressors are often called blue-collar stressors because they are more of a problem in blue-collar occupations.[9] In 1985, occupational injuries resulted in 3,750 work-related deaths in private-sector establishments

---

[8]Robert R. Holt, "Occupational Stress," in *Handbook of Stress,* ed. Leo Goldberger and Shlomo Breznitz (New York: Free Press, 1982), pp. 419–44.

[9]E. C. Poulton, "Blue-Collar Stressors," in *Stress at Work,* ed. Cary L. Cooper and Roy Payne (New York: John Wiley & Sons, 1978), pp. 51–80.

with 11 or more employees. The fatality rate was 6.2 per 100,000 full-time employees.[10] Estimates of the toll of workplace chemicals, radiation, heat stress, pesticides, and other toxic materials have led the National Institute of Occupational Safety and Health (NIOSH) to estimate that about 100,000 workers may die annually from industrial disease that could have been prevented.

Workers may become nervous and stressed by the alleged health consequences of working in such jobs as police officer, nurse, secretary, and social worker. Since the passage in 1970 of the Occupational Safety and Health Act (OSHA), some work stress has been reduced. Gains can be traced to employers' increased acceptance of OSHA regulations. In addition, many unions enthusiastically support the act. Although problems still exist, management is now being held responsible in more cases by the courts for stress that is related to the physical and general work environment. Jury compensation awards to workers have become more widespread. We expect the courts' role to become even more significant in the future.[11]

The *Exxon Valdez* disaster on March 24, 1989, is a case that involves stress, alcohol, and environmental stressors. The Close-Up discusses some of the stress factors involved in the case and touches on legal issues that have complicated its resolution.

Individual Stressors

Stressors at the individual level have been studied more than any other category presented in Figure 7–2. Role conflict is perhaps the most widely studied individual stressor.[12] **Role conflict** is present in an individual whenever compliance to one set of expectations about the job is in conflict with compliance to another set of expectations—for example, being pressured to get along well with people with whom you are not compatible. Regardless of whether role conflict results from organizational policies or from other persons, it can be a significant stressor for some individuals.

Kahn and associates' interview survey of the national sample of male wage and salary employees revealed that 48 percent experienced role conflict.[13] A study at Goddard Space Flight Center determined that about 67 percent of the employees reported some role conflict. The study also found that workers who suffered more role conflict had lower job satisfaction and higher job-related tension.[14] Researchers also found that the greater the power or authority of the people sending the conflicting role messages, the more job dissatisfaction was

ROLE CONFLICT

Stressor that arises when person receives incompatible messages regarding appropriate role behavior.

[10]Diane M. Cotter and Janet A. Macon, "Deaths in Industry, 1985: BLS Survey Findings," *Monthly Labor Review,* April 1987, pp. 45–47.

[11]John M. Ivancevich, Michael T. Matteson, and Edward P. Richards III, "Who's Liable for Stress on the Job?" *Harvard Business Review,* March–April 1985, pp. 60–62, 66, 70, 72.

[12]John R. P. French and Robert D. Caplan, "Organizational Stress and Individual Strain," in *The Failure of Success,* ed. J. Marrow (New York: AMACOM, 1973), pp. 30–66.

[13]Robert L. Kahn, D. M. Wolfe, Robert P. Quinn, J. Diedrich Snoek, and R. A. Rosenthal, *Organizational Stress: Studies in Role Conflict and Ambiguity* (New York: John Wiley & Sons, 1964), p. 94.

[14]Ibid.

EXXON VALDEZ: A COMPLICATED LEGAL CASE

Joseph Hazelwood was the captain of *Exxon Valdez*. On March 23, 1989, the ship with its cargo of 11 million barrels of crude oil began its voyage off the Alaska coast, under dangerous and stressful conditions. Chunks of ice were falling at an unprecedented rate into the shipping channels of Prince Edward Sound.

Captain Hazelwood left the controls and went to his cabin as the ship moved through the ice chunks. He placed the ship on autopilot and in control of a third mate who lacked the experience and a license to pilot a ship under such dangerous conditions. One hour after leaving port, the *Exxon Valdez* ran aground, cracking open its hull and causing the nation's worst oil spill, a clean-up nightmare that may become the most expensive and legally entangled industrial accident in U.S. history.

An alcohol and drug screen of the crew 10 hours after the grounding allegedly showed the level of alcohol in Hazelwood's blood was five times the legal level. Although he could have been drinking after the accident, Hazelwood was seen drinking shortly before taking command of the ship. His personal background revealed a history of alcohol abuse.

What role did the drinking play in the accident? Was stress a contributing factor? Who was legally responsible to clean up the Alaskan coastal waters fouled by the spill? Some captains who travel the dangerous, ice-filled waters believe that alcohol calms the nerves, reduces anxiety, and improves a captain's job performance; up to a limited amount, alcohol is accepted by many of the older captains.

Captain Hazelwood was acquitted on charges of reckless endangerment in the *Exxon Valdez* case. However, the legal aspects of the case are likely to be complex. Exxon still faces 150 pending civil suits for punitive damages. The notion that alcohol is needed to steer a ship through dangerous waters is not going to win the day in most courts. That "old captain's folklore" about alcohol and its beneficial effects was not used in the defense of Hazelwood's job performance.

Source: Leonard Moss, "Polluters Beware," *The Economist*, April 7, 1990, p. 38; "Partners for a Drug-Free Workplace," *Across the Board*, December 1989, pp. 22–31.

---

produced by role conflict. A larger and more medically oriented study found that, for white-collar workers, role conflict was related to abnormal electrocardiographic readings.[15] Chapter 8, Group Behavior, discusses role conflict, also an important part of the conflict that occurs within groups.

To perform their jobs well, employees need certain information regarding what they are expected to do and not do. They need to know their rights, privileges, and obligations. **Role ambiguity** is a person's lack of understanding about his or her rights, privileges, and obligations in doing a job. Studies have addressed the question of role ambiguity. In the study of Goddard Space Flight Center, administrators, engineers, and scientists completed a role

ROLE AMBIGUITY
Person's lack of understanding about rights, privileges, and obligations of a job.

[15]John R. P. French and Robert D. Caplan, "Organizational Stress and Individual Strain," *Industrial Medicine*, September 1970, pp. 383–97.

ambiguity stress scale. Blood samples, blood pressure, and pulse rate readings showed that role ambiguity was significantly related to low job satisfaction and to feelings of job-related threats to mental and physical well-being.[16] Furthermore, the more ambiguity a person reported, the lower the person's utilization of intellectual skills, knowledge, and leadership skills.

Everyone has experienced work *overload* at one time or another. Overload may be of two different types: quantitative or qualitative. Having too many things to do or insufficient time to complete a job is quantitative overload. Qualitative overload, on the other hand, occurs when individuals feel that they lack the ability needed to complete their jobs or that performance standards are too high.

From a health standpoint, studies as far back as 1958 established that quantitative overload might cause biochemical changes, specifically elevations in blood cholesterol levels.[17] The suggestion has also been made that overload is most harmful to those who experience the lowest job satisfaction.[18] Still another study found overload to be associated with lowered confidence, decreased work motivation, and increased absenteeism. Overload may also be indirectly responsible for decreases in decision-making quality, deteriorating interpersonal relations, and increases in accidents.[19]

One study examined the relationship of overload, underload, and stress among 1,540 executives of a major corporation. Those executives in the low and high ends of the stress ranges reported having more significant medical problems. This study suggests that the relationship between stressors, stress, and disease may be curvilinear. That is, those who are underloaded and those who are overloaded represent two ends of a continuum, each with a significantly elevated number of medical problems.[20] The underload/overload continuum is presented in Figure 7–3. The optimal stress level provides the best balance of challenge, responsibility, and reward.

Any kind of *responsibility* can be a burden for some people, but different types apparently function differently as stressors. One way of categorizing this variable is in terms of responsibility for people versus responsibility for things. The intensive care unit nurse, the neurosurgeon, and the air-traffic controller each have a high responsibility for people. One study found support for the hypothesis that responsibility for people contributes to job-related stress.[21] The more responsibility for people reported, the more likely the person was to smoke heavily, have high blood pressure, and show elevated cholesterol levels.

---

[16]Kahn et al., *Organizational Stress.*

[17]Bruce L. Margolis, William M. Kroes, and Robert P. Quinn, "Job Stress: An Untested Occupational Hazard," *Journal of Occupational Medicine,* October 1974, pp. 659–61.

[18]Stephen M. Sales, "Organizational Role as a Risk Factor in Coronary Disease," *Administrative Science Quarterly,* September 1969, pp. 325–36.

[19]S. Kasl, "Work and the Mental Health," in *Work and the Quality of Life,* ed. James O'Toole (Cambridge, Mass.: MIT Press, 1974), pp. 171–96.

[20]C. Weiman, "A Study of Occupational Stressors and the Incidence of Disease/Risk," *Journal of Occupational Medicine,* February 1977, pp. 119–22.

[21]John R. P. French and Robert D. Caplan, "Psychosocial Factors in Coronary Heart Disease," *Industrial Medicine,* September 1970, p. 387.

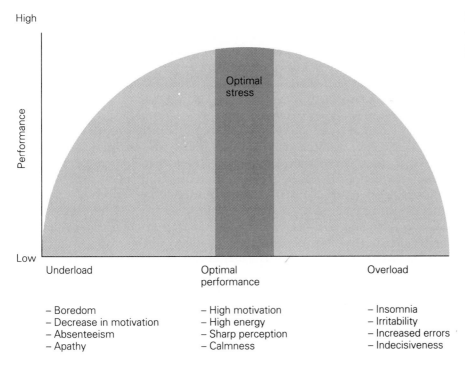

Conversely, the more responsibility for things the employee reported, the lower these indicators were.

Group Stressors

The effectiveness of any organization is influenced by the nature of the relations among groups. Group characteristics can be powerful stressors for some individuals. Behavioral scientists have suggested that maintaining good *relationships* among the members of a work group is a central factor in individual well-being.[22] Poor relations include low trust, low supportiveness, and low interest in listening to and trying to deal with the problems that confront another employee.[23] Studies in this area have reached the same conclusion: mistrust of co-workers is positively related to high role ambiguity, which leads to inadequate communications among people and low job satisfaction.

Organizational Stressors

One problem in the study of organizational stressors is identifying which are the most important ones. An important part of working within organizations

---

[22]Chris Argyris, *Integrating the Individual and the Organization* (New York: John Wiley & Sons, 1964). Also Cary L. Cooper, *Group Training and Organizational Development* (Basel, Switzerland: Karger, 1973).

[23]French and Caplan, *Psychosocial Factors*.

for some individuals is participation in decision making. *Participation* refers to the extent that a person's knowledge, opinions, and ideas are included in the decision process. Such participation can contribute to stress. Some people may be frustrated by the delays often associated with participative decision making. Others may view shared decision making as a threat to the traditional right of a supervisor or manager to have the final say.

Another stressor, *organizational structure,* has rarely been studied. One available study of trade salespersons examined the effects of tall (bureaucratically structured), medium, and flat (less rigidly structured) organizations on job satisfaction, stress, and performance. Researchers determined that salespersons in the least bureaucratically structured organizations experienced less stress and more job satisfaction and performed more effectively than did salespersons in the medium and tall structures.[24]

Several studies have examined the relationship of organizational level to health effects. The majority of these studies suggest that the risk of contracting such health problems as coronary heart disease increases with organizational level.[25] Not all research, however, supports that notion. A study of Du Pont employees found the incidence of heart disease to be inversely related to salary level.[26]

The nature of the classifications used in these studies has contributed to the confusion of the results.[27] The trend now is to look in more detail at significant job components as a way of explaining the effects of stress. Several studies, for example, have tried to assess whether inactivity or increased intellectual and emotional job demands contribute most to the increased risk of coronary heart disease. One early study found that downtown bus drivers (sedentary jobs) and conductors (active jobs) had higher coronary heart disease than did their suburban counterparts.[28] More research is needed to determine whether emotional job demands are more powerful than inactivity in explaining the incidence of health problems.

We have considered only a very small sample of the tremendous amount of behavioral and medical research on stressor, stress, and effects linkage. The information gathered, as with other organizational research, is contradictory in some cases. However, the available research implies these important points:

1. Stressors at work are related to physical, psychological, and emotional changes in individuals.

---

[24]John M. Ivancevich and James H. Donnelly, "Relation of Organizational Structure to Job Satisfaction, Anxiety-Stress, and Performance," *Administrative Science Quarterly,* June 1975, pp. 272–80.

[25]R. V. Marks, "Social Stress and Cardiovascular Disease," *Milbank Memorial Fund Quarterly,* April 1976, pp. 51–107.

[26]S. Pell and C. A. D'Alonzo, "Myocardial Infarction in a One-Year Industrial Study," *Journal of the American Medical Association,* June 1958, pp. 332–37.

[27]Cary L. Cooper and Judi Marshall, "Occupational Sources of Stress: A Review of the Literature Relating to Coronary Heart Disease and Mental Ill Health," *Journal of Occupational Psychology,* March 1976, pp. 11–28.

[28]J. N. Morris et al., "Coronary Heart Disease and Physical Activity at Work: Coronary Heart Disease in Different Occupations," *Lancet,* October 1953, pp. 1053–57.

2. The adaptive responses to stressors at work have been measured by self-rating, performance appraisals, and biochemical tests. Much more research must be done in properly measuring stress at work.

3. There is no universally acceptable list of stressors. Each organization has its own unique set that should be examined.

4. Individual differences explain why the same stressor that is disruptive and unsettling to one person is challenging to another person.

LIFE-EVENT STRESSORS

According to a commonsense proposition, when individuals undergo extremely stressful changes in their lives, their personal health eventually suffers. Research work on this intriguing proposition was initiated by Thomas Holmes and Richard Rahe.[29] Their work led to the development of the Schedule of Recent Life Events, later titled the Social Readjustment Rating Scale (SRRS). Through research and analysis, Holmes and Rahe weighted the SRRS (presented in Table 7–1). This scale asks individuals to indicate which of the listed events has happened to them in the past 12 months. Holmes and Rahe found that individuals reporting *life change units* totaling 150 points or less generally had good health the following year. However, those reporting life change units totaling between 150 and 300 points had about a 50 percent chance of developing a serious illness the following year. And among individuals scoring 300 or more points, there was at least a 70 percent chance of contracting a major illness the following year.

A premise underlying the SRRS is that life events require adaptive or coping behavior on the part of the person. Too much life change over a short period is thought to predispose one to illness: the greater the amount of total life change, the more the illness. Some researchers have challenged the notion that positive and negative life events are functionally equivalent in predisposing one to illness.[30] Other research suggests that females cope with financial difficulties, marital problems, and the death of a spouse more effectively than males.[31] It has also been determined that life change is predictive of athletic injury, especially for females.[32]

The relationships found between life change event scores and personal health problems have not been overwhelming.[33] In most studies, correlations

[29]Thomas H. Holmes and Richard H. Rahe, "Social Readjustment Rating Scale," *Journal of Psychosomatic Research,* 1967, pp. 213–18.

[30]Irwin G. Sarason, J. H. Johnson, and Judith M. Siegal, "Assessing the Impact of Life Changes: Development of the Life Experience Survey," *Journal of Consulting and Clinical Psychology,* 1978, pp. 932–40.

[31]R. C. Kessler and J. D. McLeod, "Sex Differences in Vulnerability to Undesirable Life Events," *American Sociological Review,* 1984, pp. 620–31.

[32]Charles J. Hardy and Richard E. Riehl, "An Examination of the Life Stress–Injury Relationship among Noncontract Sport Participants," *Behavioral Medicine,* Fall 1988, pp. 112–18.

[33]S. M. Monroe, "Major and Minor Life Events as Predictors of Psychological Distress: Further Issues and Findings," *Journal of Behavioral Medicine,* June 1983, pp. 189–205.

TABLE 7-1

Social Readjustment Rating
Scale

Rank	Life Event	Mean Value
1	Death of spouse	100
2	Divorce	73
3	Marital separation	65
4	Jail term	63
5	Death of close family member	63
6	Personal injury or illness	53
7	Marriage	50
8	Fired at work	47
9	Marital reconciliation	45
10	Retirement	45
11	Change in health of family member	44
12	Pregnancy	40
13	Sex difficulties	39
14	Gain of new family member	39
15	Business readjustment	39
16	Change in financial state	38
17	Death of close friend	37
18	Change to different line of work	36
19	Change in number of arguments with spouse	35
20	Mortgage over $10,000*	31
21	Foreclosure of mortgage or loan	30
22	Change in responsibilities at work	29
23	Son or daughter leaving home	29
24	Trouble with in-laws	29
25	Outstanding personal achievement	28
26	Spouse beginning or stopping work	26
27	Beginning or ending school	26
28	Change in living conditions	25
29	Revision of personal habits	24
30	Trouble with boss	23
31	Change in work hours or conditions	20
32	Change in residence	20
33	Change in schools	20
34	Change in recreation	19
35	Change in church activities	19
36	Change in social activities	18
37	Mortgage or loan less than $10,000*	17
38	Change in sleeping habits	16
39	Change in number of family get-togethers	15
40	Change in eating habits	15
41	Vacation	13
42	Christmas	12
43	Minor violations of the law	11

Note: The amount of life stress that a person has experienced in a given period of time, say one year, is measured by the total number of life change units (LCUs). These units result from the addition of the values (shown in the right-hand column) associated with events that the person has experienced during the target time period.

*In the 1990s, mortgages are usually over $10,000.

Source: Thomas H. Holmes and Richard H. Rahe, "The Social Readjustment Rating Scale," *Journal of Psychosomatic Research*, 1967, pp. 213–18.

between the total score and major health problems the following year have been relatively low.[34] Of course, individuals who are exposed to many life changes often show absolutely no subsequent health problems. That is, they are hardy enough to withstand the consequences of life changes.

A number of studies have examined the relationship between life events and illness and job performance. Negative, as opposed to positive, life changes have been found to be more strongly associated with lower levels of job satisfaction, organizational commitment, and perceived job stress.[35]

INDIVIDUAL DIFFERENCES

Stressors evoke different responses from different people. Some individuals are better able to cope with a stressor than others; they can adapt their behavior in such a way as to meet the stressor head-on. On the other hand, individuals predisposed to stress are not able to adapt to the stressor.

The model presented in Figure 7–2 suggests that various factors ("individual differences") moderate the relationship between stressors and stress. A moderator is a condition, behavior, or characteristic that qualifies the relationship between two variables. The effect may be to intensify or weaken the relationship. The relationship between the number of gallons of gasoline used and total miles driven, for example, is affected by the variable speed (a moderator). Likewise, an individual's personality may moderate or affect the extent to which that individual experiences stress as a consequence of being in contact with a particular stressor.

Type A Behavior Pattern

Cardiovascular disease is the leading cause of death in the United States. Nearly 1 million Americans die of cardiovascular disease each year, and more than 40 million Americans are afflicted with some form of the disease.[36]

In the 1950s, medical cardiologists and researchers Meyer Friedman and Ray Rosenman discovered what they called the **Type A behavior pattern (TABP)**.[37] Searching the medical literature, they found that traditional coronary risk factors such as dietary cholesterol, blood pressure, and heredity could not totally explain or predict coronary heart disease (CHD), the name given to cardiovascular diseases characterized by an inadequate supply of oxygen to the heart. Other factors seemed to be playing a major role in CHD. By interviewing and observing patients, Friedman and Rosenman began to

TYPE A BEHAVIOR PATTERN (TABP)

Name given to the behavior pattern of a person who is aggressive, driven, ambitious, competitive, task oriented, and always on the move.

---

[34]D. V. Perkins, "The Assessment of Stress Using Life Events Scales," in *Handbook of Stress,* ed. Leo Goldberger and Shlomo Breznitz (New York: Free Press, 1982), pp. 320–31.

[35]Arthur M. Nezu, Christine M. Nezu, and Sonia E. Blessett, "Sense of Humor as a Moderator of the Relations between Stressful Events and Psychologic Distress: A Prospective Analysis," *Journal of Personality and Social Psychology,* March 1988, pp. 520–25.

[36]Virginia A. Price, *Type A Behavior Pattern* (New York: Academic Press, 1982), p. 3.

[37]Meyer Friedman and Ray H. Rosenman, *Type A Behavior and Your Heart* (New York: Alfred A. Knopf, 1974).

uncover a pattern of behavior or traits that they eventually called the Type A behavior pattern. The person with TABP:

— Chronically struggles to get as many things done as possible in the shortest time period.
— Is aggressive, ambitious, competitive, and forceful.
— Speaks explosively, rushes others to finish what they are saying.
— Is impatient, hates to wait, considers waiting a waste of precious time.
— Is preoccupied with deadlines and is work oriented.
— Is always in a struggle—with people, things, events.

TYPE B BEHAVIOR PATTERN
Name given to the behavior pattern of a person who is relaxed, patient, steady, and even-tempered. Opposite of Type A.

Conversely, the individual with a **Type B behavior pattern** generally feels no pressing conflict with either time or persons. The Type B may have considerable drive, wants to accomplish things, and works hard, but a confident style allows him or her to work at a steady pace and not to race against the clock. The Type A has been likened to a racehorse, the Type B to a turtle.

As cardiologists, Friedman and Rosenman observed numerous coronary patients, most of whom were Type A's. They described one incident that highlighted what individuals with TABP were like. An upholsterer, called to fix the seats of chairs in their reception room, told them that he noticed a peculiar thing about the wear and tear on the office furniture: only the front edge of each seat was worn out. Friedman and Rosenman, after a significant period of time and being puzzled by their data, interpreted the upholstery phenomenon to indicate the impatience of their patients sitting on the edge of their seats to see the doctor.[38] Type A's waiting impatiently in an office would tend to do such things.

Type A assessment methods.   Since the early work of Friedman and Rosenman on TABP, a number of studies have examined whether Type A is a predictor of CHD.[39] The most commonly used methods to assess Type A behavior are the structured interview and a number of self-report questionnaires such as the Jenkins Activity Survey and Framingham Type A Scale.

Structured interview.   The structured interview (SI) was originally developed in 1960 to classify over 3,000 male participants in the Western Collaborative Group Study (discussed below). Respondents are asked a series of questions about their characteristic responses to a variety of situations designed to trigger competitiveness, impatience, and hostility. For example, questions probe their reactions to waiting in long lines, to driving behind slow-moving cars, and to participating in sports and other games. Some of the SI questions are deliberately presented in a manner to elicit the explosive and impatient speech response indicative of Type A. For example, one question about when

---

[38]Meyer Friedman and Diane Ulmer, *Treating Type A Behavior and Your Heart* (New York: Alfred A. Knopf, 1984), pp. 3–4.

[39]Karen A. Matthews, "Psychological Perspectives on the Type A Behavior Pattern," *Psychological Bulletin,* March 1982, pp. 293–323. Also, Michael T. Matteson and John M. Ivancevich, "The Coronary-Prone Behavior Pattern: A Review and Appraisal," *Social Science and Medicine,* July 1980, pp. 337–51.

the interviewee normally wakes up is asked in a slow, hesitant manner. The Type A person generally interrupts and answers prior to the interviewer completing the question.

The interview responses and observations result in the interviewees being placed into one of five categories: A1, a fully developed, hardcore Type A; A2, an incompletely developed Type A; X, a mixed Type A and Type B, or a person displaying characteristics of both types; B3, an incompletely developed Type B; and B4, a fully developed Type B. Interrater reliabilities for trained interviewers range from .70 to .90 in classifying interviewees.[40] Repeated interviews in the Western Collaborative Group Study found similar classifications two years apart in 80 percent of the cases.[41]

Self-report methods. Due to the need for more practical assessment instruments, the Jenkins Activity Survey (JAS) was developed.[42] Form B contains 52 questions similar to those in SI, only 21 of which are weighted substantially in the computer scoring system. Factor analysis has revealed that JAS contains three independent factors or subcomponents: H, or hard-driving competitiveness; S, or speed and impatience; and J, or job involvement.

The Framingham Type A Scale consists of 10 questions derived from a 300-item inventory administered to the Framingham study participants.[43] There are slightly different versions for employed and unemployed persons. Employed persons are asked how often they feel pressed for time, have a need to excel in most things, are dominating, and eat quickly. The scale is scored by averaging the responses to the 10 questions; it yields continuous scores ranging from 0 to 10.

These self-report measures of Type A behavior share a number of problems. Each is affected by response biases, such as social desirability of Type A qualities and gender influences on reporting male stereotype characteristics. In addition, unlike the SI format, it is not possible to provide a challenging environment to elicit Type A behavior indicators.

A limited number of studies have used SI and various self-report measures with women. The agreement between self-report measures and SI have been lower than the corresponding figures for men. For example, Anderson and Waldron reported a 54 percent agreement rate between SI and JAS among 40- to 59-year-old women.[44]

---

[40]Theodore M. Dembroski, "Reliability and Validity of Methods Used to Assess Coronary-Prone Behavior," in *Coronary Prone Behavior,* ed. Theodore M. Dembroski, Stephen M. Weiss, Jay L. Shields, et al. (New York: Springer-Verlag, 1978).

[41]Ray H. Rosenman, Meyer Friedman, R. Straus, et al., "A Predictive Study of Coronary Heart Disease," *Journal of the American Medical Association* 189 (1964), pp. 103–10.

[42]C. D. Jenkins, "A Comparative Review of the Interview and Questionnaire Methods in the Assessment of Coronary-Prone Behavior Pattern," in *Coronary Prone Behavior,* ed. Theodore M. Dembroski, Stephen M. Weiss, Jay L. Shields, et al. (New York: Springer-Verlag, 1978).

[43]S. G. Haynes, S. Levine, N. Scotch, M. Feinleib, and W. B. Kannel, "The Relationship of Psychosocial Factors to Coronary Heart Disease in the Framingham Study: I. Methods and Risk Factors," *American Journal of Epidemiology* 107 (1978), pp. 362–83.

[44]J. R. Anderson and I. Waldron, "Behavioral and Content Components of the Structured Interview Assessment of the Type A Behavior Pattern in Women," *Journal of Behavioral Medicine* 6 (1983), pp. 123–34.

The originators of the Type A construct, Friedman and Rosenman, recommend that SI be used to assess the behavior pattern. However, before using SI, managers should consider how they will use the assessment data and whether the cost and time requirements of SI warrant its use. If the assessment is to be used as a classification for training programs or as simply a feedback scale for individuals interested in examining their Type A characteristics, it probably is not worth the time, effort, or cost to use the SI. The JAS, Framingham, or other self-report measures could provide a less costly and less time-consuming general picture of a person's Type A characteristics than SI does.

Type A studies since Friedman and Rosenman.

Western Collaborative Group Study.   The first major prospective study designed to examine the coronary risk associated with Type A behavior was the Western Collaborative Group Study.[45] The study used a double-blind design: the researchers assessing Type A had no knowledge of the 3,154 men's health status; those assessing coronary heart disease risk (e.g., blood pressure, cholesterol level, triglycerides, and family history) had no knowledge of the men's Type A behavior. Structured interviews were used to assess Type A's at the beginning and also 8.5 years later. The men assessed as Type A had a risk ratio of 2.2 for development of coronary heart disease, compared to Type B's. The 2-to-1 risk ratio remained after multivariate statistical adjustment for the traditional risk factors.

Interestingly, among the 231 men in the study who had a heart attack and survived the first 24-hour period, the Type A's had a better survival rate. Thus, although heart attacks were more common in Type A's, survival rates were also better.[46]

MRFIT STUDY

Large study of 3,110 adults used as clinical trial to alter behaviors associated with traditional coronary heart disease factors.

MRFIT study.   The **Multiple Risk Factor Intervention Trial (MRFIT) study** was a large-scale clinical trial designed to alter behaviors associated with traditional coronary heart disease factors.[47] A subset of MRFIT participants (n = 3,110) was recruited to determine whether the prospective finding of the Western Collaborative Group Study would be replicated.[48] Rosenman trained and certified the SI interviewers. Eight centers from different regions of the United States followed the assessment and seven-year follow-up phases of the

---

[45]Ray H. Rosenman, R. J. Brand, C. D. Jenkins, et al., "Coronary Heart Disease in the Western Collaborative Group Study: Final Follow-Up Experience of 8 and 1/2 years," *Journal of the American Medical Association* 233 (1975), pp. 872–77.

[46]J. E. Damsdale, "A Perspective on Type A Behavior and Coronary Disease," *New England Journal of Medicine,* January 1988, pp. 110–12.

[47]Richard B. Shekelle, S. B. Hulley, J. D. Neaton, et al., "The MRFIT Behavior Pattern Study: II. Type A Behavior and Incidence of Coronary Heart Disease," *American Journal of Epidemiology* 122 (1985), pp. 559–70.

[48]Jeremiah Stamler, "Type A Behavior Pattern: An Established Major Risk Factor for Coronary Heart Disease," in *Current Controversies in Cardiovascular Disease,* ed. E. Rapaport (Philadelphia: Saunders, 1980).

study, and all assessments were done blind to the Type A behavior of participants. Final results revealed no relationship between SI-defined Type A or self-report–defined Type A and any clinical manifestations of coronary heart disease.

Subcomponent research.   The MRFIT research pointed to the need to move beyond assessing only global Type A behavior. An increasing number of researchers are attempting to determine which aspects of Type A are the most "toxic."[49] Thus, instead of examining a global Type A factor, they are assessing subcomponents of Type A or behavioral factors not associated with Type A. Redford Williams proposes that hostility and anger are the most damaging Type A components in terms of coronary heart disease.[50] He has used the Cook-Medley Ho Scale as a measure of hostility. The Ho scale consists of 50 Minnesota Multiphasic Personality Inventory items that can be answered in either a hostile or nonhostile direction. Ho scores increase as a function of increasing Type A behavior as assessed by SI. Among Duke Medical Center patients with Ho scores of 10 or less, only 48 percent had significant coronary heart disease problems. Among those with scores above 10, 70 percent had problems. The relationship of Type A to coronary heart disease is significant in both men and women.

The Duke Medical Center research is interesting, but it used participants already suspected of having coronary heart disease. Would the same findings occur with currently healthy people? Shekelle and colleagues examined data collected 27 years earlier from 1,877 middle-aged men at Western Electric.[51] They found that among men with low Ho scores the mortality rate was about 18 percent, while among those with high Ho scores the mortality rate was 30 percent. The relative risk of dying in the high-Ho versus the low-Ho groups is about 1.5. This is similar to the relative risk found in the Duke Medical Center patients, 70 percent versus 48 percent.

Certain aspects of hostility appear more important than others in leading to illness. These include cynicism, a more frequent and intense experience of anger, and the tendency to express such angry feelings in overtly aggressive behavior. When angered by interpersonal confrontations, more hostile persons have been found to show more pronounced cardiovascular responses characteristic of the fight-or-flight response.[52] It is generally accepted that an individual's degree of hostility results from the interplay between that person's genetic makeup and the environment in which he or she grows up.

The concept of *amae* has been used to describe the normal Japanese personality. It is defined as a kind of dependency on the basic good intentions of others to treat one well and with kindness. If *amae* is a part of the Japanese

---

[49]Redford B. Williams, Jr., "Type A Behavior and Coronary Heart Disease: Something Old, Something New," *Behavior Medicine Update* 6 (1984), pp. 29–33.

[50]Redford B. Williams, Jr., *The Trusting Heart* (New York: Times Books, 1989).

[51]Richard B. Shekelle, M. Gayle, Adrian M. Ostfeld, and O. Purl, "Hostility, Risk of Coronary Heart Disease, and Mortality," *Psychosomatic Medicine* 45 (1983), pp. 109–14.

[52]Linda Musante, James M. MacDougall, Theodore M. Dembroski, and Paul T. Coster, Jr., "Potential for Hostility and Dimensions of Anger," *Journal of Human Stress,* Fall 1989, pp. 343–54.

culture, then individuals in Japan should have lower Ho scores.[53] That this has been found in preliminary studies helps point out the role that environment might play in the development of hostility.

The interest and research on subcomponents of Type A behavior, such as hostility and anger, suggest that global measures of SI and the self-report measures may not be the best or most accurate predictors of subsequent health problems. The importance of anger and hostility was captured in the original comments of Friedman and Rosenman on Type A behavior. To the extent that hostility, anger, and other factors may be more predictive of coronary heart disease, future research should measure and separate out the subcomponents of Type A behavior as well as examine global Type A that is measured by SI.

Hardiness

Some researchers propose that to improve the predictability of illness or poor job performance as a consequence of stress, one needs to separate individuals into categories: those who are and are not susceptible to illness under conditions of stress. The basis of this categorization is that (*a*) stress cannot be conceived in terms of an external event independent of the individual's appraisal of the event and (*b*) some individuals are more likely than others to appraise events in such a way as to evoke a stress response.[54]

HARDINESS

Personality style that expresses commitment, control, and challenge.

Following the logic of the categorization, Kobasa has advanced the notion of **hardiness.** She interprets hardiness as a personality style that expresses commitment, control, and challenge. *Commitment* is the ability to believe in the truth, importance, and interest value of who one is and what one is doing; *control* refers to the tendency to believe and act as if one can influence the course of events; and *challenge* is based on the belief that change, rather than routine and stability, is what people seek.[55]

The theme of the hardiness approach is that among people facing significant stressors (e.g., a nagging loss, a time deadline, a negative personal life event), those high in hardiness will be significantly less likely to fall ill, either mentally or physically, than those who lack hardiness or who display alienation and powerlessness in the face of change. Hardiness facilitates a form of coping that includes:

1. Keeping specific stressors in perspective. Everything is not a life-or-death struggle.
2. Knowing that one has the creativity and resources needed to deal with stressors.
3. Seeing stressors as opportunities instead of always as threats.

---

[53]Harold Stevenson, Hiroshi Azuma, and Kenji Hakuta, eds., *Child Development and Education in Japan* (San Francisco: W. H. Freeman, 1986).

[54]Jay G. Hull, Ronald R. Van Treuren, and Suzanne Virnelli, "Hardiness and Health: A Critique and Alternative Approach," *Journal of Personality and Social Psychology,* September 1987, pp. 518–30.

[55]Suzanne C. Kobasa, "Conceptualization and Measurement of Personality in Job Stress Research," in *Occupational Stress: Issues and Developments in Research,* ed. Joseph J. Hurrell, Jr., Lawrence R. Murphy, Steven L. Sauter, and Cary L. Cooper (New York: Taylor & Francis, 1988), pp. 100–109.

The most cited study of hardiness was the initial research of Kobasa conducted at the Illinois Bell Telephone Company. Through the use of a questionnaire, 100 Bell executives reported high levels of stressful life events and high levels of general physical symptoms and illnesses, while 100 other executives with comparably high stressful life events experiences were not showing the same high illness patterns.[56]

In order to study the executives more closely, a personality survey was designed to assess all three hardiness components. The high-stress/low-illness executives did differ from high-illness counterparts on the three hardiness components. To examine the Bell executives over time, a prospective test was designed, and 259 executives from whom personality, stress, and health data had been completed earlier were studied for the next two years. Even when prior illness was controlled for, stressful life events (work and nonwork) led to an increase in debilitation, and hardiness predicted a decrease.[57] The researchers concluded that a significant stress and hardiness interaction was an indication that being hardy is especially important for health when one is undergoing an intensely stressful time.

It is premature to conclude that hardiness is a unitary phenomenon. Critics have found that commitment and control have been related to health outcomes; the challenge subcomponent has not held up in a number of studies.[58] Perhaps, we need to examine more closely the measurement properties of the three subcomponents. Until measurement and empirical issues are clarified and problems resolved, it is too early to recommend to managers that they maintain and enhance the hardiness of employees in various ways.[59] We still cannot say with confidence that by addressing hardiness managers will be taking a step toward improving the quality of work life.

Social Support

Some research indicates that **social support** reduces or buffers the adverse psychological impacts of exposure to stress and stressful situations.[60] Interaction with another person or a group is sure to involve social support if it is perceived by the recipient as esteem enhancing or if it involves stress-related interpersonal aid. The term *perceived support* refers to a generalized appraisal individuals make in various situations that they are cared for and valued, that significant others are available to them in times of need, and that they are satisfied with the relationships they have.[61]

SOCIAL SUPPORT
The appraisal of a person that he or she is cared for and valued.

---

[56]Suzanne C. Kobasa, "Stressful Life Events, Personality, and Health: An Inquiring into Hardiness," *Journal of Personality and Social Psychology*, 1979, pp. 1–11.

[57]Suzanne C. Kobasa, Salvatore R. Maddi, and S. Kahn, "Hardiness and Health: Prospective Study," *Journal of Personality and Social Psychology*, 1982, pp. 168–77.

[58]Hull et al., "Hardiness and Health."

[59]Salvatore R. Maddi and Suzanne C. Kobasa, *The Hardy Executive: Health under Stress* (Homewood, Ill.: Dow Jones-Irwin, 1984).

[60]P. A. Thoits, "Social Support Is Coping Assistance," *Journal of Consulting and Clinical Psychology*, 1986, pp. 416–23.

[61]K. Hellker, R. W. Swindle, Jr., and L. Dusenbury, "Component Social Support Processes: Comments and Integration," *Journal of Consulting and Clinical Psychology*, 1986, pp. 466–70.

The major social support hypothesis is that it buffers the impact of stressors on an individual. However, findings have been somewhat inconsistent.[62] Several studies report evidence of the buffering effect. LaRocco, House, and French reported that social support moderated the effects of stressors on health outcomes such as depression and somatic complaints, but they found no evidence of that effect on job dissatisfaction and boredom.[63] Kobasa and Puccetti reported that support from the boss buffered the effect of critical life events on illness symptoms but that support from the family did not.[64] Terry Beehr noted that work group support tended to increase the impact of role ambiguity on job dissatisfaction.[65]

The inconsistency in results may be due to various methodological shortcomings.[66] Much of the available research on social support has used a limited number of stress measures (e.g., role ambiguity and role conflict); certainly, other organizational stressors may be related to outcomes. Also, the size of samples used in most social support studies has been relatively small. Thus, obtaining statistical power sufficient to tease out interactions of typically small effect size has not been possible. Larger samples need to be studied. There is also the problem of accurately assessing who is providing the social support: supervisors, co-workers, friends, families, or strangers.

The best evidence to date on the importance of social support derives from the literature on rehabilitation, recovery, and adaptation to illness.[67] For example, better outcomes have been found in alcohol treatment programs when the alcoholic's family was supportive and cohesive.[68] Managerial use of social support research in reducing stress will be expanded as more organizationally based research is conducted.[69]

CONSEQUENCES OF STRESS

Mobilization of the body's defense mechanisms is not the only potential consequence of contact with stressors. The effects of stress are many and varied. Some, of course, are positive, such as self-motivation, stimulation to work harder, and increased inspiration to live a better life. However, many are disruptive and potentially dangerous. Cox has identified five categories of potential effects of stress:[70]

---

[62]Gregory Strayhorn, "Expectations versus Reality, Social Support, and the Well-Being of Medical Students," *Behavioral Medicine,* Fall 1989, pp. 133–39.

[63]J. M. LaRocco, James S. House, and John R. P. French, Jr., "Social Support, Occupational Stress, and Health," *Journal of Health and Social Behavior,* June 1980, pp. 202–18.

[64]Suzanne C. Kobasa and M. C. Puccetti, "Personality and Social Resources in Stress Resistance," *Journal of Personality and Social Psychology,* October 1983, pp. 839–50.

[65]T. A. Beehr, "Perceived Situational Moderators of the Relationship between Subjective Role Ambiguity and Role Strain," *Journal of Applied Psychology,* February 1976, pp. 35–40.

[66]D. C. Ganster, M. R. Fusiler, and B. T. Mazis, "Role of Social Support in the Experience of Stress at Work," *Journal of Applied Psychology,* February 1986, pp. 102–10.

[67]R. E. Mitchell, A. G. Billings, and R. M. Moos, "Social Support and Well-Being: Implications for Prevention Programs," *Journal of Primary Prevention,* February 1982, pp. 77–98.

[68]B. H. Gottlieb, *Social Support Strategies* (Beverly Hills, Calif.: Sage Publications, 1983).

[69]J. J. House, *Work Stress and Social Support* (Reading, Mass.: Addison-Wesley Publishing, 1981).

[70]T. Cox, *Stress* (Baltimore: University Park Press, 1978), p. 92.

Subjective—anxiety, aggression, apathy, boredom, depression, fatigue, frustration, loss of temper, low self-esteem, nervousness, loneliness.

Behavioral—accident proneness, alcoholism, drug abuse, emotional outbursts, excessive eating or smoking, impulsive behavior, nervous laughter.

Cognitive—inability to make sound decisions, poor concentration, short attention span, hypersensitivity to criticism, mental blocks.

Physiological—increased blood glucose levels, increased heart rate and blood pressure, dryness of the mouth, sweating, dilation of pupils, hot and cold flashes.

Organizational—absenteeism, turnover, low productivity, alienation from co-workers, job dissatisfaction, reduced organizational commitment and loyalty.

These are not all-inclusive; nor are they limited to effects for which there are universal agreement and clear scientific evidence. They merely represent some of the potential effects frequently associated with stress. It should not be inferred, however, that stress always causes the effects listed above.

The Most Costly Effects of Stress

From a managerial perspective, each of the five categories of stress effects shown in Figure 7–2 is important. However, withdrawal and nonproductive behaviors such as absenteeism, turnover, alcoholism, and drug abuse are especially troublesome in terms of lost productivity and costs.

Withdrawal.   Being absent and quitting are two forms of withdrawal behavior that can temporarily reduce job stress in some cases. Some research indicates a relationship between job stress and absenteeism and turnover. For example, one study indicated that over a 15-year period, absenteeism attributed to physical health problems increased 22 percent while absenteeism associated with psychological health problems increased 152 percent for men and 302 percent for women.[71]

A study of 175 hospital employees examined stress as a predictor of turnover. Organizational commitment, job satisfaction, and working conditions were unable to predict turnover. However, high levels of stress were a significant predictor of intentions to leave the hospital. The researchers concluded that employees with low stress levels had expectations of longer tenure at the hospital.[72]

Alcoholism.   **Alcoholism** is a disease characterized by repeated excessive drinking that interferes with an individual's health and work behavior.[73] The negative effects from drug and alcohol abuse are estimated to cost the United States $116 billion annually. Absenteeism, lower productivity, and accidents related to alcoholism are part of the cost to organizations. Experts estimate that

ALCOHOLISM
Disease characterized by repeated excessive drinking that interferes with individual's health and work behavior.

[71]J. D. Kearns, *Stress in Industry* (London: Priory Press, 1973).

[72]J. F. McKenna, P. L. Oritt, and H. K. Wolff, "Occupational Stress as a Predictor in the Turnover Decision," *Journal of Human Stress,* December 1981, pp. 12–17.

[73]Raul Cattano, "Public Opinions about Alcoholism and Its Treatment," *Journal of Studies of Alcohol,* March 1987, pp. 153–60.

ORGANIZATIONS:
CLOSE-UP

AN INSIDE LOOK AT EMPLOYEE ASSISTANCE PROGRAMS

Employee assistance programs (EAPs) began appearing in organizations around 1950, when alcohol abuse was first addressed as a major problem. The initial EAPs used "constructive confrontation" as the method of addressing the problem. Today, EAPs have a broader, more comprehensive approach. Counseling, confidentiality, and referral services are used for a wide range of problems — mental, marital, drug abuse, alcohol abuse, stress related.

General Motors may have the largest EAP. Its program, endorsed by top management and union executives, assists more than 500,000 employees in North America. Full-time union representatives, physicians, and social workers develop joint union-management committees. Each year, about 100,000 employees use the EAP for alcohol and drug abuse problems.

The EAP three-phase model presented on page 245 shows the identification, referral, and treatment phases of assistance. Note that referral can occur when a manager identifies a work performance problem or when an employee admits himself or herself to the program.

An important aspect of EAPs is the confidentiality of information. In devising an EAP, planners need to specify who will have access to what information and under what conditions. Unless personal data is confidential and the guidelines are followed, employees with problems are likely to stay away from EAPs.

Source: Steven H. Appelbaum and Barbara T. Shapiro, "The ABCs of EAPs," *Personnel*, July 1989, pp. 39–46.

approximately 9 percent of males and 5 percent of females in the U.S. population are at risk for alcoholism or serious drinking.[74] Thus, an estimated 10.5 million Americans are alcoholics.[75] Probably no one factor can cause alcoholism, which is a complex entity. The suicide rate among alcoholics is 58 times that of the general public. Rockwell International Corporation, with 100,000 employees, placed the cost of alcoholism to its operations at $250 million. The Illinois Bell Telephone Company set wage replacements due to alcoholism at $418,500.[76] To curb this cost, an increasing number of employers have been establishing alcohol control programs. Over 12,000 such programs are now being operated in organizations. Some information about employee assistance programs is provided in the Close-Up.

[74]Jack Stoltzfus, "A Soviet-American Dialogue on Alcoholism," *EAP Digest*, November–December 1988, pp. 26–32.

[75]Delores A. Rumpel, "Motivating Alcoholic Workers to Seek Help," *Management Review*, July 1989, pp. 37–39.

[76]S. H. Applebaum, "A Human Resources Counseling Model: The Alcoholic Employee," *Personnel Administrator*, August 1982, p. 35.

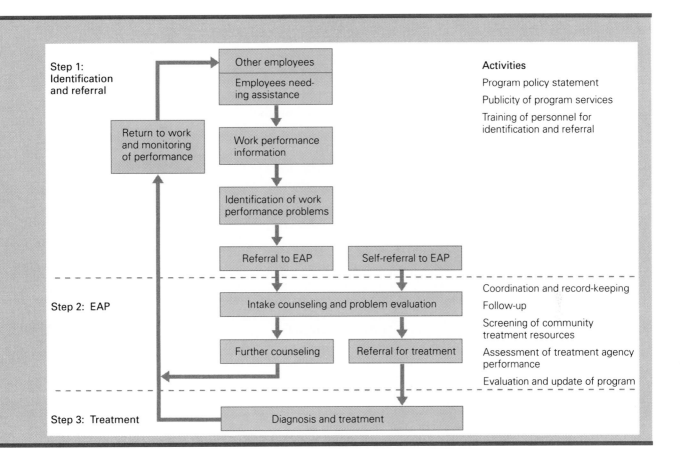

Step 1:
Identification
and referral

Other employees

Employees need-
ing assistance

Return to work
and monitoring
of performance

Work performance
information

Identification of work
performance problems

Referral to EAP   Self-referral to EAP

Step 2: EAP   Intake counseling and problem evaluation

Further counseling   Referral for treatment

Step 3: Treatment   Diagnosis and treatment

Activities

Program policy statement

Publicity of program services

Training of personnel for
identification and referral

Coordination and record-keeping

Follow-up

Screening of community
treatment resources

Assessment of treatment agency
performance

Evaluation and update of program

No correlations have been established between specific types of work stress and the use of alcohol as a response to stress. However, researchers have found that alcoholics have a high need for emotional support, make aggressive demands, show impulsivity with easy decision making, and engage in efforts at control by repression and suppression.[77] Surprisingly, alcoholism is not always accompanied by deteriorating job performance in the early stages of the disease. But as the disease progresses, both quantity and quality of job performance eventually suffer.[78]

Early identification of alcoholism is important because the prognosis for successful treatment is more favorable if treatment is initiated at the early stages of the disease. Managers can look for these signs of alcoholism:

1. Excessive absenteeism patterns: Mondays, Fridays, and days before and after holidays.

[77]J. C. Finney, D. F. Smith, D. E. Skeeters, and C. Auvenshine, "MMPI and Alcoholic Scales," *Quarterly Journal of Studies on Alcohol,* November 1971, pp. 1055–60.

[78]M. B. Sobell and L. C. Sobell, "Functional Analysis of Alcohol Problems," in *Medical Psychology: Contributions to Behavioral Medicine,* ed. C. K. Prokop and L. A. Bradley (New York: Academic Press, 1981), pp. 81–90.

2. Unexcused and frequent absences.
3. Tardiness and early departures.
4. Poor judgment and bad decisions.
5. Sloppy personal appearance.
6. Marked increase in nervousness and occasional hand tremors.
7. Marked increase in hospital-medical-surgical claims.

These signs signal problems to alert managers, who must understand that job stress can contribute to a person's need for and use of alcohol. They should also realize that professional help needs to be applied early if the individual is to be successfully treated. Furthermore, although the use of alcohol develops in response to stress and serves to alleviate it, drinking can itself become a source of stress as the pattern of use progresses into alcoholism.

Drug abuse.   As long as a significant portion of the American population takes drugs, people will continue to bring their drugs with them to work.[79] Some firms, admitting that drug abuse occurs at work, use a variety of means to combat the problem. Drug-sniffing dogs search work areas at Mobay Chemical Corporation in Baytown, Texas; Humphrey & Associates, an electrical firm in Dallas, gives blood tests to anyone who has an accident on the job; and Sunkist Products Group of Ontario, California, requires employees who behave strangely on the job to take a urine test.[80] These drug detection programs have their critics and raise serious legal questions. However, more and more organizations have been getting on the antidrug bandwagon, both for humanitarian reasons and because drug and alcohol abuse has an estimated cost of over $116 billion annually.[81]

According to most experts, cocaine, crack, and ice use is growing faster than other forms of drug abuse. At least three widespread myths have contributed to cocaine's increasing popularity. Myth 1 is that cocaine is harmless. In fact, it can cause respiratory collapse or heart failure. Myth 2 is that primitive people have used it for years to ward off cold and exhaustion. In reality, the coca leaves chewed by Bolivian Indians are not comparable in potency to the powder snorted by employees. Myth 3 is that cocaine is nonaddictive. In fact, cocaine is the most addictive of any drug that employees abuse. Cocaine changes people who had no intention of being changed.[82]

One of the causes of drug abuse is stress stemming from the job. Stimulants and hallucinogens (e.g., marijuana and cocaine), narcotics (e.g., heroin and Demerol), and sedative-hypnotics (e.g., barbiturates and Valium) are taken by

[79]Leonard Moss, "Partners for a Drug-Free Workplace," *Across the Board,* December 1989, pp. 22–31.

[80]Timothy L. Baker, "Preventing Drug Abuse at Work," *Personnel Administrator,* July 1989, pp. 56–59.

[81]Michael D. Newcomb and P. M. Bentler, "Cocaine Use among Adolescents: Long-Termed Associations with Social Context Psychopathology, and Use of Other Substances," *Addictive Behaviors,* 1986, pp. 263–73; Steven Flax, "The Executive Addict," *Fortune,* June 24, 1985, pp. 24–31.

[82]P. B. Bensinger, "Drugs in the Workplace," *Harvard Business Review,* November–December 1982, pp. 48–60.

employees across all job categories to relieve job boredom, excessive stress, and related work problems. To combat drug abuse, management has to first recognize that work-related stress can lead or contribute to drug abuse. Next, it is in management's interest to combat drug abuse with a humane and effective program.

Combating drugs requires managers to focus primarily on the effects of drug use on job performance. Other suggestions based on the experiences of companies fighting drug abuse are:

1. *Establish and communicate a clear policy on drug use.* Management must inform employees about the health and safety risks caused by drugs and the danger posed in the workplace by drug abuse. Management must also communicate that it is determined to obey the law.

2. *Reinforce the drug abuse policy.* High-level management must back supervisors who enforce the firm's drug policy.

3. *Anticipate the problem, and do not be surprised by it.* Management must be aware of the magnitude of the drug abuse problem in society, articulate its drug policy, and enforce that policy consistently.

4. *Maintain good relationships with law enforcement agencies.* In some cases, the police are needed to take action. They should be viewed as a part of the team fighting drug abuse in the workplace.

5. *Don't attempt to deal with the problem on your own; seek professional advice.*[83] Most organizations lack the investigative capability and skills needed to investigate and assemble evidence on drug abuse.

Organizations that have developed and implemented antidrug programs have accepted the role of helping employees with drug problems who are willing to seek assistance. As well as being good employee relations, such a policy is also good from an economic standpoint. Retraining, hiring, and arbitration costs are avoided, and a favorable public image results from a well-run antidrug program.[84]

Physical and Mental Health

Of the potential consequences of stress, those classified as physiological are perhaps the most controversial and organizationally dysfunctional. To hypothesize a link between stress and physical health problems is, in effect, to suggest that an emotional response is responsible for producing a physical change in an individual.[85] In fact, most medical textbooks attribute between 50 and 75 percent of illness to stress-related origins.[86]

Perhaps the most significant of the potential stress–physical illness relationships is that of coronary heart disease. Although virtually unknown in the industrialized world 60 years ago, CHD now accounts for half of all deaths in

[83]Robert F. Pritchard and Gregory C. Potter, *Fitness Inc.* (Homewood, Ill.: Dow Jones-Irwin, 1990), p. 91.

[84]William J. Judge and David Evans, "Drug-Testing Decisions: Inplications for EAPs," *EAP Digest,* September–October 1989, pp. 25–32.

[85]P. Astrand and K. Rodahl, *Textbook of Work Physiology* (New York: McGraw-Hill, 1970).

[86]M. H. Brenner, "The Stressful Price of Prosperity," *Science News,* March 18, 1978, p. 166.

the United States. The disease is so pervasive that American males who are now between the ages of 45 and 55 have one chance in four of dying from a heart attack in the next 10 years.

Traditional risk factors such as obesity, smoking, heredity, high cholesterol, and high blood pressure can account for only about 25 percent of the incidences of coronary heart disease. There is growing medical opinion that job and life stress may be a major contributor in the remaining 75 percent.[87]

Even this brief overview of the health consequences of stress would be incomplete without some mention of mental health effects. Arthur Kornhauser extensively studied the mental health of industrial workers.[88] He did not find a relationship between mental health and such factors as salary, job security, and working conditions. Instead, clear associations between mental health and job satisfaction emerged. Poor mental health was associated with frustration growing out of not having a satisfying job.

In addition to frustration, the anxiety and depression experienced by individuals under a great deal of stress may be manifested in the form of alcoholism, drug dependency, hospitalization, and, in extreme cases, suicide.[89] Even the relatively minor mental disruptions produced by stress, such as the inability to concentrate or reduced problem-solving capabilities, may prove very costly to an organization.

ORGANIZATIONAL PROGRAMS TO MANAGE STRESS

An astute manager never ignores a turnover or absenteeism problem, workplace drug abuse, a decline in performance, reduced product quality, or any other sign that the organization's performance goals are not being met. The effective manager, in fact, views these occurrences as symptoms and looks beyond them to identify and correct the underlying causes. Most managers today are still likely to search for traditional causes such as poor training, defective equipment, or inadequate instructions;[90] in all likelihood, stress is not on the list of possible problems.

The very first step in any program to manage stress so that it remains within tolerable limits is recognition that it exists. Any intervention program must first determine whether stress exists and what is contributing to its existence. A few examples of organizational programs are presented in this section.

Role Analysis and Clarification

The model presented in Figure 7–2 highlights the importance of how employees see their jobs. Employees must have a clear understanding of the

---

[87]D. C. Glass, *Behavior Patterns, Stress, and Coronary Disease* (Hillsdale, N.J.: Erlbaum & Associates, 1977), pp. 5–6.

[88]Arthur Kornhauser, *Mental Health of the Industrialized Worker* (New York: John Wiley & Sons, 1965).

[89]H. Peyser, "Stress and Alcohol," in *Handbook of Stress,* ed. Leo Goldberger and Shlomo Breznitz (New York: Free Press, 1982), p. 586.

[90]R. Payne, T. D. Jick, and R. J. Burke, "Whither Stress Research? An Agenda for the 1980s," *Journal of Occupational Medicine,* January 1982, pp. 131–45.

job; they must know what the company expects and be confident that they can fulfill these expectations. Stress occurs when employees are confused about their work roles or fear they cannot do their jobs. When excessive stress exists in a role, management can initiate adaptive responses such as these: redefine the person's role, reduce role overload by redistributing the work, and implement procedures for reducing stress when it occurs (e.g., allow the employee to have a meeting with those who are causing problems so that a solution can be worked out).[91]

Each of these methods attempts to improve the fit between the person in a particular role and the job or organizational environment. This same logic is used in job enrichment programs. Job enrichment involves redefining and restructuring a job to make it more meaningful, challenging, and intrinsically rewarding (see Chapter 14). In the context of job stress, the objective of job enrichment is to make the job more stimulating and challenging. Assigning tasks that are intrinsically rewarding improves the fit between the jobholder and the job.

Companywide Programs

Stress management programs can be offered on a companywide basis. Some indicate a specific focus: alcohol or drug abuse, job relocation, career counseling, and so forth. Others are more general: the Emotional Health Program of Equitable Life, AT&T's Total Life Concept, the Employee Assistance Center at B. F. Goodrich, the Illinois Bell Health Evaluation Program, and the Caterpillar Tractor Special Health Services. According to the National Survey of Worksite Health Promotion Activities, greater than 50 percent of the general programs were in place for fewer than five years.[92]

Originally, labels such as mental health were used. However, to get away from the connotation of serious psychiatric disease, companies have changed the names of their programs. Today, a popular label is stress management. Two prototypes of stress management programs—clinical and organizational—are in use. The former is initiated by the firm and focuses on individual problems; the latter deals with units or groups in the work force and focuses on problems of the group or the total organization.

Clinical programs.   These programs are based on the traditional medical approach to treatment. Some of the elements in the programs include:

Diagnosis. Person with a problem asks for help. Personnel in the employee health unit attempt to diagnose the problem.

Treatment. Counseling or supportive therapy is provided. If staff within the company cannot help, employee is referred to professionals in the community.

Screening. Periodic examination of individuals in highly stressful jobs detects early indications of problems.

---

[91]French and Caplan, "Organizational Stress and Individual Strain."

[92]Marjory Roberts and T. George Harris, "Wellness at Work," *Psychology Today,* May 1989, pp. 54–58.

WELLNESS AT WORK

Bonne Bell began its first official fitness program by building tennis and volleyball courts, a track, and shower and locker facilities. The company also constructed exercise rooms at both of its office locations in Ohio. To get and keep employees interested, Bonne Bell has set up generous incentives: workers can use the facilities for free, they get an extra 30 minutes at lunch if they want to exercise, and workout clothes are acceptable attire after lunch. Employees can also purchase running suits and shoes at discount prices. Its newest incentive promises a check for $250 to employees who exercise four days a week from January to June. Bonne Bell also pays $250 to employees who stop smoking for six months and $5 for each pound (up to 50) a worker loses over six months. Going back to bad health habits costs double: the company requires people who start smoking again to give $500 to the corporate charitable foundation; for every pound gained back within six months of its loss, that donation is $10.

AT&T's Total Life Concept (TLC) program began in 1983 with ambitious goals and an antistress agenda. Former corporate medical director Dorothea Johnson helped launch the TLC program at several test sites. Some 2,400 people took part in the first program. Following their progress for one year, AT&T found substantial improvements in health and morale: participants reduced their overall cholesterol levels by 10 percent, and 78 percent of the men and women who wanted to lower their blood pressure managed at least a 10 percent decrease. Of those who joined smoking cessation courses, 80 percent succeeded; half were still nonsmokers after 12 months. And, says Molly McCauley, program director of TLC, "people's attitudes changed. We sent a message to employees that said, 'We care about your health and well-being.' They got the message."

For the most part, wellness at Sara Lee is defined in local terms. In rural areas, for example, Sara Lee companies have taken advantage of open space to construct

Prevention. Education and persuasion are used to convince employees at high risk that something must be done to help them cope with stress.

Clinical programs must be staffed by competent personnel if they are to provide benefits. The trust and respect of users must be earned. This is possible if a qualified staff exists to provide diagnosis, treatment, screening, and prevention.

Organizational programs. These programs are aimed more broadly, at an entire employee population. They are sometimes extensions of the clinical program. Often, organizational programs are stimulated by problems identified in a group or a unit or by some impending change such as the relocation or closing of a plant or the installation of new equipment. Such programs are found in IBM, Dow Chemical, Control Data, and Equitable Life.

A variety of programs can be used to manage work stress. Included in a list of such organizational programs would be management by objectives, organizational development programs, job enrichment, redesigning the structure of the organization, establishing autonomous work groups, establishing variable work schedules, and providing employee health facilities. For exam-

outdoor fitness trails. In cities, where tight space makes it hard to build exercise facilities right on company grounds, Sara Lee picks up part of employees' membership fees at local health clubs. At the six Sara Lee companies based in Winston-Salem, North Carolina, where 80 percent of the employees are women, wellness programs center around women's health issues. "We asked the employees what their health concerns were," says Sara Lee's medical director Donald Hayes, "and then we put together a series of workshops on prenatal care, reproductive health, nutrition, physical conditioning, stress management, and preventive strategies for avoiding diseases such as osteoporosis."

"If we are a company of healthy people, then we will be a healthy company," says Honeywell's chairman and CEO James Renier. Honeywell starts with appraisals of cholesterol, blood pressure, and body fat, usually at no charge. The company also offers courses (costing from $5 to $50) on stress management, smoking cessation, fitness, and nutrition. Special events include annual health fairs featuring everything from proper lifting techniques to lessons in health cooking. In Freeport, Illinois, nearly 600 employees have learned cardiopulmonary resuscitation (CPR). The company also operates 40 programs to treat workers with alcohol or drug dependency problems. The payoff? Honeywell estimates that, nationally, large corporations experienced an average of 14 percent increase in the cost of health care services last year—compared to just 4 percent at major Honeywell sites. And surveys of employees over the last three years show a substantial boost to morale after they get involved in a health promotion activity.

Source: Marjory Roberts and T. George Harris, "Wellness at Work," *Psychology Today,* May 1989, pp. 54–58.

ple, such companies as Xerox, Rockwell International, Weyerhaeuser, and Pepsi-Cola are spending thousands of dollars for gyms equipped with treadmills, exercise bicycles, jogging tracks, and full-time physical education and health care staffs. One of the more impressive programs is found at Kimberly-Clark, where $2.5 million has been invested in a 7,000-square-foot health testing facility and a 32,000-square-foot physical fitness facility staffed by 15 full-time health care personnel.[93] Other examples of organizational programs are presented in the Close-Up on wellness.

INDIVIDUAL APPROACHES TO STRESS

Individual approaches to managing stress come in a vast variety. To see this, visit any bookstore and look at the self-improvement section. It is stocked with numerous "how to" books for reducing stress. Of the more popular methods of individually managing stress, we have selected a few for discussion

---

[93]John M. Ivancevich and Michael T. Matteson, *Stress & Work, A Managerial Perspective* (Glenview, Ill.: Scott, Foresman, 1980), p. 215.

because (1) some research is available on their impact, (2) they are widely cited in both the scientific and the popular press, and (3) scientifically sound evaluation of their effectiveness is under way.

Exercise

Epidemiological studies indicate that physically inactive individuals have a higher incidence of heart attacks and death than do active individuals.[94] Sachs and Buffone have compiled a bibliography of over 1,000 references pertaining to the psychology of exercise.[95] Most of the studies claim that exercise reduces depression, anxiety, and phobias. In general, evidence that exercise buffers the negative impact of stress comes from three sources: anecdotal reports, controlled laboratory studies, and a limited number of cross-sectional studies.[96]

Researchers have concluded that exercisers are less stressed and tense, more self-confident, and more optimistic. Folkins conducted a randomized study of exercise in which he assigned subjects to an exercise or a control group, paying careful attention in both groups to issues of compliance.[97] Both groups met three times weekly for 12 weeks. The exercise group showed a significant decrease in levels of stress and depression. The emphasis on compliance may have been a crucial ingredient in this study's findings. One of the problems found in many exercise studies is that control subjects frequently drop in to exercise centers and exercise even though they were assigned a different activity. This makes measurement of treatment effects more difficult.

Although it seems reasonable to assume that exercisers are less stressed and depressed and have higher morale than nonexercisers, caution is necessary. In available studies on exercise, subjects have rarely been randomly assigned to the various treatment groups. Also, exercise is usually administered or initiated with a great deal of enthusiasm and high expectations. Is it the exercise or the enthusiasm and expectations that contribute to improvements?

Relaxation

Just as stress is an adaptive response of the body, so is the adaptive antistress response, relaxation.[98] Herbert Benson reports that in this response muscle tension decreases, heart rate and blood pressure decrease, and breathing

---

[94]J. E. Dimsdale, B. S. Alpert, and N. Schneiderman, "Exercise as a Modulator of Cardiovascular Reactivity," in *Handbook of Stress, Reactivity, and Cardiovascular Disease,* ed. K. A. Matthews et al. (New York: John Wiley & Sons, 1986), pp. 365–84.

[95]Michael L. Sachs and Gary W. Buffone, "Bibliography: Psychological Considerations in Exercise, including Exercise as Psychotherapy, Exercise Dependence (Exercise Addiction), and the Psychology of Running," 1983.

[96]Johnathan D. Brown and Judith M. Siegel, "Exercise as a Buffer of Life Stress: A Prospective Study of Adolescent Health," *Health Psychology,* Winter 1988, pp. 341–53.

[97]C. Folkins, "Effects of Physical Training on Mood," *Journal of Clinical Psychology,* April 1976, pp. 385–90.

[98]Herbert Benson, *The Relaxation Response* (New York: William Morrow, 1975).

slows.[99] The stimuli necessary to produce relaxation include (*a*) a quiet environment, (*b*) closed eyes, (*c*) a comfortable position, and (*d*) a repetitive mental device.[100]

The research evidence on relaxation is limited. Self-report assessments, the lack of comparable control groups, and short time periods of study are found to be problems in most studies. Until better research designs are used, skeptical managers will probably not pay significant attention to relaxation methods.[101]

Humor

Is laughter the best response to stress? Some research indicates that humor is used by children to handle stressful home life, that professional comedians come from family backgrounds filled with uncertainty and tension, and that laughter may be good therapy for combating some illnesses.

A longitudinal study examined the development of humor in children. The children who laughed the most were those who had been exposed to tension and tough situations. In contrast, children who had been "babied" and protected from conflict had a less developed sense of humor.[102]

Research also indicates that most professional comedians tended to be funny as children and continued this style of relating to people in adulthood.[103] Carol Burnett, for example, had alcoholic parents who fought frequently. She describes using humor as a way of gaining strength rather than "buckling under" in her tension-filled home. Humor created a playful state of mind, helping her deflect her attention away from the tension.

Norman Cousins used humor to help himself recover from a serious illness. He was hospitalized for a rare, crippling disease of the connective tissue, from which he was told he would not recover. Working with a cooperative physician, he checked out of the hospital and into a hotel room. For several months, he consumed vitamin C and for hours every day watched old "Candid Camera" films and other belly-laugh–filled movies. He recovered from the incurable disease.[104]

Biofeedback

While a great deal of public interest in biofeedback has been triggered in recent years, very few people actually use biofeedback devices at home or in the

[99]Herbert Benson and R. L. Allen, "How Much Stress Is Too Much?" *Harvard Business Review,* September–October 1980, p. 88.

[100]Gregg D. Jacobs and Joel F. Lubar, "Spectral Analysis of the Central Nervous System Effects of the Relaxation Response Elected by Autogenic Training," *Behavioral Medicine,* Fall 1989, pp. 125–32.

[101]Michael T. Matteson and John M. Ivancevich, "Industrial Stress Management Interventions: Evaluation of Techniques," *Journal of Managerial Psychology,* Summer 1987, pp. 24–30.

[102]P. E. McGhee, *Humor: Its Origin and Development* (San Francisco: W. H. Freeman, 1979).

[103]William F. Fry, Jr., and Melanie Allen, *Make 'em Laugh* (Palo Alto, Calif.: Science & Behavior Books, 1975).

[104]Norman Cousins, *The Anatomy of an Illness as Perceived by a Patient: Reflections on Healing and Rejuvenation* (New York: W. W. Norton, 1979).

office. In reality, there is nothing new about biofeedback—it has been around as long as humans have. Every time you take your pulse, check your breathing rate, or place your hand on your forehead to see if you have a fever, you are using biofeedback. What is relatively new is the instrumentation, the machines that monitor bodily processes and give us information about them.

Research suggests that biofeedback may have an important role in stress management for at least two reasons. First, it helps demonstrate to the user that physiological responses can actually be voluntarily controlled and that stress does, in fact, elicit physiological responses. Second, it provides reinforcement for the user regarding progress made over time.[105]

The potential role of biofeedback as an individual stress management technique can be seen from the bodily functions that can, to some degree, be brought under voluntary control: brain waves, heart rate, muscle tension, body temperature, stomach acidity, and blood pressure. Most, if not all, of these processes are affected by stress. The potential of biofeedback, then, is its ability to help induce a state of relaxation and restore bodily functions to a nonstressed state. One advantage of biofeedback over nonfeedback techniques is that it gives precise data about body functions. By interpreting the feedback, individuals know how high their blood pressure is, for example, and through practice discover means of lowering it. When they are successful, the feedback provides instantaneous information to that effect.

As an individual stress management strategy, biofeedback not only offers some advantages but also has some disadvantages. On the positive side, a growing body of research points to its effectiveness in a wide variety of applications. Biofeedback training has been useful in reducing anxiety, lowering stomach acidity (and thus reducing the likelihood of ulcer formation), controlling both tension and migraine headaches, reducing stress-related hypertension, modifying Type A behavior, and in general reducing negative physiological manifestations of dysfunctional stress.[106] James Manuso reported on organizational applications of biofeedback at the Equitable Life Assurance Company.[107] Employees suffering from chronic tension headaches and anxiety due to stress overload were given nine weeks of biofeedback training in the company's facility. Among the positive outcomes reported by Manuso were a 50 percent reduction in headaches, a decrease (from 18 percent to 14 percent) in daily time lost due to stress symptoms, and an 80 percent reduction in visits to the health center for stress-related problems during a year.

On the negative side, however, biofeedback requires the purchase of equipment, which comes in great variety—much of it of questionable accuracy and reliability. Further complicating matters is the wide variation in equipment price, with little apparent association between price and quality (at least at the lower end of the price scale). While feedback trainers can be purchased at prices ranging from $25,000 down, much of the equipment

[105]G. E. Schwartz, "Stress Management in Occupational Settings," in *Managing Health Promotion in the Workplace,* ed. R. S. Parkinson et al. (Palo Alto, Calif.: Mayfield Publishing, 1982), p. 74.

[106]B. Brown, *New Mind, New Body* (New York: Harper & Row, 1974).

[107]James S. Manuso, "Executive Stress Management," *Personnel Administrator* 24 (1979), p. 23–26.

below $500 is severely lacking in sensitivity and accuracy. (One company sells a "biofeedback trainer" for $2.95; it is nothing more than a plastic mood ring.) Individuals interested in biofeedback should proceed carefully in the selection of instrumentation.

SUMMARY OF KEY POINTS

— Individuals establish a defense reaction to stress. It has been called the general adaptation syndrome (GAS). The three phases of GAS are alarm, resistance, and exhaustion.

— Stress at work influences a person's nonwork activities. The interrelatedness of work and nonwork stress must be considered when attempting to explain and understand employee behavior and performance.

— Three especially counterproductive effects of stress are withdrawal behaviors (absenteeism and turnover), alcoholism, and drug abuse.

— Stressors are external events that are potentially but not necessarily harmful to individuals. Stressors at work can occur in the physical environment and on the individual, group, or organizational level.

— Stressors at work evoke different responses from different people. Figure 7–2 shows a number of moderators of the stressor-stress and stress-effects relationships.

— Three publicized and scientifically studied moderators are the Type A behavior pattern (TABP), hardiness, and social support.

— Research based on medical and behavioral science suggests that TABP is associated with coronary heart disease.

— It is too early in terms of research evidence to suggest that managers need to create work settings that support hardiness to improve the quality of work life.

— The many consequences of stress can be classified as subjective, behavioral, cognitive, physiological, and organizational.

— Many organization-sponsored and -initiated programs are available for managing work stress. Some of the popular programs include role analysis and clarification practices, companywide clinical programs, and physical health facilities for employees.

— Individual intervention programs for managing stress are numerous. Some of the potentially promising programs include exercise, relaxation, humor, and biofeedback.

DISCUSSION AND REVIEW QUESTIONS

1. Discuss the components of hardiness. What has research to date shown about this moderator?

2. Would it be difficult to change or modify an individual's Type A behavior pattern to a Type B behavior pattern? Why?

3. Which subcomponents of the Type A construct appear to be the most toxic?

4. Which social support networks could possibly buffer the effects of stress?

5. What has been the overall problem with finding the best program for intervention and reducing stress?

6. Should managers be concerned about the potential health effects of job stress? Why?

7. It has been suggested that research on the immune system has significant promise for laboratory or college settings but is not meaningful for starting employees or managers. Why would such a suggestion be made?

8. Should management be concerned about and involved in drug detection in the workplace? Why?

9. Even if a manager knows that an employee had a high hostility level, could anything be done at the workplace? What?

10. Why would humor be a possible intervention that could reduce stress?

ADDITIONAL REFERENCES

Allred, K. D., and T. W. Smith. "The Hardy Personality: Cognitive and Psychological Responses to Evaluative Threat." *Journal of Personality and Social Psychology,* February 1989, pp. 257–66.

Carver, C. S.; M. F. Scheier; and J. K. Weintraub. "Assessing Coping Strategies: A Theoretically Based Approach." *Journal of Personality and Social Psychology,* February 1989, pp. 267–83.

Garzona, C. "How to Get Employees behind Your Program." *Personnel Administrator,* October 1989, pp. 60–62.

Hill, C. J., and A. J. Christensen. "Affirmative New, Different Types of Social Support, and Physical Symptoms." *Journal of Applied Social Psychology,* November 1989, pp. 1351–70.

Kahn, W. A. "Toward a Sense of Organizational Humor: Implications for Organizational Diagnosis and Change." *Journal of Applied Behavioral Science,* Winter 1989, pp. 45–63.

Manning, M. R.; J. S. Osland; and A. Osland. "Work-Related Consequences of Smoking Cessation." *Academy of Management Journal,* September 1989, pp. 606–21.

Trenk, B. S. "Corporate Fitness Programs Become Hearty Investments." *Management Review,* August 1989, pp. 33–37.

AM I A SUCCESS OR A FAILURE?

At age 46, Jim Roswell is a self-made man. Although he never graduated from college, Jim was recently promoted to vice president of operations of a manufacturing firm with annual sales of $80 million. He is known around the firm as a take-charge, no-nonsense man who likes both adults and children. Jim is very active in the Boy Scouts, Little League baseball, and local business groups. He is married, with a son in college and a daughter who is a senior in high school.

Recently, Jim has been experiencing what he calls a midlife breakdown in health. He has complained about breathing difficulties, lower back pain, insomnia, and recurring and intense headaches. His physician, who found no physiological basis for the problems, is considering asking Jim to see a psychiatrist.

Jim worked his way up through the ranks. He started with the company 23 years ago as an assembler. Due to hard work, his people skills, and his thorough way of doing things, he received one promotion after another. His last two promotions required him to move first from Miami to Atlanta and then to Colorado Springs. His wife, who had been very active in the Miami community, became quite upset with the move to Atlanta.

As Jim's responsibilities grew, he found that he had to delegate more and more authority. Since some of his subordinates were not well trained, he worked hard helping them do their jobs. This extra work took him away from his family. His wife began to experience frequent bouts of depression. Finally, under a physician's care, she began to take antidepressant medication. One of the side effects of the medication was that she was always fatigued.

Jim feels that his world is caving in around him. His son recently informed him that he was getting married and thinking about dropping out of school for a few years. His daughter has become very antagonistic about life in general, and her grades have slipped badly this year.

The situation facing Jim seems very bleak to him. He is having difficulty in justifying all the hard work he put in trying to be successful. He thinks he has been successful in the organizational world but is at a loss to explain what went wrong at home. He is really fighting against becoming a regular visitor to a psychiatrist. He feels that all his life he made adjustments, and he is puzzled about his current inability to cope with his problems.

Questions for Consideration

1. What stressors in Jim's life are having an effect on his thinking, behavior, and performance?
2. Explain how work and nonwork stressors are influencing Jim's view of the world.
3. Is Jim going to be able to solve his problems on his own? Why?

EXPERIENTIAL EXERCISE

Objectives

1. To provide each student with a view of his or her Type A behavior pattern.
2. To enable students to compare their TABP scores with those of others in the class.

Related Topics

TABP has been associated with various behavioral characteristics, such as impatience, competitiveness, and forcefulness. It has also been associated with coronary heart disease. Those with more pronounced TABP appear to have a greater chance of contracting coronary heart disease.

Starting the Exercise

Each student should complete the behavior activity profile. The instructor has the scoring key and some norms for students to use.

Completing the Exercise

Phase I (15 minutes): Individually complete and score the behavior activity profile.

Phase II (20 or more minutes): Meet in small groups (four to six people) and discuss the behavior activity profiles of all members of your group.

BEHAVIOR ACTIVITY PROFILE

Because we are all unique individuals, we have different ways of behaving and acting as well as different values, thought patterns, and approaches to relationships. The behavior activity profile is designed to access the characteristic style or approach that you exhibit in certain situations. There are no right or wrong answers. The best answer to each item is the response that most nearly describes the way you really feel, behave, or think.

Instructions

For each item in the profile, indicate which of the two alternatives offered is more descriptive of you. For some items, you may feel that the two alternatives are equally descriptive; for other items, you may feel that neither alternative is descriptive. Nonetheless, try to determine which alternative is relatively more descriptive. For each item, you have five points, which you may distribute between the two alternatives in any of the following ways:

If X is totally descriptive of you and Y is not at all descriptive, place a 5 in the X box and a 0 in the Y box.

X	Y
5	0

If X is mostly descriptive of you and Y is somewhat or reasonably descriptive, place a 4 in the X box and a 1 in the Y box.

X	Y
4	1

If X is slightly more descriptive of you than Y is, place a 3 in the X box and a 2 in the Y box.

X	Y
3	2

Each of the above three combinations can be reversed. Thus, if Y is slightly more descriptive of you than X, place a 2 under X and a 3 under Y, and so on for X = 1, Y = 4, and X = 0, Y = 5.

(Continued)

Thus, there are six possible combinations for responding to each pair of alternatives. Whatever combination you use, be sure that the total points you allocate sum to 5. Remember, answer on the basis of what you honestly feel is descriptive, not how you feel you should be or how you would like to be.

X Y

1. ☐☐

X.   I guess I'm just interested in what other people have to say. I seldom find my attention wandering when someone is talking to me.

or

Y.   Many times when someone is talking to me, I find myself thinking about other things.

X Y

2. ☐☐

X.   When I talk, I tend to accent words with increased volume and my delivery is staccato, but rapid.

or

Y.   My speech usually flows slowly in a smooth amplitude, without changes in speed.

X Y

3. ☐☐

X.   I like to enjoy whatever it is I'm doing; the more relaxed and noncompetitive I can be, the more I enjoy the activity.

or

Y.   In just about everything I do, I tend to be hard-driving and competitive.

X Y

4. ☐☐

X.   I prefer being respected for the things that I accomplish.

or

Y.   I prefer being liked for who I am.

X Y

5. ☐☐

X.   I let people finish what they are doing or saying before I respond in any way—no use in jumping the gun and making a mistake.

or

Y.   I usually anticipate what a person will do or say next; for example, I'll start answering a question before it has been completely asked.

(Continued)

X Y

6. ☐☐

    X.   Probably, my behavior is seldom or never governed by a desire for recognition and influence.

                                  or

    Y.   If I were really honest about it, I'd have to admit that a great deal of what I do is designed to bring me recognition and influence.

X Y

7. ☐☐

    X.   Frankly, I frequently get upset or angry with people even though I may not show it.

                                    or

    Y.   I rarely get upset with people; most things simply aren't worth getting angry about.

X Y

8. ☐☐

    X.   Quite candidly, I frequently feel impatient toward others either for their slowness or for the poor quality of their work.

                                    or

    Y.   While I may be disappointed in the work of others, I just don't let it frustrate me.

X Y

9. ☐☐

    X.   My job provides me with my primary source of satisfaction; I don't find other activities nearly as gratifying.

                                    or

    Y.   While I like my job, I regularly find satisfaction in numerous pursuits such as spectator sports, hobbies, friends, and family.

X Y

10. ☐☐

    X.   If I had to identify one thing that really frustrates me, it would be having to stand in line.

                                    or

    Y.   Quite honestly, I find it kind of amusing the way some people get upset about waiting in line.

X Y

11. ☐☐

    X.   I don't have to control my temper; it's just not a problem for me.

                                    or

(Continued)

    Y.   Quite frankly, I frequently find it hard to control my temper, although I usually manage to do so.

X Y

12. ☐☐

    X.   I work hard at my job because I have a very strong desire to get ahead.

or

    Y.   I work hard at my job because I owe it to my employer, who pays my salary.

X Y

13. ☐☐

    X.   It's very unusual for me to have difficulty getting to sleep because I'm excited, keyed up, or worried about something.

or

    Y.   Many times I'm so keyed up that I have difficulty getting to sleep.

X Y

14. ☐☐

    X.   I may not be setting the world on fire, but I don't really want to either.

or

    Y.   I often feel uncomfortable or dissatisfied with how well I am doing in my job or career.

X Y

15. ☐☐

    X.   It really bothers me when, for some reason, plans I've made can't be executed.

or

    Y.   Few plans I make are so important that I get upset if something happens and I can't carry them out.

X Y

16. ☐☐

    X.   Such things as achieving peace of mind or enjoyment of life are as worthy ambitions as a desire to get ahead.

or

    Y.   People who do not want to get ahead professionally or careerwise simply don't have any ambition.

BEHAVIOR WITHIN ORGANIZATIONS

Groups and Interpersonal Influence

8

Group Behavior

DOES ALLOWING WORK GROUPS MORE FREEDOM IMPROVE GROUP PERFORMANCE?*

ARGUMENT FOR

The management of a paper mill believed that autonomous work groups were a better way to utilize human resources and increase employee satisfaction. The idea was to break away from the one-person, one-machine organization and have a small group monitor several machines.

The experiment began in the chemical pulp department, with 35 workers divided into four continuous shift groups of 8 to 9 workers. Supervisors were eliminated, and the number of managers was cut in half. Workers were trained in quality control and information handling.

The experiment worked. In six years, it spread virtually throughout the plant and reduced turnover from 25 to 6 percent a year, while doubling productivity. It gave management much more flexibility in scheduling work, and enabled the plant to stay open through holiday periods.

There are a number of reasons why autonomous work groups are better than one-person operations. However, one of the most obvious is that human beings are social: people like to interact with other people. When people like each other, interact with each other, and know their job, the group structure is best. Isolation, being separated, not being able to communicate on the job, and closely supervising managers are all factors in hindering performance. Remove these obstacles and the result is likely to be productivity improvements.

ARGUMENT AGAINST

The management of a steel fabricating plant believed that autonomous work groups would improve performance. Attempts were made to break away from the one-person, one-machine organization. Workers were allowed to move among the various machines and to be responsible for some equipment maintenance.

This experiment did not work. Both workers and middle managers were hostile to the idea. In one instance, one of five workers was ill for two weeks. The remaining workers handled the five machines and in addition produced more than all five workers had done previously. Unfortunately, the experiment was halted because both workers and middle managers were unwilling to alter the basic work patterns or wage structure.

Changing work patterns that work is a strain on many employees. People like to develop a routine, a comfortable work pattern. The familiarity of setting up a job, organizing a work area, and moving freely appeals to many employees. Being an individual, with a purpose and a work assignment, becomes routine and generally gratifying. People like to be in control of their own destiny.

Too many management experts believe that the "group" or forming a group is what all employees want. Do not reach the hasty conclusions advocated by groupness philosophers and gurus. There are many employees who view themselves as experts, knowledgeable, and experienced. They are comfortable with their style, individuality, and freedom. Experiments to develop autonomous groups should not be pushed on individual thinkers, those employees who have a gratifying routine, or employees who simply like being individualistic. Why does everyone have to be a part of the herd? It does not make sense to change a successful work pattern. A good manager will think through the consequences of breaking the routine before he or she joins the groups-are-best thinkers.

*Source: *Behavioral Sciences Newsletter,* August 8, 1977, p. 1. Also see Marvin Weisbord, "Participative Work Design: A Personal Odyssey," *Organizational Dynamics,* Spring 1985, pp. 4–20; Paul F. Buller and Cecil H. Bell, Jr., "Effects of Team Building and Goal Setting on Productivity: A Field Experiment," *Academy of Management Journal,* June 1986, pp. 305–28; Toby D. Wall, Nigel J. Kemp, Paul R. Jackson, and Chris W. Clegg, "Outcomes of Autonomous Workgroups: A Long-Term Field Experiment," *Academy of Management Journal,* June 1986, pp. 280–304; Paul Chance, "Great Experiments in Team Chemistry," *Across the Board,* May 1989, pp. 19–25.

This chapter examines groups in organizations. Groups in organizations can alter the individual's motivations or needs and influence the behavior of individuals in an organizational setting. Organizational behavior is more than the logical composite of the behavior of individuals. It is also the behavior of groups that interact and the activities within groups. This chapter provides a model for understanding the nature of groups in organizations. The chapter explores various groups, the reasons for their formation, the characteristics of groups, and role conflict.

THE NATURE OF GROUPS

No generally accepted definition of a group exists. Instead, we present a range of available views developed over many years in a variety of disciplines. From these different perspectives, we develop a comprehensive definition of a group.

A Group in Terms of Perception

Many behavioral scientists believe that for a collection of individuals to be considered a group, its members must perceive their relationships to others. For example:

> A small group is defined as any number of persons engaged in interaction with one another in a single face-to-face meeting or series of such meetings, in which each member receives some impression or perception of each other member distinct enough so that he can, either at the time or in later questioning, give some reaction to each of the others as an individual person, even though it may be only to recall that the other was present.[1]

This view points out that the members of a group must perceive the existence of each member as well as the existence of the group.

---

[1] R. F. Bales, *Interaction Process Analysis: A Method for the Study of Small Groups* (Reading, Mass.: Addison-Wesley Publishing, 1950), p. 33.

A Group in Terms of Organization

Sociologists view the group primarily in terms of organizational characteristics. For example, according to a sociological definition, a group is

> an organized system of two or more individuals who are interrelated so that the system performs some function, has a standard set of role relationships among its members, and has a set of norms that regulate the function of the group and each of its members.[2]

This view emphasizes some of the important characteristics of groups, such as roles and norms, which are discussed later in this chapter.

A Group in Terms of Motivation

A group that fails to aid its members in satisfying their needs has difficulty remaining viable. Employees who are not satisfying their needs in a particular group will search for other groups to aid in important need satisfactions. This view defines a group as

> a collection of individuals whose existence as a collection is rewarding to the individuals.[3]

As pointed out in an earlier chapter, it is difficult to ascertain clearly which facets of the work organization are rewarding to individuals. The problem of identifying individual needs is a shortcoming of defining a group solely in terms of motivation.

A Group in Terms of Interaction

Some theorists assume that interaction in the form of interdependence is the core of "groupness." A view that stresses interpersonal interactions is the following:

> We mean by a group a number of persons who communicate with one another often over a span of time, and who are few enough so that each person is able to communicate with all of the others, not at second-hand, through other people, but face-to-face.[4]

All of these four views are important because they all point to key features of groups. Furthermore, if a group exists in an organization, its members:

1. Are motivated to join.
2. Perceive the group as a unified unit of interacting people.
3. Contribute in various amounts to the group processes (i.e., some people contribute more time or energy to the group).
4. Reach agreements and have disagreements through various forms of interaction.

---

[2]J. W. McDavid and M. Harari, *Social Psychology: Individuals, Groups, Societies* (New York: Harper & Row, 1968), p. 237.

[3]Bernard M. Bass, *Leadership, Psychology, and Organizational Behavior* (New York: Harper & Row, 1960), p. 39.

[4]G. C. Homans, *The Human Group* (New York: Harcourt Brace Jovanovich, 1950), p. 1.

In this textbook, a **group** is defined as

> two or more employees who interact with each other in such a manner that the behavior and/or performance of a member is influenced by the behavior and/or performance of other members.[5]

TYPES OF GROUPS

An organization has technical requirements that arise from its stated goals. The accomplishment of these goals requires that certain tasks be performed and that employees be assigned to perform these tasks.[6] As a result, most employees are members of a group based on their positions in the organization. These are formal groups. In addition, whenever individuals associate on a fairly continuous basis, groups tend to form whose activities may be different from those required by the organization. These are informal groups. Both formal groups and informal groups exhibit the same general characteristics.

Formal Groups

The demands and processes of the organization lead to the formation of two types of **formal groups:** command and task.

Command group.   The command group, which is specified by the organization chart, comprises the subordinates who report directly to a given supervisor. The authority relationship between a department manager and the supervisors or between a senior nurse and her subordinates exemplifies a command group.

Task group.   A task group comprises the employees who work together to complete a particular task or project. For example, the activities of clerks in an insurance company are required tasks. When an accident claim is filed, several clerks must communicate and coordinate with one another if the claim is to be handled properly. These required tasks and interactions facilitate the formation of a task group.[7] The nurses assigned to duty in the emergency room of a hospital usually constitute a task group, since certain activities are required when a patient is treated.

Informal Groups

Informal groups are natural groupings of people in the work situation, in response to social needs. In other words, informal groups do not arise as a result of deliberate design but rather evolve naturally. Two specific informal groups exist: interest and friendship.

GROUP

Collection of individuals in which behavior and/or performance of one member is influenced by behavior and/or performance of other members.

FORMAL GROUPS

Groups created by managerial decision to accomplish stated goals of organization.

INFORMAL GROUPS

Groups that arise from individual efforts and develop around common interests and friendships rather than deliberate design.

---

[5]Marvin E. Shaw, *Group Dynamics* (New York: McGraw-Hill, 1981).

[6]Deborah L. Gladstein, "Group in Context: A Model of Task Group Effectiveness," *Administrative Science Quarterly,* December 1984, pp. 499–517.

[7]Connie J. G. Gersick, "Marking Time: Predictable Transitions in Task Groups," *Academy of Management Journal,* June 1989, pp. 274–309.

Interest groups.   Individuals who may not be members of the same command or task group may affiliate to achieve some mutual objective. The objectives of such groups are not related to those of the organization but are specific to each group. Employees banding together to present a unified front to management for more benefits and waitresses pooling their tips are examples of interest groups.

Friendship groups.   Many groups form because the members have something in common, such as age, political beliefs, or ethnic background. These friendship groups often extend their interaction and communication to off-the-job activities.

If employees' affiliation patterns were documented, it would become readily apparent that they belong to numerous and often overlapping groups. A distinction has been made between two broad classifications of groups, formal and informal. The major difference between them is that formal command and task groups are designated by the formal organization as a means to an end. Informal interest and friendship groups are important for their own sake. They satisfy a basic human need for association.[8]

The Close-Up on avoiding apathy illustrates clearly the importance of groups and how intelligent managers recognize their importance and try to use them productively.

WHY PEOPLE FORM GROUPS

Formal and informal groups form for various reasons.[9] Some of the reasons involve needs, proximity, attraction, goals, and economics.

The Satisfaction of Needs

The desire for need satisfaction can be a strong motivating force leading to group formation.[10] Specifically, the security, social, esteem, and self-actualization needs of some employees can be satisfied to a degree by their affiliation with groups.

Security.   Without the group to lean on when various management demands are made, certain employees may assume that they are standing alone, facing management and the entire organization system. This "aloneness" leads to a degree of insecurity. By being a member of a group, the employee can become involved in group activities and discuss management demands with other members who hold supportive views. The interaction and communication among the group's members serve as a buffer to management demands. The

[8]Kerwyn K. Smith and David N. Berg, *Paradoxes of Group Life* (San Francisco: Jossey-Bass, 1987).

[9]Seth Alcorn, "Understanding Groups at Work," *Personnel,* August 1989, pp. 28–36.

[10]Linda N. Jewell and H. Joseph Reitz, *Group Effectiveness in Organizations* (Glenview, Ill.: Scott, Foresman, 1981). This is an excellent comprehensive work devoted entirely to the subject of groups in organizational settings.

AVOIDING APATHY AT PHILLIPS PAPER CORPORATION

As an employee at Phillips Paper Corporation, Gil Phillips noticed that his fellow workers lacked concern for the company's goals. Years later, when he bought the business, Phillips was determined to increase the workers' motivation and effort. He decided to try an approach that was utilized in Yugoslavia's experiments with a labor-managed economy.

Phillips gives his workers an important role in the governance of the firm. He makes stock ownership available to them, as well as membership on the board of directors. Job committees, which include all workers, are set up to oversee the firm's daily operations. The committees discuss and recommend decisions related to all facets of operations, including scheduling, equipment maintenance and purchase, record-keeping, working conditions, and other work-related decisions.

Phillips does not attend the meetings unless invited. Each committee elects a chairman, who runs the meetings and reports majority decisions to an operations committee made up of two company officers and all committee chairmen. The operations committee has the authority to make decisions in all matters suggested by the job committee. The board of directors may overrule decisions made by the operations committee, but it has never done so.

Workers at Phillips Paper report high job satisfaction, and Phillips say he has noticed marked improvement in their motivation since the days of traditional management styles. Profits are five times higher than during the earlier regime. The success of this program implies that employee apathy can be overcome by increasing their involvement in the governance of their own area of work.

Source: Reported in "Job Committees Reduce Apathy," *Pryor Report*, December 1988, p. 12.

need for a buffer may be especially strong in the case of a new employee, who may depend heavily on the group for aid in correctly performing the job.

Social.   The gregariousness of people stimulates their need for affiliation; the desire to be a part of a group points up the intensity of social needs. The need to socialize exists not only on the job but away from the workplace, as evidenced by the vast array of social, political, civic, and fraternal organizations one can join.

Esteem.   In a particular work environment, a certain group may be viewed by employees as having a high level of prestige for a variety of reasons (technical competence, outside activities, etc.). Consequently, membership in this group carries with it a certain status not enjoyed by nonmembers. For employees with high esteem needs, membership in such a group can provide much-needed satisfaction.[11]

---

[11]K. W. Mossholder, A. G. Bedeian, and A. A. Armenakis, "Group Process—Work Outcome Relationships: A Note on the Moderating Effects of Self-Esteem," *Academy of Management Journal*, September 1982, pp. 575–85.

Proximity and Attraction

Interpersonal interaction can result in group formation. Two important facets of interpersonal interaction are proximity and attraction. Proximity involves the physical distance between employees performing a job. Attraction designates the degree to which people are drawn to each other because of perceptual, attitudinal, performance, or motivational similarity.[12]

Individuals who work in close proximity have numerous opportunities to exchange ideas, thoughts, and attitudes about various on- and off-the-job activities. These exchanges often result in some type of group formation. Proximity also makes it possible for individuals to learn about the characteristics of other people. To sustain the interaction and interest, a group is often formed.

Group Goals

A group's goals, if clearly understood, can be reasons why an individual is attracted to it. For example, an individual may join a group that meets after work to become familiar with a new personal computer system that is to be implemented in the work organization over the next two years. The person who voluntarily joins the after-hours group believes that learning the new system is a necessary and important goal for employees.

Identifying group goals is not always possible. The assumption that formal organizational groups have clear goals must be tempered by the understanding that perception, attitudes, personality, and learning can distort goals.[13] For example, a new employee may never be formally told the goals of the unit that he or she has joined. By observing the behavior and attitudes of others, individuals may conclude what they believe the goals to be. These perceptions may or may not be accurate. The same can be said about the goals of informal groups.[14]

Economics

In many cases, groups form because individuals believe that they can derive greater economic benefits from their jobs if they organize. For example, individuals working at different points on an assembly line may be paid on a group incentive basis, where the production of the group determines the wages of each member. By working and cooperating as a group, the individuals may obtain higher economic benefits.

---

[12]Daniel J. Brass, "Men's and Women's Networks: A Study of Interaction Patterns and Influence in an Organization," *Academy of Management Journal,* September 1986, pp. 327–43; Connie Sitterly and Beth Duke, *A Woman's Place: Management* (Englewood Cliffs, N.J.: Prentice Hall, 1988).

[13]P. Amsa, "Organizational Culture and Work Group Behavior: An Empirical Study," *Journal of Management Studies,* May 1986, pp. 347–62.

[14]See Larry Hirschhorn, *The Workplace Within: Psychodynamics of Organizational Life* (Cambridge, Mass.: MIT Press, 1988).

In numerous other instances, economic motives lead to group formation: workers in nonunion organizations form a group to exert pressure on top management for more benefits; top executives in a corporation form a group to review executive compensation. Whatever the circumstances, the group members have a common interest—increased economic benefits—that leads to group affiliation.

STAGES OF GROUP DEVELOPMENT

Groups learn, just as individuals do. Group performance depends both on individual learning and on how well the members learn to work with one another.[15] For example, a new product committee formed for the purpose of developing a response to a competitor may evolve into a very effective team, with the interests of the company being most important; however, it may be very ineffective if its members are more concerned about their individual departmental goals than about developing a response to a competitor. This section describes some general stages through which groups evolve and points out the sequential developmental process involved.

One model of group development assumes that groups proceed through four stages of development: (1) mutual acceptance, (2) communication and decision making, (3) motivation and productivity, and (4) control and organization. Although competing models of group development exist, we believe that the model presented here is the most useful for students of organizational behavior.[16]

Mutual Acceptance

In the early stages of group formation, members are generally reluctant to communicate with one another. Typically, they are not willing to express opinions, attitudes, and beliefs. This is similar to the situation facing a faculty member at the start of a new semester. Until the class members accept and trust one another, very little interaction or class discussion is likely to occur.

Communication and Decision Making

After a group reaches the point of mutual acceptance, its members begin to communicate openly with one another. This communication results in in-

---

[15]Colleen Cooper and Mary Ploor, "The Challenges that Make or Break a Group," *Training and Development Journal,* April 1986, pp. 31–33; Connie J. G. Gersick, "Time and Transition in Work Teams: Toward a New Model of Group Development," *Academy of Management Journal,* March 1988, pp. 9–41.

[16]One early analysis of group development identified four stages similar to the ones discussed here. The author labeled the four stages very appropriately as forming, storming, norming, and performing. Each stage is characterized by features and activities similar to our approach. See B. W. Tuckman, "Development Sequence in Small Groups," *Psychological Bulletin,* November 1965, pp. 384–99.

creased confidence and even more interaction within the group. The discussions begin to focus more specifically on problem-solving tasks and on the development of alternative strategies to accomplish the tasks.[17]

Motivation and Productivity

In this stage of development, effort is expended to accomplish the group's goals. The group works as a cooperative rather than a competitive unit.

Control and Organization

At this point, group affiliation is valued, and members are regulated by group norms. The group goals take precedence over individual goals, and the norms are complied with—or sanctions are exercised. The ultimate sanction is ostracism for not complying with the group goals or norms. Other forms of control include temporary isolation from the group or harassment by the other members.

CHARACTERISTICS OF GROUPS

As groups evolve through their various stages of development, they begin to exhibit certain characteristics: structure, status hierarchy, roles, norms, leadership, cohesiveness, and conflict. Understanding group behavior requires an awareness of these general characteristics.[18]

Structure

Within any group, some type of structure evolves over a period of time. Group members are differentiated on the basis of such factors as expertise, aggressiveness, power, and status; each member occupies a position in the group. The pattern of relationships among the positions constitutes a group structure.[19] Members of the group evaluate each position's prestige, status, and importance to the group. In most cases, status differences among positions create a hierarchical group structure.

Status in formal groups is usually based on position in the formal organization, while status in informal groups can be based on anything relevant to the group (e.g. golf scores, ability to communicate with management). Other members expect the occupant of each position to enact certain behaviors. The set of expected behaviors associated with a position in the structure constitutes the role of that position's occupant.

---

[17]See Steve Buchholz, Thomas Roth, and Karen Hess, eds., *Creating the High Performance Team* (San Francisco: Jossey-Bass, 1988), for several discussions.

[18]Briance Mascarenhas, "Strategic Group Dynamics," *Academy of Management Journal,* June 1989, pp. 333–52.

[19]See Barry Wellman and S. D. Berkowitz, eds., *Social Structures: A Network Approach* (New York: Cambridge University Press, 1988), for several discussions and examples.

Status Hierarchy

Status and position are so similar that the terms are often interchangeable. The status assigned to a particular position is typically a consequence of certain characteristics that differentiate one position from other positions. In some cases, a person is assigned status because of such factors as job seniority, age, or assignment. For example, the oldest worker may be perceived as being more technically proficient and is therefore attributed status by a group of technicians. Thus, assigned status may have nothing to do with the formal status hierarchy.

Roles

Each person in the group structure has an associated role that consists of the expected behaviors of the occupant of that position.[20] The director of nursing services in a hospital is expected to organize and control the department of nursing and to assist in preparing and administering the budget for the department. A nursing supervisor, on the other hand, is expected to supervise the activities of nursing personnel engaged in specific nursing services, such as obstetrics, pediatrics, and surgery. These expected behaviors generally are agreed to not only by the occupants but also by members of the nursing group and other hospital personnel.

In addition to the *expected role,* there are a perceived role and an enacted role. The *perceived role* is the set of behaviors that a person in a position believes he or she should enact. (In some cases, the perceived role may correspond to the expected role.) As discussed in Chapter 3, in some instances, perception can be distorted or inaccurate. The *enacted role,* in contrast, is the behavior that a person actually carries out. Fairly stable or permanent groups typically foster good agreement between expected and perceived roles. But conflict and frustration may result from differences in the three roles. When the enacted role deviates too much from the expected role, the person can either become more like the expected role or leave the group.

Because of membership in different groups, individuals perform multiple roles. For example, first-line supervisors are members of the management team and also members of the group of workers they supervise. These multiple roles result in a number of expected role behaviors. In many instances, the behaviors specified by the different roles are compatible. When they are not, however, the individual experiences role conflict. There are several role conflicts and some important consequences. Role conflict is discussed later in the chapter.

Norms

Norms are the standards shared by the members of a group.[21] They have certain characteristics that are important to group members. First, norms are formed only with respect to things that have significance for the group. They

NORMS
Generally agreed-upon standards of individual and group behavior developed as result of member interaction over time.

---

[20]A good reference on this and related topics is Dennis W. Organ, *Organizational Citizenship Behavior: The Good Soldier Syndrome* (Lexington, Mass.: Lexington Books, 1988).

[21]Daniel C. Feldman, "The Development and Enforcement of Group Norms," *Academy of Management Review,* January 1984, pp. 47–53.

TABLE 8–1

Examples of Positive and
Negative Norms

Positive Norms	Negative Norms
1. It's a tradition around here for people to stand up for the company when others criticize it unfairly.	1. In our company, they are always trying to take advantage of us.
2. In our company, people always try to improve, even when they are doing well.	2. Around here, there's no point in trying harder; nobody else does.
3. Around here, people are good listeners and actively seek out the ideas and opinions of others.	3. Around here, it's dog-eat-dog and save your own skin.
4. Around here, managers and supervisors really care about the people they supervise.	4. In our company, it's best to hide your problems and avoid your supervisor.

may be written, but they can very often be verbally communicated to members. In many cases, they are never formally stated but somehow are known by group members. Second, norms are accepted in various degrees by group members. Some are accepted completely, others only partially. And third, norms may apply to every group member or to only some group members.

Both formal and informal groups may have a variety of norms. For example, most groups have loyalty norms fostering the development of a strong degree of loyalty and commitment from their members. Members are expected to do certain things (e.g., work late, accept transfers, help out other members) to prove they are loyal. Other groups have formal or informal dress norms. Company sales force members may all dress similarly to present the company's desired image to customers; people working in the operations center of a bank away from customers, however, may come to work in very casual clothing. Finally, groups have resource allocation norms and performance norms. Resource allocation norms of a formal organization relate to how status symbols, pay, and promotions should be allocated. Informal groups may also have allocation norms regarding such informal rewards as who works with whom, who gets helped and does the helping, and other informal favors. Performance norms relate to evaluating satisfactory performance. In formal groups, this may be made relatively clear by management; but as we shall see, performance norms may or may not be accepted by the informal group. In fact, informal groups may have performance norms of their own. Table 8–1 contains examples of some positive and negative norms, as expressed in one study.[22]

Leadership

The leadership role in groups is an extremely crucial group characteristic. The leader of a group exerts some influence over the members of the group. In the formal group, the leader can exercise legitimately sanctioned power. That is,

---

[22]Adapted from Robert F. Allen and Saul Plotnick, "Confronting the Shadow Organization: How to Detect and Defeat Negative Norms," *Organizational Dynamics*, Spring 1973, pp. 6–10.

the leader can reward or punish members who do not comply with directives, orders, or rules.

The leadership role is also a significant factor in an informal group. The person who becomes an informal group leader is generally a respected, high-status member who:

1. Contributes to the group in accomplishing its goals.
2. Enables members to satisfy needs.
3. Embodies the values of the group. In essence, the leader is a personification of the values, motives, and aspirations of the members.
4. Is the choice of the group members to represent their viewpoint when interacting with other group leaders.
5. Is a facilitator of group conflict, an initiator of group actions, and concerned with maintaining the group as a functioning unit.

Cohesiveness

Formal and informal groups seem to possess a closeness or commonness of attitude, behavior, and performance. This closeness, referred to as **cohesiveness,** is generally regarded as a force acting on the members to remain in a group that is greater than the forces pulling the member away from the group. A cohesive group, then, involves individuals who are attracted to one another. A group that is low in cohesiveness does not possess interpersonal attractiveness for the members.

There are, of course, numerous sources of attraction to a group. A group may be attractive to an individual because:[23]

1. The goals of the group and the members are compatible and clearly specified.
2. The group has a charismatic leader.
3. The reputation of the group indicates that the group successfully accomplishes its tasks.
4. The group is small enough to permit members to have their opinions heard and evaluated by others.
5. The members are attractive in that they support one another and help each other overcome obstacles and barriers to personal growth and development.

These five factors are related to need satisfaction. As discussed earlier, one of the reasons for group formation is to satisfy needs. If an individual is able to join a cohesive group, then the satisfaction of needs should increase through this group affiliation.

Since highly cohesive groups consist of individuals who are motivated to be together, there is a tendency to expect effective group performance. This logic is not supported conclusively by research evidence. In general, as the cohesiveness of a work group increases, the level of conformity to group norms

COHESIVENESS
Strength of group members' desires to remain in group, and their commitment to group.

---

[23]C. Cartwright and A. Zander, *Group Dynamics: Research and Theory* (New York: Harper & Row, 1968).

ORGANIZATIONS:
CLOSE-UP

PRIDE MEANS BETTER WORK AND MORE PROFITS

An employee's pride in his or her work can often translate into quality work and larger profits for the employer. Southern Services Company Inc. of Atlanta implemented PRIDE, a program designed to increase employee involvement in company operations and decisions. PRIDE offers a systematic means for getting employees involved in problem solving by providing a central resource for all groups throughout the company.

PRIDE encourages workers to provide insights about their jobs. Since teamwork is an essential component of the program, several options exist for both structured and unstructured group works. Ongoing performance teams, one-time problem-solving teams, interdepartmental task forces, and various other types of groups have been established to help employees cut through red tape and address concerns relating to work quality, productivity, and safety.

In addition to the hard savings generated by performance teams, PRIDE also offers several intangible benefits. Communication is improved because employees have ready access to managers. Employee suggestions have increased because employees have a better understanding of the company. Morale and cooperation have improved because workers believe they're making a contribution. Other benefits include improved productivity and decreased absenteeism, overtime, and errors. In essence, PRIDE is a program designed to reduce costs and improve quality by involving employees more deeply in the company's decision-making process.

Source: "Taking 'PRIDE' in Their Work," *Impact*, March 9, 1988, pp. 3–4.

also increases; the group pressures to conform are more intense in the cohesive group. But the group norms may be inconsistent with those of the organization.

The recognition of the impact of groups on performance is a vital one for managers.[24] And the question of whether managers should encourage or discourage group cohesiveness is examined later in the chapter. The Close-Up on PRIDE outlines the productive utilization of work groups toward the development of positive group norms.

Cohesiveness and performance.   The concept of cohesiveness is important for understanding groups in organizations. A group's degree of cohesiveness can have positive or negative effects, depending on how well group goals match those of the formal organization. Four distinct relationships are possible, as illustrated in Figure 8–1.

The figure indicates that if cohesiveness is high and the group accepts and agrees with formal organization goals, then group behavior will be positive

---

[24]Karen A. Brown, "Explaining Group Poor Performance: An Attributional Analysis," *Academy of Management Review*, January 1984, pp. 54–63.

		Agreement with Organizational Goals	
		Low	High
Degree of Group Cohesiveness	Low	Performance probably oriented away from organizational goals.	Performance probably oriented toward achievement of organizational goals.
	High	Performance oriented away from organizational goals.	Performance oriented toward achievement of organizational goals.

FIGURE 8–1

Relationship between Group Cohesiveness and Agreement with Organizational Goals

from the formal organization standpoint.[25] Such a situation appears to exist at Southern Services Company, featured in the Close-Up. However, if the group is highly cohesive but its goals are not congruent with those of the formal organization, then group behavior will be negative from the formal organization's standpoint.

Figure 8–1 also indicates that if a group is low in cohesiveness and the members have goals not in agreement with those of management, then the results probably are negative from the organization's standpoint. Behavior is more on an individual basis than on a group basis because of the low cohesiveness. A group can be low in cohesiveness and yet have members' goals agree with those of the formal organization. Here, the results are probably positive, although again more on an individual basis than on a group basis. The Close-Up, "Influencing Group Cohesiveness," presents some useful strategies.

Groupthink.   Highly cohesive groups are very important forces in organizational behavior. In other words, the organization should place people with many similarities in an isolated setting, give them a common goal, and reward them for performance. On the surface, this may look like a good idea. However, one author has provided a very provocative analysis of highly cohesive groups.[26] Irving Janis studied foreign policy decisions made by several presidential administrations and concluded that these groups were highly cohesive and close-knit. He labeled their decision-making process **groupthink.** Janis defines groupthink as the "deterioration of mental efficiency, reality testing, and moral judgment" in the interest of group solidarity.[27] In his book, he described the following characteristics.

Illusion of invulnerability.   Members of one group believed that they were invincible. For example, on the eve of the disastrous attempt to invade Cuba in April 1961 (the Bay of Pigs invasion), Robert Kennedy stated that, with the

GROUPTHINK

Occurs when cohesive group's desire for agreement interferes with group's consideration of alternative solutions.

[25]Also see Ned Rosen, *Teamwork and the Bottom Line: Groups Make a Difference* (Hillsdale, N.J.: Erlbaum & Associates, 1988).

[26]Irving Janis, *Victims of Groupthink: A Psychological Study of Foreign Policy Decisions and Fiascos* (Boston: Houghton Mifflin, 1973).

[27]Ibid., p. 9.

ORGANIZATIONS: CLOSE-UP

INFLUENCING GROUP COHESIVENESS

Given what we know about the concept of group cohesiveness, there may be times when you as a manager want to encourage group cohesiveness (when performance norms are positive) or discourage group cohesiveness (when performance norms are negative). Managers could use the following strategies to influence group cohesiveness.

To encourage group cohesiveness:

1. Make the group smaller.
2. Encourage agreement with group goals.
3. Stimulate competition with other groups.
4. Give rewards to the group rather than to members.
5. If possible, physically isolate the group.

To discourage group cohesiveness:

1. Make the group larger.
2. Disband the group.
3. Give rewards to individual members rather than to the group.
4. Encourage disagreement with group goals.
5. Do not physically isolate the group.

talent in the group, they could overcome whatever challenged them with "common sense and hard work" and "bold new ideas."

Tendency to moralize.   The group studied had a general tendency to view the United States as the leader of the free world. Any opposition to this view was characterized by the group's members as weak, evil, or unintelligent.

Feeling of unanimity.   Each member of the Executive Committee initially supported the president's decisions. Later on, however, members indicated that they had had serious doubts at the time the decisions were being made. For example, Arthur Schlesinger and Theodore Sorensen both reported that they had reservations about the decisions being made with respect to Southeast Asia during the Kennedy years. Both men admitted regretting their hesitancy to let their views be known at the time. However, each believed then that everyone else was in total agreement and that he had the only differing view. Rather than appear weak or soft, each kept his view to himself. This indicates how the pressure toward group solidarity can distort the judgment of individual members.

Pressure to conform.   Occasionally, President John F. Kennedy would bring in an expert to respond to questions that members of the group might have. The purpose was, in effect, to have the expert silence the critic instead of actively encouraging discussion of divergent views. Other informal pressures to conform were also used on cabinet and staff members. In one instance, Arthur Schlesinger reported, Robert Kennedy had mentioned informally to him that while he (Kennedy) could see some problems associated with a particular decision, the president needed unanimous support on the issue. There was a strong perceived need for group solidarity. Thus, groups can exert great pressure on individual members to conform.

Opposing ideas dismissed.   Any individual or outside group that criticized or opposed a decision or policy received little or no attention from the group. Even valid ideas and relevant arguments were often dismissed prematurely. Janis notes that much evidence indicated strongly that the invasion of Cuba would fail, but it was given little consideration. Thus, information conflicting with group goals can be distorted or ignored as individual members strive for agreement and solidarity.

Certainly, some level of group cohesiveness is necessary for a group to tackle a problem. If seven individuals from seven different organizational units are assigned a task, the task may never be completed effectively. The point, however, is that when it comes to cohesiveness, more may not necessarily be better. While members of task groups may redefine solving a problem to mean reaching agreement rather than making the best decision, members of cohesive groups may redefine it to mean preserving relations among group members and preserving the image of the group. The decision to invade Cuba, as described by Janis, is an example of the negative impact of group pressures on the quality of the decisions made by the group. Groupthink illustrates the impact of group dynamics and cohesiveness on group performance.[28]

The groupthink phenomenon could even explain such events as Watergate, the Iran-Contra affair, and the collusion that occurred at E. F. Hutton. It can also be applied to the Eastern bloc nations who are attempting to permit group discussions to bring about major economic reforms. In these nations (e.g., Poland, the USSR, Romania, and East Germany), groupthink has existed for too long, but breaking down old habits is painful as observations of what is occurring are brought into the public awareness.

Intergroup Conflict

An important characteristic of groups is that they frequently conflict with other groups in an organization. Groups conflict with one another for many reasons, and the consequences can be either good for the organization or extremely negative. This chapter is concerned mainly with what happens within groups: the types and characteristics of groups as they develop. What happens between groups (intergroup behavior) is the subject of the next chapter.

---

[28]Also see Glen Whyte, "Groupthink Reconsidered," *Academy of Management Review,* January 1989, pp. 40–56.

THE ROLE CONCEPT

The concept of role is very important to the understanding of group behavior. **Role** refers to the expected behavior patterns attributed to a particular position in an organization. The roles of physician and patient are familiar to everyone. Those roles are culturally defined expectations associated with particular positions.

A role may include attitudes and values as well as specific kinds of behavior. It is what an individual must do to validate his or her occupancy of a particular position. In other words, what kind of physician or patient an individual is depends a great deal on how he or she performs the culturally defined role associated with the position. Consider your own perceptions of the roles associated with law enforcement officers, military officers, politicians, college professors, and business executives.

In the formal organization, every position has certain activities that are expected. These activities constitute the role for that position from the standpoint of the organization. The organization develops job descriptions that define the activities of each particular position and how it relates to other positions in the organization. However, for both formal (task and command) and informal (interest and friendship) groups, roles may not be set forth explicitly and yet be clearly understood by group members. For example, members of the marketing department in a bank may know that only the director of marketing represents the bank at national conventions and that they have no chance of attending, even though this has never been explicitly stated. Thus, whether they are formally or informally established, status hierarchies and accompanying roles are integral parts of every organization. The role of the follower is described in the Close-Up.

Multiple Roles and Role Sets

Most of us perform **multiple roles.** We occupy many different positions in a variety of organizations—home, work, church, civic groups, and so forth; within each of these organizations, we occupy and perform certain roles. We may simultaneously be playing the role of parent, mate, supervisor, and subordinate. Each position involves different role relationships. For example, the position of college professor involves not only the role of teacher in relation to students but also numerous other roles relating the position to administrators, peers, the community, and alumni. Each group may expect different things: students may expect good classroom performance, research, and publication; the college community may expect community service; and alumni may expect help in recruiting students and athletes. This we term the **role set.** A role set refers to others' expectations for the behavior of the individual in the particular role. The more expectations, the more complex is the role set. For example, a college professor probably has a more complex role set than that of a forest ranger but one less complicated than that of an ambassador to Hungary.

Multiple roles refer to different roles, while role set refers to the different expectations associated with one role. Therefore, an individual involved in many different roles, each with a complex role set, faces the ultimate in

ORGANIZATIONS: CLOSE-UP

THE ROLE OF THE FOLLOWER

Too often, companies ignore or discourage followership. Yet, to enjoy continued success, a company needs to have a proper mix of both leaders and followers. Situations of "too many chiefs and too few Indians" can be avoided by cultivating an atmosphere in which the importance of following, as well as leading, is emphasized. Steps in cultivating effective followers include:

— Defining followership and leadership. Key traits that effective followers possess are the ability to self-manage work, to focus contributions on the important core activities of the company, to build credibility early with co-workers and bosses, and to have the courage to exercise conscience when following or leading.

— Fine-tuning followership skills. Programs designed to train employees to follow effectively should include topics on improving independent, critical thinking; self-management; disagreeing agreeably; acting responsibly toward the organization, the leader, co-workers, and oneself; and identifying similarities and differences between leadership and followership roles.

— Developing organizational structures that encourage followership. Examples of such structures are leaderless groups, where members assume equal responsibility for achieving goals; groups with temporary and rotating leadership and followership; and the delegation of more responsibility to the lowest level of employees.

Companies able to develop and implement followership programs are more likely to enjoy smooth transitions in periods of leadership changes. In addition, alliances are developed with the company, not the leader. The effective company of tomorrow will be a learning organization, one in which employees teach themselves how to analyze and solve problems. Gone will be the days when only a manager thinks of an improvement and instructs the employees to implement it. Instead, the workers themselves will be thinking, anticipating, and implementing.

Source: Robert E. Kelly, "In Praise of Followers," *Harvard Business Review,* November–December 1988, pp. 142–48; Dennis W. Organ, *Organizational Citizenship Behavior: The Good Soldier Syndrome* (Lexington Mass.: Lexington Books, 1988), chaps. 1, 2; Brian Dumaine, "What the Leaders of Tomorrow See," *Fortune,* July 3, 1989, pp. 48–57.

complexity of individual behavior. Multiple roles and role sets are important concepts because of possible complications that make defining specific roles extremely difficult, especially in organizational settings. This can often result in *role conflict* for the individual. As we saw in Chapter 7, role conflict is a major cause of individual stress in organizations.

Role Perception

Different individuals have different perceptions of the behavior associated with a given role. In an organizational setting, accuracy in role perception can have a definite impact on performance. This matter is further complicated because within the organization there may be three different perceptions of the same role: the formal organization's, the group's, and the individual's. For example, a college dean, the students, and the professors themselves have perceptions of the role of professor. But as we saw in the preceding discussion of role sets, student perceptions of the role of a professor may be very different from those of the college administrators. These differences in perception increase even further the possibility of role conflict.

The organization.   The position an individual occupies in an organization is the sum total of that person's organizationally defined roles. This includes the position in the chain of command, the amount of authority associated with the position, and the functions and duties of the position. These roles as defined by the organization relate to the position and not to a particular individual.

The group.   Role perceptions develop that relate individuals to the various groups to which they belong, both formal and informal. The expectations evolve over time and may or may not match up with the organization's perception of the role. In a group of salespeople, for example, the individual with the longest time in the field may be expected to represent the group to the district manager, although this person may not be the most successful salesperson in the company. In this respect, role relationships are similar to group norms.

The individual.   Every individual who occupies a position in an organization or group has a clearly defined perception of his or her role. This perception is influenced greatly by background and social class, since they affect the basic values and attitudes the individual brings to the organization and to the perception of his or her roles. For example, because of social class, background, and values, a newly promoted first-line supervisor may perceive his or her role as being that of a representative of the group *to* management rather than that of a representative *of* management to the group.

Role Conflict

Because of the multiplicity of roles and role sets, an individual may face a complex situation of simultaneous role requirements where the performance of one role precludes the performance of the others. When this occurs, the individual faces a situation known as **role conflict.** Several forms of role conflict can occur in organizations.

Person-role conflict.   Person-role conflict occurs when role requirements violate the basic values, attitudes, and needs of the individual occupying the position. A supervisor who finds it difficult to dismiss a subordinate with a family and an executive who resigns rather than engage in some unethical activity are examples of individuals experiencing person-role conflict.[29]

ROLE CONFLICT
Conflict that arises when a person in an organization receives incompatible messages regarding appropriate role behavior.

---

[29]For an analysis of some of the organizational implications of this type of conflict, see L. Roos and F. Starke, "Roles in Organizations," in *Handbook of Organizational Design,* ed. W. Starbuck and P. Nystrom (Oxford, England: Oxford University Press, 1980).

Intrarole conflict.   Intrarole conflict occurs when different individuals define a role according to different sets of expectations, making it impossible for the person occupying the role to satisfy all of them. This is more likely to occur when a given role has a complex role set (many different role relationships). The supervisor in an industrial situation has a rather complex role set and thus may face intrarole conflict. One the one hand, top management has a set of expectations that stresses the supervisor's role in the management hierarchy. On the other hand, the supervisor may have close friendship ties with members of the command group who may be former working peers. This is why supervisors are often described as being "in the middle."[30]

Interrole conflict.   Interrole conflict can result from facing multiple roles.[31] It occurs because individuals simultaneously perform many roles, some of which have conflicting expectations. A scientist in a chemical plant who is also a member of a management group might experience role conflict of this kind. In such a situation, the scientist may be expected to behave in accordance with the expectations of management as well as the expectations of professional chemists. A physician placed in the role of hospital administrator may also experience interrole conflict. The next chapter describes how this type of role conflict often causes conflict between groups in many organizations.

The results of role conflict.   Behavioral scientists agree that an individual confronted with role conflict experiences psychological stress that may result in emotional problems and indecision.[32] These problems were outlined in detail in Chapter 7. Research has shown that role conflict does occur frequently and with negative effects on performance over a wide spectrum of occupations.[33]

While managers can do little to avoid certain kinds of role conflict, many can be minimized. For example, some role conflict (especially intrarole conflict) can result from violations of the classical principles of chain of command and unity of command. The early management writers' rationale for these two

---

[30]For classic discussions of the conflict-laden position of foreman, see F. J. Roethlisberger, "The Foreman: Master and Victim of Double Talk," *Harvard Business Review,* September–October 1965, pp. 23ff; F. C. Mann and J. K. Dent, "The Supervisor: Member of Two Organizational Families," *Harvard Business Review,* November–December 1954, pp. 103–12.

[31]Jeffrey H. Greenhaus and Nicholas J. Beutell, "Sources of Conflict between Work and Family Roles," *Academy of Management Review,* January 1985, pp. 76–88.

[32]Susan E. Jackson, Sheldon Zedeck, and Elizabeth Summers, "Family Life Disruptions: Effects of Job-Induced Structural and Emotional Interference," *Academy of Management Journal,* September 1985, pp. 574–86.

[33]John M. Ivancevich and James H. Donnelly, Jr., "A Study of Role Clarity and Need for Clarity for Three Occupational Groups," *Academy of Management Journal,* March 1974, pp. 28–36; L. Chonko, "The Relationship of Span of Control to Sales Representatives' Experienced Role Conflict and Role Ambiguity," *Academy of Management Journal,* June 1982, pp. 452–56; P. J. Nicholson, Jr., and S. C. Goh, "The Relationship of Organization Structure and Interpersonal Attitudes to Role Conflict and Ambiguity in Different Work Environments," *Academy of Management Journal,* March 1983, pp. 148–56.

FIGURE 8–2

A Model of Group Formation and Development

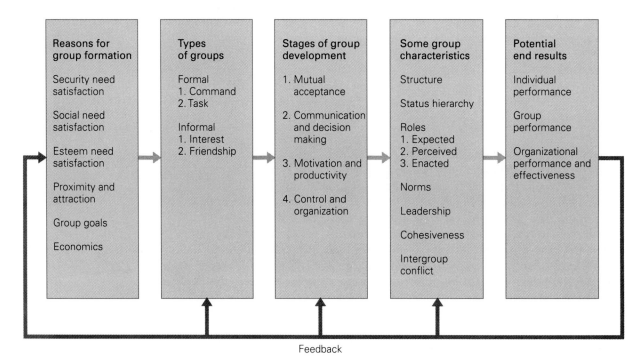

Reasons for group formation	Types of groups	Stages of group development	Some group characteristics	Potential end results
Security need satisfaction Social need satisfaction Esteem need satisfaction Proximity and attraction Group goals Economics	Formal 1. Command 2. Task Informal 1. Interest 2. Friendship	1. Mutual acceptance 2. Communication and decision making 3. Motivation and productivity 4. Control and organization	Structure Status hierarchy Roles 1. Expected 2. Perceived 3. Enacted Norms Leadership Cohesiveness Intergroup conflict	Individual performance Group performance Organizational performance and effectiveness

Feedback

principles was that violation would probably cause conflicting pressures on the individual. In other words, when individuals are faced with conflicting expectations or demands from two or more sources, the likely result is a decline in performance.

In addition, interrole conflict can be generated by conflicting expectations of formal or informal groups, with results similar to those of intrarole conflict. Thus, a highly cohesive group whose goals are not consistent with those of the formal organization can cause a great deal of interrole conflict for its members.

AN INTEGRATED MODEL OF GROUP FORMATION AND DEVELOPMENT

Figure 8–2 summarizes what has been discussed to this point. In effect, it supports both sides of the Organizational Issue for Debate by indicating that performance (positive or negative) has an important impact on group behavior. Figure 8–2 indicates all of the potential end results of group behavior: individual performances, group performances, and overall organizational effectiveness and performance. The model also includes feedback from the potential behavioral consequences and each of the other elements in the model. Note that each segment can influence each of the other segments.

SUMMARY OF KEY POINTS

— A group can be viewed in terms of perception, organization, motivation, or interaction. A group consists of employees who interact in such a manner that the behavior or performance of one group member is influenced by the behavior or performance of other group members.

— By being aware of group characteristics and behaviors, managers can be prepared for the potential positive and negative results of group activities. A manager can proactively intervene to modify the perceptions, attitudes, and motivations that influence the results.

— People are attracted to groups because of their potential for satisfying needs, their physical proximity and attraction, and the appeal of group goals and activities. In essence, people are attracted to one another; that is a natural process.

— Groups develop at different rates and with unique patterns that depend on the task, the setting, the members' individual characteristics and behavioral patterns, and the manager's style of managing.

— Characteristics of groups include structure, status hierarchy, roles, norms, leadership, cohesiveness, and intergroup conflict. These characteristics pervade all groups. In an informal group, they emerge from within the unit; in a formal group, they are established by the managerial process.

— Group characteristics provide a degree of predictability for the members that is important to the group and to the outside (e.g., management, other groups). An unstable or unpredictable group is a problem for its members and for others who interact with it.

— Each group possesses some degree of cohesiveness. This attractiveness of the group can be a powerful force in influencing individual behavior and performance.

— Research studies indicate that cohesive groups can formulate goals and norms that may or may not agree with those of management. When a group's goals and norms are incongruent with the organization's, some form of managerial intervention is necessary.

— The concept of role is vital to an understanding of group behavior. A role consists of the expected behavior patterns attributed to a particular position. Most individuals perform multiple roles, each with its own role set (others' expectations for the role). An individual involved in many different roles, each having a complex role set, faces the ultimate in complexity of individual behavior.

— In organizations, there may be as many as three perceptions of the same role: the organization's, the group's, and the individual's. When an individual faces two or more simultaneous role requirements for which the performance of one precludes the performance of the other(s), he or she experiences role conflict.

— Three different types of role conflict—person-role, intrarole, and interrole—can occur in organizational settings. Research has shown that the consequences of role conflict to the individual include increased psychological stress and other emotional reactions. Management can minimize certain types of role conflicts and should be continually aware that the consequences of conflict to the organization can include ineffective performance by individuals and groups.

DISCUSSION AND REVIEW QUESTIONS

1. Think of an informal group to which you belong. Does a status hierarchy exist in the group? On what is it based?

2. For the group you selected in question 1, can you describe any evolution or developmental process such as was outlined in the chapter? Discuss.

3. Describe some of the attitudes, beliefs, and so forth, that you held when you first joined the class in which you are using this book? Then, indicate whether you believe that they have had any impact on your behavior and performance in the class.

4. Are there any cohesive subgroups in your class? How do you know? Do you think that this has influenced the behavior or performance of their members in the class?

5. Describe some sources of person-role conflict, intrarole conflict, and interrole conflict that you have either experienced personally or watched others experience.

6. Why is it important for a manager to be familiar with concepts of group behavior?

7. Why is cohesiveness an important concept in managing group behavior?

8. How can a manager determine the degree of cohesiveness of a particular group?

9. What factors play a part in how fast or slow a group develops?

10. What group characteristics apply to your present classroom?

ADDITIONAL REFERENCES

Brockner, J., and T. Hess. "Self-Esteem and Task Performance in Quality Circles." *Academy of Management Journal,* 1986, pp. 617–22.

Hackman, J. R. "Group Influences on Individuals." In *Handbook of Industrial and Organizational Psychology,* ed. M. D. Dunnette. Skokie, Ill.: Rand McNally, 1976.

Herek, G.; I. L. Janis; and P. Huth. "Quality of U. S. Decision Making during the Cuban Missile Crisis: Major Errors in Welch's Reassessment." *Journal of Conflict Resolution,* September 1989, pp. 446–59.

Katz, J., and W. B. Gartner. "Perceptions of Emerging Organizations." *Academy of Management Review,* 1988, pp. 429–41.

May, L. *Morality of Groups: Collective Responsibility, Group-Based Harm and Corporate Rights.* Notre Dame, Ind.: Notre Dame Press, 1988.

Mitchell, R. "Team Building by Disclosure of Internal Frames of Reference." *Journal of Applied Behavioral Science,* 1986, pp. 15–28.

Schein, E. H. "Corporate Teams and Totems." *Sloan Management Review,* 1989, pp. 4–7.

Sims, H. P., and J. W. Dean. "Beyond Quality Circles: Self-Managing Teams." *Personnel,* 1985, pp. 25–32.

Tjosvold, D. "Constructive Controversy: A Key Strategy for Groups." *Personnel,* 1986, pp. 39–44.

Vancil, R. E., and C. H. Green. "Managerial Perceived Influence over Intradepartmental Decisions." *Journal of Management Studies,* 1985, pp. 155–74.

Weisbord, M. R. *Productive Workplaces: Organizing and Managing for Dignity, Meaning and Community.* San Francisco: Jossey-Bass, 1987.

Wood, R.; F. Hull; and K. Azum. "Evaluating Quality Circles: An American Application." *California Management Review,* 1986, pp. 37–53.

The "No Martini" Lunch

Jim Lyons had just completed his second month as manager of an important office of a nationwide sales organization. He believed that he had made the right choice in leaving his old company. This new position offered a great challenge, excellent pay and benefits, and tremendous opportunity for advancement. In addition, his family seemed to be adjusting well to the new community. However, in Jim's mind there was one very serious problem that he believed must be confronted immediately, or it could threaten his satisfaction in the long run.

After taking the job, Jim found out that the man he replaced had made an institution of the hard-drinking business lunch. He and a group of other key executives had virtually a standing appointment at various local restaurants. Even when clients were not present, they would have several drinks before ordering their lunches. When they returned, it was usually well into the afternoon, and they were in no condition to make decisions or take the actions that were often the pretext of the lunch in the first place. This practice had also spread to the subordinates of the various executives; it was not uncommon to see various groups of salespersons doing the same thing a few days each week.

Jim decided that he wanted to end the practice, at least for himself and the members of his group. He knew that this was not going to be easy. The drinking had become institutionalized with a great deal of psychological pressure from a central figure—the man he had replaced. Jim decided to plan his approach and then discuss the problem and his approach for solving it with his superior, Norm Landy.

The following week, Jim made an appointment with Norm to discuss the situation. Norm listened intently as Jim explained the drinking problem but did not show any surprise at learning about it. Jim then explained what he planned to do.

"Norm, I'm making two assumptions on the front end. First, I don't believe it would do any good to state strong new policies about drinking at lunch or to lecture my people about the evils of the liquid lunch. About all I'd accomplish would be to raise a lot of latent guilt that would only result in resentment and resistance. Second, I am assuming that the boss is often a role model for his subordinates. Unfortunately, the man I replaced made a practice of the drinking lunch. The subordinates close to him then conformed to his drinking habits and exerted pressure on other members of the group. Before you know it, everyone is a drinking buddy, and the practice becomes institutionalized even when one member is no longer there.

"Here is what I intend to do about it. First, when I go to lunch with the other managers, I will do no drinking. More important, however, for the members of my group, I am going to establish a new role model. For example, at least once a week, we have a legitimate reason to work through lunch. In the past, everyone has gone out anyway. I intend to hold a business lunch and have sandwiches and soft drinks sent in. In addition, I intend to make it a regular practice to take different groups of my people to lunch at a no-alcohol coffee shop.

"My goal, Norm, is simply to let my subordinates know that alcohol is not a necessary part of the workday and that drinking will not win my approval. By not drinking with the other managers, I hope sooner or later to make the point with them also. As you can see, I intend to get the message across by my behavior. There will be no words of censure. What do you think, Norm?"

Norm Landy pushed himself away from his desk, came around, and seated himself beside Jim. He then looked at Jim and whispered, "Are you crazy? I guarantee you, Jim, that you are going to accomplish nothing but cause a lot of trouble—trouble between your group and other groups if you succeed, trouble between you and your group, and trouble between you and the other managers.

Believe me, Jim, I see the problem, and I agree with you that it is a problem. But the cure might kill the patient. Will all that conflict and trouble be worth it?''

Jim thought for a moment and said, ''I think it will be good for the organization in the long run.''

Questions for Consideration

1. Do you agree with Norm Landy or with Jim Lyons? Why?
2. Do you think that anything can be done about this situation? Why? What is your opinion of Jim's plan?
3. What would you do in Jim's situation? Be specific.

PARTICIPATION IN AND OBSERVATIONS OF
GROUP PROCESSES

Objectives

1. To provide experience in participating in and observing groups undertaking a specific task.
2. To generate data that can be the focus of class discussion and analysis.

Starting the Exercise

The situation. You are appointed to a personnel committee in charge of selecting a manager for the department that provides administrative services to other departments. Before you begin interviewing candidates, you are asked to develop a list of the personal and professional qualifications the manager needs. The list will be used as the selection criteria.

Completing the Exercise

1. Select five to seven members to serve on the committee.
2. Ask the committee to rank the items in the following list in their order of importance in selecting the department head.
3. The students not on the committee should observe the group process. Some should observe the whole group, and others individual members. The observers can use observation guides A and B.
4. The observers should provide feedback to the participants.
5. The class should discuss how the committee might improve its performance.

Selection Criteria

____ Strong institutional loyalty
____ Ability to give clear instructions
____ Ability to discipline subordinates
____ Ability to make decisions under pressure
____ Ability to communicate
____ Stable personality

____ High intelligence
____ Ability to grasp the overall picture
____ Ability to get along well with people
____ Familiarity with office procedures
____ Professional achievement
____ Ability to develop subordinates

A. Group Process Observation Guide

Instructions: Observe the group behavior in the following dimensions. Prepare notes for feedback.

Group Behaviors	Description	Impact
Group Goal: Are group goals clearly defined?		

Source: Kae H. Chung and Leon C. Megginson, *Organizational Behavior* (New York: Harper & Row, 1981), pp. 241–44. Used by permission.

Group Behaviors	Description	Impact
Decision Procedure: Is the decision procedure clearly defined?		
Communication Network: What kind of communication network is used? Is it appropriate?		
Decision Making: What kind of decision process is used? Is it appropriate?		
Group Norm: Observe the degrees of cohesiveness, compatibility, and conformity.		
Group Composition: What kind of group is it?		
Other Behavior: Is there any behavior that influences the group process?		

B. Individual Role Observation Guide

Instructions: Observe one committee member. Tabulate (or note) behaviors that he or she exhibits as the group works.

Initiating Ideas: Initiates or clarifies ideas and issues.	**Confusing Issues:** Confuses others by bringing up irrelevant issues or by jumping to other issues.
Managing Conflicts: Explores, clarifies, and resolves conflicts and differences.	**Mismanaging Conflicts:** Avoids or suppresses conflicts, or creates "win-or-lose" situations.

Influencing Others: Appeases, reasons with, or persuades others.	**Forcing Others:** Gives orders or forces others to agree.
Supporting Others: Reinforces or helps others to express their opinions.	**Rejecting Others:** Deflates or antagonizes others.
Listening Attentively: Listens and responds to others' ideas and opinions.	**Showing Indifference:** Does not listen or brushes off others.
Showing Empathy: Shows the ability to see things from other people's viewpoint.	**Self-Serving Behavior:** Exhibits behavior that is self-serving.
Exhibiting Positive Nonverbal Behaviors: Pays attention to others, maintains eye contact, composure, and other signs.	**Exhibiting Negative Nonverbal Behaviors:** Tense facial expression, yawning, little eye contact, and other behaviors.

9

Intergroup Behavior and Managing Conflict

LEARNING OBJECTIVES

After completing Chapter 9, you should be able to:

DEFINE
functional conflict and dysfunctional conflict.

DESCRIBE
the impact of intergroup conflict on organizational performance.

DISCUSS
why intergroup conflict occurs.

COMPARE
the consequences of intergroup conflict within groups and between groups.

IDENTIFY
various techniques that can be used to manage intergroup conflict.

AN ORGANIZATIONAL
ISSUE FOR DEBATE   SHOULD MANAGEMENT SEEK TO ELIMINATE CONFLICT?*

ARGUMENT FOR

Some practicing managers view group conflict negatively and thus seek to resolve or eliminate all types of disputes. These managers contend that conflict disrupts the organization and prevents optimal performance. As such, conflict is a clear indication that something is wrong with the organization and that sound principles are not being applied in managing the activities of the organization.

Since their desire was to eliminate conflict, early organizational writers based their approaches on the principles of authority and unity of command. They believed that conflict could be eliminated or avoided by recruiting the right people, carefully specifying job descriptions, structuring the organization in such a way as to establish a clear chain of command, and establishing clear rules and procedures to meet various contingencies.

Some writers believe that this view is held today by the majority of practicing managers. These managers view all conflict as disruptive, and they think that their task is to eliminate it. The main fear is that intense conflict eventually results from unchecked minimal conflict. Instead of permitting such heated conflict to emerge, proactive managers must root out the problems that cause the conflict.

ARGUMENT AGAINST

Many other managers think that a more realistic view of conflict is that it cannot be avoided. They believe that conflict is inevitable and that it can result from numerous factors, including the structure of the organization itself, the performance evaluation system, and even something as seemingly unimportant as the physical design of an office and its furnishings.

In fact, these individuals believe that a certain amount of conflict is not only inevitable but that optimal organizational performance requires a moderate level of conflict. Without conflict, there would be no sensing of a need to change, and attention would not be called to problem areas.

Obviously, these individuals realize that too much conflict is undesirable. Thus, they believe that conflict can either add to or detract from organizational performance in varying degrees. In other words, conflict can be positive or negative for the organization, depending on the amount and kind. According to this viewpoint, management's task becomes one of managing the level of conflict to achieve optimal performance. This, of course, is a delicate task. It is difficult to pinpoint what is optimal. Management techniques and observation skills are stretched when attempts are made to find what is optimal. However, it is better to search and face the reality that conflict is inevitable and must be managed. The view that conflict must be eliminated is unrealistic in modern organizations.

*Early discussions of the first view are presented in C. B. Derr, *A Historical Review of Management Organization Conflict* (Boston: Graduate School of Education, Harvard University, 1972), pp. 1–22. An early discussion of the opposing view is presented in M. Olson, *The Logic of Collective Action* (Cambridge, Mass.: Harvard University Press, 1965). For recent discussions, see F. van de Vliert, "Escalative Intervention in Small Group Conflicts," *Journal of Applied Behavioral Science,* Winter 1985, pp. 19–36; K. Watkins, "When Co-Workers Clash," *Training and Development Journal,* April 1986, pp. 26–27; and W. F. G. Mastenbrock, *Conflict Management and Organizational Development* (New York: John Wiley & Sons, 1987).

For any organization to perform effectively, interdependent individuals and groups must establish working relationships across organizational boundaries, between individuals, and among groups. Individuals or groups may depend on one another for information, assistance, and coordinated action. This interdependence may foster either cooperation or conflict.

For example, the production and marketing executives of a firm may meet to discuss ways to deal with foreign competition. Such a meeting may be reasonably free of conflict. Decisions get made, strategies are developed, and the executives return to work. Thus, there is intergroup cooperation to achieve a goal. However, this may not be the case if sales decline because the firm is not offering enough variety in its product line. The marketing department desires broad product lines to offer more variety to customers, while the production department desires narrow product lines to keep production costs at a manageable level and to increase productivity. Conflict is likely to occur at this point because each function has its own goals, which in this case conflict. Thus, groups may cooperate on one point and conflict on another.

Intergroup problems are not the only conflicts that can exist in organizations.[1] Conflict between individuals, however, can usually be more easily resolved through existing mechanisms. Troublesome employees can be fired, transferred, or given new work schedules.

The focus of this chapter is on conflict occurring between groups in organizations. We begin with an examination of attitudes toward conflict. Reasons for the existence of intergroup conflict and its consequences are also presented. Finally, we outline various techniques for use in successfully managing intergroup conflict.

A REALISTIC VIEW OF INTERGROUP CONFLICT

Conflict is inevitable in organizations. However, because it can be both a positive and a negative force, management should not strive to eliminate all conflict, only that which has disruptive effects on the organization's efforts to achieve goals. Some type or degree of conflict may prove beneficial if it is used as an instrument for change or innovation. Chapter 7 stated that individuals have differing abilities to withstand stress. Thus, the critical issue appears to be not conflict itself but rather how it is managed. Using this approach, we can define conflict in terms of the *effect it has on the organization*. In this respect, we discuss both functional and dysfunctional conflict.[2]

Functional Conflict

A **functional conflict** is a confrontation between groups that enhances and benefits the organization's performance. For example, two departments in a hospital may conflict over the most efficient and adaptive method of delivering

FUNCTIONAL CONFLICT
From the organization's standpoint, confrontation between groups that results in benefits to the organization.

---

[1]Clayton Alderfer and Ken J. Smith, "Studying Intergroup Relations Embedded in Organizations," *Administrative Science Quarterly,* March 1982, pp. 35–64; P. K. Edwards, *Conflict at Work* (New York: Basil Blackwell, 1987).

[2]Stephen P. Robbins, *Managing Organizational Conflict* (Englewood Cliffs, N.J.: Prentice Hall, 1974); Robert E. Quinn, *Beyond Rational Management: Mastering the Paradoxes and Competing Demands of High Performance* (San Francisco: Jossey-Bass, 1988).

THE TEAMWORK APPROACH AT KIMBERLY-CLARK

The Kimberly-Clark plant at Coosa Pines, Alabama, typifies the once dominant position of American industry. By 1988, the 40-year-old facility needed $200 million worth of improvements to pull it up to par with competitors. Although the investment promised to improve quality, no increased productivity or market share would result without cooperation from the unions. And the plant would be no match for newer plants being built worldwide.

In order to succeed, the company and the unions had to join in common battle against domestic and foreign competitors. Darwin Smith, chief executive officer (CEO) of Kimberly-Clark, bluntly told employees that either productivity had to improve or the plant would be sold, starting a six-month effort to make the plant profitable.

In an attempt to improve production, a team approach to operating was implemented. The team approach, a common Japanese technique, divides the work force into small groups and delegates responsibility to the lowest levels. However, implementation efforts were made difficult by the antagonistic views, developed over the years, that management and the unions held toward each other. In addition, the paper industry was in the process of experiencing several strikes, lockouts, and several cases of sabotage as managements nationwide pressed for concessions from workers.

health care to low-income rural families. The two departments agree on the goal but not on the means to achieve it. Whatever the outcome, low-income rural families will probably end up with better medical care once the conflict is settled. Without such conflict in organizations, there would be little commitment to change; most groups would probably become stagnant. Thus, functional conflict can be thought of as a type of "creative tension." The Close-Up on Kimberly-Clark gives an example.

Dysfunctional Conflict

A **dysfunctional conflict** is any confrontation or interaction between groups that harms the organization or hinders the achievement of organizational goals. Management must seek to eliminate dysfunctional conflicts.

Beneficial conflicts can often turn into harmful ones. In most cases, the point at which functional conflict becomes dysfunctional is impossible to identify precisely. The very same level of stress and conflict that may create a healthy and positive movement toward goals in one group may prove extremely disruptive and dysfunctional in another group (or at a different time for the same group). A group's tolerance for stress and conflict can also depend on the type of organization it serves. Automobile manufacturers, professional sports teams, and crisis organizations such as police and fire departments would have different points at which functional conflict becomes dysfunctional

Fortunately, Kimberly-Clark acknowledged that its workers were the strength of the organization. A process of intense negotiation was started. The unions wanted to protect job security and the seniority system; the company wanted flexibility in making worker assignments and the ability to cut some jobs. By offering incentives for early retirement and stipulating that no workers would be laid off or suffer wage reductions, management was able to strike a deal with the unions. In exchange for these concessions, the unions agreed to adopt the team concept. In addition, Kimberly-Clark committed the $200 million necessary to modernize the plant.

Although Smith is quick to point out that the arrangement can't yet be called a success, he does acknowledge that it is an important beginning. Part of the modernization money will be put toward a 31,000-square-foot health center for the employees. No other mill in the world can boast of such a facility. Indeed, no other domestic paper facility can boast of having the same consensus for a team approach to management.

Source: Gary Jacobson, "A Teamwork Ultimatum Puts Kimberly-Clark's Mill Back on the Map," *Management Review*, July 1989, pp. 26–31; Wendy Zeilner, "Suddenly the UAW Is Raising Its Voice at GM," *Business Week*, November 6, 1989, pp. 96–100; Ned Rosen, *Teamwork and the Bottom Line: Groups Make a Difference* (Hillsdale, N.J.: Erlbaum & Associates, 1988).

than would organizations such as universities, research and development firms, and motion picture production firms.

Dysfunctional conflict can have a negative impact on the performance of individuals, groups, and organizations. Such a situation is illustrated vividly in the Close-Up on franchise systems.

Conflict and Organizational Performance

Conflict may have either a positive or a negative impact on organizational performance, depending on the nature of the conflict and how it is managed. For every organization, an optimal level of conflict exists that can be considered highly functional: it helps generate positive performance. On one hand, when the conflict level is *too low,* performance can suffer. Innovation and change are difficult, and the organization may have difficulty in adapting to change in its environment. If this low conflict level continues, the very survival of the organization can be threatened. On the other hand, if the conflict level becomes *too high,* the resulting chaos can also threaten the organization's survival. An example is dissension in labor unions and its impact on performance. Fighting between rival factions in the union that becomes too great can render the union less effective in pursuing its mission of furthering its members' interests. The proposed relationship between level of intergroup conflict and organizational performance is presented in Figure 9–1 and explained for three hypothetical situations.

FIGURE 9—1

Proposed Relationship
between Intergroup Conflict
and Organizational
Performance

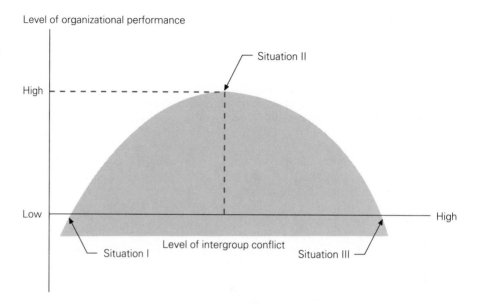

	Level of Intergroup Conflict	Probable Impact on Organization	Organization Characterized by	Level of Organizational Performance
Situation I	Low or none	Dysfunctional	Slow adaptation to environmental changes Few changes Little stimulation of ideas Apathy Stagnation	Low
Situation II	Optimal	Functional	Positive movement toward goals Innovation and change Search for problem solutions Creativity and quick adaptation to environmental changes	High
Situation III	High	Dysfunctional	Disruption Interference with activities Coordination difficult Chaos	Low

ORGANIZATIONS:
CLOSE-UP

DYSFUNCTIONAL CONFLICT IN FRANCHISE SYSTEMS

One would think franchisees of a fast-food chain that increased sales at a rate almost triple the industry average would be a happy lot. Such is not the case at Arby's. At the annual franchise meeting, more than 175 franchisees contributed $1,000 per store to finance a $1.5 million campaign to wrest control away from the franchisor and its leader, Victor Posner. Unhappiness with Posner's firing of a popular CEO and fears that the company was being used as a cash cow for Posner's other operations led to this situation.

While perhaps the most heated, the conflict at Arby's is by no means the only battle shaping up between franchisees and franchisors. Burger King franchisees recently blocked an attempt by its parent company, Pillsbury, to spin off the fast-food subsidiary as a defense against a takeover bid by Grand Metropolitan PLC. The action led to a successful acquisition by Grand Met. Marriott was thwarted in its effort to sell the Straw Hat Pizza chain to Pizza Hut. Franchisees objected and ultimately bought out the chain from Marriott.

Franchisees of Eastern Onion, a singing telegram service, spent more than four years in litigation and more than $4 million in legal fees after Eastern Onion filed for bankruptcy protection under Chapter 11. The franchisor sued the franchisees for withholding royalty payments, and the franchisees countersued, charging mismanagement and other abuses. A co-op of 28 franchisees now licenses the Eastern Onion trademark.

Battles between franchisees and franchisors are spreading. Franchising has always attracted "mom-and-pop" operators because it offers a relatively cheap way to own a business. Traditionally, the franchisees have been at the mercy of the franchisors, whose decisions about new products, marketing, and capital spending can determine whether the franchisee's life savings go up in smoke. Increasingly, however, franchisees are fighting back. They are forming associations to represent their views to franchisors, lawmakers, and judges. Many of the disagreements center around the recent flurry of spin-offs, mergers, and restructurings on the part of the franchisor.

Do all relationships have to be hostile? The answer is no. Dunkin' Donuts has found that franchisees are powerful allies. They have banded together with the franchisor to oppose a hostile takeover attempt. In the case of this company, growing strength and activism on the part of franchisees is good news.

Source: Gail DeGeorge, "Fed-Up Franchisees: They're Mad as Hell And . . . ," *Business Week*, November 13, 1989, pp. 83–84; Joseph M. Winski, "The Man Who Stood Up to Victor Posner," *Advertising Age*, November 27, 1989, pp. 4, 98.

Views on Intergroup Conflict in Practice

Some organizational researchers contend that dysfunctional conflict should be eliminated and functional conflict encouraged. However, this is not what actually happens in most organizations. In practice, most managers attempt to eliminate all types of conflict, whether dysfunctional or functional. Why is this the case? Some reasons are:

1. Anticonflict values have historically been reinforced in the home, school, and church. Traditionally, conflict between children or between children and parents has, for the most part, been discouraged. In school systems, conflict was discouraged; teachers had all the answers, and both teachers and children were rewarded for orderly classrooms. Finally, most religious doctrines stress peace, tranquillity, and acceptance without questioning.

2. Managers are often evaluated on and rewarded for the lack of conflict in their areas of responsibility. Anticonflict values, in fact, become part of the culture of the organization. Harmony and satisfaction are viewed positively, while conflicts and dissatisfaction are viewed negatively. Under such conditions, managers seek to avoid conflicts—functional or dysfunctional—that could disturb the status quo.

WHY INTERGROUP CONFLICT OCCURS

Every group comes into at least partial conflict with every other group with which it interacts. In this section, we examine four factors that contribute to group conflict: work interdependence, differences in goals, differences in perceptions, and the increased demand for specialists.

Work Interdependence

Work interdependence occurs when two or more organizational groups must depend on one another to complete their tasks. The conflict potential in such situations is high. Three distinct types of interdependence among groups have been identified.[3]

POOLED INTERDEPENDENCE
Interdependence that requires no interaction among groups except through total organization.

Pooled interdependence.   **Pooled interdependence** requires no interaction among groups because each group, in effect, performs separately. However, the pooled performances of all the groups determine how successful the organization is. For example, the staff of an IBM sales office in one region may have no interaction with their peers in another region; similarly, two bank branches have little or no interaction. In both cases, however, the groups are interdependent because the performance of each must be adequate if the total organization is to thrive. The conflict potential in pooled interdependence is relatively low, and management can rely on standard rules and procedures developed at the main office for coordination.

SEQUENTIAL INTERDEPENDENCE
Interdependence that requires one group to complete its task before another can complete its task, thereby increasing likelihood of conflict.

Sequential interdependence.   **Sequential interdependence** requires one group to complete its task before another group can complete its task. Tasks are performed in a sequential fashion. In a manufacturing plant, for example, the product must be assembled before it can be painted. Thus, the assembling department must complete its task before the painting department can begin painting.

[3]J. Thompson, *Organizations in Action* (New York: McGraw-Hill, 1967).

Under such circumstances, in which the output of one group serves as the input for another, conflict between the groups is more likely to occur. Coordinating sequential interdependence involves effective planning by management.[4]

Reciprocal interdependence.   **Reciprocal interdependence** requires the output of each group to serve as input to other groups in the organization. Consider the relationships among the anesthesiology staff, nursing staff, technicians, and surgeons in a hospital operating room; such relationships create a high degree of reciprocal interdependence. The same interdependence exists among groups involved in space launchings. Another example is the interdependence between airport control towers, flight crews, ground operations, and maintenance crews. Clearly, the potential for conflict is great in any of these situations. Effective coordination involves management's skillful use of the organizational processes of communication and decision making.

All organizations have pooled interdependence among groups. Complex organizations also have sequential interdependence. The most complicated organizations experience pooled, sequential, and reciprocal interdependence among groups. The more complex the organization, the greater is the potential for conflict and the more difficult is the task facing management. The Close-Up illustrates the concept of interdependence in team sports.

> RECIPROCAL INTERDEPENDENCE
> Interdependence that requires each group's output to serve as other groups' input, thereby providing basis for great potential conflict.

Differences in Goals

As the subunits of organization become specialized, they often develop dissimilar goals. A goal of a production unit may include low production costs and few defective products. A goal of the research and development unit may be innovative ideas that can be converted into commercially successful new products. These different goals can lead to different expectations among the members of each unit: production engineers may expect close supervision, while research scientists may expect a great deal of participation in decision making. Because of the different goals, conflict can result when these two groups interact. Finally, marketing departments usually have a goal of maximum gross income; in contrast, credit departments seek to minimize credit losses. Depending on which department prevails, different customers might be selected. Here again, conflict can occur because each department has a different goal. Because of differences in goals, certain conditions foster intergroup conflict:

Limited resources.   When limited resources must be allocated, mutual dependencies increase, and any differences in group goals become more apparent. If money, space, labor force, and materials were unlimited, each group could pursue (at least to a relative degree) its own goals. But in virtually all cases, resources must be allocated or shared. What often occurs in limited-resource situations is a win-lose competition that can easily result in dysfunctional conflict.

---

[4]For example, see C. B. Chapman, D. F. Cooper, and M. J. Page, *Management for Engineers* (New York: John Wiley & Sons, 1987).

ORGANIZATIONS:
CLOSE-UP

INTERDEPENDENCE IN SPORTS

Sports teams are good examples of organizations where members must depend on one another if the entire group is to succeed. Examples of work interdependence in three team sports are shown in the table.

	Baseball Team	Football Team	Basketball Team
1. What is the nature (and degree) of task-based interaction among unit members?	Pooled (low).	Sequential (moderate).	Reciprocal (high).
2. What is the geographical distribution of unit members?	Widely dispersed.	Somewhat clustered.	Highly concentrated.
3. Given team objectives and constraints, where does autonomy reside?	Within each unit member.	Above the unit (that is, within unit management).	Among unit members (that is, within the unit as a whole).
4. How is coordination achieved?	Through unit design in which the sum of individual unit members' objectives approximates unit objectives.	Through complex protocols that clearly and tightly specify the roles and responsibilities of each unit member.	Through continuous self-regulation and responsibility sharing among unit members.
5. What sports expression metaphorically sums up the operating management task?	Fill out (revise) the lineup card.	Prepare (execute) the game plan.	Influence the game's flow.

Source: Adapted from Robert W. Keidel, "Baseball, Football and Basketball: Models for Business," *Organizational Dynamics*, Winter 1984, pp. 12–14.

Reward structures. Intergroup conflict is more likely to occur when the reward system is related to individual group performance rather than to overall organizational performance. When rewards are aimed at individual groups, performance is viewed as an independent variable even while the performance of the group is in reality very interdependent. For example, in the marketing versus credit situation just described, suppose that the marketing group is rewarded for sales produced and that the credit group is rewarded for minimizing credit losses. In such a situation, competition is directly reinforced and dysfunctional conflict inadvertently rewarded.

Intergroup conflict arising from differences in goals, not only dysfunctional to the organization as a whole, may also be dysfunctional to third-party groups—usually the clients the organization serves. An example of this is the conflict in many teaching hospitals between meeting the goals of quality health care for patients and meeting the learning needs of future physicians.

Differences in Perceptions

Differences in goals can be accompanied by differing perceptions of reality; disagreements over what constitutes reality can lead to conflict. For instance, a problem in a hospital may be viewed in one way by the administrative staff and in another way by the medical staff; or alumni and faculty may have different perceptions concerning the importance of a winning football program. Many factors cause groups in organizations to form differing perceptions of reality.[5] The major factors include different goals, different time horizons, status incongruency, and inaccurate perceptions.

Different goals.   Differences in group goals are an obvious contributor to differing perceptions. For instance, if the goal of marketing is to increase the market shares and sales throughout the world, that department's personnel certainly view a reorganization task force goal to reduce expansion of the company's products to the Pacific Rim differently. Marketing perceives the Pacific Rim as important, and the task force perceives the Pacific Rim as too far from the home office to control and manage.

Different time horizons.   Time perspectives influence how a group perceives reality. Deadlines influence the priorities and importance that groups assign to their various activities. Research scientists working for a chemical manufacturer may have a time perspective of several years, while the same firm's manufacturing engineers may work within time frames of less than a year. A bank president might focus on 5- and 10-year time spans, while middle managers might concentrate on much shorter spans. With such differences in time horizons, problems and issues deemed critical by one group may be dismissed as unimportant by another, setting the stage for conflict.

Status incongruency.   Usually, many different status standards, rather than an absolute one, are found in an organization. The result is many status hierarchies. Conflicts concerning the relative status of different groups are

---

[5]Karen A. Brown and Terence R. Mitchell, "Influence of Task Interdependence and Number of Poor Performers on Diagnosis of Causes of Poor Performance," *Academy of Management Journal,* June 1986, pp. 412–23; Reed E. Nelson, "The Strength of Strong Ties: Social Networks and Intergroup Conflict in Organizations," *Academy of Management Journal,* June 1989, pp. 377–401.

ORGANIZATIONS:
CLOSE-UP   THE TOP MANAGEMENT—EVERYBODY ELSE CONFLICT

CEOs across the nation have gone to their employees with the rallying cry, "We're a team. We're all in this together." However, employees on all levels of the company are increasingly reluctant to respond. They look at the differences between their pay and benefits and the CEO's, asking themselves, "Is this togetherness?" And as the diversity in pay widens, resentment and mistrust grow. Unlike traditional employee conflicts, this battle is not between salaried and hourly employees. Rather, it pits the top managers of a company against all others—middle managers, supervisors, salespeople, and technical, clerical, and hourly workers.

Sources of conflict are not just limited to issues of pay and working conditions. Recent polls have shown a growing "perception gap" between what employees want and what top management thinks they want. Top management believes that employees rank job security as their main concern. In reality, employees list higher standards of management ethics, increased recognition of employee contributions, and closer, more honest communication between employees and senior management as the real issues to be dealt with.

What has caused this discontent? Experts point to management's fear of regularly auditing their employees' views and concerns. Many CEOs still believe that asking for opinions is equivalent to letting employees run the workplace.

Even those companies that do conduct surveys often conceal results or don't inform employees of how policy changes are related to the survey findings. The result often is a situation where management talks and employees don't listen. In a recent survey, 82 percent of Fortune 500 executives stated that their corporate strategy was understood by "everyone who needs to know." However, a poll of employees found that less than one third said that management provides clear goals and direction.

Suggestions offered for resolving this conflict are many and diverse. Having a truly open-door policy where employees can talk to the CEO at any time is working at Rubbermaid. Preston Trucking, a $594 million carrier, uses surveys and bottom-up communication tools that last year succeeded in generating 4,412 money-saving suggestions. Genetech issues pocket-size brochures containing the company's goals and credos. Du Pont, even in down times, retains a high level of loyalty and commitment by giving as much warning as possible of bad news. What is important is that top management realize that a conflict may exist and have a plan ready for resolving any actual or perceived problems.

Source: Alan Franham, "The Trust Gap," *Fortune*, December 4, 1989, pp. 56–78; Theodore Caplow, *Managing an Organization*, 2nd ed. (New York: Holt, Rinehart & Winston, 1988).

common and influence perceptions. For example, status conflicts are often created by work patterns—which group initiates the work and which group responds. A production department may perceive a change as an affront to its status because it must accept a salesperson's initiation of work. This status conflict may be aggravated deliberately by the salesperson. In another example, involving the academic snobbery that is certainly a fact of campus life at

TABLE 9—1

Common Causes of
Line/Staff Conflict

— *Perceived diminution of line authority.* Line managers fear that specialists will encroach on their jobs and thereby diminish their authority and power. As a result, specialists often complain that line executives do not make proper use of staff specialists and do not give staff members sufficient authority.

— *Social and physical differences.* Often, major differences exist between line managers and staff specialists with respect to age, education, dress, and attitudes. In many cases, specialists are younger than line managers and have higher educational levels of training in a specialized field.

— *Line dependence on staff knowledge.* Since line generalists often do not have the technical knowledge necessary to manage their departments, they are dependent on the specialist. The resulting gap between knowledge and authority may be even greater when the staff specialist is lower in the organizational hierarchy than the manager, which is often the case. As a result, staff members often complain that line managers resist new ideas.

— *Different loyalties.* Divided loyalties frequently exist between line managers and staff specialists. The staff specialist may be loyal to a discipline, while the line manager may be loyal to the organization. The member of the product development group may be a chemist first and a member of the organization second. The production manager's first loyalty, however, may be to the organization. When loyalties to a particular function or discipline are greater than loyalties to the overall organization, conflict is likely to occur.

many colleges and universities, members of a particular academic discipline perceive themselves, for one reason or another, as having a higher status than others.

Inaccurate perceptions.   Inaccurate perceptions often cause one group to develop stereotypes about other groups. While the differences between groups may actually be small, each group tends to exaggerate them. Thus, you hear that "all women executives are aggressive" or "all bank officers behave alike." When the differences between the groups are emphasized, the stereotypes are reinforced, relations deteriorate, and conflict develops. The "Top Management–Everybody Else" Close-Up provides a good example of conflict caused by inaccurate perceptions.

Increased Demand for Specialists

Conflicts between staff specialists and line generalists are probably the most common intergroup conflict. Line and staff persons simply view one another and their roles in the organization from different perspectives. With the growing necessity for technical expertise in all areas of organizations, staff roles can be expected to expand, and line and staff conflicts can be expected to increase. Table 9–1 summarizes some causes of conflict between staff specialists and generalists.[6] The increased sophistication, specialization, and complex-

[6]Line-staff conflict has been the subject of a great deal of research for over four decades. For some representative examples, see J. A. Balasco and J. A. Alutto, "Line and Staff Conflicts: Some Empirical Insights," *Academy of Management Journal*, March 1969, p. 469–77; J. E. Sorenson and T. L. Sorenson, "The Conflict of Professionals in Bureaucratic Organizations," *Administrative Science Quarterly*, March 1974, pp. 98–106.

ity in most organizations make line-staff conflicts a major concern in the management of organizational behavior.

CONSEQUENCES OF DYSFUNCTIONAL INTERGROUP CONFLICT

Behavioral scientists have spent more than four decades researching and analyzing how dysfunctional intergroup conflict affects those who experience it.[7] They have found that groups placed in a conflict situation tend to react in fairly predictable ways, in changes that occur within groups and between groups as a result of dysfunctional intergroup conflict.

Changes within Groups

Many changes are likely to occur within groups involved in intergroup conflict. Unfortunately, these changes generally result in either continuance or escalation of the conflict.

Increased group cohesiveness.   Competition, conflict, or external threat usually results in group members putting aside individual differences and closing ranks. Members become more loyal to the group, and group membership becomes more attractive.

Rise in autocratic leadership.   In extreme conflict situations, when threats are perceived, democratic methods of leadership are likely to become less popular; the members want strong leadership. Thus, leaders are likely to become more autocratic. In the Major League Baseball Players Association lockout in 1990, the head of the union, Donald Fehr, had tremendous authority. He was granted full authority by the players to negotiate in their best interest. Fehr had full power and authority to do what he believed was best for the major league baseball players.

Focus on activity.   When a group is in conflict, its members usually emphasize doing what the group does and doing it very well. The group becomes more task oriented. Tolerance for members who "goof off" is low, and there is less concern for individual member satisfaction. The emphasis is on accomplishing the group's task and defeating the "enemy" (the other group in conflict).

Emphasis on loyalty.   Conformity to group norms tends to become more important in conflict situations. Group goals take precedence over individual satisfaction, as members are expected to demonstrate their loyalty. In major

---

[7]The classic work is Muzafer Sherif and Carolyn Sherif, *Groups in Harmony and Tension* (New York: Harper & Row, 1953). In a study conducted among groups in a boys' camp, they stimulated conflict between the groups and observed the changes that occurred in group behavior.

conflict situations, interaction with members of "the other group" may be outlawed.

Changes between Groups

During conflicts, certain changes occur between the groups involved.

Distorted perceptions.   During conflicts, the perceptions of each group's members become distorted. Group members develop stronger opinions of the importance of their units. Each group sees itself as superior in performance to the other and as more important to the survival of the organization than other groups. In a conflict situation, nurses may conclude that they are more important to a patient than physicians, while physicians may consider themselves more important than hospital administrators. The marketing group in a business organization may think, "Without us selling the product, there would be no money to pay anyone else's salary." The production group meanwhile says, "If we don't make the product, there is nothing to sell." Ultimately, none of these groups is more important, but conflict can cause their members to develop gross misperceptions of reality.

Negative stereotyping.   As conflict increases and perceptions become more distorted, all of the negative stereotypes that may have ever existed are reinforced. A management representative may say, "I've always said these union guys are just plain greedy. Now they've proved it." The head of a local teacher's union may say, "Now we know all that politicians are interested in is getting reelected, not the quality of education." When negative stereotyping is a factor in a conflict, the members of each group see fewer differences within their unit than actually exist and greater differences between the groups than actually exist.

Decreased communication.   Communication between the groups in conflict usually breaks down. This can be extremely dysfunctional, especially where sequential interdependence or reciprocal interdependence relationships exist. The decision-making process can be disrupted, and customers or others whom the organization serves can be affected. Consider the possible consequences to patients, for instance, if a conflict between hospital technicians and nurses continues until it lowers the quality of health care.

While not the only dysfunctional consequences of intergroup conflict, these are the most common, and they have been well documented in the research literature.[8] Other consequences, such as violence and aggression, are less common but also occur. When intergroup conflicts take place, some form of managerial intervention is usually necessary. How managers can deal with these situations is the subject of the next sections.

---

[8]Edgar Schein, "Intergroup Problems in Organizations," in *Organization Development: Theory, Practice, Research,* 2nd ed., ed. Wendell French, Cecil Bell, and Robert Zawacki (Plano, Tex.: Business Publications, 1983), pp. 106–10.

MANAGING INTERGROUP CONFLICT THROUGH RESOLUTION

Since managers must live with intergroup conflict, they need to confront the problem of managing it.[9] This section presents techniques used successfully in resolving intergroup conflicts that have reached levels dysfunctional to the organization.[10]

Problem Solving

The confrontation method of problem solving seeks to reduce tensions through face-to-face meetings of the conflicting groups. The purpose of the meetings is to identify conflicts and resolve them. The conflicting groups openly debate various issues and bring together all relevant information until a decision is reached. For conflicts resulting from misunderstandings or language barriers, the confrontation method has proved effective. For solving more complex problems, (e.g., conflicts where groups have different value systems), the method has been less successful.

Superordinate Goals

SUPERORDINATE GOALS
Goals that cannot be achieved without cooperation of conflicting groups.

In the resolution of conflicts between groups, the **superordinate goals** technique involves developing a common set of goals and objectives that cannot be attained without the cooperation of the groups involved. In fact, they are unattainable by one group singly and supersede all other goals of any of the individual groups involved in the conflict.[11] For example, several unions in the automobile and airline industries have in recent years agreed to forgo increases and in some cases to accept pay reductions, because the survival of their firm or industry was threatened. When the crisis was over, demands for higher wages were again made.

Expansion of Resources

As noted earlier, a major cause of intergroup conflict is limited resources. Whatever one group succeeds in obtaining is gained at the expense of another group. The scarce resource may be a particular position (e.g., the presidency of the firm), money, space, or so forth. Expansion of resources may be one way of solving such problems. For example, when one major publishing firm decided to expand by establishing a subsidiary firm, most observers believed that the major reason for the expansion was to allow the firm to become involved in other segments of the market. While this was partially correct, a

---

[9]William L. Ury, Jeanne M. Brett, and Stephen Goldberg, *Getting Disputes Resolved: Designing Systems to Cut the Costs of Conflict* (San Francisco: Jossey-Bass, 1988).

[10]Also see Robbins, *Managing Organizational Conflict*, pp. 67–77; M. Afzalur Rahim, ed., *Managing Conflict: An Interdisciplinary Approach* (New York: Praeger Publishers, 1989).

[11]Muzafer Sherif and Carolyn Sherif, *Social Psychology* (New York: Harper & Row, 1969), pp. 228–62. Sherif and Sherif conducted sociopsychological experiments to determine effective ways of resolving conflict. Based on this research, they developed the concept of superordinate goals.

stronger reason was to enable the firm to stem the exit of valued personnel. By establishing the subsidiary, the firm was able to double its executive positions because the subsidiary needed a president, various vice presidents, and other executives. Expanding resources is potentially a very successful technique for solving conflicts in many cases, since this technique may enable almost everyone to be satisfied. In reality, however, resources are usually not expanded.

Avoidance

Frequently, some way can be found to avoid conflict. While avoidance may not bring any long-run benefits, it certainly can work as a short-run solution. Avoiding a conflict neither effectively resolves it nor eliminates it. Eventually, the conflict has to be faced. But in some circumstances, avoidance may be the best temporary alternative.

Smoothing

The technique known as smoothing emphasizes the common interests of the conflicting groups and de-emphasizes their differences. The basic belief behind smoothing is that stressing shared viewpoints on certain issues facilitates movement toward a common goal. If the differences between the groups are serious, smoothing—like avoidance—is at best a short-run solution.

Compromise

Compromise is a traditional method for resolving intergroup conflicts. With compromise, there is no distinct winner or loser, and the decision reached is probably not ideal for either group. Compromise can be used very effectively when the goal sought (e.g., money) can be divided equitably. If this is not possible, one group must give up something of value as a concession. Compromise may also involve third-party interventions, as well as total group or representative negotiating and voting.[12] The process of negotiation will be examined in detail later in the chapter.

Authoritative Command

The use of authority may be the oldest, most frequently used method for resolving intergroup conflict. Using this method, management simply resolves the conflict as it sees fit and communicates its desires to the groups involved. Subordinates usually abide by a superior's decision, whether or not they agree with it. Thus, authoritative command usually works in the short run. As with avoidance, smoothing, and compromise, however, it does not focus on the cause of the conflict but rather on the results of it. If the causes remain, conflict will probably recur.

---

[12]M. A. Neale and Max H. Bazerman, "The Effects of Framing and Negotiator Overconfidence on Bargaining Behavior and Outcomes," *Academy of Management Journal*, March 1985, pp. 34–49.

Altering the Human Variable

Altering the human variable involves trying to change group members' behavior. This method focuses on the cause or causes of the conflict and on the attitudes of the people involved. While the method is certainly difficult, it does center on the cause of the conflict. Part VI of this book focuses specifically on changing behavior. In it, we show that, although slower than other methods and often costly, the results of altering the human variable can be significant in the long run.

Altering the Structural Variables

Another way to resolve intergroup disputes is to alter the structural variables. This involves changing the formal structure of the organization. Structure refers to the fixed relationships among the jobs of the organization and includes the design of jobs and departments. Altering the structure of the organization to resolve intergroup conflict involves such things as transferring, exchanging, or rotating members of the groups or having a coordinator, liaison, or go-between who keeps groups communicating with one another.

Identifying a Common Enemy

In some respects, identifying a common enemy is the negative side of superordinate goals. Groups in conflict may temporarily resolve their differences and unite to combat a common enemy. The common enemy may be a competitor that has just introduced a clearly superior product. Conflicting groups in a bank may suddenly work in close harmony when government bank examiners make a visit. The common-enemy phenomenon is very evident in domestic conflicts. Most police officers prefer not to become involved in heated domestic conflicts because, in far too many cases, the combatants close ranks and turn on the police officer.

The most commonly used methods for managing intergroup conflict each have strengths and weaknesses and are effective or ineffective under different conditions and situations. What this chapter has said thus far about intergroup conflict is summarized in Figure 9–2. The figure illustrates the relationship between causes and types of intergroup conflict, the consequences of intergroup conflict, and techniques for resolution.

Whatever the techniques utilized to deal with intergroup conflict (and there undoubtedly are others), the important point is that managers must learn how to recognize both the existence and the causes of intergroup conflict. They must also develop skills to deal with it.

MANAGING INTERGROUP CONFLICT THROUGH NEGOTIATION

A widely used yet often less recognized method of managing intergroup conflict is through the process of negotiation. Despite its importance, the process is often misunderstood and badly carried out.[13] It entails having two sides, with differing or conflicting interests, come together to forge an

---

[13]D. A. Lax and J. K. Sebenius, *The Manager as Negotiator* (New York: Free Press, 1986), chap. 1.

FIGURE 9—2

An Overview of Intergroup Conflict

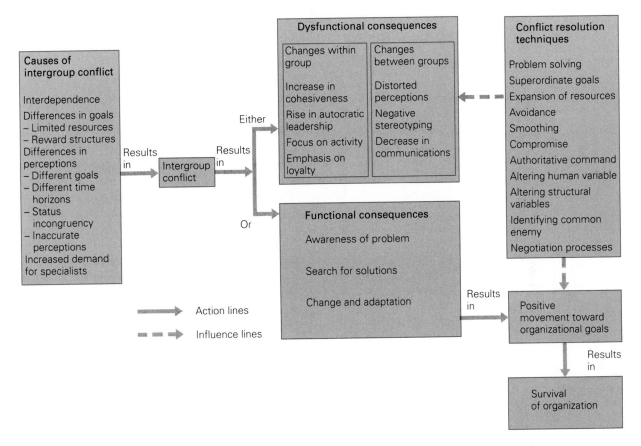

agreement. Usually, each side will bring to the process a series of proposals that then are discussed and acted upon. Everyone is familiar with the importance of bargaining to settle union disputes, formulate trade pacts, handle hostage situations, and reach arms agreements. Managers in organizations perform the same function on a continuing basis, negotiating with subordinates, superiors, vendors, and customers daily.

Group Negotiations

Group negotiations take place whenever the work of one group is dependent on the cooperation and actions of another group over which the first group's manager has no control.[14] Negotiations between marketing and production functions regarding order deliveries, between finance and engineering over research and development funding, and between maintenance and manufacturing over machine maintenance are all examples of the group process.

---

[14]Ibid.

Negotiation differs from compromise in that the only really successful negotiations are those in which all the affected parties walk away feeling like they have won.[15] Several tasks and tactics can be undertaken by managers prior to and during the negotiation process in order to increase the probability of achieving mutually beneficial results.

Prenegotiation Tasks

Understanding the other side.   Prior to sitting down and negotiating with managers and/or representatives of other groups, managers must thoroughly understand the other side's needs and positions regarding the issues to be resolved.[16] A product manager who desperately wants a customer order filled by manufacturing within the next two weeks should be aware of other obligations currently being placed on manufacturing. Likewise, a sales group negotiating with a customer over a major purchase should know how the customer uses the product/service, how important it is to the customer's business, what elements of the purchase (e.g., delivery date, training, warranty, price) are critical to the customer, and what other alternatives are available to the customer. Regardless of whether the customer is internal (a more frequent occurrence as a result of divisionalization and decentralization efforts undertaken by organizations) or external to the organization, the same procedures apply.

To gain this information, the manager must ask questions. Although positions are usually up-front, underlying interests or problems often are not.[17] A manager's goal should be to come to the negotiations with a full appreciation of the values, beliefs, and wants that drive the other side's actions. By freely exchanging information with the other group and performing as much outside or third-party research as possible, the manager can come prepared for the process. The element of surprise, which can prove to be of value in many business tactics, only serves to delay and hinder the negotiation process.

Knowing all the options.   Perhaps more important than the accumulation of information is its use in developing, understanding, and evaluating options available to resolve the conflict. Although the same issue may be negotiated over and over again, the outcomes may differ, depending on the parties involved or the timing of the negotiations.[18] One instance of a negotiation between two groups in an organization would be the funding of a capital investment. For example, discussions between finance and manufacturing may lead to the funds becoming available immediately, contingent on manufacturing's formulation of a detailed spending plan. A second outcome may consist of the funds being allocated over time, with the capital investment project being completed on a piecemeal basis. A third possible outcome would be the

---

[15]M. Zetlin, "The Art of Negotiating," *Success!,* June 1986, pp. 34–39.

[16]R. Dawson, "Resolving Angry Disagreements," *Supervisory Management,* January 1989, pp. 13–16.

[17]J. Grenig, "Better Communication Spells Success in Negotiations," *Impact,* December 2, 1985, pp. 6–7.

[18]Zetlin, "The Art of Negotiating."

allocation of a certain percentage of the funding, with the remainder coming from the sale of the assets being replaced. The important point is that the greater the number of options that can be identified, the greater is the likelihood that both groups can benefit from the negotiation process.

Negotiation Tactics

A countless number of specific negotiation tactics can be employed by managers involved in the process.[19] Several of the most often used ones will be discussed.

1. *Good-guy/bad-guy team.* Anyone who has read a detective story or seen a television police show is familiar with this tactic. The bad-guy member of the negotiating group advocates positions so much out of line that whatever the good guy says sounds reasonable.

2. *The nibble.* This tactic involves getting an additional concession or perk after an agreement has been reached. An example would be the request for an additional staff position by a marketing manager after an agreement was reached between his or her group and another marketing group regarding the division of market research duties.

3. *Joint problem solving.* A manager should never assume that the more one side wins, the more the other loses. Feasible alternatives not yet considered may exist. For instance, can manufacturing provide earlier completion dates on products if the sales department increases the order size and reduces the order frequency?

4. *Power of competition.* Tough negotiators use competition to make opponents think they don't need them. A line manager may use this tactic by threatening that his or her group will procure computer services outside the organization if the headquarters computer staff doesn't comply with demands. The most effective defense against this tactic is for a manager to remain objective. Do not commit quickly to unfavorable terms because of the fear of quick action on the other group's part.

5. *Splitting the difference.* This can be a useful technique when two groups come to an impasse. Managers should be careful, however, when the other group offers to split the difference too early. It may mean the other group has already gotten more than it thinks it deserves.

6. *Low-balling.* Ridiculously low offers and/or concessions are often used to lower the other group's expectations. A manager should not let this type of offer lower his or her expectations or goals; nor should the manager walk out assuming the other group's position is inflexible. The communications process should continue.

Different situations call for different tactics. A manager should be aware of the options available and strive to understand the rationale behind the options.

The Impact of Personalities on the Negotiation Process

The process of negotiating is a very people-oriented experience. In addition to understanding the goals, needs, and wants of the other side, the successful negotiator tries to understand the relevant personality traits of the other

---

[19]Ibid.

individual(s) negotiating.[20] Attitudes, opinions, emotions, and temperament all affect behavioral actions. Knowledge of these traits allows the manager to "read" and understand the opposing side, a valuable planning and operational tool in negotiations.

Four of the most common types of personalities a manager will face at the negotiation table are:[21]

1. *The power seeker*—task and results oriented, seeking challenges and opportunities, and potentially confrontational. A good decision maker.
2. *The persuader*—outgoing, socially oriented, ambitious, and tough under a cloak of amiability, likability, and affability. A dangerous opponent at the negotiating table.
3. *The reliable performer*—solid, dependable, comfortable in supportive surroundings, and resistant to sudden change. Dependent on past precedents for confidence in decision making.
4. *The limited performer*—lacking in self-confidence, in need of a sheltered environment, nondecisive, and introverted. Likely to crack under pressure.

The degree of a manager's ability to successfully understand and handle people will ultimately determine his or her success at negotiating.

The Role of Trust

Previously in the chapter, functional conflict was defined as a confrontation between groups that enhances and benefits the organization's effectiveness. In the negotiation process, there will be a greater likelihood of a beneficial outcome for the organization if a high degree of trust exists between the conflicting groups. Negotiators tend to regard making statements about their group's needs, wants, and priorities as risky and therefore are only willing to make them if there is mutual trust (i.e., they believe that the other side is also cooperatively motivated).[22] A high level of trust between the two conflicting parties will lead to greater openness and sharing of information.

A good negotiator will never place the other party in a position from which he or she can't move without losing face.[23] By offering choices between alternatives (sometimes done by following mild demands with stronger ones), the other side will be more likely to view the process as cooperative and thus be more willing to reach an agreement.

Alternatives to Direct Negotiations

Occasionally, groups are unable to resolve their differences through direct negotiations. Likely candidates are groups that conflict often or are led by

---

[20]C. W. Barlow and G. P. Eisen, *Purchasing Negotiations* (Boston: CBI Publishing, 1983), chap. 5.
[21]Ibid.
[22]D. G. Pruitt, J. M. Magenau, E. Konar-Goldband, and P. J. Carnevale, "Effects of Trust, Aspiration, and Gender on Negotiation Tactics," *Journal of Personality and Social Psychology* 38, no. 1 (1980), pp. 9–22.
[23]Grenig, "Better Communication."

managers of equal rank. Groups can reach a point where they feel stuck in disagreement. Rather than letting the conflict evolve into a long nasty battle, the two sides should seek outside help. A third party, often a CEO or other top executive, can be called in to mediate the dispute.[24] Use of a mediator allows an impartial person to work with the two sides to reach an agreement that benefits both sides and the organization as a whole. Bringing in a mediator early enough in the process allows conflicts to be resolved before group hostilities set in, which could lead to dysfunctional results.

An option to mediation is arbitration, in which groups are bound by the arbitrator's decision. Some companies set up formal committees of high-ranking executives whose sole purpose is to resolve disputes between groups.[25] These committees have the authority either to render a clear-cut decision in favor of one group, to provide for a mutually agreeable resolution, or to ask the involved parties to collect more information before a decision is reached. A benefit of this approach is that disagreeing parties don't have to compromise themselves in order to settle an issue. Once a decision is reached, both groups are able to return to a cooperative status.

MANAGING INTERGROUP CONFLICT THROUGH STIMULATION

Throughout this chapter, we have stressed that some conflict is beneficial. This point is made again in Figure 9–2, which focuses on some of the functional consequences of intergroup conflict. The figure indicates that, out of conflict, change can develop from an awareness of problems and from a creative search for alternative solutions. We have already examined a situation where conflict is dysfunctional because it is too high and requires resolution. It is also possible, however, that intergroup conflict may be too low and require stimulation to generate action. This section examines techniques that have successfully stimulated conflict to a functional level, where it contributes positively to organizational performance.[26]

Communication

By intelligent use of the organization's communication channels, a manager can stimulate beneficial conflict. Information can be placed carefully into formal channels to create ambiguity, reevaluation, or confrontation. Information that is threatening (e.g., a proposed budget cut) can stimulate functional conflict in a department and improve performance. Carefully planted rumors can also serve a useful purpose. For example, a hospital administrator may start a rumor about a proposed reorganization of the hospital. The purpose is

---

[24]L. G. Greenhaigh, "Secrets of Managing People Much, Much More Effectively," *Boardroom Reports*, November 1, 1989, pp. 13–14.

[25]B. Rodgers, *The IBM Way: Insights into the World's Most Successful Organization* (New York: Harper & Row, 1986).

[26]Robbins, *Managing Organizational Conflict*, chap. 9.

twofold: (1) to stimulate new ideas on how to more effectively carry out the mission of the hospital and (2) to reduce apathy among the staff.

Bringing Outside Individuals into the Group

A technique widely used to bring a stagnant organization or subunit of an organization "back to life" is to hire or transfer in individuals whose attitudes, values, and backgrounds differ from those of the group's present members. Many college faculties consciously seek new members with different backgrounds, often discouraging the hiring of graduates of their own programs. This is to ensure a diversity of viewpoints on the faculty. The technique of bringing in outsiders is also widely used in government and business. Recently, a bank president decided not to promote from within for a newly created position of marketing vice president. Instead, he hired a highly successful executive from the very competitive consumer products field. The bank president felt that while the outsider knew little about marketing financial services, her approach to and knowledge of marketing were what the bank needed to become a strong competitor.

Altering the Organization's Structure

Changing the structure of the organization not only helps resolve intergroup conflict; it also *creates* conflict. For example, suppose a school of business has one large department. The Department of Business Administration includes all of the faculty members who teach courses in management, marketing, finance, and production management. Accordingly, the department is rather large, with 32 members under one department chairperson, who reports to the dean. A new dean has recently been hired, and he is considering dividing the business administration unit into several separate departments (e.g., marketing, finance, management), each with five or six members and a chairperson. The reasoning is that reorganizing in this manner will create competition among the groups for resources, students, faculty, and so forth, where none existed before because there was only one group. The dilemma is whether this restructuring will improve performance.

Stimulating Competition

Many managers utilize various techniques to stimulate competition among groups. Incentives, such as awards and bonuses for outstanding performance, often stimulate competition. If properly utilized, such incentives help maintain a healthy atmosphere of competition that may result in a functional level of conflict. Incentives can be given for least defective parts, highest sales, best teacher, most new customers, or in any area where increased conflict is likely to lead to more effective performance.

Managing intergroup conflict through stimulation is a difficult challenge for a manager. It can easily backfire and very quickly become dysfunctional conflict.

SUMMARY OF KEY POINTS

— Conflict between groups is inevitable in organizations. This conflict may be positive or negative, depending on its impact on the organization's goal achievement.

— Functional conflict represents a confrontation between groups that enhances and benefits the organization's performance.

— Dysfunctional conflict results from a confrontation or interaction between groups that hinders the achievement of organizational goals.

— While most managers try to eliminate conflict, evidence indicates that for most organizations an optimal level of conflict can positively influence organizational performance.

— Intergroup conflict results from such factors as work interdependence, differences in goals, differences in perceptions, and the increasing demand for specialists.

— Dysfunctional conflict causes changes to take place within and between the groups involved. Within the group, there may be an increase in group cohesiveness, a rise in autocratic leadership, a focus on the task, and an emphasis on loyalty. Changes occurring between the groups include distorted perceptions, negative stereotyping, and a decrease in communication.

— One of the difficult tasks a manager must confront is diagnosing and managing intergroup conflict. Some useful techniques for resolving intergroup conflict include problem solving, superordinate goals, expansion of resources, avoidance, smoothing, compromise, authority, changing either the people or the organization's structure, and identifying a common enemy. The process of negotiation is also a valuable conflict management technique. Each of these techniques is useful in specific situations and circumstances.

— Conflict management techniques also exist for situations where the manager diagnoses a level of conflict that is dysfunctional because it is too low. Conflict stimulation techniques include using the communication channels, hiring or transferring in differently oriented individuals, changing the organization's structure, and stimulating competition. The important point is that effective conflict management involves both resolution and stimulation.

DISCUSSION AND REVIEW QUESTIONS

1. When trying to get into a closed class during registration, have you ever visited the faculty member's office in an attempt to convince him or her to let you in the class? Was it a process of negotiation? If so, discuss your experience.

2. Discuss a situation in which your group was involved in a conflict with another group. Describe any changes that took place within your group and between the two groups.

3. Some individuals believe that compromise is not a good conflict resolution technique, because there is no distinct winner and the decision reached is probably not ideal for either group. What are your beliefs about compromise as a conflict resolution technique?

4. In purchasing your last automobile, what kind of a negotiator was the seller? What technique did he or she use?

5. From your personal experiences, describe situations where conflict was functional and situations where it was dysfunctional.

6. Is the competition for grades among students functional or dysfunctional? Why?

7. Some individuals believe that conflict is necessary in order for change to take place. Comment.

8. Identify an intergroup conflict situation at your school. Is the conflict functional or dysfunctional? Why? If dysfunctional, what conflict management technique would you recommend to either resolve it or stimulate it?

9. Assume that you were chosen by the president of your school to recommend strategies for eliminating student apathy. What would your recommendation be?

10. What is meant when it is said that a manager must be able to diagnose intergroup conflict situations? How can a manager obtain these diagnostic skills?

ADDITIONAL REFERENCES

Barone, F. S. "Can Conflicting Values on the Change Team Work?" *Training and Development Journal,* 1986, pp. 50–53.

Benfield, C. J. "Problem Performers: The Third Party Solution." *Personnel Journal,* 1985, pp. 96–101.

Boulding, E. "Further Reflections on Conflict Management." In *Power and Conflict in Organizations,* ed. R. Kahn and E. Boulding. New York: Basic Books, 1964.

Kabaroff, B. "Potential Influence Structures as Sources of Interpersonal Conflict in Groups and Organizations." *Organizational Behavior and Human Decision Processes,* 1985, pp. 113–41.

Karambayya, R., and J. M. Brett. "Managers Handling Disputes: Third Party Roles and Perceptions of Fairness." *Academy of Management Journal,* 1989, pp. 685–704.

Kimberly, J. R., and R. E. Quinn, eds. *Managing Organizational Transitions.* Homewood, Ill.: Richard D. Irwin, 1984.

Mastenbrock, W. F. G. *Conflict Management and Organizational Development.* New York: John Wiley & Sons, 1987.

Pritchett, P. *After the Merger: Managing the Shockwaves.* Homewood, Ill.: Dow Jones-Irwin, 1985.

Sullivan, J.; R. Peterson; N. Kameda; and J. Shimada. "The Relationship between Conflict Resolution Approaches and Trust—A Cross-Cultural Study." *Academy of Management Journal,* 1981, pp. 803–15.

CHANGING WORK INTERDEPENDENCE AT FORD

The Taurus and Sable are two of Ford Motor Co.'s most successful entries into the highly competitive automobile marketplace. Why have these two models proved so successful? Ford believes that one of the reasons is the way the Taurus and Sable are built.

In the past, Ford followed a sequential approach in producing its cars. Each group completed its task before passing the vehicle on to the next group. Ford executives believe the sequential process stifled communication and reinforced the "not invented here" syndrome.

Formerly, the first stop in the new-car process was the styling department, which designed the overall appearance of the car. Next, engineers made the mechanics fit the designed shape. Then, manufacturing engineers determined how to stamp the sheet metal, build the chassis and components, and tool the assembly lines. Various supply firms then built specific components. Finally, after four or five years, workers were assigned the task of putting it all together.

Ford management concluded that allowing each group to work in virtual isolation was often the cause of problems. Designers and stylists might design a fender or bumper that was difficult for the manufacturing engineers to stamp. Engineers might mount spark plugs so that they are difficult for a mechanic to reach. Suppliers could rarely provide feedback, either to correct problems or suggest ideas or improvements, since they did not become involved until after the design was complete.

The Team Taurus concept operates on a total continuum where all groups were involved right from the start. Ford calls this "upstream-downstream involvement." Team members make visits to other Ford plants to identify the problems workers faced while building the cars the Taurus and Sable would replace. In one situation, this resulted in a design change that cut in half the number of workers needed to install a windshield. The Team Taurus concept encourages ideas from external suppliers, with very positive results and features that would not have otherwise been included in the cars.

Questions for Consideration

1. What do you think Ford means by the "not invented here" syndrome?
2. Ford has been building cars successfully for decades, using a sequential interdependence process. Can you give any reasons why problems with this process have apparently developed recently?
3. Do you foresee any potential problems with the Team Taurus concept?

"WE'LL JUST LET THEM SHOW THEIR STUFF"

Seven months ago, Captain Jon Shea announced that he would retire as police chief of Bay Ridge in one year. This advance notice was to allow Mayor Foster Taff and the city commissioners time to initiate the search and selection process for his replacement. Captain Shea had come to Bay Ridge six years earlier from a much larger city in Florida, where he had served as assistant police chief for five years.

During his term as chief, Shea has initiated many changes in the department. For the most part, the changes have been accepted, and nearly everyone agrees that Shea has done a fine job. The crime rate is below the national average; citizen-police relations appear good; and the morale of the police officers seems high. The Bay Ridge Police Association (BRPA), the organization that represents the police officers, occasionally has had minor disagreements with the chief and the city administration. However, these conflicts are small compared to the conflicts taking place in other cities. During the last five years, salaries for foot patrol officers surpassed the national average for cities the size of Bay Ridge.

Many Bay Ridge citizens have been quite surprised at Shea's relative success. The "outside candidate" for the job, he was selected over two veteran members of the force. The two inside candidates had engaged in bitter infighting that had divided the department at that time. One of them subsequently took a chief's position elsewhere. One city commissioner recently stated off the record, "I don't know how Shea did it. I didn't give him a snowball's chance six years ago. I thought he was crazy for taking the job and jumping into that hornet's nest. I guess being 1,000 miles away, he may not have known what he was getting into. But he sure has done one helluva job."

During the last seven months, an intensive search has been conducted. Applications have been received from all over the country. The search committee is made up of city officials. In addition, three professors from the management department of a local university were hired as an advisory committee to the search committee.

A total of 12 candidates were invited to interview personally for the job. Each was interviewed intensively by both committees. Surprisingly, both committees agree on the top three choices, although not in the same order. They are:

Philip Kinney.   23 years on the Bay Ridge Police Force. Holds the rank of captain and has been the head of the Robbery Division for three years. Excellent record in the Robbery Division. Holds every departmental commendation. He is 51 years old, married, with three grown children. He is a graduate of Bay Ridge High School and was one of the final two inside candidates in the search seven years ago. According to inside sources, he barely missed getting appointed.

Anthony Jackson.   Holds the rank of lieutenant in the Narcotics Division. Has had an outstanding record of accomplishment since becoming the first black person on the police force 15 years ago. Extremely popular in the black community and credited by the press with being instrumental in improving relations between the department and the black community. In fact, many black civic leaders have encouraged him to take a leave of absence to run for political office. He is 39 years old, married, with two young children. He holds a B.S. degree in law enforcement. He ran unsuccessfully for president of the BRPA in the last election.

Paul Stephens.   20 years in the department. Holds the rank of captain in the Homicide Division. Considered to be one of the top homicide detectives in this region of the country, often serving as a consultant to police departments in other cities on difficult cases. Holds every departmental commendation. He is single at present, with one child by an earlier marriage. He holds a B.S. degree in law enforcement and is president of the BRPA.

The candidates are presented to Mayor Taff by City Manager Bill Joslin, with the recommendation that he select one of the three to replace Shea. Joslin's first comment to Taff is, "Shea must have developed some good people while he was here. None of the outside candidates made the cut."

"Who does Shea like?" the mayor asks. "He's not saying," Joslin replies. "He says that since he won't have to work for the guy, he shouldn't influence the selection. That's also why he declined to serve on the search committee. He also told that to the press this morning. Apparently, someone leaked the names of the three finalists to a TV station. Reporters cornered Shea on the way out of his house this morning."

"Which one do you like?" asks Joslin, adding, "I think you should announce your choice as soon as you've made it."

"No," says the mayor. "I think I'll wait. We've got about five months." "Why wait?" asks Joslin. After a short silence, the mayor replies, "We'll just let them show their stuff."

Questions for Consideration

1. What do you think of the mayor's decision to wait? Why?
2. What are the advantages of waiting? The disadvantages?
3. Could the mayor's decision have any positive or negative impact outside the department? Discuss.

EXPERIENTIAL EXERCISE

THE OLD STACK PROBLEM

Objectives

1. To closely examine the dynamics of intergroup competition.
2. To illustrate how effectively a group is in developing a solution to a problem.

Starting the Exercise

Step 1: Group problem solving (30 minutes). Divide into groups of from four to six persons each. Each group member should read "The Problem" below. The best procedure is for each person to develop a solution independently and for the group to spend a period of time discussing these solutions without evaluating them. Then the solutions should be evaluated and the best solution adopted.

The problem may be assigned in advance of class in order to give students more time to develop solutions. However, the final discussion and selection process should be done as a group in the classroom.

Step 2: Select judges and spokespeople (5 minutes). Each group should select one member to serve on a panel of judges to select the best solution. A spokesperson must also be selected to present the solution to the panel of judges.

Step 3: Present solutions (15 minutes). Spokespeople for each group will present their group's solution to the judges and the remainder of the class. A chalkboard or flip chart should be used to illustrate the solution along with the spokesperson's explanation. The explanation should be brief and concise, and spokespeople may not criticize other solutions. The spokespeople should provide quality arguments in support of their solutions.

Step 4: Straw vote (5 minutes). After all group solutions have been presented, the judges may think about the solutions for one or two minutes, then judges will state in turn which solution they prefer. *Judges must make their judgments independently, without discussion among themselves.* Judges are asked simply to state the solution they prefer. They do not explain their reasons for voting. The instructor should record the number of votes given to each solution on the chalkboard or flip chart next to that solution.

Step 5: Modified problem solving (10 minutes). Student groups re-form and discuss their approach. Judges and spokespeople return to their original groups. At this time, the groups may not change the basic strategy of their solution, but they may provide refinements. Groups are encouraged to compare their solution to other solutions at this point and may instruct the spokesperson to present weaknesses in other solutions as well as strengths of their own. The group also has the freedom to nominate a new spokesperson or judge at this time.

Step 6: Restate solutions (10 minutes). The group spokespeople briefly restate the solutions using the earlier illustration. Minor modifications can be made. Spokespeople are encouraged to point out the strengths of their group's solutions and to criticize other solutions. The goal of the spokespeople is to persuade the judges that their group's solution is best.

The original source for this exercise could not be identified.

Step 7: Final vote.   The judges are given one or two minutes to individually decide which solution to vote for. Judges may not discuss the solutions among themselves, and they must state their vote out loud. The instructor will indicate the number of votes next to each solution's illustration. The solution that receives the most votes is the winner.

Step 8: Discussion (15 minutes).   The class as a whole should reflect on their experience and discuss what happened. Students are encouraged to be self-reflective about their feelings toward their own group's solution, toward the judges, and so on. Judges are encouraged to express their feelings about any pressures they felt from the group to vote in a certain way. The instructor or student may also wish to compare their observations to theories of intergroup behavior as illustrated in lectures or readings. The following questions may help guide that discussion.

1. Did any examples of scapegoating occur? Did losing groups express dissatisfaction or unfairness with the judges or the evaluation process?

2. Did any groups put pressure on the judges to act as a representative of their group rather than to vote in an unbiased fashion? Did judges feel pressure to represent their group even if pressure was not overtly expressed?

3. Did any groups develop a superiority complex, wherein they truly believed that their own group solution was best although from an objective perspective the solution may not have been best?

4. What was the reaction of winning versus losing groups? Did winners seem happy and satisfied while losers seemed discontented with one another or with the exercise?

5. During the second round of presentations, were certain solutions singled out for more criticism? Were these solutions the ones that received the most votes in the straw ballot, as if people were trying to tear down the strongest contender?

6. How does this group exercise compare to functioning of groups in the real world? These groups existed temporarily, while groups in the real world engage in real competitions and have strong and lasting commitments. Would representatives of real-world groups tend to reflect group wishes or to reach unbiased decisions? How might intergroup difficulties be overcome in organizations?

The Problem

An explosion has ripped a hole in a brick smokestack. The stack appears to be perfectly safe, but a portion of the access ladder has been ripped away and the remainder loosened. Your engineers need to inspect the damage immediately to determine whether the stack may collapse. How do you get one of your engineers up to inspect the hole safely and efficiently?

The smokestack is 140 feet high. The structure next to the smokestack is a water tower. In your solution you should use only those materials shown in Exhibit 1, including what you assume to be in the truck and sporting goods store.

EXHIBIT 1

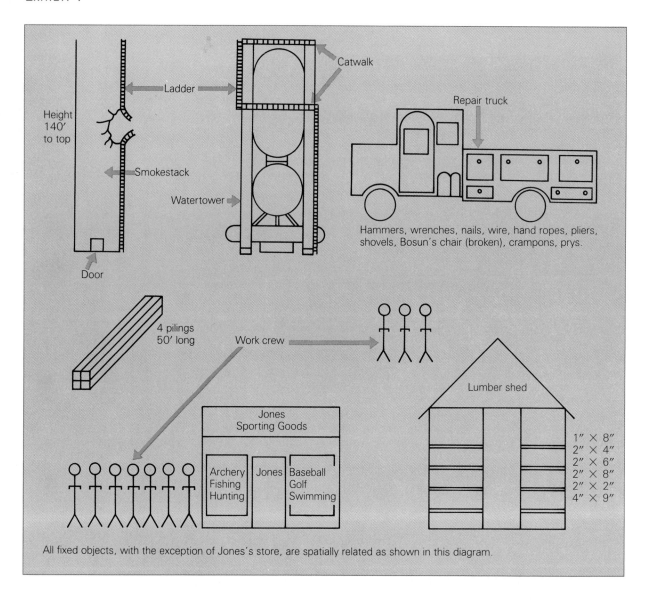

Height 140′ to top

Door

Ladder

Smokestack

Watertower

Catwalk

Repair truck

Hammers, wrenches, nails, wire, hand ropes, pliers, shovels, Bosun's chair (broken), crampons, prys.

4 pilings 50′ long

Work crew

Jones Sporting Goods

Archery Fishing Hunting

Jones

Baseball Golf Swimming

Lumber shed

1″ × 8″
2″ × 4″
2″ × 6″
2″ × 8″
2″ × 2″
4″ × 9″

All fixed objects, with the exception of Jones's store, are spatially related as shown in this diagram.

10

Power and Politics

LEARNING OBJECTIVES

After completing Chapter 10, you should be able to:

DEFINE
what is meant by the expression "two faces of power."

DESCRIBE
the five interpersonal power bases.

DISCUSS
how subunits within an organization acquire and use power.

COMPARE
the tactics used in the insurgency and counterinsurgency political games.

IDENTIFY
the reasons why an illusion of power can influence a person's behavior.

AN ORGANIZATIONAL
ISSUE FOR DEBATE   SHARING OF POWER: POSSIBLE OR IMPOSSIBLE?*

ARGUMENT FOR

In this chapter, we discuss the sharing of power—that is, involving others in decision making. Power in the United States has traditionally resided with the ownership of property, so the owner theoretically is the one who has to share power. Realistically, however, most power in American organizations is in the hands of professional managers. These managers must initiate the steps needed to share power with subordinates.

Managers today realize that the sharing of power is important to many workers. An example of a novel power-sharing idea took place in 1982, when General Motors and the United Auto Workers (UAW) union agreed to encourage labor-management cooperation. The contract was a step by the General Motors management to share power with the union. The chairman of General Motors declared, "It moves us in a new direction—away from confrontation and toward cooperation. . . . It seeks to directly involve the union and its members in the effort to make GM more competitive."

Contracts like that of General Motors and a new wave of management enthusiasm about power sharing are assumed to be good for business. To compete and to remain productive, management must share more of its decision-making power with subordinates. An adversarial relationship between management and nonmanagement employees is costly, disruptive, and not at all conducive to long-term success.

Management has taken decades to realize that the sharing of power is a necessity. Today, managers who refuse to share power are faced with an alienated work force, employees who are likely to withhold productivity, and even employees who turn to unionization as an answer to powerlessness.

Arguments for the sharing of power are so convincing with regard to productivity and satisfaction that it is a matter not of sharing power but of when and how much power will be shared.

ARGUMENT AGAINST

Top management sharing power with others by involving others in decision making is a dream, a myth. There must be a power center or focal point in any organization. Sharing power creates confusion and a vacuum in an organization. Managers should control power so that order and efficiency are built into the organization. Some individuals cite the 1982 General Motors contract with the UAW as an example of power sharing. Others disagree with this viewpoint. In fact, on the day the contract granting union concessions was announced, GM also announced an enhanced executive bonus plan. Management was considered, by some, not to be sharing but to be lining its own pockets with concessions.

Management cannot share power, because it must make rapid and tough decisions. People have to be transferred, fired, passed over for promotion, and so on. You cannot keep passing the buck on these kinds of tough business decisions. Democracy, participation, and power sharing are worthy goals when everything is operating smoothly and according to forecasts. However, this kind of dream world doesn't exist at U.S. Steel, Texas Instruments, General Motors, or any other firm.

Some individuals claim that increased foreign competition encourages power sharing. Again, this seems to be a misguided claim. What is needed to combat foreign competition is strong management decision makers who take decisive action and who can make decisions without always attempting to reach a consensus. You just cannot respond to any kind of competition if your hands are tied by worrying about sharing power with others.

Power sharing is like other theories; it raises some interesting points but is not very practical. Proponents of power sharing are just not able to support their assumptions and wishes with factual information. In the real organizational world, power sharing costs more than the benefits it generates. It costs in terms of slow decision making, clumsy decision making, and a management by consensus orientation. These costs are too much for any organization in a competitive, quick-moving environment to bear.

*Related discussions can be found in A. Kakabadse and C. Parker, eds., *Power, Politics and Organizations* (New York: John Wiley & Sons, 1984); Trudy Heller, "Changing Authority Patterns: A Cultural Perspective," *Academy of Management Review*, July 1985, pp. 488–95; Robert Kuttner, "Sharing Power at Eastern Airlines," *Harvard Business Review*, May–June 1985, pp. 91–102; Fred E. Jandt, *Win-Win Negotiation* (New York: John Wiley & Sons, 1987).

Power is a pervasive part of the fabric of organizational life.[1] Both managers and nonmanagers use it. They manipulate power to accomplish goals and, in many cases, to strengthen their own positions. A person's success or failure at using or reacting to power is largely determined by understanding power, knowing how and when to use it, and being able to anticipate its probable effects.

Behavioral scientist Warren Bennis has said about power: "It is the organization's last dirty secret." Power is considered dirty because some use it to hurt other people or to achieve self-serving purposes. But when power is used in an ethical and fair way, there is nothing dirty about it. The purpose of this chapter is to explain power and its uses in organizational settings. We examine the bases of power, how power is used, the need for power, and the relationship between power and organizational politics. The chapter indicates that power is not a dirty secret but is actually a mechanism used continually to achieve organizational, group, and individual goals.

POWER AND AUTHORITY

The study of power and its effects is important to understanding how organizations operate. Every interaction and every social relationship in an organization involve an exercise of power.[2] How organizational subunits and individuals are controlled is related to the issue of power. **Power** is simply the

POWER
Ability to get someone to do something one wants done.

[1]See Iain Mangham, *Power and Performance in Organizations* (New York: Basil Blackwell, 1988), for a discussion of power in organizations.

[2]Anthony T. Cobb, "Political Diagnosis: Applications in Organizational Development," *Academy of Management Review*, July 1986, pp. 482–96.

ability to get things done the way one wants them to be done. The power of a manager who wants increased financial resources is her ability to get the desired resources. The power of a salesperson who wants his sales territory expanded is his ability to get the larger territory.

Power involves a relationship between two or more people. Robert Dahl, a political scientist, captures this important relational focus when he defines power as: "A has power over B to the extent that he can get B to do something B would not otherwise do."[3] A person or group cannot have power in isolation; power has to be exercised or have the potential for being exercised in relation to some other person or group.

The Organizational Issue for Debate points out that some people feel that power can be used in isolation or by one person over other people. We agree with the power-sharing argument that unless some power is shared, adversarial attitudes and relationships will increase. However, this raises the problem of determining how power sharing can be implemented. Power sharing is a process that requires some time to develop within an organization's culture. It cannot be forced on people. Time is needed to develop (1) better lines of communication, (2) more trust, and (3) openness between the power sharers—managers and subordinates or subunits. Since organizations have for many years relied on authority hierarchies to accomplish goals, it is unreasonable to expect managers simply to begin sharing their power with others without some resistance.[4]

In the literature, a distinction is made between power and authority. Max Weber called attention to differences between these two concepts.[5] He believed that power involved force and coercion. Authority, however, is a subset of power. Much narrower in scope, authority does not carry the implication of force. Rather, it involves a "suspension of judgment" on the part of its recipients. **Authority** is the formal power that a person has because of the position that he or she holds in the organization. Directives or orders from a manager in an authority position are followed because they must be followed. That is, persons in higher positions have legal authority over subordinates in lower positions. In the authority hierarchy, the chief executive officer (CEO) is above the district manager, who is above the salesperson. Today, authority is considered to have the following properties:

1. It is invested in a person's position. An individual has authority because of the position that he or she holds, not because of any specific personal characteristics.

2. It is accepted by subordinates. The individual in a legal authority position exercises authority and can gain compliance because he or she has a legitimate right.

3. Authority is used vertically. Authority flows from the top down in the hierarchy of an organization.

AUTHORITY

Formal power a person holds because of his or her position in the organizational hierarchy.

---

[3]Robert Dahl, "The Concept of Power," *Behavioral Science,* July 1957, pp. 202–3.

[4]J. Lawrence French and Joseph Rosenstein, "Employee Ownership, Work Attitudes, and Power Relationships," *Academy of Management Journal,* December 1984, pp. 861–69.

[5]Max Weber, *Theory of Social and Economic Organization* (New York: Free Press, 1947), pp. 324–28.

Influence is a word that one often comes across when studying power. We agree with Henry Mintzberg and others that making a distinction between influence and power adds little to understanding.[6] Therefore, we use the terms *influence* and *power* interchangeably throughout this chapter.

Power can be derived from many sources. How it is obtained in an organization depends to a large extent on the type of power being sought. Power can be derived from interpersonal, structural, and situational bases.

INTERPERSONAL POWER

John French and Bertram Raven suggested five interpersonal bases of power: legitimate, reward, coercive, expert, and referent.[7]

Legitimate Power

Legitimate power is a person's ability to influence because of position. A person at a higher level has power over people below. In theory, organizational equals (e.g., all first-line supervisors) have equal legitimate power. However, each person with legitimate power uses it with a personal flair. Legitimate power is similar to Weber's concept of authority.

Subordinates play a major role in the exercise of legitimate power. If subordinates view the use of power as legitimate, they comply. However, the culture, customs, and value systems of an organization determine the limits of legitimate power. A company president who suggests that all employees should vote for a particular political candidate may find that only some people comply with the suggestion.

LEGITIMATE POWER
A person's ability to influence others because of being in a more powerful position.

Reward Power

A person derives power from the ability to reward compliance. **Reward power** is used to back up the use of legitimate power. If followers value the rewards or potential rewards that the person can provide (recognition, a good job assignment, a pay raise, additional resources to complete a job), they may respond to orders, requests, and directions. For example, a sales manager who can reward salespeople with cash bonuses, expanded client lists, or additional entertainment funds can exert reward power.

REWARD POWER
The ability one has to reward the behavior of others.

Coercive Power

The opposite of reward power is **coercive power,** the power to punish. Followers may comply because of fear. A manager may block a promotion or transfer a subordinate for poor performance. These practices, and the fear that they will be used, are coercive power. Although punishment may result in

COERCIVE POWER
Capability to punish noncompliance of followers.

---

[6]Henry Mintzberg, *Power in and around Organizations* (Englewood Cliffs, N.J.: Prentice Hall, 1983), p. 5; Henry Mintzberg, "Power and Organization Life Cycles," *Academy of Management Review,* April 1984, pp. 207–24.

[7]John R. P. French and Bertram Raven, "The Basis of Social Power," in *Studies in Social Power,* ed. D. Cartwright (Ann Arbor: Institute for Social Research, University of Michigan, 1959), pp. 150–67.

BOSSES WHO RELY ON TWO TYPES OF POWER

Today, more and more chief executives rely on two kinds of personal power: expertise and referent. This use of personal power stems from changes in the direction in which corporate America is heading. Mobile work forces, the flattening of organizations, changes in employee attitudes, forced compensation systems, affirmative action laws, and circumscribed obligations have forced CEOs to rely less and less on the traditional kinds of power — reward, punishment, and authority. Instead, top executives are finding that they can actually wield more power by spreading it around.

To confer power on subordinates without giving up personal responsibility for the organization's performance, the CEO must do three things: (1) unambiguously and loudly delegate authority, (2) implement a rigorous planning system, and (3) develop a strong communications system.

Ralph Stayer, CEO of Johnsonville Foods, gives volunteers from the shop floor the power to develop manufacturing budgets. Another group of workers designs the manufacturing line. Employees are responsible for developing discounted cash flow projections to back up capital investment requests. Stayer's objective is to have goals set as far down in the company as possible, giving top management time for prioritizing goals. Does the system work? Johnsonville has doubled its return on assets, and sales are rising at 15 percent a year.

some unexpected side effects (discussed in Chapter 6), it is a form of coercive power that is still being used to bring about compliance or to correct nonproductive behavior in organizations.

Expert Power

EXPERT POWER
The power to influence others because of possessing special expertise.

A person who possesses special expertise that is highly valued has **expert power.** Experts have power even when their rank is low. An individual may possess expertise on technical, administrative, or personal matters. The more difficult it is to replace the expert, the greater is the degree of expert power that he or she possesses.

Expert power is a personal characteristic, while legitimate, reward, and coercive power are largely prescribed by the organization. A secretary who has a relatively low-level organizational position may have high expert power because he or she knows the details of operating the business — where everything is or how to handle difficult situations.

Referent Power

REFERENT POWER
Power based on charisma due to personality or style of behavior.

Many individuals identify with and are influenced by a person because of the latter's personality or behavioral style. The charisma of the person is the basis of **referent power.** A person with charisma is admired because of his or her personality. The strength of a person's charisma is an indication of his or her referent power. Charisma is a term often used to describe the magnetic personalities of some politicians, entertainers, or sports figures. Some managers are also regarded by their subordinates as extremely charismatic.

At Heinz, variations on the philosophies of management by objectives and management by exception flourish. Most divisions are run on management-by-exception principles, using variances from projections to provide clues on plans going awry. Both yearly and quarterly goals are communicated and well understood by managers. Managers won't make decisions inconsistent with those goals. When problems develop, they are clearly seen and acted upon. Managers have much incentive to accept major responsibilities. Under the regime of current CEO J. F. O'Reilly, employee ownership of Heinz stock has risen from 4 percent of the total to 16 percent.

Communication is seen as the most important source of personal power. T. Boone Pickens, Jr., CEO of Mesa Petroleum, believes "talking is the natural way to do business": writing is for keeping records and pinning down details, but talk generates ideas. Smart CEOs realize that they have to actively encourage communication. J. Carter Fox, CEO of Chesapeake Corp., requires his division heads to take turns making presentations to the board. Heinz promotes communication through interdepartmental task forces that share knowledge and make policy. Colgate has advisory groups that serve as channels of communication, as well as sources of specialized expertise.

Source: Thomas A. Stewart, "New Ways to Exercise Power," *Fortune,* November 6, 1989, pp. 52–64; T. Boone Pickens, Jr., *Boone* (Boston: Houghton Mifflin, 1987).

The five bases of interpersonal power can be divided into two major categories: organizational and personal. Legitimate, reward, and coercive power are primarily prescribed by the organization, the position, formal groups, or specific interaction patterns. A person's legitimate power can be changed by transferring the person, rewriting the job description, or reducing the person's power by restructuring the organization. In contrast, expert and referent power are very personal. A person has expertise, or he or she develops a set of credentials or the image characteristic of an expert. A person has or does not have charisma. It cannot be tampered with, modified, or developed through training programs. It is a personal style that is quite individualized.

The five types of interpersonal power are not independent. On the contrary, a person can use these power bases effectively in various combinations. Also, the use of a particular power base can affect the others. For example, a manager who uses coercive power to punish a subordinate may lose his referent power. The Close-Up focuses on managers who rely heavily on two types of power.

Need for Power

Throughout history, human beings have been fascinated by power. In ancient Chinese writings, concern about power is clearly expressed—the taming power of the great, the power of light, the power of the dark. Early religious writings also contain numerous references to persons who possess or acquire power. Historical records show differences in the extent to which individuals have pursued, feared, enjoyed, and misused power. Currently, the image of those who seek power is, for the most part, quite negative. For example, power seekers have been portrayed as:[8]

> Neurotics who are covering up feelings of inferiority, anxiety, or hatred.
>
> Persons substituting power for lack of affection, being alone, or being deprived of friendship.
>
> Those attempting to compensate for some childhood deprivation.

The power seeker has been labeled as weak, neurotic, and troubled. This, of course, may be true for some (e.g., Adolf Hitler), but to place every power seeker in this category seems too sweeping and general.

NEED FOR POWER (N POW)
Desire to influence others.

David McClelland proposes that power can be responsibly sought and used.[9] In addition to examining the need for achievement (discussed in Chapter 4), McClelland examined the **need for power,** or (as he refers to it) n Pow. McClelland defines *n Pow* as the desire to have an impact on others. This type of impact may be shown basically in three ways: (1) by strong action, by giving help or advice, by controlling someone; (2) by action that produces emotion in others; and (3) by a concern for reputation.

Research has attempted to determine how people high in n Pow behave as contrasted with people low in n Pow. In general, individuals high in n Pow (1) are competitive and aggressive, (2) are interested in prestige possessions (e.g., an expensive car), (3) prefer action situations, and (4) join a number of groups. Research on n Pow conducted by McClelland and his associates reveals that the most effective organizational managers share these characteristics:[10]

- They have a high n Pow.
- They use their power to achieve organizational goals.
- They practice a participative or "coaching" style when interacting with followers.
- They do not concentrate on developing close relations with others.

The effective managers in McClelland's research were designated as *institutional managers* because they used their power to achieve organizational (institutional) goals. The institutional managers were more effective than the *personal power managers,* who used their power for personal gain, and the *affiliative managers,* who were more concerned with being liked than with using their power. Figure 10–1 summarizes the responses of subordinates of managers who were perceived as using the three different power styles.

McClelland also found that managers who score high in n Pow, low in need for affiliation, and high in self-control are very effective. Young managers who displayed these characteristics when they entered AT&T were more likely to

---

[8]David Kipnis, *The Powerholders* (Chicago: University of Chicago Press, 1976), pp. 149–56. Kipnis doesn't present these characteristics as fitting all power seekers but only as a summarization of the negative face of power seekers.

[9]David C. McClelland, *Power: The Inner Experience* (New York: Irvington, 1975), p. 7.

[10]David C. McClelland and David H. Burnham, "Power Is the Great Motivator," *Harvard Business Review,* March–April 1976, pp. 100–110.

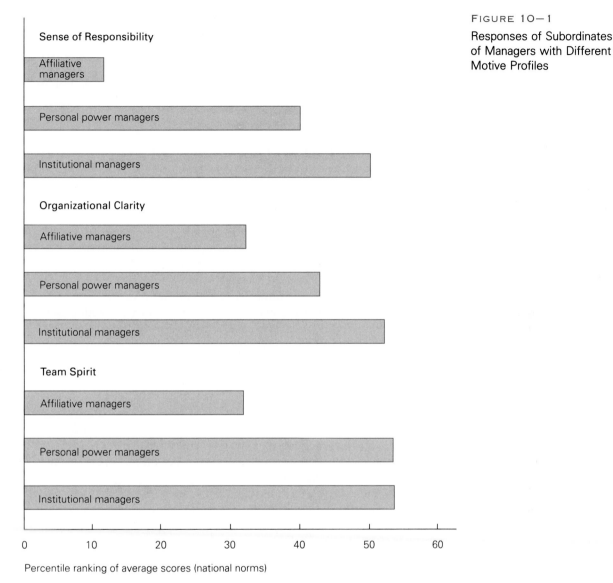

FIGURE 10–1

Responses of Subordinates
of Managers with Different
Motive Profiles

Percentile ranking of average scores (national norms)

Source: Reprinted by permission of the *Harvard Business Review.* An exhibit from David C. McClelland
and David H. Burnham, "Power Is the Great Motivator," *Harvard Business Review,* March–April 1976.
Copyright © 1976 by the President and Fellows of Harvard College; all rights reserved.

have been promoted to high management levels in the company after 16 years
than were those who did not display these characteristics.[11]

The research stimulated and conducted by McClelland presents evidence
that is contrary to the negative image historically attached to all power seekers.

---

[11]David C. McClelland, "Understanding Psychological Man," *Psychology Today,* May 1982,
pp. 55–56.

Stating that all power seekers are weak, neurotic, and troubled is as inaccurate as stating that all power seekers are effective, well adjusted, and highly motivated. McClelland refers to the "two faces of power." One face depicts power seekers in negative terms; the other suggests that power can be used to accomplish goals, use resources efficiently, and help followers feel more powerful themselves.[12]

STRUCTURAL AND SITUATIONAL POWER

Power is primarily prescribed by the structure of the organization,[13] which is the control mechanism by which the organization is governed. The organization's structural arrangements allocate decision-making discretion to various positions. Structure also establishes the patterns of communication and the flow of information. Thus, organizational structure creates formal power and authority by specifying certain individuals to perform specific job tasks and make certain decisions. Structure also encourages informal power through its effect on information and communication within the system.

We have already discussed how formal position is associated with power and authority. Certain rights, responsibilities, and privileges accrue from a person's position. Other forms of structural power exist because of resources, decision making, and information.[14]

Resources

Rosabeth Kanter argues quite convincingly that power stems from (1) access to resources, information, and support and (2) the ability to get cooperation in doing necessary work.[15] Power occurs when a person has open channels to resources—money, workers, technology, materials, and customers. In organizations, vital resources are allocated downward along the lines of the hierarchy.[16] The top-level manager has more power to allocate resources than do managers further down in the managerial hierarchy. The lower-level manager receives resources that are granted by top-level managers. To ensure compliance with goals, top-level managers (e.g., presidents, vice presidents, directors) allocate resources on the basis of performance and compliance. Thus, a top-level manager usually has power over a lower-level manager, who must receive resources from above to accomplish goals.

---

[12]For a different look at this issue, see Shoshana Zuboff, *In the Age of the Smart Machine: The Future of Work and Power* (New York: Basic Books, 1988).

[13]Jeffrey Pfeffer, *Power in Organizations* (Marshfield, Mass.: Pitman Publishing, 1981), p. 117; Dean Tjosvold, "Power and Social Context in Superior-Subordinate Interaction," *Organizational Behavior and Human Decision Processes,* Summer 1985, pp. 281–93.

[14]Pfeffer, *Power,* pp. 104–22; Rosabeth M. Kanter, "Power Failures in Management Circuits," *Harvard Business Review,* July–August 1979, pp. 65–75; Hugh R. Taylor, "Power at Work," *Personnel Journal,* April 1986, pp. 42–49.

[15]Kanter, "Power Failures."

[16]David Ulrich and Jay B. Barney, "Perspectives in Organizations: Resource Dependence, Efficiency, and Population," *Academy of Management Review,* July 1984, pp. 471–81.

The *dependency* relationship exists because of limited resources and division of labor.[17] The division of labor (e.g., positions in the hierarchy) grants upper management, by position, the privilege of allocating limited resources.[18] Without adequate compliance with top management's goals and requests, a lower-level manager cannot receive the necessary resources to do the job.

Decision-Making Power

The degree to which individuals or subunits (e.g., a department or a special project group) can affect decision making determines their level of power. A person or subunit with power can influence how the decision-making process occurs, what alternatives are considered, and when a decision is made. For example, when Richard J. Daley was mayor of Chicago in the 1960s and 70s, he was recognized as a power broker. He not only influenced the decision-making process but also had the power to decide which decision would be given priority in the city council and when decisions would be made.[19] He was a powerful politician because he was considered to be an expert at controlling each step in making important decisions.[20] His son was elected mayor of Chicago in 1989 and does not have the level of power that his father possessed and used.

Information Power

Having access to relevant and important information gives power. Information is the basis for making effective decisions. Thus, those who possess information needed to make optimal decisions have power. The accountant's position in the organization structure may not accurately portray the power that he or she wields. Accountants do not generally have a particularly strong or apparent interpersonal power base in an organization; they have power because they control important information. A true picture of a person's power is provided not only by the person's position but also by the person's access to relevant information.

Many organizational situations illustrate how different sources can create powerful and powerless managers. Powerful managers exist because they allocate required resources, make crucial decisions, and have access to important information. They are likely to make things happen. Powerless managers, however, lack the resources, information, and decision-making prerogatives needed to be productive. Table 10-1 presents some of the common symptoms

---

[17]For a study of dependency between organizations, see Steven S. Skinner, James H. Donnelly, Jr., and John M. Ivancevich, "Effects of Transactional Form on Environmental Linkages and Power-Dependence Relations," *Academy of Management Journal,* September 1987, pp. 577–88.

[18]For a discussion of the resource issue in a nonbusiness setting, see William McKinley, Joseph L. C. Cheng, and Allen G. Schnick, "Perception of Resource Criticality in Times of Resource Scarcity: The Case of University Departments," *Academy of Management Journal,* September 1986, pp. 621–31.

[19]Mike Royko, *Boss: Richard J. Daley of Chicago* (New York: E. P. Dutton, 1971).

[20]Also see Susan L. Carpenter and W. J. D. Kennedy, *Managing Public Disputes* (San Francisco: Jossey-Bass, 1988).

TABLE 10—1

Symptoms and Sources of
Powerlessness

Position	Symptoms	Sources
First-line supervisors (e.g., line supervisor)	Supervise too closely. Fail to train subordinates. Not sufficiently oriented to the management team. Inclined to do the job themselves.	Routine, rule-minded jobs. Limited lines of communication. Limited advancement opportunities for themselves and their subordinates.
Staff professionals (e.g., corporate lawyer, personnel/human resources specialists)	Create islands and set themselves up as experts. Use professional standards as basis for judging work that distinguishes them from others. Resist change and become conservative risk-takers.	Routine tasks are only adjuncts to real line job. Blocked career advancement. Replaced by outside consultants for nonroutine work.
Top-level managers (e.g., chief executive officer, vice president)	Have short-term time horizon. Emphasize top-down communication systems. Reward followers to think like the manager; do not welcome bearers of bad news.	Uncontrollable lines of supply. Limited or blocked lines of information about lower managerial levels. Diminished lines of support because of challenges to legitimacy.

Source: Reprinted by permission of the Harvard Business Review. Adapted from "Power Failures in Management Circuits," by Rosabeth Moss Kanter (July–August 1979), p. 73. Copyright © 1979 by the President and Fellows of Harvard College, all rights reserved.

and sources of powerlessness of first-line supervisors, staff professionals, and top-level managers. The table indicates that a first-line manager may display a number of symptoms of powerlessness, such as supervising very closely and not showing much concern about training or developing subordinates. If these symptoms persist, the individual is probably powerless.

UPWARD FLOW OF POWER

Most people think of power as being exerted in a downward direction. It is true that individuals in positions at the lower end of the power hierarchy generally have less power than do individuals in higher-level positions. However, power can also be exercised up the organization.[21] In sociological terms, a person exerting power-upward has personal power but no authority. The power-sharing argument in the opening Organizational Issue for Debate suggests that power should flow not only downward but also upward if optimal performance is to be accomplished.[22]

---

[21]Gary Yukl and Tom Taber, "The Effective Use of Managerial Power," *Personnel*, March–April 1983, pp. 37–44; Henry Mintzberg, "The Organization of Political Arena," *Journal of Management Studies*, March 1985, pp. 135–54.

[22]Keith G. Provan, "Recognizing, Measuring, and Interpreting the Potential/Enacted Power Distinction in Organizational Research," *Academy of Management Review*, October 1980, pp. 549–59; K. Macher, "The Politics of Organization," *Personnel Journal*, February 1986, pp. 80–86.

The discussion of legitimate authority suggests that individuals in higher-level positions (supervisors) can exert only as much power as individuals in lower-level positions (subordinates) accept. The concept of subordinate power can be linked to expertise, location, and information. Significant upward power or influence can sometimes be exerted by a relatively low-ranking secretary, computer programmer, or clerk who possesses expertise, is in a position to interact with important individuals, or has access to and control of important information.[23] Expertise, location, and information control are important determinants of the power potential of employees at lower levels of the hierarchy.

Two important sources of upward influence have been referred to as manipulative persuasion and manipulation.[24] *Manipulative persuasion* is a person's direct attempt to disguise the true persuasion objective. This is the hidden-agenda ploy. Through persuasive skills, the individual accumulates power to gain an objective. For example, a manager who is trying to have a poor worker transferred may present only the strengths of the worker to a project manager looking for people for a new assignment. Although the manager's true objective is to unload the worker on someone else, that objective is hidden within the manager's persuasive presentation of the employee's strengths.

Manipulation refers to the form of influence in which both the objective and the attempt are concealed. For example, instead of providing customer complaints to a manager as they are received, the clerk receiving the complaints may arrange them in such a way as to place other employees or a department in a more or less favorable light.[25] If the clerk arranges the incoming complaints so that the manager in charge reprimands a departmental supervisor whom the clerk doesn't like, the clerk's action would be considered manipulation in the upward direction. The Close-Up examines employee stock ownership plans (ESOPs), a possible future form of significant upward power.

INTERDEPARTMENTAL POWER

To this point, the primary focus has been on individual power and how it is obtained. However, interdepartmental power is also important. Even though all vice presidents of departments at the same level in the managerial hierarchy are supposed to have the same amount of power, this is not usually the case. Some vice presidents have more power by virtue of being

[23]Lyman W. Porter, Robert W. Allen, and H. L. Angee, "The Politics of Upward Influence in Organizations," in *Research in Organizational Behavior,* ed. Larry L. Cummings and Barry M. Staw (Greenwich, Conn.: JAI Press, 1981), pp. 181–216.

[24]For excellent discussions of upward influence, see Richard T. Mowday, "The Exercise of Upward Influence in Organizations," *Administrative Science Quarterly,* March 1978, pp. 137–56; Richard S. Blackburn, "Lower Participant Power: Toward a Conceptual Integration," *Academy of Management Review,* January 1981, pp. 127–31.

[25]For an interesting discussion of this and related topics, see Robert C. Liden and Terence R. Mitchell, "Ingratiating Behaviors in Organizational Settings," *Academy of Management Review,* October 1988, pp. 572–87.

WILL ESOPS INCREASE UPWARD POWER?

Across America, a major change in the way companies are owned and operated is quietly taking place. Corporate America is rushing to embrace the idea of employee stock ownership plans (ESOPs). What was once unthinkable by corporate executives, the giving up of billions of dollars of equity and the margin of power to employees, is now occurring with regularity. Large companies—including ITT, Xerox, Delta, Procter & Gamble, J. C. Penney, Anheuser-Busch, Texaco, U.S. West, and Polaroid—have instituted ESOPs. Predicts Polaroid CEO MacAllister Booth: "Twenty years from now, we'll find that employees have a sizable stake in every American corporation."

Why have ESOPs become so popular? Answers to this question are as varied as the companies that have instituted ESOPs. For some companies, ESOPs cut the tax bill and establish a lid on pension and medical costs. For others, an ESOP provides an effective defense against hostile takeover attempts. In addition, an ESOP can serve to increase employee morale. To date, most companies have allowed financial and tax issues to dominate management thinking. However, evidence is mounting that ESOPs are a means by which gains in productivity can occur. At Brunswick, sales per employee have jumped nearly 50 percent since an ESOP was set up in 1983.

But with the gains come uncertainties. Productivity increases are not guaranteed. Some studies have shown that ESOPs help little unless management is willing to

in a particular unit or department. In an early study, Charles Perrow surveyed managers in 12 industrial firms to consider subunit power.[26] He was concerned about power differences in the production, sales and marketing, research and development, and finance and accounting departments. Perrow's survey results indicated that sales and marketing units had the most power. The subunit rank-ordering from most powerful to least powerful was (1) sales and marketing, (2) production, (3) finance and accounting, and (4) research and development.

STRATEGIC CONTINGENCY
Event or activity of crucial importance to complete project or accomplish goal.

The strategic contingency theory developed by D. J. Hickson focused on subunit power. A **strategic contingency** is an event or activity that is extremely important for accomplishing organizational goals.[27] Michel Crozier, a French sociologist, provided insight into the idea of strategic contingencies. He studied the relationships between workers in the production and maintenance departments of French tobacco processing plants. Crozier found that the production workers enjoyed job security because of tenure, were protected against unfair disciplinary action, and were not replaced or transferred arbitrarily. The production workers were less skilled than the maintenance workers. The maintenance workers were highly skilled; they were recruited and selected only after going through a rigorous screening process.

---

[26]Charles Perrow, "Departmental Power and Perspective in Industrial Firms," in *Power in Organizations,* ed. M. N. Zald (Nashville, Tenn.: Vanderbilt University Press, 1970), pp. 59–89.

[27]Michel Crozier, *The Bureaucratic Phenomenon* (Chicago: University of Chicago Press, 1964).

give workers a genuine role in running things. ESOPs present a risk to current management. Managers who alienate the owner-employees just might end up being thrown out in favor of a raider. ESOPs also can present a risk to employees. The more an employee relies on an ESOP for pension income, the more dependent that employee is on the price of the company's stock. This leaves employees dependent on Wall Street as well as vulnerable to management mistakes. Finally, Congress could change the tax rules governing ESOPs as budget pressures intensify.

Procter & Gamble serves as a role model for other companies. With its new ESOP, employees will eventually own 20 percent of the company. The company already has a profit sharing plan in place and serves as a leader in workplace innovation. In many of its plants, products are produced by teams of hourly workers who, for most practical purposes, manage themselves.

The future of ESOPs, in a large way, is dependent on the willingness of management to actively encourage employee involvement. If management puts ESOPs in place solely as a means for establishing a tax shelter, the opportunity for lasting productivity gains will be lost.

Source: Christopher Farrell and John Hoerr, "ESOPs: Are They Good for You?" *Business Week*, May 15, 1989, pp. 116–23; Sylvia Nasar, "The Foolish Rush to ESOPs," *Fortune*, September 25, 1989, pp. 141–50.

The production workers were dependent on the maintenance workers. This power differential was explained in terms of the control exercised by the maintenance workers over an important contingency. If machines were shut down, the entire plant came to a halt. Efficiently functioning machines were needed to accomplish output goals. Since they repaired machines at the request of the production workers, the maintenance workers possessed significant power.

When machines were down, the job performance of the production workers suffered. Stoppages totally disrupted the work flow and the output of the production workers. Crozier proposed that the maintenance workers controlled a strategically contingent factor in the production process. Crozier's study provided clear evidence of interdepartmental power differences. The study also stimulated other studies that eventually resulted in a strategic contingencies explanation of power differences.[28]

Hinnings and associates studied the strategic contingency explanation of power in 28 subunits of seven manufacturing organizations in Canada and the

---

[28]The strategic contingency theory was developed by D. J. Hickson and his colleagues. Other theorists and researchers have modified and discussed this approach. However, readers are urged to use the original sources for a discussion of the complete and unmodified theory. See D. J. Hickson, C. R. Hinnings, C. A. Lee, R. E. Schneck, and J. M. Pennings, "A Strategic Contingency Theory of Intraorganizational Power," *Administrative Science Quarterly*, June 1971, pp. 219–29; C. R. Hinnings, D. J. Hickson, J. M. Pennings, and R. E. Schneck, "Structural Conditions of Intraorganizational Power," *Administrative Science Quarterly*, March 1974, pp. 22–44.

FIGURE 10—2

A Strategic Contingency
Model of Subunit Power

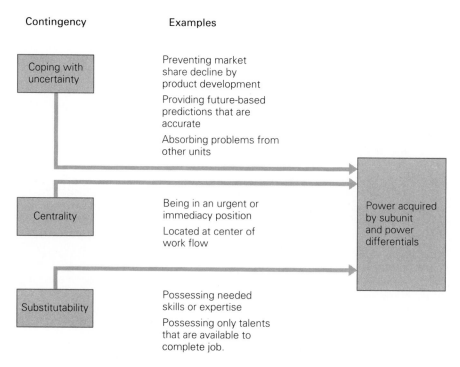

Contingency

Examples

Coping with uncertainty

Preventing market share decline by product development

Providing future-based predictions that are accurate

Absorbing problems from other units

Centrality

Being in an urgent or immediacy position

Located at center of work flow

Substitutability

Possessing needed skills or expertise

Possessing only talents that are available to complete job.

Power acquired by subunit and power differentials

Source: This figure is based on the detailed research work conducted by D. J. Hickson, C. R. Hinnings, C. A. Lee, R. E. Schneck, and J. M. Pennings. See Hickson et al., "A Strategic Contingency Theory of Intraorganizational Power," *Administrative Science Quarterly,* June 1971, pp. 216–29; C. R. Hinnings, D. J. Hickson, J. M. Pennings, and R. E. Schneck, "Structural Conditions of Intraorganizational Power," *Administrative Science Quarterly,* March 1974, pp. 22–44.

United States.[29] Engineering, marketing, production, and accounting departments were studied. Each subunit interacted with the three others. The researchers examined various indicators of power, such as substitutability (ability of the subunit to obtain alternative performance for its activities), work flow pervasiveness (the degree to which the work flows of a subunit were linked to the work flows of other subunits), uncertainty (the lack of information about future events), and work flow immediacy (the speed and severity with which the work flow of a subunit affected the final outputs of the organization). Researchers found that only a combination of high values on all the power indicators gave a subunit dominant, first-rank power. Thus, being able to deal with uncertainty alone or possessing substitutability power alone does not provide a subunit with dominant power over other subunits.

Based on the work of Crozier and of Hickson and associates, a concise explanation of strategic contingencies is possible. The model presented in Figure 10–2 suggests that subunit power, the power differential between subunits, is influenced by (1) the ability to cope with uncertainty, (2) the centrality of the subunit, and (3) the substitutability of the subunit.

---

[29]Hinnings et al., "Structural Conditions," p. 41.

Coping with Uncertainty

Unanticipated events can create problems for any organization or subunit. Therefore, the subunits most capable of coping with uncertainty typically acquire power:

> Uncertainty itself does not give power; coping gives power. If organizations allocate to their various subunits task areas that vary in uncertainty, then those subunits that cope most effectively with the most uncertainty should have the most power within the organization.[30]

Coping activities comprise three types. In *coping by prevention,* a subunit works at reducing the probability that some difficulty will arise. For example, designing a new product to prevent lost sales because of new competition in the marketplace is a coping technique. Another example would be to hire two individuals when only one is actually needed, because of expected turnover.

Coping by information is another type. The use of forecasting is an example. Possessing timely forecasting information enables a subunit to deal with such events as competition, strikes, shortages of materials, and consumer demand shifts. Planning departments conducting forecasting studies acquire power when their predictions prove accurate.

Coping by absorption, the third type, involves dealing with uncertainty as it impacts the subunit. For example, one subunit might take a problem employee from another subunit and then attempt to retrain and redirect that employee. This is done as a favor, so that the other subunit does not have to go through the pain of terminating or continuing to put up with the employee. The subunit that takes in the problem employee gains the respect of other subunits, which results in an increase in power.

Regarding the relation of coping with uncertainty to power, Hinnings said, "The more a subunit copes with uncertainty, the greater its power within the organization."[31]

Centrality

The subunits that are most central to the flow of work in an organization typically acquire power. No subunit has zero centrality since all are somehow interlinked with other subunits. A measure of centrality is the degree to which the work of the subunit contributes to the final output of the organization.[32] A subunit in a position to affect other subunits has some degree of centrality and, therefore, power.

A subunit also possesses power if its activities have a more immediate or urgent impact than that of other subunits. For example, Ben Taub is a major public hospital in Houston. The emergency and trauma treatment subunit is

---

[30]Hickson et al., "Strategic Contingency Theory," pp. 219–20.

[31]Hinnings et al., "Structural Conditions," p. 39.

[32]Richard L. Daft, *Organization Theory and Design* (St. Paul, Minn.: West Publishing, 1983), pp. 392–98. This source contains an excellent discussion of the strategic contingency perspective in terms of managerial and organizational theory. Daft's discussion is a concise and informative presentation of the original Hickson et al. theory and research.

extremely important and crucial. Because failures in this subunit could result in the death of emergency victims, it possesses significant power within the hospital. The psychiatric subunit does important work that is not as crucial and immediate. Therefore, it has significantly less subunit power than the emergency and trauma treatment subunit.

The two main centrality propositions offered by Hinnings and associates are:[33]

> The higher the pervasiveness of the work flows of a subunit, the greater is its power within the organization.
> The higher the immediacy of the work flows of a subunit, the greater is its power with the organization.

Substitutability

Substitutability refers to the ability of other subunits to perform the activities of a particular subunit. If an organization has or can obtain alternative sources of skill, information, and resources to perform the job done by a subunit, the subunit's power is diminished. On one hand, training subunits lose power if training work can be done by line managers or outside consultants. On the other hand, a subunit with unique skills and competencies (e.g., the maintenance workers in Crozier's study) is hard to duplicate or replace; this increases the subunit's power over other subunits.

Changes in the labor market may result in changes in a subunit's power. Today, there is a shortage of robotic technical specialists. Since robotic technicians are difficult to replace, train, and substitute for, the robotic subunit of an organization possesses inordinate power. Of course, other reasons exist for the emergence of powerful robotic subunits, such as their access to technical information, their centrality, and the productivity improvements that they bring about.

Hinnings and associates captured the importance of substitutability power when they proposed that the lower the substitutability of the activities of a subunit, the greater is its power within the organization.[34]

THE ILLUSION OF POWER

Admittedly, some individuals and subunits have vast amounts of power to get others to do things the way they want them done. However, there are also illusions of power. Imagine that one afternoon your supervisor asks you to step into his office. He starts the meeting: "You know we're really losing money using that Beal stamping machine. I'd like you to do a job for the company. I want you to destroy the machine and make it look like an accident." Would you comply with this request? After all, this is your supervisor, and he is in charge of everything—your pay, your promotion

---

[33]Hinnings et al., "Structured Conditions," p. 41.

[34]Ibid., p. 40.

opportunities, your job assignments. You might ask, "Does my supervisor have this much power over me?"

Where a person's or a subunit's power starts and stops is difficult to pinpoint. One might assume that the supervisor in the hypothetical example has the specific power to get someone to do this unethical and illegal "dirty work." However, even individuals who seemingly possess only a little power can influence others. A series of studies conducted by Stanley Milgram focused on the illusion of power.

Milgram conducted highly controversial experiments on "obedience to authority."[35] The subjects in the experiments were adult men drawn from a variety of occupations and social positions in the New Haven, Connecticut, area. Upon arriving at the laboratory, each subject was introduced to his supposed cosubject, a man of about 50 who was actually working with Milgram. The two were asked to draw lots to determine who would be the "teacher" and who the "learner." The drawing was rigged. The real subject always became the teacher.

The experiment was ostensibly designed to find out about the effects of punishment on learning. Whenever the learner made a mistake, he was to be punished with an electric shock. A shock-generating machine was used. It had 30 switches on it, the first delivering 15 volts, the second 30, and so on up to 450 volts, where the switch was labeled, "Danger—Severe Shock—XXX."

The teacher (the real subject) then took his place at the shock-generating machine, where he could not see the learner (Milgram's confederate). The plan was for the learner to make many mistakes in repeating words given to him by the teacher. With each mistake, the teacher was told to increase the shocks. At 75 volts, the teacher could hear grunts coming from the learner, who was actually faking as instructed by Milgram. At 150 volts, the learner shouted, "Let me out," and said his heart couldn't stand the pain. He began to yell. He let out an agonizing scream at 285 volts and refused to go on, but seemingly kept trying and made even more mistakes.

Most of the teachers became very upset. Some asked the experimenter whether it was proper to continue. No matter what the teacher asked or how he protested, the experimenter only said, "The experiment requires that we go on." The subjects were also told, "You have no other choice; you must go on." Milgram wanted to know how many subjects would defy the orders to go on and how many would continue. Before these experiments were conducted, 40 psychiatrists were asked their opinions about whether the subjects would quit. Only 4 percent of the subjects, the psychiatrists predicted, would continue to shock learners who failed to respond. But look at Figure 10–3 to see what actually happened.

Out of a total of 40 subjects, 26 (65 percent) obeyed the experimenter all the way to the very highest voltage level on the shock generator (XXX). These men were not abnormal. In fact, most showed extreme signs of emotional

[35]Stanley Milgram, "Behavioral Study of Obedience," *Journal of Abnormal and Social Psychology,* October 1963, pp. 371–78; Stanley Milgram, *Obedience to Authority* (New York: Harper & Row, 1974). For a more recent discussion of the concept of obedience, see N. Woolsey, B. Gary, and G. Hamilton, "The Power of Obedience," *Administrative Science Quarterly,* December 1984, pp. 540–49.

FIGURE 10-3

Results of Milgram's Classic
Experiment on Obedience

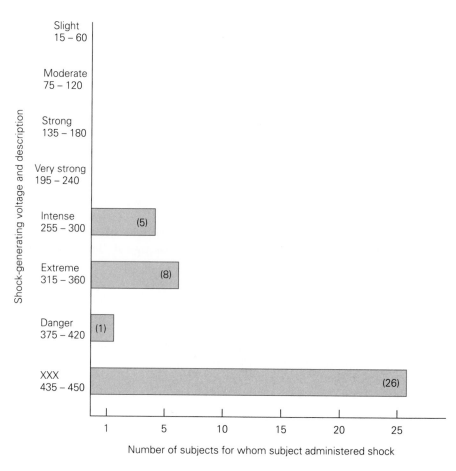

Number of subjects for whom subject administered shock

Source: Based on descriptions and data presented in Stanley Milgram, "Behavioral Study of Obedience," *Journal of Abnormal and Social Psychology,* October 1963, pp. 371–78.

strain and psychological conflict during the experiment. They trembled, bit their lips, and dug their fingernails into the palms of their hands. They repeatedly asked for the experimenter's permission to stop. Yet, they continued increasing the voltage. Milgram stated:

> I observed a mature and initially poised businessman enter the laboratory, smiling and confident; within 20 minutes he was reduced to a twitching, stuttering wreck, who was rapidly approaching a point of nervous collapse, . . . yet he continued to respond to every word of the experimenter and obeyed to the end.[36]

After the experiment, the subjects were all told the truth. The shock-generating machine delivered "nothing at all"; it was a sham. During the experiment, however, every subject was convinced that the learner was another subject like himself. Milgram's experiments have produced much controversy over the ethics of the procedure. Some opponents of this type of

---

[36]Milgram, "Behavioral Study," p. 377.

research maintain that many of the subjects suffered long-term psychological harm. Milgram flatly rejects this idea and points out that his sessions all ended with a complete briefing.

Why did the subjects obey the experimenter? Although he possessed no specific power over the subjects, he appeared to be a powerful person. The experimenter created an illusion of power: he dressed in a white lab coat, was addressed by others as "doctor," and was very stern. The subjects perceived him as possessing legitimacy to conduct the study. The experimenter apparently did an excellent job of projecting the illusion of having power.

The Milgram experiments indicate that exercising power in an authoritative way is not the only way that power can be exerted. Power is often exerted by individuals who have only minimum or no actual power. An individual may be able to significantly influence others simply because he or she is perceived to have power. The "eye of the beholder" plays an important role in the exercise of power.[37] The Close-Up examines some specific guidelines for identifying where the power really is.

POLITICAL STRATEGIES AND TACTICS

Individuals and subunits continually engage in **political behavior.** By political behavior, we mean:

1. Behavior that is usually outside the legitimate, recognized power system.
2. Behavior that is designed to benefit an individual or subunit, often at the expense of the organization in general.
3. Behavior that is intentional and is designed to acquire and maintain power.

As a result of political behavior, the formal power that exists in an organization is often sidetracked or blocked.

> POLITICAL BEHAVIOR
> Behavior outside the normal power system, designed to benefit an individual or a subunit.

Research on Politics

A number of studies have explored political behavior and perceptions in organizations.[38] An early study of 142 purchasing agents examined their political behavior.[39] The job objective of the purchasing agents was to negotiate and fill orders in a timely manner. However, the purchasing agents also viewed their jobs as being a crucial link with the environment— competition, price changes, market shifts. Thus, the purchasing agents

---

[37]K. Macher, "The Politics of People," *Personnel Journal,* January 1986, pp. 50–53.

[38]Dan L. Madison, Robert W. Allen, Lyman W. Porter, Patricia A. Renwick, and Bronston T. Mayes, "Organizational Politics: An Exploration of Managers' Perceptions," *Human Relations,* February 1980, pp. 79–100; Jeffrey Gantz and Victor V. Murray, "The Experience of Workplace Politics," *Academy of Management Journal,* June 1980, pp. 237–51; Robert W. Allen, Dan L. Madison, Lyman W. Porter, Patricia A. Renwick, and Bronston T. Mayes, "Organizational Politics: Tactics and Characteristics of Its Actors," *California Management Review,* 1979, pp. 77–83.

[39]George Strauss, "Tactics of the Lateral Relationship: The Purchasing Agent," *Administrative Science Quarterly,* 1962, pp. 161–86.

ORGANIZATIONS:
CLOSE-UP

WHO REALLY HOLDS THE POWER?

Supposedly, the higher one is in the organization, the more power one is presumed to hold. People at the top give orders; people at the bottom obey them. Anyone who has worked in an organization knows, however, that matters are not that simple. People who are supposed to be powerful often are not, and people without formal positions of authority often carry a great deal of weight. How does a newcomer learn where people really fit in an organization's power hierarchy? Four issues can make the difference: (1) who controls the resources, (2) who holds a central position, (3) who makes decisions, and (4) who has the best reputation.

New employees can gain this essential information by asking a series of questions related to the four issues.

1. *Resources:* What kinds of resources are most important to the members—funds, equipment, personnel, information?

2. *Centrality:* What technical and administrative processes are vital to everyday operations? To organizational success?

3. *Influence on decision making:* Who participates in key (both formal and informal) decision-making forums? Who has access to top decision makers? Whose views dominate major decisions? Who has come out on top in power struggles?

4. *Reputation:* Which units and individuals are especially powerful? Which units do people join who want to get ahead?

Answers to these questions tell who really wields the actual power in organizations.

Source: David A. Whetten and Kim Cameron, *Developing Managerial Skills* (Glenview, Ill.: Scott, Foresman, 1984), pp. 250–59; Michael I. Harrison, *Diagnosing Organizations: Methods, Models, and Processes* (Beverly Hills, Calif.: Sage Publications, 1989).

considered themselves information processors. This vital link between each purchasing agent and the external environment placed them in conflict with the engineering department. As a result of the conflict, attempts to influence the engineering subunit were a regular occurrence.

This study found a variety of political tactics used by the purchasing agents:

1. *Rule evasion*—evading the formal purchase procedures in the organization.

2. *Personal-political*—using friendships to facilitate or inhibit the processing of an order.

3. *Educational*—attempting to persuade engineering to think in purchasing terms.

4. *Organizational*—attempting to change the formal or informal interaction patterns between engineering and purchasing.

These four political tactics (1) were outside the legitimate power system, (2) occasionally benefited the purchasing agent at the expense of the rest of the

Tactic	Combined Groups	Chief Executive Officers	Staff Managers	Supervisors
Attacking or blaming others	54.0%	60.0%	50.0%	51.7%
Use of information	54.0	56.7	57.1	48.3
Image building/ impression management	52.9	43.3	46.4	69.0
Developing base of support	36.8	46.7	39.3	24.1
Praising others, ingratiation	25.3	16.7	25.0	34.5
Power coalitions, strong allies	25.3	26.7	17.9	31.0
Associating with the influential	24.1	16.7	35.7	20.7
Creating obligations/reciprocity	12.6	3.3	14.3	30.7

TABLE 10−2

Managerial Perceptions of Organizational Political Behavior

Source: R. W. Allen, D. L. Madison, L. W. Porter, P. A. Renwick, and B. T. Mayes, "Organizational Politics: Tactics and Characteristics of Its Actors." Copyright 1979 by the Regents of the University of California. Reprinted from *California Management Review*, December 1979, p. 79, by permission of the Regents.

organization, and (3) were intentionally developed so that more power was acquired by the purchasing agent.

Another study of political behavior was conducted in the electronics industry in southern California.[40] A total of 87 managers (30 chief executive officers, 28 higher-level staff managers, 29 supervisors) were interviewed and asked about political behavior. Table 10−2 summarizes the eight categories of political tactics (behavior) mentioned most frequently by the three managerial groups. The managers were also asked to describe the personal characteristics of the individuals who used political behavior effectively. Thirteen personal characteristics were identified as important; these are presented in Table 10−3.

The managers in this study were aware of political behavior because it was a part of their organizational experiences. As the researchers noted, the research was not designed to praise or disparage political behavior. Instead, it was intended to show that politics is a fact of organizational existence.

Playing Politics

If anything, the available (albeit scanty) research indicates that politics exists in organizations and that some individuals are very adept at political behavior. Herbert Mintzberg and others describe these adept politicians as playing games.[41] The games that managers and nonmanagers engage in are intended to (1) resist authority (e.g., the insurgency game), (2) counter the resistance to

---

[40]Allen et al., "Organizational Politics."

[41]For a complete and interesting discussion of political games, refer to Mintzberg, *Power in and around Organizations,* chap. 13, pp. 171−271.

TABLE 10–3

Personal Characteristics of
Effective Politicians

Personal Characteristics	Combined Groups	Chief Executive Officers	Staff Managers	Supervisors
Articulate	29.9%	36.7%	39.3%	12.8%
Sensitive	29.9	50.0	21.4	17.2
Socially adept	19.5	10.0	32.1	17.2
Competent	17.2	10.0	21.4	20.7
Popular	17.2	16.7	10.7	24.1
Extroverted	16.1	16.7	14.3	17.2
Self-confident	16.1	10.0	21.4	17.2
Aggressive	16.1	10.0	14.3	24.1
Ambitious	16.1	20.0	25.0	3.4
Devious	16.1	13.3	14.3	20.7
"Organization person"	12.6	20.0	3.6	13.8
Highly intelligent	11.5	20.0	10.7	3.4
Logical	10.3	3.3	21.4	6.9

Source: R. W. Allen, D. L. Madison, L. W. Porter, P. A. Renwick, and B. T. Mayes, "Organizational Politics: Tactics and Characteristics of Its Actors." Copyright 1979 by the Regents of the University of California. Reprinted from *California Management Review,* December 1979, p. 78, by permission of the Regents.

authority (e.g., the counterinsurgency game), (3) build power bases (e.g., the sponsorship game and coalition-building game), (4) defeat rivals (e.g., the line versus staff game), and (5) effect organizational change (e.g., the whistle-blowing game). In all, Mintzberg describes and discusses 13 political games. Six are briefly presented here.

Insurgency game.   This game is played to resist authority. For example, suppose that a plant supervisor is instructed to reprimand a particular worker for violating company policies. The reprimand can be delivered according to the supervisor's feelings and opinions about its worth and legitimacy. A reprimand delivered in a halfhearted manner will probably have no noticeable effect. However, if delivered aggressively, it may be effective. Insurgency in the form of not delivering the reprimand as expected by a higher-level authority would be difficult to detect and correct. Insurgency as a game to resist authority is practiced in organizations at all levels.

Counterinsurgency game.   Often, a person in an authority position fights back when faced with insurgency. The supervisor's superior may have to carefully monitor whether policies concerning the reprimand are being followed. One tactic is to occasionally (not always) follow up requests given to subordinates with a detailed checking system. For example, the person with ultimate authority could ask the supervisor on occasion whether the reprimand had been given, when it was given, what the person's reaction was, and how the supervisor would make presentation improvements in the future. The superior could also check with the person reprimanded to determine when and how the reprimand was given. The purpose of periodic monitoring is to encourage the supervisor to deliver the reprimand according to company procedures.

HARD WORK MAY NOT BE ENOUGH

If you're one of those people who always thought that getting in with the teacher or boss paid off as much as hard work, consider yourself somewhat vindicated. A recent study of 124 enlisted men and women in the army found a high correlation between those who engaged in ingratiatory behavior and those who had favored in-group status with the powers that be.

The researcher's recommendations for scoring points with the boss include:

— *Flattery.* Carefully identify a co-worker or superior of your boss who interacts often with him or her, and say good things about your boss. It will be passed on.

— *Opinion conformity.* Intentionally disagree with your boss, only to yield gracefully later. Bosses feel good if they can persuade you to change your mind.

— *Self-presentation.* Present yourself as what you perceive to be your boss's ideal employee. Self-deprecation, for example, works with leaders who view an admission of weakness by an employee as a bond of trust.

Does ingratiation make for a more efficient organization? It appears to be a matter of degree. Moderate doses of puff give a boss a heightened sense of confidence, which in all likelihood will result in more responsibility being delegated to the employee. The boss tends to offer members of the in-group more desirable work assignments, place greater value on their ideas, and be more willing to offer help when the employee faces work difficulty. A usually flattered boss is also less likely to be upset when the employee argues a different point of view. Other studies have shown that in-group employees are more committed to their jobs than others and are more willing to extend their responsibilities.

Source: "Sucking Up Pays Off," *Fortune,* December 18, 1989, p. 12; Dave Day, "Beating the In Group–Out Group Problem," *Supervisory Management,* August 1989, pp. 17–21.

Sponsorship game. In this rather straightforward game, a person attaches himself or herself to someone with power. The sponsor is typically the person's boss or someone else with higher power and status. Typically, individuals attach themselves to someone who is on the move. A few rules are involved in playing this game: First, the person must be able to show commitment and loyalty to the sponsor. Second, the person must follow each sponsor-initiated request or order. Third, the person must stay in the background and give the sponsor credit for everything. Finally, the person must be thankful and display gratitude to the sponsor. The sponsor is not only a teacher and trainer but also a power base. Some of the sponsor's power tends to rub off on the person through association.

The "Hard Work" Close-Up indicates that playing politics may help a manager sell an idea or get ahead in the organization.

Coalition-building game. A subunit such as a personnel/human resources department or a research and development department may be able to increase its power by forming an alliance, or coalition, with other subunits. The strength-in-numbers idea is encouraged by coalition building.[42] When such alliances are formed within the organization, common goals and common interests are emphasized. However, forming coalitions with groups outside the organization can also enhance the power of a subunit.

Acquiring power by building an internal coalition is illustrated by the example that follows. In most organizations, the personnel/human resources department typically has limited power. However, litigation involving employee relations and employee health problems associated with disability triggered by job stress is becoming a costly expense. Consequently, legal staffs in organizations have acquired power. These legal staffs do not have the information, daily contact with employees, and records needed to serve the firm's legal needs. Skills, abilities, and information to cope with employee-based uncertainties are more in the domain of the personnel/human resources department. Therefore, an alliance between the legal staff and the personnel/human resources department would enhance both their power bases. The coalition would enable the organization to effectively address legal issues.

Building a coalition with an external group can also enhance the power of various groups. The alumni office of most state universities interacts with alumni in fund-raising, projecting a positive image, and providing service on community projects. Because alumni donations are extremely important for funding and supporting research programs conducted within a university, the alumni office would acquire more power by forming an alliance with major donors who actively support their alma mater. The university would be hard pressed to ignore requests that major donors made to the administration to support the alumni office, the implication being that failing to support the alumni office and its personnel would cause these donors to withhold funds.

Line versus staff game.   The line manager versus the staff adviser game has existed for years in organizations. In essence, this game pits line authority to make operating decisions against the expertise possessed by staff advisers. There are also value differences and a clash of personality. On one hand, line managers are typically more experienced, more oriented to the bottom line, and more intuitive in reaching decisions. On the other hand, staff advisers tend to be younger, better educated, and more analytical decision makers. These differences result in the two groups viewing the organizational world from slightly different perspectives.

Withholding information, having access to powerful authority figures, creating favorable impressions, and identifying with organizational goals are tactics used by line and staff personnel. The line versus staff clash must be controlled in organizations before it reaches the point at which, because of the disruption, organizational goals are not being achieved.

Whistle-blowing game.   This game is played to bring about organizational change. It takes place when a person in an organization identifies a behavior that violates his or her sense of fairness, morals, ethics, or law and then blows

---

[42]William B. Stevenson, Jane L. Pearce, and Lyman W. Porter, "The Concept of Coalition in Organization Theory and Research," *Academy of Management Review,* April 1985, pp. 256–68.

the whistle. **Whistle-blowing** means that the person informs someone—a newspaper reporter, a government representative, a competitor—about an assumed injustice, irresponsible action, or violation of the law.

The whistle-blower, who may come from any level in the organization, attempts to correct the behavior or practice by bypassing the authority system within the organization. This is viewed in a negative light by managers who possess position power. For example, when an Eastern Air Lines pilot complained to management first and then to the public about defects in his plane's automatic pilot mechanisms, his complaints were attacked by management as being groundless. An engineer complained about the O-rings of the *Challenger* booster rockets—which later cracked, and led to the death of seven astronauts. The engineer's complaints were not given a high priority to check out. In another example, a biologist reported to the Environmental Protection Agency that his consulting firm had submitted false data to the agency on behalf of an electric utility company; he was fired. In still another publicized case, an engineer at Ford complained about the faulty design of the Pinto. Unfortunately, this whistle-blower was demoted. Many of the legal costs and settlements from Pinto crash victims might have been avoided if the whistle-blower's message had been taken more seriously.[43] Often, whistle-blowing is done secretly so that retribution by the authority system is avoided.

ETHICS, POWER, AND POLITICS

Issues of power and politics often involve ethical issues as well. For example, if power is used within the formal boundaries of a manager's authority and within the framework of organizational policies, job descriptions, procedures, and goals, it is really nonpolitical power and most likely does not involve ethical issues. But the use of power outside the bounds of formal authority, politics, procedures, job descriptions, and organizational goals is political in nature. When this occurs, ethical issues are likely to be present. Some examples might include bribing government officials, lying to employees and customers, polluting the environment, and a general "ends justify the means" mentality.

Managers confront ethical dilemmas in their jobs because they frequently use power and politics to accomplish their goals. Each manager, therefore, has an ethical responsibility. Recently, researchers have developed a framework that allows a manager to integrate ethics into political behavior. Researchers recommend that a manager's behavior must satisfy certain criteria to be considered ethical.[44]

WHISTLE-BLOWING
Informing someone about an organizational practice or behavior that violates the law or conflicts with a personal opinion, value, or belief.

[43]See Alice L. Priest, "When Employees Think Their Company Is Wrong," *Business Week,* November 24, 1980, p. 2; Andy Pasztor, "Speaking Up Gets Biologist into Big Fight," *The Wall Street Journal,* November 26, 1980, p. 29; Janelle Brinker Dozier and Marcia P. Miceli, "Potential Predictors of Whistle-Blowing: A Prosocial Behavior Perspective," *Academy of Management Review,* October 1985, pp. 823–36.

[44]Gerald F. Cavanagh, Denis J. Moberg, and Manuel Velasquez, "The Ethics of Organizational Politics," *Academy of Management Review,* July 1981, pp. 363–74; Manuel Velasquez, Denis J. Moberg, and Gerald F. Cavanagh, "Organizational Statesmanship and Dirty Politics." Also see "Collegians Speak Out on Ethical Issues," *Collegiate Edition Marketing News,* January 1988, pp. 1,4.

1. *Utilitarian outcomes:* The manager's behavior results in the optimal satisfaction of people both inside and outside the organization. In other words, it results in the greatest good for the greatest number of people.

2. *Individual rights:* The manager's behavior respects the rights of all affected parties. In other words, it respects basic human rights of free consent, free speech, freedom of conscience, privacy, and due process.

3. *Distributive justice:* The manager's behavior respects the rules of justice. It does not treat people arbitrarily but rather equitably and fairly.

What does a manager do when a potential behavior cannot pass the three criteria? Researchers suggest that it may still be considered ethical in the particular situation if it passes the criterion of *overwhelming factors*. To be justified, the behavior must be based on tremendously overwhelming factors in the nature of the situation, such as conflicts among criteria (e.g., the manager's behavior results in both positive and negative results), conflicts within the criteria (e.g., a manager uses questionable means to achieve a positive result), and/or an incapacity to employ the first three criteria (e.g., the manager acts with incomplete or inaccurate information).

SUMMARY OF KEY POINTS

— Power is defined as the ability to get things done in the way that one wants them to be done.

— Authority is a much narrower concept than power. Authority is a form of power that is made legitimate because it is accepted by subordinates or followers.

— French and Raven introduced the notion of five interpersonal power bases—legitimate (position based), reward, coercive (punishment based), expert, and referent (charismatic). These five bases can be divided into two major categories: organizational and personal. Legitimate, reward, and coercive power are primarily prescribed by an organization, while expert and charismatic power are based on personal qualities.

— Structural and situational power bases also exist. An organization's structural arrangement establishes patterns of communication and information flow that play an important role in power formation and use.

— Historically, power seekers have been presented in negative terms. They have been portrayed as weak, neurotic, and troubled. However, research by McClelland on the need for power paints a different picture. McClelland has found that some managers with a high need for power are effective, use their power to accomplish organizational goals, and are involved heavily in coaching subordinates.

— Power and influence can flow from the bottom to the top in an organization. Lower-level employees can have significant power because of expertise, location, and access and control of information. Some lower-level employees acquire power through persuasion and manipulation skills.

— Subunits within organizations acquire and use power. The strategic contingency approach addresses subunit power. A strategic contingency is an event or activity that is extremely important for accomplishing organizational goals. The strategic contingency factors that have been disclosed by research include coping with uncertainty, centrality, and substitutability. Coping with uncertainty is extremely important for acquiring, retaining, and using power.

— Individuals can sometimes exercise power because of illusion. The Milgram "obedience to authority" experiments involving faked electric shocks illustrate how the illusion of power can bring about compliance.

— Politics is present in all organizations. Politics comprises those activities used to acquire, develop, and use power and other resources to obtain one's preferred outcome when there is uncertainty or disagreement about choices.

— Mintzberg introduced the notion of political game playing. Examples of political games are the insurgency and counterinsurgency games, the sponsorship game, the coalition-building game, the line versus staff game, and the whistle-blowing game.

— Issues of power and politics often involve ethical issues, especially when the use of power is political in nature.

DISCUSSION AND REVIEW QUESTIONS

1. Describe an organization with which you are familiar. Select an individual who you believe has power in that organization. Why do you believe this individual has power?

2. The word *power* has negative connotations to many people. Are you one of those people? Why or why not?

3. Some cynics comment that the golden rule is "Those who have the gold make the rules." Discuss this statement in light of your understanding of the various power bases.

4. Why would it be important to share power with others?

5. What changes in an organization's or subunit's environment would bring about changes in strategic contingencies?

6. Why is it unrealistic to assume that little or no political game playing exists in an organization such as McDonald's Corporation or Chrysler Corp.?

7. Power and politics are two terms that elicit negative reactions. However, we believe that it is more accurate to regard power and politics as neutral terms. Why?

8. Charisma is a term used to explain the referent power base. Do you believe it is possible to increase or improve a person's charisma? How?

9. What power and political tactics are used to give an illusion of power? Is it ethical to create an illusion of power?

10. It has been claimed that when managers are faced with uncertainties in making decisions, they tend to do more political maneuvering and jockeying. Do you agree? Why?

ADDITIONAL REFERENCES

Cobb, A. T. "An Episodic Model of Power: Toward an Integration." *Academy of Management Review,* 1984, pp. 482–93.

Davidson, K. M. *Megamergers.* Cambridge, Mass.: Ballinger Publishing, 1985.

Ewing, D. L. *Do It My Way or You're Fired.* New York: John Wiley & Sons, 1983.

Ferrell, O. C., and S. J. Skinner. "Ethical Behavior and Bureaucratic Structure in Marketing Research Organizations." *Journal of Marketing Research,* 1988, pp. 103–9.

Gray, B., and S. S. Ariss. "Politics and Strategic Change across Organizational Life Cycles." *Academy of Management Review,* 1985, pp. 707–23.

Gray, B., and T. Hopper. "Political Limits to Interorganizational Consensus and Change." *Journal of Applied Behavioral Science,* 1986, pp. 95–112.

Hosmer, L. T. *The Ethics of Management.* Homewood, Ill.: Richard D. Irwin, 1987.

———."The Institutionalization of Unethical Behavior." *Journal of Business Ethics,* 1987, pp. 439–47.

Jackson, C. N., and D. C. King. "The Effects of Representatives' Power within Their Own Organizations on the Outcome of a Negotiation." *Academy of Management Journal,* 1983, pp. 178–85.

Jansen, E., and M. A. von Glinow. "Ethical Ambivalence and Organizational Reward Systems." *Academy of Management Review,* 1985, pp. 814–22.

Loucks, V. R. "A CEO Looks at Ethics." *Business Horizons,* 1987, p. 4.

Margulies, N., and A. P. Raia. "The Politics of Organization Development." *Training and Development Journal,* 1984, pp. 20–23.

Mathews, M. C. "Codes of Ethics: Organizational Behavior and Misbehavior." In *Research in Corporate Social Performance and Policy,* ed. W. C. Frederick. Greenwich, Conn.: JAI Press 1987, pp. 107–30.

Mitroff, I. *Business Not as Usual.* San Francisco: Jossey-Bass, 1987.

Modic, S. J. "Movers and Shakers." *Industry Week,* 1988, p. 47.

Molander, E. A. "A Paradigm for Design, Promulgation, and Enforcement of Ethical Codes." *Journal of Business Ethics,* 1987, pp. 619–31.

Mueller, R. K. *Behind the Boardroom Door.* New York: Crown Publishers, 1984.

Provan, K. G. "Interorganizational Cooperation and Decision Making Autonomy in a Consortium Multi-Hospital System." *Academy of Management Review,* 1984, pp. 494–504.

Provan, K., and S. Skinner. "Interorganizational Dependence and Control as Predictors of Opportunism in Dealer-Supplier Relations." *Academy of Management Journal,* 1989, pp. 202–12.

Quinn, R., and P. Lees. "Attraction and Harassment: Dynamics of Sexual Politics in the Workplace." *Organizational Dynamics,* 1984, pp. 34–46.

Rubin, I. M., and D. E. Berlew. "The Power Failure in Organizations." *Training and Development Journal,* 1984, pp. 34–39.

The Power Center at Geico Corporation

John J. Byrne is chairman of Geico Corporation, the Washington, D.C., auto insurer. He took over in 1976, when the firm was on the verge of bankruptcy. Within a few years, he succeeded in building a culture at Geico based on consensus management and inflexible operator rules. He found, however, that one of his inflexible rules stood in the way of Geico's sales growth. Byrne could have used his authority as chief executive to change the rule, but instead he chose to "muddle." That way, it took four years to bring about a change that, from his position of power, he could have commanded with a one-page memo.

Byrne's career began at Lincoln National Life as a roving reinsurance actuary. In 1967, he moved to Traveler's Insurance and in six years was promoted to executive vice president. He describes himself as a pusher, a driver who sometimes pushes his ideas too hard.

During his first few months at Geico, Byrne was putting out fires and not really concerned about building a productive work culture. He went strictly by the books and relied on his position power to do the job. That is, he influenced others by the use of legitimate, reward, and coercive power bases—the position power prescribed by the organization. He hired, fired, and put together his own Geico management team.

Byrne describes his muddling style as a blend of management by objectives and consensus management. He believes that top management should not make policy decisions by itself. Instead, it should create a company culture and style in which power is shared and subordinates are trusted to perform well.

Byrne is considered a politician by some managers. He has tailored Geico's culture to fit his personality. Although he can yield and bend to group decisions, he stays in control of the decision-making process. Long before any major issue is put to the group, Byrne moves from office to office, gently nudging group members, listening, and getting to know what group members are thinking and feeling. He is jockeying for advice, coaxing, and letting others know what he thinks.

Byrne uses "challenge sessions" as a tool to stimulate and prod other managers. This is how they work. Each manager circulates copies of his or her proposed budget and goals for the year to a group of other managers. Each manager must sit alone at the front of the room presenting his or her proposal. The other managers then attack the proposals from every direction. It is not acceptable to simply "rubber-stamp" another manager's proposal. Managers are expected to sell their proposals to others. The challenge sessions last 12 to 16 hours a day, five days a week, for three weeks. At the end, each manager has accepted responsibility for a one-year corporate operating plan.

Byrne is firm about not rewarding with a bonus any manager who fails to meet his or her goals. If managers hold back and try to set lower goals at the challenge sessions, Byrne has a knack for spotting this and letting the manager know it. He wants his managers to perform and pushes them to set realistic, challenging objectives. His philosophy is that results are the key to success at Geico. As long as the employee gets results, he states, "I don't care if he shines his shoes with a brick."

Indoctrinated in Byrne's style of managing, Geico managers are cost cutters and realistic goal setters, and they perform their jobs with zeal. Byrne has pushed, led by example, subtly coerced, and motivated the Geico management team. In addition, he listens and shares power through the muddling process. Byrne is patient, and he waits for managers to finally see the light.

Byrne prides himself on creating a corporate culture that permits power to be shared. The sharing has facilitated trust, internal communication, and realistic targets.

Instead of relying on power, fear, and coercion, Byrne has taken another route. When he perceives a need for major changes, he waits for the lieutenants to see the need rather than issuing orders.

Questions for Consideration

1. Some critics of Byrne's muddling style claim that it can work in insurance but not in a more volatile and unpredictable industry such as computers, automobiles, or clothing, where competition would simply pass Byrne by. What do you think?
2. Which power bases does Byrne actually rely on to perform his job as chairman at Geico?
3. Why would a manager making a formal presentation at a "challenge session" tend to feel powerless?
4. How does Byrne combine power and politics to perform his job?

OCCUPATIONAL POWER DIFFERENCES AND TACTICS

Objectives

1. To examine the power bases of various occupations.
2. To illustrate the difference in opinions about power bases.

Starting the Exercise

Phase I (5 minutes).   Individually rank the following occupations according to the overall power that they would generally possess in their organizations. Place a 1 in front of the occupation that you feel to be the most powerful in its particular organization, a 15 in front of the occupation that you feel to be the least powerful in its particular organization, and numbers 2 through 14 in front of the remaining occupations.

_____ Nurse in hospital
_____ President of major university
_____ Chief executive officer of major firm
_____ Medical technologist in hospital
_____ Counselor in personnel unit of major firm
_____ College professor in major university
_____ Machinist in major firm
_____ Accountant in hospital
_____ District sales manager in major firm
_____ Research and development scientist in high-technology firm
_____ Police officer
_____ Navy ensign
_____ Homemaker (full-time)
_____ Secretary to president of major firm
_____ U.S. senator

Phase II (15 minutes).   Decide which of the occupations listed would have the strongest legitimate, reward, and coercive power bases. Write a 50-word explanation of why you selected each of the occupations as the most powerful in each of the three categories of interpersonal power.

Phase III (10 minutes).   Select the least powerful occupation from your ranking, and develop a brief list of power and political tactics that could be used to enhance the power of this occupation.

Phase IV (15 minutes).   The instructor will form small groups of four, six, or eight students to discuss the rankings, the brief reports on power bases, and the lists of power and political tactics.

Phase V (5–10 minutes).   The instructor will wrap up the session by briefly discussing the findings of the small groups.

11

Leadership
Theories and Models

LEARNING OBJECTIVES

*After completing Chapter 11,
you should be able to:*

DEFINE
the term *leadership.*

DESCRIBE
why the trait approach to
leadership has not provided a
universal set of characteristics associated with effective
leaders.

DISCUSS
whether leaders are really
needed in work settings.

COMPARE
the situational factors used in
discussions of the contingency and path-goal
approaches to leadership.

IDENTIFY
the specific leadership style
for each of the eight situations in Fiedler's contingency
model.

ARE LEADERS REALLY NEEDED?

ARGUMENT FOR

Most countries yearn for leaders to step forward to resolve economic and social crises, to motivate employees, and to chart the best course for the future. Certainly, some leaders openly abuse their leadership power, status, and authority. However, most serve as examples of our society's cherished values. They have a significant role in creating a state of mind. They serve as symbols of the moral unity of the society. Leaders express the work ethic and values that hold the society together.

The leaderless work organization is nothing more than pie-in-the-sky propaganda or a Hollywood portrayal of the good life. The reality in management practice is that leaderless teams of workers, left on their own, lack direction and discipline; they accomplish very few goals. Every group or team needs an emergent or assigned leader. Even teams using a participative approach to problem solving cherish the counseling, guidance, and prodding that can only be provided by a respected leader.

No single factor provides more benefits to an organization than effective leadership. Leaders are needed to set objectives, to allocate scarce resources, to focus attention on the goals of the firm, to coordinate change, to provide a common interpersonal contact with followers, and to chart the correct or best course when failures occur. It is simply a fact of life that groups with leaders can do these things more efficiently and more correctly than any leaderless group.

Instead of talking about having no need for leaders, it would be more beneficial to search for and seek out individuals who have the potential to lead. Selecting, training, and motivating leaders present some major problems. However, these complexities should not stop or retard the search for leaders. Our society needs more, not fewer, effective leaders in medicine, education, industry, government, and military service.

ARGUMENT AGAINST

The belief that leadership is not necessary in organizations is gaining ground. Some scientific and professional experts believe that a person who influences others, a leader, is not needed to solve or identify problems—that problems can actually be solved by expert technical advice or action. In fact, the very notion of leadership is at odds with the ideals of a free society: by definition, a leader is in a superior or higher status position than others in the group. Finally, so-called leaders are associated with such distasteful goals as gaining power and earning excess profits.

Instead of identifying leader traits, training individuals to be leaders, and rewarding leaders, organizations need to build and nurture teams of workers to do jobs as a unit. Teams can run their own operations, discipline members as needed, and be responsible for quality and quantity of output. Why waste money for the selection, retention, and unnecessary development of leaders?

The image of the corporate leader, the college president, or the political leader has too many unattractive features. Leaders must compromise their convictions daily, they must work long hours to retain and use their power, and they must force their values on others. With such results, it is about time to do away with finding leaders. Organizations would simply be better off without them.

The 21st century will usher in the era of leaderless work organizations. There will be less hierarchy and more participation, because people demand such an arrangement. Recent events in Eastern Europe—Poland, Czechoslovakia, and Romania—illustrate that people's demands are being heard and are now forces in fostering change. The major change as we come into the next century will be the elimination of leaders and the increase in the team approach to producing products and services effectively.

In each of the groups to which you have belonged—family, sports, social, study, work—one person typically was more influential than the others and was probably called a leader. Leaders are extremely important in a variety of organizational settings. Indeed, organizations would undoubtedly be less efficient without leaders and, in extreme cases, would be unable to accomplish purposeful goals. For these and similar reasons, theorists, researchers, and practitioners have centered their attention on leadership.

Although leadership is important and has been studied by behavioral scientists for decades, it remains something of a mystery. Even after thousands of studies, the experts still lack consensus on exactly what leadership is and how it should be analyzed. This and the next chapter examine leadership in organizational settings. Several somewhat distinct perspectives of leadership are presented. Each is explored theoretically, empirically, and from the standpoint of its application value. This type of exploration suggests that (1) leadership is not the same as management; (2) leadership is a complex concept; (3) leadership attributes can be developed through experience, training, and analysis; (4) leadership effectiveness depends primarily on the fit between the leader, followers, and situations; and (5) leadership is substituted for in various settings and situations—that is, in some situations, leadership is neither an important nor a significant influence.[1]

Leadership is a narrower concept than management. A manager in a formal organization is responsible for and entrusted with such functions as planning, organizing, and controlling. However, leaders in informal groups are not always formal managers performing managerial functions required by the organization. Consequently, leaders may or may not be managers.

The concept of role was clarified in Chapter 8, which dealt with group behavior. In the formal organization, roles often have specific responsibilities associated with them. For example, the first-line supervisory role may be one in which the role occupant is responsible for the level and quality of production generated by a particular group of employees. Exactly how the supervisor fulfills the responsibility involves personal style. Some first-line supervisors rely on the *authority* of the position to secure compliance with performance standards, while others use a more *participative* approach that involves joint decision making on the part of the leader (manager) and followers (subordinates).

A hierarchy of roles also exists in informal groups. The informal leader is accepted as the person to carry out the duties of the position. Once again, how

---

[1]J. A. Klein and P. A. Posey, "Good Supervisors Are Good Supervisors—Anywhere," *Harvard Business Review,* November–December 1986, pp. 125–28.

ORGANIZATIONS:
CLOSE-UP

THE GROWING NUMBER OF WOMEN IN LEADERSHIP POSITIONS: A FACT OF LIFE

The 1990s have been referred to as the "decade of women in leadership." Twenty years ago, women who worked as managers and executives were decidedly in the minority. But the 1990s have ushered in a new era. Today, women are starting new businesses at twice the rate of men.

Women hold about 39 percent of the 14.2 million executive, administrative, and management jobs. More than one third of Procter & Gamble's marketing executives are women. An average 35 percent of Arthur Andersen & Co. recruits are women. At Apple Computer, 30 percent of the managers are women. The Small Business Association (SBA) reports that 30 percent of small businesses are owned by women.

The leaders emerging today are not the order-giving, hard-driving, cigar-smoking, noisy type that predominated in the 60s, 70s, and early 80s. The leader is more a teacher, facilitator, coach, and mentor. Women, as well as men, can serve as effective coaches.

The largest source of coaches, facilitators, and teachers is the estimated 14 million nonworking women who will enter the labor force in the 1990s. Flexible work schedules and day care support will lure more women into the labor force. In statistical terms, women will take two thirds of all jobs created in the 1990s. Even in

the leader brings about compliance from followers depends largely on the leadership style used. What is effective for one leader may not be for another. This, in essence, is the crux of the leadership issue: what constitutes effective leadership?

What is effective leadership? Are more women becoming leaders? Are leaders necessary? As indicated in the opening debate, there are no simple answers to these important questions. The Close-Up points out that more and more women are in leadership positions.

LEADERSHIP DEFINED

LEADERSHIP

The ability to influence the motivation or competence of other individuals in a group.

When one individual attempts to affect the behavior of others in a group without using the coercive form of power, we describe the effort as **leadership.** More specifically, the *Handbook of Leadership* defines leadership as "an interaction between members of a group. Leaders are agents of change, persons whose acts affect other people more than other people's acts affect them. Leadership occurs when one group member modifies the motivation or competencies of others in the group."[2]

This definition implies that leadership involves the use of influence and that all relationships can involve leadership. A second element in the definition

[2]Bernard M. Bass, *Stogdill's Handbook of Leadership* (New York: Free Press, 1982), p. 16.

Japan, there is a massive influx of women into the work force. Japanese women in leadership positions are still not as common as in the United States, Canada, or Britain, but the times are changing. There are about 50,000 Japanese women in managerial positions, which is still a small number, but it has doubled in the past decade.

Women leaders as role models can be found in business organizations, politics, education, health care, and the law. The personal leadership styles of women can be autocratic, democratic, charismatic, or transformational. Each woman, like each man, has her own personal style.

Excluding women from leadership positions makes no sense in any area, industry, or situation. Women are needed more than ever to deal with sweeping international changes. The "old boy" network or the "glass ceiling blocking women from top jobs" is not going to be effective in an era of leadership shortages and global competition. Organizations need the best leaders available. In at least 50 percent of the cases, these leaders will be women in the 1990s.

Source: John Naisbitt and Patricia Aburdene, *Megatrends 2000* (New York: William Morrow, 1990), pp. 216–40.

involves the importance of being a change agent—able to affect the behavior and performance of followers. Last, the definition focuses on the accomplishment of goals. The effective leader may have to deal with individual, group, and organizational goals. Leader effectiveness is typically measured by the accomplishment of one or a combination of these goals. Individuals may view the leader as effective or ineffective according to the satisfactions they derive from the total work experience. In fact, acceptance of a leader's directives or requests rests largely on the followers' expectations that a favorable response can lead to an attractive outcome.

In a hierarchical organization, the appointed manager may direct, instruct, or command; but unless followers have some choice to follow or not follow, there is no leadership. If followers have no choice, there is domination and intimidation. Leadership results when a person influences followers to accept his or her requests without any apparent exertion of power. Through an ability to influence, the leader creates and uses the power and authority received from followers.

The literature of leadership has progressed along several paths. Initially, most of the definitions and writing focused on the use of power and authority as portrayed in Machiavelli's *The Prince*. Then, attention shifted to the traits of leaders and the behavioral styles (e.g., autocratic, participative) of leaders. Another path emphasized the situation and how the leader, followers, and situation interact and work.

Yukl has presented a model (see Figure 11–1) that includes the various traits, behavioral styles, and situational paths that have been identified in

FIGURE 11—1
Yukl's Overarching Model

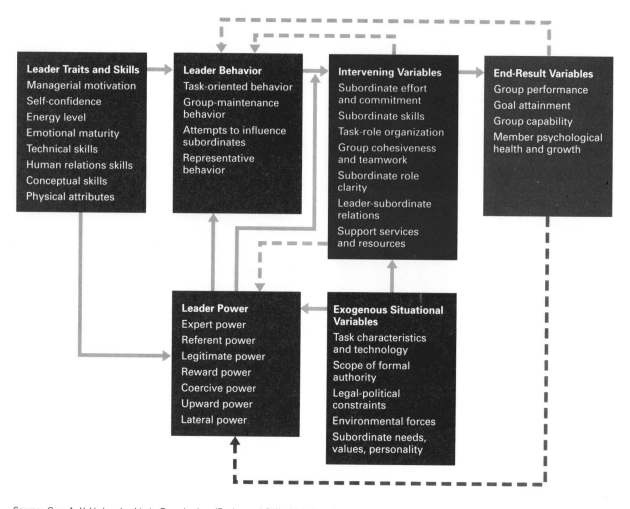

Source: Gary A. Yukl, *Leadership in Organizations* (Englewood Cliffs, N.J.: Prentice Hall, 1981), p. 270.

historically tracing the leadership construct. In this and the following chapters, many of the variables presented in Yukl's overarching view of leadership will be discussed, debated, and, in some cases, modified.

IS LEADERSHIP IMPORTANT?

As Figure 11–1 suggests, a leader can make a difference in terms of end-result factors—performance, goal attainment, and individual growth and development. However, the degree of difference and the process of using leadership to make a difference are somewhat ambiguous. Some theorists and researchers offer cautious advice about the impact of leadership.

Empirical evidence of the magnitude of the effects of leadership on performance is modest. A number of reasons have been cited for the observed modest effects of leaders on performance and other organizational outcomes.[3] First, those selected as leaders are similar in background, experience, and qualifications. The similarity across selected individuals reduces the range of characteristics exhibited by leaders. The similarity of leaders also can produce a self-selection bias: leaders select individuals similar to themselves. Second, leaders at even the highest levels do not have unilateral control over resources. Major decisions require approval, review, and suggested modification by others. Third, many factors cannot be controlled or modified by a leader. Labor markets, environmental factors, and policies are often outside a leader's direct control. External factors may be overwhelming and uncontrollable, no matter how astute, insightful, and influential a leader may be in a job situation.

Some research has specified only a modest effect of leadership on performance. One study of 167 business firms in 13 industries over a 20-year period found that the administration factor (i.e., a combination of leadership and managership) had a limited effect on sales, profits, and profit margins.[4] Reanalysis of the same data found that leadership accounted for more variance in performance than did many of the other variables studied.[5]

A report by Sember on Brazilian managers again raises doubts about the effect of leaders.[6] Sember believes that democracy, profit sharing, and information are more important than a management hierarchy, a power base headed by a leader, or the specialization of work. Instead, employee involvement, salaries instead of wages, circles instead of management hierarchies, and job rotation make leaders almost unnecessary. Sember refers to his organization as Brazil's largest marine and food-processing machinery manufacturer that manages to be profitable without managers.

Despite some studies that dispute the claim that leadership makes a difference, evidence does exist that leadership can have an impact on performance. Leaders do not always make a difference, but they can and do in enough cases. Did Iacocca make a difference at Chrysler? Did John F. Kennedy make a difference in his short tenure as president? Can Mikhail Gorbachev make a difference in the Soviet Union? In these and similar cases, there is no clear-cut answer. However, a majority of people would probably conclude that Iacocca, Kennedy, and Gorbachev were leaders, and they did make a difference.

---

[3]Jeffrey P. Pfeffer, "The Ambiguity of Leadership," *Academy of Management Journal*, January 1977, pp. 104–12.

[4]S. Lieberson and J. F. O'Conner, "Leadership and Organization Performance: A Study of Large Corporations," *American Sociological Review*, 1972, pp. 117–30.

[5]Nan Weiner and Thomas A. Mahoney, "A Model of Corporate Performance as a Function of Environmental, Organizational, and Leadership Influences," *Academy of Management Journal*, June 1981, pp. 453–70.

[6]Ricardo Sember, "Managing without Managers," *Harvard Business Review*, September–October 1989, pp. 76–84.

ORGANIZATIONS:
CLOSE-UP

FLEXIBILITY: A LEADERSHIP SUBSTITUTE AT
HARBOR SWEETS

Substitutes for direct leadership come in many forms. Take the case of Billie Phillips, who works for Salem, Massachusetts–based Harbor Sweets, Inc. She is able to work at a job, take work home, take calls at home, and leave work when her children are sick. The company has attracted and retains loyal and qualified employees because flexibility in scheduling is the rule. Flexibility means that close supervision is out and self-management is in. The employees want flexibility in their schedule, and that's what they get. This results in trust, respect, and loyalty.

Harbor Sweets pays only $5 an hour and does not pay for medical or other insurance for the part-time workers who make up most of the work force. Part-timers have no pension plan, no 401(k), and no paid sick days. They do get paid vacations, profit sharing that averages about 5 percent of wages, and a discount on the company's product: top-of-the-line, handmade chocolates.

Founder and chief executive officer Beneville Strohecker, who is practicing substitute leadership, probably never read or heard about the concept. He assumed that an ideal work force would be well educated and responsible and would not require leaders or someone to tell them how to do a job. He didn't want machines or a rigid leadership structure. He wanted to create a feeling of trust, respect, and loyalty. He now has 114 production employees who work at their own pace, on their own schedule, for at least 20 hours per week.

SUBSTITUTES FOR LEADERSHIP

Leadership substitutes have been identified as task, organizational, or subordinate characteristics that render relationship- and/or task-oriented leadership as not only impossible but also unnecessary. A related concept is called a leadership neutralizer—something that makes it impossible for leadership to make a difference.[7]

Researchers have identified a wide variety of individual, task, environmental, and organizational characteristics as leadership substitute factors that influence relationships between leader behavior and follower satisfaction and performance. Some of these variables (e.g., follower expectations of leader behavior) appear to influence which leadership style will enable the leader to motivate and direct followers. Others, however, function as **substitutes for leadership.** Substitute variables tend to negate the leader's ability to either increase or decrease follower satisfaction or performance.[8]

At Harbor Sweets, Inc., leadership substitutes have been used effectively. The Close-Up illustrates that the philosophy of the founder of Harbor Sweets emphasizes substitutes.

SUBSTITUTES FOR
LEADERSHIP

Task, organizational, and subordinate characteristics that can substitute for leader behaviors. Leader will have little or no effect if certain situations, skills, or tasks exist.

---

[7]Jan P. Howell, Peter W. Dorfman, and Steven Kerr, "Moderator Variables in Leadership Research," *Academy of Management Review*, January 1986, pp. 88–102.

[8]Steven Kerr and John M. Jermier, "Substitutes for Leadership: Their Meaning and Measurement," *Organizational Behavior and Human Performance*, December 1978, pp. 376–403.

The Harbor Sweets emphasis on flexibility and no rigid control is made obvious by these features and philosophy:

— *No assembly line.* Part-timers work as teams at their self-imposed pace.
— *Part-time workers.* If there is demand, hire a work force.
— *Cross-training.* Workers learn several jobs so that demand can be met on time.
— *Flexible schedule.* If employees plan to be absent, they let the company know. (In the order department, they must arrange for someone to cover the shift that will be missed.)

The Harbor Sweets philosophy is expressed well by Strohecker: "If you're not having fun, you'll probably quit, because you're surely not depending on a part-time job at Harbor Sweets for survival." Harbor Sweets substitutes flexibility for management control, close supervision, and long lists of dos and don'ts. In this firm, the substitute seems to work very well.

Source: Martha E. Mangesdord, "Managing the New Work Force," *Inc.*, January 1990, pp. 78–83.

Substitutes for leadership are claimed to be prominent in many organizational settings. However, the dominant leadership approaches fail to include substitutes for leadership in discussing the leader behavior–follower satisfaction and performance relationship.

Table 11–1, based on previously conducted research, provides substitutes for only two of the more popular leader behavior styles—relationship oriented and task oriented. For each of these styles, Kerr and Jermier present substitutes (characteristics of the subordinate, the task, or the organization) that neutralize the style.[9] For example, an experienced, well-trained, and knowledgeable employee does not need a leader to structure the task (e.g., a task-oriented leader). Likewise, a job (task) that provides its own feedback does not require a task-oriented leader to inform the employee how he or she is doing. Also, an employee in a close-knit, cohesive group does not need a supportive, relationship-oriented leader. The group substitutes for this leader.[10]

Admittedly, we do not fully understand the leader-follower relationship in organizational settings. We need to continue searching for guidelines and principles. Such searching now seems to be centered on more careful analysis of a situational perspective of leadership and on issues such as the cause-effect question, the constraints on leader behavior, and substitutes for leadership. We

[9]Ibid.

[10]C. C. Manz, "Self-Leadership: Toward an Expanded Theory of Self-Influence Processes in Organizations," *Academy of Management Review*, July 1986, pp. 585–600.

TABLE 11—1

Substitutes for Leadership

	Neutralizes	
Characteristic	Relationship-Oriented Leadership	Task-Oriented Leadership
Of the subordinate:		
1. Ability, experience, training, knowledge		X
2. Need for independence	X	X
3. "Professional" orientation	X	X
4. Indifference toward organizational rewards	X	X
Of the task:		
5. Unambiguous and routine		X
6. Methodologically invariant		X
7. Provides its own feedback concerning accomplishment		X
8. Intrinsically satisfying	X	
Of the organization:		
9. Formalization (explicit plans, goals, and areas of responsibility)		X
10. Inflexibility (rigid, unbending rules and procedures)		X
11. Highly specified and active advisory and staff functions		X
12. Close-knit, cohesive work groups	X	X
13. Organizational rewards not within the leader's control	X	X
14. Spatial distance between superior and subordinates	X	X

Source: Adapted from Steven Kerr and John M. Jermier, "Substitutes for Leadership: Their Meaning and Measurement," *Organizational Behavior and Human Performance*, December 1978, p. 378.

feel that it is better to study leaders and substitutes for leaders than to use catchy descriptions to identify leaders. Such study and analysis can result in the development of programs to train, prepare, and develop employees for leadership roles.

TRAIT THEORIES

Much of the early discussions and research on leadership focused on identifying the traits of effective leaders. This approach assumed that a finite number of individual traits of effective leaders could be found. The research was designed to identify intellectual, emotional, physical, and other personal traits of successful leaders. To a significant extent, the personnel testing component of scientific management supported the **trait theory of leadership.**[11] In addition to being studied by personnel testing, the traits of leaders have been studied by observation of behavior in group situations, by choice of associates (voting), by nomination or rating by observers, and by analysis of biographical data.

TRAIT THEORY OF LEADERSHIP

Theory that attempts to identify specific characteristics (physical, mental, personality) associated with leadership success. Relies on research that relates various traits to certain success criteria.

---
[11]Ralph M. Stogdill, "Historical Trends in Leadership Theory and Research," *Journal of Contemporary Business*, Autumn 1974, p. 4.

Intelligence

In a review of 33 studies, Ralph Stogdill found that leaders were more intelligent than followers.[12] One of the most significant findings was that extreme intelligence differences between leaders and followers might be dysfunctional. For example, a leader with a relatively high IQ attempting to influence a group whose members have average IQs may be unable to understand why the members do not comprehend the problem. In addition, such a leader may have difficulty in communicating ideas and policies. Being too intelligent would be a problem in some situations.

Personality

Some research results suggest that such personality traits as alertness, originality, personal integrity, and self-confidence are associated with effective leadership.[13] Edwin Ghiselli reported several personality traits associated with leader effectiveness.[14] For example, he found that the ability to initiate action independently was related to the respondent's level in the organization. The higher the person went in the organization, the more important this trait became. Ghiselli also found that self-assurance was related to hierarchical position in the organization. Finally, he found that persons who exhibited individuality were the most effective leaders.

Some writers argue that personality is unrelated to leadership. This view is too harsh, considering how personality has been found to be related to perception, attitudes, learning, and motivation. The problem is finding valid ways to measure personality traits. Although this goal has been difficult to achieve, progress, albeit slow, is being made.[15]

Physical Characteristics

Studies of the relationship between effective leadership and physical characteristics such as age, height, weight, and appearance provide contradictory results. Being taller and heavier than the average of a group is certainly not advantageous for achieving a leader position.[16] However, many organizations believe a physically large person is needed to secure compliance from followers. This notion relies heavily on coercive power. Nonetheless, Truman, Gandhi, Napoleon, and Stalin are examples of individuals of small stature who rose to powerful positions of leadership.

---

[12]Ralph M. Stogdill, *Handbook of Leadership* (New York: Free Press, 1974), pp. 43–44.

[13]Chris Argyris, "Some Characteristics of Successful Executives," *Personnel Journal,* June 1955, pp. 50–63; J. A. Hornaday and C. J. Bunker, "The Nature of the Entrepreneur," *Personnel Psychology,* Spring 1970, pp. 47–54.

[14]Edwin E. Ghiselli, "The Validity of Management Traits in Relation to Occupational Level," *Personnel Psychology,* Summer 1963, pp. 109–13.

[15]R. W. Lundin, *Personality* (New York: Macmillan, 1974); L. Krasner and L. P. Ullman, *Behavior Influence and Personality* (New York: Holt, Rinehart & Winston, 1973).

[16]Ralph M. Stogdill, "Personal Factors Associated with Leadership," *Journal of Applied Psychology,* January 1948, pp. 35–71.

A LEADERSHIP TRAIT: THE QUADRACCI RISK-TAKING APPROACH AT QUAD/GRAPHICS

Is risk-taking an important leadership trait? Is it something that can be taught, or is a person born to be a risk-taker? Harry V. Quadracci is called a leader, a risk-taker, and a tremendous manager. He is the founder and president of the Pewaukee, Wisconsin–based commercial printer Quad/Graphics. The small business he started in 1971 now has over $400 million in annual sales and more than 3,500 employees.

Quadracci prides himself on taking risks. He likes to be thought of as a "hunchman." He believes that leaders must be doers, be listeners, and take the risk in some situations by being a "hunchman." His philosophy, as he calls it, is "MPYPIDK: My plan, your plan, I don't know. Let's just lead followers and see what happens." Quadracci assumes that too much is made out of complicated theories and approaches to leadership.

The Quadracci style of leadership emphasizes doing things out of the ordinary. He prefers to not practice management by walking around, the method recommended in the best-seller *In Search of Excellence*. He practices management by walking away. He lets people do it their way; he practices coordination, not control; and he wants all his bosses to be considered sponsors and mentors. Procedural manuals,

Supervisory Ability

Using the leaders' performance ratings, Ghiselli found a positive relationship between supervisory ability and level in the organizational hierarchy.[17] The supervisor's ability is defined as the "effective utilization of whatever supervisory practices are indicated by the particular requirements of the situation."[18] Once again, a valid measurement of the concept is needed, and this is a difficult problem to resolve.

A summary of a number of the most researched traits of leaders is presented in Table 11–2. These are some of the traits that have been found most likely to be characteristic of successful leaders. Some studies have reported that these traits contribute to leadership success. However, leadership success is neither primarily nor completely a function of these or other traits.[19] The Close-Up comments on risk-taking as a leadership trait.

Although in some studies traits such as those listed in Table 11–2 have differentiated effective from ineffective leaders, many contradictory research findings still exist, for a number of possible reasons. First, the list of potentially important traits is endless. Every year, new traits—such as the sign under

---

[17]Edwin E. Ghiselli, *Exploration in Managerial Talent* (Santa Monica, Calif.: Goodyear Publishing, 1971).

[18]Ibid., p. 19.

[19]D. A. Kenny and S. J. Zaccaro, "An Estimate of Variance Due to Traits in Leadership," *Journal of Applied Psychology,* November 1983, pp. 678–85.

time clocks, and specified work flow procedures are outlawed. Let people think for themselves and be responsible.

In May each year, Quad/Graphics holds its Spring Fling. That's the day when management plays hooky, leaving the rank and file in charge. It is a morale booster, a vote of confidence. Quadracci believes that Spring Fling encourages people to take risks, to do what is needed to operate the company. Skeptics believed that Spring Fling could ruin Quad/Graphics, but Quadracci considered it a low risk. He wanted to fire up his employees, and he has by taking one risk after another and waiting for the results. He challenges everyone, and coddling is not permitted. If you are a poor performer, you don't survive at Quad/Graphics.

Quadracci is called a hunchman, a risk-taker, a manager who walks away. He is also called a "Houdini" of leadership, a leader with style, a leader who performs, and a successful entrepreneur. Would his style work elsewhere? He doesn't really care about elsewhere. Quadracci leadership works at Quad/Graphics. Ask the market, the customers, or the employees about Quadracci leadership.

Source: Daniel M. Kehrer, "The Miracle of Theory Q," *Business Month,* September 1989, pp. 45–49.

which a person is born, handwriting style, and order of birth—are added to personality, physical characteristics, and intelligence. This continual "adding on" results in more confusion among those interested in identifying leadership traits. Second, trait test scores are not consistently predictive of leader effectiveness. Leadership traits do not operate singly, to influence followers, but in combination. This interaction influences the leader-follower relationship. Third, the patterns of effective behavior depend largely on the situation: the leadership behavior that is effective in a bank may be ineffective in a laboratory. Finally, the trait approach fails to provide insight into what the effective leader does on the job. Observations are needed that describe the behavior of effective and ineffective leaders.

Despite its shortcomings, the trait approach is not completely invalid. Stogdill concisely captures the value of the trait approach: "The view that leadership is entirely situational in origin and that no personal characteristics are predictive of leadership . . . seems to overemphasize the situational and underemphasize the personal nature of leadership."[20]

However, after years of speculation and research on leadership traits, we are not even close to identifying a specific set of such traits. Thus, the trait approach appears to be interesting but not very effective for identifying and predicting leadership potential.

---

[20]Stogdill, "Personal Factors," p. 72.

TABLE 11—2

Traits Associated with
Leadership Effectiveness

Intelligence	Personality	Abilities
Judgment	Adaptability	Ability to enlist cooperation
Decisiveness	Alertness	Cooperativeness
Knowledge	Creativity	Popularity and prestige
Fluency of speech	Personal integrity	Sociability (interpersonal skills)
	Self-confidence	Social participation
	Emotional balance and control	Tact, diplomacy
	Independence (nonconformity)	

Source: Adapted from Bernard M. Bass, *Stogdill's Handbook of Leadership* (New York: Free Press, 1982),
pp. 75–76.

PERSONAL–BEHAVIORAL THEORIES

In the late 1940s, researchers began to explore the notion that how a person
acts determines that person's leadership effectiveness. Instead of searching for
traits, these researchers examined behaviors and their impact on the performance and satisfaction of followers. A number of well-known **personal-
behavioral leadership theories** have resulted.

**PERSONAL-BEHAVIORAL
LEADERSHIP THEORIES**
Theories based primarily on personal and behavioral characteristics of leaders. Focus is on *what*
leaders do and/or *how* they behave in carrying out leadership
function.

The University of Michigan Studies: Job-Centered and Employee-Centered Leadership

In 1947, Rensis Likert began studying how best to manage the efforts of
individuals to achieve desired performance and satisfaction objectives.[21] The
purpose of most of the leadership research of the Likert-inspired team at the
University of Michigan (UM) was to discover the principles and methods of
effective leadership. The effectiveness criteria used in many of the studies
included:

Productivity per work hour, or other similar measures of the organization's
success in achieving its production goals.

Job satisfaction of members of the organization.

Turnover, absenteeism, and grievance rates.

Costs.

Scrap loss.

Employee and managerial motivation.

Studies were conducted in a wide variety of organizations: chemical, electronics, food, heavy machinery, insurance, petroleum, public utilities, hospitals,
banks, and government agencies. Data were obtained from thousands of
employees doing different job tasks, ranging from unskilled work to highly
skilled research and development work.

Through interviewing leaders and followers, the researchers identified two
distinct styles of leadership, referred to as *job centered* and *employee centered*. The
job-centered leader practices close supervision so that subordinates perform

JOB-CENTERED LEADER
A person who closely supervises
and observes the work of others.

[21]Rensis Likert, *New Patterns of Management* (New York: McGraw-Hill, 1961).

their tasks using specified procedures. This leader relies on coercion, reward, and legitimate power to influence the behavior and performance of followers. Concern for people is viewed as an important luxury that a leader cannot always afford.

The **employee-centered leader** believes in delegating decision making and aiding followers in satisfying their needs by creating a supportive work environment. The employee-centered leader is concerned with followers' personal advancement, growth, and achievement. These actions are assumed to be conducive to group formation and development.

EMPLOYEE-CENTERED
LEADER
A person who only generally supervises the work of others. He or she attempts to permit others to sense autonomy and support.

The UM series of studies does not clearly show that one particular style of leadership is always the most effective. Moreover, it only examines two aspects of leadership—task and people behavior.

The Ohio State University Studies: Initiating Structure and Consideration

Among the several large leadership research programs that developed after World War II, one of the most significant was headed by Fleishman and his associates at Ohio State University (OSU). This program resulted in the development of a two-factor theory of leadership.[22] A series of studies isolated two leadership factors, referred to as initiating structure and consideration. **Initiating structure** involves behavior in which the leader organizes and defines the relationships in the group, tends to establish well-defined patterns and channels of communication, and spells out ways of getting the job done. The leader with a high initiating structure tendency focuses on goals and results. **Consideration** involves behavior indicating friendship, mutual trust, respect, warmth, and rapport between the leader and the followers. The leader with a high consideration overview supports open communication and participation.

INITIATING STRUCTURE
Leadership acts that imply structuring of job tasks and responsibilities for followers.

CONSIDERATION
Acts of leader that show supportive concern for followers in group.

These dimensions are measured by two separate questionnaires. The Leadership Opinion Questionnaire (LOQ) assesses how leaders think they behave in leadership roles. The Leader Behavior Description Questionnaire (LBDQ) measures the perceptions of subordinates, peers, or superiors.

The initiating structure and consideration scores derived from the responses to the questionnaires provide a way to measure leadership style. Figure 11–2 provides a view of the behaviors of five different leaders. Individual 1 is high on both initiating structure and consideration; individual 4 is low on both dimensions.

The original premise was that a high degree of consideration and a high degree of initiating structure (High-High) was the most desirable. Since the original research undertaken to develop the questionnaire, there have been numerous studies of the relationship between these two leadership dimensions and various effectiveness criteria. In a study at International Harvester,

---

[22]For a review of the studies, see Stogdill, *Handbook of Leadership,* chap. 11. Also see E. A. Fleishman, "The Measurement of Leadership Attitudes in Industry," *Journal of Applied Psychology,* June 1953, pp. 153–58; C. L. Shartle, *Executive Performance and Leadership* (Englewood Cliffs, N.J.: Prentice Hall, 1956); E. A. Fleishman, E. F. Harris, and H. E. Burtt, *Leadership and Supervision in Industry* (Columbus: Bureau of Educational Research, Ohio State University, 1955).

FIGURE 11—2

Scores of Five Leaders:
Initiating Structure and
Consideration

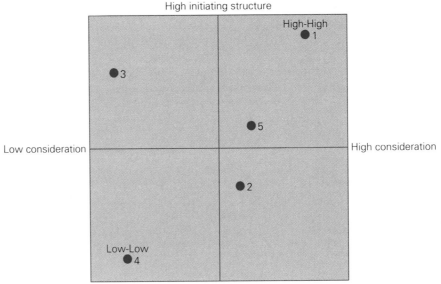

researchers began to find some more complicated interactions of the two dimensions. Supervisors that scored high on initiating structure not only had high proficiency ratings (ratings received from superiors) but also had more employee grievances. A high consideration score was related to lower proficiency ratings and lower absences.[23]

Other studies have examined how male and female leaders utilize initiating structure and consideration. A literature review of such studies found that male and female leaders exhibit equal amounts of initiating structure and consideration and have equally satisfied followers.[24]

The OSU personal-behavioral theory has been criticized for simplicity (e.g., only two dimensions of leadership), lack of generalizability, and reliance on questionnaire responses to measure leadership effectiveness. Researchers have cautioned against reliance on questionnaire measures of leadership initiating factors. One convincing argument is that when raters know about a leader's performance, their ratings of his or her behavior may be substantially distorted. Hence, correlations between past performance and rated behavior may reflect performance-induced distortions in behavioral ratings as well as real causal effects of past behavior on performance.[25]

The simplicity of the initiating structure and consideration view of leadership is appealing. However, most researchers believe that environmental

[23]Fleishman et al., *Leadership and Supervision.*

[24]G. H. Dobbins and S. J. Platz, "Sex Differences in Leadership: How Real Are They?" *Academy of Management Review,* January 1986, pp. 118–27.

[25]Robert G. Lord, "An Information Processing Approach to Social Perceptions, Leadership, and Behavioral Measurement in Organizations," *Research in Organizational Behavior,* ed. Larry L. Cummings and Barry M. Staw (Greenwich, Conn.: JAI Press, 1985), p. 117.

TABLE 11—3

A Review of Two Personal-Behavioral Leadership Approaches

Leadership Factors	Prime Initiator(s) of the Theory	Method of Measurement	Subjects	Principal Conclusions
Employee-centered and job-centered.	Likert.	Interview and questionnaire responses of groups of followers.	Formal leaders and followers in public utilities, banks, hospitals, manufacturing, food, government agencies.	Employee-centered and job-centered styles result in production improvements. However, after a brief period of time, the job-centered style creates pressure that is resisted through absenteeism, turnover, grievance, and poor attitudes. The best style is *employee-centered*.
Initiating structure and consideration.	Fleishman, Stogdill, and Shartle.	Questionnaire responses of groups of followers, peers, the immediate superior, and the leader.	Formal leaders and followers in military, education, public utilities, manufacturing, and government agencies.	The combination of initiating structure and consideration behavior that achieves individual, group, and organizational effectiveness depends largely on the situation.

variables play some role in leadership effectiveness. For example, when successful initiating structure behavior is found, what other variables in the environment are at work? A worker who prefers to have a structured job and needs to have a job is likely to perform effectively under high initiating structure. What situational variables need to be considered? The Ohio State approach does not point out environmental factors.

Synopsis of the Personal-Behavioral Theories

A review of the two prominent personal-behavioral theories and related research indicates several common themes. Each theory attempts to isolate broad dimensions of leadership behavior. The logic of this appears to be that multidimensions confound the interpretation of leadership behavior and complicate the research designs developed to test the particular theory.

The measurement of leadership style for the two theories is accomplished typically through paper-and-pencil questionnaire responses. This method of measurement is, of course, limited and controversial.

The common bases of the personal-behavioral theories are presented in Table 11–3. These approaches have provided practitioners with information on what behaviors leaders should possess. This knowledge has resulted in the establishment of training programs for individuals who perform leadership tasks. Each approach is also associated with highly respected theorists, researchers, or consultants, and each has been studied in different organizational settings. Yet, the linkage between leadership and such important performance indicators as production, efficiency, and satisfaction has not been conclusively resolved by either of the two personal-behavioral theories.

SITUATIONAL THEORIES

SITUATIONAL THEORIES OF
LEADERSHIP
Approach to leadership which
advocates that leaders understand their own behavior, behavior of subordinates, and situation
before utilizing particular leadership style. Requires leader to
have diagnostic skills in human
behavior.

The search for the "best" set of traits or behavior has failed to discover an effective leadership mix and style for all situations. Thus, **situational-theories of leadership** evolved that suggest leadership effectiveness depends on the fit between personality, task, power, attitudes, and perceptions.[26] A number of situation-oriented leadership approaches have been publicized and researched. Two of the earlier ones are the Fiedler contingency model and the path-goal theory.

Only after inconclusive and contradictory results evolved from much of the early trait and personal-behavioral research was the importance of the situation studied more closely by those interested in leadership. Eventually, researchers recognized that the leadership behavior needed to enhance performance depends largely on the situation: what is effective leadership in one situation may be disorganized incompetence in another. The situational theme of leadership, while appealing, is certainly a challenging orientation to implement.[27] Its basic foundation suggests that an effective leader must be flexible enough to adapt to the differences among subordinates and situations.

Deciding how to lead other individuals is difficult and requires an analysis of the leader, the group, and the situation.[28] Managers who are aware of the forces they face are more readily able to modify their styles to cope with changes in the work environment. Three factors of particular importance are forces within the managers, forces in the subordinates, and forces in the situation.[29] Tannenbaum and Schmidt state the situational theme in this way:

> Thus, the successful manager of men can be primarily characterized neither as a strong leader nor as a permissive one. Rather, he is one who maintains a high batting average in accurately assessing the forces that determine what his most appropriate behavior at any given time should be and in actually being able to behave accordingly.[30]

As the importance of situational factors and leader assessment of forces became more recognized, leadership research became more systematic, and contingency models of leadership began to appear in the organizational behavior and management literature. Each model has its advocates, and each attempts to identify the leader behaviors most appropriate for a series of leadership situations. Also, each model attempts to identify the leader-situation patterns important for effective leadership.

---

[26]E. A. Fleishman, "Twenty Years of Consideration and Structure," in *Current Developments in the Study of Leadership*, ed. E. A. Fleishman and J. C. Hunt (Carbondale: Southern Illinois University Press, 1973).

[27]G. Bellman, *The Quest for Staff Leadership* (Glenview, Ill.: Scott, Foresman, 1986).

[28]D. K. Carew, E. Parisi-Carew, and K. H. Blanchard, "Group Development and Situational Leadership: A Model for Managing Groups," *Training and Development Journal*, June 1986, pp. 46–50.

[29]The discussion that follows is based on R. Tannenbaum and W. H. Schmidt, "How to Choose a Leadership Pattern," *Harvard Business Review*, May–June 1973, pp. 162–80.

[30]Ibid., p. 180.

CONTINGENCY LEADERSHIP MODEL

Developed by Fiedler,[31] the contingency model of leadership effectiveness postulates that the performance of groups is dependent on the interaction between leadership style and situational favorableness. Leadership is viewed as a relationship based on power and influence.

Important Considerations

Two important questions are considered in the contingency model: (1) To what degree does the situation provide the leader with the power and influence needed to be effective? Or, how favorable are the situational factors? (2) To what extent can the leader predict the effects of his or her style on the behavior and performance of followers?

Leader's style.   Fiedler was concerned about measuring the leadership orientation of an individual. He developed the **Least-Preferred Co-Worker (LPC) Scale** to measure two leadership styles: (1) task (controlling, structuring) leadership and (2) relationship (passive, considerate) leadership. Figure 11–3 presents a sample of the LPC scale.

LEAST-PREFERRED CO-WORKER SCALE

A questionnaire used by Fiedler to assess the task and relationship leadership tendencies (style) of a person.

Respondents to the complete LPC scale sum their ratings on 18 bipolar scores to obtain a score between 18 and 144. According to Fiedler, someone with a score of 64 or higher is a high-LPC person, one who can work with difficult people. The high-LPC person is sensitive to others' needs and is classified as a "relationship-motivated" leader.

A score of 57 or lower indicates a low-LPC leader. This person tends to classify the least-preferred co-worker in negative terms. The low-LPC person is a "task-motivated" leader. A score of 58–63 indicates a mix of motivation in your leadership style.

Fiedler proposes three situational factors that determine whether a high-LPC or low-LPC leader is more likely to be effective: leader-member relations, task structure, and position power. From a theoretical as well as an intuitive point of view, interpersonal leader-follower relationships are likely to be the most important variable that determines power and influence. The **leader-member relations** factor refers to the degree of confidence, trust, and respect that the followers have in the leader. This situational variable reflects the acceptance of the leader. The leader's influence depends in part on acceptance by the followers. If others are willing to follow because of charisma, expertise, or mutual respect, the leader has little need to rely on task structure or position power. If, however, the leader is not trusted and is viewed negatively by the followers, the situation is considered less favorable in Fiedler's theory.

LEADER-MEMBER RELATIONS

Factor in Fiedler contingency model that refers to degree of confidence, trust, and respect leader obtains from followers.

The second most important measure of situational favorableness is referred to as **task structure.** This dimension includes the following components:

— *Goal clarity*—the degree to which the tasks and duties of the job are clearly stated and known to the people performing the job.

TASK STRUCTURE

Factor in Fiedler contingency model that refers to how structured job is with regard to requirements, problem-solving alternatives, and feedback on job success.

---

[31]Fred E. Fiedler, *A Theory of Leadership Effectiveness* (New York: McGraw-Hill, 1967).

FIGURE 11—3

Least-Preferred Co-Worker
(LPC) Scale

Throughout your life, you work in many groups with a wide variety of different people—on your job, in social groups, in church organizations, in volunteer groups, on athletic teams, and in many other situations. Some of your co-workers may have been very easy to work with in attaining the group's goals, while others were less so.

Think of all the people with whom you have ever worked and then think of the person with whom you could work *least well*. He or she may be someone with whom you work now or with whom you have worked in the past. This does not have to be the person you liked least, but should be the person with whom you had the most difficulty getting a job done, the *one* individual with whom you could work *least well*.

Describe this person on the scale that follows by placing an X in the appropriate space. Look at the words at both ends of the line before you mark your X. *There are no right or wrong answers*. Work rapidly; your first answer is likely to be the best. Do not omit any items, and mark each item only once.

Now describe the person with whom you can work least well.

										Scoring
Pleasant	__	__	__	__	__	__	__	__	Unpleasant	__
	8	7	6	5	4	3	2	1		
Friendly	__	__	__	__	__	__	__	__	Unfriendly	__
	8	7	6	5	4	3	2	1		
Rejecting	__	__	__	__	__	__	__	__	Accepting	__
	1	2	3	4	5	6	7	8		
Tense	__	__	__	__	__	__	__	__	Relaxed	__
	1	2	3	4	5	6	7	8		

— *Goal-path multiplicity*—the degree to which problems encountered in the job can be solved by a variety of procedures. An assembly-line worker solves problems within a systematic framework, while a scientist has many different ways to solve a problem.

— *Decision verifiability*—the degree to which the "correctness" of the solutions or decisions typically encountered in a job can be demonstrated by appeal to authority, by logical procedures, or by feedback. A quality control inspector can show defective parts and clearly indicate why a part is sent back for reworking.

— *Decision specificity*—the degree to which there is generally more than one correct solution. An accountant preparing a balance sheet has few choices, while a research scientist may have numerous potentially correct alternatives to choose from.

POSITION POWER

Factor in Fiedler contingency model that refers to power inherent in leadership position.

Position power in the contingency model refers to the power inherent in the leadership position. To determine leader position power, questions such as the following are asked:[32]

Can the supervisor recommend subordinate rewards and punishments to the boss?

Can the supervisor punish or reward subordinates on his or her own?

Can the supervisor recommend promotion or demotion of subordinates?

---

[32]Fred E. Fiedler and M. M. Chemers, *Leadership and Effective Management* (Gleniew, Ill.: Scott, Foresman, 1974).

Fiedler contends that such questions provide a profile of high or low position power.

Favorableness of the situation. The three situational factors that seem to be the most important in determining a leader's power and influence are: (1) whether leader-member relations are good or poor, (2) whether the task is relatively structured or unstructured, and (3) whether the position power is relatively strong or weak. A few examples show how Fiedler would determine the *favorableness* of the situation for a particular leader.

Office manager. This individual has eight subordinates who like her. She structures the job by making work assignments and by setting goals for required outputs. She is also responsible for reviewing the work of subordinates and is the main spokesperson for and evaluator of the employees at merit review time.

Project engineer. This individual was appointed as the leader of a five-person project study group. None of the assigned members really wants to serve in the group; they have other, more pressing jobs. As the appointed leader, the project engineer was actually given no power. His calls for meetings are generally unanswered. And when he gets the assigned members together, they are rather hostile, negative, and discourteous.

Registered nurse (supervisor). This individual is well liked by her subordinates, but the physicians have taken almost total control of the work. They will not give permission for the registered nurse to perform what she feels are nursing activities. This nurse is in a constant battle with the physicians to let her do the job and to stop interfering.

The classification of these three individuals according to Fiedler is shown in Figure 11–4. The office manager is in situation I, in which she is liked, has a structured task, and position power. The project engineer is in situation VIII, with poor leader-member relations, low task structure, and weak position power. The registered nurse is in situation IV. She is well liked, but she has no task-structure opportunities and no position power because of the physicians. The situation is more favorable for the situation I leader than for the situation VIII leader.

Fiedler contends that a permissive, more lenient (relationship-oriented) style is best when the situation is moderately favorable or moderately unfavorable. Thus, if a leader were moderately liked and possessed some power and the job tasks for subordinates were somewhat vague, the leadership style needed to achieve the best results would be relationship oriented.

In contrast, when the situation is highly favorable or highly unfavorable, a task-oriented approach generally produces the desired performance. The well-liked office manager, who has power and has clearly identified the performance goals, is operating in a highly favorable situation. The project engineer, who is faced with a group of suspicious and hostile subordinates and has little power and vague task responsibilities, needs to be task oriented in this highly unfavorable situation.

FIGURE 11—4

Summary of Fiedler's Situational Variables and Their Preferred Leadership Styles

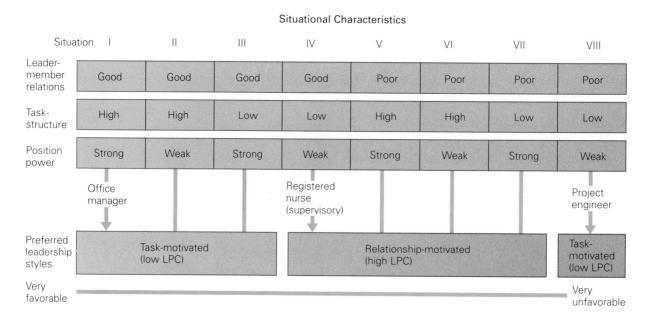

Fiedler recommends that leaders do something about their situations. He suggests that leaders can make changes that result in more favorable situations. Table 11–4 presents some of his suggestions for changing particular situational factors.

Research on Fiedler's Model

Over the past two decades, Fiedler and advocates of the contingency model have studied military, educational, and industrial leaders. In a summary of 63 studies based on 454 separate groups, Fiedler suggests the kind of leadership that is the most appropriate for the situational conditions.[33] Figure 11–5 summarizes his analysis. The situational characteristics are shown at the bottom of the figure. The vertical axis indicates the correlation between a leader's LPC score and the group's performance. A median correlation above the midline shows that the relationship-oriented leaders tend to perform better than the task-oriented leaders. A median correlation below the midline indicates that the task-oriented leaders perform better than the relationship-oriented leaders.

The data presented in Figure 11–5 imply two things about effective leaders. First, task-oriented leaders perform better than relationship-oriented leaders in situations that are very favorable (I, II, III) and in situations that are unfavorable

[33]Fred E. Fiedler, "How Do You Make Leaders More Effective: New Answers to an Old Puzzle," *Organizational Dynamics,* Autumn 1972, pp. 3–8.

TABLE 11-4

Leadership Actions to
Change Situations

Modifying Leader-Member Relations

1. Spend more—or less—informal time (lunch, leisure activities, etc.) with your subordinates.
2. Request particular people for work in your group.
3. Volunteer to direct difficult or troublesome subordinates.
4. Suggest or effect transfers of particular subordinates into or out of your unit.
5. Raise morale by obtaining positive outcomes (e.g., special bonuses, time off, attractive jobs) for subordinates.

Modifying Task Structure

If you wish to work with less structured tasks:
1. Ask your boss, whenever possible, to give you the new or unusual problems and let you figure out how to get them done.
2. Bring the problems and tasks to your group members and invite them to work with you on the planning and decision-making phases of the tasks.

If you wish to work with more highly structured tasks:
1. Ask your superior to give you, whenever possible, the tasks that are more structured or to give you more detailed instructions.
2. Break the job down into smaller subtasks that can be more highly structured.

Modifying Position Power

To raise your position power:
1. Show your subordinates "who's boss" by exercising fully the powers that the organization provides.
2. Make sure that information to your group gets channeled through you.

To lower your position power:
1. Call on members of your group to participate in planning and decision-making functions.
2. Let your assistants exercise relatively more power.

(VIII). Second, relationship-oriented leaders perform better than task-oriented leaders in situations that are intermediate in favorableness (IV, V, and VII).[34] These findings support the notion that each type of leader is effective in certain situations.

Can leaders be trained? Changing a leader's style through training is an extremely difficult task, as Fiedler states: "Fitting the man to the leadership job by selection and training has not been spectacularly successful. It is surely easier to change almost anything in the job situation than [to change] a man's personality and his leadership style."[35] Fiedler contends that training programs and experience can improve a leader's power and influence if the situational favorableness is high. This means a training program that improves a leader's power and influence may benefit the relationship-oriented person but could be detrimental to the task-oriented person.

[34]J. K. Kennedy, Jr., "Middle LPC Leaders and the Contingency Model of Leadership Effectiveness," *Organizational Behavior and Human Performance*, August 1982, pp. 1–14.

[35]Fred E. Fiedler, "Engineering the Job to Fit the Manager," *Harvard Business Review*, September–October 1965, p. 115. Also see Fred E. Fiedler, "The Effects of Leadership Training and Experience: A Contingency Model Interpretation," *Administrative Science Quarterly*, December 1972, pp. 453–70.

FIGURE 11—5

A Summary of Contingency Model Research

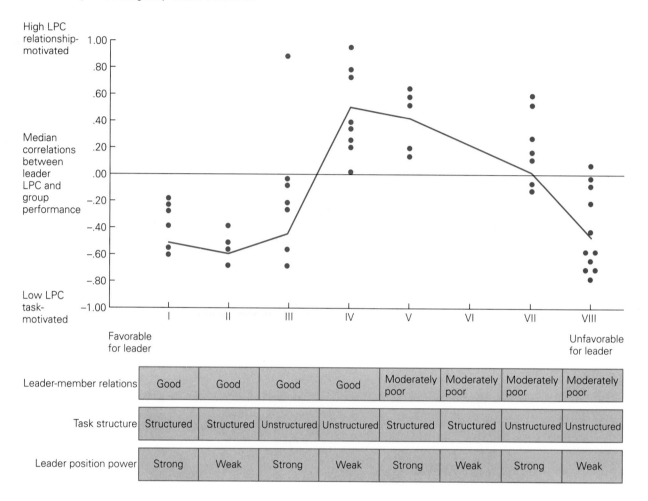

A practical application of Fiedler's contingency approach is the training program LEADER MATCH.[36] Most training programs try to change the leader's personality to fit the situation; but this programmed learning system trains leaders to modify their leadership situation to fit their personalities. In LEADER MATCH training, participants read a workbook, complete the LPC scale, discuss and analyze leadership situations, and evaluate their performance in analyzing the situations. To date, LEADER MATCH has been used with managers, military personnel, and students. In the majority of studies, the leaders trained with LEADER MATCH rated more highly than untrained leaders.

[36]Fred E. Fiedler and M. M. Chemers, *Improving Leadership Effectiveness: The LEADER MATCH Concept* (New York: John Wiley & Sons, 1984).

One study used computer simulations to examine the accuracy of LEADER MATCH prescriptions concerning which leadership style should be used. The researchers found that leadership situations classified by the LEADER MATCH text differ from the prescribed leadership styles in Fiedler's traditional model (see Figure 11–4).[37] This potential inaccuracy in suggesting which optimal leadership style to use can result in faulty applications.

Critique of the Contingency Model

Fiedler's model and research have elicited pointed criticisms and concerns. First, Graen and associates present evidence that research support for the model is weak, especially if studies conducted by researchers not associated with Fiedler are examined.[38] The earlier support and enthusiasm for the model came from Fiedler and his students, who conducted numerous studies of leaders. Second, researchers have called attention to the questionable measurement of the LPC. These researchers claim that the reliability and validity of the LPC questionnaire measure are low.[39] Third, the meaning of the variables presented by Fiedler is not clear. For example, at what point does a "structured" task become an "unstructured" task? Who can define or display this point? Finally, critics claim that Fiedler's theory can accommodate nonsupportive results. This point is specifically made by one critic who states: "Fiedler has revealed his genius twice; first, in devising the model, which stands like calculus to arithmetic compared with previous leadership models, and second, in his ability to integrate new findings into his models."[40]

Despite these incisive criticisms, Fiedler's contingency model has made significant contributions to the study and application of leadership principles. Fiedler called direct attention to the situational nature of leadership. His view of leadership stimulated numerous research studies and much-needed debate about the dynamics of leader behavior. Certainly, Fiedler has played one of the most prominent roles in encouraging the scientific study of leadership in work settings. He pointed the way and made others uncomfortably aware of the complexities of the leadership process.

PATH–GOAL MODEL

Like the other situational or contingency leadership approaches, the **path-goal leadership model** attempts to predict leadership effectiveness in different situations. According to this model, developed by Robert J. House, leaders are effective because of their positive impact on followers' motivation, ability to

PATH-GOAL LEADERSHIP MODEL

Theory that suggests leader needs to influence followers' perception of work goals, self-development goals, and paths to goal attainment.

[37]A. G. Jago and J. W. Ragan, "The Trouble with LEADER MATCH Is That It Doesn't Match Fiedler's Contingency Model," *Journal of Applied Psychology,* 1986, pp. 555–59.

[38]G. Graen, J. B. Orris, and K. M. Alvares, "Contingency Model of Leadership Effectiveness: Some Experimental Results," *Journal of Applied Psychology,* June 1971, pp. 196–201.

[39]C. A. Schriesheim, B. D. Bannister, and W. H. Money, "Psychometric Properties of the LPC Scale: An Extension of Rice's Review," *Academy of Management Review,* April 1979, pp. 287–90.

[40]J. Kelly, *Organizational Behavior: Its Data, First Principles, and Applications* (Homewood, Ill.: Richard D. Irwin, 1980), p. 367.

perform, and satisfaction. The theory is designated path-goal because it focuses on how the leader influences the followers' perceptions of work goals, self-development goals, and paths to goal attainment.[41]

The foundation of path-goal theory is the expectancy motivation theory, discussed in Chapter 5. Some early work on the path-goal theory asserts that leaders become effective by making rewards available to subordinates and by making those rewards contingent on the subordinates' accomplishment of specific goals.[42] It is argued that an important part of the leader's job is to clarify for subordinates the behavior most likely to result in goal accomplishment. This activity is referred to as *path clarification.*

This early path-goal work led to the development of a complex theory involving four specific leader behaviors (directive, supportive, participative, and achievement) and three subordinate attitudes (job satisfaction, acceptance of the leader, and expectations about effort-performance-reward relationships.)[43] The *directive leader* tends to let subordinates know what is expected of them. The *supportive leader* treats subordinates as equals. The *participative leader* consults with subordinates and considers their suggestions and ideas before reaching a decision. The *achievement-oriented* leader sets challenging goals, expects subordinates to perform at the highest level, and continually seeks improvement in performance.

A study of professional employees from research and development organizations examined the path-goal model.[44] The results indicated that need for clarity moderated the relationship between a leader's path clarification and employees' satisfaction. The higher the need for clarity among subordinates, the stronger the relationship between the leader's initiating structure and job satisfaction.

Research studies also suggest that these four behaviors can be practiced by the same leader in various situations. These findings are contrary to the Fiedler notion concerning the difficulty of altering style. The path-goal approach suggests more flexibility than the Fiedler contingency model.

The Main Path-Goal Propositions

The path-goal theory has led to the development of two important propositions:[45]

---

[41]Robert J. House, "A Path-Goal Theory of Leadership Effectiveness," *Administrative Science Quarterly,* September 1971, pp. 321–39; Robert J. House and Terence R. Mitchell, "Path-Goal Theory of Leadership," *Journal of Contemporary Business,* Autumn 1974, pp. 81–98.

[42]M. G. Evans, "The Effects of Supervisory Behavior on the Path-Goal Relationship," *Organizational Behavior and Human Performance,* May 1970, pp. 277–98.

[43]Robert J. House and G. Dessler, "The Path-Goal Theory of Leadership: Some Post Hoc and A Priori Tests," in *Contingency Approaches to Leadership,* ed. J. G. Hunt (Carbondale: Southern Illinois University Press, 1974).

[44]Robert T. Keller, "A Test of the Path-Goal Theory of Leadership with Need for Clarity as a Moderator in Research and Development Organizations," *Journal of Applied Psychology,* April 1989, pp. 208–12.

[45]House and Mitchell, "Path-Goal Theory," p. 84.

1. Leader behavior is effective to the extent that the subordinates perceive such behavior as a source of immediate satisfaction or as instrumental to future satisfaction.

2. Leader behavior is motivational to the extent that it makes satisfaction of subordinates' needs contingent on effective performance and that it complements the environment of subordinates by providing the guidance, clarity of direction, and rewards necessary for effective performance.

According to the path-goal theory, leaders should increase the number and kinds of rewards available to subordinates. In addition, the leader should provide guidance and counsel to clarify the manner in which these rewards can be obtained. This means that the leader should help subordinates clarify realistic expectancies and reduce the barriers to the accomplishment of valued goals. For example, counseling employees on their chances for promotion and helping them eliminate skill deficiencies so that a promotion becomes a more realistic possibility are appropriate leadership behaviors. The leader works at making the path to goals as clear as possible for subordinates. The style best suited to accomplish this is selected and applied. Thus, the path-goal approach requires flexibility from the leader to use whichever style is appropriate in a particular situation.

Situational Factors

Two situational, or contingency, variables are considered in the path-goal theory: *personal characteristics of subordinates* and *environmental pressures and demands* with which subordinates must cope to accomplish work goals and derive satisfaction.

An important personal characteristic is subordinates' *perceptions of* their own *ability.* The higher the degree of perceived ability relative to the task demands, the less likely the subordinate is to accept a directive leader style. This directive style of leadership would be viewed as unnecessarily close. In addition, a person's *locus of control* also affects responses. Individuals with an internal locus of control (they believe that rewards are contingent upon their efforts) are generally more satisfied with a participative style, while individuals who have an external locus of control (they believe that rewards are beyond their personal control) are generally more satisfied with a directive style.[46]

Environmental variables include factors that are not within the control of the subordinate but are important to satisfaction or to the ability to perform effectively.[47] These include the tasks, the formal authority system of the organization, and the work group. Any of these environmental factors can motivate or constrain the subordinate. Environmental forces may also serve as reward for acceptable levels of performance. For example, the subordinate could be motivated by the work group and receive satisfaction from co-workers' acceptance for doing a job according to group norms.

---

[46]Ibid.

[47]Ibid., p. 87.

FIGURE 11—6
The Path-Goal Model

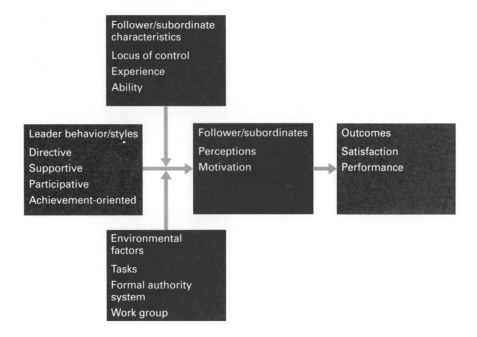

The path–goal theory proposes that leader behavior is motivational to the extent that it helps subordinates cope with environmental uncertainties. A leader who reduces the uncertainties of the job is considered to be a motivator because he or she increases the subordinates' expectations that their efforts lead to desirable rewards.

Figure 11–6 presents the features of the path-goal approach. The total path-goal approach has not been subjected to a complete test. Parts of the model, however, have been examined in field settings. One study found that when task structure (the repetitiveness or routineness of the job) was high, directive leader behavior was negatively related to satisfaction; when task structure was low, directive leader behavior was positively related to satisfaction. Also, when task structure was high, supportive leadership was positively related to satisfaction; under low task structure, there was no relationship between supportive leader behavior and satisfaction.[48]

Critique of the Path-Goal Model

There is some question about the predictive power of the path-goal model. One researcher suggested that subordinate performance might be the cause of changes in leader behavior instead of, as predicted by the model, the other way around.[49] A review of the path-goal approach suggested that the model had resulted in the development of only a few hypotheses. These reviewers also point to the record of inconsistent research results associated with the model.

---

[48]House and Dessler, "The Path-Goal Theory."

[49]C. Greene, "Questions of Causation in the Path-Goal Theory of Leadership," *Academy of Management Journal,* March 1979, pp. 22–41.

	Fiedler's Contingency Model	House's Path-Goal Model
Leadership qualities	Leaders are task or relationship oriented. The job should be engineered to fit the leader's style.	Leaders can increase followers' effectiveness by applying proper motivational techniques.
Assumptions about followers	Followers prefer different leadership styles, depending on task structure, leader-member relations, and position power.	Followers have different needs that must be fulfilled with the help of a leader.
Leader effectiveness	Effectiveness of the leader is determined by the interaction of environment and personality factors.	Effective leaders are those who clarify for followers the paths or behaviors that are best suited.
History of research: problems	If investigations not affiliated with Fiedler are used, the evidence is contradictory on the accuracy of the model.	Model has generated very little research interest in last decade.

TABLE 11–5

Summary Comparison of Two Important Situational Models of Leadership

They agree that research has consistently shown that the higher the task structure of subordinate jobs, the higher the relationship between supportive leader behavior and subordinate satisfaction. However, they maintain that the second main hypothesis of the path-goal model has not received consistent support. This hypothesis—the higher the task structure, the lower the relationship between directive leader behavior and subordinate satisfaction—has received only some support.[50]

On the positive side, one must admit that the path-goal model is an improvement over the trait and personal-behavioral theories. It attempts to indicate which factors affect the motivation to perform. In addition, the path-goal approach introduces both situational factors and individual differences when examining leader behavior and outcomes such as satisfaction and performance. The approach makes an effort to explain why a particular style of leadership works best in a given situation. As more research accumulates, this type of explanation will have practical utility for those interested in the leadership process in work settings.

COMPARING THE SITUATIONAL APPROACHES

The two models for examining situation leadership have some similarities and some differences. They are similar in that they (1) focus on the dynamics of leadership, (2) have stimulated research on leadership, and (3) remain controversial because of measurement problems, limited research testing, or contradictory research results.

The themes of each model are summarized in Table 11–5. Fiedler's model, the most tested, is perhaps the most controversial. His view of leader behavior

[50]C. A. Schriesheim and A. DeNisi, "Task Dimensions as Moderators of the Effects of Instrumental Leadership: A Two-Sample Replicated Test of Path-Goal Leadership Theory," *Journal of Applied Psychology*, October 1981, pp. 589–97.

centers on task- and relationship-oriented tendencies and how these interact with task and position power. The path-goal approach emphasizes the instrumental actions of leaders and four styles for conducting these actions—directive, supportive, participative, and achievement oriented.

The situational variables discussed in each approach differ somewhat. There is also a different view of outcome criteria for assessing how successful the leader behavior has been: Fiedler discusses leader effectiveness, and the path-goal approach focuses on satisfaction and performance.

SUMMARY OF KEY POINTS

— As the ability to influence followers, leadership involves the use of power and the acceptance of the leader by the followers. This ability to influence followers is related to the followers' need satisfaction.

— The trait approach has resulted in attempts to predict leadership effectiveness from physical, sociological, and psychological traits. The search for traits has led to studies involving effectiveness and such factors as height, weight, intelligence, and personality.

— There continues to be a great deal of semantic confusion and overlap in the definition of leadership behavior. Such terms as *employee centered, job centered, initiating structure,* and *consideration* are classified as personal-behavioral descriptions of what the leader does.

— The personal-behavioral approaches suggest that leaders should seriously consider situational variables such as the follower's expectations, skills, role clarity, and previous experiences. Leaders can do little to improve effectiveness unless they can properly modify these variables or change their style of leadership.

— The *situational approach* emphasizes the importance of forces within the leader, the subordinates, and the organization. These forces interact and must be properly diagnosed if effectiveness is to be achieved.

— The *contingency model* proposes that the performance of groups is dependent on the interaction of leadership style and situational favorableness. The three crucial situational factors are leader-member relations, task structure, and position power.

DISCUSSION AND REVIEW QUESTIONS

1. Suppose that you, an undergraduate in a business school, found yourself appointed to lead a group of Ph.D. scientists in a research laboratory of a large pharmaceutical firm. Would you need to lead such a group of subordinates? Explain.

2. In what kind of work situations would a leader not be needed to help motivate a group or a team? Think of three situations and explain why a leader is not usually needed.

3. Present a path-goal explanation of a mother attempting to help her daughter improve her college study habits and grade performance.

4. Why is measurement such a crucial issue when discussing the Ohio State approach to leadership?

5. Can management or organizational behavior courses be used to train leaders how to lead followers? Explain.

6. Why has the trait approach failed to present a universally acceptable set of effective leadership traits?

7. According to the contingency theory, an alternative to modifying the style of leadership through training is changing the favorableness of the situation. What is meant by changing the favorableness of the situation?

8. Would a leader (on an assembly line) from Eastern Europe (Poland or Romania) be able to lead French workers on an assembly line in France? Explain.

9. Why should a leader examine the substitutes for leadership?

10. Why would a leader be replaced in a formal organizational group? In an informal group?

After reviewing this book, please take a minute to give us your opinion. We appreciate your comments.

Title: GIBSON ORG
Book No.: 08-1022-07   0-256-08046-1   Qty: 1

CAT	REFER	DATE	ST	SCH	PROF	SRC	O/L
08	221123	10/25/90	43	420	015	1	

1. Is this book suitable for your course(s)?

   Yes _____

   No _____

2. If yes, do you plan to adopt this book?

   Yes _____ Class size? _____

   No _____

MEDICAL U OF SO CAROLINA
     PROF ANNE O KILPATRICK
COL OF HEALTH RELATED PRO
171 ASHLEY AVENUE
CHARLESTON SC 29425

3. Please identify some of the features that caused you to select this text for your course(s).

   a.) _____

   b.) _____

   c.) _____

4. If you have chosen not to adopt this text, please explain any deficiencies you may have encountered:

   Content _____ Comprehension Level/Too High _____

   Presentation _____ Comprehension Level/Too Low _____

   Comments: _____

   _____

5. What book(s) are you now using in your course?

   _____

   _____

   Why did you choose this book?

   _____

   _____

6. If you have not yet adopted a textbook for your course, what is your decision date? _____

7. Can we quote your comments?   Yes ☐   No ☐

   Your comments are appreciated.

Please write: Marketing Department   **Or Call:** Faculty Services
                   RICHARD D. IRWIN, INC.   (800)-323-4560   (Continental U.S.)
                   1818 Ridge Road   (708)-798-6000 (Outside U.S.)
                   Homewood, IL 60430

Would you be willing to discuss this questionnaire with us? If so, please indicate your phone number. _____

_____

Fold, moisten and mail.

Meeting your needs is our business. You can help us meet these needs by sharing your opinions with us. This *IRWIN* text has been sent to you with our compliments. We hope you'll share in our enthusiasm over this excellent text. Please share your opinions with us.

▼ Times Mirror
◢ Books

BUSINESS REPLY MAIL

FIRST CLASS   PERMIT NO. 17   HOMEWOOD, IL

POSTAGE WILL BE PAID BY ADDRESSEE

MARKETING DEPARTMENT
RICHARD D. IRWIN, INC.
1818 Ridge Road
Homewood, IL 60430-9986

ADDITIONAL REFERENCES

Bass, B. M., and R. M. Stogdill. *Bass and Stogdill's Handbook of Leadership.* New York: Free Press, 1990.

Gardner, J. W. *On Leadership.* New York: Free Press, 1990.

Jacques, E. "In Praise of Hierarchy." *Harvard Business Review,* January–February 1990, pp. 127–33.

Kraut, A. I.; P. R. Pedigo; D. D. McKenna; and M. D. Dunnette. "The Role of the Manager: What's Really Important in Different Management Jobs." *Academy of Management Executive,* November 1989, pp. 286–93.

Posner, B. G. "Owner's Rights." *Inc.,* January 1990, p. 114.

Zaleznik, A. "The Leadership Gaps." *Academy of Management Executive,* February 1990, pp. 7–22.

CASE FOR ANALYSIS

A NEW LEADERSHIP POSITION

Dancey Electronics Company is located in a suburb of Dallas. Management forecasts have indicated that the company should enjoy moderate growth during the next 10 years. This growth rate would require the promotion of three employees into newly created general manager positions. These individuals would then be required to spend most of their time working with departmental managers and less time on production, output, and cost issues.

A majority of the candidates for the three new positions have been with the company for at least 15 years. They are all skilled in the production aspects of operations. Company vice president Don Kelly believed, however, that none of the candidates has the training or overall insight into company problems to move smoothly into the general manager positions. Despite these anticipated problems, the board of directors decided that the three new general managers would be recruited from within Dancey.

In attempting to find the best candidates for the new positions, Dancey hired a consulting firm, Management Analysis Corporation (MAC), to perform an internal search for qualified individuals. Through interviews, testing, and a review of company records, the consulting firm generated a list of six candidates.

One of the candidates found by MAC was Joe Morris. The analysis used to assess Joe involved the study of environmental variables and his current style of leadership. Exhibit 1 presents a profile of Joe's leadership style and various environmental factors that have some impact on this style.

EXHIBIT 1

Morris Profile of Leadership

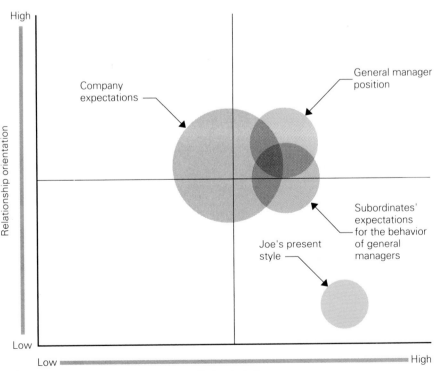

Joe's present leadership style, which is high in task orientation and low in relationship orientation, is similar to the leadership styles of the other five general manager candidates. The expectations of the company, the potential subordinates of the general manager, and the new position of general manager are not consistent with any of the candidates' present leadership styles. The shaded, intersecting area indicates where the expectations of the company, the new position, and the subordinates would be consistent. According to MAC, this is the ideal leadership style for candidates to use as the general managers. If Joe or any of the other candidates were to accept the general manager job, they would have to significantly increase their relationship orientation. If they did not change their orientation, the probability of failure, according to the consulting firm, would be high.

Don Kelly was adamant about not going outside Dancey to find three potentially successful new general managers. He and the entire board of directors wanted to utilize a recruitment-from-within policy to secure the three best general managers. It was Don's belief that a leader could modify his or her style of leadership to meet new situational demands. This belief and the internal recruitment plan led Don to call a meeting to discuss a program to improve the compatibility between the three general managers finally selected — Joe Morris, Randy Cooper, and Gregg Shumate — and the environmental factors: the company, the subordinates, and the requirements of the new position.

Questions for Consideration

1. Do you believe that the diagnosis and resulting profile prepared by Management Analysis Corporation were a necessary step in the process of finding a potentially successful group of general managers? Explain.

2. What alternatives are available to modify the potential effectiveness of Joe Morris in the new general manager position?

3. Why will it be difficult for Joe Morris to modify his style of leadership?

ADAPTING LEADERSHIP SKILLS TO PEOPLE PROBLEMS

Objectives

1. To determine if a particular style of leadership could be used to solve the problem.
2. To identify how a leader must proceed in a delicate situation involving employees, organization culture, and work performance.

Related Topics

Motivation, work rules, and organization etiquette are all issues covered in this exercise.

Starting the Exercise

Each class member is to read the case involving Bob and Nancy.

Case: What to Do with Bob and Nancy?

Dave Simpson was sitting at his desk, wondering how the devil to handle this situation. In engineering school, they don't tell you what to do when you think two of your key subordinates are having an affair! Dave knew a lot about the relative conducting properties of metals, but what about the properties of people?

Dave was engineering manager of a division in a large corporation situated on the East Coast. The division comprised 3 engineering supervisors, 5 lead engineers, and approximately 55 engineers (see Exhibit 1). The past two years had seen several reductions in work force due to a temporary decline in the business base. The remaining men and women in the organization were "cream of the crop," all hard workers with a professional attitude about their jobs; any deadwood was long gone. The division had just won a large contract which would provide for long-term growth but would also require a heavy workload until new people could be hired and trained.

The work of the organization was highly technical and required considerable sharing of ideas within and between the individual groups. This need for internal cooperation and support had been amplified because the organization was still understaffed.

Dave's previous secretary had transferred to an outplant location just before the new contract award, and it had taken a long time to find a suitable replacement. Because of a general shortage within the company, Dave had been forced to hire temporary help from a secretarial service. After several months, he found Nancy and felt very fortunate to have located an experienced secretary from within the company. She was in her mid-30s, was attractive, had a pleasant disposition, and was very competent.

In the electronic design group was an enthusiastic, highly respected lead engineer named Bob. Bob and Dave had been close friends for several years, having started with the company at the same time. They shared several common interests, which had led to spending a fair amount of time together away from work.

Bob was struggling to get into management, and Dave's more rapid advancement had put a strain on the friendship. Dave had moved up from co-worker to being his boss and finally to being his boss's boss. Dave felt they could still be good friends at work, but he could not show Bob any favoritism. Bob understood the situation.

From Nancy's first day on the job, Bob began to hang around her desk. He would go out of his way to start conversations and draw her attention. This was not a surprise, since Nancy was attractive and Bob had gained a reputation over the years as being a bit of a "wolf." He was always the first on the scene when an attractive new female joined the program.

Before long, Bob and Nancy began eating lunch together. As time passed, the lunch dates became a regular routine, as did their trips together to the coffee machine. Their conversations during the working day also became more frequent. Dave felt slightly concerned about the wasted time, but since the quality and quantity of their work was not suffering in any measurable way, he did not say anything to either person. Furthermore, it was not unreasonable for Bob to be having numerous conversations with her since she had been instructed to provide typing and clerical support to the engineers whenever she had idle time. (Bob's section was temporarily looking for a secretary, and the engineers were developing several new documents.)

After a few months, Bob and Nancy introduced their spouses to each other, and the two couples began to get together for an increasing number of social gatherings. Bob and Nancy continued their frequent lunch dates, now leaving the plant for lunch and occasionally returning late. This was not considered a major rule infraction if the lateness was infrequent and if the time were made up in the long run. This tolerance policy was generally respected by all, including Bob and Nancy. On balance, the company seemed to be receiving at least a full week's work from both of them, since they often worked late.

Table of Organization   Exhibit 1

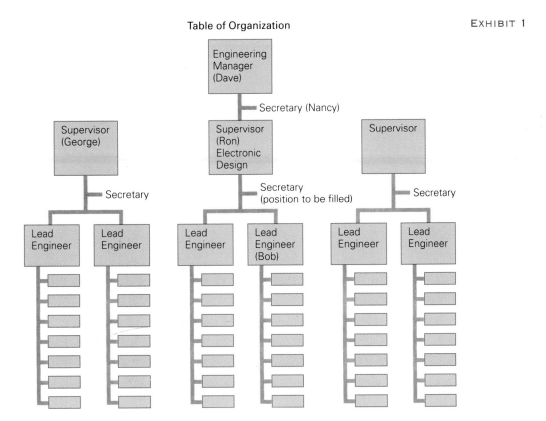

What was also going on (but Dave didn't learn about until later) was that Bob and Nancy were calling each other on the phone during the workday even though they worked in the same general area, just desks apart. They would wait until Dave had left the office and then chat on the phone. However, Nancy's work performance was not visibly affected.

Of course, the internal grapevine was at work, and occasionally Dave would be asked about the situation between Bob and Nancy. "Do you know they've been seen having cocktails together in the evening?" "Did you know Nancy was having marital problems?" "Does Bob's wife know what's going on?"

It was apparent that Bob and Nancy were starting to have an affair, but how serious it was, and how long it would last, wasn't known. They were being very careful around Dave, and almost all of what Dave knew was based upon second- and third-hand information and rumors. At this point, about four months after Nancy had started work, Dave did speak to Ron, Bob's supervisor, about it; but Ron was anxious to downplay the whole thing. He was willing to talk to Bob about the late lunches but unwilling to discuss anything else. This seemed appropriate since, from the company's standpoint, employees' private lives were their own business. Ron was new to the organization, and this factor contributed to his reluctance to discuss a delicate issue.

Dave decided not to confront Bob directly. If their relationship had been as close as it had been in years past, he might have spoken to Bob about the rumors going around, but during this period the friendship had further deteriorated. They were talking on a less personal level, and Bob was spending less off-hour time with old friends. Furthermore, Dave knew from previous discussions that Bob was particularly sensitive about private matters. "He probably wouldn't welcome my advice," thought Dave.

Dave did speak to Nancy about the need to be back in the office at the end of the lunch hour, but he had not made an issue out of it. Even though it was a definite annoyance when she was not there to answer the phone or type a memo, her performance had not declined. Dave certainly did not want to bring up the issue of an affair to Nancy. He imagined what might arise: tears, defensive denial (much of what Dave thought was going on would be difficult to substantiate if Nancy were to challenge his assessment), and even potential legal ramifications if the situation were handled improperly. Bob and Nancy could claim that their reputations or careers had been damaged. (Dave also didn't want to raise this issue with Personnel; it might permanently tarnish both of their records.)

During this same time frame, there was a dramatic change in Bob's personal appearance. Instead of his usual coat-and-tie attire, he started wearing open-front shirts and a beaded necklace in an attempt to acquire the current "macho" look. Although perhaps acceptable in a southern California business office, it certainly was out of place in the Northeast with the more conservative environment of the company. As a lead engineer, Bob directed, and often presented to management, the work of 12 other engineers. The custom was for all engineers and managers to wear a coat and tie, especially since they might be called upon, with little notice, to meet with a customer or higher management. Even though Bob's attire was considered unprofessional, there was nothing in the company's written dress code requirement to forbid it.

Up to this point, there had been no serious violation of company rules by either Bob or Nancy, although rules were being bent and tolerance policies abused.

Then the situation took a turn for the worse while Dave was on a two-week company trip with Ron. Bob and Nancy used the opportunity to go out for a very long lunch. When they returned just before quitting time, George, one of the other supervisors, called Bob into his office and suggested that he "clean up his act."

George told Bob that he was being foolish in chasing Nancy and that, among other things, he was jeopardizing his career opportunities with the company. Bob denied being anything more than friends with Nancy and politely told George to stay out of his private affairs.

When Dave returned from his trip and heard of the incident, he told Ron to reprimand Bob and make it clear to him that "his actions are unacceptable and that further long lunch periods will not be tolerated." Bob apologized, said he would make up the time, and that it wouldn't happen again.

Dave spoke to Nancy, and she also promised that there would be no more long lunches. But this was not the end of their noontime, outplant lunch dates, and before long, Nancy's husband Ted got involved. Ted was a salesman for the company and worked in the same building. He began to drop by at lunchtime to question the engineers about Nancy's whereabouts. In addition, he started calling Dave after work, wanting to know when Nancy had left and expressing concern that she had not yet arrived home. This questioning was an unpleasant experience for everybody.

By now, the entire organization was well aware of the irregular relationship and was growing disrespectful of both Bob and Nancy. This was a difficult situation for the engineers. The attitudes of the organization had always been very professional, and the success of each group depended upon teamwork and strong leadership from its lead engineer. Bob had been highly respected for his technical competence and ability to direct. In addition, the members of his group knew Bob's family and had always considered him to be a good family man. Now, this image had been destroyed. From a technical standpoint, Bob was still an excellent engineer and a vital resource on the new contract. But with the group's declining respect, Bob was becoming less effective as a leader. Bob's own engineers felt very uncomfortable about the situation. They believed that Bob's real interests at work were more with Nancy than with them.

The situation had now deteriorated to the point where total organization effectiveness was being measurably affected. Something had to be done to remedy this situation. But what to do?

Completing the Exercise

After individually reviewing the case, the class will divide into groups of four to eight members. In a 20- to 30-minute period, the group will discuss what actions Dave should take and why. Each group will then report its proposal strategies to the entire class.

12

Leadership
Emerging Concepts and Approaches

AN ORGANIZATIONAL
ISSUE FOR DEBATE   ARE THERE SIGNIFICANT DIFFERENCES IN MEN AND
WOMEN LEADERS?

ARGUMENT FOR*

Since the early 70s, more and more women have entered the work force and moved upward in management. Despite their progress, however, the evidence is still convincing that women differ from men as leaders. Research has shown that women fear success. How can a person lead others if she fears being successful?

There are also reports that women do not possess the emotional stability needed to serve in leadership roles. When faced with pressure, the hard and fast activities of daily confrontations, and the need to stand up to a "bully" colleague, they fall apart, cry, or run away.

Women state that they want to be treated like men, but do they really? They want time off for personal reasons. Women do not want some of the more difficult jobs, such as evening shifts, frequent travel, and managing rowdy, undisciplined, physically threatening employees.

In terms of leadership charisma, transformational skills, and serving as role models, women come up short. Certainly, there are some women who are better leaders than men. There are also some women who control their emotions, who can do any difficult job, and who enthusiastically seek success. However, these women, a small minority, number very few in organizations.

Today, it is popular to be on the side of similarities. However, finding female leaders who are respected by men and women co-workers, who are strong role models for society, and who are effective performers is a difficult task. We can continue to search for similarities, and we will occasionally find women suited for some leadership positions. However, to conclude that men and women leaders are generally alike in terms of style, motivation, interpersonal competence, and philosophy is unrealistic. Instead of always searching for similarities, researchers should permit the scientific evidence to accumulate before reaching a conclusion.

Women are different than men in work organization. Let's identify situations in which these differences can be used effectively to achieve better performance. Researchers who attempt to force the notion that men and women leaders are similar are missing an important opportunity. That opportunity is to match women leaders and men leaders with jobs, groups, and situations that are best suited to the characteristics possessed by the individual.

ARGUMENT AGAINST

Despite comments, anecdotes, and folklore, there is really little difference in the leadership style and effectiveness of women and men. Throughout history, according to the norms of particular cultures, the roles of men and women in society have tended to be different. The nature of these roles is gradually changing in Western economies. More and more women are completing university work, starting businesses, moving into leadership positions.

The so-called reports about women being too emotional and fearful of success are not scientifically validated. They are simply reports, myths, unsubstantiated folklore. Where are the scientific studies? They do not exist, because they were never conducted. There is no scientific evidence that suggests that men are better leaders than women.

The issue of men and women in leadership roles is a loaded one. Some individuals honestly believe that women do not have the capacity to lead. But very few have concerned themselves with the question of whether *men* in general make good leaders. Why then should the question of whether women make good leaders be so frequently asked?

As the number of women within organizations increases, nothing positive results from unsubstantiated comments about flaws in emotional stability, style, and interpersonal competence. The time has come to end the debate, the political posturing about men versus women in leadership positions. Discrimination based on sex is illegal and will damage the prospects of the United States ever regaining the competitive edge in the area of internationalization. Women are going to be needed more than ever to serve as leaders and role models.

Some women make outstanding leaders, and some are failures. The same can be said about men. Research results indicate that female leaders are similar in most respects to their male counterparts. If there is one major difference, it is that women are entering markets that are not traditionally male dominated. Thus, a larger number of female leaders are being reported in the service industry and small businesses. The growth of women-owned businesses is a reflection of a changing society. The fact that more examples of women leaders are to be found in retailing and services reflects greater opportunities for women.

The argument that the public identifies with few female leaders is true. However, that is not because female leaders do not exist. They exist but in smaller numbers than males, because females have for years been blocked and discouraged from leadership positions. The times are rapidly changing, and the issue of whether men and women leaders are similar is no longer relevant. Female leaders have intelligence, self-confidence, charisma, and interpersonal competence—the same attributes possessed by male leaders.

*Source: Based on Sue Birley, Ann M. Morrison, and Mary Ann von Glinow, "Women and Minorities in Management," *American Psychologist,* February 1990, pp. 200–208; "Female Entrepreneurs: Are They Really Different?" *Journal of Small Business Management,* January 1989, pp. 32–37; Burt Nenus, *The Leader's Edge* (Chicago: Contemporary Books, 1989).

A frequently heard complaint about the study of leadership is that it is simply a list of traits, behaviors, and situational concepts. Chapter 12 presents some of the theories and research that have stimulated the criticisms. The scarcity and ambiguities of leadership have fueled the problem. There is a scarcity when we compare our present-day leaders to statesmen, executives, and social leaders of yesterday: Abraham Lincoln, Winston Churchill, Gandhi, Susan B. Anthony, and Alfred Sloan.

In order to develop more precision about leadership as we know it today, a number of approaches have been proposed. They do not answer the past versus today leadership comparisons. However, the approaches are more informative, meaningful, and realistic in that they often use job-related or task-oriented settings and examples. This chapter will examine what we refer to as emerging leadership models, research, and applications. Are these approaches the final answer, the most refined, or the most rigorously studied views of leadership? No. They are, however, interesting, progressive, and integrative explanations of leadership.

SILENCE IS NOT A GOLDEN VIRTUE FOR LEADERS

A good follower is hard to find today. To be classified as a good follower takes courage, honesty, and risky communication. A good follower must tell the truth. Followers who speak the truth and leaders who listen are ahead of most others.

Movie mogul Samuel Goldwyn had a philosophy about sound backtalk or follower opinion. After a series of box-office losers, Mr. Goldwyn called his brain trust together and told them: "I want you to tell me exactly what's wrong with me and MGM, even if it means losing your job." The yes-man or -woman is not what Goldwyn was asking for. He was talking about having followers who tell you accurately what your strengths and weaknesses are and how you are really doing.

Speaking back, giving an honest opinion, is vital if the work unit is to learn how to improve. The follower's obligation is to share opinions, feelings, and ideas with the leader. Only if accurate information is received can leaders be sure that they are doing what is best. The fortunate leaders are those that have courageous and honest followers.

Some advocates suggest that dissent should be rewarded and encouraged. Remaining silent causes stress, strain, and dishonesty to flourish. Taking a risk and speaking out is what effective leaders want and need. What job is worth the stress and strain of following a leader who values loyalty in the narrowest sense?

At a Washington press club gathering over 30 years ago, Soviet prime minister Nikita Khrushchev was asked a question: "Today, you talked about the hideous rule of your predecessor, Stalin. You were one of his closest aides and colleagues during those years. What were you doing all that time?" Khrushchev's face grew red. "Who asked that?" he shouted out. No one answered. "Who asked that?" he repeated firmly. Again, there was total silence. "That's what I was doing," Khrushchev said. Silence will not help a leader improve.

Source: Warren Bennis, "Followers Make Good Leaders Good," *New York Times,* December 31, 1989, p. 3.

As the discussion in this chapter will illustrate, leaders can command respect, transform organizations from also-rans to successful units, and find the best combination of persuasion and authority to complete the job. The discussion also shows that effective leaders are good at diagnosing situations and listening to followers. A leader that does not encourage communication is at a disadvantage. The Close-Up on "Silence" emphasizes what is found throughout the chapter: that a leader needs subordinates who will speak up and needs to work at listening to what they communicate.

As you review each of the approaches presented in this chapter, think about the role that diagnosis and listening play. In using the Vroom–Yetton, attribution, or transformational approach, the effective leader must be skilled in diagnosis and communication. Do you possess these skills?

VROOM–JAGO REVISED LEADERSHIP MODEL

Victor Vroom and P. Yetton initially developed a leadership and decision-making model that indicates the situations in which various degrees of participative decision making are appropriate.[1] In contrast to Fred Fiedler, Vroom and Yetton attempted to provide a *normative model* that a leader can use in making decisions. Their approach assumes that no one particular leadership style is appropriate for each situation. Unlike Fiedler, they assume that leaders must be flexible enough to change their leadership styles to fit situations. It was Fiedler's contention that the situation must be altered to fit an individual's leadership style.

In developing their model, Vroom and Yetton made these assumptions:

1. The model should be of value to leaders or managers in determining which leadership styles they should use in various situations.
2. No single leadership style is applicable to all situations.
3. The main focus should be the problem to be solved and the situation in which the problem occurs.
4. The leadership style used in one situation should not constrain the styles used in other situations.
5. Several social processes influence the amount of participation by subordinates in problem solving.

Applying these assumptions resulted in the initial model that was concerned with leadership and decision making. The **Vroom-Yetton leadership model** generated interest among researchers, practitioners, and trainers. However, to improve the accuracy and predictability of the initial model, Vroom and Jago have developed a modified model.[2]

Nature of the Vroom-Jago Model

The new model shares two key features with its predecessor. First, it employs the same decision processes as those used in the discussion of the original Vroom-Yetton model. The terms for describing decision processes—AI, AII, CI, CII, and GII, with the addition of GI and DI for individual problems—are carried over intact from the previous model. These are presented in Table 12–1.

Second, the new model also retains the criteria against which the effects of participation are evaluated. Like the earlier model, the new model is concerned with evaluating the effects of participation on decision quality, decision acceptance, subordinate development, and time.

Decision effectiveness. The new model retains the concept of decision effectiveness (D_{Eff}). As shown in the following equation, D_{Eff} is dependent on decision quality (D_{Qual}) and decision commitment (D_{Comm}):

VROOM-YETTON MODEL
Leadership model that specifies leadership decision-making procedures most effective in each of several different situations: two autocratic (AI, AII); two consultative (CI, CII); one oriented toward joint decisions of the leader and group (GII).

---

[1] Victor Vroom and P. Yetton, *Leadership and Decision Making* (Pittsburgh: University of Pittsburgh Press, 1973).

[2] Victor H. Vroom and Arthur G. Jago, *The New Leadership: Managing Participation in Organizations* (Englewood Cliffs, N.J.: Prentice Hall, 1988).

TABLE 12—1

Decision Styles for
Leadership: Individuals and
Groups

Individual Level	Group Level
AI. You solve the problem or make the decision yourself, using information available to you at that time.	**AI.** You solve the problem or make the decision yourself, using information available to you at that time.
AII. You obtain any necessary information from the subordinate, then decide on the solution to the problem yourself. You may or may not tell the subordinate what the problem is while getting the information. The role played by your subordinate in making the decision is clearly one of providing specific information that you request, rather than generating or evaluating alternative solutions.	**AII.** You obtain any necessary information from subordinates, then decide on the solution to the problem yourself. You may or may not tell the subordinates what the problem is in getting the information from them. The role played by your subordinates in making the decision is clearly one of providing specific information that you request, rather than generating or evaluating solutions.
CI. You share the problem with the relevant subordinate, getting ideas and suggestions. Then *you* make the decision. This decision may or may not reflect your subordinate's influence.	**CI.** You share the problem with the relevant subordinates individually, getting their ideas and suggestions without bringing them together as a group. Then *you* make the decision. This decision may or may not reflect your subordinates' influence.
GI. You share the problem with one of your subordinates, and together you analyze the problem and arrive at a mutually satisfactory solution in an atmosphere of free and open exchange of information and ideas. You both contribute to the resolution of the problem, with the relative contribution of each being dependent on knowledge rather than formal authority.	**CII.** You share the problem with your subordinates in a group meeting. In this meeting, you obtain their ideas and suggestions. Then *you* make the decision, which may or may not reflect your subordinates' influence.
DI. You delegate the problem to one of your subordinates, providing him or her with any relevant information that you possess, but giving him or her responsibility for solving the problem alone. Any solution the person reaches receives your support.	**GII.** You share the problem with your subordinates as a group. Together, you generate and evaluate alternatives and attempt to reach a consensus on a solution. Your role is much like that of chairperson, coordinating the discussion, keeping it focused on the problem, and making sure that the critical issues are discussed. You do not try to influence the group to adopt "your" solution, and you are willing to accept and implement any solution that has the support of the entire group.

$$D_{Eff} = D_{Qual} + D_{Comm} - D_{TP}$$

However, there is a third term in the equation. D_{TP} stands for *decision time penalty.* This term acknowledges that having sound thinking and a committed group to implement the decision is often not all that is needed to produce effective decisions. Decisions must also be made in a timely manner. Many decisions are made under severe time constraints. For example, an air-traffic controller has limited time to place airplanes in various zones before increasing the risk of an accident. D_{TP} takes on a value of zero whenever no stringent time constraints limit the process chosen.

Decision effectiveness is the criterion to use if there were no values attached to either time or to development or if those values were completely unknown. However, a more comprehensive criterion called *overall effectiveness* (O_{Eff}) is introduced. O_{Eff} is greatly influenced by decision effectiveness, but, as shown in the following equation, its values reflect the remaining two criteria affected by degree of participation. Both consequences pertain to effects of the decision process on available "human capital." Independent of the effectiveness of the decisions produced, a decision process can have effects, either positive or negative or both, on the energy and talent available for subsequent work.

$$O_{Eff} = D_{Eff} - Cost + Development$$

Negative effects on human capital occur because decision processes use up time and energy, even in the absence of a time constraint. An executive group meeting including a senior executive and five subordinates and lasting two hours would consume 12 work hours. The value of that time is certainly not zero, although its precise cost varies with the opportunity costs of the meeting. Which other activities had to be forsaken by each of the managers to participate in that meeting? When critically important activities are not carried out because of time spent in meetings, costs are incurred that must, at the very least, be "traded off" against the benefits of the meeting. In the above equation, cost represents the value of time lost through use of a given decision process.

On the other hand, participation can *contribute* to human capital. Participation in decision making can build teamwork, strengthen commitment to organizational goals, and contribute to the development of participants' technical and managerial skills. In the O_{Eff} equation, development is intended to represent organizational benefits that extend beyond the individual decision under consideration.

Situational variables. One of the biggest differences between the traditional Vroom-Yetton model and the new one lies in the problem attributes. Vroom-Yetton used seven problem attributes; the new model continues the use of these seven and adds five.

The most important additional problem attribute takes into consideration the information and expertise possessed by subordinates. This additional attribute pertaining to information was included because the original Vroom-Yetton model performed somewhat better in accounting for differences in the acceptance of decisions than it did in predicting decision quality.[3] Incorporating information possessed by subordinates and that possessed by the leader is expected to improve predictions about the quality of decisions and to further enhance the validity, or batting average, of the model.

A second new problem attribute pertains to the existence of stringent time constraints that could restrict opportunities to involve subordinates. The third involves geographical restrictions on interactions among subordinates. The

---

[3]See Victor H. Vroom, "Can Leaders Learn to Lead?" *Organizational Dynamics,* Winter 1976, pp. 17–28; Victor H. Vroom and Arthur G. Jago, "On the Validity of the Vroom-Yetton Model," *Journal of Applied Psychology,* April 1978, pp. 151–62; R. H. G. Field, "A Test of the Vroom-Yetton Normative Model of Leadership," *Journal of Applied Psychology,* October 1982, pp. 523–32; Victor H. Vroom and Arthur G. Jago, "Decision Making as a Social Process: Normative and Descriptive Models of Leader Behavior," *Decision Sciences,* October 1974, pp. 743–69; Arthur G. Jago and Victor H. Vroom, "Predicting Leader Behavior from a Measure of Behavior Intent," *Academy of Management Journal,* December 1978, pp. 715–21; R. H. G. Field, "A Critique of the Vroom-Yetton Contingency Model of Leadership Behavior," *Academy of Management Review,* April 1979, pp. 249–57; Arthur G. Jago and Victor H. Vroom, "Perceptions of Leadership Style: Superior and Subordinate Descriptions of Decision-Making Behavior," in *Leadership Frontiers,* ed. J. G. Hunt and L. L. Larson (Carbondale: Southern Illinois University Press, 1975), pp. 103–20.

original Vroom-Yetton model envisioned managers and subordinates located, if not in adjacent offices, at least sufficiently proximate to one another so that interaction could take place relatively easily. Thus, the Vroom-Yetton model prescribed group meetings of managers separated by thousands of miles. Without denigrating the usefulness of such meetings, the benefits that the Vroom-Yetton model predicted from joint decision making may not outweigh the costs of assembling far-flung managers in one central location. The revised model addresses this issue by ascertaining not only the existence of geographical constraints but also whether the expected benefits might outweigh the costs.

Finally, the other two new attributes concern the importance of time and development. In the new model, these are not either-or judgments introduced after the fact to guide the choice among equally feasible alternatives. Instead, they are independent judgments obtained simultaneously with judgments of other problem attributes; taken together, they affect the benefits and costs of employing participative methods.

Continuous scales.   The original Vroom-Yetton model utilized dichotomous (yes-no) judgments in generating the prescriptions of the model: Do you have enough information to make a high-quality decision? If you were to make the decision by yourself, is it reasonably certain that it would be accepted by your subordinates? Do subordinates share the organizational goals to be gained in this problem? These and other questions had to be answered either yes or no to be of any use to the model. "Maybe" responses, or even numerical probability estimates, were not recognized as admissible responses.

Of the 12 problem attributes in the new model, 10 have been designed to be expressed as five-point scales. The four attributes dealing with importance (quality, commitment, time, and development) are answered on scales ranging from "no importance" to "critical importance." Another six attributes (leader information, problem structure, commitment probability, goal congruence, conflict, and subordinate information) are expressed as probability estimates. For example, the question "Do you have sufficient information to make a high-quality decision?" can now be answered no, probably no, maybe, probably yes, or yes. Table 12–2 shows 4 of the 12 attributes, the questions used to measure them, and the permissible responses for each.

Application of the New Model

For a given situation, the new Vroom-Jago model predicts the components of decision effectiveness (D_{Eff}) and overall effectiveness (O_{Eff}) from additional mathematical formulas too complex to describe here. Using the manager's analysis of the situation represented by that manager's responses to the diagnostic questions, the formulas predict the most appropriate way of handling the situation, the second-best way, and so forth. However, the complexity of the equations precludes their pencil-and-paper application.

Vroom and Jago offer two alternatives for the application of their new model to actual managerial problems. The first is a computer program that guides the manager through the analysis of the situation and, with speed and accuracy, solves the relevant equations. The second method, more familiar to users of the original Vroom-Yetton model, employs decision trees that

TABLE 12—2

Problem Attributes in the
Vroom-Jago Model

QR: Quality Requirement

How important is the technical quality of this decision?

(1)	(2)	(3)	(4)	(5)
No Import	Low Import	Average Import	High Import	Critical Import

LI: Leader Information

Do you have sufficient information to make a high-quality decision?

(1)	(2)	(3)	(4)	(5)
No	Probably No	Maybe	Probably Yes	Yes

ST: Problem Structure

Is the problem well structured?

(1)	(2)	(3)	(4)	(5)
No	Probably No	Maybe	Probably Yes	Yes

TC: Time Constraint

Does a critically severe time constraint limit your ability to involve subordinates?

(1)		(5)
No		Yes

represent the operation of the complex equations if certain simplifying assumptions are made.[4]

Figure 12–1 shows one of these decision trees. The first simplifying assumption is that each problem attribute can be given a clear yes or no (or high or low) response. This restricts the application of the model to relatively unambiguous situations. The second simplifying assumption is that 4 of the 12 problem attributes are held constant. Severe time constraints and the geographical dispersion of subordinates (relatively infrequent occurrences) are assumed not to exist. Additionally, it is assumed that the manager's motivation to conserve time and to develop subordinates does not change. Figure 12–1 depicts what Vroom and Jago label the "time-driven" decision tree, applied to the manager's problem depicted in the Close-Up on a manufacturing manager. It is designed for the manager who places maximum weight on saving time and minimum weight on developing subordinates.

Other decision trees exist for managers who weight time and development differently. The important point is that each tree accurately reproduces the prescriptions of the complex equations and formulas if the simplifying assumptions are made.

---

[4]Victor H. Vroom and Arthur G. Jago, *The New Leadership: Cases and Manuals for Use in Leadership Training* (New Haven, Conn.: 1987). Authors retain all rights for decision trees, cases, and computer software.

FIGURE 12–1

Time-Driven Decision Tree

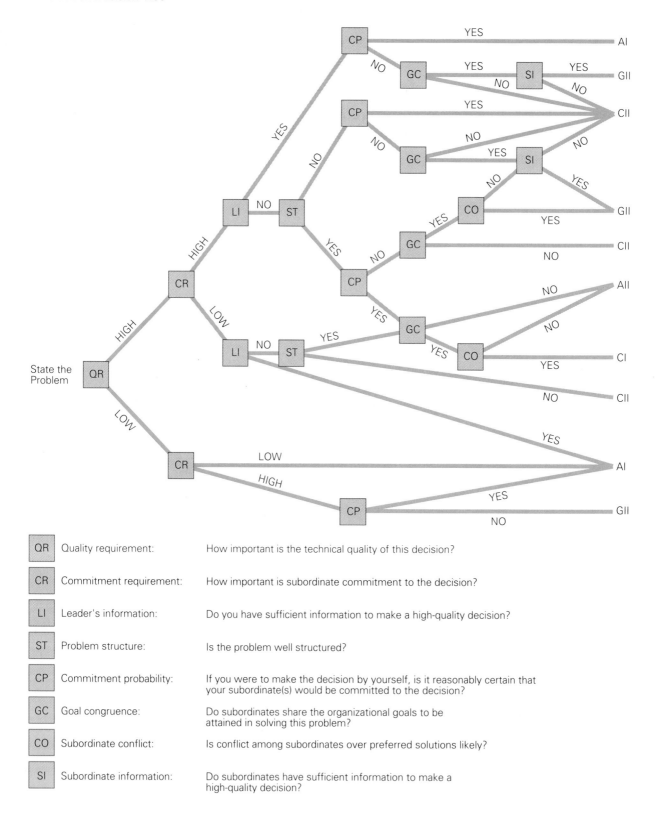

QR	Quality requirement:	How important is the technical quality of this decision?
CR	Commitment requirement:	How important is subordinate commitment to the decision?
LI	Leader's information:	Do you have sufficient information to make a high-quality decision?
ST	Problem structure:	Is the problem well structured?
CP	Commitment probability:	If you were to make the decision by yourself, is it reasonably certain that your subordinate(s) would be committed to the decision?
GC	Goal congruence:	Do subordinates share the organizational goals to be attained in solving this problem?
CO	Subordinate conflict:	Is conflict among subordinates over preferred solutions likely?
SI	Subordinate information:	Do subordinates have sufficient information to make a high-quality decision?

Validity of the Vroom-Jago Model

As was the case with the original Vroom-Yetton model when it was first introduced, the revised model currently lacks complete empirical evidence establishing its validity. Certainly, the model is thought to be consistent with what we now know about the benefits and costs of participation. Moreover, it represents a direct extension of the original 1973 model, for which ample validation evidence now does exist.[5] Nonetheless, without extensive evidence that the use of the new model can improve decision effectiveness—and, by extension, leadership success—its value as a theoretical contribution and as a practical tool remains open to question.

International research. A valuable aspect of the Vroom-Yetton and Vroom-Jago approaches to leadership is that research has been conducted both in and outside of the United States. In an increasingly interdependent world it is increasingly important not to reach conclusions about a theory or an approach, based solely on domestic samples of leaders.

One study of Austrian managers, used real decisions made by the participants.[6] Small discussion groups of managers reviewed each situation and provided (1) the decision process used by the manager and (2) an analysis of the problem attributes present in the situation. The study results indicated that small-group judgments were more accurate than a single person's judgments in analyzing written descriptions of the situations.

Another study looked at owner-operated cleaning franchises in the United States and Canada.[7] The leadership behavior of the American and Canadian owner-managers was assessed through the use of problem sets (one- to two-page scenarios similar to the "Manufacturing Manager" Close-Up). The results indicated that U.S. and Canadian managers who had above-average conformity to what the model prescribes had significantly more profitable businesses and more satisfied employees.

Limitations of the model. After a thorough review of leadership theories, models, and concepts, one behavioral scientist concluded that the Vroom-Yetton approach is unsurpassed in terms of scientific validity and practical usefulness.[8] Nevertheless, the model has some limitations.

The model forces a person to make a definite response. Because it fails to permit a "probably yes" or a "probably no," a yes or no response must be made. Work situations are not that easy to categorize; in many situations, neither yes nor no is accurate.

The model is also criticized for being too complex. It includes decision trees, ratings, problem sets. Although the model is complex, we believe this

---

[5]Ibid.

[6]W. Bohnisch, Arthur G. Jago, and G. Reber, "Zur interkulturellen Validitat des Vroom/Yetton Models," *Bebriebsivirtschaft*, 1987, pp. 85–93.

[7]C. Margerison and R. Gluf, "Leadership Decision-Making: An Empirical Test of the Vroom and Yetton Model," *Journal of Management Studies*, 1979, pp. 45–55.

[8]John B. Miner, "The Validity and Usefulness of Theories in an Emerging Science," *Academy of Management Review*, 1984, pp. 296–306.

ORGANIZATIONS:
CLOSE-UP

MANUFACTURING MANAGER

You are a manufacturing manager in a large electronics plant. The company's management has always been searching for ways of increasing efficiency. Recently, they installed new machines and put in a new, simplified work system. To the surprise of everyone, including yourself, the expected increase in productivity was not realized. In fact, production has begun to drop, quality has fallen off, and the number of employee separations has risen.

You do not believe there is anything wrong with the machines. You have had reports from other companies using them that confirm this opinion. You also have had representatives from the firm that built the machines go over them; they reported the machines are operating at peak efficiency.

You suspect that some parts of the new work system may be responsible for the change. This view is not widely shared among your immediate subordinates, four first-level supervisors and the supply manager. The drop in production has been variously attributed to poor training of the operators, lack of an adequate system of financial incentives, and poor morale. Clearly, this is an issue about which there is considerable depth of feeling within individuals and potential disagreement among your subordinates.

This morning you received a phone call from your division manager. He had just received your production figures for the last six months and was calling to express his concern. He indicated that the problem was yours to solve in any way that you think best, but that he would like to know within a week what steps you plan to take.

You share your division manager's concern with the falling productivity and know that your people are also concerned. The problem is to decide which steps to take to rectify the situation.

criticism is not warranted. The model is precise and specific, which means that some complexity is likely to be needed. Instead of discussing complexity, we might better state that the model, like most leadership explanations, simplifies how managers think and process stimuli.

Finally, organizational life is complex, and the way individual managers think is complex. The model, according to some critics, fails to deal with the realities today's managers face in terms of change, technological advancement, and international competition. Can any model deal with every contingency of leading and remain understandable and useful? Perhaps critics are expecting too much.

ATTRIBUTION THEORY OF LEADERSHIP

Attribution theory suggests that a leader's understanding of and ability to predict how people will react to events around them are enhanced by knowing their causal explanations for those events. Kelley stresses that attribution theory is mainly concerned with the cognitive processes by which a person

Attribute	Analysis	Ratings on Scales	For Use in Decision Tree
Quality requirement	Critical importance	(QR = 5)	High
Commitment requirement	High importance	(CR = 4)	High
Leader information	Probably no	(LI = 2)	No
Problem structure	No	(ST = 1)	No
Commitment productivity	Probably no	(CP = 2)	No
Goal congruence	Yes	(CG = 4)	Yes
Subordinate conflict	Yes	(CO = 5)	Yes
Subordinate information	Maybe yes	(SI = 3)	Yes
Time constraints	No	(TC = 1)	Held constant
Geographical dispersion	No	(GD = 1)	Held constant
Motivation — time	Critical importance	(MT = 5)	
Motivation — development	No importance	(MD = 1)	
Highest overall effectiveness (leadership style choice): GII			

The decision tree requires conversion of the scale to yes-no responses. Also, so that the decision tree does not become overly complex, the time constraint and geographical dispersion factors are held constant.

interprets behavior as being caused by (attributed to) certain cues in the relevant environment.[9] The emphasis of **attribution leadership theory** is on *why* some behavior has occurred. Since most causes of subordinate, or follower, behaviors are not directly observable, determining causes requires reliance on perception. In attribution theory, individuals are assumed to be rational and to be concerned about the causal linkages in their environments.

The attributional approach starts with the position that the leader is essentially an *information processor.*[10] In other words, the leader searches for informational cues as to "why" something is happening and then attempts to construct causal explanations that guide his or her leadership behavior. The process in simple terms appears to be follower behavior → leader attributions → leader behavior.

ATTRIBUTION LEADERSHIP THEORY

Theory of relationship between individual perception and interpersonal behavior. Suggests that understanding of and ability to predict how people will react to events are enhanced by knowing their causal explanations for those events.

[9]H. H. Kelley, "Attribution Theory in Social Psychology," in *Nebraska Symposium on Motivation,* ed. D. Levine (Lincoln: University of Nebraska Press, 1967).

[10]S. G. Green and Terence R. Mitchell, "Attributional Processes of Leaders in Leader-Member Interactions," *Organizational Behavior and Human Performance,* June 1979, pp. 429–58.

Leader's Attributions

Kelley suggests that the primary attributional task of the leader is to categorize the causes of follower, or subordinate, behavior into one of three source dimensions: person, entity, or context. That is, for any given behavior, such as poor quality of output, the leader's job is to determine whether the poor quality was caused by the person (e.g., inadequate ability), the task (entity), or some unique set of circumstances surrounding the event (context).

The leader seeks three types of information when forming attributions about a follower's behavior: distinctiveness, consistency, and consensus. For any behavior, the leader first attempts to determine whether the behavior is *distinctive* to a task—that is, whether the behavior occurs on this task but not on other tasks. Next, the leader is concerned about *consistency,* or how frequently the behavior occurs. Finally, the leader estimates *consensus,* the extent to which others behave in the same way. A behavior unique to one follower has low consensus; if it is common to other followers, this reflects high consensus.

Leader's Perception of Responsibility

The judgment of responsibility moderates the leader's response to an attribution. Clearly, the more a behavior is seen as caused by some characteristic of the follower (i.e., an internal cause) and the more the follower is judged to be responsible for the behavior, the more likely the leader is to take some action toward the follower. For example, an outcome (e.g., poor performance) may be attributed to factors outside the control of a person, such as not having the tools to do the job well, or to internal causes, such as lack of effort.

Attributional Leadership Model

Attribution theory offers a framework for explaining leader behavior more insightfully than either trait or personal-behavioral theories. Attribution theory attempts to explain *why* behaviors are happening;[11] trait and personal-behavioral theories are more descriptive and do not focus on the why issue. Furthermore, attribution theory can offer some predictions about a leader's response to a follower's behavior.

Figure 12–2 presents an attributional leadership model that emphasizes two important linkages. At the first linkage point, the leader attempts to make attributions about poor performance. These attributions are moderated by the three information types: distinctiveness, consistency, and consensus. The second linkage point suggests that the leader's behavior, or response, is determined by the attributions that he or she makes. This relationship between attribution and leader behavior is moderated by the leader's perception of responsibility. Is the responsibility internal or external?

---

[11]Terence R. Mitchell, S. C. Green, and Robert E. Wood, "An Attributional Model of Leadership and the Poor Performing Subordinate: Development and Validation," in *Research in Organizational Behavior,* ed. Barry M. Staw and Larry L. Cummings (Greenwich, Conn.: JAI Press, 1981).

FIGURE 12—2

An Attributional Leadership Model

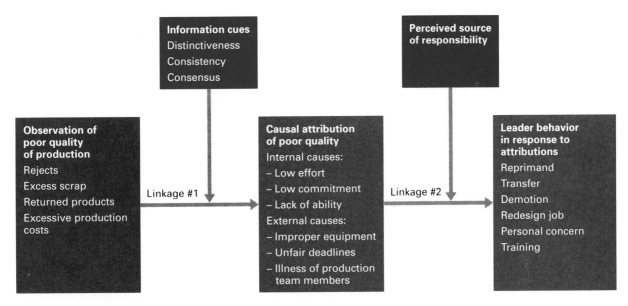

Source: Adapted from Terence R. Mitchell and Robert E. Wood, "An Empirical Test of an Attributional Model of Leader's Responses to Poor Performance," *Academy of Management Proceedings*, ed. Richard C. Huseman, 1979, p. 94.

One empirical test of attribution leadership theory examined nursing supervisors who were considered leaders. Distinctiveness, consistency, and consensus did influence the leader's attributions. Leaders who made attributions of internal causes (e.g., lack of effort) tended to use more punitive behaviors, and leaders tended to make more internal attributions and to respond more harshly when the problems were serious.[12]

An interesting research approach has been to include sex effects in the attributional model of leadership. Research regarding the sex of the leader and the sex of the subordinate has been largely neglected. A study of college students examined whether the sex of the leader, the sex of the subordinate, and the interaction between these two factors would affect both the attributions made for employees' poor performance and the corrective action taken by leaders.[13] The researchers concluded that the sex composition of the leader-subordinate dyad was a critical and neglected variable in attributional research.

---

[12]Terence R. Mitchell and Robert E. Wood, "An Empirical Test of an Attributional Model of Leader's Responses to Poor Performance," in *Academy of Management Proceedings,* ed. Richard C. Huseman, 1979, pp. 94–98.

[13]G. H. Dobbins, E. C. Pence, J. A. Orban, and J. A. Sgro, "The Effects of Sex of the Leader and Sex of the Subordinate on the Use of Organizational Control Policy," *Organizational Behavior and Human Performance,* December 1983, pp. 325–43.

Currently, research support for the attributional theory of leadership is limited. There is a need to test the theory in more organizational settings.[14] Understanding the causes of leader behavior or at least searching for these causes seems more promising for managerial use than does simply adding another trait or descriptive theory to the leadership literature.[15]

Leader Behavior: Cause or Effect?

We have implied that leader behavior has an effect on the follower's performance and job satisfaction. However, a sound basis exists for proposing that follower performance and satisfaction cause the leader to vary his or her leadership style. It has been argued that people develop positive attitudes toward objects that are instrumental to the satisfaction of their needs.[16] This argument can be extended to leader-follower relationships. For example, organizations reward leaders (managers) based on the performance of followers (subordinates). Leaders might then be expected to develop positive attitudes toward high-performing followers. Let us say that employee Joe's outstanding performance enables his boss, Mary, to receive the supervisory excellence award, a bonus of $1,000. The expectation then is that Mary would think highly of Joe and reward him with a better work schedule or job assignment. In this case, Joe's behavior leads to Mary's being rewarded, and she in turn rewards Joe.

In a field study, data were collected from first-line managers and from two of each manager's first-line supervisors. The purpose of this research was to assess the direction of causal influence in relationships between leader and follower variables. The results strongly suggested that (1) leader consideration behavior caused subordinate satisfaction and (2) follower performance caused changes in the leader's emphasis on both consideration and the structuring of behavior-performance relationships.[17]

Research on the cause-effect issue is still quite limited. To conclude that all leader behavior or even a significant portion of such behavior is a response to follower behavior would be premature. However, an examination of the leader-follower relationship in terms of **reciprocal causation** is needed. In reciprocal causation, leader behavior causes follower behavior, and follower behavior causes leader behavior.

Japanese management techniques suggest that the reciprocal causation view has some validity. Leaders and followers are emphasized in the Japanese consensus approach to managing. The Close-Up points out some crucial Japanese leadership principles.

RECIPROCAL CAUSATION

Argument that follower behavior impacts leader behavior and leader behavior influences follower behavior.

[14]John A. Pearce and A. S. DeNisi, "Attribution Theory and Strategic Decision Making: An Application to Coalition Formation," *Academy of Management Journal,* March 1983, pp. 119–28.

[15]D. A. Giola and H. P. Sims, Jr., "Cognitive-Behavior Connections: Attribution and Verbal Behavior in Leader-Subordinate Interactions," *Organizational Behavior and Human Decision Processes,* April 1986, pp. 197–229.

[16]D. Katz and E. Stotland, "A Preliminary Statement to a Theory of Attitude Structure and Change," in *A Study of Science,* ed. S. Koch (New York: McGraw-Hill, 1959).

[17]C. N. Greene, "The Reciprocal Nature of Influence between Leader and Subordinate," *Journal of Applied Psychology,* April 1975, pp. 187–93.

IMPORTING JAPANESE LEADERSHIP

Approximately 250,000 Americans are now working for Japanese firms in the United States. Matsushita employs 8,000; Sony has 7,000; and Nissan Motors employs 3,300. Can Americans work for Japanese leaders? These firms and a growing number of other Japanese firms investing in the United States think so.

Americans are going to encounter some ingrained leadership preferences in the Japanese. The following principles of work and leadership point up some differences in how leaders from Japan think.

1. The Japanese like teams of workers to be group oriented—that is, to self-lead whenever possible. However, if a person becomes a team leader, he or she accepts the responsibility to help motivate team members.

2. Among the Japanese, expertise and seniority are what leaders seek in employees.

3. Japanese value patience. Thus, leaders must be trained to wait patiently for followers to join in and work to accomplish goals.

4. Being respected and valued by a team leader in a Japanese firm is important for receiving promotions.

5. In Japanese firms, the team leader sets the pace and the time when the team stops. A team member is expected not to leave a job or to stop working until the team leader does so.

6. Japanese leaders do not like confrontation and conflict with followers. They tend to be annoyed over conflicts involving job assignments, pay increases, and promotion choices.

These and other characteristics of Japanese leaders are being imported into Japanese-owned firms in the United States. Although major cultural differences exist, the individualistic Americans are learning more about the Japanese style of leadership. If estimates are correct, an additional 800,000 to 1 million Americans will be working in Japanese firms in the United States in the next decade.

Source: B. Powell, B. Martin, D. Lewis, B. Turque, G. Rain, and B. Cohn, "Where the Jobs Are and How to Win Over a Japanese Boss," *Newsweek*, February 2, 1987, pp. 42–48.

CHARISMATIC LEADERSHIP

Individuals such as John F. Kennedy, Winston Churchill, Mikhail Gorbachev, and Walt Disney possess an attractiveness that enables them to make a difference with citizens, employees, or followers. Their leadership approach is referred to as **charismatic leadership.** Max Weber suggested that some leaders have a gift of exceptional qualities—a charisma—that enables them to motivate followers to achieve outstanding performance.[18] Such a charismatic leader is depicted as being able to play a vital role in creating change.

CHARISMATIC LEADERSHIP
Ability to influence followers based on supernatural gift and powers that are attractive. Followers enjoy being with charismatic leader because they feel inspired, correct, and important.

[18]Max Weber, *The Theory of Social and Economic Organization*, trans. A. M. Henderson and T. Parsons (New York: Free Press, 1947, originally published 1924).

Lee Iacocca is considered by some to have charismatic qualities. He worked for a one-dollar salary his first year at Chrysler, helped salvage bankruptcy at the firm by obtaining a large, government-backed loan that he paid back ahead of schedule, permitted the union to have representation on the company's board of directors, and worked tirelessly to produce advertisements in which he served as the company's main spokesperson. He used some unconventional tactics to win over his followers at Chrysler. To some, he is the embodiment of charisma.

Steven Jobs, cofounder of Apple Computers, provided another example of how charisma works to inspire others. Job's impact, attraction, and inspiration when he was with the firm were described as follows:

> When I walked through the Macintosh building with Steve, it became clear that he wasn't just another general manager bringing a visitor along to meet another group of employees. He and many of Apple's leaders weren't managers at all; they were impresarios. . . . Not unlike the director of an opera company, the impresario must cleverly deal with the creative temperaments of artists. . . . His gift is to merge powerful ideas with the performance of his artists.[19]

Defining Charismatic Leadership

Charisma is a Greek word meaning "gift." Powers that could not be clearly explained by logical means were called charismatic. Presently, no definitive answer has been given on what constitutes charismatic leadership behavior. House suggests that charismatic leaders are those who have charismatic effects on their followers to an unusually high degree.[20]

Conger's model.   Jay Conger has proposed a model that illustrates how charisma evolves.[21] Figure 12–3 presents his four-stage model of charismatic leadership. In stage one, the leader continuously assesses the environment, adapts, and formulates a vision of what must be done. The leader's goals are established. In stage two, the leader communicates his or her vision to followers, using whatever means are necessary. The stage-three segment is highlighted by working on trust and commitment. Doing the unexpected, taking risk, and being technically proficient are important in this stage. In stage four, the charismatic leader serves as a role model and motivator. The charismatic leader uses praise and recognition to instill within followers the belief that they can achieve the vision.

What constitutes charismatic leadership behavior?   What behavioral dimensions distinguish charismatic leaders from noncharismatic leaders? A criticism of the early work on charismatic leadership is that the explanations of it lacked specificity. Some limited attempts have been made to develop and test specific

---

[19]John Sculley, "Sculley's Lessons from inside Apple," *Fortune,* September 14, 1987, pp. 108–11.

[20]Robert J. House, "A 1976 Theory of Charismatic Leadership," in *Leadership: The Cutting Edge,* ed. J. G. Hunt and L. L. Larson (Carbondale: Southern Illinois University Press, 1977), pp. 189–207.

[21]His views of charismatic leadership are clearly presented in Jay A. Conger, *The Charismatic Leader* (San Francisco: Jossey-Bass, 1989).

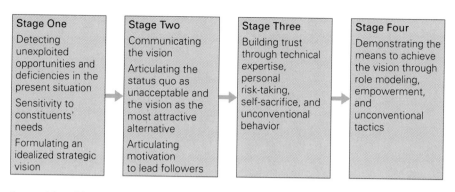

Stage One	Stage Two	Stage Three	Stage Four
Detecting unexploited opportunities and deficiencies in the present situation	Communicating the vision	Building trust through technical expertise, personal risk-taking, self-sacrifice, and unconventional behavior	Demonstrating the means to achieve the vision through role modeling, empowerment, and unconventional tactics
Sensitivity to constituents' needs	Articulating the status quo as unacceptable and the vision as the most attractive alternative		
Formulating an idealized strategic vision	Articulating motivation to lead followers		

FIGURE 12–3

Stages in Charismatic Leadership

Source: Adapted from Jay A. Conger and Rabindra N. Kanungo, "Behavioral Dimensions of Charismatic Leadership," in *Charismatic Leadership*, ed. Jay A. Conger, Rabindra N. Kanungo, and associates (San Francisco: Jossey-Bass, 1988), p. 27.

charismatic qualities such as vision, acts of heroism, and the ability to inspire.[22] However, in most cases, clarifying what specifically constitutes charismatic behavior has been generally ignored.

A number of empirical studies have examined behavior and attributes of charismatic leaders, such as articulation ability, affection for the leader, ability to inspire, dominating personality, and need for influence.[23] However, no specific set of behaviors and attributes is universally accepted by theorists, researchers, and practitioners. A descriptive behavioral framework that builds upon empirical work has been offered. The framework, presented in Table 12–3, assumes that charisma must be viewed as an attribution made by followers within the work context.

Two Types of Charismatic Leaders

In most discussions of charismatic leadership, the term *vision* is highlighted. It is argued that the first requirement for exercising charismatic leadership is expressing a shared vision of what the future could be. Through communication ability, the visionary, charismatic leader links followers' needs and goals to job or organizational goals. Linking followers with the organization's direction, mission, and goals is easier if they are dissatisfied or not challenged by the current situation.

Crisis-based charismatic leaders have an impact when the system must handle a situation for which existing knowledge, resources, and procedures are not adequate.[24] The crisis-produced charismatic leader communicates clearly

---

[22]See A. R. Willner, *The Spellbinders: Charismatic Political Leadership* (New Haven, Conn.: Yale University Press, 1984).

[23]Bernard M. Bass, *Leadership Performance beyond Expectations* (New York: Academic Press, 1985); Warren G. Bennis and Burt Nanes, *Leaders* (New York: Harper & Row, 1985); Robert J. House and M. L. Baetz, "Leadership: Some Empirical Generalizations and New Research Directions," in *Research in Organizational Behavior*, ed. Barry M. Staw (Greenwich, Conn.: JAI Press, 1979), pp. 399–401.

[24]J. M. Bryson, "A Perspective on Planning and Crisis in the Public Sector," *Strategic Management Journal*, 1981, pp. 181–96.

TABLE 12–3

Behavioral Components of Charismatic and Noncharismatic Leaders

Component	Charismatic Leader	Noncharismatic Leader
Relation to status quo	Essentially opposed to status quo and strives to change it (Steve Jobs at Apple).	Essentially agrees with status quo and strives to maintain it.
Future goal	Idealized vision highly discrepant from status quo (Tom Monaghan with the Domino's Pizza concept).	Goal not too discrepant from status quo.
Likableness	Shared perspective and idealized vision makes him or her a likable and honorable hero worthy of identification and imitation (Lee Iacocca in first three years at Chrysler).	Shared perspective makes him or her likable.
Expertise	Expert in using unconventional means to transcend the existing order (Al Davis, owner of the Los Angeles Raiders).	Expert in using available means to achieve goals within the framework of the existing order.
Environmental sensitivity	High need for environmental sensitivity for changing the status quo (Edgar Woolard at Du Pont).	Low need for environmental sensitivity to maintain status quo.
Articulation	Strong articulation of future vision and motivation to lead (Ross Perot at EDS).	Weak articulation of goals and motivation to lead.
Power base	Personal power, based on expertise, respect, and admiration for a unique hero (Jan Carlzon at Scandinavian Airlines System—SAS).	Position power and personal power (based on reward, expertise, and liking for a friend who is a similar other).
Leader-follower relationship	Elitist, entrepreneur, an exemplary (Mary Kay Ash of Mary Kay Cosmetics).	Egalitarian, consensus seeking, or directive.
	Transforms people to share the radical changes advocated (Edward Land, inventor of Polaroid camera).	Nudges or orders people to share his or her views.

Source: Adapted from Jay A. Conger and Rabindra Kanungo, "Toward a Behavioral Theory of Charismatic Leadership in Organizational Settings," *Academy of Management Review*, October 1987, pp. 637–47.

and specifically what actions need to be taken and what will be the consequences of the actions.

A number of crisis situations have required immediate action on the part of leaders. Do you recall some of them?

— In 1978, the Three Mile Island nuclear power plant accident.
— In 1982, the contamination of Tylenol capsules with cyanide, causing the deaths of eight people and a loss of $100 million in recalled packages for Johnson & Johnson. In 1986, a second poisoning incident caused the recall of packages and another loss of $150 million.

— In 1984, the worst industrial accident in history in Bhopal, India, killing 3,000 people and injuring another 300,000.

— In 1985, the deadly bacteria found in Jalisco cheese that caused the deaths of 84 people.

— In 1986, a tragic explosion of the space shuttle *Challenger,* costing the lives of 7 astronauts.

— In 1989, a 10 million–gallon oil spill into Prince William Sound near Valdez, Alaska, by an Exxon oil tanker.

— In 1990, 72 million bottles of Perrier water were recalled by the company because of possible benzene contamination.

These events caught the attention of everyone. Each day, smaller but still significant crises occur throughout the world.

Crisis management is a growing field of study and inquiry.[25] The crises managers face enable charismatic leadership to emerge. First, under conditions of stress, ambiguity, and chaos, followers give power to individuals who have the potential to correct the crisis situation. The leader is empowered to do what is necessary to correct the situation or solve the problem. In many cases, the leader is unconstrained and is allowed to use whatever he or she thinks is needed.[26]

A crisis also permits the leader to promote nontraditional actions by followers. The crisis-based charismatic leader has greater freedom to encourage followers to search for ways to correct the crisis. Some of the methods, procedures, and tactics adopted by followers may be disorderly, chaotic, and outside the normal boundary of actions. However, the charismatic leader in a crisis situation encourages, supports, and usually receives action from followers.[27]

The present state of knowledge about charismatic leadership is still relatively abstract and ambiguous. Despite Weber's concept of charismatic authority, Conger's framework of how charismatic leadership evolves, House's definition and propositions about the characteristics of charismatic leaders, and some limited research results, much more theoretical and research work needs to be done. There is a void in understanding about whether charismatic leaders can be harmful in expressing visions that are unrealistic or inaccurate or in the way they attack a crisis problem. Management scholar and writer Peter Drucker claims that "charisma becomes the undoing of leaders." How accurate is Drucker? No one knows at this time. However, evidence suggests that charismatic leaders (e.g., Hitler, Stalin, Jim Jones) can secure greater commitment to failing, personally demeaning, and tragic goals than can the average leader.[28] In the business world, John DeLorean was able to raise hundreds of millions of dollars for his failed automobile venture because of his powers of

---

[25]S. Fink, *Crisis Management* (New York: AMACOM, 1986); Ian I. Mitroff, Paul Shrivastava, and Firdaus E. Udivadia, "Effective Crisis Management," *Academy of Management Executive,* November 1987, pp. 283–92.

[26]N. Roberts, "Transforming Leadership: A Process of Collective Action," *Human Relations,* 1985, pp. 1023–46.

[27]B. Hedberg, "How Organizations Learn and Unlearn," in *Handbook of Organizational Design,* ed. P. C. Nystrom and W. H. Starbuck (London: Oxford University Press, 1980), pp. 3–27.

[28]Conger, *Charismatic Leader,* p. 137.

persuasion and impression management. He promoted himself as an innovative genius.

The positive and negative aspects of charismatic leadership need to be studied. Studying each theory of leadership with regard to its positive and negative impact on followers and situations should be a top priority. We raise questions here about the dark side of charismatic leadership; but to be thorough, we must also ask whether there is a dark side to the other theories we present in Chapters 11 and 12.

TRANSACTIONAL AND TRANSFORMATIONAL LEADERSHIP

Each of the leadership theories discussed emphasizes the point that leadership is an exchange process. Followers are rewarded by the leader when they accomplish agreed-upon objectives. The leader serves to help followers accomplish the objectives.

Transactional Leadership

TRANSACTIONAL LEADERSHIP

Leader identifies what followers want or prefer and helps them achieve level of performance that results in rewards that satisfy them.

The exchange role of the leader has been referred to as *transactional*. Figure 12–4 presents the **transactional leadership** roles. The leader helps the follower identify what must be done to accomplish the desired results: better-quality output, more sales or services, reduced cost of production. In helping the follower identify what must be done, the leader takes into consideration the person's self-concept and esteem needs. The transactional approach uses the path-goal concepts as its framework.

In using the transaction style, the leader relies on contingent reward and on management by exception. Research shows that when contingent reinforcement is used, followers exhibit an increase in performance and satisfaction:[29] followers believe that accomplishing objectives will result in their receiving desired rewards. Using management by exception, the leader will not be involved unless objectives are not being accomplished.

Transactional leadership is not often found in organizational settings. One national sample of U.S. workers showed that only 22 percent of the participants perceived a direct relationship between how hard they worked and how much pay they received.[30] That is, the majority of workers believed that good pay was not contingent on good performance. Although workers prefer a closer link between pay and performance, it was not present in their jobs. Why? There are probably a number of reasons, such as unreliable performance appraisal systems, subjectively administered rewards, poor managerial skills in showing employees the pay-performance link, and conditions outside the manager's control. Also, managers often provide records that are not perceived by followers to be meaningful or important.

---

[29]P. M. Podsakoff, W. D. Tudor, and R. Skov, "Effect of Leader Contingent and Non-Contingent Reward and Punishment Behaviors on Subordinate Performance and Satisfaction," *Academy of Management Journal*, 1982, pp. 810–21.

[30]D. Yankelovich and J. Immerivoki, *Putting the Work Ethic to Work* (New York: Public Agenda Foundation, 1983).

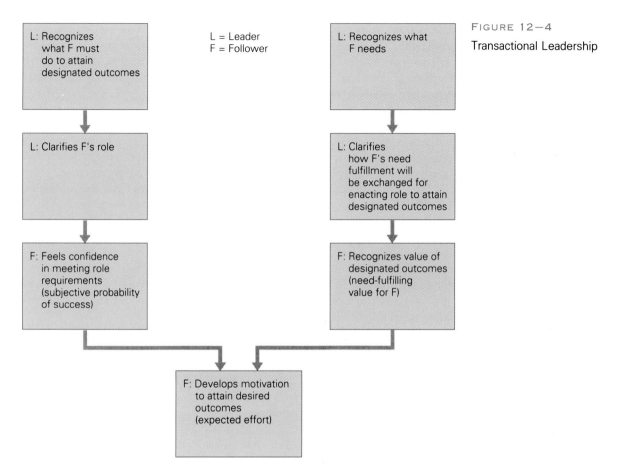

FIGURE 12—4

Transactional Leadership

Source: Bernard M. Bass, *Leadership and Performance beyond Expectations* (New York: Free Press, 1985), p. 12.

A small pay increase, a personal letter from the boss, or a job transfer may not be what employees want in the form of a contingent reward. Until managers understand what the employee wants, administer the rewards in a timely manner, and emphasize the pay-performance link, there is likely to be confusion, uncertainty, and minimal transactional impact in leader-follower relationships.

The Transformational Theme

An exciting new kind of leader, referred to as the transformational leader,[31] motivates followers to work for transcendental goals instead of short-term self-interest and for achievement and self-actualization instead of security.[32] In

---

[31]James M. Burns, *Leadership* (New York: Harper & Row, 1978).

[32]Brice J. Avolio and Bernard M. Bass, "Transformational Leadership, Charisma, and Beyond," in *Emerging Leadership Vistas,* ed. James G. Hunt, B. Rajaram Baliga, H. Peter Dachler, and Chester A. Schriesheim (Lexington, Mass.: Lexington Books, 1988), pp. 29–49.

TRANSFORMATIONAL
LEADERSHIP
Ability to inspire and motivate
followers to achieve results
greater than originally planned
and for internal rewards.

transformational leadership, viewed as a special case of transactional leadership, the employee's reward is internal. By expressing a vision, the transformational leader persuades followers to work hard to achieve the goals envisioned. The leader's vision provides the follower with motivation for hard work that is self-rewarding (internal).

Transactional leaders will adjust goals, direction, and mission for practical reason. Transformational leaders, on the other hand, make major changes in the firm's or unit's mission, way of doing business, and human resource management in order to achieve their vision. The transformational leader will overhaul the entire philosophy, system, and culture of an organization.

Names that come to mind when we think about transformational leaders are Michael Eisner at Walt Disney, Jack Welch at General Electric, and, of course, Lee Iacocca at Chrysler. Under Eisner's leadership, for example, Disney has moved into movies (some R-rated), syndicated a business show for television, introduced a television channel, introduced new cartoon characters, and licensed new apparel products. Eisner took risks and pushed the company along a path that was unheard of for 40 years. He transformed Walt Disney Company from a conservative into an assertive, proactive company.[33]

A framework that helps describe how Eisner, Welch, and Iacocca transformed their organizations is presented in Figure 12–5. Note that the transactional approach is incorporated into the transformational leadership model. As noted by Tosi, most successful charismatic/transforming leaders have the ability to transact with subordinates the day-to-day routine requirements and actions.[34] The transformational leader must possess transactional leadership skills.

The development of transformational leadership factors has evolved from research by Bass.[35] He identified five factors (first three apply to transformational and last two apply to transactional leadership) that describe transformational leaders. They are:

Charisma. The leader is able to instill a sense of value, respect, and pride and to articulate a vision.

Individual attention. The leader pays attention to followers' needs and assigns meaningful projects so that followers grow personally.

Intellectual stimulation. The leader helps followers rethink rational ways to examine a situation. Encourages followers to be creative.

Contingent reward. The leader informs followers about what must be done to receive the rewards they prefer.

Management by exception. The leader permits followers to work on the task and does not intervene unless goals are not being accomplished in a reasonable time and at a reasonable cost.

---

[33]Jay Clarke, "Disney World Grows like Pinocchio's Nose," *Houston Chronicle,* March 6, 1988, p. 9.

[34]Henry J. Tosi, Jr., "Toward a Paradigm Shift in the Study of Leadership," in *Leadership: Beyond Establishment Views,* ed. James G. Hung, V. Sekaran, and Chester A. Schriesheim (Carbondale: Southern Illinois University Press, 1982), pp. 222–23.

[35]Bass, *Leadership Performance.*

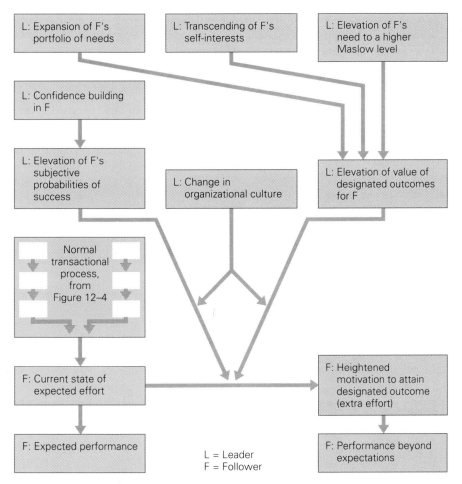

FIGURE 12—5

Transformation Leadership

Source: Bernard M. Bass, *Leadership and Performance beyond Expectations* (New York: Free Press, 1985), p. 23.

One of the most important characteristics of the transformational leader is charisma. However, charisma by itself is not enough for successful transformational leadership, as Bass clearly states:

> The deep emotional attachment which characterizes the relationship of the charismatic leader to followers may be present when transformational leadership occurs, but we can distinguish a class of charismatics who are not at all transformational in their influence. Celebrities may be identified as charismatic by a large segment of the public. Celebrities are held in awe and reverence by the masses who are developed by them. People will be emotionally aroused in the presence of celebrities and identify with them in their fantasy, but the celebrities may not be involved at all in any transformation of their public. On the other hand, with charisma, transformational leaders can play the role of teacher, mentor, coach, reformer, or revolutionary. Charisma is a necessary ingredient of transformational leadership, but by itself it is not sufficient to account for the transformational process.[36]

---

[36]Ibid., p. 31.

In addition to charisma, transformational leaders need assessment skills, communication abilities, and a sensitivity to others. They must be able to articulate their vision, and they must be sensitive to the skill deficiencies of followers.

LEADERSHIP THEORIES: THE NEED FOR RESEARCH

In any discussion of leadership, invoking names such as Gandhi, Churchill, King, and Kennedy generates attention. We assume, based on such examples, that leaders are heroic, inspiring, articulate. (Some skeptics refer to this elevation of the leadership function as a "romance."[37]) However, as critics have so aptly stated, the leadership field's array of theories and limited research are beset with scientific deficiencies, illusion, and myths. Attempts to understand and evaluate charismatic, transactional, and transformational leadership theories inevitably seem to reach a dead end, due to the scarcity of scientific research into each of these approaches.

To have validity for use, each of the theories and explanations of leadership presented in Chapters 11 and 12 must be based on scientific inquiry. There is a definite lack of such research on charismatic, transactional, and transformational leadership. They need more thorough testing in organizations, using male and female samples, employing American and non-American leaders, and incorporating rigorous longitudinal designs.

Until this happens, these approaches should be used cautiously. Discussing charisma and transformational leadership prescriptions may be intriguing, but managers do not have enough scientific evidence to apply the prescriptions effectively. It is premature to develop and implement training, selection, and reward programs based on them.

---

[37]James R. Meindl, Stanford B. Ehilich, and Janet M. Dukerich, "The Romance of Leadership," *Administrative Science Quarterly*, March 1985, pp. 78–102.

SUMMARY OF KEY POINTS

— Vroom and Yetton originally, and Vroom and Jago more recently, have developed a leadership model to select the amount of group decision-making participation needed in a variety of problem situations. The model suggests that the amount of subordinate participation depends on the leader's skill and knowledge, whether a quality decision is needed, the extent to which the problem is structured, and whether acceptance by subordinates is needed to implement the decision.

— The Vroom-Yetton-Jago explanations are criticized for being too complex. Because leadership is a complex process, a more accurate criticism perhaps is that the explanation is too simplistic with regard to managerial

cognition about how to lead and the consequences of leadership behaviors.

— The attribution theory of leadership suggests that a leader's ability to predict how followers will react is enhanced by knowing how the followers explain their behavior and performance.

— Leaders attribute the causes of followers' behaviors to the person, the task, or a unique set of circumstances called the context.

— The word *charisma* comes from a Greek word meaning "gift." The ability to influence people that can not be clearly explained by logical means is called charisma.

— Charisma evolves over a period of time. By assessing, adapting, and formulating goals and actions, articulating a vision, and building and reinforcing commitment, the leader builds his or her charismatic profile.

— Two types of charismatic leaders have been suggested: one that articulates a vision and one that exercises leadership in a crisis situation.

— Transactional leadership involves engaging in an exchange role in which the leader helps followers accomplish meaningful objectives to achieve satisfactory rewards.

— The transformational leader makes major changes in mission, the way of doing business, and how human resources are managed, in order to achieve a vision.

— The transactional approach is involved in the more expansive transformational leadership framework. Three main characteristics of transformational leadership are charisma, individual attention to followers, and intellectual stimulation of followers.

— There is insufficient research evidence available to promote charismatic, transactional, or transformational practices in organizations. The romantic aspects of being charismatic or transformational have not been supported with research evidence. Explanations are interesting but not yet sufficiently supported with scientific facts.

DISCUSSION AND REVIEW QUESTIONS

1. Does Ronald Reagan or George Bush possess charismatic qualities? Explain.

2. Compare the available research on the Vroom-Yetton-Jago model of leadership to the transactional explanation. What research is needed in both of these theories of leadership?

3. How does charisma play a role in transformational leadership?

4. Why is it considered romantic to examine leadership in various settings—politics, business, military, and even street gangs?

5. As you progress in this course, what attributions do you make about what you are learning?

6. How could a leader use attribution theory to explain the poor performance of a group of followers?

7. Collect information on Lee Iacocca's work history at Chrysler. After reviewing your sources, write a brief report indicating which type of leader he was and currently is in the company? Does charisma best explain his early successes at Chrysler? Explain your answers.

8. Which of the theories explained in this chapter would be the most useful in explaining to someone from Hungary what leadership approaches will be needed to make Hungary more competitive in the international marketplace?

9. Can a woman be charismatic to male employees? Explain and give some political, business, and family examples.

10. Why is communication such an important skill in the charismatic, transactional, and transformational explanations of leadership?

ADDITIONAL REFERENCES

Aslund, A. *Gorbachev's Struggle for Economic Reform.* Ithaca, N.Y.: Cornell University Press, 1989.

Block, P. *The Empowered Manager.* San Francisco: Jossey-Bass, 1987.

Gardner, J. W. *On Leadership.* New York: File Press, 1989.

McCall, M. W., Jr.; M. M. Lombardo; and A. M. Morrison. *The Lessons of Experience.* Lexington, Mass.: Lexington Books, 1988.

Nanus, B. *The Leader's Edge.* Chicago: Contemporary Books, 1989.

Vries, de Kets M. *Prisoners of Leadership.* New York: John Wiley & Sons, 1989.

SIX SIGMA AT MOTOROLA: ALL ABOUT BEING THE BEST IN INTERNATIONAL MARKETS

Who is Robert W. Galvin? And why do the Japanese respect his views on management, quality control, and marketing?

Galvin, as chief executive officer of Motorola, Inc., is the main leader in one of the world's leading high-tech companies. He is a charismatic leader who has not been afraid to take on the Japanese or anyone else competing in the international marketplace.

Galvin has instilled a competitive spirit throughout Motorola—a "can do" attitude that permeates the entire firm. The company intends to become the best manufacturer of electronic hardware in the world. Wristwatch pagers, cellular phones, and other electronic devices are some of the products with which Motorola intends to beat everyone in the marketplace. Under the guidance of Galvin, the company has upgraded quality, improved manufacturing processes to cut costs, and aggressively pursued specific markets. It has also supported research and development consortiums and working with other firms to gain new footholds in foreign markets. Motorola is also becoming a major force in Japan's home markets by offering high-quality products and forcefully marketing the company.

Galvin travels to Washington, D.C., regularly to brief legislators on the realities of international competition. The foreign competition is no longer free from Galvin's lobbying, comments, and observations. The playing field of international competition has leveled off because Galvin is unrelenting, convincing, and honest. He only wants to compete fairly, which is the message he constantly delivers.

Like the Japanese, Motorola has discovered that better quality pays for itself. High quality costs less because floor space, equipment, and people used for nothing cost money. Motorola attempts to stay lean and to keep its eye on the hidden cost of poor quality.

Promotions, bonuses, and raises at Motorola are as important as in any firm. Each, however, is tied to quality improvement. Workers now see and believe that better quality means more rewards. They are convinced that they can be number one in any market Motorola enters. They are convinced that teamwork, vision, and rewards are important to that goal.

Can one man make a difference? Can leaders be trained to be Galvin-like in style? There are no empirical studies to support the idea that one man's ideas, vision, and passion can inspire, motivate, and direct people. However, the Motorola approach seems to be working. The firm is a major competitor and a world leader in various markets. From Scandinavia to Japan to South America, Galvin's company is on the move.

Of course, Motorola's competitors are not sitting around. A proposed merger of world-class giants General Electric and Ericcson could give Motorola some stiff competition. Not willing to settle for second best, Motorola is committed to fight. The goals of a tenfold reduction in defects, teamwork, and the Six Sigma quality plan have provided Motorola employees with a cause, a mission. (Six Sigma is statistical jargon for near-perfect manufacturing—a rate of just 3.4 defects per million products.)

Motorola is not satisfied with any defects. All employees have wallet-size cards stating Motorola's Six Sigma goals in 11 languages. At officers' meetings, Six Sigma and quality are the first topics discussed. Motorola, at the direction of Galvin, has

Source: Based on Thomas A. Stewart, "How to Manage in the New Era," *Fortune,* January 15, 1990, pp. 58–72; Lois Therrien, "The Rival Japan Respects," *Business Week,* November 13, 1989, pp. 108–18; John Hillkerk, "Top Quality Is Behind Comeback," *USA Today,* March 28, 1989, pp. 1–2B.

increased its spending on employee training: about 40 percent, or $40 million, is spent on developing skills to sustain and improve on the Six Sigma goals.

Galvin believes that Motorola can produce products that are virtually perfect. His vision of the perfect product is now embedded in the culture at Motorola. The Galvin crusade has resulted in attention, awards, and international respect for Motorola and each of the 105,000 employees.

Questions for Consideration

1. What charismatic qualities and characteristics does Robert W. Galvin project?
2. What behaviors and skills of Galvin's suggest that he is not only a manager but also a leader?
3. Can it be concluded that Galvin is a transformational leader at Motorola? Why?

LEADERSHIP STYLE ANALYSIS

Objectives

1. To learn how to diagnose different leadership situations.
2. To learn how to apply a systematic procedure for analyzing situations.
3. To improve understanding of how to reach a decision.

Related Topics

Decision making and problem solving when given facts about a situation.

Starting the Exercise

Review the decision process flowchart in Figure 12–1. Also examine the "Manufacturing Manager" Close-Up on page 410. The instructor will then form groups of four to five people to analyze each of the following cases. Try to reach a group consensus on which decision style is best for the particular case. Select the best style, based on use of the modified model, available decision styles, and decision rules. Each case should take between 30 and 45 minutes to analyze.

Case I: R&D Director

You are the head of a research and development (R&D) laboratory in the nuclear reactor division of a large corporation. Often, whether a particular piece of research has potential commercial interest or is merely of academic interest to the researchers is not clear. In your judgment, one major area of research has advanced well beyond the level at which operating divisions pertinent to the area could possibly assimilate or make use of the data being generated.

Recently, two new areas with potentially high returns for commercial development have been promised by one of the operating divisions. The team working in the area referred to in the previous paragraph is ideally qualified to research these new areas. Unfortunately, both of the new areas are relatively devoid of scientific interest, while the project on which the team is currently engaged is of great scientific interest to all members.

At the moment, this team is, or is close to being, your best research team. It is very cohesive, has a high level of morale, and has been very productive. You are concerned not only that team members would not want to switch their effort to these new areas but also that forcing them to concentrate on these two new projects could adversely affect their morale, their good intragroup working relations, and their future productivity both as individuals and as a team.

You have to respond to the operating division within the next two weeks, indicating which resources, if any, can be devoted to working on these projects. It would be possible for the team to work on more than one project, but each project would need the combined skills of all the members of the team, so fragmentation of the team is not technically feasible. This fact, coupled with the fact that the team is very cohesive, means that a solution that satisfies any team member would very probably go a long way to satisfying everyone on the team.

Attribute	Analysis	Ratings on Scales
Quality requirement	High importance	(QR = 4)
Commitment requirement	High importance	(CR = 4)
Leader information	Probably yes	(LI = 4)
Problem structure	Yes	(ST = 5)
Commitment probability	No	(CP = 1)
Goal congruence	Probably no	(CG = 2)
Subordinate conflict	Probably no	(CO = 2)
Subordinate information	No	(SI = 1)
Time constraints	No	(TC = 1)
Geographical dispersion	No	(GD = 1)
Motivation — time	No importance	(MT = 1)
Motivation — development	Critical importance	(MD = 5)

Highest overall effectiveness (leadership style choice): _____

Case II: U.S. Coast Guard Cutter Captain

You are the captain of a 210-foot, medium-endurance U.S. Coast Guard cutter, with a crew of nine officers and 65 enlisted personnel. Your mission is general at-sea law enforcement and search and rescue. At 2 A.M. this morning, while enroute to your home port after a routine two-week patrol, you received word from the New York Rescue Coordination Center that a small plane had ditched 70 miles offshore. You obtained all the available information concerning the location of the crash, informed your crew of the mission, and set a new course at maximum speed for the scene.

You have now been searching for survivors and wreckage for 20 hours. Your search operation has been increasingly impaired by rough seas, and a severe storm is building to the southwest. The atmospherics associated with the deteriorating weather have made communications with the New York Rescue Center impossible. A decision must be made shortly about whether to abandon the search and place your vessel on a northeasterly course to ride out the storm (thereby protecting the vessel and your crew but relegating any possible survivors to almost certain death from exposure) or continuing a potentially futile search and taking the risks it would entail.

You have contacted the weather bureau for up-to-date information on the severity and duration of the storm. While your crew is extremely conscientious about its responsibility, you believe that the members would be divided on the decision of leaving or staying.

Attribute	Analysis	Ratings on Scales
Quality requirement	Critical importance	(QR = 5)
Commitment requirement	High importance	(CR = 4)
Leader information	Yes	(LI = 4)
Problem structure	Yes	(St = 5)
Commitment probability	Yes	(CP = 5)
Goal congruence	Yes	(GC = 5)
Subordinate conflict	Yes	(CO = 5)

Attribute	Analysis	Ratings on Scales
Subordinate information	Maybe	(SI = 3)
Time constraints	No	(TC = 1)
Geographical dispersion	No	(GD = 1)
Motivation — time	High importance	(MT = 4)
Motivation — development	No importance	(MD = 1)
Highest overall effectiveness (leadership style choice): _____		

Completing the Exercise

Phase I: 10–15 minutes.   Individually read each case and select the proper decision style, using the Vroom-Jago model.

Phase II: 30–45 minutes.   Join a group appointed by the instructor and reach group consensus.

THE STRUCTURE AND DESIGN OF ORGANIZATIONS

13

Organization Structure

AN ORGANIZATIONAL
ISSUE FOR DEBATE   ARE ORGANIZATION CHARTS NECESSARY FOR EFFECTIVE
MANAGEMENT?

ARGUMENT FOR

Those who believe that organization charts are necessary to ensure effective management point out that confusion develops without them. Individuals do not understand their jobs—what they must do, how they are to do it, and with whom they should work. Managers of different organizational subunits, such as departments and divisions, do not understand how their work fits into the work of other subunits. In the absence of an organization chart to clarify relationships, illogical and confusing ones will develop. In fact, the very process of charting the organization is a good test of its soundness, because any relationship that cannot be charted is likely to be unsound and therefore confusing to those working in it.

The most vocal proponents believe that management should supplement organization charts with written specifications of essential requirements of each level of management, each department, each committee, and each job or group of similar jobs. These materials provide individuals and groups with additional information to help them understand how their efforts correlate with the efforts of others. They can therefore devote their full energies to effective discharge of their proper duties, avoiding duplication of effort with other individuals and units.

Another argument for organization charts draws on the analogy between management and engineering, pointing out that design comes first in the engineering process. To construct a social machine that will get work done, management must design it according to principles rather than personalities. An organization that tries to get along without a definite organization plan and chart will inevitably turn to politics and favoritism on matters of promotion and advancement. Moreover, without clear descriptions of job duties, there can be no bases for training others to do the jobs of those who are promoted. One individual cannot be trained to take over another's personal experience.

The argument that organization charts are necessary only when the organization becomes too big for any one individual to manage does not hold. In many instances, small firms that do rather well in the early stages of their development begin to fail when the founders can no longer manage in their personal styles. The transition from successful small firm to successful large firm is impaired because the employees are doing jobs that fit their personality and unique skills rather than jobs necessary for organizational performance. Organization charts and supporting documents are necessary from the very beginning of a firm's existence, not just when it gets too big for one person to manage.

ARGUMENT AGAINST

Organization charts do not show the important relationships among individuals and units. In fact, what they do show may be misleading. For example, they do not show informal lines of communication and influence. The hierarchical drawing of a chart depicts an intended chain of communication and authority; but in practice, many channels of communication and authority exist. Communications flow horizontally and diagonally as individuals interact and share information. This is especially true because telephones and computer networks enable people to contact others quickly and effectively.

The organization chart shows a hierarchy of positions, implying that positions above are more important and influential than those below. This is clearly inaccurate, as some individuals are important and influential in some decisions but not in others. The first-line supervisor can have the last word on a decision involving the use of overtime in his or her department. For that matter, departmental workers can have the last word on overtime. The organization chart also fails to show the relative influence of individuals at the same level; it would seem to indicate that they have the same influence. In fact, that is incorrect. For example, the marketing manager can override the production manager if the decision depends on market research rather than production planning.

Perhaps the most damaging criticism of organization charts is that they encourage individuals to take a very narrow view of their jobs. Job definitions imply what people will not do as well as clarifying what they will do. The result is an organization that is not responsive to change, that lacks flexibility. The organization chart and all the supporting documentation (job descriptions and manuals) become substitutes for action and creative responses. In fact, some managers adamantly oppose the creation of organization charts even when employees complain that they need some direction to understand what they should do. These managers respond by saying that it is better to go ahead and fail than to do nothing.

The focus of this chapter is organizational structure, one of the three main topics of the entire book. The discussion will reflect the ideas depicted in Figure 13–1. Organization structure results from managerial decisions about four important attributes of all organizations: division of labor, bases for departmentalization, size of departments, and delegation of authority. The decisions managers make are influenced by job design factors and organization design factors such as individual differences, task competence, technology, environmental uncertainty, strategy, and certain characteristics of managers themselves. The attributes of the structure determine the extent to which the organization reflects the dimensions of formalization, complexity, and centralization. The structure of the organization contributes to organizational effectiveness, and that relationship justifies our interest. This chapter focuses on the four decisions and their relationships with the three dimensions. Chapter 14 analyzes the issues associated with job design, and Chapter 15 analyzes organizational design issues.

THE CONCEPT OF ORGANIZATIONAL STRUCTURE

Organizational **structure** is an abstract concept. No one has ever actually seen one. What we see is the evidence of structure; and from that evidence, we infer that structure is present. We therefore need to identify what we mean when we discuss structure in this and subsequent chapters.

STRUCTURE

Pattern of jobs and groups of jobs in organization. An important cause of individual and group behavior.

Structure as an Influence on Behavior

In Chapter 1, we noted the importance of organizational structure as an influence on the behavior of the individuals and groups who make up the organization. The importance of that relationship is so widely accepted that

FIGURE 13–1

Organization Structure

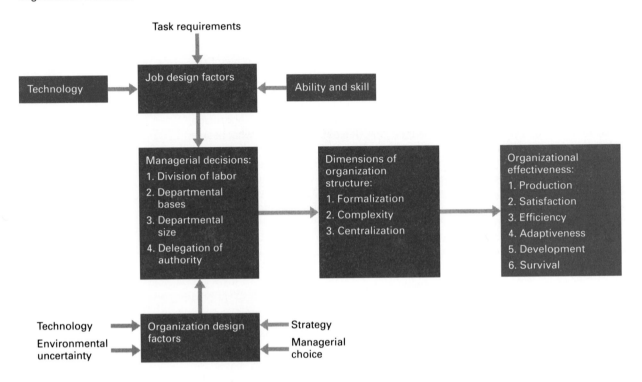

some experts define structure in these terms: "Organizational structure for our purposes will be defined broadly as those features of the organization that serve to control or distinguish its parts."[1] All of us have worked in organizations (we were one of its "parts"), and we have experienced the way our behavior was controlled. We did not simply go to work and do what we wanted to do; we did what the organizations wanted, and paid, us to do. We gave up free choice when we undertook the work necessitated by the jobs we held. Jobs are important features of any organization.

All organizations have a structure of jobs. In fact, the existence of structure distinguishes organizations. While the most visible evidence of structure is the familiar organizational chart, the Organizational Issue for Debate causes us to consider the possibility that charts are not always necessary or sufficient to describe the structure. For example, some small organizations can get along very well without them as long as all employees understand what they are to do and with whom they are to do it.

But jobs are not the only features of an organization. Again, from experience, we know that organizations consist of departments, divisions, units, or any of a number of terms that denote groups of jobs. No doubt, the

---

[1]Robert H. Miles, *Macro Organizational Behavior* (Santa Monica, Calif.: Goodyear Publishing, 1980), p. 18.

college or university you attend is made up of a number of academic departments—management, accounting, economics if you are in a business school. Each of these departments contains individuals performing different jobs, which combine to produce a larger outcome than is possible from the efforts of any single job or department. When you graduate, your education will have been made possible by the combined efforts of individual departments.

The point here is not that these departments combine the effects of many different jobs. Rather, we are noting the effect of the departments on the behavior of the individuals in them. As members of departments, individuals necessarily must abide by commonly held agreements, policies, and rules and thereby give up the freedom to act with complete autonomy.

One seemingly innocent characteristic of organizational units—the number of individuals they comprise—has important implications for controlling the behavior of group members. The specific number of individuals in a group is the number of individuals that must be managed—the manager's span of control. As the span of control decreases, the manager can exert greater supervision and consequently greater control over subordinates. But the price for additional control is an increase in the number of managers (and in managers' salaries). Conversely, the number of managers can be reduced by increasing the span of control—that is, by increasing the number of individuals within groups in the organization. As a result, of course, managers will be less able to exert close supervision of the group. So we see that the issue of achieving control through manipulating the size of a department involves balancing the relative benefits and costs of at least two desirable outcomes: control and efficiency. Controlling the behavior of employees is but one of those outcomes.

Structure as Recurring Activities

A second perspective on organizational structure must be introduced to provide a complete understanding of the concept. It focuses on the activities performed as consequences of the structure. From this perspective, "The concept of structure . . . implies a configuration of activities that is characteristically enduring and persistent; the dominant feature of organizational structure is its patterned regularity."[2] Note that this definition says nothing about the reason for the patterned regularity, only that it exists—that within organizations certain activities can be counted on to occur routinely. For example, people come to work each morning at 8 o'clock, clock in, go to their workstations, and begin doing the same work they did the day before. They talk to the same people, they receive information from the same people, they are periodically but predictably evaluated for promotion and raises. Without these predictable activities, the work of the organization could not be achieved.

Definitions that focus on regularly occurring organizational activities emphasize the importance of what, in this book, we term *organizational*

---

[2]Stewart Ranson, Bob Hinings, and Royston Greenwood, "The Structuring of Organizational Structures," *Administrative Science Quarterly,* March 1980, p. 1.

processes. In Part V of the book, we will discuss the processes involved in communication, decision making, and career and socialization. These processes occur with considerable regularity, and analyzing the patterns of communication, decision making, and other processes is certainly possible and even useful. But distinguishing between activity (or processes) and the causes of that activity is also useful. Thus, when we discuss structure in the following pages, we refer to a relatively stable framework of jobs and departments that influences the behavior of individuals and groups toward organizational goals.[3]

Structure Is Purposeful and Goal Directed

Organizations are purposeful and goal oriented. It follows that the structure of the organization is likewise purposeful and goal directed.[4] Our concept of organizational structure will take into account the existence of purposes and goals, and our attitude will be that management should think of structure in terms of its contribution to organizational effectiveness.

The statement that organizational structures facilitate the achievement of organizational goals assumes that managers know how to match organizational structures and goals and that they desire to do so. In many instances, however, organizational structures do not contribute positively to organizational performance, because managers are unable by training or intellect to design a structure that guides the behavior of individuals and groups to achieve high levels of production, efficiency, satisfaction, adaptiveness, and development. And in some instances, organizational structures reflect and contribute to the personal goals of managers at the expense of the goals of the organization. Thus, to say that organizational structures contribute *positively* to organizational effectiveness requires assumptions about the abilities and motivations of those who have power to design them. The structure of an organization is, without doubt, related to the achievement of organizational effectiveness, even though the exact nature of the relationship is inherently difficult to know.[5]

THE IMPORTANCE OF ORGANIZATION STRUCTURE

Business historians will have every reason to describe the 1980s as the era of "reorganization." Headline after headline in *The Wall Street Journal, Business Week, Forbes, Fortune,* and countless other periodicals and newspapers reported how America's great corporations reorganized to be more effective competitors in their markets. Such headlines invite us to read and learn how IBM and

[3]Danny Miller, "The Genesis of Configuration," *Academy of Management Review,* October 1987, pp. 691–92.

[4]George P. Huber and Reuben R. McDaniel, "The Decision-Making Paradigm of Organizational Design," *Management Science,* May 1986, p. 573.

[5]Dan R. Dalton, William D. Todor, Michael J. Spendolini, Gordon J. Fielding, and Lyman W. Porter, "Organization Structure and Performance: A Critical Review," *Academy of Management Review,* January 1980, pp. 49–64.

IBM REORGANIZES

January 28, 1986, was a significant date in a significant year at IBM. On that date, IBM boss John F. Akers announced a massive reorganization that some have described as nothing less than reinventing IBM. After three years of slumping sales and profit, Akers decided that the situation required what he termed a drastic change. IBM's organization at that time could best be described as a centralized structure in which major decisions were made in a headquarters office. Local managers were unable to act on market and technological developments because they did not have the authority to do so. Their behavior was restricted by the way IBM was structured.

The first step in getting IBM back on track was to delegate authority for products and markets to six general managers who were closer to the action than corporate headquarters. More than 20,000 people were affected by the decision, as they moved into new jobs in new locations. Individual jobs changed; many were eliminated. (IBM permitted early retirements and job transfers to dampen the effects of job eliminations.)

The most visible evidence of the reorganization is five autonomous product groups: personal computer systems, midrange systems, mainframes, communications, and chip technology. The groups have nearly complete authority to develop and market products and services within their sphere of activity. Structurally, they are the initial points of departure. Akers noted at the time of the reorganization that other groups could emerge as market and technology forces dictate the necessity for change.

Source: "Big Changes at Big Blue," *Business Week*, February 15, 1988, pp. 92–98.

U.S. Shoe decentralized, how General Motors reduced the number of managers and increased the span of control, how Procter & Gamble increased the number of managers by superimposing another level of management on the existing management, and how Kodak redefined the bases for grouping jobs. Evidently, the way jobs are organized to achieve control and coordination has important implications for attaining organizational effectiveness.

No American corporation enjoys wider name recognition than IBM. This corporation led the way in developing applications of computer technology. It is also well known for its strong commitment to employee well-being. When IBM does something, it gets considerable notice. The Close-Up on IBM describes some of the reorganization "Big Blue" undertook in the late 1980s.

Reports of IBM's reorganization have used many of the terms and themes of this and the following two chapters. We can see that organization structure has something to do with jobs, groups of jobs, and delegated authority. Those terms recur throughout IBM's story. We also see that IBM's chief executive officer (CEO) must have believed that organization structure has important effects on individual and group behavior. In fact, he must have believed that these effects can be either positive or negative, depending on the specific configuration of jobs, groups of jobs, and delegated authority.

EFFECTS OF STRUCTURE ON INDIVIDUAL AND GROUP BEHAVIOR

The behavior of individuals and groups in organizations is affected in significant ways by the jobs they perform. Jobs themselves provide powerful stimuli for individual behavior: the demands on and expectations of individuals can result in high levels of personal satisfaction or stress, anxiety, and physiological dysfunctions.[6] People's jobs require them to perform activities in combination with other people in the organization. The activities can be routine or nonroutine; they can require high or low levels of skill; they can be perceived as challenging or as trivial. The required relationships can be with co-workers, managers, clients, suppliers, or buyers; they can result in feelings of friendship, competition, cooperativeness, and satisfaction, or they can be causes of stress and anxiety.

Structure also affects the behavior and functioning of groups in organizations.[7] Depending on the specific configuration of jobs and departments, groups can be either more or less cohesive, more or less communicative. For example, in a business firm, a department that contains 10 individuals performing the same job will act quite differently from one that contains 10 individuals, each performing a different job. The group containing people doing the same jobs will be less cohesive, less open to new ideas, and less communicative than the group of people doing different jobs.

DESIGNING AN ORGANIZATIONAL STRUCTURE

ORGANIZATIONAL DESIGN
Management decisions and actions that result in specific organization structure.

Managers who set out to design an organizational structure face difficult decisions. They must choose among a myriad of alternative frameworks of jobs and departments. The process by which they make these choices is termed **organizational design**, and it means quite simply the decisions and actions that result in an organizational structure.[8] This process may be explicit or implicit, it may be "one shot" or developmental, it may be done by a single manager or by a team of managers.[9] However the actual decisions come about, the order of the decisions is always the same. The first decision focuses on individual jobs; the next two decisions focus on departments, or groups of

---

[6]Greg R. Oldham and J. Richard Hackman, "Relationships between Organizational Structure and Employee Reactions: Comparing Alternative Frameworks," *Administrative Science Quarterly,* March 1981, pp. 66–83; John M. Ivancevich and James H. Donnelly, Jr., "Relation of Organizational Structure to Job Satisfaction, Anxiety-Stress, and Performance," *Administrative Science Quarterly,* June 1975, pp. 272–80; Larry L. Cummings and Chris J. Berger, "Organization Structure: How Does It Influence Attitudes and Performance?" *Organizational Dynamics,* Autumn 1976, pp. 34–49.

[7]John A. Pearce II and Fred R. David, "A Social Network Approach to Organizational Design and Performance," *Academy of Management Review,* July 1983, pp. 436–44.

[8]Hugh C. Willmott, "The Structuring of Organizational Structures: A Note," *Administrative Science Quarterly,* September 1981, pp. 470–74.

[9]Ronald A. Heiner, "Imperfect Decisions in Organizations: Toward a Theory of Internal Structures," *Journal of Economic Behavior and Organization,* January 1988, pp. 25–44.

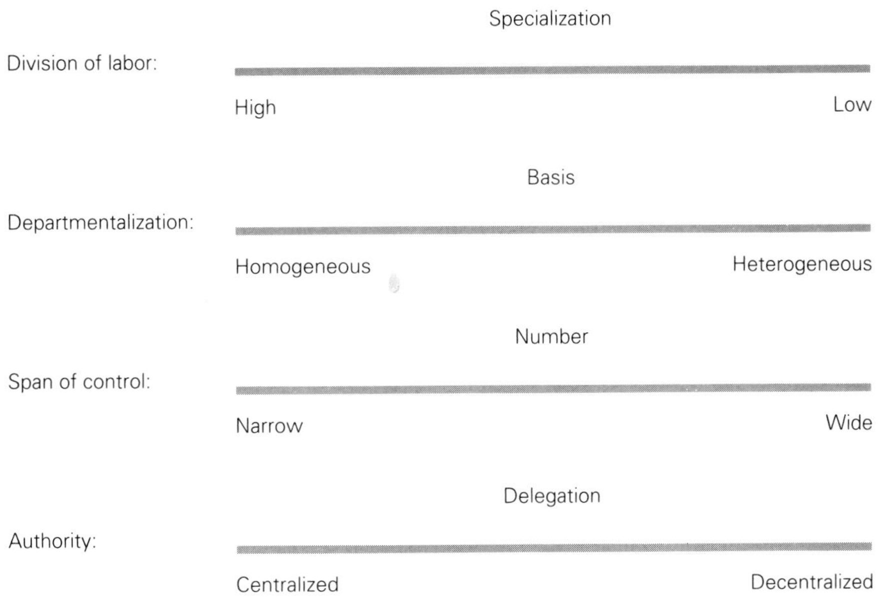

FIGURE 13—2
The Four Key Design
Decisions

Specialization

Division of labor:

High   Low

Basis

Departmentalization:

Homogeneous   Heterogeneous

Number

Span of control:

Narrow   Wide

Delegation

Authority:

Centralized   Decentralized

jobs; the fourth decision considers the issue of delegation of authority throughout the structure.

1. Managers decide how to split the overall task into successively smaller jobs, dividing the total activities of the task into smaller sets of related activities. The effect of this decision is to define jobs in terms of specialized activities and responsibilities. Although jobs have many characteristics, the most important one is their degree of specialization.

2. Managers decide the bases by which individual jobs are to be grouped together. This decision, much like any other classification decision, can result in groups containing jobs that are relatively homogeneous or heterogeneous.

3. Managers decide the appropriate size of the group reporting to each superior. As we have already noted, this decision involves determining whether spans of control should be relatively narrow or wide.

4. Managers distribute authority among the jobs. Authority is the right to make decisions without approval by a higher manager and to exact obedience from designated other people. All jobs contain some degree of right to make decisions within prescribed limits, but not all jobs contain the right to exact obedience from others. The latter aspect of authority distinguishes managerial from nonmanagerial jobs. Managers can exact obedience, nonmanagers cannot.

Thus, organizational structures vary, depending on the choices that managers make. If we consider each of the four design decisions to be a continuum of possible choices, the alternative structures can be depicted as in Figure 13–2. Generally speaking, organizational structures tend toward one extreme or the other along each continuum. Structures situated on the left are characterized by a number of terms including classical, formal, structured, bureaucratic, System 1, and mechanistic. Structures on the right are termed neoclassical, informal, unstructured, nonbureaucratic, System 4, and organic.[10] Exactly where along the continuum an organization finds itself has implications both for its performance and for individual and group behavior.[11]

DIVISION OF LABOR

DIVISION OF LABOR
Process of dividing work into relatively specialized jobs to achieve advantages of specialization.

Division of labor concerns the extent to which jobs are specialized. Managers divide the total work of the organization into specific jobs having specified activities. The activities are defined by what the person performing the job is to accomplish. For example, the activities of the job of accounting clerk can be defined in terms of the methods and procedures required to process a certain quantity of transactions during a period of time. Different accounting clerks could use the same methods and procedures to process different types of transactions: one could be processing accounts receivable, while the others process accounts payable. Thus, jobs can be specialized both by method and by application of the method.

The economic advantages of dividing work into specialized jobs provide the principal historical reasons for the creation of organizations.[12] As societies became more and more industrialized and urbanized, craft production gave way to mass production. Mass production depends on the ability to obtain the economic benefits of specialized labor, and the most effective means for obtaining specialized labor is through organizations. Although managers are concerned with more than the economic implications of jobs, they seldom lose sight of specialization as the rationale for dividing work among jobs.[13]

Division of labor in organizations can occur in three ways:[14]

1. Work can be divided into different *personal* specialties. Most people think of specialization in the sense of occupational and professional specialties. Thus, we think of accountants, engineers, scientists, physicians, and the myriad of other specialties that exist in organizations and everyday life.

2. Work can be divided into different activities necessitated by the natural sequence of the work the organization does. For example, manufacturing plants often divide work into fabricating, assembly, and finishing; individuals will be assigned to do the work of one of these three activities. This particular method of division of work is termed *horizontal* specialization.

3. Finally, work can be divided along the *vertical* plane of an organization. All organizations have a hierarchy of authority from the lowest-level manager to the highest-level manager. The work of the CEO is different from that of the shift supervisor.

---

[10]Henry Tosi, *Theories of Organization* (New York: John Wiley & Sons, 1984).

[11]Oldham and Hackman, "Relationship between Organizational Structure."

[12]Richard E. Kopelman, "Job Redesign and Productivity: A Review of the Literature," *National Productivity Review,* Summer 1985, p. 239.

[13]Donald J. Campbell, "Task Complexity: A Review and Analysis," *Academy of Management Review,* January 1988, pp. 40–52.

[14]Judith R. Gordon, *A Diagnostic Approach to Organizational Behavior* (Boston: Allyn & Bacon, 1983), p. 407.

The determination of what each job in the organization should do is a key managerial decision. While the next chapter contains a more complete discussion of the decision, the important point here is that jobs vary along a general dimension of specialization, with some jobs more highly specialized than others. Managers can change the way an organization is structured by changing the degree of job specialization.

One dramatic effect of the trend toward downsizing organizations during the 1980s has been to despecialize managerial jobs, particularly those of middle managers. General Electric has aggressively pursued a policy of reducing the number of managers in the hierarchy. As a result, managers have more to do (their jobs are less specialized) as their spans of control have increased.[15]

The process of defining the activities and authority of jobs is analytical. That is, the total work of the organization is broken down into successively smaller tasks. Then, management must combine the divided tasks into groups or departments based on some criterion and containing a specified number of individuals or jobs. We will discuss these two decisions relating to departments in that order.

DEPARTMENTALIZATION BASES

The rationale for grouping jobs rests on the need to coordinate them. The specialized jobs are separate, interrelated parts of the total task, the accomplishment of which requires completion of each of the jobs. These jobs must be performed in the specific manner and sequence defined by management. As the number of specialized jobs in an organization increases, a point comes when they can no longer be effectively coordinated by a single manager. Thus, to create a manageable number of jobs, they are combined into smaller groups in a process called **departmentalization**. And a new job is defined, that of manager of the group.

DEPARTMENTALIZATION
Process in which organization is structurally divided by combining jobs in departments according to some shared characteristic, or basis.

The crucial managerial consideration when creating departments is determining the basis for grouping jobs, particularly the departments that report to the top management position. Numerous bases are used throughout an organization, but what is used at the highest level determines critical dimensions of the organization. Some of the more widely used departmentalization bases are described in the following sections.[16]

Functional Departmentalization

Every organization must undertake certain activities in order to do its work. Those necessary activities are the organization's functions. Managers can combine jobs according to these functions.

The necessary functions of a manufacturing firm include production, marketing, finance, accounting, and personnel—all activities necessary to

---

[15]"Caught in the Middle," *Business Week,* September 12, 1988, pp. 80–88.

[16]Mariann Jelinek, "Organization Structure: The Basic Conformations," in *Organization by Design,* ed. Mariann Jelinek, Joseph A. Litterer, and Raymond E. Miles (Plano, Tex.: Business Publications, 1981), pp. 293–302.

create, produce, and sell a product. The necessary functions of a commercial bank include taking deposits, making loans, and investing the bank's funds. The functions of a hospital include surgery, psychiatry, housekeeping, pharmacy, nursing, and personnel.[17] Each of these functions can be a specific department, and jobs can be combined according to them. The functional basis is often used in relatively small organizations that provide a narrow range of products and services. It is also widely used as the basis in divisions of large, multiproduct organizations.

Manufacturing organizations are typically structured on a functional basis, as depicted in Figure 13–3. The functions are engineering, manufacturing, reliability, distribution, finance, personnel, public relations, and purchasing. Organization charts for a commercial bank and a hospital structured along functional lines are also depicted in Figure 13–3. The functional basis has wide application in service as well as in manufacturing organizations. The specific configuration of functions that appear as separate departments varies from organization to organization.

The principal advantage of the functional basis is its efficiency. To have a department that consists of experts in a particular field such as production or accounting seems logical. Such departments of specialists are highly efficient units. An accountant is generally more efficient when working with other accountants and other individuals who have similar backgrounds and interests. They can share expertise to get the work done. General Motors attracted considerable attention when it combined its traditional product divisions into two functional departments—production and sales. The driving force behind GM's reorganization was to reduce the cost of developing and marketing automobiles by realizing the efficiencies of function-based organization structure.[18]

A major disadvantage of the functional basis is that because specialists are working with and encouraging each other in their area of expertise and interest, the organizational goals may be sacrificed in favor of departmental goals. Accountants may see only their problems and not those of production or marketing or the total organization. In other words, departmental culture and ties are often stronger than identification with the organization and its culture.

Territorial Departmentalization

Another basis for departmentalizing is to establish groups according to geographical area. The logic is that all activities in a given region should be under one manager. In large organizations, territorial arrangements are advantageous because physical separation of activities makes centralized coordination difficult. For example, it is extremely difficult for someone in New York to manage salespeople in Kansas City. Assigning the managerial job to someone in Kansas City makes sense.

---

[17]Peggy Leatt and Rodney Schneck, "Criteria for Grouping Nursing Subunits in Hospitals," *Academy of Management Journal*, March 1984, pp. 150–64.

[18]Richard B. Chase and David A. Tansik, "The Customer Contact Model for Organization Design," *Management Science*, September 1983, pp. 1037–50.

FIGURE 13—3

Functional-Base Organization in Three Settings

A. Manufacturing

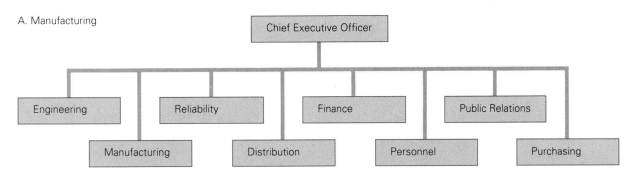

B. Banking

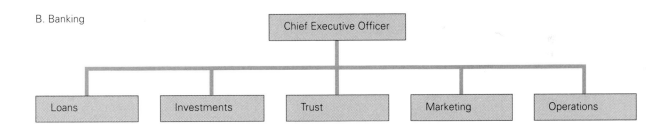

C. Hospital

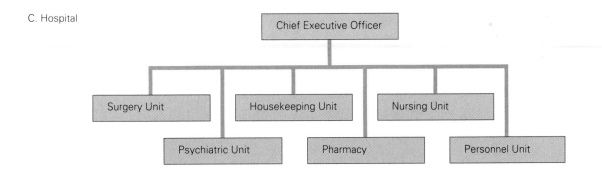

Large retail stores are often organized along territorial lines, as depicted in Figure 13–4. The divisions of the department store reflect the locations of Macy stores in the several states in which they operate. The managers of individual stores in a specific city report to a regional president. For example, the manager of the Sacramento outlet reports to the president of the California Division. The headquarters units, organized on a functional basis, provide technical support and expertise to the managers of the local stores.

Territorial departmentalization provides a training ground for managerial personnel. The company is able to place managers in territories and then assess

R. H. Macy & Co., Inc.: Organizational Structure

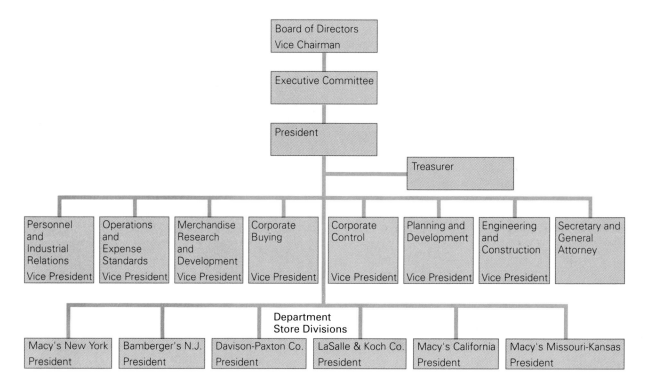

their progress in that region. The experience that managers acquire in a territory away from headquarters provides valuable insights about how products and/or services are accepted in the field.

Product Departmentalization

Managers of many large, diversified companies group jobs on the basis of product. All the jobs associated with producing and selling a product or product line will be placed under the direction of one manager. Product becomes the preferred basis as a firm's product line grows. Coordinating the various functional departments gets increasingly difficult, and product units become advantageous. This form of organization allows the product group's personnel to develop total expertise in researching, manufacturing, and distributing a product line. Concentrating authority, responsibility, and accountability in a specific product department allows top management to coordinate actions.

The Consumer Products Division of Kimberly-Clark reflects product departmentalization. The specific product groups shown in Figure 13–5 include feminine hygiene, household, and commercial products. Within each of these units, we would find production and marketing personnel. Since

FIGURE 13–5

Consumer Products Division, Kimberly-Clark Corporation: Organizational Structure

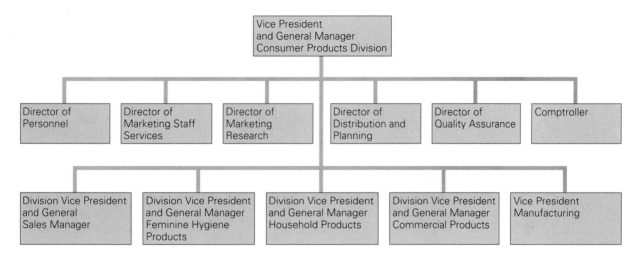

managers of product divisions coordinate sales, manufacturing, and distribution of a product, they become the overseers of a profit center. In this manner, profit responsibility is implemented in product-based organizations. Managers are often asked to establish profit goals at the beginning of a time period and then to compare actual profit with planned profit.

Product-based organizations foster initiative and autonomy by providing division managers with the resources necessary to carry out their profit plans. But such organizations face the difficult issue of deciding how much redundancy is necessary. Divisional structures contain some degree of redundancy because each division wants its own research, engineering, marketing, production, and all other functions necessary to do business. Thus, technical and professional personnel are found throughout the organization at the division levels. The cost of this arrangement can be exorbitant. 3M has attempted to deal with the problem by organizing the R&D function as described in the Close-Up.

Customer Departmentalization

Customers and clients can be a basis for grouping jobs.[19] Examples of customer-oriented departments are the organization structures of educational institutions. Some institutions have regular (day and night) courses and extension divisions. In some instances, a professor will be affiliated solely with the regular division or extension division. In fact, the title of some faculty positions often specifically mentions the extension division.

---

[19]Frank Cornish, "Building a Customer-Oriented Organization," *Long Range Planning,* June 1988, pp. 105–7.

3M'S ORGANIZATION OF THE R&D FUNCTION

3M has a divisional structure, with 89 divisions responsible for producing and marketing some 60,000 types and sizes of products. The divisions are grouped into sectors, and sector managers report to corporate headquarters. The company has found that coordinating product research and development in such a structure presents staggering problems.

To manage the function, the company created a structure that distinguishes between different R&D activities. Research and development personnel at the divisional level concentrate attention on the existing products and markets. They are expected to investigate opportunities for modifying products the division has already developed and placed on the market. R&D personnel at the sector level function in scientific research laboratories and concentrate on the hard sciences, particularly chemistry. Their product development research is limited to those scheduled for introduction within five years. The third R&D group, located at corporate headquarters, conducts primary research on state-of-the-arts technology.

An advantage of splitting a seemingly homogeneous function such as R&D is that differences in usage can be identified for each level of the organization. In addition, the sector-level personnel act as coordinators of the day-to-day needs of division-level research and the blue-sky activities of the corporate researchers.

Source: Alicia Johnson, "3M: Organized to Innovate," *Management Review,* July 1986, pp. 38–39.

Another form of customer departmentalization is the loan department in a commercial bank. Loan officers are often associated with industrial, commercial, or agricultural loans. The customer will be served by the appropriate category of loan officer.

Some clothing retailers are departmentalized to some degree on a customer basis. They have groupings such as university shops, men's clothing, and boys' clothing. They have bargain floors that carry a lower quality of university, men's, and boys' clothing. Organizations with customer-based departments are better able to satisfy customer-identified needs than organizations that base departments on noncustomer factors.[20]

The Matrix Organization: Combining Bases

MATRIX ORGANIZATION
Organization design that super-imposes product- or project-based design on existing function-based design.

An emerging organization design, termed the **matrix organization**, attempts to maximize the strengths and minimize the weaknesses of both the functional and product bases. In practical terms, the matrix design combines functional and product departmental bases.[21] American Cyanamid, Avco, Carborun-

---

[20]Jay R. Galbraith and Robert K. Kazanjian, "Organizing to Implement Strategies of Diversity and Globalization: The Role of Matrix Organizations," *Human Resource Management,* Spring 1986, pp. 37–54.

[21]Kenneth Knight, "Matrix Organization: A Review," *Journal of Management Studies,* May 1976, p. 111.

Projects, Products	Functions			
	Manufacturing	Marketing	Engineering	Finance
Project or product A				
Project or product B				
Project or product C				
Project or product D				
Project or product E				

FIGURE 13—6

Matrix Organizations

dum, Caterpillar Tractor, Hughes Aircraft, ITT, Monsanto Chemical, National Cash Register, Prudential Insurance, TRW, and Texas Instruments are only a few of the users of matrix organization. Public sector users include public health and social service agencies.[22] Although the exact definition of a matrix organization is not well established, it most typically is seen as a balanced compromise between functional and product organization, between departmentalization by function and by product.[23]

Matrix organizations achieve the desired balance by superimposing, or overlaying, a horizontal structure of authority, influence, and communication on the vertical structure. In the arrangement shown in Figure 13–6, personnel assigned in each cell belong not only to the functional department but also to a particular product or project. For example, manufacturing, marketing, engineering, and finance specialists are assigned to work on one or more of projects/products A, B, C, D, and E. As a consequence, employees report to two managers, one in their functional department and one in the project or product unit. The existence of a *dual authority* system is a distinguishing characteristic of matrix organization.

Matrix structures are found in organizations that require responses to rapid change in two or more environments (e.g., technology and markets), that face uncertainties that generate high information processing requirements; and that must deal with financial and human resources constraints.[24] Managers confronting these circumstances must obtain certain advantages that are most likely to be realized with matrix organization.[25]

Matrix organization facilitates the utilization of highly specialized staff and equipment. Each project/product unit can share the specialized resource with other units rather than duplicating it to provide independent coverage for each. This is a particular advantage when projects require less than the full-time efforts of the specialist. For example, a project may require only half a

---

[22]Ibid., p. 114.

[23]Paul R. Lawrence, Harvey F. Kolodny, and Stanley M. Davis, "The Human Side of the Matrix," *Organizational Dynamics,* September 1977, p. 47.

[24]The following discussion is based on Knight, "Matrix Organization."

[25]Christopher A. Bartlett and Sumantra Ghosal, "Organizing for Worldwide Effectiveness: The Transactional Solution," *California Management Review,* Fall 1988, pp. 54–74.

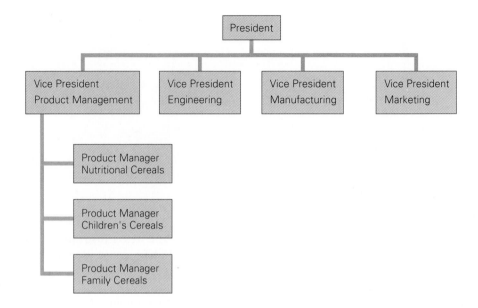

computer scientist's time. Rather than having several underutilized computer scientists assigned to each project, the organization can keep fewer of them fully utilized by shifting them from project to project.

Such flexibility results in quicker response to competitive conditions, technological breakthroughs, and other environmental conditions. Also, these interactions encourage cross-fertilization of ideas, such as when a computer scientist must discuss the pros and cons of electronic data processing with a financial accounting expert. Each specialist must be able to listen, understand, and respond to the views of the other. At the same time, specialists maintain ongoing contact with members of their own discipline because they are also members of a functional department.

A fully developed matrix organization has product management departments along with the usual functional departments. Figure 13–7 depicts an organization with a product manager reporting to top management and with subproduct managers for each product line. In some instances, the subproduct managers are selected from specific functional departments and would continue to report directly to their functional managers. In other instances, the product managers are permanently assigned to the product management department. There is considerable diversity in the application of matrix organization, yet the essential feature is the creation of overlapping authority and the existence of dual authority.

Departmentalization in Multinational Corporations

MULTINATIONAL
CORPORATIONS (MNCs)

Firms that do business in more than one country.

Corporations that cross national boundaries must decide how to include the foreign activity in the organization, how to coordinate the international activities. In fact, the foreign activities of **multinational corporations (MNCs)** are but extensions of the domestic businesses and coordination involves issues similar to those of local activities. The outstanding success of Japanese corporations in international markets has initiated great interest in the ways firms can and should organize to compete successfully with the Japanese. The discussion centers on which departmental basis is appropriate under which circumstances.[26]

The most prevalent departmental basis is *territory*. The arrangement has national and regional managers reporting to a headquarters in the same national or regional area. Territory-based organizations for MNCs have the same characteristics as those for domestic organizations. Each national or regional office has all the resources necessary to produce and market the product or service. This organizational form is suitable for organizations that have limited product lines, such as ITT and Charles Pfizer Corporation.

MNCs having a diversified product line will find certain advantages in the *product*-based organization structure. This structure assigns worldwide responsibility for a product or product line to a single corporate office, and all foreign and domestic units associated with that product report to the corporate product office.[27] Kodak Company uses the product-based structure to assign responsibility for worldwide research and development, manufacturing, marketing, and distribution of its products. The basic product unit, called a line of business (LOB), makes its own decisions and succeeds or fails accordingly. Kodak believes this structure enables managers to respond more quickly to market conditions.

MNCs with relatively few product lines, such as firms in the extractive industry, will use the *function* approach. According to this structure, a corporate office for each business function (e.g., production, marketing, and finance) has authority over those functions wherever they take place throughout the world. Thus, the production personnel in Europe, South America, and North America will report to corporate officials in charge of production.

The Close-Up describes the changes undertaken at Bayer AG, a major multinational corporation, to meet changing circumstances.

The degree of coordination that management achieves greatly depends on having appropriate departmentalization bases at each level in the organization. As illustrated by the Bayer AG experience, appropriate bases may change with time and circumstances. The changes at Bayer AG reflect the relative importance of obtaining efficiency and production (functional departments), the increasing importance of making and selling different products (specialist committees), and adaptation to the special needs of different segments of the market (product divisions).[28]

Departmentalization is a key decision in organization design. An equally important decision is the determination of each manager's span of control.

---

[26]David J. Lemak and Jeffrey A. Bracker, "A Strategic Contingency Model of Multinational Corporate Structure," *Strategic Management Journal,* September–October 1988, pp. 521–26.

[27]Wilber J. Prezzano, "Kodak Sharpens Its Focus on Quality," *Management Review,* May 1989, pp. 39–41.

[28]Christopher A. Bartlett, "How Multinational Organizations Evolve," *Journal of Business Strategy,* Winter 1982, pp. 20–32.

REORGANIZATION AT BAYER AG

One managerial reaction to growth is reorganization. Bayer AG of Leverkusen, Germany, has over 175,000 employees and is one of the largest chemical and health care organizations in the world. Since its founding in 1863, the company has diversified into many products and regions of the world. It recently announced a structural reorganization, which company management states is a natural evolution in response to the pressures of growth.

Until 1965, Bayer was organized along functional lines: production, sales, research, personnel, and finance. This structure worked well until the company's product line became so extensive that product coordination began to suffer. In 1965, to counter that problem, Bayer established a number of "specialist committees," which consisted of the managers of product-related units in each of the functional units. These committees were organized along product lines such as organic chemicals, dyes, rubber, and fiber. Then, in 1971, the company adopted a form of divisional structure in which the specialist committees became product divisions. These divisions included production, sales, research, and engineering units. Other support units were retained at corporate headquarters and made available on an as-needed basis.

The most recently announced reorganization establishes the product divisions as relatively independent business units with access to all but the most highly specialized functions, which remain at corporate level.

Source: Heinrich Vossberg, "Bayer Reorganizes in Response to Growth," *Long Range Planning,* December 1985, pp. 15–20.

SPAN OF CONTROL

SPAN OF CONTROL
Number of individuals who report to specific manager.

The determination of appropriate bases for departmentalization establishes the *kinds* of jobs that will be grouped together. But that determination does not establish the *number* of jobs to be included in a specific group, or the **span of control**. Will the organization be more effective if the span of control is relatively wide or narrow? Generally, the issue comes down to how many people a manager can oversee; what volume of interpersonal relationships the department's manager is able to handle. Moreover, the span of control must be defined to include not only formally assigned subordinates but also those who have access to the manager. A manager may not only be responsible for immediate subordinates but may also be the chairperson of several committees and task groups that take time.[29]

The number of potential interpersonal relationships between a manager and subordinates increases geometrically as the number of subordinates increases arithmetically. This relationship holds because managers potentially contend with three types of interpersonal relationships: (1) direct single, (2) direct

---

[29]William G. Ouchi and John B. Dowling, "Defining the Span of Control," *Administrative Science Quarterly,* September 1974, pp. 357–65.

group, and (3) cross. Direct single relationships occur between the manager and each subordinate individually, in a one-on-one setting. Direct group relations occur between the manager and each possible combination of subordinates. Finally, cross-relationships occur when subordinates interact with one another.

The critical consideration in determining a manager's span of control is not the number of potential relationships. Rather, the frequency and intensity of the actual relationships are important. Not all relationships will occur, and those that do will vary in importance. If we shift our attention from potential to actual relationships as the bases for determining optimum span of control, at least three factors appear to be important.

Required Contact

In research and development, medicine and production work, frequent contact and a high degree of coordination between superior and subordinates are needed. The use of conferences and other forms of consultation often aids in the attainment of goals within a constrained time period. For example, the R&D team leader may have to consult frequently with team members so that a project is completed within a time period that will allow the organization to place a product on the market. Thus, instead of relying on memos and reports, the organization would do best to have as many in-depth leader-team contacts as possible. A wide span of control, which would preclude contacting subordinates so frequently, could have detrimental effects on completing the project. In general, the greater the inherent ambiguity that exists in an individual's job, the greater the need for contact (supervision) to avoid conflict and stress.[30]

Degree of Specialization

How specialized employees are is a critical consideration in establishing the span of control at all levels of management. A manager at the lower organizational level can generally be expected to oversee more subordinates, because work at the lower level is more specialized and less complicated than at higher levels of management. Management can combine highly specialized and similar jobs into relatively large departments because the employees may not need close supervision.

Ability to Communicate

Instructions, guidelines, and policies must be communicated verbally to subordinates in most work situations. The need to discuss job-related factors influences the span of control. The individual who can clearly and concisely communicate with subordinates is able to manage more people than one who cannot do so.

---

[30]Lawrence B. Chonko, "The Relationship of Span of Control to Sales Representatives, Experienced Role Conflict and Role Ambiguity," *Academy of Management Journal,* June 1982, pp. 452–56.

ORGANIZATIONS:
CLOSE-UP

SPANS OF CONTROL AT DANA CORPORATION

When Dana Corporation of Toledo, Ohio, underwent some changes in its organizational structure, one of top management's objectives was to reduce the total number of managerial jobs. A promising approach to achieving that goal was to increase spans of control. According to John M. Toth, communications manager, top management encouraged plant managers to organize according to how many people a manager could supervise rather than by what functions coincided with a manager's title. Plant managers evaluated the supervisory skills of each manager and assigned a correspondingly appropriate number of individuals.

Thus, at Dana, a quality control manager may supervise people involved in maintenance and shipping, for example, instead of only six or so quality control inspectors. The people who perform work other than quality control can be assigned to the manager because of his or her supervisory skill. The concept that underlies Dana Corporation's approach is that management should be defined in terms of control rather than as boxes on an organizational chart.

Source: John M. Toth, "How Dana Is Reducing Number of Managers Despite Its Growth," *Management Review*, November–December 1982, pp. 29, 36.

The Close-Up describes the importance of span of control in Dana Corporation's organization structure. Even though identifying some of the specific factors related to optimal spans of control is possible, the search for the full answer continues.[31]

DELEGATION OF AUTHORITY

DELEGATION OF AUTHORITY
Process of distributing authority downward in organization.

Managers decide how much authority is to be delegated to each job and each jobholder. **Delegation of authority** refers specifically to making decisions, not to doing work. As we have noted, authority refers to the right of individuals to make decisions without approval by higher management and to exact obedience from others. A sales manager can be delegated the right to hire salespersons (a decision) and the right to assign them to specific territories (obedience). Another sales manager may not have the right to hire but may have the right to assign territories. Thus, the degree of delegated authority can be relatively high or relatively low with respect to both aspects of authority. And any particular job involves a range of alternative configurations of authority delegation. Managers must balance the relative gains and losses of these alternatives.

---

[31]Robert D. Dewar and Donald P. Simet, "A Level-Specific Prediction of Spans of Control Examining the Effects of Size, Technology, and Specialization," *Academy of Management Journal*, March 1981, pp. 5–24.

Reasons to Decentralize Authority

Relatively high delegation of authority encourages the development of professional managers. No doubt, Philip G. Barach, CEO of U.S. Shoe Corporation, had this point in mind when he described his management style as organized anarchy because he tends to leave his day-to-day managers alone without any direction from his office—until things go wrong![32] As decision-making authority is pushed downward (delegated) in the organization, managers have opportunities to make significant decisions and to gain skills that enable them to advance in the company. By having the right to make decisions on a broad range of issues, managers develop expertise that enables them to cope with problems of higher management. Managers with broad decision-making power often make difficult decisions; consequently, they are trained for promotion into positions of even greater authority and responsibility. Upper management can readily compare managers on the basis of actual decision-making performance. The advancement of managers on the basis of demonstrated performance can eliminate favoritism and personality conflicts in the promotion process.

Second, greater delegation of authority can lead to a competitive climate within the organization. Managers are motivated to contribute, since they are compared with their peers on various performance measures. A competitive environment in which managers compete on how well they achieve sales, cost reduction, and employee development targets can be a positive factor in overall organizational performance. Competitive environments can also produce destructive behavior if the success of one manager occurs at the expense of another. But whether positive or destructive in effect, significant competition exists only when individuals have authority to do those things that enable them to win.

Finally, managers with relatively high authority are able to exercise more autonomy and thus satisfy their desire to participate in problem solving. This autonomy can lead to managerial creativity and ingenuity, which contribute to the adaptiveness and development of the organization and managers. As we have seen in earlier chapters, opportunities to participate in setting goals can be positive motivators. But a necessary condition for goal setting is authority to make decisions. Many organizations, large and small, choose to follow the policy of decentralization of authority. One such instance is reported in the "Clairson International" Close-Up.

Reasons to Centralize

Decentralization of authority has its benefits, but these benefits are not without costs. Organizations unable or unwilling to bear these costs will find reasons to centralize authority. First, managers must be trained to make the decisions that go with delegated authority. The expense of formal training programs can more than offset the benefits.

Second, managers accustomed to making decisions may resist delegating authority to their subordinates. Consequently, they may perform at lower

---

[32]"Why U.S. Shoe Is Looking Down at the Heel," *Business Week,* July 4, 1988, p. 60.

**ORGANIZATIONS:
CLOSE-UP**

DECENTRALIZATION AT CLAIRSON INTERNATIONAL

Clairson International, headquartered in Ocala, Florida, manufactures household and commercial wire storage products. It employs 1,700 people at 15 sites located in Florida, Georgia, Nevada, California, and Iowa. The two major divisions, household products and commercial products, are headed by two presidents who meet each year to go through an annual and strategic planning cycle. In conjunction with the corporation's executive committee, the presidents hammer out the budgeting and action plans for the year. Once the executive committee approves the plans, the presidents are free to implement them without further review. The two divisions have sufficient autonomy to carry out their plans, and the corporate executive committee intervenes only in unusual circumstances.

The company was not always run as a decentralized organization. In its early days, all decisions were made at the corporate level. But as the company grew and the product line expanded into distant markets, centralized control proved unworkable, and a process of decentralization was undertaken. The only centralized functions are benefits, compensation review, affirmative action, and equal employment opportunity compliance. All other administrative matters are handled in the divisions at the plant levels.

Source: Marlene C. Piturro, "Decentralization: Rebuilding the Corporation," *Management Review,* August 1988, pp. 31–34.

---

levels of effectiveness because they believe that delegation of authority involves losing control.

Third, when authority is delegated, administrative costs are incurred. New or altered accounting and performance systems must be developed to provide top management with information about the effects of their subordinates' decisions. When authority is delegated to lower levels of management, top managers must have some means of reviewing the use of that authority. Consequently, they typically create reporting systems that inform them.

Fourth, and perhaps the most pragmatic reason to centralize, is that decentralization means duplication of functions. To be independent, each autonomous unit must be truly self-supporting. But that involves a potentially high cost of duplication. The Close-Up reports Hewlett-Parkard's recent move toward centralization.

Decision Guidelines

As with most managerial issues, the degree to which authority should be delegated cannot be resolved simply. Whether to centralize or decentralize authority can only be guided by general questions.[33] Managers faced with the issue can ask and answer the following four questions:

---

[33]Barry A. Liebling, "Is It Time to (De)Centralize?" *Management Review,* September 1981, pp. 14–20.

ORGANIZATIONS:
CLOSE-UP

HEWLETT-PACKARD BEGINS TO CENTRALIZE

In 1985, Hewlett-Packard (HP) began to reverse its long-standing practice of allowing its units to operate as minicompanies, each with its own manufacturing, marketing, finance, and personnel staffs. The impetus for the reversal was the increasing cost of duplication at the local level. For example, each HP unit produced the circuit boards for its own products, even though the circuit boards were interchangeable. This arrangement enabled local managers to have control and flexibility over volume and quality. But the cost of duplication became intolerable as competition forced down the prices of HP products. Circuit board production is now consolidated in a few manufacturing sites and under the direction of a single manager.

Prior to centralization, HP manufactured three different computers in three autonomous divisions. The computers were incompatible even though marketed to the same professional and office markets. The three units acted as though they were in competition. In 1987, HP consolidated the three divisions under the direction of one manager, with the mandate that the computers were to be made technologically compatible.

Source: "IBM's Plan to Decentralize May Set a Trend—But Imitation Has a Price," *The Wall Street Journal*, February 19, 1988, p. 17.

1. *How routine and straightforward are the job's or unit's required decisions?* The authority for routine decisions can be centralized. For example, fast-food restaurants such as Kentucky Fried Chicken centralize the decision of food preparation to ensure consistent quality at all the stores. However, the decision to hire and dismiss employees is decentralized to the store level. This question points out the importance of the distinction between deciding and doing. The food is prepared at the local store, but the decision as to how it will be prepared is made at headquarters.

2. *Are individuals competent to make the decision?* This question implies that the delegation of authority can differ from individual to individual, depending on each one's ability to make the decision. Even if the decision is nonroutine, as in the case of hiring employees, the decision will necessarily be centralized if the local manager is not competent to make it.

3. *Are individuals motivated to make the decision?* Capable individuals are not always motivated individuals. We discussed the issues of motivation and individual differences in earlier chapters. Decision making can be difficult and stressful, thus discouraging some individuals from accepting authority for that task. It can also involve a level of commitment to the organization that is beyond the willingness of the individual to make. For whatever reasons, motivation must accompany competency to create conducive conditions for decentralization.

4. Finally, return to the points we made earlier. *Do the benefits of decentralization outweigh its costs?* This question is perhaps the most difficult one to answer, because so many of the benefits and costs are assessed in

ORGANIZATIONS:
CLOSE-UP

DECENTRALIZATION AT DOMINO'S PIZZA

According to the president of Domino's Pizza Distribution Corporation, the advantages of decentralized authority far exceed the disadvantages. The company, headquartered in Ann Arbor, Michigan, had nearly 4,000 Domino's Pizza Stores in 1987. Almost 95 percent of the stores bought their food supplies and equipment from the distribution company even though only the 35 percent that were company owned were required to do so. But the president believes that the reason all the others count on the distribution company for supplies is its reputation for reliability. The worst sin in the company is to force a store to close because it has inadequate supplies to meet customer demand.

The distribution company's profits increased from a negative $330,000 in 1978 to $13.7 million in 1986. This record of success reflects the benefits of decentralization as practiced at Domino's. All employees of the distribution company are given sufficient autonomy to achieve specific goals consistent with the company's mission. To reinforce its commitment to decentralization, the company insists that employees be willing to use their own minds to solve problems. There are no formal job titles; each employee is referred to as a "team member." Beyond that, the company places little importance on job titles and encourages individuals to refer to themselves in whatever terms reflect their duties. Employees must assume a large amount of responsibility and can count on very little hand-holding from headquarters. The company motto "Do anything to get the job done" accounts for its record of reliable delivery.

Source: Donald J. Vlcek, Jr., "Decentralization: What Works and What Doesn't," *Journal of Business Strategy*, Fall 1987, pp. 71–74.

subjective terms. Nevertheless, managers should at least attempt a benefit-cost analysis.[34]

The Close-Up describes how Domino's Pizza has used decentralization to the benefit of the company.

DIMENSIONS OF STRUCTURE

The four design decisions (division of labor, delegation of authority, departmentalization, and span of control) result in the organization's structure. Researchers and practitioners of management have attempted to develop their understanding of relationships between structures and performance, attitudes, satisfaction, and other variables thought to be important. Understanding has been hampered not only by the complexity of the relationships themselves but also by the difficulty of defining and measuring the concept of organizational structure.

Although universal agreement of a common set of dimensions by which to measure differences in structure is neither possible nor desirable, some

[34]Richard S. Blackburn, "Dimensions of Structure: A Review and Reappraisal," *Academy of Management Review*, January 1982, pp. 59–66.

suggestions can be made. At the present time, the three dimensions often used in research and practice to describe structure are formalization, centralization, and complexity.[35]

Formalization

Formalization refers to the extent to which expectations regarding the means and ends of work are specified and written. In a highly formalized organization structure, rules and procedures are available to prescribe what each individual should be doing. Such organizations have written standard operating procedures, specified directives, and explicit policy. In terms of the four design decisions, formalization is the result of high specialization of labor, high delegation of authority, the use of functional departments, and wide spans of control:[36]

FORMALIZATION
Extent to which organization relies on written rules and procedures to predetermine actions of employees.

1. High specialization of labor, such as in the auto industry, facilitates the development of written work rules and procedures. The jobs are so specialized as to leave little to the discretion of the jobholder.

2. High delegation of authority creates the need to have checks on its use. Consequently, the organization will write guidelines for decision making and will insist on reports that describe the use of authority.

3. Functional departments are made up of jobs that have great similarities, such as accountants, engineers, machinists, and the like. Because of the similarity of the jobs and the rather straightforward nature of the department's activities, management can develop written documents to govern the department's activities.

4. Wide spans of control discourage one-on-one supervision, because there are simply too many subordinates for managers to deal with on that basis. Consequently, managers will require written reports to inform them.

Although formalization is defined in terms of the existence of written rules and procedures, understanding how they are viewed by the employees is important. Some organizations may have all the appearances of formalization, complete with thick manuals of rules, procedures, and policies, but employees do not perceive them as affecting their behavior. Thus, rules and procedures must be enforced if they are to affect behavior.[37]

Centralization

Centralization refers to the location of decision-making authority in the hierarchy of the organization. More specifically, the concept refers to the delegation of authority among the jobs in the organization. Researchers and

CENTRALIZATION
Degree to which top management delegates authority to make decisions.

[35]James P. Walsh and Robert D. Dewar, "Formalization and the Organizational Life-Cycle," *Journal of Management Studies,* May 1987, pp. 215–32.

[36]For a discussion of formalization in relation to centralization, see Peter H. Grinyear and Masoud Yasai-Ardekani, "Dimensions of Organizational Structure: A Critical Replication," *Academy of Management Journal,* September 1980, pp. 405–21.

[37]Eric J. Walton, "The Comparison of Measures of Organization Structure," *Academy of Management Review,* January 1981, pp. 155–60.

practitioners typically think of centralization in terms of (1) decision making and (2) control.

Despite its apparent simplicity, the concept can be complex. This complexity derives from three sources. First, people at the same level can have different decision-making authority. Second, not all decisions are of equal importance in organizations. For example, a typical management practice is to delegate authority for making routine operating decisions (decentralization) but to retain authority for making strategic decisions (centralization). Third, individuals may not perceive that they really have authority, even though their job descriptions include it. Thus, objectively they have authority, but subjectively they do not.[38]

Centralization generally relates to the four design decisions as follows:

1. The higher the specialization of labor, the greater the centralization. This relationship holds because highly specialized jobs do not require the discretion that authority provides.

2. The less authority delegated, the greater the centralization. By definition, centralization involves retaining authority in the top management jobs rather than delegating it to lower levels in the organization.

3. The greater the use of functional departments, the greater the centralization. The use of functional departments requires that the activities of the several interrelated departments be coordinated. Consequently, authority to coordinate them will be retained in top management.

4. The wider the spans of control, the greater the centralization. Wide spans of control are associated with relatively specialized jobs, which (as we have seen) have little need for authority.

Complexity

COMPLEXITY

Number of different job titles and authority levels in organization.

The direct outgrowth of dividing work and creating departments, **complexity** specifically refers to the number of distinctly different job titles, or occupational groupings, and the number of distinctly different units, or departments, in an organization. The fundamental idea is that organizations with a great many different kinds and types of jobs and units create more complicated managerial and organizational problems than those with fewer jobs and departments.

Complexity, then, relates to differences among jobs and units. Not surprisingly, therefore, differentiation is often used synonymously with complexity. Moreover, it has become standard practice to use the term *horizontal differentiation* to refer to the number of different units at the same level,[39] while *vertical differentiation* refers to the number of levels in the organization. Complexity (horizontal and vertical differentiation) and the four design decisions are generally related as follows:

1. The greater the specialization of labor, the greater the complexity. Specialization is the process of creating different jobs and thus more complexity. It contributes primarily to horizontal differentiation.

---

[38]Jeffrey D. Ford, "Institutional versus Questionnaire Measures of Organizational Structure," *Academy of Management Journal,* September 1979, pp. 601–10.

[39]Richard L. Daft and Patricia J. Bradshaw, "The Process of Horizontal Differentiation: Two Models," *Administrative Science Quarterly,* September 1980, pp. 441–56.

Dimensions	Decisions
High formalization	1. High specialization 2. Functional departments 3. Wide spans of control 4. Delegated authority
High centralization	1. High specialization 2. Functional departments 3. Wide spans of control 4. Centralized authority
High complexity	1. High specialization 2. Territorial, customer, and product departments 3. Narrow spans of control 4. Delegated authority

TABLE 13—1

Organization Dimensions in Relation to Organizational Decisions

2. The greater the delegation of authority, the greater the complexity of the organization. Delegation of authority is typically associated with a lengthy chain of command—that is, with a relatively large number of managerial levels. Thus, delegation of authority contributes to vertical differentiation.

3. The greater the use of territorial, customer, and product bases, the greater the complexity. These bases involve the creation of self-sustaining units that operate much like freestanding organizations. Consequently, there must be considerable delegation of authority, which creates considerable complexity.[40]

4. Narrow spans of control are associated with high complexity. This is true because narrow spans are necessary when the jobs to be supervised are quite different one from another. A supervisor can manage more people in a simple organization than in a complex organization. The apparently simple matter of span of control can have profound effects on both organizational and individual behavior. Hence, we should expect the controversy that surrounds it.

The relationships among dimensions of organizational structure and the four design decisions are summarized in Table 13–1. The table notes only the causes of *high* formalization, centralization, and complexity. However, the relationships are symmetrical: the causes of low formalization, centralization, and complexity are the opposite of those shown in the table.

[40]Dennis S. Mileti, Doug A. Timmer, and David F. Gillespie, "Intra- and Interorganizational Determinants of Decentralization," *Pacific Sociological Review,* April 1982, pp. 162–83.

SUMMARY OF KEY POINTS

— The structure, or anatomy, of an organization consists of relatively fixed and stable relationships among jobs and groups of jobs. The primary purpose of organization structure is to influence the behavior of individuals and groups so as to achieve effective performance.

— Four key managerial decisions determine organization structures. These decisions are dividing work, departmentalizing jobs into groups, determining spans of control, and delegating authority. The four key decisions are interrelated and interdependent, although each has certain specific problems that can be considered apart from the others.

— Dividing the overall work into smaller related tasks, or jobs, which is called division of labor, depends initially on the technical and economic advantages of specialization of labor.

— The grouping of jobs into departments requires the selection of common bases, such as function, territory, product, or customer. Each departmentalization basis has advantages and disadvantages that must be evaluated in terms of overall effectiveness. The matrix form of organization provides opportunities to realize the advantages of function and product as combined bases for departments. The principal disadvantage is the creation of dual reporting channels for members for product departments and groups.

— The optimal span of control is not a specific number of subordinates. Although the number of potential relationships increases geometrically as the number of subordinates increases arithmetically, the important consideration is the frequency and intensity of the actual relationships.

— Delegated authority enables an individual to make decisions and to exact obedience without approval by higher management. Similar to other organizing issues, delegation of authority is a relative, not absolute, concept. All individuals, managers and nonmanagers, in an organization have some authority. The question is whether they have enough to do their jobs.

— Organizational structures differ as a consequence of the four management decisions. To measure these differences it is necessary to identify measurable attributes, or dimensions, of structure. Three often-used dimensions are formalization, centralization, and complexity. Formalization is the extent to which policies, rules, and procedures exist in written form; centralization is the degree to which authority is retained in the jobs of top management; complexity refers to the extent to which the jobs in the organization are relatively specialized.

DISCUSSION AND REVIEW QUESTIONS

1. Explain how you would go about determining the organization structure for a small retail firm that does not have an organization chart.

2. Compare functional and product departmentalization in terms of relative efficiency, production, satisfaction, adaptiveness, and development. Consider particularly the possibility that one basis may be superior in achieving one aspect of effectiveness, yet inferior in achieving another.

3. Why would an organization find it necessary to use various departmental bases at different levels of the structure?

4. Discuss the statement: To manage effectively, a person must have the authority to hire subordinates, assign them to specific jobs, and reward them on the basis of performance. Interview any chairperson of an academic department and determine whether he or she has this authority.

5. The terms *responsibility, authority,* and *accountability* appear in the management and organization literature. What is your understanding of these terms? Are they different?

6. How can a manager know that the organizational design is ineffective? Is there any difference between designing and changing organizational structure? Explain.

7. Discuss the relationship between delegation of authority and bases for departmentalization. In particular, is it desirable to create product-based divisions without delegating considerable authority to the managers of those divisions? Explain.

8. Explain how you could use the three dimensions of structure to compare two organizations.

9. Describe managerial skills and behaviors that would be required to manage effectively in a functional department. Are these skills and behaviors different from those required in a product department? Explain.

10. What circumstances would cause managers of an organization to consider a matrix organization structure? What would cause managers of an organization to consider abandoning a matrix structure?

ADDITIONAL REFERENCES

Burn, L. R. "Matrix Management in Hospitals: Testing Theories of Matrix Structure and Development." *Administrative Science Quarterly,* 1989, pp. 349–68.

Burns, J. N. "The Impact of Information Technology on Organizational Structure." *Information and Management,* 1989, pp. 1–10.

Carlisle, K. E. *Analyzing Jobs and Tasks.* Englewood Cliffs, N.J.: Educational Technology Publications, 1986.

Collins, P. D., and F. Hull. "Technology and Span of Control: Woodward Revisited." *Journal of Management Studies,* 1986, pp. 143–65.

Dess, G. G., and D. W. Beard. "Dimensions of Organizational Task Environments." *Administrative Science Quarterly,* 1984, pp. 52–73.

Egelhoff, W. G. *Organizing the Multinational Enterprise.* Cambridge, Mass.: Ballinger, 1988.

Ettlie, J. E. *Taking Charge of Manufacturing: How Companies Are Combining Technological and Organizational Innovation to Compete Successfully.* San Francisco: Jossey-Bass, 1988.

Keats, B. A., and M. A. Hitt. "A Causal Model of Linkages among Environmental Dimensions, Macro-Organizational Characteristics and Performance." *Academy of Management Journal,* 1988, pp. 570–98.

Kolodny, H. F., and B. Dresner. "Linking Arrangements and New Work Designs." *Organizational Dynamics,* 1986, pp. 33–51.

Kralewski, J. E.; L. Pitt; and D. Shatin. "Structural Characteristics of Medical Group Practices." *Administrative Science Quarterly,* 1985, pp. 34–45.

Larsson, R., and D. E. Bowen. "Organization and the Customer: Managing Design and Coordination of Services." *Academy of Management Review,* 1989, pp. 213–34.

Lawler, E. E., III. "Substitutes for Hierarchy." *Organizational Dynamics,* 1988, pp. 4–15.

Mansfield, R. *Company Strategy and Organizational Design.* New York: St. Martin's Press, 1986.

March, J. G. *Decisions and Organizations.* New York: Basil Blackwell, 1988.

Mintzberg, H. *Structure in Fives: Designing Effective Organizations.* Englewood Cliffs, N. J.: Prentice Hall, 1983.

Nosek, J. T. "Organization Design Strategies to Enhance Information Resource Management." *Information and Management,* 1989, pp. 81–92.

Nystrom, P. C., and W. H. Starbuck. *Handbook of Organizational Design,* vols. 1 and 2. New York: Oxford University Press, 1983.

Pasmore, W. A. *Designing Effective Organizations.* New York: John Wiley & Sons, 1988.

Perkins, D. N. T.; V. F. Nieva; and E. E. Lawler III. *Managing Creation: The Challenge of Building a New Organization.* New York: John Wiley & Sons, 1983.

RESTRUCTURING AT MOTOROLA

Competitive pressures from home and abroad have forced many business firms to consider ways to cut costs and eliminate waste. At the same time firms sought ways to cut costs, they also looked for ways to increase the flow of innovative ideas. Many companies responded to these twin challenges in the 1980s by reducing the levels of management and increasing the spans of control. These flatter structures had the advantages of reducing costs by eliminating managerial jobs (and salaries) and increasing the flow of ideas by giving individuals more authority to make decisions. Many reports of the positive results of these restructuring efforts filled the popular press.

Some of the more notable success stories include Ford Motor Co.'s acknowledgment that its 12 layers of management should be reduced and brought more in line with Toyota's 7 and Xerox Corporation's reduction in middle management. Even those firms with records of efficient operations announced that they were attempting to do better by reducing the managers in their organizations. Dana Corporation, for example, an acknowledged efficiency leader, announced its intention to reduce its five levels of management to four. These success stories came to the attention of Motorola, Inc.'s top management, who instructed the company's human resource professionals to evaluate potential gains through flattening the structure.

Motorola's top management was particularly concerned with how any efforts to reduce managerial personnel would affect the company's long-standing commitment to certain values. The company enjoyed the reputation of treating employees with respect and dignity, including protecting employees who had served the company well in the past. Any restructuring effort to eliminate managerial jobs would have to be consistent with the company's reputation. Top management was also concerned with how managers themselves would respond to efforts to reduce managerial jobs. Would they see such efforts as threats, particularly if it meant reducing personnel in their own departments?

Aware of these issues, human resource professionals devised the following strategy for dealing with the necessity to cut costs and, at the same time, to adhere to people-first values. The process consisted of five steps involving the managers and human resource professionals in joint activities:

Step 1: Data gathering. Each top manager drew an organization chart showing every reporting relationship down to the direct-labor level. These hand-drawn charts showed what really went on in the unit, as distinct from what was supposed to go on.

Step 2: Analysis. Human resource professionals analyzed the charts and identified issues for discussion with the managers. The analysis indicated instances of too many managerial levels, too narrow spans of control, and overlapping responsibilities.

Step 3: Discussion. The analyses of the human resource professionals were presented to the managers for discussion. Managers were given opportunities to explain and clarify the relationships shown on the charts.

Step 4: Goals negotiation. As discussions between managers and the human resources staff revealed problems, managers were asked to propose solutions. When managers disagreed with the staff, they were challenged to present their own analyses and solutions.

Step 5: Implementation and tracking. As managers implemented the changes in organizational structure, they documented the resultant cost savings. The sources of

Source: Based on Phil Nienstedt and Richard Wintermantel, "Motorola Restructures to Improve Productivity," *Management Review*, January 1987, pp. 47–49.

these savings were salaries of managers not replaced on retirement or transfer. A second source of savings was the replacement of a manager with a nonmanager at a lower salary.

Thus, through elimination of some jobs and redefinition of others, Motorola succeeded in its efforts to reduce costs by restructuring its organization. The restructuring has caused Motorola's managers to constantly ask themselves whether they each can effectively direct one more employee. They ask: "If I manage five, why not six?" The results of the restructuring have been impressive in economic terms, with savings in excess of $4.3 million in the first year. Other results included improved vertical communications, more effective managerial selection and training, and greater participation in decision making by all employees.

Questions for Consideration

1. Evaluate Motorola's decision to restructure from a tall to a flat organization.

2. If Motorola had not been pressured by competition, would it have restructured its organization? Explain your answer.

3. Based on the experience of Motorola, can you make the case for flat organizations being relatively more effective than tall organizations in dealing with competitive pressures? Explain your answer.

EXPERIENTIAL EXERCISE

DESIGNING THE NEW VENTURE

Objective

To provide students with firsthand experience in organizing a new business venture.

Related Topics

Organizational design necessitates making assumptions about the market, competition, labor resources, scheduling, and profit margins, to name just a few areas. There is no one best design that should be regarded as a final answer.

Starting the Exercise

Read the scenario presented. Then the instructor will set up teams of five to eight students to serve as organizational design experts who will provide the Gammons brothers with the best structure for their new venture.

Scenario

Some years ago, George Ballas got so frustrated trying to keep his lawn neatly trimmed around the roots of oak trees that he developed what is now called the Weed Eater. The original Weed Eater was made from a popcorn can that had holes in it and was threaded with nylon fishing line. Weed Eater sales in 1972 totaled $568,000; by 1978, sales were in excess of $100 million. Twenty or so similar devices are now on the market.

Two brothers from Pittsburgh, George and Jim Gammons, are starting a new venture called Lawn Trimmers, Inc. They are attempting to sell trimmers that do not wear out for over 2,000 trimming applications. The Weed Eater and similar products often have breaks in the nylon lines that require the user to turn off the trimmer and readjust the line. The Gammons have developed a new type of cutting fabric that is not physically harmful and cuts for over 2,000 applications.

In order to sell the Lawn Trimmers, the Gammons brothers will have to market their products through retail establishments. They will make the products in their shop in Pittsburgh and ship them to the retail establishments. The profits will come entirely from the sales of the Lawn Trimmers to retail establishments. The price of the product is already set, and it appears that there will be sufficient market demand to sell at least 6,000 Lawn Trimmers annually.

Completing the Exercise

Each group should:

1. Establish a design that would be feasible for the Gammons at this stage in their venture.
2. Select a spokesperson to make a short presentation of the group's organizational design for the Gammons.

The class should compare the various designs and discuss why there are similarities and differences in what is presented.

14

Job Design

AN ORGANIZATIONAL
ISSUE FOR DEBATE   JOB REDESIGN AT GENERAL FOODS: WAS IT SUCCESSFUL?*

ARGUMENT FOR

General Foods Corporation's pet-food plant in Topeka, Kansas, was designed to minimize supervision by delegating authority to workers to make job assignments, schedule coffee breaks, interview prospective employees, and decide pay raises. The system, installed in the plant by a company task force with the assistance of Richard E. Walton of Harvard University, assigned three areas of responsibility — processing, packaging and shipping, and office duties — to self-managing teams of 7 to 14 workers.

The teams, directed by "team leaders," share responsibility for a variety of tasks, including those typically performed by staff personnel (e.g., equipment maintenance and quality control). Team members rotate between dreary and meaningful jobs. Pay is related to the number of tasks each individual masters. The teams perform much of the work assigned to managerial and staff personnel. According to J. W. Bevans, Jr., manager of organizational development, the system attempts "to balance the needs of the people with the needs of the business."

The success of the program is unquestionable, according to the former manager of pet-food operations, Layman D. Ketchum: "From the standpoint of humanistic working life and economic results, you can consider it a success." As evidence of the claim, the plant's unit costs are 5 percent less than comparable sites, amounting to an annual savings of $1 million. Employee turnover is only 8 percent, and the plant went almost four years before experiencing a lost-time accident.

ARGUMENT AGAINST

Whether General Foods' experience with job redesign was successful depends on whom you talk to. One employee states emphatically: "The system went to hell. It didn't work." According to critics, problems arose because the system came up against the company's bureaucracy. Lawyers, fearing reactions from the National Labor Relations Board, opposed allowing workers to vote on pay raises. Personnel managers opposed the idea of workers making hiring decisions; engineers resented workers doing engineering work. These resentments resulted in power struggles among and between corporate level staff, plant managers, and workers. Several managers, including three from the pet-food plant itself, quit General Foods.

As a consequence of such pressures, the Topeka system began to change: workers participated less, job classifications were added, and supervisors supervised. These changes were perceived as a weakening of management's commitment to the philosophy underlying the system. Quality dipped, teams had fewer team meetings, and competition among shifts increased. A major contribution to competition was jealousy, particularly as reflected in pay decisions. Workers found it especially difficult to discard their subjective judgments of friends when considering work performance. Workers at Topeka have also argued that they should share in the financial success of Topeka through the provision of bonuses tied to cost savings.

Critics observe that negative evaluations of the Topeka system must have merit, because General Foods no longer permits reporters inside the Topeka plant despite the fact that management once encouraged publicity. Critics also point out that the Topeka system has not been implemented in any other General Foods plant. One manager has predicted that "the future of that plant (Topeka) is to conform to the company norm."

*Source: Based on Richard E. Walton, "The Topeka Work System: Optimistic Visions, Pessimistic Hypotheses, and Reality," in *The Innovative Organization*, ed. Robert Zager and Michael P. Rosow (New York: Pergamon Press, 1982), pp. 260–87; Tomasz Mroczkowski and Paul Champagne, "Job Redesign in Two Countries: A Comparison of the Topeka and Kalmar Experiences," *Industrial Management*, November–December 1984, pp. 17–22.

Individual, group, and organizational effectiveness has many causes. A major cause is the job performance of employees. **Job design** refers to the process by which managers decide individual job tasks and authority. Apart from the very practical issues associated with job design—that is, issues that relate to effectiveness in economic, political, and monetary terms—we can appreciate its importance in social and psychological terms. As noted in earlier chapters, jobs can be sources of psychological stress and even mental and physical impairment. On a more positive note, they can provide income, meaningful life experiences, self-esteem, esteem from others, regulation of our lives, and association with others. Thus, the well-being of both the organization and the people in it depends on how well management is able to design jobs.

This chapter describes some of the many theories and practices that deal with job design and redesign. Job design should be viewed as a dynamic process. A particular job comes into being when an organization discovers the need for the task to be completed. And at that point in time, the job is designed. With the passage of time and the development of new tools and processes, management's expectations for that job will change. It will be redesigned.

In the context of our discussion, **job redesign** means that management has decided to reconsider what employees are expected to do and to get done while on the job. In some instances, the redesign effort may be nothing more than requiring the individual to use a computer rather than a calculator to do clerical work. In other instances, the redesign effort may require the individual to work with other employees in a team effort rather than to work alone on the task.

> **JOB DESIGN**
> The process by which managers decide individual job tasks and authority.

> **JOB REDESIGN**
> The process by which managers reconsider what employees are expected to do.

JOB DESIGN AND QUALITY OF WORK LIFE

In recent years, the issue of designing jobs has gone beyond the determination of the most efficient way to perform tasks. The term **quality of work life (QWL)** is now widely used to refer to "a philosophy of management that enhances the dignity of all workers; introduces changes in an organization's culture; and improves the physical and emotional well-being of employees (e.g., providing opportunities for growth and development)."[1] In some

> **QUALITY OF WORK LIFE (QWL)**
> Management philosophy that enhances employee dignity, introduces cultural change, and provides opportunities for growth and development.

---

[1] Richard E. Kopelman, "Job Redesign and Productivity: A Review of the Evidence," *National Productivity Review*, Summer 1985, p. 239.

organizations, QWL programs are intended to increase employee trust, involvement, and problem solving so as to increase both worker satisfaction and organizational effectiveness.[2] Thus, the concept and application of QWL are broad and involve more than jobs, but the jobs that people do are important sources of satisfaction. Not surprisingly, the quality of work life concept embodies theories and ideas of the human relations movement of the 1950s and the job enrichment efforts of the 60s and 70s.

As America moves into the 1990s, the challenge to managers is to provide both for quality of work life and for improved production and efficiency through revitalization of business and industry. At the present time, the trade-offs between the gains in human terms from improved quality of work life and the gains in economic terms from revitalization are not fully known. Some believe that it will be necessary to defer quality of work life efforts so as to make the American economy more productive and efficient.[3] Others observe that the sense of urgency to become more competitive in domestic and overseas markets presents opportunities to combine quality of life and reindustrialization efforts.[4] To those ends, job design and redesign techniques can play a vital role.

Job design and redesign techniques attempt (1) to identify the most important needs of employees and the organization and (2) to remove obstacles in the workplace that frustrate those needs. Managers hope the results are jobs that (1) fulfill important individual needs and (2) contribute to individual, group, and organizational effectiveness. The Organizational Issue for Debate that opened this chapter illustrates that managers are, in fact, redesigning jobs and job settings, but whether the outcome of those managerial actions are positive is debatable. Obviously, designing and redesigning jobs is complex.

The remainder of this chapter reviews the important theories, research, and practices of job design. As will be seen, contemporary management has at its disposal a wide range of techniques that facilitate the achievement of personal and organizational performance.

CONCEPTUAL MODEL OF JOB DESIGN

The conceptual model depicted in Figure 14–1 is based on the extensive research literature that has appeared in the last 20 years. The model includes the various terms and concepts seen in the current literature. Linked together, these concepts describe the important determinants of job performance and organizational effectiveness.

---

[2]Harry C. Katz, Thomas A. Kochan, and Mark R. Weber, "Assessing the Effects of Industrial Relations Systems and Efforts to Improve the Quality of Working Life on Organizational Effectiveness," *Academy of Management Journal*, September 1985, pp. 514–15.

[3]Amitai Etzioni, "Choose America Must—Between 'Reindustrialization and Quality of Life,'" *Across the Board*, October 1980, pp. 43–49; Marvin R. Weisbord, *Productive Workplaces: Organizing and Managing for Dignity, Meaning and Community* (San Francisco: Jossey-Bass, 1987).

[4]D. J. Skrovan, ed., *Quality of Work Life* (Reading, Mass.: Addison-Wesley Publishing, 1983); Noel M. Tichy and David Ulrich, "The Challenge of Revitalization," *New Management*, Winter 1985, pp. 53–59.

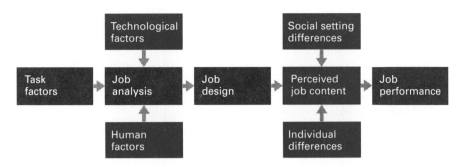

FIGURE 14—1

Conceptual Model of Job
Design and Job Performance

The model takes into account a number of sources of complexity. It recognizes that individuals react differently to jobs: while one person may derive satisfaction from a job, another may not. It also recognizes the difficult trade-offs between organizational and individual needs. For example, the technology of manufacturing (an environmental difference) may dictate that management adopt assembly-line, mass production methods and low-skill jobs to achieve optimal efficiency. Such jobs, however, may result in great unrest and worker discontent. Perhaps these costs could have been avoided by a more careful balancing of organizational and individual needs.

The ideas reflected in Figure 14–1 are the bases for this chapter. We will present each important factor that is the cause or the effect of job design.

JOB ANALYSIS

The purpose of **job analysis** is to provide an objective description of the job itself.[5] Individuals who perform job analysis gather information about three aspects of all jobs: (1) job content, (2) job requirements, and (3) job context. Many different job analysis methods exist to help managers identify the three aspects. One study suggests that these methods can be classified into four categories: mechanistic, motivational, biological, and perceptual-motor, depending on the primary focus and intent.[6] We are concerned here, however, only with an understanding of the three general aspects of all jobs.[7]

Defining the Three Universal Job Aspects

Job content. **Job content** refers to the activities required in the job. Depending on the specific job analysis method used, this description can be either broad or narrow in scope. It can vary from general statements of job

JOB ANALYSIS

Providing a description of how one job differs from another in terms of demands, activities, and skills required.

JOB CONTENT

Specific activities required in a job.

---

[5]Stephen E. Bemis, Ann Holt Belenky, and Dee Ann Soder, *Job Analysis: An Effective Management Tool* (Washington, D.C.: Bureau of National Affairs, 1983), p. 2.

[6]Michael A. Campion and Paul W. Thayer, "Job Design: Approaches, Outcomes, and Tradeoffs," *Organizational Dynamics,* Winter 1987, pp. 66–79; Michael A. Campion, "Interdisciplinary Approaches to Job Design: A Constructive Replication with Extensions," *Journal of Applied Psychology,* August 1988, pp. 467–81.

[7]Bemis et al., *Job Analysis,* pp. 1–2.

FUNCTIONAL JOB
ANALYSIS (FJA)

Method of job analysis that focuses on specific activities, machines, methods, and required
output.

activities to highly detailed statements of each and every hand and body motion required to do the job. One widely used method, **functional job analysis (FJA),** describes jobs in terms of:

1. What the worker does in relation to data, people, and jobs.
2. Methods and techniques the worker uses.
3. Machines, tools, and equipment the worker uses.
4. Materials, products, subject matter, or services the worker produces.

The first three dimensions relate to job *activities.* The fourth relates to job *performance.* FJA provides job descriptions that can be the bases for classifying jobs according to any one of the four dimensions. In addition to defining what activities, methods, and machines make up the job, FJA also defines what the individual doing the job should produce. FJA can, therefore, be the basis for defining standards of performance.

FJA is the most popular and widely used of the job analysis methods.[8] In addition, it is the basis for the most extensive available list of occupational titles.[9]

JOB REQUIREMENTS

Factors such as education, experience, degrees, licenses, and
other personal characteristics
required to perform job.

POSITION ANALYSIS
QUESTIONNAIRE (PAQ)

Method of job analysis that takes
into account human characteristics as well as task and technological factors.

Job requirements.   **Job requirements** refer to factors such as education, experience, degrees, licenses, and other personal characteristics thought to be required of an individual in order to perform the job content. In recent years, the idea has emerged that job requirements should also identify skills, abilities, knowledge, and other personal characteristics required to perform the job content in the particular setting. One widely used method, the **Position Analysis Questionnaire (PAQ),** takes these human factors into account[10] through analysis of the following job dimensions:

1. Information sources critical to job performance.
2. Information processing and decision making critical to job performance.
3. Physical activity and dexterity required of the job.
4. Interpersonal relationships required of the job.
5. Reactions of individuals to working conditions.

The PAQ method can be adapted to jobs of all types, including managerial jobs.[11]

JOB CONTEXT

Physical environment and other
working conditions, along with
other factors considered to be
extrinsic to job.

Job context.   **Job context** refers to factors such as the physical demands and working conditions of the job, the degree of accountability and responsibility, the extent of supervision required or exercised, and the consequences of error.

---

[8]Marc J. Wallace, Jr., N. Frederic Crandall, and Charles H. Fay, *Administering Human Resources* (New York: Random House, 1982), p. 196; Roger J. Plachy, "Writing Job Descriptions that Get Results," *Personnel,* October 1987, pp. 56–63.

[9]U.S. Department of Labor, *Dictionary of Occupational Titles,* 4th ed. (Washington, D.C.: U.S. Government Printing Office, 1977).

[10]E. J. McCormick, *Job Analysis: Methods and Applications* (New York: AMACOM, 1979); E. J. McCormick, P. R. Jeanneret, and R. C. Mecham, "A Study of Job Characteristics and Job Dimensions as Based on the Position Analysis Questionnaire (PAQ)," *Journal of Applied Psychology,* August 1972, pp. 347–68.

[11]Bemis et al., *Job Analysis,* p. 34.

Job context describes the environment within which the job is to be performed.

Numerous methods exist to perform job analysis, and different methods can give different answers to important questions such as "How much is the job worth?"[12] Thus, the selection of a method of job analysis, far from trivial, is one of the most important decisions to be made in job design.[13] As we noted, PAQ and FJA appear to be two of the most popular ones in practice. A recent survey of the opinions of expert job analysts bears out this popularity.[14]

Job Analysis in Different Settings

People perform their jobs in a variety of settings. Rather than discuss them all, which is impossible, we will focus on two significant job settings: the factory and the office. One has historical significance, the other has future significance.

Factory.   Job analysis began in the factory. Industrialization created the setting in which individuals perform many hundreds of specialized jobs. The earliest attempts at job analysis followed the ideas advanced by the proponents of scientific management. They were industrial engineers who, at the turn of the 20th century, began to devise ways to analyze industrial jobs. The major theme of scientific management is that objective analyses of facts and data collected in the workplace could provide the bases for determining the *one best way* to design work.[15] Frederick W. Taylor stated the essence of scientific management:[16]

> First: Develop a science for each element of a man's work which replaces the old rule-of-thumb method.
>
> Second: Scientifically select and then train, teach, and develop the workman, whereas in the past he chose his own work and trained himself as best he could.
>
> Third: Heartily cooperate with the men so as to insure all of the work being done in accordance with the principles of the science which has been developed.

---

[12]Robert M. Madigan and David J. Hoover, "Effects of Alternative Job Evaluation Methods on Decisions Involving Pay Equity," *Academy of Management Journal,* March 1986, pp. 84–100; Edward E. Lawler III, "What's Wrong with Point-Factor Job Evaluation," *Personnel,* January 1987, pp. 38–44; Howard W. Risher, "Job Evaluation: Validity and Reliability," *Compensation and Benefits Review,* January–February 1989, pp. 22–36.

[13]Philip C. Grant, "What Use Is a Job Description?" *Personnel Journal,* February 1988, pp. 44–65.

[14]Jai V. Ghorpade, *Job Analysis: A Handbook for the Human Resource Director* (Englewood Cliffs, N.J.: Prentice Hall, 1988); Edward L. Levine, Ronald A. Ash, Hardy Hall, and Frank Sistrunk, "Evaluation of Job Analysis Methods by Experienced Job Analysts," *Academy of Management Journal,* June 1983, pp. 339–48.

[15]The literature of scientific management is voluminous. The original works and subsequent criticisms and interpretations would make a large volume. Of special significance are the works of the principal authors, including Frederick W. Taylor, *Principles of Scientific Management* (New York: Harper & Row, 1911); Harrington Emerson, *The Twelve Principles of Efficiency* (New York: Engineering Magazine, 1913); Henry L. Gantt, *Industrial Leadership* (New Haven, Conn.: Yale University Press, 1916); Frank B. Gilbreth, *Motion Study* (New York: Van Nostrand Reinhold, 1911); Lillian M. Gilbreth, *The Psychology of Management* (New York: Sturgis & Walton, 1914).

[16]Taylor, *Principles,* pp. 36–37.

ORGANIZATIONS:
CLOSE-UP

FLEXIBLE JOBS AT MOTOROLA

In 1985, Motorola won an antidumping suit against Japanese manufacturers of cellular phones. But that did not solve Motorola's underlying problem of poor quality. The company's product was simply not up to standards of competition, and product quality improvement became the most important management problem to be solved. Management responded by shifting responsibility for quality control from inspectors at the end of the assembly line to individual production workers. Then, to encourage individual workers to learn to understand and do all the jobs on the line so as to recognize potential and actual sources of quality failures, Motorola revised its compensation plan to reward individuals who learned a variety of jobs. The effect was to increase the content and requirements of the production workers' jobs and to decrease the rate of product failure by 77 percent.

Source: Norm Alster, "What Flexible Workers Can Do," *Fortune*, February 13, 1989, p. 63.

Fourth: There is almost an equal division of the work and the responsibility between the management and the workmen. The management takes over all work for which they are better fitted than the workmen, while in the past, almost all of the work and the greater part of the responsibility were thrown upon the men.

These four principles underlie scientific management methods. Management should take into account task and technology to determine the best way for each job; then they should train people to do the job according to that way.

Scientific management produced many techniques still in use. Motion and time study, work simplification, and standard methods are at the core of job analysis in factory settings. Although the mechanistic approach to job analysis is widespread in industry, many manufacturers are turning away from the idea of one person doing one specialized job, as noted in the Close-Up on job flexibility. As we will discuss later in the chapter, many manufacturing firms are now analyzing jobs to determine the extent to which content and requirements can be changed to tap a larger portion of individual employees' talents and abilities.

Office.   In the short time since the advent of scientific management, the American economy has shifted from factory-oriented to office-oriented work. The fastest-growing segment of jobs is secretarial, clerical, and information workers. The growth of these jobs is due to technological breakthroughs in both settings.

Technological breakthroughs in automation, robotics, and computer-assisted manufacturing have reduced the need for industrial jobs and increased the need for office jobs. The modern office, however, is no mere extension of the traditional factory; it reflects the new computer technology. Its most striking feature is the replacement of paper with some electronic medium, usually a video display terminal (VDT). One individual uses the VDT to do a

ORGANIZATIONS:
CLOSE-UP

WORK MODULES IN BANKING

The First National Bank of Chicago reported increases in profitability, productivity, customer satisfaction, and staff morale as a consequence of its approach to job design in the bank's unit that issues letters of credit. The unit employs 110 people who traditionally had performed fragmented tasks on what they referred to as their paperwork assembly line. Over a period of six months, the employees of the unit participated with management in designing their jobs around whole jobs that required greater skill and talent. The newly designed jobs were different in content, requirements, and context. The additional content meant that employees had to undergo training to meet the expanded activities and responsibilities, but the result is that they are now being paid more because they are more productive.

Source: F. K. Plous, Jr., "Redesigning Work," *Personnel Administrator,* March 1987, p. 99.

variety and quantity of tasks that in earlier times would have required many individuals. A significant aspect of job analysis in modern offices is the creation of work modules, interrelated tasks that can be assigned to a single individual. The Close-Up describes how a Chicago bank designed work around the concept of work modules.

In recent times, managers and researchers have found that human factors must be given special attention when analyzing jobs in the electronic office. VDT operators, for example, report that they suffer visual and postural problems such as headaches, "burning" eyes, shoulder pain, and backaches.[17] The source of these problems seems to be in the design of the workplace, particularly the interaction between the individual and the VDT. The tendency is to overemphasize the technological factor—in this case, the computer,—and to analyze jobs only as extensions of the technology. As was true of job analysis in factories, dealing with the relatively fixed nature of tasks and technology is easier than dealing with variable human nature.[18]

JOB DESIGNS

Job designs result from job analysis. They specify three characteristics of jobs: range, depth, and relationships.

---

[17]Barbara S. Brown, Key Dismukes, and Edward J. Rinalducci, "Video Display Terminals and Vision of Workers: Summary and Review of a Symposium," *Behavior and Information Technology,* April–June 1982, pp. 121–40.

[18]David A. Buchanan and David Boddy, "Advanced Technology and the Quality of Working Life: The Effects of Word Processing on Video Typists," *Journal of Occupational Psychology,* March 1982, pp. 1–11; Walter B. Kleeman, "The Future of the Office," *Environment and Behavior,* September 1982, pp. 593–610.

Range and Depth

JOB RANGE

Number of tasks person is expected to perform while doing job. The more tasks required, the greater the job range.

JOB DEPTH

Degree of influence or discretion that individual possesses to choose how job will be performed.

The **range** of a job refers to the number of tasks a jobholder performs. The individual who performs eight tasks to complete a job has a wider job range than a person performing four tasks. In most instances, the greater the number of tasks performed, the longer it takes to complete the job.

A second job characteristic is **depth,** the amount of discretion an individual possesses to decide job activities and job outcomes. In many instances, job depth relates to personal influence as well as delegated authority. Thus, an employee with the same job title and at the same organizational level as another employee may possess more, less, or the same amount of job depth because of personal influence.

Job range and depth distinguish one job from another not only within the same organization but also among different organizations. To illustrate how jobs differ in range and depth, Figure 14–2 depicts the differences for selected jobs of business firms, hospitals, and universities.

For example, business research scientists, hospital chiefs of surgery, and university presidents generally have high job range and significant depth. Research scientists perform a large number of tasks and are usually not closely supervised. Chiefs of surgery have significant job range in that they oversee and counsel on many diverse surgical matters. In addition, they are not supervised closely, and they have the authority to influence hospital surgical policies and procedures. University presidents have a large number of tasks to perform. They speak to alumni groups, politicians, community representatives, and students. They develop, in consultation with others, policies on admissions, fund-raising, and adult education. They can alter the faculty recruitment philosophy and, thus, the course of the entire institution. For example, a university president may want to build an institution that is noted for high-quality classroom instruction and for providing excellent services to the community. This thrust may lead to recruiting and selecting professors who want to concentrate on these two specific goals. In contrast, another president may want to foster outstanding research and high-quality classroom instruction. Of course, another president may attempt to develop an institution that is noted for instruction, research, and service. The critical point is that university presidents have sufficient depth to alter the course of a university's direction.

Examples of jobs with high depth and low range are packaging machine mechanics, anesthesiologists, and faculty members. Mechanics perform the limited tasks that pertain to repairing and maintaining packaging machines. However, they can decide how breakdowns on the packaging machine are to be repaired. The discretion means that the mechanics have relatively high job depth. Anesthesiologists also perform a limited number of tasks. They are concerned with the rather restricted task of administering anesthetics to patients. However, they can decide the type of anesthetic to be administered in a particular situation, a decision indicative of high job depth. University professors specifically engaged in classroom instruction have relatively low job range. Teaching involves comparatively more tasks than the work of the anesthesiologist, yet fewer tasks than that of the business research scientist. However, professors' job depth is greater than that of graduate student

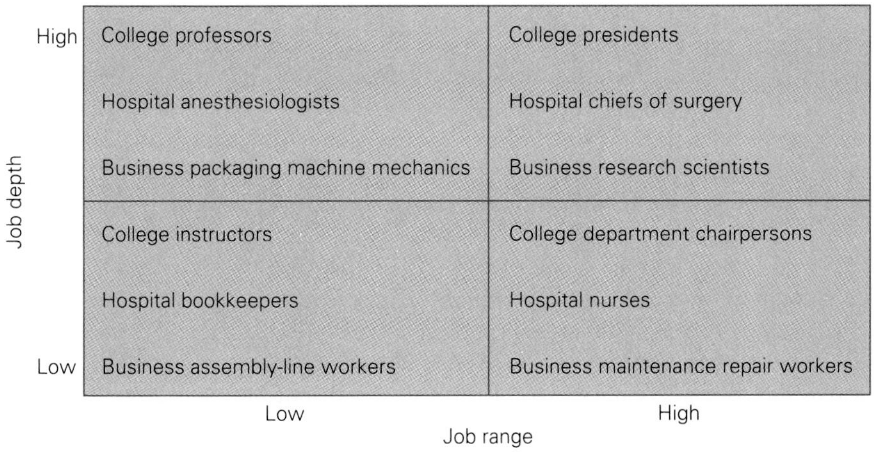

FIGURE 14—2

Job Depth and Range:
Differences in Selected Jobs

instructors. This follows from the fact that the professors determine how they will conduct the class, what materials will be presented, and the standards to be used in evaluating students. Graduate students typically do not have complete freedom in the choice of class materials and procedures; professors decide these matters for them.

Highly specialized jobs are those having few tasks to accomplish and prescribed means by which to accomplish them. Such jobs are quite routine; they also tend to be controlled by specified rules and procedures (low depth). A highly despecialized job (high range) has many tasks to accomplish within the framework of discretion over means and ends (high depth). Within an organization, great differences in both range and depth typically exist among jobs. Although managers have no precise equations to use to decide job range and depth, they can ask this guideline question: Given the economic and technical requirements of the organization's mission, goals, and objectives, what is the optimal point along the continuum of range and depth for each job?

Job Relationships

Managers' decisions regarding departmentalization bases and spans of control determine job relationships. And a manager becomes responsible to coordinate the resulting groups toward organization purposes. These job relationship decisions also determine the nature and extent of jobholders' interpersonal **relationships,** individually and within groups. As we already have seen in the earlier discussion of groups in organizations, group performance is affected in part by group cohesiveness, which depends on the quality and kind of interpersonal relationships of jobholders assigned to a task or command group.

The wider the span of control, the larger the group and consequently the more difficult it is to establish friendship and interest relationships. People in larger groups are less likely to communicate (and interact sufficiently to form interpersonal ties) than people in smaller groups. Without the opportunity to communicate, people will be unable to establish cohesive work groups. Thus,

JOB RELATIONSHIPS
Interpersonal relationships required or made possible on job.

an important source of satisfaction may be lost for individuals who seek to fulfill social and esteem needs through relationships with co-workers.

The departmentalization basis that management selects also has important implications for job relationships. The functional basis places jobs with similar depth and range in the same groups, while product, territory, and customer bases group jobs with dissimilar depth and range. Thus, in functional departments, people will do much the same specialty. Product, territory, and customer departments, however, comprise quite heterogeneous jobs. Individuals who work in such departments experience feelings of dissatisfaction, stress, and involvement more intensely than those in homogeneous, functional departments. People with homogeneous backgrounds, skills, and training have more common interests than those with heterogeneous ones. Thus, they more easily establish satisfying social relationships with not only less stress but also less involvement in the department's activities.

Job designs describe the *objective* characteristics of jobs. That is, job analysis techniques enable managers to design jobs in terms of required activities to produce a specified outcome. But, before we can understand the relationship between jobs and performance, another factor must be considered: perceived job content.

PERCEIVED JOB CONTENT

Taylor proposed that the way to improve work—that is, to make it more efficient—is to determine (1) the "best way" to do a task (motion study) and (2) the standard time for completion of the task (time study). Motion study determines preferred work activities in relation to raw materials, product design, order of work, tools, equipment, and workplace layout; time study determines the preferred time for performing each job activity. Through motion and time studies, scientific management practitioners design jobs solely in terms of technical data.

The belief that job design can be based solely on technical data ignores the very large role played by the individual who performs the job. Individuals differ profoundly, as we have noted in Chapter 3. They come to work with different backgrounds, needs, and motivations. Once on the job, they experience in unique ways the social setting in which the work is performed. It is not surprising then to find that different individuals perceive jobs differently.

Perceived job content refers to characteristics of a job that define its general nature as perceived by the jobholder. It is important to distinguish between the *objective* and *subjective* properties of jobs as reflected in the perceptions of people who perform them.[19] Managers cannot understand the causes of job performance without considering individual differences such as

PERCEIVED JOB CONTENT

Specific job activities and general job characteristics as perceived by individual performing job. Two individuals doing same job may have same or different perceptions of job content.

---

[19]Kenneth R. Brousseau, "Toward a Dynamic Model of Job-Person Relationships: Findings, Research Questions and Implications for Work System Design," *Academy of Management Review*, January 1983, pp. 33–45.

personality, needs, and span of attention.[20] Nor can managers understand the causes of job performance without considering the social setting in which the job is performed.[21] According to Figure 14–1, perceived job content precedes job performance. Thus, if managers desire to increase job performance by changing perceived job content, they can change job design, individual differences, or social settings—all causes of perceived job content.

Measuring Perceived Job Content

To understand perceived job content, management must have some method for measuring it.[22] In response to this need, organization behavior researchers have attempted to measure perceived job content in a variety of work settings. The methods researchers use rely on questionnaires that jobholders complete and that measure their perceptions of certain job characteristics.

Job characteristics. Pioneering efforts to measure perceived job content through employee responses to a questionnaire resulted in the identification of six characteristics: variety, autonomy, required interaction, optional interaction, knowledge and skill required, and responsibility.[23] The index of these six characteristics is the Requisite Task Attribute Index (RTAI). The original RTAI has been extensively reviewed and analyzed.

One important development was the review by Hackman and Lawler, who revised the index to include the six characteristics shown in Table 14–1.[24] Variety, task identity, and feedback are perceptions of job range; autonomy is the perception of job depth; and dealing with others and friendship opportunities reflect perceptions of job relationships. Employees sharing similar perceptions, job designs, and social settings should report similar job characteristics. Employees with different perceptions, however, report different job characteristics of the same job. For example, an individual with a high need for social belonging would perceive "friendship opportunities" differently than an individual with a low need for social belonging.

Current approaches to measurement. Two approaches currently exist to measure perceived job content. The Job Characteristics Index (JCI) attempts to

---

[20]Donald P. Schwab and Larry L. Cummings, "A Theoretical Analysis of the Impact of Task Scope on Employee Performance," *Academy of Management Review,* April 1976, pp. 31–32.

[21]James W. Dean and Daniel J. Brass, "Social Interaction and the Perception of Job Characteristics in an Organization," *Human Relations,* June 1985, pp. 571–82.

[22]Thomas W. Ferratt, Randall B. Dunham, and Jon L. Pierce, "Self-Report Measures of Job Characteristics and Affective Responses: An Examination of Discriminant Validity," *Academy of Management Journal,* December 1981, pp. 780–94.

[23]Eugene F. Stone and Hal G. Gueuthal, "An Empirical Derivation of the Dimensions along which Characteristics of Jobs Are Perceived," *Academy of Management Journal,* June 1985, pp. 376–96, identifies Arthur N. Turner and Paul R. Lawrence, *Industrial Jobs and the Worker: An Investigation of Response to Task Attributes* (Cambridge, Mass.: Harvard University Press, 1965), as the source of contemporary measures of perceived job characteristics.

[24]J. Richard Hackman and Edward E. Lawler III, "Employee Reactions to Job Characteristics," *Journal of Applied Psychology,* 1971, pp. 259–86; J. Richard Hackman and Greg R. Oldham, "Development of the Job Diagnostic Survey," *Journal of Applied Psychology,* 1975, pp. 159–70.

TABLE 14–1

Six Characteristics of
Perceived Job Content

Characteristic	Description
Variety	Degree to which a job requires employees to perform a wide range of operations in their work, and/or degree to which employees must use a variety of equipment and procedures in their work.
Autonomy	Extent to which employees have a major say in scheduling their work, selecting the equipment they use, and deciding on procedures to be followed.
Task identity	Extent to which employees do an entire or whole piece of work and can clearly identify with the results of their efforts.
Feedback	Degree to which employees, as they are working, receive information that reveals how well they are performing on the job.
Dealing with others	Degree to which a job requires employees to deal with other people to complete their work.
Friendship opportunities	Degree to which a job allows employees to talk with one another on the job and to establish informal relationships with other employees at work.

Source: Henry P. Sims, Jr., Andrew D. Szilagyi, and Robert T. Keller, "The Measurement of Job Characteristics," *Academy of Management Journal,* June 1976, p. 197.

measure jobholders' perceptions of the six characteristics shown in Table 14–1.[25] A more widely used approach is the Job Diagnostic Survey (JDS),[26] which measures variety, autonomy, task identity, feedback, and significance. Unlike the JCI, which includes job relationship dimensions, the JDS attempts to measure only the "core" dimensions of perceived job content. In doing so, it includes an additional dimension, significance, which reflects the perceived importance of the work to the organization or to others. The JDS has been widely used by researchers.[27]

Some evidence exists that the JCI is an alternative measure;[28] but a recent examination of the JDS's validity lends support to its continued use to measure jobholders' perceptions of job content.[29] Future studies will no doubt improve the measurement of perceived job content, but it is doubtful that any perceptual measurement will ever eliminate the effects of individual differences.

---

[25]Henry P. Sims, Jr., Andrew Szilagyi, and Robert T. Keller, "The Measurement of Job Characteristics," *Academy of Management Journal,* June 1976, pp. 195–212.

[26]Hackman and Oldham, "Development of the Job Diagnostic Survey."

[27]K. H. Roberts and William H. Glick, "The Job Characteristics Approach to Task Design: A Critical Review," *Journal of Applied Psychology,* 1981, pp. 193–217; Ramon J. Aldag, Steve H. Barr, and Arthur P. Brief, "Measurement of Perceived Task Characteristics," *Psychological Bulletin,* November 1981, pp. 415–31.

[28]Jon L. Pierce and Randall B. Dunham, "The Measurement of Perceived Job Characteristics: The Job Diagnostic Survey versus the Job Characteristics Inventory," *Academy of Management Journal,* March 1978, pp. 123–28.

[29]Carol T. Kulik, Greg R. Oldham, and Paul H. Langner, "Measurement of Job Characteristics: Comparison of the Original and the Revised Job Diagnostic Survey," *Journal of Applied Psychology,* August 1988, pp. 462–66.

Individual Differences

The effect of individual differences is to "provide filters such that different persons perceive the same objective stimuli in different manners."[30] For example, individual differences in need strength, particularly growth needs, have been shown to influence the perception of task variety. Employees with relatively weak higher-order needs are less concerned with performing a variety of tasks than are those with relatively strong growth needs. Thus, managers expecting higher performance to result from increased task variety would be disappointed if the jobholders did not have strong growth needs. Even individuals with strong growth needs cannot respond continuously to the opportunity to perform more and more tasks. At some point, performance declines as these individuals reach the limits imposed by their abilities and time. The relationship between performance and task variety, even for individuals with high growth needs, is likely to be curvilinear.[31]

Social Setting Differences

Differences in social settings of work also affect perceptions of job content. Examples of such differences include leadership style[32] and what other people say about the job.[33] As more than one research study has shown, how one perceives a job is greatly affected by what other people say about it. Thus, if one's co-workers say their jobs are boring, one is likely to state that his or her job is also boring. If an individual perceives the job as boring, job performance will no doubt suffer.

JOB PERFORMANCE OUTCOMES

Job performance includes a number of outcomes. This section discusses performance outcomes that have value to both the organization and the individual.

Objective Outcomes

Quantity and quality of output, absenteeism, tardiness, and turnover are objective outcomes that can be measured in quantitative terms. For each job, implicit or explicit standards exist for each of these objective outcomes. Industrial engineering studies establish standards for daily quantity, and quality

[30]Randall B. Dunham, Ramon J. Aldag, and Arthur P. Brief, "Dimensionality of Task Design as Measured by the Job Diagnostic Survey," *Academy of Management Journal,* June 1977, p. 222.

[31]Joseph E. Champoux, "A Three Sample Test of Some Extensions to the Job Characteristics Model of Work Motivation," *Academy of Management Journal,* September 1980, pp. 466–78.

[32]Ricky W. Griffin, "Supervisory Behavior as a Source of Perceived Task Scope," *Journal of Occupational Psychology,* September 1981, pp. 175–82.

[33]Joe Thomas and Ricky W. Griffin, "The Social Information Processing Model of Task Design: A Review of the Literature," *Academy of Management Review,* October 1983, pp. 672–82; Ricky W. Griffin, "Objective and Subjective Sources of Information in Task Redesign: A Field Experiment," *Administrative Science Quarterly,* June 1983, pp. 184–200; Jeffrey Pfeffer, "A Partial Test of the Social Information-Processing Model of Job Attitudes," *Human Relations,* July 1980, pp. 457–76.

control specialists establish tolerance limits for acceptable quality. These aspects of job performance account for characteristics of the product, client, or service for which the jobholder is responsible. But job performance includes other outcomes.

Personal Behavior Outcomes

The jobholder reacts to the work itself by either attending regularly or being absent, by staying with the job or by quitting. Moreover, physiological and health-related problems can result from job performance. Performance-related stress can contribute to physical and mental impairment; accidents and occupationally related disease can also ensue.

Intrinsic and Extrinsic Outcomes

Job outcomes include intrinsic and extrinsic work outcomes. The intrinsic-extrinsic distinction is important for understanding the reactions of people to their jobs. In a general sense, intrinsic outcomes are objects or events that follow from the worker's own efforts, not requiring the involvement of any other person. More simply put, they are outcomes clearly related to action on the worker's part. Such outcomes typically are thought to be solely in the province of professional and technical jobs; yet, all jobs potentially have opportunities for intrinsic outcomes. Such outcomes involve feelings of responsibility, challenge, and recognition and result from such job characteristics as variety, autonomy, identity, and significance.

Extrinsic outcomes, however, are objects or events that follow from the workers' own efforts in conjunction with other factors or persons not directly involved in the job itself. Pay, working conditions, co-workers, and even supervision are objects in the workplace that are potential job outcomes but are not a fundamental part of the work. Dealing with others and friendship interactions are sources of extrinsic outcomes.

Because most jobs provide opportunities for both intrinsic and extrinsic outcomes, understanding the relationship between the two is important. Generally, when the individual can attribute the source of the extrinsic reward to his or her own efforts, extrinsic rewards reinforce intrinsic rewards positively. For example, receiving a pay raise (extrinsic reward) increases feeling good about oneself if the cause of the pay raise is thought to be one's own efforts and competence and not favoritism extended by the boss. This line of reasoning explains why some individuals get no satisfaction out of sharing in the gains derived from group rather than individual effort.[34]

Job Satisfaction Outcome

JOB SATISFACTION
Individual's attitude about job. Attitude may be positive (satisfaction) or negative (dissatisfaction).

Job satisfaction depends on the levels of intrinsic and extrinsic outcomes and how the jobholder views those outcomes, which have different values for different people. For some people, responsible and challenging work may have

[34]Hugh J. Arnold, "Task Performance, Perceived Competence, and Attributed Causes of Performance as Determinants of Intrinsic Motivation," *Academy of Management Journal,* December 1985, pp. 876–88.

neutral or even negative value. For others, such outcomes may have high positive values. People also differ in the importance they attach to job outcomes. These value differences alone would account for different levels of job satisfaction for essentially the same job tasks.

Another important individual difference is job involvement.[35] People differ in the extent to which (1) work is a central life interest, (2) they actively participate in work, (3) they perceive work as central to self-esteem, and (4) they perceive work as consistent with self-concept. Persons who are not involved in their work cannot be expected to realize the same satisfaction as those who are. This variable accounts for the fact that two workers could report different levels of satisfaction for the same performance levels.

A final individual difference is the perceived equity of the outcome in terms of what the jobholder considers a fair reward. If the outcomes are perceived to be unfair in relation to those of others in similar jobs requiring similar effort, the jobholder will experience dissatisfaction and seek means to restore the equity, either by seeking greater rewards (primarily extrinsic) or by reducing effort.

Job performance includes many potential outcomes. Some are of primary value to the organization—the objective outcomes, for example. Other outcomes, such as job satisfaction, are of primary importance to the individual. Thus, we can see that job performance is without doubt a complex variable that depends on the interplay of numerous factors. Managers can make some sense of the issue by understanding the motivational implications of jobs. The field of organization behavior has advanced a number of suggestions for improving the motivational properties of jobs. Invariably the suggestions, termed job redesign strategies, attempt to improve job performance through changes in actual job characteristics.[36] In the next sections, the more significant of these strategies are reviewed.

REDESIGNING JOB RANGE: JOB ROTATION AND JOB ENLARGEMENT

The earliest attempts to redesign jobs date to the scientific management era. Efforts at that time emphasized efficiency criteria. As a result, the individual tasks that make up a job were designed to be limited, uniform, and repetitive. This practice led to narrow job range and, consequently, high reported levels of job discontent, turnover, absenteeism, and dissatisfaction. Accordingly, managers devised strategies that resulted in wider job range through increasing the requisite activities of jobs. Two of these approaches are job rotation and job enlargement.

Job Rotation

Managers of organizations such as Western Electric, Ford, Bethlehem Steel, and TRW Systems have utilized different forms of the **job rotation** strategy. This practice involves rotating an individual from one job to another. In so

JOB ROTATION

Practice of moving individuals from job to job to reduce potential boredom and increase potential motivation and performance.

---

[35]S. D. Saleh and James Hosek, "Job Involvement: Concepts and Measurements," *Academy of Management Journal,* June 1976, pp. 213–24.

[36]William H. Glick, G. Douglas Jenkins, Jr., and Nina Gupta, "Method versus Substance: How Strong Are Underlying Relationships between Job Characteristics and Attitudinal Outcomes?" *Academy of Management Journal,* September 1986, pp. 441–64.

doing, the employee is expected to complete more job activities, since each job includes different tasks.[37] Job rotation involves increasing the range of jobs and the perception of variety in the job content. Increasing task variety should, according to expectancy theory, increase the intrinsic valence associated with job satisfaction. However, the practice of job rotation does not change the basic characteristics of the assigned jobs.

Some relatively small firms have successfully used job rotation to good effect as suggested in the Close-Up on that subject. However, critics state that job rotation often involves nothing more than having people perform several boring and monotonous jobs rather than one. An alternative strategy is job enlargement.

Job Enlargement

A pioneering study by Charles Walker and Robert Guest dealt with social and psychological problems associated with mass production jobs in automobile assembly plants.[38] Walker and Guest found many workers were dissatisfied

[37]Allan W. Farrant, "Job Rotation Is Important," *Supervision,* August 1987, pp. 14–16.
[38]Charles R. Walker and Robert H. Guest, *The Man on the Assembly Line* (Cambridge, Mass.: Harvard University Press, 1952).

ORGANIZATIONS:
CLOSE-UP

JOB ENLARGEMENT IN A RETAIL STORE

Lechmere Inc., a 27-store retail chain owned by Dayton Hudson, opened an outlet in Sarasota, Florida, in 1987. Because unemployment in the area was less than 4 percent and entry-level people were in short supply, the store faced the unusual circumstance of being unable to employ its typical work force of part-timers such as teenagers and homemakers. Retailers such as Lechmere rely on part-time employees, using them at the times and hours of peak activity.

In the absence of a part-time work force, Lechmere adopted a different approach, designing jobs that included considerable range of activities. They hired full-time employees and then rewarded them for learning and doing many different "jobs." Cashiers learned to sell merchandise; sporting goods salespeople learned to operate forklifts in the warehouse. The company increased the job range by increasing content and context.

Using this system, management can shift individuals from job to job as the need arises. The Sarasota store employs 60 percent full-timers, compared to 30 percent for the entire chain. Moreover, the store has higher productivity records than other stores.

Source: Norm Alster, "What Flexible Workers Can Do," *Fortune*, February 13, 1989, p. 62.

with their highly specialized jobs, in particular the mechanical pacing, repetitiveness of operations, and lack of a sense of accomplishment. The researchers also found a positive relationship between job range and job satisfaction.

The findings of this research gave early support for those motivation theories that predict that increases in job range will increase job satisfaction and other, objective job outcomes. **Job enlargement** strategies focus on the opposite of dividing work; they are a form of despecialization, or increasing the number of tasks an employee performs. For example, a job is redesigned to include six tasks instead of three.

JOB ENLARGEMENT
Practice of increasing number of tasks for which individual is responsible. Increases job range, not depth.

Although in many instances an enlarged job requires a longer training period, job satisfaction usually increases because boredom is reduced. The implication, of course, is that job enlargement also leads to improvement in other performance outcomes.

The concept and practice of job enlargement have become considerably more sophisticated. In recent years, effective job enlargement involves more than simply increasing task variety. Management must also redesign certain other aspects of job range, including replacing machine-paced control with worker-paced control.[39] Each change involves balancing the gains and losses of varying degrees of division of labor. Contemporary applications of job enlargement involve training individuals to perform several different jobs,

[39]Kae H. Chung and Monica F. Ross, "Differences in Motivational Properties between Job Enlargement and Job Enrichment," *Academy of Management Review*, January 1977, pp. 114–15.

each of which requires considerable skill. The Close-Up on page 487 tells about such an application in a retail store.

Some employees cannot cope with enlarged jobs because they cannot comprehend complexity. Moreover, they may not have a long enough attention span to stay with and complete an enlarged set of tasks. However, if employees are amenable to job enlargement and if they have the requisite ability, then job enlargement should increase satisfaction and product quality and decrease absenteeism and turnover. These gains are not without costs, including the likelihood that employees will demand larger salaries in exchange for their performance of enlarged jobs. Yet, these costs must be borne if management desires to implement the redesign strategy that enlarges job depth: job enrichment. Job enlargement is a necessary precondition for job enrichment.

REDESIGNING JOB DEPTH: JOB ENRICHMENT

The impetus for redesigning job depth was provided by Herzberg's two-factor theory of motivation.[40] The basis of his theory is that factors that meet individuals' needs for psychological growth—especially responsibility, job challenge, and achievement—must be characteristic of their jobs. The application of his theory is called **job enrichment.**

JOB ENRICHMENT

Practice of increasing discretion individual can use to select activities and outcomes. Increases job depth and accordingly fulfills growth and autonomy needs.

Job enrichment is realized through direct changes in job depth. Managers can provide employees with greater opportunities to exercise discretion by implementing the following:

1. *Direct feedback.* The evaluation of performance should be timely and direct.
2. *New learning.* A good job enables people to feel that they are growing. All jobs should provide opportunities to learn.
3. *Scheduling.* People should be able to schedule some part of their own work.
4. *Uniqueness.* Each job should have some unique qualities or features.
5. *Control over resources.* Individuals should have some control over their job tasks.
6. *Personal accountability.* People should be provided with an opportunity to be accountable for the job.

As defined by the executive in charge of a pioneering job enrichment program at Texas Instruments (TI), job enrichment is a process that (1) encourages employees to behave like managers in managing their jobs and (2) redesigns the job to make such behavior feasible.[41] The process as implemented at TI is continuous and pervades the entire organization: every job is subject to analysis to determine if it can be enriched to include managerial

---

[40]Frederick Herzberg, "The Wise Old Turk," *Harvard Business Review,* September–October 1974, pp. 70–80.

[41]M. Scott Myers, *Every Employee a Manager* (New York: McGraw-Hill, 1970), p. xii.

JOB ENRICHMENT AT CITIBANK

Citibank extensively changed the ways its employees did their work, after a customer survey indicated that the bank scored very low on "customer service." Examining the causes of the problem, bank management concluded that the reason for the problem was that its employees didn't "feel like somebody." They were dissatisfied with their rather mundane jobs, created in part by an earlier decision of the bank to introduce automatic teller machines.

Building on the idea that everybody wants to feel like somebody, the bank undertook extensive changes designed to recognize the individuality of employees as well as customers. Among the many changes implemented were the following:

— Encouraging communications between the functional departments— operations, marketing, and servicing.

— Decentralizing operations so that one person could handle an entire transaction from the time it comes into the bank until it leaves.

— Putting the employees who do the job in direct contact with the customers and the computers.

— Asking the people who do the job what is boring and/or troublesome before automating.

— Undertaking considerable training and education for the entire work force.

These changes in job design, made over a two-year period, were accompanied by training sessions that taught the new skills. It was also necessary to develop new attitudes among the management personnel, including the attitude that employee opinions are valuable and desirable inputs into decisions.

Source: Roy W. Walters, "The Citibank Project: Improving Productivity through Work Design," in *How to Manage Change Effectively*, ed. Donald L. Kirkpatrick (San Francisco: Jossey-Bass, 1985), pp. 195–208.

activities and thereby made more meaningful. Moreover, as the jobs of nonmanagerial personnel are redesigned to include greater depth, the jobs of managers also must be redesigned. The redesigned managerial jobs emphasize training and counseling of subordinates and de-emphasize control and direction. Job enrichment in a nonmanufacturing setting is illustrated in the Citibank Close-Up.

As the theory and practice of job enrichment have evolved, managers have learned that successful applications require numerous changes in the way work is done. Some of the more important changes include delegating greater authority to workers to participate in decisions, to set their own goals, and to evaluate their (and their work groups') performance. Job enrichment also involves changing the nature and style of managers' behavior. Managers must be willing and able to delegate authority. The significant changes that take place in managerial jobs, coupled with changes in nonmanagerial jobs, suggest the importance of a supportive work environment as a prerequisite for successful job enrichment efforts.[42]

Given the ability of employees to carry out enriched jobs and the willingness of managers to delegate authority, gains in performance can be expected. These positive outcomes are the result of increasing employees' expectancies that efforts lead to performance, that performance leads to intrinsic and extrinsic rewards, and that these rewards have power to satisfy needs.

REDESIGNING JOB RANGE AND DEPTH: COMBINED APPROACH

Job enrichment and job enlargement are not competing strategies. Job enlargement, rather than job enrichment, may be compatible with the needs, values, and abilities of some individuals. Yet job enrichment, when appropriate, necessarily involves job enlargement. A promising new approach to job redesign, the job characteristic model, attempts to integrate the two approaches. Richard Hackman and associates devised the approach and based it on the Job Diagnostic Survey, cited in an earlier section.[43]

The model attempts to account for the interrelationships among (1) certain job characteristics, (2) psychological states associated with motivation, satisfaction, and performance, (3) job outcomes, and (4) growth need strength. Figure 14–3 describes the relationships among these variables. According to this model, although variety, identity, significance, autonomy, and feedback do not completely describe perceived job content, they sufficiently describe those aspects that management can manipulate to bring about gains in productivity.

The steps management can take to increase the core dimensions include:

— Combining task elements.
— Assigning whole pieces of work (i.e., work modules).
— Allowing discretion in selection of work methods.
— Permitting self-paced control.
— Opening feedback channels.

These actions increase task variety, identity, and significance. Consequently, the "experienced meaningfulness of work" psychological state is increased. By permitting employee participation and self-evaluation and creating autonomous work groups, the feedback and autonomy dimensions are increased along with the psychological states "experienced responsibility" and "knowledge of actual results."

---

[42]Gerald R. Ferris and David C. Gilmore, "The Moderating Role of Work Context in Job Design Research: A Test of Competing Models," *Academy of Management Journal,* December 1984, pp. 885–92.

[43]J. Richard Hackman, Greg R. Oldham, Robert Janson, and Kenneth Purdy, "New Strategy for Job Enrichment," *California Management Review,* Summer 1975, pp. 57–71; J. Richard Hackman and Greg R. Oldham, "Development of the Job Diagnostic Survey," *Journal of Applied Psychology,* April 1975, pp. 159–70.

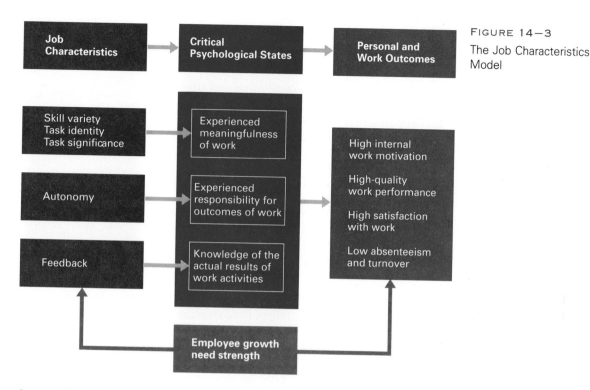

FIGURE 14–3

The Job Characteristics Model

Source: J. Richard Hackman and Greg R. Oldham, "Development of the Job Diagnostic Survey," *Journal of Applied Psychology,* 1975, pp. 159–70.

Implementing the job characteristics in a particular situation begins with a study of existing job perceptions by means of the Job Description Survey. Hackman and Oldham have reported numerous applications of the model in a variety of organizations.[44] They have also compiled normative data for a variety of job categories, so that managers and practitioners can compare the responses of their own employees to those of a larger population.

The positive benefits of these redesign efforts are moderated by individual differences in the strength of employees' growth needs. That is, employees with strong needs for accomplishment, learning, and challenge will respond more positively than those with relatively weak growth needs. In other, more familiar terms, employees who have high need for self-esteem and self-actualization are more likely candidates for job redesign. Employees forced to participate in job redesign programs when they lack either the need strength or the ability to perform redesigned jobs may experience stress, anxiety, adjustment problems, erratic performance, turnover, and absenteeism.

Available research on the interrelationships between perceived job content and performance is meager. One recent study of 30 actual applications of job redesign strategies confirms that failures are as frequent as successes.[45]

---

[44]J. Richard Hackman and Greg R. Oldham, *Work Redesign* (Reading, Mass.: Addison-Wesley Publishing, 1980).

[45]Kopelman, "Job Redesign and Productivity," p. 239.

Managers apparently must cope with significant problems in matching employee needs and differences with organizational needs.[46] The problems associated with job redesign include:

1. The program is time-consuming and costly.

2. Unless lower-level needs are satisfied, people will not respond to opportunities to satisfy higher-level needs. And even though our society has been rather successful in providing food and shelter, these needs regain importance when the economy moves through periods of recession and inflation.

3. Job redesign programs are intended to satisfy needs typically not satisfied in the workplace. As workers are told to expect higher-order need satisfaction, they may raise their expectations beyond what is possible. Dissatisfaction with the program's unachievable aim may displace dissatisfaction with the jobs.

4. Finally, job redesign may be resisted by labor unions that see the effort as an attempt to get more work for the same pay.

Practical efforts to improve productivity and satisfaction through implementation of job redesign strategy have emphasized autonomy and feedback. Relatively less emphasis has been placed on identity, significance, and variety.[47] Apparently, providing individuals with greater responsibility for the total task and with increased feedback is easier than changing the essential nature of the task itself. To provide identity, significance, and variety often requires enlarging the task to the point of losing the benefits of work simplification and standardization. Within the economic constraints imposed by the logic of specialization, however, work can be designed to give individuals complete responsibility for its completion and, at the same time, to provide supportive managerial monitoring.

In general, job redesign approaches are relatively successful in increasing quality of output, but only if the reward system already satisfies lower-level needs. If it does not, employees cannot be expected to experience upper-level need satisfaction (intrinsic rewards) through enriched jobs. In particular, managers cannot expect individuals with relatively low growth needs to respond as positively as those with relatively high growth needs.[48]

Successful job redesign efforts are the result of the circumstances that initiate the effort and the process undertaken to manage the effort. Organizations under considerable external pressure to change have a better chance of successfully implementing job redesign than those not under such pressure. Moreover, successful efforts are accompanied by broad-scale participation of both managers and employees.

---

[46]William E. Zierden, "Congruence in the Work Situation: Effects of Growth Needs, Management Style, and Job Structure on Job-Related Satisfactions," *Journal of Occupational Behavior,* October 1980, pp. 297–310.

[47]Kopelman, "Job Design and Productivity," p. 253.

[48]Lisa R. Berlinger, William H. Glick, and Robert C. Rodgers, "Job Enrichment and Performance Improvement," in *Productivity in Organizations,* ed. John P. Campbell and Richard J. Campbell (San Francisco: Jossey-Bass, 1988), pp. 219–54.

Since a primary source of organizational effectiveness is job performance, managers should design jobs according to the best available knowledge.[49]

JOB DESIGN, TECHNOLOGY, AND SOCIOTECHNICAL SYSTEM DESIGN

Job design strategy focuses on jobs in the context of individuals' needs for economic well-being and personal growth. A somewhat broader perspective is provided by sociotechnical theory, which focuses on jobs in the context of work systems. Both perspectives recognize the imperative of achieving organizational effectiveness. Sociotechnical theory and application of job design developed from studies undertaken in English coal mines from 1948 to 1958.[50] The studies were widely publicized for demonstrating the relationship between the social system and the technical system of organizations, revealed when economic circumstances forced management to change the way the coal was mined (the technical system). Historically, the technical system consisted of small groups of miners (the social system) working together on "short faces," or seams of coal. Then, technological advancements improved roof control and safety and made longwall mining possible. The new technical system required a change in the social system: groups were disbanded in favor of one-person, one-task jobs. Despite the efforts of management and even the union, the miners eventually devised a social system that restored many of the characteristics of the group system. This experience, completely described in organizational behavior literature, has stimulated much research and application.

Sociotechnical theory and job redesign theory are quite compatible. Their compatibility relates to the demands of modern technology for self-directed and self-motivated job behavior. Such job behavior is made possible in jobs that are designed to provide autonomy and variety. In practice, such jobs are parts of self-regulating work teams responsible for completing whole tasks. The **work module** concept pervades applications of sociotechnical theory.[51] Perhaps the most publicized application of sociotechnical design theory has been ongoing in Volvo Corporation, described in the Close-Up.

Numerous applications of sociotechnical design are reported in the literature.[52] Some of the most influential industrial and service organizations have confronted the necessity to redesign jobs to take advantage of the rapid pace of technological advance.

WORK MODULES
Whole pieces of work assigned to individuals.

---

[49]William A. Pasmore, "Overcoming the Roadblocks in Work-Restructuring Efforts," *Organizational Dynamics,* Spring 1982, pp. 54–67.

[50]Eric Trist, "The Evolution of Sociotechnical Systems," Ontario Quality of Working Life Centre (Occasional Paper, June 1981).

[51]Harvey F. Kolodny and Barbara Dresner, "Linking Arrangements and New Work Designs," *Organizational Dynamics,* Winter 1986, pp. 33–51.

[52]Louis E. Davis and James C. Taylor, eds., *Design of Jobs* (Santa Monica, Calif.: Goodyear Publishing, 1979); Marc Bassin, "A Special Blend of Teamwork," *Personnel Journal,* May 1988, p. 62; Roger Smith, "The U.S. Must Do What GM Has Done," *Fortune,* February 13, 1989, pp. 70–73.

JOB REDESIGN AT VOLVO CORPORATION

When Pehr Gyllenhammar joined Volvo in 1971 as its managing director, performance indicators such as productivity, absenteeism, and turnover were unsatisfactory. Gyllenhammar took a keen interest in experiments by Ingvar Barrby, head of Volvo's upholstery department, in job rotation (termed job alternation in Volvo). The reduction in turnover from 35 percent to 15 percent encouraged the new managing director to adopt other aspects of job redesign. For example, group management and work modules are used at the Torslanda car assembly plant. Employees, in groups, follow the same auto body for seven or eight workstations along the line (for 20 minutes).

Job redesign at Volvo reached a major milestone when the Kalmar assembly plant opened. Gyllenhammar had been personally and visibly behind the design and construction phases of the new plant to assure that opportunities to provide job enrichment were part of the physical and technological layout. The plant incorporates an assembly technology in which overhead carriers move the auto body, chassis, and subassemblies to assembly team areas. There, work teams of 20 to 25 employees complete major segments of auto assembly—electrical systems, instrumentation, finishing, and so on. Each group is responsible for a whole piece of work. They function as autonomous units, much as those at the truck assembly plant.

Source: Berth Jonsson and Alden G. Lank, "Volvo: A Report on the Workshop on Production Technology and Quality of Working Life," *Human Resource Management,* Winter 1985, pp. 455–65; "Volvo's Radical New Plant," *Business Week,* August 28, 1989.

SUMMARY OF KEY POINTS

— Job design involves managerial decisions and actions that specify objective job depth, range, and relationships to satisfy both the organizational requirements and the social and personal requirements of the jobholders.

— Contemporary managers must consider the issue of quality of work life when designing jobs. This issue reflects society's concern for work experiences that contribute to the personal growth and development of employees.

— Strategies for increasing the potential of jobs to satisfy the social and personal requirements of jobholders have gone through an evolutionary process. Initial efforts were directed toward job rotation and job enlargement. These strategies produced some gains in job satisfaction but did not change primary motivators such as responsibility, achievement, and autonomy.

— During the 1960s, job enrichment became a widely recognized strategy for improving quality of work life

factors. This strategy, based on Herzberg's motivation theory, involves increasing the depth of jobs through greater delegation of authority to jobholders. Despite some major successes, job enrichment is not universally applicable because it does not consider individual differences.

— Individual differences are now recognized as crucial variables to consider when designing jobs. Experience, cognitive complexity, needs, values, valences, and perceptions of equity are some of the individual differences that influence the reactions of jobholders to the scope and relationships of their jobs. When individual differences are combined with environmental, situational, and managerial differences, job design decisions become increasingly complex.

— The most recently developed strategy of job design emphasizes the importance of core job characteristics as perceived by jobholders. Although measurements of individual differences remain a problem, managers should be encouraged to examine ways to increase positive perceptions of variety, task identity, significance, autonomy, and feedback. By doing so, the potential for high-quality work performance and high job satisfaction is increased, given that jobholders possess relatively high growth need strength.

— Many organizations, including Volvo, Citibank, General Motors, and General Foods, have attempted job redesign with varying degrees of success. The current state of research knowledge is inadequate for making broad generalizations regarding the exact causes of

success and failure in applications of job redesign. Managers must diagnose their own situations to determine the applicability of job redesign in their organizations.

— Sociotechnical theory combines technological and social issues in job redesign practice. Sociotechnical theory is compatible with job redesign strategy and, in fact, emphasizes the practical need to design jobs that provide autonomy, feedback, significance, identity, and variety.

DISCUSSION AND REVIEW QUESTIONS

1. Why are jobs the building blocks of organizations? What are the costs to the organizations if the building blocks are poorly designed?

2. Explain the relationships among job depth, job range, job relationships, and job characteristics that influence the critical psychological states of the job characteristics model.

3. Explain how differences in social settings can account for differences in perceived job content.

4. Why do electronic offices pose special job design issues? Which of the job redesign approaches should management consider first in these job settings? Why?

5. What characteristics of jobs cannot be enriched? Do you believe that management should ever consider any job incapable of enrichment? Why?

6. Explain the relationship between feedback as a job content factor and personal goal setting. Is personal goal setting possible without feedback? Explain.

7. The Organizations: Close-Ups throughout the chapter describe instances of job design in service and manufacturing organizations. In which type of organization is job enrichment likely to be more effective as a strategy for increasing motivation and performance? Explain.

8. Which of the core dimensions do you now value most highly? Explain, and list them in rank order of importance to you.

9. Is it possible for American auto assembly plants to adopt job redesign strategies similar to those adopted in the Volvo plants? Explain.

10. In your opinion, was the General Foods experience with job redesign a success or a failure? Explain.

ADDITIONAL REFERENCES

Abdel-Halin, A. A. "Effects of Role Stress—Job Design—Technology Interaction on Employee Work Satisfaction." *Academy of Management Journal*, 1981, pp. 260–73.

Algera, J. A. "Objective and Perceived Task Characteristics as a Determinant of Reactions by Task Performers." *Journal of Occupational Psychology*, 1983, pp. 95–107.

Becherer, R. C. "The Job Characteristics of Industrial Salespersons: Relationship to Motivation and Satisfaction." *Journal of Marketing*, 1982, pp. 125–35.

Blau, G. J., and R. Katerberg. "Toward Enhancing Research with the Social Information Processing Approach to Task Design." *Academy of Management Review*, 1982, pp. 543–50.

Carlisle, K. E. *Analyzing Jobs and Tasks.* Englewood Cliffs, N.J.: Educational Technology Publications, 1986.

Cellar, D. F.; M. C. Kernan; and G. V. Barrett. "Conventional Wisdom and Ratings of Job Characteristics: Can Observers Be Objective?" *Journal of Management*, 1985, pp. 131–38.

Crystal, J. C., and R. S. Deems. "Redesigning Jobs." *Training and Development Journal,* 1983, pp. 44–46.

Dainoff, M. J. "Occupational Stress Factors in Visual Display Terminal (VDT) Operations: A Review of Empirical Research." *Behavior and Information Technology,* 1982, pp. 141–76.

Gomez–Mejia, L. R.; R. C. Page; and W. W. Turnow. "Comparison of the Practical Utility of Traditional, Statistical, and Hybrid Job Evaluation Approaches." *Academy of Management Journal,* 1982, pp. 790–809.

Grant, P. C. *Multiple Use Job Descriptions.* Westport, Conn.: Quorum Books, 1989.

————. *Task Design.* Glenview, Ill.: Scott, Foresman, 1982.

Griffin, R. W.; T. S. Bateman; S. J. Wayne; and T. C. Head. "Objective and Social Factors as Determinants of Task Perceptions and Responses: An Integrated Perspective and Empirical Investigation." *Academy of Management Journal,* 1987, pp. 501–23.

Hedge, A. "The Open-Plan Office: A Systematic Investigation of Employee Reactions to Their Work Environment." *Environment and Behavior,* 1982, pp. 519–42.

Hutton, M., and R. Collins. "Job Design: Australian Practice and Prospects." *Practising Manager,* 1983, pp. 11–15.

Kopelman, R. E. *Managing Productivity in Organizations: A Practical People-Oriented Perspective.* New York: McGraw-Hill, 1986.

Lawler, E. E., III, and G. E. Ledford, Jr. "Productivity and the Quality of Work Life." *National Productivity Review,* 1982, pp. 25–36.

Lewis, C. T. "Assessing the Validity of Job Evaluation." *Public Personnel Journal,* 1989, pp. 45–64.

Manese, W. R. *Occupational Job Evaluation: A Research Based Approach to Job Classification.* Westport, Conn.: Quorum Books, 1988.

Mecham, R. C. "Quantitative Job Evaluation Using the Position Analysis Questionnaire." *Personnel Administrator,* 1983, pp. 82–88, 124.

Montagno, R. V. "The Effects of Comparison Others and Prior Experience on Responses to Task Design." *Academy of Management Journal,* 1985, pp. 491–98.

O'Connor, E. J.; C. J. Rudolph; and L. H. Peters. "Individual Differences and Job Design Reconsidered: Where Do We Go from Here?" *Academy of Management Review,* 1980, pp. 249–54.

Passmore, W. A. *Designing Effective Organizations: The Sociotechnical Systems Perspective.* New York: John Wiley & Sons, 1988.

Patten, T. H. *Fair Play: The Managerial Challenge of Comparable Job Worth and Job Analysis.* San Francisco: Jossey-Bass, 1988.

Shaw, J. B. "An Information-Processing Approach to the Study of Job Design." *Academy of Management Review,* 1980, pp. 41–48.

Wall, T. "What's New in Job Design?" *Personnel Management,* 1984, pp. 28–29.

Weisbord, M. R. "Participative Work Design: A Personal Odyssey." *Organizational Dynamics,* 1985, pp. 4–20.

WORK REDESIGN IN AN INSURANCE COMPANY

The executive staff of a relatively small life insurance company is considering a proposal to install an electronic data processing system. The proposal is being presented by the assistant to the president, John Skully. He has been studying the feasibility of the equipment after a management consultant recommended a complete overhaul of the jobs within the company.

The management consultant had been engaged by the company to diagnose the causes of high turnover and absenteeism. After reviewing the situation and speaking with groups of employees, the consultant recommended that the organization structure be changed from a functional to a client basis. The change in departmental basis would enable management to redesign jobs to reduce the human costs associated with highly specialized tasks.

The present organization includes separate departments to issue policies, collect premiums, change beneficiaries, and process loan applications. Employees in these departments complained that their jobs were boring, insignificant, and monotonous. They had stated that the only reason they stayed with the company was because they liked the small-company atmosphere. They felt that management had a genuine interest in their welfare but that the trivial nature of their jobs contradicted that feeling. As one employee said, "This company is small enough to know almost everybody. But the job I do is so boring that I wonder why they even need me to do it." This and similar comments had led the consultant to believe that the jobs must be altered to provide greater motivation. Recognizing that work redesign opportunities were limited by the organization structure, he recommended that the company change to a client basis. In such a structure, each employee would handle every transaction related to a particular policyholder.

When the consultant presented his views to the members of the executive staff, they were very much interested in his recommendation. In fact, they agreed that his recommendation was well founded. They noted, however, that a small company must pay particular attention to efficiency in handling transactions. The functional basis enabled the organization to achieve the degree of specialization necessary for efficient operations. The manager of internal operations stated: "If we move away from specialization, the rate of efficiency must go down because we will lose the benefit of specialized effort. The only way we can justify redesigning the jobs as suggested by the consultant is to maintain our efficiency; otherwise, there won't be any jobs to redesign because we will be out of business."

The internal operations manager explained to the executive staff that despite excessive absenteeism and turnover, he was able to maintain acceptable productivity. The narrow range and depth of the jobs reduced training time to a minimum. It was also possible to hire temporary help to meet peak loads and to fill in for absent employees. "Moreover," he said, "changing the jobs our people do means that we must change the jobs our managers do. They are experts in their own functional areas, but we have never attempted to train them to oversee more than two operations."

A majority of the executive staff believed that the consultant's recommendations should be seriously considered. At that point, the group directed John Skully to evaluate the potential of electronic data processing (EDP) as a means of obtaining efficient operations in combination with the redesigned jobs. He has completed the study and is presenting his report to the executive staff.

"The bottom line," Skully says, "is that EDP will enable us to maintain our present efficiency, but with the redesigned jobs we will not obtain any greater gains. If my analysis is correct, we will have to absorb the cost of the equipment out of earnings, because there will be no cost savings. So it comes down to what price we are willing and able to pay for improving the satisfaction of our employees."

Questions for Consideration

1. Which core characteristics of the employees' jobs will be changed if the consultant's recommendations are accepted? Explain.
2. Which alternative redesign strategies should be considered? For example, job rotation and job enlargement are possible alternatives. What are the relevant considerations for these and other designs in the context of this company?
3. What would be your decision in this case? What should the management be willing to pay for employees' satisfaction? Defend your answer.

PERSONAL PREFERENCES

Objectives

1. To illustrate individual differences in preferences about various job design characteristics.
2. To illustrate how your preferences may differ from those of others.
3. To examine the most important and least important job design characteristics and how managers would cope with them.

Related Topics

This exercise is related to intrinsic and extrinsic reward topics. The job design characteristics considered could be viewed as either intrinsic or extrinsic job issues.

Starting the Exercise

First, you will respond to a questionnaire asking about your job design preferences and how you view the preferences of others. After you have worked through the questionnaire *individually,* small groups will be formed. In the groups, discussion will focus on the individual differences in preferences expressed by group members.

The Facts

Job design is concerned with a number of attributes of a job. Among them are the job itself, the requirements of the job, the interpersonal interaction opportunities on the job, and performance outcomes. Individuals prefer certain attributes: some prefer job autonomy, while others prefer to be challenged by different tasks. Obviously, individual differences in preferences would be an important consideration for managers. An exciting job for one person may be a demeaning and boring job for another person. Managers could use this information in attempting to create job design conditions that match organizational goals with individual goals and preferences.

   The Job Design Preferences form is presented below. Please read it carefully and complete it after considering each of the characteristics listed. Due to space limitations, not all job design characteristics are included for your consideration. Use only those included on the form.

Completing the Exercise

Phase I: 15 minutes.   Individually complete the A and B portions of the Job Design Preferences form.

Phase II: 45 minutes.

1. The instructor will form groups of four to six students.
2. Discuss the differences in the ranking individuals made on the A and B parts of the form.
3. Present each of the A rank orders of group members on a flip chart or the blackboard. Analyze the areas of agreement and disagreement.
4. Discuss what implications the A and B rankings would have to a *manager* who would have to supervise a group such as the one you are in. What could a manager do to cope with the individual differences displayed in the above steps?

JOB DESIGN PREFERENCES

A. Your Job Design Preferences

Decide which of the following characteristics is most important to you. Place a *1* in front of the most important characteristic. Then decide which characteristic is the second most important to you and place a *2* in front of it. Continue numbering the items in order of importance until the least important is ranked *10*. There are no right answers, since individuals differ in their job design preferences. Do not discuss your individual rankings until the instructor forms groups.

_____ Variety in tasks
_____ Feedback on performance from doing the job
_____ Autonomy
_____ Working as a team
_____ Responsibility
_____ Developing friendships on the job
_____ Task identity
_____ Task significance
_____ Having the resources to perform well
_____ Feedback on performance from others (e.g., the manager, co-workers)

B. Others' Job Design Preferences

In the A section, you have provided your job design preferences. Now number the items as you think others would rank them. Consider others who are in your course, class, or program—that is, who are also completing this exercise. Rank the factors from 1 (most important) to 10 (least important).

_____ Variety in tasks
_____ Feedback on performance from doing the job
_____ Autonomy
_____ Working as a team
_____ Responsibility
_____ Developing friendships on the job
_____ Task identity
_____ Task significance
_____ Having the resources to perform well
_____ Feedback on performance from others (e.g., the manager, co-workers)

15

Organizational Design

ARGUMENT FOR

Since the groundbreaking studies of Joan Woodward, the view that technology *determines* structure has been debated. According to this view, an optimal organizational design exists for each technological type; managers therefore should match the design with the technology. Woodward's studies indicated that the mechanistic design proposed by classical theorists is optimal only for mass production technology; the organic design strategy is appropriate for job order and process technologies. These studies cast considerable doubt on the view that there is one universally best way to organize.

As other researchers tested Woodward's findings in other settings, evidence that technology is the compelling force behind design decisions accumulated. Although subsequent research studies differed in some respects, the conclusions were consistent. Studies of industrial organizations in the Minneapolis–St. Paul area, for example, confirmed that when management failed to match structure with technology, additional costs were incurred that resulted in lower organizational performance.

The finding that technology determines structure has prompted theorists to devise explanations for the relationship. Their theories attempt to provide general frameworks for thinking about the relationships between structure and technology. Thus, it is possible to argue that in nonmanufacturing as well as manufacturing business firms, technology is the most important determinant of optimal organizational structure.

ARGUMENT AGAINST

Research indicates that although technology is important, other considerations must be taken into account in organization design. The most compelling counterargument is that technology is the important variable for designing organizational units that directly produce the product or service. Thus, the production department or division should be designed to meet technological demands, but other units in the organization face different, nontechnological demands. Organizations must deal with various subenvironments, each posing different constraints.

The view that technology is the primary influence on structure is not borne out by studies of very large organizations. Woodward's studies, and those of supportive researchers, included firms of relatively small size. The impact of technology is more noticeable in small firms than in large ones, since larger firms create staff units—research, marketing, and information, for example—to deal with nonproduction environments. The larger the organization, the less influential technology becomes. Thus, according to one counterargument, size rather than technology is the principal determinant of structure.

Organizational design refers to managerial decisions that determine the structure and processes that coordinate and control the jobs of the organization. The outcome of organizational design decisions is a system of jobs and work groups, including the processes that link them. These linking processes include authority relationships and communication networks in addition to specific planning and controlling techniques. In effect, organization design creates a superstructure within which the work of the organization takes place.

Organization design has been at the core of managerial work since the earliest efforts to develop management theory. The importance of design decisions has stimulated a great deal of interest in the issue. Managers and organizational behavior theorists and researchers have contributed to what is now a considerable body of literature. The manager who faces the necessity of designing an organizational structure is at no loss for ideas. Quite the contrary, the literature of organizational design contains numerous and conflicting ideas about how an organization should be designed to achieve optimal effectiveness.

The Organizational Issue for Debate that opens this chapter summarizes some of the arguments for and against the view that technology is the most important factor in design decisions. As this chapter discusses, however, technology is only one of numerous design factors. Other factors include the nature of the work itself, the characteristics of people who will do the work, the demands of the environment in which the organization exists, the necessity to receive and process information from that environment, and the overall strategy the organization chooses for relating to its environment.

To make some sense of this apparent complexity, we first describe two general models of organization design: mechanistic and organic. Next, we examine three important factors that managers must take into account when designing the structure: technology, environmental uncertainty, and information processing requirements. Finally, we integrate the discussion of this and the previous two chapters in a model of organizational design.

MECHANISTIC AND ORGANIC MODELS OF ORGANIZATION DESIGN

The two models of organizational design described in this section are important in management theory and practice; they receive considerable theoretical and practical attention. Despite this, there is little uniformity in the terms used to designate the two models. The two terms we use here, mechanistic and organic, are relatively descriptive of the important features of the models.[1]

Mechanistic Model

During the early part of the 20th century, a body of literature emerged that considered designing the structure of an organization as only one of a number of managerial tasks, including planning and controlling. These writers wanted to define *principles* that could guide managers in the performance of their tasks. An early writer, Henri Fayol, proposed a number of principles he had found

---

[1]Tom Burns and G. M. Stalker, *The Management of Innovation* (London: Tavistock Publications, 1961), are largely responsible for the terms *mechanistic* and *organic*.

MECHANISTIC MODEL
Organization design emphasizing importance of achieving high levels of production and efficiency through extensive use of rules and procedures, centralized authority, and high specialization of labor.

useful in the management of a large coal mining company in France.[2] Some of Fayol's principles dealt with the management function of organizing, and four are relevant for understanding the **mechanistic model:**

Principle of specialization.   Fayol saw specialization as the best means for making use of individuals and groups of individuals. At the time of his writings, the limit of specialization (i.e., the optimal point) had not been defined. As stated in the previous chapter, scientific management popularized a number of methods for implementing specialization of labor. These methods, such as work standards and motion and time studies, emphasized technical rather than behavioral dimensions of work.

Principle of unity of direction.   According to this principle, jobs should be grouped by specialty. Engineers should be grouped with engineers, salespeople with salespeople, accountants with accountants. The departmentalization basis that most nearly implements this principle is the functional basis.

Principle of authority and responsibility.   Fayol believed that a manager should be given sufficient authority to carry out his or her assigned responsibilities. Because the assigned responsibilities of top managers are considerably more important to the future of the organization than those of lower management, the application of the principle inevitably leads to centralized authority. Centralized authority is a logical outcome not only because of top managements' larger responsibilities but also because of the more complex work at this level, the greater number of workers involved, and the remote relationship between actions and results.

Scalar chain principle.   The natural result of implementing the preceding three principles is a graded chain of managers from the ultimate authority to the lowest ranks. The scalar chain is the route for all vertical communications in an organization. All communications from the lowest level must pass through each superior in the chain of command; communications from the top must pass through each subordinate until they reach the appropriate level.

Fayol's writings became part of a literature that, although each contributor made unique contributions, had a common thrust. Writers such as James Mooney and Allan Reiley,[3] Mary Follet,[4] and Lyndall Urwick[5] all shared the common objective of defining the principles that should guide the design and management of organizations. Here, we will discuss the ideas of one individual who made important contributions to the mechanistic model: Max Weber,

[2]Henri Fayol, *General and Industrial Management,* trans. J. A. Conbrough (Geneva: International Management Institute, 1929). The more widely circulated translation is that of Constance Storrs (London: Pitman Publishing, 1949).

[3]James D. Mooney and Allan C. Reiley, *Onward Industry* (New York: Harper & Row, 1939); subsequently revised under the authorship and title James D. Mooney, *The Principles of Organization* (New York: Harper & Row, 1947).

[4]Henry C. Metcalf and Lyndall Urwick, eds., *Dynamic Administration: The Collected Papers of Mary Parker Follett* (New York: Harper & Row, 1940).

[5]Lyndall Urwick, *The Elements of Administration* (New York: Harper & Row, 1944).

who described applications of the mechanistic model and coined the term *bureaucracy*.

Bureaucracy has various meanings. The traditional usage is the political science concept of government by bureaus but without participation by the governed. In lay terms, bureaucracy refers to the negative consequences of large organizations, such as excessive "red tape," procedural delays, and general frustration.[6] In Max Weber's writings, however, bureaucracy refers to a particular way to organize collective activities.[7] Weber's interest in bureaucracy reflected his concern for the ways society develops hierarchies of control so that one group can, in effect, dominate other groups.[8] Organizational design involves domination in the sense that authority involves the legitimate right to exact obedience from others. His search for the forms of domination that evolve in society led him to the study of bureaucratic structure.

According to Weber, the bureaucratic structure is "superior to any other form in precision, in stability, in the stringency of its discipline and its reliability. It thus makes possible a high degree of calculability of results for the heads of the organization and for those acting in relation to it."[9] The bureaucracy compares with other organizations "as does the machine with nonmechanical modes of production."[10] These words capture the essence of the mechanistic model of organization design.

To achieve the maximum benefits of the bureaucratic design, Weber believed that an organization must have the following characteristics and practices:

1. All tasks will be divided into highly specialized jobs. Through specialization, jobholders become expert in their jobs, and management can hold them responsible for the effective performance of their duties.

2. Each task is performed according to a system of abstract rules to ensure uniformity and coordination of different tasks. This practice enables the manager to eliminate uncertainty in task performance due to individual differences.

3. Each member or office of the organization is accountable for job performance to one, and only one, manager. Managers hold their authority because of their expert knowledge and because it is delegated from the top of the hierarchy. An unbroken chain of command exists.

4. Each employee of the organization relates to other employees and clients in an impersonal, formal manner, maintaining a social distance with subordinates and clients. The purpose of this practice is to assure that personalities and favoritism do not interfere with the efficient accomplishment of the organization's objectives.

---

[6]Michael Crozier, *The Bureaucratic Phenomenon* (Chicago: University of Chicago Press, 1964), p. 3.

[7]Max Weber, *The Theory of Social and Economic Organization,* trans. A. M. Henderson and Talcott Parsons (New York: Oxford University Press, 1947).

[8]Richard M. Weiss, "Weber on Bureaucracy: Management Consultant or Political Theorist?" *Academy of Management Review,* April 1983, pp. 242–48.

[9]Weber, *The Theory of Social and Economic Organization,* p. 334.

[10]H. H. Gerth and C. W. Mills, eds. and trans., *Max Weber: Essays in Sociology* (New York: Oxford University Press, 1946), p. 214.

ORGANIZATIONS:
CLOSE-UP

PROCTER & GAMBLE'S MECHANISTIC STRUCTURE

Procter & Gamble (P&G) innovated the brand management system in which each brand of a product has its own advocate within the organization. The brand manager of Camay soap would compete against the Ivory soap manager as if he or she were an external competitor. P&G's system became the standard of the industry, and nearly every major competitor used some form of brand management organization. In recent years, P&G has done away with the system in a sweeping reorganization that company officials describe as the most important management change in the past 30 years. The reorganization does not abolish the brand managers, but it makes them accountable to a new type of manager, one who manages a category of products. The intent of the reorganization is to exert greater coordination in the planning and marketing of the individual brands through a higher level of management.

The organization that adopts category management moves toward a mechanistic structure by adding complexity and centralization to the existing structure. In effect, the chain of command is lengthened, because brand managers are now accountable to an additional layer of management (the category managers). The mechanistic structure enables P&G to obtain more efficient results in product development and marketing by eliminating some of the duplication of effort that occurred at the brand manager level.

Source: "The Marketing Revolution at Procter & Gamble," *Business Week*, July 25, 1988, pp. 72–73, 76.

5. Employment in the bureaucratic organization is based on technical qualifications and protected against arbitrary dismissal. Similarly, promotions are based on seniority and achievement. Employment in the organization is viewed as a lifelong career, and a high degree of loyalty is engendered.

These five characteristics of bureaucracy describe organizations of the kind Fayol believed to be most effective. Both Fayol and Weber described the same type of organization: one that functions in a machinelike manner to accomplish the organization's goals very efficiently. Thus, the term *mechanistic* aptly describes such organizations. The Close-Up describes the reorganization of Procter & Gamble into a structure that has mechanistic characteristics.

The mechanistic model achieves high levels of efficiency due to its structural characteristics. It is:

1. Highly complex because of its emphasis on specialization of labor.
2. Highly centralized because of its emphasis on authority and accountability.
3. Highly formalized because of its emphasis on function as the basis for departments.

These organizational characteristics and the practices discussed earlier in this section underlie a widely used organizational model. But the mechanistic model is not the only one to be used.

Organic Model

The **organic model** of organization design stands in sharp contrast to the mechanistic model because of their distinctly different organizational characteristics and practices. The most obvious differences result from the different effectiveness criteria each seeks to maximize. While the mechanistic model seeks to maximize efficiency and production, the organic model seeks to maximize flexibility and adaptability.

The organic organization is flexible and adaptable to changing environmental demands because its design encourages greater utilization of the human potential. Managers are encouraged to adopt practices that tap the full range of human motivations through job design that stresses personal growth and responsibility. Decision making, control, and goal-setting processes are decentralized and shared at all levels of the organization. Communications flow throughout the organization, not only down the chain of command. These practices are intended to implement a basic assumption of the organic model: an organization will be effective to the extent that its structure is "such as to ensure a maximum probability that in all interactions and in all relationships with the organization, each member, in the light of his background, values, desires, and expectations, will view the experience as supportive and one which builds and maintains a sense of personal worth and importance."[11]

An organization design that provides individuals with this sense of personal worth and motivation and that facilitates flexibility and adaptability would be:

1. Relatively simple because of its de-emphasis of specialization and its emphasis on increasing job range.
2. Relatively decentralized because of its emphasis on delegation of authority and increasing job depth.
3. Relatively informal because of its emphasis on product and customer as bases for departments.

An 84-year-old insurance company recently reorganized from a mechanistic to an organic structure, as described in the Close-Up.

One leading spokesperson and developer of ideas supporting applications of the organic model is Rensis Likert. The studies Likert carried out at the University of Michigan led him to argue that organic organizations (Likert uses the term *System-4*) differ markedly from mechanistic organizations (*System-1*) along a number of structural dimensions.[12] The important differences are shown in Table 15–1.

Without question, Likert's views are widely shared by researchers and practitioners. The literature is filled with reports of efforts to implement organic designs in actual organizations.[13] Likert himself reported many of

ORGANIC MODEL
Organization design emphasizing importance of achieving high levels of adaptiveness and development through limited use of rules and procedures, decentralized authority, and relatively low degrees of specialization.

---

[11]Rensis Likert, *New Patterns of Management* (New York: McGraw-Hill, 1961); Rensis Likert, *The Human Organization* (New York: McGraw-Hill, 1967).

[12]Likert, *New Patterns of Management*, p. 103.

[13]See particularly A. J. Marrow, D. G. Bowers, and S. E. Seashore, eds., *Strategies of Organization Change* (New York: Harper & Row, 1967); William F. Dowling, "At General Motors: System 4 Builds Performance and Profits," *Organizational Dynamics*, Winter 1975, pp. 23–28.

AID ASSOCIATION FOR LUTHERANS' ORGANIC STRUCTURE

Aid Association for Lutherans (AAL) is a fraternal society that operates a huge insurance business. It has transformed its organization from a mechanistic to an organic structure in order to take advantage of the benefits of the self-directed team concept. Prior to reorganization, AAL was structured according to the traditional functions of the insurance industry, and employees were highly trained for specific functions, such as processing, underwriting, valuations, and premium services. The specialization resulted in considerable efficiency in dealing with customers requiring the attention of one of the functions. But when multiple functions were involved, the organization got bogged down.

After exploring the potential benefits, AAL's management established teams of employees that could handle all details of a customer transaction, whether health, life, or casualty insurance. The teams, once responsible for functions, are now responsible for customers. They take initiative that once required management prodding. As a result of each team's assumption of responsibility for managing itself, three levels of management have been eliminated from the organization. AAL's organization, simpler and more decentralized than before, is therefore more organic and less mechanistic.

Source: "Work Teams Can Rev Up Paper-Pushers, Too," *Business Week,* November 28, 1988, pp. 64, 68, 72.

these studies.[14] Also without question, proponents of the organic organization believe it is universally applicable; that is, the theory is proposed as the "one best way" to design an organization. In this regard, the mechanistic and organic models' proponents are equally zealous in their advocacy.

CONTINGENCY DESIGN THEORIES

A current trend in management research and practice is to design organizations to be congruent with the demands of the situation,[15] which are termed contingencies. Accordingly, neither the mechanistic nor the organic organization design is necessarily more effective. Which one is the better approach depends on the situation. The contingency point of view provides the opportunity to get away from the dilemma of choosing between the mechanistic and the organic models. As such, it is an evolution of ideas, the bases for which can be found in the work of earlier writers.

---

[14]Likert, *New Patterns of Management;* Likert, *The Human Organization.*

[15]W. Alan Randolph and Gregory G. Dess, "The Congruence Perspective of Organization Design: A Conceptual Model and Multivariate Research Approach," *Academy of Management Review,* January 1984, pp. 114–27; Robert Drazin and Andrew H. Van de Ven, "Alternative Forms of Fit in Contingency Theory," *Administrative Science Quarterly,* December 1985, pp. 514–39.

Process	Mechanistic Structure	Organic Structure
1. Leadership	Includes no perceived confidence and trust. Subordinates do not feel free to discuss job problems with their superiors, who in turn do not solicit their ideas and opinions.	Includes perceived confidence and trust between superiors and subordinates in all matters. Subordinates feel free to discuss job problems with their superiors, who in turn solicit their ideas and opinions.
2. Motivation	Taps only physical, security, and economic motives, through the use of fear and sanctions. Unfavorable attitudes toward the organization prevail among employees.	Taps a full range of motives through participatory methods. Attitudes are favorable toward the organization and its goals.
3. Communication	Information flows downward and tends to be distorted, inaccurate, and viewed with suspicion by subordinates.	Information flows freely throughout the organization—upward, downward, and laterally. The information is accurate and undistorted.
4. Interaction	Closed and restricted. Subordinates have little effect on departmental goals, methods, and activities.	Open and extensive. Both superiors and subordinates are able to affect departmental goals, methods, and activities.
5. Decision	Relatively centralized. Occurs only at the top of the organization.	Relatively decentralized. Occurs at all levels through group process.
6. Goal setting	Located at the top of the organization, discouraging group participation.	Encourages group participation in setting high, realistic objectives.
7. Control	Centralized. Emphasizes fixing of blame for mistakes.	Dispersed throughout the organization. Emphasizes self-control and problem solving.
8. Performance goals	Low and passively sought by managers, who make no commitment to developing the human resources of the organization.	High and actively sought by superiors, who recognize the necessity for full commitment to developing, through training, the human resources of the organization.

TABLE 15—1

Comparison of Mechanistic and Organic Structures

Source: Adapted from Rensis Likert, *The Human Organization* (New York: McGraw-Hill, 1967), pp. 197–211.

The essence of the **contingency design** approach is expressed by the question: Under what circumstances and in what situations is either the mechanistic or the organic relatively more effective? To answer this question, the manager has to specify the factors in a situation that influence the relative effectiveness of a particular design. Obviously, the contingency approach is quite complicated because of the need to consider so many factors.[16] Technology is one of the more important factors to consider.

CONTINGENCY DESIGN THEORY

Organization design approach that emphasizes importance of fitting design to demands of situation, including technology, environmental uncertainty, and strategic choice.

---

[16]Sang M. Lee, Fred Luthans, and David L. Olson, "A Management Science Approach to Contingency Models of Organizational Structure," *Academy of Management Journal*, September 1982, pp. 553–66.

TECHNOLOGY AND ORGANIZATION DESIGN

The effects of **technology** on organization structure can be readily understood at an abstract level of analysis. Although various definitions of technology exist, it is generally understood as "the *actions* that an individual performs upon an object with or without the aid of tools or mechanical devices, in order to make *some change* in that object."[17] A compatible yet even broader definition is that "technology is the application of knowledge to perform work."[18] Thus, organization structures reflect technology in the ways that jobs are designed (division of labor) and grouped (departmentalization).

In this sense, the current state of knowledge regarding the appropriate actions to change an object acts as a constraint on management. The state of technological knowledge has increased exponentially in recent years, as computers and robots have entered the workplace. One effect of this new knowledge has been to increase the interest of managers in the relationship between organization structure and technology.

The organization theory literature includes a number of studies that examine the relationship between technology and organization structure. Rather than survey all these studies, which would take considerable space and would go beyond the intent of our discussion, we will briefly review one classic study. Joan Woodward's research, which stimulated a number of follow-up studies, has become quite important in the literature of organization design.

Woodward's Classic Study

Joan Woodward gained considerable attention when she released the findings of her analyses of the organization structures of 100 manufacturing firms in southern England.[19] She and her colleagues had sought to answer a number of questions regarding the contributions of organization structure to organizational effectiveness. Their conclusions about technology and structure are widely acclaimed.

Woodward and her team of researchers looked for possible structural differences between the more and the less effective firms. Using a number of measures of effectiveness, they classified the firms into three categories: above average, average, and below average. When no consistent pattern emerged within each category, the team began analyzing the information relating to technology ("the methods and processes of manufacture").[20] They measured technology in terms of three related variables: "(1) stages in the historical

---

[17]Charles Perrow, "A Framework for the Comparative Analysis of Organizations," *American Sociological Review,* April 1967, p. 195. See Michael Withey, Richard L. Daft, and William H. Cooper, "Measures of Perrow's Work-Unit Technology: An Empirical Assessment and a New Scale," *Academy of Management Journal,* March 1983, pp. 45–63.

[18]Denise M. Rousseau, "Assessment of Technology in Organizations: Closed versus Open Systems Approaches," *Academy of Management Review,* October 1979, p. 531.

[19]Joan Woodward, *Industrial Organization: Theory and Practice* (London: Oxford University Press, 1965).

[20]Ibid., p. 35.

development of production processes, (2) the interrelationship between the items of equipment used for these processes, and (3) the extent to which the operations performed in the processes were repetitive or comparable from one production cycle or sequence to the next."[21] Applying the measure to information about a firm's manufacturing methods resulted in a continuum with job order manufacturing and process manufacturing methods at the extremes, separated by mass production manufacturing.

Classifying the firms according to the three categories of technology, the research team discovered that the organizational structures of firms within each category were different in comparison to other categories. The important differences were:[22]

1. The organizations at each end of the continuum were more flexible. That is, they resembled the organic model, with job duties and responsibilities being less clearly defined. Organizations in the middle of the continuum were more specialized and formalized. That is, they resembled the mechanistic model.

2. The organizations at each end of the continuum made greater use of verbal than written communications; organizations in the middle made greater use of written communications and were more formalized. This pattern is also consistent with distinctions between organic and mechanistic models of design.

3. The managerial positions were more highly specialized in mass production than in either job order or process manufacturing. First-level supervisors engaged primarily in direct supervision, leaving the technical decisions to staff personnel. In contrast, managers in job order firms were expected to have greater technical expertise, and managers in process manufacturing were expected to have greater scientific expertise.

4. Consistent with the above point, the actual control of production in the form of scheduling and routing was separated from supervision of production in mass production firms. Those two managerial functions were more highly integrated in the role of the first-level supervisor in organizations at the extremes of the continuum.

Thus, the data indicated sharp organizational differences due to technological differences.

Other Evidence

Subsequent research on the effect of technology on structure has produced mixed results. The most complete replication was undertaken by William Zwerman, whose findings lend support to Woodward's.[23] Another supportive

---

[21]J. J. Rackham, "Automation and Technical Change—The Implications for the Management Process," in *Organizational Structure and Design,* ed. Gene W. Dalton, Paul R. Lawrence, and Jay W. Lorsch (Homewood, Ill.: Richard D. Irwin, 1970), p. 299.

[22]Joan Woodward, *Management and Technology, Problems of Progress in Industry,* no. 3 (London: Her Majesty's Stationery Office, 1958), pp. 4–30; Gary A. Yukl and Kenneth N. Wexley, eds., *Readings in Organizational and Industrial Psychology* (New York: Oxford University Press, 1971), p. 19.

[23]William L. Zwerman, *New Perspectives in Organization Theory* (Westport, Conn.: Greenwood, 1970).

study, completed by Edward Harvey, found that as fewer product changes occurred over time, there was an *increase* in the number of specialized subunits, the number of managerial levels, the ratio of managerial to nonmanagerial personnel, and the extent of formalized rules and communication channels.[24] Other studies of relationships between technology and structure have produced inconsistent results.

The mixed results can be explained, at least partially. Critical reviews of the literature on technology and structure have produced several explanations.[25] First, there is confusion over level of analysis. Some studies focus on the effects of technology on the individual task, while other studies focus on effects of technology on groups and organizations.[26] Second, researchers tend to define technology only in terms of the conversion phases of a technical system, with little regard to either the input or output phases.[27] Finally, distinguishing technology as a *cause* of structural differences from technology as the *effect* of such differences is inherently difficult. For example, by increasing the degree of participation in decision making (decentralization of authority), a human services organization changed the manner in which clients are treated (technology).[28] These research and theoretical issues must be taken into account when attempting to reconcile studies of technology and structure.

Recent studies have indicated that at least two factors moderate the relationship between technology and structure, *size* and *managerial choice*. Size affects impact of technology on the total organization structure. This relationship was noted in the Aston studies[29] and subsequently in those by Peter Blau and his associates.[30] The structures of small organizations do not permit the

---

[24]Edward Harvey, "Technology and the Structure of Organizations," *American Sociological Review,* 1968, pp. 247–59.

[25]Donald Gerwin, "The Comparative Analysis of Structure and Technology: A Critical Appraisal," *Academy of Management Review,* January 1979, pp. 41–51; Louis W. Fry, "Technology-Structure Research: Three Critical Issues," *Academy of Management Journal,* September 1982, pp. 532–52.

[26]Louis W. Fry and John W. Slocum, Jr., "Technology, Structure and Work Group Effectiveness: A Test of a Contingency Model," *Academy of Management Journal,* June 1984, pp. 221–46; Judith W. Alexander and W. Alan Randolph, "The Fit between Technology and Structure as a Predictor of Performance in Nursing Subunits," *Academy of Management Journal,* December 1985, pp. 844–60.

[27]Rousseau, "Assessment of Technology," pp. 531–42; Peter K. Mills and Dennis J. Moberg, "Perspectives on the Technology of Service Organizations," *Academy of Management Review,* July 1982, pp. 467–78.

[28]Charles A. Glisson, "Dependence of Technological Routinization on Structural Variables in Human Service Organizations," *Administrative Science Quarterly,* September 1978, pp. 383–95.

[29]The original Aston studies were carried out from 1961 to 1973 by the Industrial Administration Unit of the University of Aston in Birmingham, England. The significant papers of this research are presented in Derek S. Pugh and David J. Hickson, *Organizational Structure in Its Context* (Westmead, England: Saxon House, D. C. Heath, 1976); Derek S. Pugh and Charles R. Hinings, *Organizational Structure: Extensions and Replications* (Westmead, England: Saxon House, D. C. Heath, 1976). A recent review of the Aston Group's measure of structure is Peter H. Grinyer and Masoud Yasai-Ardekani, "Some Problems with the Measurement of Macro-Organizational Structure," *Organization Studies* 2, no. 3 (1981), pp. 287–96.

[30]Peter M. Blau, Cecilia M. Falbe, William McKinley, and K. Tracy Phelps, "Technology and Organization in Manufacturing," *Administrative Science Quarterly,* March 1976, pp. 20–30; John B.

creation of support units such as engineering, research and development, product development, and public relations. Consequently, the effect of technology on structure is more apparent in firms having a larger number of subunits whose goals and functions are related to the production process.[31]

Managerial choice involves the range of options that managers have in designing an organization.[32] Choices are constrained by factors such as technology and economies of scale, but managers have considerable discretion within those constraints.[33] This point of view confirms the importance of management decision making for organizational performance. More important, it identifies technology as only one, albeit an important one, factor in the organization's environment.

Understanding the Technology-Structure Relationship

An understanding of the relationship between technology and organizations can be based on the natural business functions: product development, production, and marketing.

The job order firm produces according to customer specifications; the firm must secure the order, develop the product, and manufacture it. The cycle begins with marketing and ends with production. This sequence requires the firm to be especially adept at sensing market changes and adjusting to those changes. More important, the product development function holds the key to the firm's success. This function must convert customer specifications into products acceptable to both the customer and the production personnel. Various approaches exist to facilitate the kinds of interactions and communication patterns required to meet the market and product development problems associated with job order or unit production. The more complicated approaches involve interactions better managed in organic types of structures.[34]

Cullen, Kenneth S. Anderson, and Douglas D. Baker, "Blau's Theory of Structural Differentiation Revisited: A Theory of Structural Change or Scale?" *Academy of Management Journal,* June 1986, pp. 203–29; W. Graham Astley, "Organization Size and Bureaucratic Structure," *Organization Studies* 6, no. 3 (1985), pp. 201–28.

[31]Bernard C. Reimann, "Organizational Structure and Technology in Manufacturing: System versus Work Flow Level Perspectives," *Academy of Management Journal,* March 1980, pp. 61–77; Robert M. Marsh and Hiroshi Mannari, "Technology and Size as Determinants of the Organization Structures of Japanese Firms," *Administrative Science Quarterly,* March 1981, pp. 33–57; Nancy M. Carter, "Computerization as a Predominate Technology: Its Influence on the Structure of Newspaper Organizations," *Academy of Management Journal,* June 1984, pp. 247–70.

[32]John R. Montanari, "An Expanded Theory of Structural Determination: An Empirical Investigation of the Impact of Managerial Discretion on Organization Structure" (D.B.A. dissertation, University of Colorado, 1976); Donald C. Hambrick, "Environment, Strategy and Power within Top Management Teams," *Administrative Science Quarterly,* June 1981, pp. 253–76.

[33]H. Randolph Bobbitt and Jeffrey D. Ford, "Decision-Maker Choice as a Determinant of Organizational Structure," *Academy of Management Review,* January 1980, pp. 13–23; Jeffrey D. Ford and W. Harvey Hegarty, "Decision Makers' Beliefs about the Causes and Effects of Structure: An Exploratory Study," *Academy of Management Journal,* June 1984, pp. 271–91.

[34]James W. Dean, Jr., and Gerald I. Susman, "Organizing for Manufacturing Design," *Harvard Business Review,* January–February 1989, pp. 28–32, 36.

At the other extreme of the technological continuum lies the process manufacturer. In such firms, the cycle begins with product development. The key to success is the ability to discover, through scientific research, a new product (e.g., a new chemical, gasoline additive, or fabric) that can be manufactured by already existing facilities or by new facilities once a market is established. The development, marketing, and production functions in process manufacturing all tend to demand scientific personnel and specialized competence at the highest levels in the organization. Since the success of these firms depends upon adjustment to new scientific knowledge, the organic design is more effective than the mechanistic design.

The mechanistic design is effective for firms that use mass production technology. The market exists for a more or less standardized product (autos, foods, clothing), and the task is to manufacture the product efficiently and economically through fairly routine means. Workers tend machines designed and paced by engineering standards. Actual control of the work flow is separated from supervision of the work force. In such organizations, the ideas of scientific management and mechanistic design are applicable.

This explanation of the relationship between technology and structure rests on traditional views of manufacturing technology. Recent advances in computers and robots have initiated a new understanding of manufacturing possibilities and of organization structures compatible with those advances.

Flexible Manufacturing Technology

FLEXIBLE MANUFACTURING TECHNOLOGY (FTM)

Modern manufacturing methods that combine computer and robotry to achieve high levels of production as well as high levels of flexibility.

Flexible manufacturing technology (FMT) enables management to use the computer to integrate marketing, design, manufacturing, inventory control, materials handling, and quality control into a continuous operation.[35] FMT increases manufacturing flexibility through the ability (1) to transfer information, material, and other resources throughout the organization, (2) to design products quickly in consultation with customers, manufacturing personnel, and marketing personnel, and (3) to set up machines to manufacture only the needed quantity of parts and components, thus reducing the need for inventory.

With flexible manufacturing technology, organizations can combine the positive attributes of job order, mass production, and process technology in ways not previously contemplated. Its major effect on organization structure is to challenge the case for mechanistic designs in mass production firms. FMT in mass production settings creates managerial problems similar to those in job order and process manufacturing settings. The principal managerial challenge is to manage interdependent activities that must respond to rapidly changing conditions. But the possibilities are unlimited, including the ability to be more responsive to changing customer needs and preferences.[36] Organic structures begin to emerge as the preferred structure in mass producers who move into the flexible manufacturing era, as described in the Close-Up on Ford Motor Co.

---

[35]Patricia L. Nemetz and Louis W. Fry, "Flexible Manufacturing Organizations: Implications for Strategy Formulation and Organization Design," *Academy of Management Review,* October 1988, pp. 627–38.

[36]Richard B. Chase and David A. Garvin, "The Service Factory," *Harvard Business Review,* July–August 1989, pp. 61–69.

TURNAROUND AT FORD MOTOR CO.

Ford Motor Co. is back in business after losing more than $3 billion during the first three years of the 1980s. It is back because people are buying Ford automobiles manufactured in plants organized in vastly different ways from those of earlier Ford plants. The biggest changes have occurred in the jobs that Ford workers perform: the jobs are bigger, with greater range and depth. Nonmanagerial personnel are performing traditional managerial tasks such as work scheduling and controlling quality.

Even as nonmanagerial jobs changed, so did managerial jobs. Ford acknowledged the importance of training managers to perform in an organization structure very different from the one in which they had learned to manage. The more organic structure required managers to accept change as an everyday fact of life, made possible by the new technology of car making.

One of Ford's applications of the flexible manufacturing technology is taking place in Romeo, Michigan. This plant is designed to be able to build engines in several different configurations in response to changes in demand and competition. The technology has characteristics of mass production (efficiency), job order (customization), and process (continuous flowthrough). The adoption of FMT, with its required changes to a more organic organization, is one reason people are buying Fords again.

Source: Beverly Geber, "The Resurrection of Ford," *Training*, April 1989, pp. 23–30; "A Dozen Motor Factories under One Roof," *Business Week*, November 20, 1989, pp. 90, 94.

The paradox of FMT and other revolutionary developments in manufacturing is that they enable different parts of the company to become more independent of one another even as they become more dependent.[37] The effect of this paradox is to emphasize the importance of integrating the activities of these interdependent yet independent units. The integration concept is a key element in discussions of the relationship between environmental uncertainty and organization design.

ENVIRONMENT AND ORGANIZATION DESIGN

The relationship between technology and effective organization design is firmly established. Yet, as we have seen, interpreting this relationship requires that the environment of the organizations be taken into account. Thus, it may be argued, a more basic explanation for differences in organization is differences in the environment. This line of reasoning has been pursued by a number of researchers, and we will review a classic study of environment and organization design in this section.

---

[37]Robert H. Hayes and Ramchandran Jaikumar, "Manufacturing Crises: New Technologies, Obsolete Organizations," *Harvard Business Review*, September–October 1988, pp. 77–85.

Lawrence and Lorsch's Classic Study

Paul Lawrence and Jay Lorsch based their findings on detailed case studies of firms in the plastics, food, and container industries.[38] In an initial exploratory study of six firms operating in the plastics industry, Lawrence and Lorsch attempted to answer the following questions:[39]

1. How do environmental demands facing various organizations differ, and how do environmental demands relate to the design of effective organizations?

2. Is it true that organizations in certain, stable environments make more exclusive use of centralized authority to make key decisions? If so, why? Is it because fewer key decisions are required or because in certain, stable environments these decisions can be made more effectively at higher organization levels or by fewer people?

3. Is the same degree of specialization and differences in orientation among individuals and groups found in organizations in different industrial environments?

4. If greater specialization and differences among individuals and groups are found in different industries, does this influence the problems of coordinating the organizations' parts? Does it influence the organizations' means of achieving integration?

To arrive at answers to these four questions, Lawrence and Lorsch undertook their research of structure in the three industries. In the course of their investigation, they coined three terms that have since become widely used in the theory and practice of organization design: *differentiation, integration,* and *environment.*

Differentiation. The "state of segmentation of the organizational system into subsystems, each of which tends to develop particular attributes in relation to the requirements posed by its relevant external environment" is termed **differentiation.**[40] This concept refers in part to the idea of specialization of labor, specifically to the degree of departmentalization. But it is broader and also includes the behavioral attributes of employees in these subsystems, or departments. The researchers were interested in three behavioral attributes:

DIFFERENTIATION
Degree of differences among units of organization due to individual and structural differences.

1. They believed that the employees of some departments would be more or less task- or person-oriented than employees in other departments. This belief reflects the ideas found in Fiedler's situational theory of leadership.

2. They proposed that the employees of some departments would have longer or shorter time horizons than members of other departments and that these differences could be explained by different environmental attributes, specifically the length of time between action and the feedback of results.

---

[38]Paul R. Lawrence and Jay W. Lorsch, "Differentiation and Integration in Complex Organizations," *Administrative Science Quarterly,* June 1967, pp. 1–47; Jay W. Lorsch, *Product Innovation and Organization* (New York: Macmillan, 1965); Paul R. Lawrence and Jay W. Lorsch, *Organization and Environment* (Homewood, Ill.: Richard D. Irwin, 1969); Paul R. Lawrence, "The Harvard Organization and Environment Research Program," in *Perspectives on Organization Design and Behavior,* ed. Andrew H. Van de Ven and William Joyce (New York: Wiley Interscience, 1981), pp. 311–37.

[39]Lawrence and Lorsch, *Organization and Environment,* p. 16.

[40]Lawrence and Lorsch, "Differentiation and Integration," pp. 3–4.

3. They expected to find some employees more concerned with the goals of their department than with the goals of the total organization.

The organization of each department in the six firms was classified along a continuum from mechanistic to organic. The employees in mechanistically organized departments were expected to be more oriented toward tasks and have shorter time horizons than employees in organic departments.

Integration. The "process of achieving unity of effort among the various subsystems in the accomplishment of the organization's task" is defined as **integration,** and it can be achieved in a variety of ways.[41] Proponents of the mechanistic model argue for integration through the creation of *rules and procedures* to govern the behavior of the subsystem members. But this method of integration can be effective only in relatively stable and predictable situations.[42] Rules and procedures lose their effectiveness as the environment becomes more unstable; thus, integration by *plans* takes on greater significance. As we approach the highly unstable environment, integration is achieved by *mutual adjustment.* Mutual adjustment requires a great deal of communication through open channels throughout the organization, a characteristic of organically designed organizations. In terms of the Lawrence and Lorsch research, the type of integrative devices managers use should be related to the degree of differentiation. Highly differentiated organizations would use mutual adjustment as a means of achieving integration. The greater the differentiation, the greater is the importance and difficulty of achieving integration.

INTEGRATION
Achieving unity of effort among different organizational units and individuals through rules, planning, and leadership.

Environment. The independent variable, *environment,* was conceptualized from the perspective of the organization members as they looked outward. Consequently, the researchers assumed that a basic reason for differentiating into subsystems is to deal more effectively with subenvironments. Lawrence and Lorsch identified three main subenvironments: market, technical-economic, and scientific. These three subenvironments correspond to the sales, production, and research and development functions within organizations. Most organizations create separate departments for these functions. The departments represent parts of the total organization, or (in researchers' terms) "subsystems of the total system."

The researchers believed that the degree of differentiation within each subsystem would vary, depending upon specific attributes of the relevant subenvironment. Specifically, the subenvironment could vary along three dimensions: (1) the rate of change of conditions over time, (2) the certainty of information about conditions at any particular time, and (3) the time span of feedback on the results of employee decisions.[43]

Figure 15–1 illustrates the idea that an organization consists of separate parts, usually departments, that must deal with different aspects of the total environment. Lawrence and Lorsch identify the organizational parts, or

---

[41]Ibid., p. 4.

[42]James D. Thompson, *Organizations in Action* (New York: McGraw-Hill, 1967), p. 56.

[43]Lawrence and Lorsch, "Differentiation and Integration," pp. 7–8.

FIGURE 15—1

Conceptualization of the
Lawrence and Lorsch Model

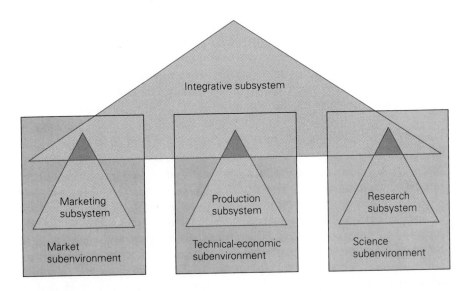

subsystems, as marketing, production, and research. They identify the environmental parts, or subenvironments, as market, technical-economic, and science. The subsystems must be organized in such a way as to deal effectively with their relevant subenvironments. The greater the differences among the three subenvironments in terms of rate of change, certainty of information, and time span of feedback, the greater will be the differences among the three subsystems in terms of organization structure and behavioral attributes. The greater these differences—that is, the more differentiated the three subsystems are—the more important is the task of integrating the three subsystems.

Other Evidence

Other studies have established the relationship of environmental factors to organizational structure.[44] But inconsistencies and contradictions appear in these studies. The causes are similar to those associated with studies of technology and organizational structure. For example, studies may have used qualitative measures of environmental uncertainty, quantitative measures, questionnaire responses as completed by participants in the organization, or objective indexes of uncertainty.[45] Studies reporting environmental effects

---

[44]Lawrence G. Hrebiniak and Charles C. Snow, "Industry Differences in Environmental Uncertainty and Organizational Characteristics Related to Uncertainty," *Academy of Management Journal,* December 1980, pp. 750–59; Howard L. Smith, Stephen M. Shortell, and Borje O. Saxberg, "An Empirical Test of the Configurational Theory of Organizations," *Human Relations,* August 1979, pp. 667–88.

[45]H. Kirk Downey and R. Duane Ireland, "Quantitative versus Qualitative Environmental Assessment in Organizational Studies," *Administrative Science Quarterly,* December 1979, pp. 630–37; Richard Blackburn and Larry L. Cummings, "Cognitions of Work-Unit Structure," *Academy of Management Journal,* December 1982, pp. 836–54; Masoud Yasai-Ardekani, "Structural Adaptation to Environments," *Academy of Management Review,* January 1986, pp. 9–21.

must be evaluated critically before any final conclusions are drawn. Considering in detail the precise effects of environmental uncertainty on the organization is also necessary. One approach is to evaluate the effects of uncertainty on the organization's information processing requirements.

Understanding the Environmental Uncertainty–Structure Relationship

The differentiation-integration approach is based on the fundamental viewpoint that organizations must be designed to cope with environmental demands. Further, different organization designs can and often do exist within a single large organization. A manufacturing firm may find it necessary to design its production department quite differently from its research and development department. In some instances, in mass production for example, the production department must be designed according to the mechanistic model, but the research and development department may be designed according to the organic model. Design differences result from the differences in the degree of environmental uncertainty each department confronts. In the relatively certain production environment, there is no need to stress adaptability; the department can be designed to achieve high levels of efficiency. The research and development environment, however, is likely to be highly uncertain, with considerable need for flexibility to cope with unforeseen changes.

The process of departmentalizing creates the necessity for integrating the activities of the departments. The integration of separate yet interdependent activities is a familiar problem in the management of organizations. Mechanistic design proponents believe that integration can be achieved through the creation of rules, procedures, plans, and a hierarchical chain of command that places managers in the position of integrators. The solutions of organic design proponents are different. They believe that committees, task groups, cross-functional teams, integrators, and group-centered decision making are better approaches. In fact, according to Lawrence and Lorsch, either approach may be appropriate, depending on the situation.

Environmental Uncertainty and Organization Design in the Service Sector

The growing importance of the service sector of the economy has stimulated much interest in understanding how to design service firms for optimal performance.[46] An increasingly promising approach uses the concept of environmental uncertainty to identify the optimal design. One variation of this approach focuses on the relative uncertainty of two customer attributes: diversity of customer demand for services and variation in customer disposition to participate in the delivery of the service.[47] According to this perspec-

---

[46]James L. Heskett, *Managing in the Service Economy* (Boston, Mass.: Harvard Business School Press, 1986).

[47]Rikard Larsson and David E. Bowen, "Organization and Customer: Managing Design and Coordination of Services," *Academy of Management Review,* April 1989, pp. 213–33.

tive, whether a service firm organizes in relatively mechanistic or organic forms depends on the degree of uncertainty in these two attributes.

Service organizations whose customers demand relatively homogeneous services and have little disposition to participate in the delivery of those services can be managed according to mechanistic principles. Examples of such organizations include banks, insurance firms, and airlines. Mechanistic designs provide appropriate channels for integrating the activities of relatively undifferentiated functions.

At the other extreme are those types of service firms whose customers demand a diverse array of services and are predisposed to participating in the service delivery. Such organizations include providers of medical care, legal advice, and higher education. These organizations are better able to integrate the activities of highly differentiated jobs through organic organization designs. The organic structure works better because it is better able to provide the flexibility required to handle the highly uncertain environment characteristic of customers demanding quite different services and desiring to play an active part in their delivery.

Between these two extremes lie intermediate levels of uncertainty. The appropriate organization designs would be less mechanistic and organic than the extremes and tailored to deal with different degrees of services demanded and participation expected.

The idea that organization structure should give customers access to the firm's services can be applied at the subunit level as well as at the overall organizational level. For instance, banks are examples of organizations whose customers demand relatively homogeneous services and who are not disposed to participate in the delivery of those services. At the level of the overall organization, the "typical" customer of a bank may well be so characterized. Within the bank, however, different units' customers may require more or less diverse services and desire more or less participation in the delivery of those services. The trust unit of a bank, which serves very affluent customers with diverse financial and personal needs, is quite different from the installment loan unit, which serves customers desiring short-term credit only and whose sole participation in the delivery of the service is to provide credit-scoring information. The implication for organizational design is that the trust division should reflect relatively more organic characteristics than the installment loan unit.

SYNTHESIZING RELATIONSHIPS: ADAPTIVE DESIGN STRATEGIES

The relationships among environment, technology, and organization structure can be synthesized. The key concept is *information,* and the key idea is that organizations must effectively receive, process, and act on information to achieve performance.[48] Information flows into the organization from the subenvironments. It enables the organization to respond to market, techno-

---

[48]The development of theory relating information processing and organization structure has been discussed in various sources. The more recent and most publicized sources are Jay Galbraith, *Designing Complex Organizations* (Reading, Mass.: Addison-Wesley Publishing, 1973); Jay Galbraith, *Organization Design* (Reading, Mass.: Addison-Wesley Publishing, 1977).

logical, and resource changes. The more rapid the changes, the greater the necessity for and availability of information.[49]

To integrate the behavior of subunits, organizations in relatively certain and unchanging environments rely on hierarchical control, rules and procedures, and planning. These integrative methods, fundamental features of classical organization designs, are effective as long as the environment remains stable and predictable. Information processing requirements are relatively modest in such environments. For example, firms manufacturing and selling paper containers can plan production schedules with relative assurance that sudden shifts in demand, resource supply, or technology will not disrupt the schedule. Information requirements consist almost solely of projections from historical sales, cost, and engineering data.

Organizations in dynamic and complex environments, however, cannot rely upon traditional information processing and control techniques. Changes in market demand, resource supplies, and technology disrupt plans and require adjustments *during* task performance. On-the-spot adjustments to production schedules and task performance disrupt the organization. Coordination becomes more difficult because it is impossible to preplan operations and to devise rules and procedures. To acquire information that reflects environmental changes is imperative; "the greater the uncertainty, the greater the amount of information that must be processed among decision makers during task completion in order to achieve a given level of performance."[50]

From a managerial perspective, the effect of environmental uncertainty and increased flow of information is to overload the organization with exceptional cases. As a greater number of nonroutine, consequential events occur in the organization's environment, managers are more and more drawn into day-to-day operating matters. Problems develop as plans become obsolete and as the various functions' coordinative efforts break down. Some organizations are designed from their inception to deal with information processing demands; most, however, must confront the problem some time after their creation. For organizations that find their present design incapable of dealing with the demands of changing environments, the problem becomes one of selecting an appropriate adaptive strategy. The two general approaches are (1) to reduce the need for information and (2) to increase the capacity to process information.

Strategies to Reduce the Need for Information

Managers can reduce the need for information by reducing (1) the number of exceptions that occur and (2) the number of factors to be considered when exceptions do occur. These two ends can be achieved by creating slack resources or by creating self-contained units.[51]

---

[49]Jay R. Galbraith, "Designing the Innovative Organization," *Organizational Dynamics,* Winter 1982, pp. 5–25; William G. Egelhoff, "Strategy and Structure in Multinational Corporations: An Information Processing Approach," *Administrative Science Quarterly,* September 1982, pp. 453–58; Jay R. Galbraith and Robert K. Kazanjian, "Organizing to Implement Strategies of Diversity and Globalization: The Role of Matrix Design," *Human Resource Management,* Spring 1986, pp. 37–54.

[50]Jay Galbraith, "Organization Design: An Information Processing View," *Interfaces,* May 1974, p. 28.

[51]William F. Joyce, "Matrix Organization: A Social Experiment," *Academy of Management Journal,* September 1986, pp. 536–61.

Creating slack resources.   Slack resources include stockpiles of materials, manpower, and other capabilities that enable the organization to respond to uncertainty. Other examples include lengthened planning periods, production schedules, and lead times; these limit the number of exceptional cases by increasing the time span within which a response is necessary. For example, job order manufacturers can intentionally overestimate the time required to complete a customized product, thus allowing time to deal with any difficulties that arise.

An additional effect of slack resources is to reduce the interdependence between units within the organization. If inventory is available to meet unexpected sales, no interaction is required between production and sales units. If inventory is not available, production and sales units must necessarily interact and coordinate their activities. Obviously, creating slack resources has cost implications. Excess inventory (safety stocks, buffer stocks) represents money that can be invested; thus, carrying costs will increase. Extended planning, budgeting, and scheduling time horizons also lower expected performance. Whether the strategy of creating slack resources is optimal depends upon careful balancing of the relevant costs and benefits.

Creating self-contained units.   Creating slack resources can be done within the present organization structure. Creating self-contained units involves a complete reorganization, from a functional base toward product, customer, or territorial bases. Each unit is provided its own resources—manufacturing, personnel, marketing, and engineering. Ordinarily, accounting, finance, and legal functions would remain centralized and be made available to the new units on an as-needed basis. Reorganization around products, customers, or territories enables the organization to achieve desired flexibility and adaptability but at the cost of lost efficiency.

In terms of information processing, self-contained units inherently face less environmental uncertainty than the larger whole. They deal with a complementary grouping of products or customers and do not have to coordinate activities with other units. With reduced coordination requirements, the units have less information to process. As an additional benefit, self-contained units can be the bases for product innovation in environments that demand such innovation, as noted in the Close-Up on innovation at IBM.

Strategies to Increase Information Processing Capacity

Instead of reducing the amount of information needed, managers may choose to increase the organization's capacity to process it. Two strategies accomplish this objective: (1) invest in vertical information systems and (2) create lateral relationships.

Investing in vertical information systems.   Increased environmental uncertainty results in information overload. Managers are simply inundated with information requiring action of some kind. A strategic response to the problem is to invest in information processing systems, which may include computers, clerks, and executive assistants. These systems process information more quickly and format the data in more efficient language.

HOW 3M INNOVATES

How does an old-line manufacturing firm whose base products are sandpaper and tape become and remain a recognized leader in product innovation? 3M's success has inspired others to emulate its management practices and organizational structure. Although the firm uses many strategies to stimulate and reward innovative behavior throughout the firm, a cornerstone is its policy of keeping divisions small, with average sales of about $200 million each. The norm within these small divisions is to share information and resources. Informal information-sharing and brainstorming sessions can crop up at any time, any place within the divisions, and they often include customers.

Innovation occurs when individuals have information and encouragement. 3M provides both ingredients. Employees can spend up to 15 percent of their time on ideas that hold promise for becoming new products. And the firm has the policy that each division's sales revenue must be generated by products developed within the past five years. Other innovative firms such as Rubbermaid, Hewlett-Packard, and General Electric have similar policies and practices.

At the core of 3M's success as an innovator however, is its practice of maintaining relatively small, self-contained units that can deal effectively with information relevant to their success.

Source: ''Masters of Innovation,'' *Business Week*, April 10, 1989, pp. 58–63.

Creating lateral relationships.   As the need for increased coordination among functional units intensifies, decisions must be made that cross authority lines. Introducing lateral relationships facilitates joint decision making among the functional units, without the loss of efficiency that accompanies specialization. The cost of creating lateral relationships is an increase in the number of managers who deal with the environment. Managers in **boundary-spanning roles** have particularly demanding jobs; the success of this strategy depends on how effectively the role occupants perform.

Employees in boundary-spanning roles perform two functions: (1) to gather information and (2) to represent the organization.[52] Sales personnel, purchasing agents, lobbyists, public relations personnel, market researchers, and personnel recruiters are a few of the job titles that gather information and represent the organization. Roles of this type exist at the interface between the organization and its environment; they can be termed *external boundary roles*.

Internal boundary roles, in contrast, exist within the organization at the interface between subunits, such as functional and product departments. Product managers, expediters, integrators, and liaisons exemplify roles that exist between subunits. As we have seen, organizations cope with environ-

BOUNDARY-SPANNING
ROLES

Jobs that require employees to relate to people in different units, both inside and outside organization.

---

[52]Howard Aldrich and Diane Herker, "Boundary Spanning Roles and Organization Structure," *Academy of Management Review*, April 1977, p. 218; Michael L. Tushman and Thomas J. Scanlan, "Boundary Spanning Individuals: Their Role in Information Transfer and Antecedents," *Academy of Management Journal*, June 1981, pp. 289–305.

mental uncertainty and increase information by establishing these types of roles. Their functions are similar to those of external boundary roles, except that they include gathering information that facilitates joint decision making.

The demands on those who perform boundary-spanning positions are qualitatively different from demands on others in the organization. Their uniqueness results from the fact that the role occupant must deal with other conflicting expectations but does not have the authority to settle the disagreement.[53]

Role conflict.   Boundary spanners are often caught between people who expect different, often incompatible behaviors. Product managers must balance the interests of marketing personnel who want high-quality products and production personnel who desire manufacturing efficiency; having authority over neither group, they must balance these interests and reach effective decisions through informal influence based on expertise. The company negotiator must deal simultaneously with the demands of fellow managers and union spokespersons.

Each segment of the environment or the organization has its own set of goals, beliefs, and values. To the extent that there are great differences among these sets, the boundary-spanning role is made more difficult. People with high tolerance for ambiguity and the desire for relative freedom from close supervision—that is, autonomy—would have the greatest chance of performing effectively because they would be able to cope with the conflict.

Lack of authority.   Boundary spanners do not have position power; that is, authority is not delegated to them. They must achieve their performance levels through other means. An industrial salesperson, for example, can attempt to influence customer demand by becoming extremely knowledgeable about customers' technical and production methods. By doing so, he or she is able to influence the customers' decisions with respect to purchasing the organization's products.

Agents of change.   Some boundary-spanning positions are created to facilitate change and innovation. For example, key roles in research and development labs are those that link the lab to the various informational sources in the environment.[54] We have already noted the manner in which organizations respond to the necessity for new product innovation by creating product task forces, teams, and managers. Indeed, the need to innovate arises coincidentally with environmental and technological pressures and demands. Yet, the fact that boundary spanners are advocates for change places them in conflict with organizational subunits that desire stable operations, such as manufacturing, data processing, and personnel departments.

The adaptation of organizations to increasing uncertainty combined with the need for information requires some changes in organization structure. Managers can choose to cope with information processing demands either by

---

[53]Marc J. Dollinger, "Environmental Boundary Spanning and Information Processing Effects on Organizational Performance," *Academy of Management Journal*, June 1984, pp. 351–68.

[54]Michael L. Tushman, "Special Boundary Roles in the Innovation Process," *Administrative Science Quarterly*, December 1977, pp. 587–605.

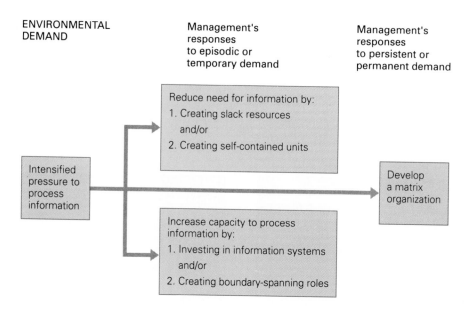

ENVIRONMENTAL
DEMAND

Management's
responses
to episodic or
temporary demand

Management's
responses
to persistent or
permanent demand

FIGURE 15—2

Management's Responses to
Environmental Demands for
Increased Information
Processing

Intensified
pressure to
process
information

Reduce need for information by:
1. Creating slack resources
   and/or
2. Creating self-contained units

Increase capacity to process
information by:
1. Investing in information systems
   and/or
2. Creating boundary-spanning roles

Develop
a matrix
organization

reducing the need or by increasing the organization's capability to process it. These adaptations are effective when the environmental pressure is episodic or temporary. Persistent and permanent environmental pressure calls for more complete solutions. In particular, management will begin to develop a matrix organization. As we indicated in Chapter 13, matrix organizations are effective structures for adapting to and coping with environmental uncertainty, regardless of organizational type[55] or national boundaries.[56] Figure 15–2 depicts the relationships among environmental uncertainty, information requirements, and managerial responses.

AN INTEGRATIVE FRAMEWORK FOR ORGANIZATION DESIGN

Many complex factors and variables go into the design of an optimal organization structure. The most important of these considerations are shown in Figure 15–3. The material presented in Chapters 13, 14, and 15 reflects the current state of knowledge regarding the issues of organization design. As we have seen, the *key design decisions* are division of labor, departmentalization, spans of control, and delegation of authority. These decisions reflect *environmental* and *managerial* interactions of these factors, and the key decisions are complex; managers do not have the luxury of designing a one best way structure. Instead, the optimal design depends on the situation as determined

---

[55]Lawton R. Burns, "Matrix Management in Hospitals: Testing Theories of Matrix Structure and Development," *Administrative Science Quarterly,* September 1989, pp. 349–68; William H. Straub and Richard E. Latchaw, "The Matrix Organization," *Administrative Radiology,* July 1988, pp. 22–26.

[56]David J. Lemak and Jeffrey S. Bracker, "A Strategic Contingency Model of Multinational Corporate Structure," *Strategic Management Journal,* September–October 1988, pp. 521–26.

FIGURE 15–3

Integrative Framework for Organizational Design

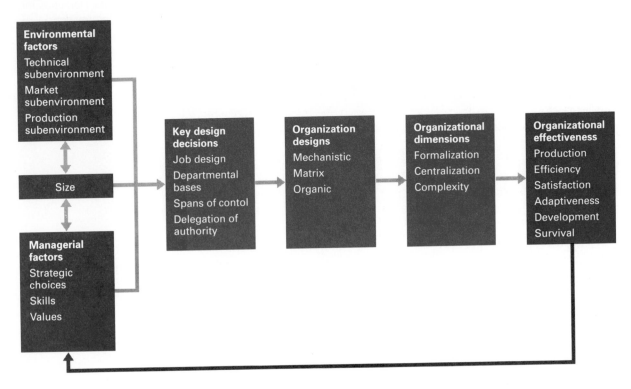

by the interaction of size, environmental, and managerial factors. Matching the appropriate structure to these factors is the essence of *contingency design* theory and practice.

The overall structure of tasks and authority that results from the key decisions is a specific *organization design*. Alternative designs range along a continuum, with mechanistic design at one extreme and organic at the other. The matrix design, at the midpoint, represents a balance between the two extremes.

Organization structures differ on many dimensions, the more important being shown in Figure 15–3. In general, mechanistic organizations are more formalized, centralized, and specialized than organic organizations. They are also less differentiated and achieve integration through hierarchy, rules and procedures, and planning. Organic organizations, however, must achieve integration through more complex methods, including boundary-spanning roles, task groups, committees, and other forms of mutual adjustment. Regardless of the specific configuration of organization dimensions and integration strategies, the overriding purpose of organization design is to channel behavior of individuals and groups into patterns that contribute to effective organization performance.

Managerial decision making plays a key role in organizational design.[57] In fact, much of what has been stated in this section can be summarized in the idea

---

[57]James W. Frederickson, "The Strategic Decision Process and Organizational Structure," *Academy of Management Review,* April 1986, pp. 280–97.

that structure follows strategy[58] and that maximum performance is achieved when there is congruence between strategy and structure.[59] Managerial strategy involves the choice of what products and services the organization will supply to which customers and markets. Thus, managers who decide to supply a single product to a specific set of customers can be expected to design a far simpler organizational structure than a manager of a highly diversified company serving multiple markets with multiple products and services.[60] Moreover, the strategic choice affects not only organizational design but also job design[61] and, apparently, leadership behavior[62] as well.

Organizational design remains an important issue in the management of organizational behavior and effectiveness. In the 1990s, organizational design will become even more important. Strategies that have been successful in the past will prove ineffectual in the face of the new international competition, technological change, and the shifting patterns of industrial development.[63] And as organizations experiment with new strategies, they will be forced to experiment with new organizational designs. These designs will bear closer resemblance to organic designs than to mechanistic designs.[64]

---

[58]Alfred Chandler, *Strategy and Structure* (Cambridge, Mass.: MIT Press, 1962).

[59]A number of studies have analyzed this relationship, including Richard Rumelt, *Strategy, Structure and Economic Performance* (Boston, Mass.: Division of Research, Harvard Business School, 1974); more recently, Peter Grinyer, Shawki Al-Bazzaz, and Masoud Yasai-Ardekani, "Strategy, Structure, the Environment, and Financial Performance in 48 United Kingdom Companies," *Academy of Management Journal,* June 1980, pp. 193–220.

[60]Jay R. Galbraith and Daniel A. Nathanson, *Strategy Implementation: The Role of Structure and Process* (St. Paul, Minn.: West Publishing, 1978).

[61]Jon L. Pierce, Randall B. Dunham, and Richard S. Blackburn, "Social System Structure, Job Design, and Growth Need Strength: A Test of the Congruence Model," *Academy of Management Journal,* June 1979, pp. 223–40.

[62]Ricky W. Griffin, "Relationships among Individual, Task Design, and Leader Behavior Variables," *Academy of Management Journal,* December 1980, pp. 665–83.

[63]Raymond E. Miles, "Adapting to Technology and Competition: A New Industrial Relations System for the 21st Century," *California Management Review,* Winter 1989, pp. 9–28.

[64]Raymond E. Miles and Charles C. Snow, "Organizations: New Concepts for New Forms," *California Management Review,* Spring 1986, pp. 62–73; Tom Peters, "Restoring American Competitiveness: Looking for New Models of Organizations," *Academy of Management Executive,* May 1988, pp. 103–9.

SUMMARY OF KEY POINTS

— Task and authority relationships among jobs and groups of jobs must be defined and structured according to rational bases. Practitioners and theorists have recommended two specific yet contradictory theories for designing organizational structures.

— One theory, termed *mechanistic design,* is based on the assumption that the more effective organizational structure is characterized by highly specialized jobs, homogeneous departments, narrow spans of control, and relatively centralized authority. The bases for these

assumptions are to be found in the historical circumstances within which this theory developed. It was a time of fairly rapid industrialization that encouraged public and private organizations to emphasize the production and efficiency criteria of effectiveness. To achieve these ends, classical design theory proposes a single best way to structure an organization.

— Beginning with the human relations era of the 1930s and sustained by the growing interest of behavioral scientists in the study of management and organization, an alternative to mechanistic design theory developed. This alternative theory, termed *organic design,* proposes that the more effective organization has relatively despecialized jobs, heterogeneous departments, wide spans of control, and decentralized authority. Such organizational structures, it is argued, achieve not only high levels of production and efficiency but also satisfaction, adaptiveness, and development.

— The design of an effective organizational structure cannot be guided by a "one best way" theory. Rather, the manager must adopt the point of view that either the mechanistic or the organic design is more effective for the total organization or for subunits within its organization.

— The manager must identify and describe the relevant subenvironments of the organization. These subenvironments determine the relationships within units, among units, and between units and their subenvironments.

— The manager must evaluate each subenvironment in terms of its rate of change, relative certainty, and time

span of feedback. These conditions are the key variables for determining the formal structure of tasks and authority.

— Each subunit structure is designed along the mechanistic-organic continuum in a manner consistent with the state of environmental conditions. Specifically, slower rates of change, greater certainty, and shorter time spans of feedback are compatible with the mechanistic design; the converse is true for the organic design.

— Concurrent with the design of subunit structures is the design of integrative techniques. The appropriate techniques, whether rules, plans, or mutual adjustment, depend on the degree of subunit differentiation. The greater the differentiation, the greater is the need for mutual adjustment techniques. The smaller the differentiation, the greater is the need for rules and plans.

— Information processing is required for all organizations, given their size, technology, and environments. Thus, information processing, as a concept, summarizes the contingency theory of organizational design.

DISCUSSION AND REVIEW QUESTIONS

1. Explain the rationale for the argument that there is one best way to design an organization. What are the basic flaws in the arguments of those who propose that there is one best way to organize?

2. What is the basis for the argument that mechanistic organization is the one best way to organize? Do you agree? What is the basis for the argument that organic organization is the one best way to organize? Do you agree?

3. Which would be easier: to change an organization from a mechanistic to organic or from organic to mechanistic? Explain.

4. Explain why organizations that previously competed in regulated industries, such as banking and transportation, have found it necessary to change their organization structures since the deregulation of these industries.

5. Do you believe that any real-world organizations can be termed organic? Do you believe any "ideal" type of bureaucracies exists? If not, of what use are these theories?

6. Use the characteristics of mechanistic and organic organization to describe two different organizations

you know about. After you have determined the organizational design differences, see if you can relate the differences to technological and environmental differences.

7. Think of the classic market, technical-economic, and scientific subenvironments of an organization. What are the counterparts in a university? A hospital? A professional football team?

8. What criteria of effectiveness were used in the Woodward research? Compare these with the criteria used in the Lawrence and Lorsch research.

9. Discuss the manner in which technology and environmental certainty interact to determine the most effective organization.

10. Based upon whatever information is at your disposal, rank from high to low the environmental uncertainty of a college of arts and sciences, a college of engineering, a college of business, and a college of education. What does your ranking suggest about the integration techniques that would be appropriate in each college?

ADDITIONAL REFERENCES

Ackoff, R. L. "The Circular Organization: An Update." *Academy of Management Executive,* 1989, pp. 11–16.

Aldrich, H.; W. McKelvey; and D. Ulrich. "Design Strategy from the Population Perspective." *Journal of Management,* 1984, pp. 67–86.

Barley, S. R. "Technology as an Occasion for Structuring: Evidence from Observations of CT Scanners and the Social Order of Radiology Departments." *Administrative Science Quarterly,* 1986, pp. 78–108.

Bartlett, C. A., and S. Ghoshal. "Organizing for Worldwide Effectiveness: The Transnational Solution." *California Management Review,* 1988, pp. 54–74.

Birnbaum, P. H., and Gilbert Y. Y. Wong. "Organizational Structure of Multinational Banks in Hong Kong from a Culture-Free Perspective." *Administrative Science Quarterly,* 1985, pp. 262–77.

Bozeman, B., and M. Crow. "Organization Theory and State Government Structures: Are There Lessons Worth Learning?" *State Government,* 1986, pp. 144–51.

Chase R. B., and D. A. Tansik. "The Customer Contact Model for Organization Design." *Management Science,* 1983, pp. 1037–50.

Collins, P. D., and F. Hull. "Technology and Span of Control: Woodward Revisited." *Journal of Management Studies,* 1986, pp. 143–65.

Daniels, J. D.; R. A. Pitts; and M. J. Tretter. "Strategy and Structure of U.S. Multinationals: An Exploratory Study." *Academy of Management Journal,* 1984, pp. 292–307.

Dess, G. G., and D. W. Beard. "Dimensions of Organizational Task Environments." *Administrative Science Quarterly,* 1984, pp. 52–73.

Donaldson, L. "Organization Design and the Life-Cycle of Products." *Journal of Management Studies,* 1985, pp. 25–37.

Driver, M. J. "A Human Resource Data–Based Approach to Organizational Design." *Human Resource Planning,* 1983, pp. 169–82.

Egelhoff, W. G. *Organizing the Multinational Enterprise.* Cambridge, Mass.: Ballinger, 1988.

Frombrun, C. J., and S. Wally. "Structuring Small Firms for Rapid Growth." *Journal of Business Venturing,* 1989, pp. 107–22.

Geeraerts, G. "The Effect of Ownership on the Organizational Structure in Small Firms." *Administrative Science Quarterly,* 1984, pp. 232–37.

Gillen, D. J., and S. J. Carroll. "Relationship of Managerial Ability to Unit Effectiveness in More Organic versus More Mechanistic Departments." *Journal of Management Studies,* 1985, pp. 668–76.

Hanna, D. P. *Designing Organizations for High Performance.* Reading, Mass.: Addison-Wesley Publishing, 1988.

Hartman, E. *Conceptual Foundations of Organization Theory.* Cambridge, Mass.: Ballinger, 1988.

Jelinek, M., and M. Burstein. "The Production Administrative Structure." *Academy of Management Review,* 1982, pp. 242–51.

Kralewski, J. E.; L. Pitt; and D. Shatin. "Structural Characteristics of Medical Group Practices." *Administrative Science Quarterly,* 1985, pp. 34–45.

Mansfield, R. *Company Strategy and Organizational Design.* New York: St. Martin's Press, 1986.

Mills, P. K., and D. J. Moberg. "Perspectives on the Technology of Service Organizations." *Academy of Management Review,* 1982, pp. 467–78.

Mintzberg, Henry. "Organization Design: Fashion or Fit?" *Harvard Business Review,* 1981, pp. 103–16.

Nosek, J. T. "Organization Design Strategies to Enhance Information Resource Management." *Information and Management,* 1989, pp. 81–92.

Pasmore, W. A. *Design Effective Organizations.* New York: John Wiley & Sons, 1988.

Pearce, J. A., II, and F. R. David. "A Social Network Approach to Organization Design—Performance." *Academy of Management Review,* 1983, pp. 436–44.

Routamaa, V. "Organizational Structuring: An Empirical Analysis of the Relationships and Dimensions of Structures in Certain Finnish Companies." *Journal of Management Studies,* 1985, pp. 498–522.

Stebbins, M. W., and A. B. Shani. "Organization Design: Beyond the 'Mafia' Model." *Organizational Dynamics,* 1989, pp. 18–30.

Voge, L. H., and I. Patterson. "Strategy and Structure: A Case Study of the Implications of Strategic Planning for Organizational Structure and Managerial Practice." *Administration in Social Work,* 1986, pp. 53–66.

DEFINING THE ROLE OF A LIAISON OFFICER

Recently, the governor of a southeastern state created a Department for Human Resources. It combined many formerly distinct state agencies that carried out health and welfare programs. The department's organization chart is shown in Exhibit 1. The functions of each of the bureaus were described in the governor's press release:

> *The Bureau for Social Insurance* will operate all income maintenance and all income supplementation programs of the Department for Human Resources. That is, it will issue financial support to the poor, unemployed, and needy, and it will issue food stamps and pay for medical assistance.
> *The Bureau for Social Services* will provide child welfare services, foster care, adoptions, family services, and all other general counseling in support of families and individuals who require assistance for successful and adequate human development.
> *The Bureau for Health Services* will operate all departmental programs that provide health service, including all physical and mental health programs. This bureau will take over the functions of the Department of Health, the Department of Mental Health, and the Commission for Handicapped Children.
> *The Bureau for Manpower Services* will operate all labor force development and job placement programs of the department, including all job recruitment and business liaison functions, job training, worker readiness functions, and job counseling and placement.
> *The Bureau for Administration and Operations* will consolidate numerous support services, such as preaudits, accounting, data processing, purchasing, and duplicating, now furnished by 19 separate units.

Very soon after the department began to operate in its reorganized form, major problems arose that were traceable to the Bureau for Administration and Operations (BAO). Prior to reorganization, each department had had its own support staff for data processing, accounting, personnel, and budgeting. Those staffs and equipment had all been relocated and brought under the direction of the BAO commissioner. Employees who had once specialized in the work of one area, such as mental health, were now expected to perform work for all the bureaus. In addition, they had to revise forms, procedures, computer programs, accounts, and records to conform to the new department's policies.

EXHIBIT 1

Department for Human Resources: Organization Chart

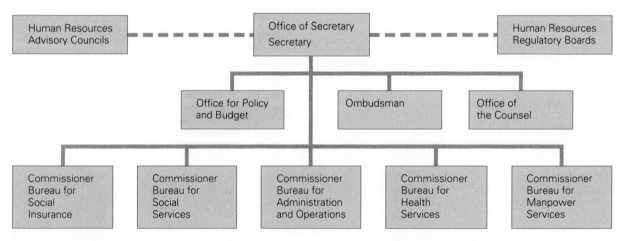

Consequently, the department began to experience administrative problems. Payrolls were late and inaccurate; payments to vendors and clients were delayed; and personnel actions got lost in the paperwork. Eventually, the integrity of the department's service programs was in jeopardy.

The executive staff of the department, consisting of the secretary, commissioner, and administrator of the Office for Policy and Budget, soon found itself spending more time dealing with these administrative problems than with policy formulation. Apparently, the department's effectiveness would depend on its ability to integrate the functions of BAO with the needs of the program bureaus. Also, the executive staff was not the appropriate body to deal with these issues. Aside from the inordinate amount of time spent on the administrative problems, a great deal of interpersonal conflict was generated among the commissioners.

The BAO commissioner was instructed by the secretary to give his full-time attention to devising a means for integrating the administrative functions. After consultation with his staff, the idea of an administrative liaison officer was formulated. The BAO commissioner presented the staff paper that described this new job (Exhibit 2) to the executive staff for discussion and adoption. According to the commissioner, there was simply no procedural or planning means for integrating the administrative functions. Rather, it would continue to be a conflict-laden process requiring the undivided attention of an individual assigned to each of the four bureaus.

EXHIBIT 2

Description of Responsibilities, Administrative Liaison Officer

Introduction

Executive Order 86–777 abolished the former human resources agencies and merged their functions into a new, single department. A prime element in the organizational concept of the new department is the centralization of administrative and support activities into a Bureau for Administration and Operations, which supports the four program bureaus of the department. While the centralization of these administrative and support activities only included those functions that were located in centralized administrative units in the former human resources agencies, the size of the Department for Human Resources dictates that extra levels of effort be applied to ensure close coordination and cooperation between the four program bureaus and the Bureau for Administration and Operations.

As one element in the comprehensive range of efforts now being applied to ensure a high level of responsiveness and cooperation between the Bureau for Administration and Operations and each program bureau, there will be created within the office of the Commissioner for Administration and Operations four positions for administrative liaison officers, one of which will be assigned responsibility for liaison with each program bureau.

Responsibilities

1. Each administrative liaison officer will provide, to the program bureau commissioner and other officials of the program bureau to which assigned, assistance in the following areas:
   a. Identification and definition of the administrative and operational support needs of that program bureau.
   b. Determination of the relative priorities of those needs for services.
   c. Identification of programmatic and operational requirements of the program bureau that may be assisted by the enforcement of administrative regulations by the Bureau for Administration and Operations.
   d. Identification of resources available within the Bureau for Administration and Operations that may be of value to the program bureau.
   e. Coordination of the delivery of services by the various divisions of the Bureau for Administration and Operations to the program bureau.

      f. Interpretation of data and information provided by the Bureau for Administration and Operations.

      g. Interpretation and distribution of administrative regulations and procedures issued by the Bureau for Administration and Operations with respect to its responsibilities under policies delineated by the secretary and the commissioners of the Department for Human Resources.

2. Each administrative liaison officer will provide assistance to the Commissioner for Administration and Operations and other officials of the Bureau for Administration and Operations in the following areas:

      a. Development of strategies for providing the maximum possible quality and quantity of support services that can be made available to the officer's particular program bureau within budgetary and policy constraints.

      b. Understanding of special needs and problems of respective program bureaus.

      c. Identification of new procedures and systems whereby services rendered to the program bureau can result in improved coordination between all organizational units of the Department for Human Resources.

      d. Identification of inadequacies or gaps in presently available services provided by the Bureau for Administration and Operations.

      e. Direction and/or coordination of task forces and other temporary organizational units created within the Bureau for Administration and Operations assigned to provide resources specific to the program bureau.

      f. Supervision of all personnel of the Bureau for Administration and Operations that may be on a temporary duty assignment to the program bureau to which the officer is assigned.

Operational Arrangement

1. The administrative liaison officer will be appointed to a position within the Office of the Commissioner for Administration and Operations.

2. The assignment of an administrative liaison officer to a program bureau will require the concurrence of the commissioner of that program bureau.

3. The Office of the Administrative Liaison Officer will be physically located within the suite of offices of the program bureau commissioner to whom the officer is assigned.

4. The administrative liaison officer will attend all staff meetings of the commissioner of the program bureau to which assigned and all staff meetings of the Commissioner for Administration and Operations.

Questions for Consideration

1. Evaluate the concept of "administrative liaison officer" as a strategy for achieving integration. Is this an example of the mutual adjustment strategy?

2. How will the officers achieve integration when they will have no authority over either the administrative functions or the programs that are to be integrated?

3. What would be the most important personal characteristics to look for in an applicant for these positions?

IDENTIFYING AND CHANGING ORGANIZATION DESIGN

Objectives

To increase the reader's understanding of different organization designs.

Related Topics

Chapters 13, 14, and 15 provide the reader with sufficient information to complete the analysis.

Starting the Exercise

The instructor will form groups of five to eight individuals toward the end of a class meeting. Each group will meet for 5–10 minutes and select a specific organizational unit, within the college or university they attend, that will be the focus of the group's analysis. The unit can be an academic department, division, or college or a non-academic unit such as the athletic department, business affairs office, student housing, or any other formally recognized campus unit.

Before the next class meeting, each group will complete the six steps of the exercise and prepare a report to present to the class.

Completing the Exercise

1. What is the primary purpose of the unit? What functions must be performed to accomplish the mission? What customers does the unit serve with what products or services? What are the primary environments that influence the unit's performance?
2. Describe the unit's primary technology, the relative uncertainty of the primary environments, and the primary information that must be processed.
3. Describe the existing organization structure in terms of the characteristics that distinguish between mechanistic and organic designs.
4. Which organization design more accurately describes the existing organization structure?
5. If the organization structure were changed to be more mechanistic or more organic, what would be the effects on jobs, departmental bases, and delegation of authority?
6. Is the existing organization design appropriate for the mission of the unit, given its mission, functions, customers, products/services, and environment? Justify your answer.

THE PROCESSES OF ORGANIZATIONS

16

Communication Processes

AN ORGANIZATIONAL ISSUE FOR DEBATE   IS GOSSIP GOOD?*

ARGUMENT FOR

Ask employees to pick the most believable and reliable source of information in an organization—top, middle, or first-line management or the office grapevine—and, according to a recent survey, employees will resoundingly pick the grapevine. The grapevine—the gossip chain—is the speediest, most efficient channel of communication in an organization. According to research, it is also highly accurate. At least 75 percent of the gossip that travels through the grapevine is true. As such, the grapevine is a useful channel of communication in organizations.

Gossiping (the grapevine in action) provides several benefits for the organization and the people in it. First, the grapevine can serve as an early warning system for employees, serving up bad news long before any formal announcement is made. Thus, the grapevine gives employees time to think about the situation and to consider how they will respond if the ill rumors are true. Second, because people gossip about other people and usually in groups of only two or three, such let-your-hair-down conversing can promote a closeness among employees. Gossiping also provides an outlet for those with little power in organizations to express their anger and frustration at the more powerful. It's an effective way to let off steam and alleviate a lot of stress. Gossiping also enables employees to hone their observation skills and even improve their understanding of people.

For managers, the grapevine provides an opportunity to float trial balloons (e.g., concerning a plan they are considering putting into action) and thus receive early indications of subordinates' reactions. Gossip can also serve as a medium for building and maintaining a company's culture. Via gossip, company war stories and those stories that communicate the culture's values can be told.

In sum, the grapevine and gossip serve useful, even healthy functions in organizations. However, those who participate in the gossip chain should be alert to certain obligations that come with participation: to pass along information that improves relationships in the organization and builds others' reputations and, likewise, to stamp out gossip that is unjustly detrimental to reputations and personal relationships.

ARGUMENT AGAINST

Gossip may serve some positive purposes in organizations. However, the grapevine also carries a quite costly downside—its potent, negative impact on productivity. Gossip hinders productivity because gossiping takes time and often saps employee morale.

Although 75 percent of grapevine gossip may be true, the remaining 25 percent carries false and often destructive rumors that employees spend costly time worrying about. Many managers also spend a disproportionate amount of time dealing with situations caused by rumors and gossip, not reality.

Because of its destructive impact, gossip must be minimized in organizations. Management can work toward this end by observing employees to estimate the amount of time that people spend gossiping. Some companies have surveyed employees anonymously to determine the degree to which gossip is affecting productivity. Management should then educate employees about the costs of gossip by conducting a seminar or formal training session on the topic. Any educational program should utilize group discussion to enable people to talk about the consequences of gossip.

Perhaps the best way to minimize gossip is to improve the other forms of communication in the organization and to tell employees what is really going on. Well-informed employees have less need to rely on gossip. Management should also respond to rumors quickly and accurately. In this regard, some companies have established a "rumor box," where employees can anonymously report rumors that they've heard. A quick response by management encourages employees to reveal what they've heard, and it prevents any further damage that destructive rumors may cause to morale and productivity.

Whatever the approach, management should strive to minimize gossip in the grapevine. Its ill effects are ongoing, and they translate to the bottom line.

*Source: Stanley J. Modic, "Grapevine Rated Most Believable; Management Say It's Talking More, But . . . ," *Industry Week*, May 15, 1989, pp. 11–12; Marilyn M. Kennedy, "Office Wars," *Executive Female*, January–February 1989, pp. 24ff; Walter Kiechel III, "In Praise of Office Gossip," *Fortune*, August 19, 1985, pp. 253ff; Elizabeth Danziger, "Minimize Office Gossip," *Personnel Journal*, November 1988, pp. 31–33.

As the Organizational Issue for Debate notes, the grapevine is a primary and always very active channel of communication in organizations. However, communication in organizations encompasses far more than grapevine gossip. Communicating pervades organizational activity; it is the process by which things get done in organizations. Every employee is continually involved in and affected by the communications process. For managers, effective communicating is a critical skill because the manager's planning, organizing, and controlling functions become operationalized only through communicative activity. Because of its importance in organizations, we devote a chapter to providing an understanding of the communication process and to the task of understanding how to become a better communicator.

THE IMPORTANCE OF COMMUNICATION

"You said to get to it as soon as I could. How did I know you meant now?" "How did I know she was really serious about resigning?" In these and similar situations, someone usually ends up saying, "What we have here is a failure to communicate." This statement has meaning for everyone, because each of us has faced situations in which the basic problem was communication. Whether on a person-to-person or nation-to-nation basis, in organizations, or in small groups, breakdowns in communication are pervasive.

Finding an aspect of a manager's job that does not involve communication would be extremely difficult. Serious problems arise when directives are misunderstood, when casual kidding in a work group leads to anger, or when informal remarks by a top-level manager are distorted. Each of these situations results from a breakdown somewhere in the process of communication.

Accordingly, the pertinent question is not whether managers engage in communication, because communication is inherent to the functioning of an organization. Rather, the real issue is whether managers communicate well or poorly. In other words, communication itself is unavoidable in an organization's functioning; but *effective* communication is avoidable. *Every manager must be a communicator.* In fact, everything a manager does communicates something in some way to somebody or some group. The only question is, "With what effect?" While this may appear an overstatement at this point, it will become apparent as you proceed through the chapter.

Despite the tremendous advances in communication and information technology, communication among people in organizations leaves much to be desired.[1] Communication among people depends not on technology but rather on forces in people and their surroundings. It is a *process* that occurs "within" people.

THE COMMUNICATION PROCESS

The general process of communication is presented in Figure 16–1. The process contains five elements: the communicator, the message, the medium, the receiver, and feedback. It can be simply summarized as: Who . . . says what, . . . in which way, . . . to whom, . . . with which effect?[2] To appreciate each element in the process, we must examine how communication works.

COMMUNICATION
Transmitting information and understanding, using verbal or nonverbal symbols.

Experts tell us that effective communication is the result of a common understanding between the communicator and the receiver. Communication is successful only if the communicator transmits that understanding to the receiver. In fact, the word **communication** is derived from the Latin *communis,* meaning "common": the communicator seeks to establish a "commonness" with a receiver. Hence, we can define communication as the *transmission of information and understanding through the use of common symbols.* The common symbols may be verbal or nonverbal. We shall see later that in the context of an organizational structure, information can flow up and down (vertical), across (horizontal), and down and across (diagonal).

A Contemporary Model

The most widely used contemporary model of the process of communication has evolved mainly from the early work of Shannon and Weaver, and Schramm.[3] These researchers were concerned with describing the general process of communication in a way that could be useful in all situations. The model that evolved from their work aids our understanding of communication. The basic elements include a communicator, an encoder, a message, a

---

[1]Klaus Krippendorf, "An Epistemological Foundation for Communication," *Journal of Communication,* Summer 1984, pp. 21–36.

[2]These five questions were first suggested in H. D. Lasswell, *Power and Personality* (New York: W. W. Norton, 1948), pp. 37–51.

[3]Claude Shannon and Warren Weaver, *The Mathematical Theory of Communication* (Urbana: University of Illinois Press, 1948); Wilbur Schramm, "How Communication Works," in *The Process and Effects of Mass Communication,* ed. Wilbur Schramm (Urbana: University of Illinois Press, 1953), pp. 3–26. These works are considered classics in the field of communication.

FIGURE 16—1

The Communication Process

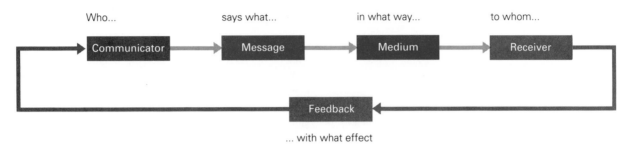

... with what effect

FIGURE 16—2

A Communication Model

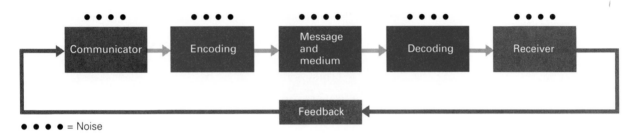

● ● ● ● = Noise

medium, a decoder, a receiver, feedback, and noise. The model is presented in Figure 16–2. Each element in the model can be examined in the context of an organization.

Communicator.   In an organizational framework, the communicator is an employee with ideas, intentions, information, and a purpose for communicating.

Encoding.   Given the communicator, an encoding process must take place that translates the communicator's ideas into a systematic set of symbols—into a language expressing the communicator's purpose. The major form of encoding is language. For example, a manager often takes accounting information, sales reports, and computer data and translates them into one message. The function of encoding, then, is to provide a form in which ideas and purposes can be expressed as a message.

Message.   The result of the encoding process is the message. The purpose of the communicator is expressed in the form of the message—either *verbal* or *nonverbal.* Managers have numerous purposes for communicating, such as to have others understand their ideas, to understand the ideas of others, to gain acceptance of themselves or their ideas, or to produce action.

Not as obvious, however, are *unintended messages* that can be sent by silence or inaction on a particular issue as well as decisions of which goals and objectives not to pursue and which methods not to utilize. For example, a

HOW FAXING IS CHANGING BUSINESS COMMUNICATION

Few innovations in business communication have caught on as fast as the facsimile machine. Since its debut in the early 1980s, faxing has become a very popular way for businesses to communicate everything from delivery orders and contracts to takeover notices. It is projected that in 1990 over 2 million fax machines will be sold; that annual number should increase to 3.2 million by 1993. Today, the fax machine has even replaced the White House's hot line to Moscow, the red phone.

Of course, faxing has greatly increased the speed of transmitting written communication. Depending on machine quality, fax machines can transmit a page of material over telephone lines in 10 to 30 seconds. Faxing also subtly affects business communication in other ways:

Fax potatoes.   Communication researchers project that fax machines will spawn a new generation of "fax potatoes," employees who, because of their workload, time pressures, or simply the machine's sheer convenience, will fax messages and documents to other departments rather than walking down the hall and delivering them in person. The result: a probable decline in the amount of interpersonal communication between employees that often occurs when an employee takes that walk down the hall.

Less "think time."   Faxing has reduced the amount of time available to think about messages you've sent or received, such as a contract offer. Explained one

decision to utilize one performance evaluation method rather than another may send a message to certain people; an instructor's decision not to give a final examination may send an unintended message to certain students that the course is too easy. This is what we meant earlier when we said that everything a manager does communicates.

The message, then, is what the individual hopes to communicate to the intended receiver, and the exact form it takes depends to a great extent on the medium used to carry the message. Decisions relating to the two are inseparable.

Medium.   The medium is the carrier of the message, the means by which the message is sent. Organizations provide information to members in a variety of ways, including face-to-face communication, telephone conversations, group meetings, fax messages, memos, policy statements, reward systems, production schedules, and video teleconferences.

The medium is sometimes a neglected element of the communication process; often, managers don't adequately consider the impact of the choice of medium on a communication's effectiveness. However, as a three-year study of managerial communication indicates,[4] the selection of the appropriate medium can have a major impact on communication effectiveness and even managerial performance. In the study, the researchers hypothesized that

---

[4]Robert H. Lengel and Richard L. Daft, "The Selection of Communication Media as an Executive Skill," *Academy of Management Executive*, August 1988, pp. 225–32.

lawyer, "When you are sending something or you've received something important in the mail, the expectation is that you have some time to think about the matter. The nature of mail gives you that little extra time. If something is faxed to you in 10 minutes, the expectation often is that you'll get back to them in a matter of minutes. Faxing gives you less time for second thoughts."

Too many faxes. Speed tends to encourage too much faxing. To ensure that employees aren't going overboard with fax enthusiasm, Robert Half International Inc., a personnel services firm based in San Francisco, recently issued a corporate memo—sent by mail—announcing the company's new "fax etiquette." The rules require that employees send faxes only if clients request them or give prior approval to receiving them. Because faxes suggest urgency, Robert Half views them as more intrusive than letters and not to be used for what clients see as routine communication. The company also requires that all faxes be followed up by mail. The reasons: people dislike the slick feel of fax paper, and faxes often "have less shelf life" than do documents on bond.

Source: Frederick H. Katayama, "Who's Fueling the Fax Frenzy," *Fortune,* October 23, 1989, pp. 151ff; Jolie Solomon, "Business Communication in the Fax Age," *The Wall Street Journal,* October 27, 1988, p. B1.

effective communication requires the correct match between the medium and content of the message. "Rich" media (such as face-to-face communication, which provides immediate feedback, a personal focus, and exposes sender and receiver to many cues of information) are best for nonroutine and complex messages. "Lean" media (such as memos and flyers on bulletin boards, which provide no feedback to the sender or no personal focus and afford limited information cues) are best for routine, simple messages.

The researchers examined the performance appraisal records of "media sensitive" executives, who demonstrated a consistent ability to accurately match the medium with the message, and "media insensitive" executives, who utilized media randomly without considering message content. They found that far more media-sensitive managers (87 percent) than media insensitive managers (47 percent) were high performers; also, over half the media-insensitive managers (53 percent) were low performers, compared to only 13 percent of the media-sensitive managers.

Recently, a new medium has gained growing acceptance in organizations and is effecting a change in the nature and content of communication. The Close-Up discusses this new medium: facsimile machines.

Decoding/receiver. For the process of communication to be completed, the message must be decoded so it is relevant to the receiver. *Decoding,* a technical term for the receiver's thought processes, involves interpretation. Receivers interpret (decode) the message in light of their own previous experiences and frames of reference. Thus, a salesperson will probably decode a memo from the company president differently than a production manager will. A nursing supervisor may decode a memo from the hospital administrator differently than the chief of surgery does. The closer the decoded message comes to the intent desired by the communicator, the more effective is the communication. This underscores the importance of the communicator being "receiver oriented."

Feedback.   *One-way* communication processes do not allow receiver-to-communicator feedback, increasing the potential for distortion between the intended message and the received message. Provision for feedback in the communication process is desirable.[5] A feedback loop provides a channel for receiver response that enables the communicator to determine whether the message has been received and has produced the intended response. *Two-way* communication processes provide for this important receiver-to-communicator feedback.

For the manager, communication feedback may come in many ways. In face-to-face situations, *direct* feedback through verbal exchanges is possible, as are such subtle means of communication as facial expressions of discontent or misunderstanding. In addition, *indirect* means of feedback (such as declines in productivity, poor production quality, increased absenteeism or turnover, and poor coordination and/or conflict between units) may indicate communication breakdowns.

Noise.   In the framework of human communication, noise can be thought of as all factors that distort the intended message. Noise may occur in each of the elements of communication. For example, a manager under a severe time constraint may be forced to act without communication or may communicate hastily with incomplete information. Or a subordinate may attach a different meaning to a word or phrase than was intended by the manager. These are examples of noise in the communication process.

The elements discussed in this section are essential for communication to occur. They should not, however, be viewed as separate. They are, rather, descriptive of the acts that must be performed for any communication to occur. The communication may be vertical (superior-subordinate, subordinate-superior) or horizontal (peer-peer), or it may involve one individual and a group, but the elements discussed here must be present.

Nonverbal Messages

The information a communicator sends that is unrelated to the verbal information—that is, nonverbal messages, or **nonverbal communication**—is an area of growing research interest among behavioral scientists.[6] One researcher has found that only 7 percent of a message's impact comes from its

---

[5]Susan Ashford, "Feedback-Seeking in Individual Adaptation: A Resource Perspective," *Academy of Management Journal,* September 1986, pp. 465–87.

[6]Dale A. Level, Jr., and William P. Galle, Jr., *Managerial Communications* (Plano, Tex.: Business Publications, 1988).

verbal content; the rest of the impact is nonverbal: 38 percent from vocal inflection and content and 55 percent from facial content.[7] When a sender's communication is contradictory (the nonverbal message contradicts the verbal message), the receiver places more weight on the nonverbal content of the overall communication.[8]

Vocal inflection means how a message is transmitted: loudly or softly, quickly or slowly, with controlled or uncontrolled inflection, or with a high or low pitch. The method of transmission adds meaning to the receiver, who assesses these cues. Body expressions are another important source of nonverbal communication. Ekman and Friesen have classified body language into five types of expression: emblems, illustrators, regulators, adaptors, and affect displays.[9]

Emblems are gestures much like sign language (the hitchhiker's thumb, the "OK" sign with thumb and forefinger, the "V" sign for victory). These movements quickly convey an understood word or phrase. *Illustrators* are gestures that give a picture of what is being said (a raised forefinger to indicate the first point of a sender's position, extended hands to illustrate the size of an object). *Regulators* are movements that regulate a conversation. For example, an upraised palm from the receiver tells a sender to slow down, an arched eyebrow can convey a request for the sender to clarify what has been said, and a nod of the head indicates understanding. Emblems, illustrators, and regulators are consciously used by individuals.

Adapters and affect displays, on the other hand, are often subconsciously communicated and can reveal much about both sender's and receiver's feelings and attitudes. *Adapters* are expressions used to adjust psychologically to the interpersonal climate of a particular situation.[10] Usually learned early in life, adapters are frequently used to deal with stress in an interpersonal situation. Drumming fingers on a table, tugging a strand of hair, or jiggling a leg or foot are all ways of releasing some degree of stress. *Affect displays,* usually subconscious, directly communicate an individual's emotions. Most affect displays are facial expressions, which are particularly important communicators of a person's feelings. There is a long-held assumption that a person's emotions are mirrored in the face and that these emotions can be "read" with a great deal of accuracy. Affect displays are also expressed in body positions. For example, a "closed posture" (arms folded across the chest, legs crossed) communicates defensiveness and often dislike. Interestingly, body positions can visibly convey a high degree of rapport between the sender and receiver. Communication researchers have found that when rapport exists, the two individuals mirror each other's movements—shifting body position, dropping a hand, or making some other movement at the same time. If a rapport is abruptly ended in a conversation, the "mirror" is quickly broken.[11]

---

[7]Albert Mehrabian, *Silent Messages* (Belmont, Calif.: Wadsworth, 1971).

[8]John Keltner, *Interpersonal Speech—Communication* (Belmont, Calif.: Wadsworth, 1970).

[9]Paul Ekman and W. V. Friesen, *Unmasking the Face* (Englewood Cliffs, N.J.: Prentice Hall, 1975).

[10]Level and Galle, *Managerial Communications,* p. 66.

[11]Michael B. McCaskey, "The Hidden Messages Managers Send," *Harvard Business Review,* November–December 1979, pp. 135–48.

Reading an individual's body language can be a challenging exercise because it involves subjectively evaluating nonverbal communication. The task becomes more difficult for American employees who work in international environments, where the meanings of nonverbal cues often differ strikingly from those back home. Consider, for example, a nod of the head, which means "yes" in the United States but "no" in Bulgaria. The OK sign with thumb and forefinger means "money" in France, "worthless" in Japan, and something very obscene in Brazil. Waving, a greeting or farewell in the United States, is a grave insult in Greece and Nigeria.[12]

COMMUNICATING WITHIN ORGANIZATIONS

Directions of Communication

The design of an organization should provide for communication in four distinct directions: downward, upward, horizontal, and diagonal. These four directions establish the framework within which communication in an organization takes place. Briefly examining each one will enable us to better appreciate the barriers to effective organizational communication and the means to overcome these barriers.

DOWNWARD COMMUNICATION
Communication that flows from higher to lower levels in an organization; includes management policies, instructions, and official memos.

Downward communication flows from individuals in higher levels of the hierarchy to those in lower levels. The most common forms of downward communication are job instructions, official memos, policy statements, procedures, manuals, and company publications. In many organizations, downward communication often is both inadequate and inaccurate, as reflected in the often heard statement among organization members that "we have absolutely no idea what's happening." Such complaints indicate inadequate downward communication and the need individuals have for information relevant to their jobs. The absence of job-related information can create unnecessary stress among organization members.[13] A similar situation is faced by a student who has not been told the requirements and expectations of an instructor.

UPWARD COMMUNICATION
Communication flowing from lower to higher levels in an organization; includes suggestion boxes, group meetings, and grievance procedures.

An effective organization needs **upward communication** as much as it needs downward communication. However, achieving effective upward communication—getting open and honest messages from employees to management—is an especially difficult task, particularly in larger organizations.[14] Some studies suggest that of the four formal communication channels, upward communication is the most ineffective. Upper-level managers often don't respond to messages sent from lower-level employees, and lower-level employees often are reluctant to communicate upward, especially if the

---

[12]C. Barnum and N. Wolniansky, "Taking Cues from Body Language (International Business Transactions)," *Management Review,* June 1989, pp. 59–60.

[13]Nicholas Smeed, "A Boon to Employee Communications: Letters of Understanding," *Personnel,* April 1985, pp. 50–53.

[14]Charles E. Beck and Elizabeth A. Beck, "The Manager's Open Door and the Communication Climate," *Business Horizons,* January–February 1986, pp. 15–19.

message contains bad news.[15] However, upward communication is often necessary for sound decision making.

Some of the most common upward communication devices are suggestion boxes, group meetings, and appeal or grievance procedures. In their absence, people somehow find ways to adapt to nonexistent or inadequate upward communication channels. One such strategy is the emergence of "underground" employee publications in many large organizations.[16]

Often overlooked in the design of organizations is provision for **horizontal communication.** In a college of business administration, when the chairperson of the accounting department communicates with the chairperson of the marketing department concerning the course offerings, the flow of communication is horizontal. Although vertical (upward and downward) communication flows are the primary considerations in organizational design, effective organizations also need horizontal communication. Horizontal communication—for example, communication between production and sales in a business organization and among the different departments or colleges within a university—is necessary for the coordination and integration of diverse organizational functions.

Since mechanisms for assuring horizontal communication ordinarily do not exist in an organization's design, its facilitation is left to individual managers. Peer-to-peer communication is often necessary for coordination and can also provide social need satisfaction.

Diagonal communication, while probably the least used channel of communication in organizations, is important in situations where members cannot communicate effectively through other channels. For example, the comptroller of a large organization may wish to conduct a distribution cost analysis. One part of that task may involve having the sales force send a special report directly to the comptroller rather than going through the traditional channels in the marketing department. Thus, the flow of communication would be diagonal as opposed to vertical (upward) and horizontal. In this case, a diagonal channel is most efficient in terms of time and effort for the organization.

HORIZONTAL COMMUNICATION
Communication that flows across functions in an organization; necessary for coordinating and integrating diverse organizational functions.

DIAGONAL COMMUNICATION
Communication that cuts across functions and levels in an organization; important when members cannot communicate through upward, downward, or horizontal channels.

The Grapevine: An Informal Communication Channel

As the Organizational Issue for Debate suggests, the grapevine is a powerful means of communication that cuts across formal channels of communication. Though the nature of its impact on organizational effectiveness is debatable, there is no denying that its impact is real. Many if not most of an organization's employees listen to the grapevine and to the assortment of facts, opinions, suspicions, and rumors it provides, information that normally does

---

[15]Allan D. Frank, "Trends in Communication: Who Talks to Whom?" *Personnel,* December 1985, pp. 41–47.

[16]For two excellent examples of company efforts to enhance communication (and the pitfalls of such attempts), see Ruth G. Newman, "Polaroid Develops a Communications System—but Not Instantly," *Management Review,* January 1990, pp. 34–39; M. M. Petty, James F. Cashman, Anson Seers, Robert L. Stevenson, Charles W. Barker, and Grady Cook, "Better Communication at General Motors," *Personnel Journal,* September 1989, pp. 40ff.

not travel through the organization's formal channels. According to research, an organization has several grapevine systems, information traveling in a grapevine does not follow an orderly path, and (as the Organizational Issue for Debate notes) the grapevine is at least 75 percent accurate.[17]

The grapevine is so much a part of organizational life that management attempts to eliminate it as an informal channel are somewhat futile. However, a manager must recognize that a grapevine that serves as a constant source of rumors can be troublesome. Rumors are an everyday part of business and management; an estimated 33 million–plus rumors are generated in U.S. businesses every day.[18]

A rumor is an unverified belief that is in general circulation inside the organization (an internal rumor) or in the organization's external environment (an external rumor).[19] A rumor has three components: The *target* is the object of the rumor. For example, in the late 1970s, McDonald's was the object of the rumor that it put red worms into its hamburger meat to boost the protein content. The *allegation* is the rumor's point about the target (putting worms in the hamburger meat). The rumor has a *source,* the original communicator of the rumor. Often, individuals will attribute a rumor to a prestigious or authoritative source to give the rumor more credibility.[20]

Some grapevine rumors are true; some are not. Regardless of validity, rumors tend to flourish if their content is entertaining, important, and/or ambiguous. *Entertaining* rumors have staying power because people find them interesting. For example, the rumor in the late 1970s that Life Savers Bubble Yum chewing gum was infected with spider eggs was logically nonsensical. However, entertainment value gave the rumor much clout. Life Savers spent over $100,000 on advertising to squelch the story. *Important* rumors have staying power because the information concerns people. For example, rumors run rampant in a company shortly after it has been acquired by another firm. Many rumors are believed because the information is important to the acquired employees, who seek to reduce their anxiety about their jobs and the acquired company's future. *Ambiguous* rumors have staying power because their lack of clarity makes it difficult to quickly refute and dismiss the rumor.[21]

Grapevines, rumors, and gossip are deeply ingrained in organizational life, so managers must be tuned in and listening to what is being said. Falsified facts traveling through the rumor mill can be corrected by feeding accurate information to primary communicators or liaison individuals. Also, informal communication systems such as the grapevine can provide yet another, albeit weak, communication vehicle to keep the work force informed about job-related matters.

---

[17]K. M. Watson, "An Analysis of Communication Patterns: A Method for Discriminating Leader and Subordinate Roles," *Academy of Management Journal,* June 1982, pp. 107–22.

[18]Robert Levy, "Tilting at the Rumor Mill," *Dun's Review,* December 1981, pp. 52–54.

[19]R. L. Rosnow, "Psychology in Rumor Reconsidered," *Psychological Bulletin,* May 1980, pp. 578–91.

[20]Frederick Koenig, *Rumor in the Marketplace* (Dover, Mass.: Auburn House, 1985).

[21]Roy Rowan, "Where Did That Rumor Come From?" *Fortune,* August 13, 1979, pp. 130ff.

Interpersonal Communications

Within an organization, communication flows from individual to individual in face-to-face and group settings. Such flows, termed **interpersonal communications,** can vary from direct orders to casual expressions. Interpersonal communication is the primary means of managerial communication; on a typical day, over three fourths of a manager's communications occur in face-to-face interactions.[22]

The problems that arise when managers attempt to communicate with other people can be traced to *perceptual differences* and *interpersonal style differences.* We know from Chapter 3 that each manager perceives the world according to his or her background, experiences, personality, frame of reference, and attitude. Managers relate to and learn from the environment (including the people in that environment) primarily through information received and transmitted. And the way in which managers receive and transmit information depends in part on how they relate to two very important *senders* of information, *themselves* and *others.*

Interpersonal styles. **Interpersonal style** refers to *the way in which an individual prefers to relate to others.* The fact that much of any interpersonal relationship involves communication indicates the importance of interpersonal style.

Let us begin by recognizing that information is held by oneself and by others but that not one of us fully has or knows that information. The different combinations of knowing and not knowing relevant information are shown in Figure 16–3. The figure, popularly known as the Johari Window, identifies four combinations, or regions, of information known and unknown by the self and others.[23]

The arena. The region most conducive to effective interpersonal relationships and communication is termed the *arena.* In this setting, both the communicator (self) and the receivers (others) know all of the information necessary to carry on effective communication. For a communication attempt to be in the arena region, the parties involved must share identical feelings, data, assumptions, and skills. Since the arena is the area of common understanding, the larger it becomes, the more effective communication is.

The blind spot. When relevant information is known to others but not to the self, a *blind spot* results. This constitutes a handicap for the self, since one can hardly understand the behaviors, decisions, and potentials of others without having the information on which these are based. Others have the advantage of knowing their own reactions, feelings, perceptions, and so forth,

INTERPERSONAL COMMUNICATIONS
Communications that flow between individuals in face-to-face and group situations.

INTERPERSONAL STYLE
Manner in which we relate to other persons.

---

[22]Fred Luthans and Janet K. Larsen, "How Managers Really Communicate," *Human Relations* 39, no. 2 (1986), pp. 161–78. See also Larry E. Penley and Brian Hawkins, "Studying Interpersonal Communication in Organizations: A Leadership Application," *Academy of Management Journal,* June 1985, pp. 309–26.

[23]Joseph Luft, "The Johari Window," *Human Relations and Training News,* January 1961, pp. 6–7. The discussion here is based on a later adaptation. See James Hall, "Communication Revisited," *California Management Review,* Fall 1973, pp. 56–67.

FIGURE 16—3

The Johari Window:
Interpersonal Styles and
Communications

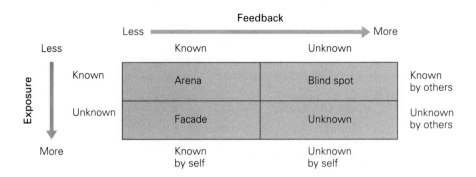

while the self is unaware of these. Consequently, interpersonal relationships and communications suffer.

The facade. When information is known to the self but unknown to others, a person (self) may react to superficial communications—that is, present a "false front," or facade. Information that we perceive as potentially prejudicial to a relationship or that we keep to ourselves out of fear, desire for power, or whatever, makes up the *facade*. This protective front, in turn, serves a defensive function for the self. Such a situation is particularly damaging when a subordinate "knows" and an immediate supervisor "does not know." The facade, like the blind spot, diminishes the arena and reduces the possibility of effective communication.

The unknown. This region constitutes that portion of the relationship where relevant information is known by neither the self nor other parties. As is often stated, "I don't understand them, and they don't understand me." It is easy to see that interpersonal communication is poor under such circumstances. Circumstances of this kind often occur in organizations when individuals in different specialties must communicate to coordinate what they do.

Interpersonal strategies. Figure 16—3 indicates that an individual can improve interpersonal communications by utilizing two strategies, exposure and feedback:

Exposure. Increasing the arena area by reducing the facade area requires that the individual be open and honest in sharing information with others. The process that the self uses to increase the information known to others is termed *exposure* because it sometimes leaves the self in a vulnerable position. Exposing one's true feelings by "telling it like it is" often involves risks.

Feedback. When the self does not know or understand, more effective communications can be developed through feedback from those who do know. Thus, the blind spot can be reduced, with a corresponding increase in the arena. Of course, whether feedback can be used depends on the individual's willingness to "hear" it and on the willingness of others to give it. Thus, the individual has less control over the provision of feedback than over the provision of exposure. Obtaining feedback is dependent on the active cooperation of others, while exposure requires the active behavior of the communicator and the passive listening of others.

Managerial styles.   The day-to-day activities of managers are closely tied to effective interpersonal communications. Managers provide *information* (which must be *understood*), they give *commands* and *instructions* (which must be *obeyed* and *learned*), and they make *efforts to influence* and *persuade* (which must be *accepted* and *acted on*). Thus, the way in which managers communicate, both as senders and receivers, is crucial to effective performance.

Theoretically, managers who desire to communicate effectively can use both exposure and feedback to enlarge the area of common understanding, the arena. As a practical matter, such is not the case. Managers differ in their ability and willingness to use exposure and feedback. At least four different managerial styles can be identified.

Type A.   Managers who use neither exposure nor feedback are said to have a **Type A** style. The unknown region predominates in this style because such managers are unwilling to enlarge the area of their own knowledge or the knowledge of others. Type A managers exhibit anxiety and hostility and give the appearance of aloofness and coldness toward others. In an organization with a large number of such managers in key positions, one would expect to find poor and ineffective interpersonal communications and a loss of individual creativity. Type A managers often display the characteristics of autocratic leaders.

Type B.   Some managers desire some degree of satisfying relationships with their subordinates. Because of their personalities and attitudes, however, these managers are unable to open up and express their feelings and sentiments. Since they cannot use exposure, they must rely on feedback. The facade is the predominant feature of interpersonal relationships when managers overuse feedback to the exclusion of exposure. Subordinates probably distrust such managers, realizing these managers are holding back their own ideas and opinions. **Type B** behavior is often displayed by managers who desire to practice some form of permissive leadership.

Type C.   Managers who value their own ideas and opinions but not the ideas and opinions of others use exposure at the expense of feedback. The consequence of this style is the perpetuation and enlargement of the blind spot. Subordinates soon realize that such managers are not particularly interested in communicating, only in telling, and are mainly interested in maintaining their own sense of importance and prestige. Consequently, **Type C** managers usually have subordinates who are hostile, insecure, and resentful.

Type D.   The most effective interpersonal communication style balances exposure and feedback. Managers who are secure in their positions feel free to expose their own feelings and to obtain feedback from others. To the extent that a manager practices **Type D** behavior successfully, the arena region becomes larger, and communication becomes more effective.

To summarize, the importance of interpersonal styles in determining the effectiveness of interpersonal communication cannot be overemphasized. The

TYPE A

Managers who are autocratic leaders, typically aloof and cold; often poor interpersonal communicators.

TYPE B

Managers who seek good relationships with subordinates but are unable to openly express feelings; often ineffective interpersonal communicators.

TYPE C

Managers interested only in their own ideas, not ideas and opinions of others; usually not effective communicators.

TYPE D

Managers who feel free to express feelings to others and to have others express feelings; most effective interpersonal communicators.

ORGANIZATIONS:
CLOSE-UP

FOR BETTER COMMUNICATING, HIRE A COACH

Because effective interpersonal communication is such a critical managerial skill, many organizations provide seminars in public speaking and assertiveness training to help managers enhance their communicative abilities. However, a growing number of organizations have decided to forgo the seminars and instead hire private coaches to help managers hone their skills.

These coaches can be an attractive alternative because they work one-on-one, providing customized service to alleviate a manager's specific weaknesses. Many coaches, such as consultants at Motivational Systems Inc., of West Orange, New Jersey, identify a manager's weak areas through paper-and-pencil tests, interviews with the manager's boss and peers, and observations of the manager communicating with employees. Often, they videotape the manager to identify patterns in communicative behavior. Communication skills are then strengthened by watching ''videomodels'' who demonstrate effective communication approaches and by role-playing, where the manager practices communicating with the coach. Special attention is also devoted to body language, a telling aspect of communication that many managers ignore.

This approach to improving communication skills sounds very involved, and it is. Utilizing coaches is also very expensive, averaging $10,000 in fees per client. Nevertheless, the coaching business is booming. A manager's interpersonal communication skills have become more critical than ever, due to the growing emphasis on teamwork in organizations, which gives people with good interpersonal skills an edge. Also, because thousands of upper-management jobs were eliminated by downsizing in the 1980s, managers must now compete for fewer upper-level positions. As a result, many managers hire coaches on their own and foot the bill themselves, realizing that every tool is useful in the intensified competition in getting ahead.

Source: Claudia H. Deutsch, "To Get Ahead, Consider a Coach," *New York Times*, January 4, 1990, p. 29.

primary determinant of effectiveness of interpersonal communication is the attitude of managers toward exposure and feedback. The most effective approach is that of the Type D manager. Type A, B, and C managers resort to behaviors that are detrimental to the effectiveness of communication and to organizational performance. Recently, a new approach to improving interpersonal communication skills has emerged in organizations: the communications coach, which is the subject of the Close-Up.

BARRIERS TO EFFECTIVE COMMUNICATION

A manager has no greater responsibility than to develop effective communications.[24] Why then does communication break down? On the surface, the answer is relatively easy. We have identified the elements of communication as

---

[24]Walter D. St. John, "You Are What You Communicate," *Personnel Journal*, October 1985, pp. 40–43.

the communicator, encoding, the message, the medium, decoding, the receiver, and feedback. If noise exists in these elements *in any way,* complete clarity of meaning and understanding do not occur. In this section, we discuss the following barriers to effective communications: frame of reference, selective listening, value judgments, source credibility, semantic problems, filtering, in-group language, status differences, proxemic behavior, time pressures, and communication overload. These sources of noise can exist in both organizational and interpersonal communications.

Frame of Reference

Different individuals can interpret the same communication differently, depending on previous experiences that result in variations in the encoding and decoding processes. Communication specialists agree that this is the most important factor that breaks down the "commonness" in communications. When the encoding and decoding processes are not alike, communication tends to break down. Thus, while the communicator actually speaks the "same language" as the receiver, the message conflicts with the way the receiver "catalogs" the world. This problem is depicted in Figure 16–4. The interior areas in this diagram represent the accumulated experiences of the participants in the communication process. If they share a large area, effective communication is facilitated. If a large area is not shared—if there has been no common experience—then communication becomes impossible, or at best highly distorted. Communicators can encode and receivers can decode only in terms of their experiences.

Distortion often occurs because of participants' differing frames of reference. Teenagers perceive things differently than do their parents; college deans perceive problems differently than do faculty members. People in various organizational *functions* can also interpret the same situation differently. A business problem may be viewed differently by the marketing manager than by the production manager; an efficiency problem in a hospital is viewed by the nursing staff from their frames of reference and experiences, which may result in interpretations different from those of the physicians. Different *levels* in the organization also have different frames of reference. First-line supervisors' frames of reference differ in many respects from those of vice presidents. Their different positions in the organization structure influence their frames of reference.[25] As a result, their needs, values, attitudes, and expectations differ, often resulting in unintentional distortion of communication. Neither group can be labeled wrong or right. In any situation, individuals choose the part of their own past experiences that relates to the current experience and that helps them form conclusions and judgments. Unfortunately, incongruencies in encoding and decoding are barriers to effective communication. Many of the other barriers examined in this section also result from variations in encoding and decoding.

Selective Listening

In this form of selective perception, the individual tends to block out new information, especially if it conflicts with existing beliefs. Thus, in a directive

---

[25]Watson, "An Analysis of Communication Patterns," p. 111.

FIGURE 16—4

Overlapping Fields of Experience

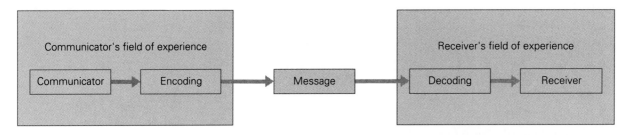

from management, the receiver notices only things that reaffirm his or her beliefs. Things that conflict with preconceived notions are either ignored or distorted to confirm those preconceptions.

For example, a notice may be sent to all operating departments that costs must be reduced if the organization is to earn a profit. The communication may not achieve its desired effect because it conflicts with the perceived "reality" of the receivers. Thus, operating employees may ignore or be amused by such information in light of the large salaries, travel allowances, and expense accounts of some executives. Whether such preconceptions are justified is irrelevant; what is important is that they result in breakdowns in communication. In other words, if we only hear what we want to hear, our "reality" cannot be disturbed.

Value Judgments

In every communication situation, the receiver makes value judgments. This basically involves assigning an overall worth to a message prior to receiving the entire communication. Value judgments may be based on the receiver's evaluation of the communicator or previous experiences with the communicator or on the message's anticipated meaning. For example, a hospital administrator may pay little attention to a memorandum from a nursing supervisor who is "always putting too much emphasis on patient comfort." A college professor, perceiving the department chairperson as not being concerned enough about teaching quality, may consider a merit evaluation meeting with the chairperson as "going through the motions." A cohesive work group may form negative value judgments concerning all actions by management.

Source Credibility

Source credibility is the trust, confidence, and faith that the receiver has in the words and actions of the communicator. The level of credibility that the receiver assigns to the communicator in turn directly affects how the receiver views and reacts to the communicator's words, ideas, and actions. Thus their evaluation of their manager affects how subordinates view a communication from him or her. This, of course, is heavily influenced by previous experiences with the manager.

Again, we see that everything done by a manager communicates. A hospital medical staff that views the hospital administrator as less than honest, manipulative, and not to be trusted is apt to assign nonexistent motives to any communication from the administrator. Union leaders who view management as exploiters and managers who view union leaders as political animals are likely to engage in little real communication.

Semantic Problems

Communication has been defined as the transmission of *information* and *understanding* through the use of *common symbols*. Actually, we cannot transmit understanding. We can only transmit information in the form of words, which are the common symbols. Unfortunately, the same words may mean entirely different things to different people. The understanding is in the receiver, not in the words.

Because different groups use words differently, communication can often be impeded. This is especially true with abstract or technical terms or phrases. "Cost-benefit study" would have meaning to those involved in the administration of the hospital but would probably mean very little to the staff physicians. In fact, it might even carry a negative meaning. Such concepts as "trusts," "profits," and "Treasury bills" may have concrete meaning to bank executives but little or no meaning to bank tellers. Thus, because words mean different things to different people, a communicator may speak the same language as a receiver but still not transmit understanding.

Filtering

Filtering, a common occurrence in upward communication in organizations, refers to the manipulation of information so that the receiver perceives it as positive. For example, subordinates "cover up" unfavorable information in messages to their superiors. The reason for such filtering should be clear; this is the direction (upward) that carries control information to management. Management makes merit evaluations, grants salary increases, and promotes individuals based on what it receives by way of the upward channel. The temptation to filter is likely to be strong at every level in the organization.

In-Group Language

Each of us at some time has undoubtedly been subjected to highly technical jargon, only to learn that the unfamiliar words or phrases described very simple procedures or very familiar objects. For example, many students are asked by researchers to "complete an instrument as part of an experimental treatment." The student soon learns that this involves nothing more than filling out a paper-and-pencil questionnaire.

Occupational, professional, and social groups often develop words or phrases that have meaning only to members. Such special language can serve many useful purposes. It can provide members with feelings of belongingness,

ORGANIZATIONS:
CLOSE-UP

BUSINESS LINGO

Over time, almost every organization develops a lingo—words and phrases for people, situations, events, and things—in short, a language distinctly the company's own. Some examples follow:

IBM. At Big Blue, a "hipo" is someone who has high potential and is quickly moving up through the organizational hierarchy. An "alpo" is an employee with low potential. When people disagree, they "nonconcur." Someone who nonconcurs frequently but for constructive reasons is a "wild duck."

Walt Disney. At Walt Disney, all employees are called "cast members." They're "onstage" when they're working and "offstage" when at lunch or taking a break. When the company treats guests for lunch or throws a party or other functions for employees, the treat is "on the mouse." Any situation or event that's positive is a "good Mickey." Anything less is a "bad Mickey."

Newsweek. Employees at *Newsweek* call each issue's leading national story the "*violin,*" so named because the story reflects the tone of the news. The top editors

cohesiveness, and (in many cases) self-esteem; it can also facilitate effective communication *within* the group. The use of in-group language can, however, result in severe communication breakdowns when outsiders or other groups are involved. This is especially the case when groups use such language in an organization, not for the purpose of transmitting information and understanding but rather to communicate a mystique about the group or its function. The Close-Up looks at popular lingo used in a number of prominent companies.

Status Differences

Organizations often express hierarchical rank through a variety of symbols (titles, offices, carpets, etc.). Such status differences can be perceived as threats by persons lower in the hierarchy, and this can prevent or distort communication. Not wanting to look incompetent, a nurse may remain quiet instead of expressing an opinion or asking a question of the nursing supervisor.

Many times, superiors, in an effort to utilize their time efficiently, make the status barriers more difficult to surmount. The governmental administrator or bank vice president may be accessible only by appointment or by passing the careful quizzing of a secretary. This widens the communication gap between superiors and subordinates.

Isolation from accurate feedback is particularly acute at the top levels of an organization. There, an executive of a company of 20,000 employees or so may have direct relationships with only 10 or 15 individuals. The personality of the highly successful executive further discourages honest feedback: an executive demeanor of total confidence and command doesn't easily invite

are called "*Wallendas*," named after the legendary aerial acrobatic troupe, the Flying Wallendas. The reason: their jobs are hectic, responsibilities are immense, and job security is nonexistent. The "*Wallendas*" work in their offices, the "*Wallendatorium.*"

Other companies sport imaginative lingos. At McDonald's, dedicated employees have "ketchup in their veins." At Eastman Kodak, committed, hard-working employees "work for the great yellow father." And when employees at Prudential Life Insurance Co. of America throw a birthday party for a colleague or celebrate some other occasion, they have a "*desk*" for the employee. The term comes from the company's tradition of decorating an employee's desk on special occasions. Although today the parties are held in conference rooms, the event is still called a *desk*.

According to communication experts, lingo serves a purpose in an organization. It makes the organization more distinctive and unique, and it tends to build employees' identity with and commitment to the company. It is also an efficient way to communicate inside the organization. But used with associates outside the company who don't know the jargon, lingo can hinder communication.

Source: Adapted from Michael W. Miller, "At Many Firms, Employees Speak a Language that's All Their Own," *The Wall Street Journal*, December 29, 1987, p. 15.

criticism from subordinates; an abrasive style with subordinates has the same effect.[26] Upper-level executives also often take on an exaggerated importance. For example, one executive once casually wondered aloud how a proposed law would affect the company, knowing that the bill stood little chance of being passed. Later, he discovered that his subordinates had responded to the casual remark with a thorough, costly—and ultimately useless—analysis of the bill's impact. From then on, the executive was cautious with his comments.[27]

Some organizations are de-emphasizing status and power differences to encourage more open supervisor-subordinate communication. At Honda Motors Co. in Marysville, Ohio, for example, visible differences in status and power have been intentionally avoided. The plant has no executive cafeteria or washroom and no special parking spaces, and executives work in open offices with no frills. Management believes that these actions reduce communication barriers between managers of all levels and their subordinates.

Proxemic Behavior

An important but often overlooked element of nonverbal communication is *proxemics,* defined as an individual's use of space when interpersonally communicating with others. According to Edward Hall, a prominent researcher of proxemics, people have four zones of informal space, spatial distances they

---

[26]Robert E. Kaplan, Wilfred H. Drath, and Joan R. Kofodimos, "Why Some Managers Don't Get the Message," *Across the Board,* September 1985, pp. 63–69.

[27]William Hennefrund, "Fear of Feedback," *Association Management,* March 1986, pp. 80–83.

maintain when interacting with others: the intimate zone (from physical contact to 18 inches); the personal zone (from 18 inches to 4 feet); the social zone (from over 4 to 12 feet); and the public zone (more than 12 feet).[28] For Americans, manager-subordinate relationships begin in the social zone and progress to the personal zone after mutual trust has developed.[29] An individual's personal and intimate zones make up a "private bubble" of space that is considered private territory, not to be entered by others unless invited.

Proxemics creates a significant communication barrier when the proxemic behavior of the sender and receiver differs. For example, assume that, like most Americans, you stand in the social zone while interacting at a social gathering such as a cocktail party. However, in the South American culture, a personal-zone distance is considered more natural in such situations. When a South American businessperson you are talking with at a cocktail party assumes a personal-zone distance, how do you feel? Typically in such a situation, an individual feels so uncomfortable with the person standing "too close" that any verbal communication is not heard. Conflicting proxemic behavior can also affect each individual's perceptions of the other: you may view the South American as pushy and aggressive; he may see you as cold and impolite.

Time Pressures

The pressure of time presents an important barrier to communication. An obvious problem is that managers do not have the time to communicate frequently with every subordinate. However, time pressures can often lead to far more serious problems than this. *Short-circuiting* is a failure of the formally prescribed communication system that often results from time pressures. What it means is simply that someone has been left out of the formal channel of communication who would normally be included. For example, suppose a salesperson needs a rush order for a very important customer and goes directly to the production manager with the request, since the production manager owes the salesperson a favor. Other members of the sales force who get word of this become upset over this preferential treatment and report it to the sales manager. Obviously, the sales manager would know nothing of the "deal," having been short-circuited.

In some cases, going through formal channels is extremely costly or even impossible from a practical standpoint. Consider the impact on a hospital patient if a nurse had to report a critical malfunction in life support equipment to the nursing team leader, who in turn had to report it to the hospital engineer, who would instruct a staff engineer to make the repair.

Communication Overload

One vital task performed by a manager is decision making. One of the necessary factors in effective decisions is *information*. Because of the advances in communication technology, the difficulty does not lie in generating information. In fact, the last decade has often been described as the "Information Era"

---

[28]Edward Hall, *The Hidden Dimension* (Garden City, N.Y.: Doubleday Publishing, 1966).

[29]Phillip L. Hunsaker, "Communicating Better: There's No Proxy for Proxemics," *Business,* March–April 1980, pp. 41–48.

FIGURE 16—5

Barriers to Effective Communication

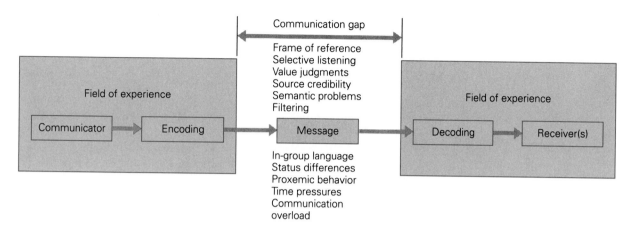

or the "Age of Information." Managers often feel buried by the deluge of information and data to which they are exposed. As a result, people cannot absorb or adequately respond to all of the messages directed to them. They "screen out" the majority of messages, which in effect means that these messages are never decoded. Thus, the area of organizational communication is one in which "more" is not always "better."

The barriers to communication discussed here, while common, are by no means the only ones. Figure 16–5 illustrates the impact of these barriers on the process of communication. Examining each barrier indicates that they are either *within individuals* (e.g., frame of reference, value judgments) or *within organizations* (e.g., in-group language, filtering). This point is important because attempts to improve communication must of necessity focus on changing people and/or changing the organization structure.

IMPROVING COMMUNICATION IN ORGANIZATIONS

Managers striving to become better communicators must accomplish two separate tasks. First, they must improve their *messages*—the information they wish to transmit. Second, they must seek to improve their own *understanding* of what other people try to communicate to them. In other words, they must become better encoders and decoders. *They must strive not only to be understood but also to understand.*[30] The following techniques can help accomplish these two important tasks.

Following Up

This technique involves assuming that you are misunderstood and, whenever possible, attempting to determine whether your intended meaning was actually received. As we have seen, meaning is often in the mind of the

---

[30]Ernest G. Bormann, "Symbolic Convergence Theory: A Communication Formulation," *Journal of Communication,* Fall 1985, pp. 128–38.

receiver. For example, an accounting unit leader in a government office passes on to accounting staff members notices of openings in other agencies. While longtime employees may understand this as a friendly gesture, a new employee might interpret it as an evaluation of poor performance and a suggestion to leave.

Regulating Information Flow

Regulating communication can ensure an optimum flow of information to managers, thereby eliminating the barrier of "communication overload." Communication can be regulated in both quality and quantity. The idea is based on the *exception principle* of management, which states that only significant deviations from policies and procedures should be brought to the attention of superiors. In formal communication, then, superiors should be communicated with only on matters of exception and not for the sake of communication.

As we saw in the section on the structure of organizations, certain organizational structures would be more amenable to this principle than would others. For example, in an organic organization, with its emphasis on free-flowing communication, this principle would not apply. However, mechanistic organizations would find the principle useful.

Utilizing Feedback

Earlier in the chapter, feedback was identified as an important element in effective two-way communication. It provides a channel for receiver response that enables the communicator to determine whether the message has been received and has produced the intended response.[31] In face-to-face communication, direct feedback is possible. In downward communication, however, inaccuracies often occur because of insufficient opportunity for feedback from receivers. Distributing a memorandum about an important policy to all employees does not guarantee that communication has occurred.

One might expect that feedback in the form of upward communication would be encouraged more in organic organizations, but mechanisms that encourage upward communication are found in many different organizational designs. A healthy organization needs effective upward communication if its downward communication is to have any chance of being effective. The point is that developing and supporting mechanisms for feedback involve far more than following up on communications.

Empathy

Empathy is the ability to put oneself in the other person's role and to assume that individual's viewpoints and emotions. This involves being receiver oriented rather than communicator oriented. The form of the communication

---

[31]Robert C. Liden and Terence R. Mitchell, "Reactions to Feedback: The Role of Attributions," *Academy of Management Journal,* June 1985, pp. 291–308.

should depend largely on what is known about the receiver. Empathy requires communicators to place themselves in the shoes of the receiver to anticipate how the message is likely to be decoded.

Managers must understand and appreciate the process of decoding. In decoding the message is "filtered" through the receiver's perceptions. For vice presidents to communicate effectively with supervisors, for faculty to communicate effectively with students, and for government administrators to communicate effectively with minority groups, empathy is often an important ingredient. Empathy can reduce many of the barriers to effective communication that have been discussed. Remember that the greater the gap between the experiences and background of the communicator and the receiver, the greater the effort that must be made to find a common ground of understanding—where fields of experience overlap.

Repetition

Repetition is an accepted principle of learning. Introducing repetition or redundancy into communication (especially that of a technical nature) ensures that if one part of the message is not understood, other parts carry the same message. New employees are often provided with the same basic information in several different forms. Likewise, students receive much redundant information when first entering a university. This ensures that registration procedures, course requirements, and new terms such as matriculation and quality points are communicated.

Encouraging Mutual Trust

Time pressures often mean that managers cannot follow up communication and encourage feedback or upward communication every time they communicate. Under such circumstances, an atmosphere of mutual confidence and trust between managers and their subordinates can facilitate communication. Subordinates judge for themselves the quality of their perceived relationship with their superiors. Managers who develop a climate of trust find that following up on each communication is less critical. Because they have fostered high source credibility among subordinates, no loss in understanding results from a failure to follow up on each communication. Some organizations initiate formal programs designed to encourage mutual trust.

Effective Timing

Individuals are exposed to thousands of messages daily. Because of the impossibility of taking in all the messages, many are never decoded and received. Managers must realize that while they are attempting to communicate with a receiver, other messages are being received simultaneously. Thus, the message that the manager sends may not be "heard." Messages that do not compete with other messages are more likely to be understood.

Because of this problem, many organizations use "retreats" when important policies or changes are being made. A group of executives may be sent to a resort to resolve an important corporate policy issue, or a college department's faculty may retreat to an off-campus site to design a new curriculum.

On an everyday basis, effective communication can be facilitated by properly timing major announcements. The barriers discussed earlier often arise from poor timing that results in distortions and value judgments.

Simplifying Language

Complex language has been identified as a major barrier to effective communication. University students often suffer when their teachers use technical jargon that transforms simple concepts into complex puzzles. Government agencies are also known for their often incomprehensible communications. And we have already noted instances where professional people use in-group language in attempting to communicate with individuals outside their group. Managers must remember that effective communication involves transmitting *understanding* as well as information. If the receiver does not understand, then there has been no communication. In fact, many of the techniques discussed in this section have as their sole purpose the promotion of understanding. Managers must encode messages in words, appeals, and symbols that are meaningful to the receiver.

Effective Listening

To improve communication, managers must not only seek to be understood but also to *understand*. This involves listening. One method of encouraging someone to express true feelings, desires, and emotions is to listen. Just listening is not enough; one must listen with understanding. Can managers develop listening skills? Numerous pointers have been given for effective listening in organizational settings. For example, one writer cites "Ten Commandments for Good Listening": stop talking; put the speaker at ease; show the speaker you want to listen; remove distractions; empathize with the speaker; be patient; hold your temper; go easy on argument and criticism; ask questions; and stop talking.[32] Note that "stop talking" is both the first and the last commandment.

Such guidelines can be useful to managers. More important, however, is the *decision to listen*. Guidelines are useless unless the manager makes the conscious decision to listen. Only after the realization that effective communication involves understanding as well as being understood can guidelines for effective listening become useful.

In conclusion, to find any aspect of a manager's job that does not involve communication would be hard. If everyone in the organization had common points of view, communicating would be easy. Unfortunately, such is not the case: each member comes to the organization with a distinct personality, background, experience, and frame of reference. The structure of the organization itself influences status relationships and the distance (levels) between individuals, which in turn influence the ability of individuals to communicate.

---

[32]Keith Davis, *Human Behavior at Work* (New York: McGraw-Hill, 1980), p. 394.

FIGURE 16-6

Improving Communication in Organizations (Narrowing the Communication Gap)

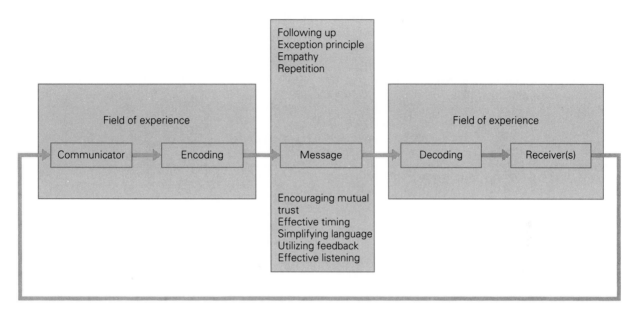

In this chapter, we have described the basic elements in the process of communication and what it takes to communicate effectively. These elements are necessary whether the communication is face-to-face or written and communicated vertically, horizontally, or diagonally within an organizational structure. We discussed several common communication barriers and several means to improve communication. Figure 16–6 shows techniques that facilitate more effective communication. Often, time does not permit managers to utilize many of the techniques for improving communication, and skills such as empathy and effective listening are not easy to develop. The figure does, however, illustrate the challenge of communicating effectively and suggest what is required. It shows that communicating involves both transmitting and receiving. Managers must be effective at both: they must understand as well as be understood.

SUMMARY OF KEY POINTS

— Communication is the transmission of information and understanding through the use of common symbols.

— The communication process consists of certain basic elements that must always be present if effective communication is to result. These elements are the communicator, the message, the medium, the receiver, and feedback.

— Nonverbal communication is an important source of information about a sender's or receiver's thoughts and feelings. The voice, body expressions, and proxemics are all important mechanisms of nonverbal communication.

— Organizational design and the communication process are inseparable. The design of an organization must provide for communication in three distinct directions:

— vertical (downward and upward), horizontal, and diagonal.

— The grapevine is an informal communication channel that pervades organizations. Typically, organizations have numerous grapevine systems through which information travels that is rarely communicated through formal channels.

— Rumors, carried through the grapevine, are an everyday part of organizational life. Regardless of validity, they tend to flourish when they are viewed by the receiver as important, entertaining, and/or ambiguous.

— Communication effectiveness is enhanced when both the sender and receiver utilize feedback and exposure. Balanced use of both is the most effective approach.

— To alleviate the numerous barriers to communication in organizations, managers should follow up on their messages, regulate information flow, utilize feedback, develop empathy, utilize message repetition, encourage mutual trust, simplify their language, effectively time the delivery of their messages, and become effective listeners.

DISCUSSION AND REVIEW QUESTIONS

1. Of all the barriers to communication discussed in the chapter, which are the most difficult to eliminate? Explain.

2. Do you tend to be a Type A, B, C, or D person when you engage in interpersonal communication? What are the strengths and shortcomings of your communication style?

3. Think of a situation in which you have been the receiver in a one-way communication process. Describe the situation. Can you think of some reasons why certain individuals might not like it? Name them. Why might some people prefer it?

4. Discuss why organizational design and communication flow are so closely related.

5. Suppose you are a manager. You want to design your office to facilitate open, effective communication. Explain how you would use the concept of proxemics to achieve your goal.

6. In your own experience, which element of the communication process has most often been the cause of your failures to communicate? Explain.

7. In a classroom situation, do you prefer one-way communication or two-way communication between the instructor and the class? Why? Can you think of reasons why someone else might prefer the opposite? Name them.

8. What, if anything, can managers do to remove barriers to communication that are beyond their control?

9. In your opinion, how can an individual develop skills in "reading" a communicator's nonverbal cues?

10. Think of a classroom situation in terms of the elements of communication: communicator, encoding, message, medium, decoding, receiver, and feedback. Identify each element and discuss the activities involved. For example, define who the communicator is, what the message is, and who the receiver is. Is effective communication occurring? Why? Identify where, if at all, breakdowns are occurring and why.

ADDITIONAL REFERENCES

Baytosh, C. M., and B. H. Kleiner. "Effective Business Communication for Women." *Equal Opportunities International,* 1989, pp. 16–19.

Buetzkow, H. "Communication in Organizations." In *Handbook of Organizations,* ed. J. G. March. Skokie, Ill.: Rand McNally, 1965.

Foxman, L. D., and W. L. Polsky. "Communication Motivates Employees." *Personnel Journal,* 1990, pp 23–24.

Kenton, S. B. "Speaker Credibility in Persuasive Business Communication: A Model which Explains Gender Differences." *Journal of Business Communication,* 1989, pp. 143–57.

Mignon, G. "Listening Is a Vital Part of the Communications Process." *Journal of Compensation and Benefits,* 1990, pp. 308–11.

Mills, G. E., and R. W. Pace. "What Effects Do Practice and Video Feedback Have on the Development of Interpersonal Communication Skills?" *Journal of Business Communication,* 1989, pp. 159–76.

Nichols, D. "Bottom-Up Strategies: Asking the Employees for Advice." *Management Review,* 1989, pp. 44–49.

Putti, J. M.; S. Aryee; and J. Phua. "Communication Relationship, Satisfaction, and Organizational Commitment." *Group and Organizational Studies,* 1990, pp. 44–52.

Reilly, B. J., and J. A. DiAngelo, Jr. "Communication: A Cultural System of Meaning and Value." *Human Relations,* 1990, pp. 129–40.

Roberts, K. H., and C. A. O'Reilly III. "Some Correlates of Communication Roles in Organizations." *Academy of Management Journal,* 1979, pp. 42–57.

Schilit, W. K., and E. Locke. "A Study of Upward Influence in Organizations." *Administrative Science Quarterly,* 1982, pp. 304–16.

Tobias, L. L. "Twenty-Three Ways to Improve Communication." *Training and Development Journal,* 1989, pp. 75–77.

Wiener, N. *Cybernetics: or, Control and Communication in the Animal and Machine.* New York: John Wiley & Sons, 1948.

Zaremba, A. "Management in a New Key: Communication Networks." *Industrial Management,* 1989, pp. 6–11.

CASE FOR ANALYSIS

Leigh Randell is supervisor of in-flight services at the Atlanta base of Omega Airlines. Omega Airlines is a very successful regional air carrier with routes throughout the South and Southwest. In addition to Atlanta, it has bases in six major cities.

Randell's job involves supervision of all in-flight services and personnel at the Atlanta base. She has been with the airline for seven years and in her present job for two years. After having served as a flight attendant for five years, she was asked to assume her present management position. While preferring flying to a permanent ground position, she decided to try the management position. In her job, she reports directly to Kent Davis, vice president of in-flight services.

During the last year, Randell has observed what she believes is a great deal of duplication of effort between flight attendants and passenger service personnel in the terminal with respect to the paperwork procedures for boarding passengers. This, she believes, has resulted in unnecessary delays in the departures of many flights. That has especially appeared to be the case with through flights, those that do not originate or terminate in Atlanta. Since most of Omega's flights of this type are in Atlanta, Randell believes that such delayed departures are probably not a major problem at Omega's other bases or at smaller airports. Thus, she has decided to try to coordinate the efforts of flight attendants and passenger service personnel with a simpler, more efficient boarding procedure, thereby reducing ground time and increasing passenger satisfaction through closer adherence to departure times.

In this respect, she has, on three occasions during the last two months, written memos to Tom Ballard, passenger services representative of Omega at the Atlanta base. Each time, Randell has requested information regarding specific procedures, time, and costs for the boarding of passengers on through flights. She has received no reply from Tom Ballard. His job involves supervision of all passenger service personnel. He has been with Omega for five years, having joined its management training program immediately after graduating from college. He reports directly to Alan Brock, vice president of passenger services at the Atlanta base. Exhibit 1 presents the organizational structure for the Atlanta base.

Last week, Leigh wrote a memo to Kent Davis in which she stated:

> For several months, I have been trying to develop a new method for facilitating the boarding of passengers on through flights by more closely coordinating the efforts of In-Flight Services and Passenger Services. The results would be a reduction in clerical work, costs, and ground time and closer adherence to departure times for through flights. Unfortunately, I have received no cooperation at all in my efforts from the passenger services representative. I have made three written requests for information, each of which has been ignored. Needless to say, this has been very frustrating to me. While I realize that my beliefs may not always be correct, in this instance I am only trying to initiate something that will be beneficial to everyone involved: Passenger Services, In-Flight Services, and, most important, Omega Airlines. I would like to meet with you to discuss this matter and the possibility of my transferring back to flight duty.

Kent Davis summoned Alan Brock and Tom Ballard to a hastily called conference. Tom Ballard was mildly asked why he had not furnished the information that Randell had requested.

"Too busy," he said. "Her questions were out of sight. There was no time for me to answer this sort of request. I've got a job to do. Besides, I don't report to her."

"But Tom, you don't understand," Kent Davis said, "All Leigh Randell is trying to do is improve the present system of boarding passengers on through flights. She has taken the initiative to work on something that might benefit everyone."

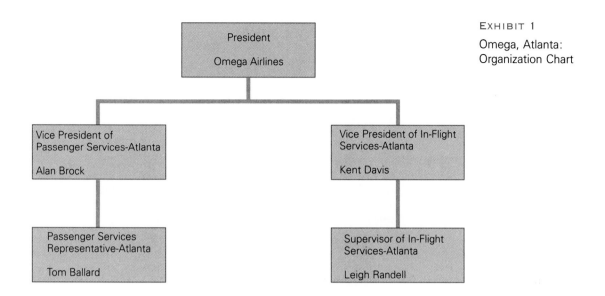

EXHIBIT 1

Omega, Atlanta:
Organization Chart

Tom Ballard thought for a moment. "No," he replied, "it didn't look like that to me. You know I've also had ideas on how to improve the system for quite some time. Anyway, she's going about it all wrong."

Questions for Consideration

1. What barriers to effective communication do you detect in this case?
2. Is anyone "wrong" in this situation? By what other means could Randell have requested the information from Tom Ballard? What do you think of Tom Ballard's reaction? Why?
3. While communicating information vertically up or down the organization does not present a major problem, why is horizontal and diagonal communication more difficult to attain? What would you recommend that the management of Omega Airlines do to remedy this situation? Why do you believe that your recommendations would improve communication in the organization?

EXPERIENTIAL EXERCISE

Objective

To illustrate how people perceive the same situation differently through the process of selective perception.

Related Topics

This exercise aptly demonstrates the wide variety of perceptual differences among people when considering a situation where little factual information is provided. The exercise should also indicate that most people selectively perceive the information they are comfortable with in analyzing a situation. Many will also subconsciously fill in gaps of information with assumptions they suppose are facts.

Starting the Exercise

The instructor will divide the class into groups of four students each. Students will then, as individuals, complete the following quiz. Group members should not converse until everyone in the class has finished.

Quiz: The Robbery

The lights in a store had just been turned off by a businessman when a man appeared and demanded money. The owner opened a cash register. The contents of the cash register were scooped up, and the man sped away. A member of the police force was notified promptly.

Answer the following questions about the story by circling T *for true,* F *for false, or* ? *for unknown.*

1. A man appeared after the owner turned off his store lights.   T F ?
2. The robber was a man.   T F ?
3. The man who appeared did not demand money.   T F ?
4. The man who opened the cash register was the owner.   T F ?
5. The store owner scooped up the contents of the cash register and ran away.   T F ?
6. Someone opened a cash register.   T F ?
7. After the man who demanded money scooped up the contents of the cash register, he ran away.   T F ?
8. While the cash register contained money, the story does not state how much.   T F ?
9. The robber demanded money of the owner.   T F ?
10. A businessman had just turned off the lights when a man appeared in the store.   T F ?
11. It was broad daylight when the man appeared.   T F ?
12. The man who appeared opened the cash register.   T F ?
13. No one demanded money.   T F ?
14. The story concerns a series of events in which only three persons are referred to: the owner of the store, a man who demanded money, and a member of the police force.   T F ?
15. The following events occurred: someone demanded money, a cash register was opened, its contents were scooped up, and a man dashed out of the store.   T F ?

Source: William V. Haney, *Communication and Interpersonal Relations: Text and Cases* (Homewood, Ill.: Richard D. Irwin, 1979), pp. 250–51.

Completing the Exercise

1. Your instructor will provide the answers to the 15 questions. Score your responses.
2. As a group, discuss your members' responses. Focus your discussion on the following questions:
   a. Why did perceptions differ across members? What factors could account for these differences?
   b. Many people don't perform very well with this quiz. Why? What other factors beyond selective perception can adversely affect performance?

17

Decision-Making Processes

AN ORGANIZATIONAL ISSUE FOR DEBATE

EXPERT SYSTEMS FOR BUSINESS APPLICATIONS

ARGUMENT FOR*

Computers have been tools for making decisions for three decades. Almost all routine, repetitive decisions that deal with quantitative data and that have a definite decision procedure are programmed. The states of a decision, programmed or nonprogrammed, depend very much on whether the decision is "unstructured" or "structured."

When no standard method exists for handling a problem or when its precise nature and structure are elusive or complex, the decision will be unstructured. Highly unstructured decisions are rarely programmed. An unstructured decision might become programmable if data can be quantified, definite decision procedures can be found, and the alternative courses of action are clarified.

In business, some routine, repetitive decisions are made by using the rule of thumb or reasoning instead of computing, because data are not quantifiable. Most of these decisions are structured but not programmed.

Recently, the success of some expert systems has caught the attention of business executives. Expert systems are software systems designed to mimic the way human experts make decisions. In one sense, building expert systems is a form of intellectual cloning. The designer builds into the system a knowledge base and an inference system. The knowledge base is derived from the expert's knowledge and experience in the field. There are two types of knowledge: (1) the facts of domain (widely shared knowledge, commonly agreed upon among practitioners) and (2) heuristic knowledge (the knowledge of good practice and good judgment in a field). The latter is the knowledge that a human expert acquires over years of work.

ARGUMENT AGAINST

Very few expert systems can be applied to organizational situations. In most cases, such situations involve behavioral variables, which can slow down acceptance of the systems. Also, organizational environments change very rapidly; managers often have to handle the unanticipated. The expert-system technology itself, behavioral variables, and other characteristics of managerial decisions all limit the development of expert systems for organizational applications.

Consider the frequent need for unstructured decisions. It takes more than experiential knowledge to make such decisions. Unstructured decisions involve decision processes that have not been encountered in quite the same form and for which no predetermined and explicit set of ordered responses exists in the organization. It is very unlikely that expert systems for highly unstructured decisions can be built, because experts have insufficient experience to provide relevant knowledge for the knowledge base in the expert system.

Organizational applications involve consideration of individual needs, perceptions, goals, and values. The heuristic knowledge that leads to good judgment of such human behavior is hard to define. As a result, mining knowledge out of the manager's head is difficult.

In the knowledge base of the computer, knowledge that is well defined must be represented as a set of if-then rules. But certain kinds of knowledge cannot be easily translated into if-then rules. Using these kinds of knowledge to build an expert system for any business application would be virtually impossible.

*There is much debate about how expert systems can be applied. See discussions in *MIS Quarterly, Planning Review, Journal of Systems Management,* and *Information Systems Management.*

This chapter focuses on decision making. The quality of managerial decisions is the yardstick of the manager's effectiveness.[1] Thus, the flow of the preceding chapters leads logically to a discussion of decision making: that is, people behave as *individuals* and as members of *groups,* within an *organizational structure,* and they *communicate* for many reasons. One of the most important reasons is to *make decisions.* This chapter, therefore, describes and analyzes decision making in terms of the ways in which people decide as a consequence of the information they receive both through the organizational *structure* and through the *behavior* of important persons and groups.

TYPES OF DECISIONS

While managers in various organizations may be separated by background, lifestyle, and distance, sooner or later they must all make decisions.[2] As discussed throughout this book, debate continues on whether managers should encourage subordinates to participate in the process of decision making.[3] However, regardless of one's stand on this issue, managers are ultimately responsible for decision outcomes. That is, they face a situation involving several alternatives, and their decision involves a comparison of alternatives and an evaluation of the outcome. In this section, our purpose is to move beyond a general definition of a decision and to present a system for classifying various decisions.

Specialists in decision making have developed several ways of classifying decisions. Similar for the most part, these systems differ mainly in terminology. We shall use the widely adopted system suggested by Herbert Simon.[4] It distinguishes between two types of decisions:

1. **Programmed decisions**. If a particular situation occurs often, a routine procedure usually can be worked out for solving it. Thus, decisions are

PROGRAMMED DECISIONS
Specific procedures developed for repetitive and routine problems.

---

[1]Bernard M. Bass, *Organizational Decision Making* (Homewood, Ill.: Richard D. Irwin, 1983).

[2]Danny Samson, *Managerial Decision Making* (Homewood, Ill.: Richard D. Irwin, 1988).

[3]For a recent study, see John L. Cotton, David A. Vollrath, and Kirk L. Froggatt, "Employee Participation: Diverse Forms and Different Outcomes," *Academy of Management Review,* January 1988, pp. 8–22.

[4]Herbert A. Simon, *The New Science of Management Decision* (New York: Harper & Row, 1960), pp. 5–6.

ORGANIZATIONS:
CLOSE-UP

DECISION MAKING IN THE INTERNATIONAL ENVIRONMENT

American companies' decisions on whether to operate in East Asia may hinge on their ability to forge business relationships without violating U.S. ethics laws. Although East Asia is the world's fastest-growing region, business ethics differ greatly from practices found in the West. In Thailand, payoffs are taken for granted. In China, widespread corruption among government officials has fueled public protests. The exit of Marcos from the Philippines has not stopped others from carrying on business in a corrupt fashion. In Malaysia, companies routinely turn out blatant copies of American products, even going so far as stamping U.S. logos on the goods.

The Foreign Corrupt Practices Act, passed in 1977, is aimed at deterring the use of payoffs by American companies in their efforts to win business. Many companies argue that the law has placed American companies at a severe disadvantage in operating overseas, because other Western countries consider such business dealings not only legal but tax deductible. The United States hoped that other countries would follow its example with similar laws. However, none have. Some companies, convinced that it's impossible to compete in this disadvantageous situation, don't even bother to try. Other companies either try to circumvent the laws

---

NONPROGRAMMED
DECISIONS

Decisions required by unique and complex management problems.

programmed to the extent that problems are repetitive and routine and a definite procedure has been developed for handling them.

2. **Nonprogrammed decisions**. Decisions are *nonprogrammed* when they are novel and unstructured. No established procedure exists for handling the problem, either because it has not arisen in exactly the same manner before or because it is complex or extremely important. Such problems deserve special treatment.

These two classifications, while broad, make important distinctions. On one hand, organization managers face great numbers of programmed decisions in their daily operations. Such decisions should be treated without expending unnecessary organizational resources on them. On the other hand, nonprogrammed decisions must be properly identified as such, since they form the basis for allocating billions of dollars of resources in our economy every year. Table 17–1 breaks down the different types of decisions, with examples of each type in different organizations. It indicates that programmed and nonprogrammed decisions apply to distinctly different problems and require different procedures.

As managers become more and more involved in international business, they find that what works at home may not work elsewhere. The Close-Up provides some interesting insights into decision making in the international environment.

Unfortunately, we know the least about the human process involved in unprogrammed decisions.[5] Traditionally, to make programmed decisions,

---

[5]Neil M. Agnew and John L. Brown, "Executive Judgment: The Intuition/Rational Ratio," *Personnel*, December 1985, pp. 48–54.

by enlisting intermediaries to take care of these local business practices or else cope with the situation as best they can while operating under the spirit of the law.

American Motors, now part of Chrysler Corp., found that signing contracts is only the beginning of negotiations in China. A stipulation added after a contract was signed to open and operate a plant was that Chinese managers be paid as much as American managers. While American managers may make, on average, $40,000 per year, Chinese executives normally take home no more than $100 a month. Hundreds of thousands of dollars per year were going to pay effectively phony salaries that ended up in the pocket of government officials.

While business in Asia may seem confusing and unfair to Americans, Far Easterners argue that it is only a matter of perspective. An Indonesian businessman poses the following question: Which is more corrupt, the American practice of hiring lobbyists and public relations firms to use their connections to influence legislation and public attitudes or the Asian practice of taking officials out to dinner and giving them gifts?

Source: Ford S. Worthy, "When Somebody Wants a Payoff," *Fortune*, Fall 1989, pp. 117–22; Jim Mann, "One Company's China Debacle," *Fortune*, November 6, 1989, pp. 145–52.

managers use rules, standard operating procedures, and the structure of the organization that develops specific procedures for handling problems. More recently, operations researchers have facilitated such decisions through the development of mathematical models. In contrast, managers make nonprogrammed decisions by general problem-solving processes, judgment, intuition, and creativity.[6] Unfortunately, the advances in modern management techniques have not improved nonprogrammed decision making nearly as much as they have programmed decision making.[7]

Ideally, top management's main concern should be nonprogrammed decisions, while first-level managers should be concerned with programmed decisions. Middle managers in most organizations concentrate mostly on programmed decisions, although in some cases they participate in nonprogrammed decisions. In other words, the nature, frequency, and degree of certainty surrounding a problem should dictate at what level of management the decision should be made.

Obviously, problems arise in organizations where top management expends much time and effort on programmed decisions. One unfortunate result is a neglect of long-range planning. It is subordinated to other activities whether the organization is successful or is having problems. Success justifies continuing the policies and practices that achieved it; if the organization experiences

---

[6]Stephen D. Brookfield, *Developing Critical Thinkers: Challenging Adults to Explore Alternative Ways of Thinking* (San Francisco: Jossey-Bass, 1987).

[7]Weston Agor, "The Logic of Intuition: How Top Executives Make Important Decisions," *Organizational Dynamics*, Winter 1986, pp. 5–18.

TABLE 17—1

Comparison of Types of
Decisions

	Programmed Decisions	Nonprogrammed Decisions
Problem	Frequent, repetitive, routine. Much certainty regarding cause and effect relationships.	Novel, unstructured. Much uncertainty regarding cause and effect relationships.
Procedure	Dependence on policies, rules, and definite procedures.	Necessity for creativity, intuition, tolerance for ambiguity, creative problem solving.
Examples:		
Business firm	Periodic reorders of inventory.	Diversification into new products and markets.
University	Necessary grade point average for good academic standing.	Construction of new classroom facilities.
Health care	Procedure for admitting patients.	Purchase of experimental equipment.
Government	Merit system for promotion of state employees.	Reorganization of state government agencies.

difficulty, its current problems have first priority and occupy the time of top management. In either case, long-range planning ends up being neglected. The neglect of long-range planning usually results in an overemphasis on short-run control and, therefore, less delegation of authority to lower levels of management. This often has adverse effects on employee motivation and satisfaction.

THE DECISION–MAKING PROCESS

DECISION

Means to achieve some result or to solve some problem; outcome of a process influenced by many forces.

Decisions should be thought of as *means* rather than ends. They are the *organizational mechanisms* by which an attempt is made to achieve a desired state. They are, in effect, an *organizational response* to a problem. Every decision is the outcome of a dynamic process that is influenced by a multitude of forces. Although this process is diagrammed in Figure 17–1, it is not a fixed procedure. It is a sequential process rather than a series of steps.[8] This enables us to examine each element in the normal progression that leads to a decision.

Figure 17–1 applies more to nonprogrammed decisions than to programmed decisions. Problems that occur infrequently, with a great deal of uncertainty surrounding the outcome, require that the manager utilize the entire process. For problems that occur frequently, the entire process is not necessary. If a policy is established to handle such problems, managers do not need to develop and evaluate alternatives each time a problem of this kind arises.

Establishing Specific Goals and Objectives and Measuring Results

Organizations need goals and objectives in each area where performance influences effectiveness. Adequately established goals and objectives will dictate which results must be achieved and which measures indicate whether or not those results have been achieved.

---

[8]Paul C. Nutt, "Types of Organizational Decision Processes," *Administrative Science Quarterly,* September 1984, pp. 414–50; S. Pokras, *Strategic Problem Solving and Decision Making* (Los Altos, Calif.: Crisp Publications, 1989).

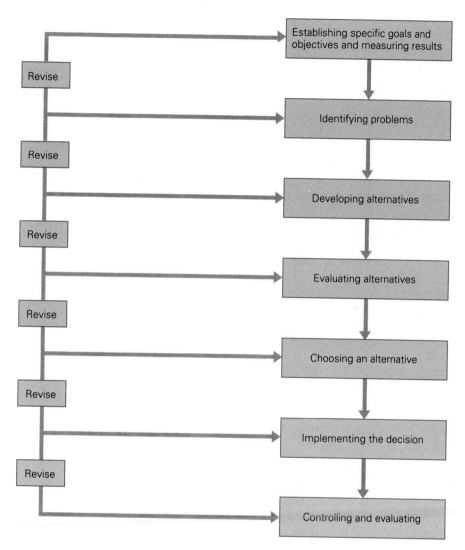

FIGURE 17—1

The Decision-Making Process

Identifying Problems

A necessary condition for a decision is a problem.[9] That is, if problems did not exist, there would be no need for decisions. This underscores the need to establish goals and objectives, because the existence of a problem is indicated by the gap between the organization's goals and objectives and the levels of actual performance. Thus, a gap of 20 percent between a sales volume objective and the volume of sales actually achieved signifies that some problem exists.

That some kind of problem exists is apparent when a gap occurs between desired results and actual results. However, identifying the exact problem can be hindered by certain factors:

1. *Perceptual problems.* As noted in Chapter 3, our individual perceptions may protect or defend us from unpleasant facts. Negative information may be

---

[9]Russell L. Ackoff, *The Art of Problem Solving* (New York: John Wiley & Sons, 1987).

selectively perceived to distort its true meaning; it may also be totally ignored. For example, a college dean may fail to identify increasing class sizes as a problem while at the same time being sensitive to problems faced by the president of the university in raising funds for the school.

2. *Defining problems in terms of solutions.* This is really a form of jumping to conclusions. For example, a sales manager may say, "The decrease in profits is due to our poor product quality," which suggests a particular solution: the improvement of product quality in the production department. Certainly, other solutions may be possible. Perhaps the sales force has been inadequately selected or trained. Perhaps competitors have a less expensive product.

3. *Identifying symptoms as problems.* "Our problem is a 32 percent decline in orders." While it is certainly true that orders have declined, the decline is really only a symptom of the true problem. The manager must identify the *cause* of the decline in orders to find the real problem.

Problems are usually of three types: opportunity, crisis, and routine. Crisis and routine problems present themselves and must be attended to by the managers.[10] Opportunities, in contrast, must usually be found; they await discovery. Often they go unnoticed and are eventually lost by an inattentive manager. Because most crises and routine problems, by their very nature, demand immediate attention, a manager may spend a great deal of time handling them and not have time to pursue important new opportunities. Many well-managed organizations try to draw attention away from crises and routine problems and toward longer-range issues through planning activities and goal-setting programs.

Developing Alternatives

Before a decision is made, feasible alternatives (potential solutions to the problem) should be developed, and the possible consequences of each alternative should be considered. For example, a sales manager may identify an inadequately trained sales force as the cause of declining sales. The sales manager would then identify possible alternatives for solving the problem, such as (1) a sales training program conducted at the home office by management, (2) a sales training program conducted by a professional training organization at a site away from the home office, and (3) more intense on-the-job training.

Developing alternatives is really a search process in which the relevant internal and external environments of the organization are investigated to provide information that can be developed into possible alternatives. Obviously, this search is conducted within certain time and cost constraints; only so much effort can be devoted to developing alternatives.[11]

Evaluating Alternatives

Once alternatives have been developed, they must be evaluated and compared. In every decision situation, the objective in making a decision is to select the

---

[10]Dean Tjosvold, "Effects of Crisis Orientation on Managers' Approach to Controversy in Decision Making," *Academy of Management Journal,* March 1984, pp. 130–38.

[11]Paul Shrivastava, "Knowledge Systems for Strategic Decision Making," *Journal of Applied Behavioral Science,* Winter 1985, pp. 95–108.

alternative that will produce the most favorable outcomes and the least unfavorable outcomes. This again points up the need for objectives and goals. In selecting among alternatives, the decision maker should be guided by previously established goals and objectives. The alternative–outcome relationship is based on three possible conditions:

1. *Certainty.* The decision maker has complete knowledge of the probability of the outcome of each alternative.
2. *Uncertainty.* The decision maker has absolutely no knowledge of the probability of the outcome of each alternative.
3. *Risk.* The decision maker has some probabilistic estimate of the outcomes of each alternative.

Decision making under conditions of risk is probably the most common situation.[12] It is in evaluating alternatives under these conditions that statisticians and operations researchers have made important contributions to decision making. Their methods have proved especially useful in the analysis and ranking of alternatives.

Choosing an Alternative

The purpose in selecting an alternative is to solve a problem to achieve a predetermined objective. This point is an important one. It means that a decision is not an end in itself but only a means to an end. While the decision maker chooses the alternative that is expected to result in the achievement of the objective, the selection of that alternative should not be seen as an isolated act. If it is, the factors that led to and lead from the decision are likely to be excluded. Specifically, the steps following the decision should include implementation, control, and evaluation. The critical point is that decision making is more than an act of choosing; it is a dynamic process.

Unfortunately for most managers, an alternative rarely achieves the desired objective without having some positive or negative impact on another objective. Situations often exist where two objectives cannot be fully achieved simultaneously. If one objective is *optimized,* the other is *suboptimized.* For example, if production in a business organization is optimized, employee morale may be suboptimized, or vice versa. A hospital superintendent may optimize a short-run objective such as maintenance costs at the expense of a long-run objective such as high-quality patient care. Thus, the multiplicity of organizational objectives complicates the real world of the decision maker.

In certain situations, an organizational objective may also be at the expense of a societal objective. This can be clearly seen in the rise of ecology groups, environmentalists, and the consumerist movement. Apparently, these groups question the priorities (organizational as against societal) of certain organizational decision makers. In any case, whether an organizational objective conflicts with another organizational objective or with a societal objective, the values of the decision maker strongly influence the alternative chosen. Individual values were discussed earlier, and their influence on the decision-making process should be clear.

---

[12]Kenneth R. MacCrimmon and Donald A. Wehrung, *The Management of Uncertainty: Taking Risks* (New York: Free Press, 1986).

In managerial decision making, optimal solutions are often impossible. The decision maker cannot possibly know all of the available alternatives, the consequences of each alternative, and the probability of these consequences occurring.[13] Thus, rather than being an optimizer, the decision maker is a *satisficer,* selecting the alternative that meets an acceptable (satisfactory) standard.

Implementing the Decision

Any decision that is not implemented is little more than an abstraction. In other words, a decision must be effectively implemented to achieve the objective for which it was made. It is entirely possible for a "good" decision to be hurt by poor implementation. In this sense, implementation may be more important than the actual choice of the alternative.

Since in most situations implementing decisions involves people, the test of the soundness of a decision is the behavior of the people affected by the decision. Subordinates cannot be manipulated in the same manner as other resources. A technically sound decision can easily be undermined by dissatisfied subordinates. Thus, a manager's job is not only to choose good solutions but also to transform such solutions into behavior in the organization. This is done by effectively communicating with the appropriate individuals and groups.[14]

Control and Evaluation

Effective management involves periodic measurement of results. Actual results are compared with planned results (the objective), and changes must be made if deviations exist. Here again, we see the importance of measurable objectives. Without them, there is no way to judge performance. Changes, if necessary, must be made in the solution chosen, in its implementation, or in the original objective if it is deemed unattainable. If the original objective must be revised, then the entire decision-making process is reactivated. The important point is that once a decision is implemented, a manager cannot assume that the outcome will meet the original objective. Some system of control and evaluation is needed to make sure the actual results are consistent with the results planned for when the decision was made. The Close-Up provides examples of what some companies are doing to help managers facilitate the process of decision making.

BEHAVIORAL INFLUENCES ON INDIVIDUAL DECISION MAKING

Several behavioral factors influence the decision-making process. Some affect only certain aspects of the process, while others influence the entire process. However, each may have an impact and therefore must be understood to fully appreciate the decision-making process in organizations. Four individual

---

[13]Paul Shrivastava and I. I. Mitroff, "Enhancing Organizational Research Utilization: The Role of Decision Makers' Assumptions," *Academy of Management Review,* January 1984, pp. 18–26.

[14]Charles R. Schwenk, *The Essence of Strategic Decision Making* (Lexington, Mass.: Lexington Books, 1988).

FACILITATING THE DECISION-MAKING PROCESS

Too often, centralized organizational structures have hindered middle management's ability to make decisions. Advocates of decentralization point to the benefits inherent in placing decision-making power at the lowest possible level in an organization. Given autonomy and authority, middle managers can make decisions quickly instead of having to wait for weeks as the process works its way up through the many layers of the corporation. However, along with this authority comes risk. Managers can no longer shield themselves by forming committees and task forces to deal with difficult issues.

Systems are evolving in which managers are treated more as entrepreneurs and evaluated as such. PepsiCo encourages managers to make decisions on their own and make them fast. Top management believes that the only way a manager will grow strong is by taking risks. Wayne Calloway, chief executive officer (CEO) of PepsiCo, states that the best time to take risks is when everything seems to be going well. Managers are evaluated on what they do to make a big difference in the business. If a manager doesn't contribute to the business in his or her first year, efforts are undertaken to find out why, and help is offered. After a year or two, however, results are expected. Those who succeed can look forward to high salaries, quick promotions, and lucrative perks. Those who fail are out.

Procter & Gamble places power in the hands of the managers closest to the customer. Well known for its brand management structure, P&G has recently created a category management system. Brand managers report to a category manager responsible for an entire product line (e.g., laundry products, which include competing brands such as Tide, Cheer, and Ivory Flakes). Within this system, category managers have the power and capacity to make quick decisions and the authority to spend up to $1 million per project. Decisions that used to take up to a year can now be made on the spot. With authority comes responsibility. As part of the decentralization process, P&G has switched from a bonus system based on corporate performance to one based on individual results.

Source: Seth Allcorn, "The Self-Protective Actions of Managers," *Supervisory Management*, January 1989, pp. 3–7; Brian Dumaine, "Those Highflying PepsiCo Managers," *Fortune*, April 10, 1989, pp. 78–86; Brian Dumaine, "P&G Rewrites the Marketing Rules," *Fortune*, November 6, 1989, pp. 34–48.

behavioral factors—values, personality, propensity for risk, and potential for dissonance—are discussed in this section. Each has a significant impact on the decision-making process.

Values

In the context of decision making, **values** are the guidelines a person uses when confronted with a situation in which a choice must be made. Values are acquired early in life and are a basic (often taken for granted) part of an individual's thoughts. The influence of values on the decision-making process is profound:

> In *establishing objectives*, value judgments must be made regarding the selection of opportunities and the assignment of priorities.

VALUES

Basic guidelines and beliefs that decision maker uses when confronted with a situation requiring choice.

In *developing alternatives,* value judgments about the various possibilities are necessary.

In *choosing an alternative,* the values of the decision maker influence which alternative is chosen.

In *implementing a decision,* value judgments are necessary in choosing the means for implementation.

In the *control* and *evaluation* phase, value judgments cannot be avoided when corrective action is decided on and taken.

Clearly, values pervade the decision-making process. They are reflected in the decision maker's behavior before making the decision, in making the decision, and in putting the decision into effect.[15]

Personality

Decision makers are influenced by many psychological forces, both conscious and subconscious. One of the most important of these forces is personality. Decision makers' personalities are strongly reflected in the choices they make. Studies that have examined the effect of personality on the process of decision making have generally focused on the following types of variables:[16]

1. *Personality variables*—the attitudes, beliefs, and needs of the individual.
2. *Situational variables*—external, observable situations in which individuals find themselves.
3. *Interactional variables*—the momentary state of the individual that results from the interaction of a specific situation with characteristics of the individual's personality.

The most important conclusions concerning the influence of personality on the decision-making process are:

— One person is not likely to be equally proficient in all aspects of the decision-making process. Some people do better in one part of the process, while others do better in another part.
— Such characteristics as intelligence are associated with different phases of the decision-making process.
— The relation of personality to the decision-making process may vary for different groups on the basis of such factors as sex and social status.

In general, the research determined that the personality traits of the decision maker combine with certain situational and interactional variables to influence the decision-making process.

[15]Linda Klebe Trevino, "Ethical Decision Making in Organizations: A Person-Situation Interactional Model," *Academy of Management Review,* July 1986, pp. 601–17.

[16]P. A. Renwick and H. Tosi, "The Effects of Sex, Marital Status, and Educational Background on Selected Decisions," *Academy of Management Journal,* March 1978, pp. 93–103; A. A. Abdel-Halim, "Effects of Task and Personality Characteristics on Subordinate Responses to Participative Decision Making," *Academy of Management Journal,* September 1983, pp. 477–84. For an interesting cross-cultural study, see Frank Heller, Peter Drenth, Paul Koopman, and Veljko Rus, *Decisions in Organizations: A Three Country Comparative Study* (Newbury Park, Calif.: Sage, 1988).

ONE MAN'S ATTITUDE TOWARD RISK

ORGANIZATIONS:
CLOSE-UP

Walter Wriston is the ex-chairman of the board of Citicorp. From 1967 to 1984, while he was chairman, Wriston transformed a local, New York City–oriented financial institution into the world's most outstanding privately owned bank, with total assets of $173.6 billion and almost 3,000 branches all over the world. Wriston believes that had he failed to take risks, the organization would not be where it is today. He believes that managers fear risk but that they must have the courage to face it. Without it, an organization can go nowhere.

Source: Walter Wriston, *Risk and Other Four-Letter Words* (New York: Harper & Row, 1986).

Propensity for Risk

From personal experience, we are all undoubtedly aware that decision makers vary greatly in their propensity for taking risks. This one specific aspect of personality strongly influences the decision-making process, as indicated in the Close-Up on attitude toward risk.

A decision maker with a low aversion to risk establishes different objectives, evaluates alternatives differently, and selects different alternatives than a decision maker in the same situation who has a high aversion to risk. The latter attempts to make choices where the risk or uncertainty is low or where the certainty of the outcome is high. As we will discuss later in the chapter, many people are bolder and more innovative and advocate greater risk-taking in groups than as individuals. Apparently, such people are more willing to accept risk as members of a group. The Close-Up on Amstrad PLC tells of a successful British firm's experience with risk.

Potential for Dissonance

Much attention has focused on the forces that influence the decision maker before a decision is made and on the decision itself. Only recently has attention been given to what happens after a decision has been made. Specifically, behavioral scientists have focused attention on the occurrence of postdecision anxiety.

Such anxiety is related to what Leon Festinger called **cognitive dissonance** over 30 years ago.[17] Festinger's theory states that there is often a lack of consistency, or harmony, among an individual's various cognitions (attitudes, beliefs, etc.) after a decision has been made. As a result, the decision maker has doubts and second thoughts about the choice. In addition, the intensity of the anxiety is likely to be greater in the presence of any of the following conditions:

COGNITIVE DISSONANCE
Anxiety that occurs when there is conflict between individual's beliefs and reality. Most individuals are motivated to reduce dissonance and achieve consonance.

1. The decision is psychologically or financially important.
2. There are a number of forgone alternatives.
3. The forgone alternatives have many favorable features.

---

[17]Leon Festinger, *A Theory of Cognitive Dissonance* (New York: Harper & Row, 1957), chap. 1.

ORGANIZATIONS:
CLOSE-UP

THE BRITISH FIRM THAT TOOK ONE RISK TOO MANY

Amstrad PLC, a British consumer electronics company, enjoyed phenomenal success during most of the 1980s. Perennially a major force in the European personal computer market, Amstrad's key to success was its ability to get products onto store shelves quickly. Alan M. Sugar, head of Amstrad, revealed the secret of the company's success. Amstrad took daring shortcuts by not testing newly designed parts before going into mass production.

For years, this strategy worked well. However, in 1989, the company took one risk too many. Amstrad tried to expand beyond its usual line of simple IBM clones by introducing more powerful models. Within a few months after the new models appeared in stores, defects started materializing. Ultimately, the computers had to be recalled. By the time the models were relaunched, the company had lost a year's worth of sales. For 1989, profits fell more than 50 percent; the stock price dropped 83 percent in 15 months. Sugar's personal stake in the company, once worth $925 million, is now valued at $157 million.

In retrospect, one could easily say that Amstrad miscalculated and shouldn't have used customers and retailers as a testing ground for new products. However, some experts point to the value of lessons learned from failure. Gerald Meyers, former CEO at American Motors, believes that failure is a part of progress, testing limits and creativity. A study comparing 20 successful Fortune 500 executives with 20 whose careers had derailed found that all had made major mistakes at one time or another. The difference is that those who learned from their mistakes ultimately succeeded. In the case of Alan Sugar and Amstrad, only time will tell.

Source: Mark Maremount, "Cutting Corners Is Cutting into Amstrad's Bottom Line," *Business Week*, December 11, 1989, pp. 109–10; Gerald C. Meyers, "How to Master Change (It Won't Be Painless)," *Business Month*, September 1989, pp. 73–75; Elisa Mambrino, "To Err Is Divine," *Success!*, October 1986, p. 26.

Dissonance can, of course, be reduced by admitting that a mistake has been made. Unfortunately, many individuals are reluctant to admit that they have made a wrong decision. These individuals are more likely to reduce their dissonance by using one or more of the following methods:

1. Seek information that supports the wisdom of their decisions.
2. Selectively perceive (distort) information in a way that supports their decisions.
3. Adopt a less favorable view of the forgone alternatives.
4. Minimize the importance of the negative aspects of the decisions and exaggerate the importance of the positive aspects.

While each of us may resort to some of this behavior in our personal decision making, a great deal of such behavior could easily be extremely harmful to organizational effectiveness.

Personality, specifically the level of self-confidence and persuasibility, influences heavily potential for dissonance. In fact, all of the behavioral influences are closely interrelated and are only isolated here for purposes of discussion.[18]

GROUP DECISION MAKING

Until now, this chapter has focused on individuals making decisions. In most organizations, however, a great deal of decision making is achieved through committees, teams, task forces, and other groups. Managers frequently face situations in which they must seek and combine judgments in group meetings. This is especially true for nonprogrammed problems, which are novel and involve much uncertainty regarding the outcome. In most organizations, decisions on such problems are rarely made by one individual on a regular basis. The increased complexity of many of these problems requires specialized knowledge in numerous fields, usually not possessed by one person. This requirement, coupled with the reality that the decisions made must eventually be accepted and implemented by many units throughout the organization, has increased the use of the collective approach to the decision-making process. The result for many managers has been endless time spent in meetings of committees and other groups. Many managers spend as much as 80 percent of their working time in committee meetings.

Individual versus Group Decision Making

Considerable debate has taken place over the relative effectiveness of individual versus group decision making. Groups usually take more time to reach a decision than individuals do, but bringing specialists and experts together has benefits, since the mutually reinforcing impact of their interaction results in better decisions. In fact, a great deal of research has shown that consensus decisions with five or more participants are superior to individual decision making, majority, vote, and leader decisions.[19]

Unfortunately, open discussion can be negatively influenced by behavioral factors, such as the pressure to conform. Such pressure may be the influence of a dominant personality in the group; or "status incongruity" may cause lower-status participants to be inhibited by higher-status participants and to "go along" even though they believe that their own ideas are superior; or certain participants may attempt to exert influence based on the perception that they are experts in the problem area.[20]

---

[18]J. Richard Harrison and James C. March, "Decision Making and Postdecision Surprises," *Administrative Science Quarterly,* March 1984, pp. 26–42. Also see James G. March, *Decisions and Organizations* (New York: Basil Blackwell, 1988).

[19]For examples, see Barry M. Staw, "The Escalation of Commitment to a Course of Action," *Academy of Management Review,* October 1981, pp. 577–88; Max H. Bazerman and Alan Appelman, "Escalation of Commitment in Individual and Group Decision Making," *Organizational Behavior and Human Decision Processes,* Spring 1984, pp. 141–52; Barbara Bird, "Implementing Entrepreneurial Ideas: The Case for Intention," *Academy of Management Review,* July 1988, pp. 442–53.

[20]Richard A. Guzzo and James A. Waters, "The Expression of Affect and the Performance of Decision Making Groups," *Journal of Applied Psychology,* February 1982, pp. 67–74; Dean

ORGANIZATIONS:
CLOSE-UP   FORCING THE BOARD TO TAKE CHARGE

In the past, boards of directors of American corporations served simply as a rubber stamp on their CEOs' ideas and decisions. Recently, however, more and more boards are getting involved in corporate governance.

Most of the credit for this change must go to outside forces. The number of lawsuits charging directors with dereliction of duty has been steadily growing. The threat of hostile takeovers has prompted directors to concentrate on maximizing shareholder value. Institutional investors, once a passive force, are starting to demand changes as they come to own a larger percentage of publicly traded stock. Boards across the country are waking up to the realization that their main job is to protect shareholders, not solely to support the CEO.

The past two years have seen an influx of outside directors named to corporate boards as shareholders begin to flex their muscles. These new directors are quick to show their assertiveness. At Alcoa, the board engineered the ouster of then CEO Charles W. Parry due to Parry's unwillingness to refocus on aluminum. At Mellon Bank, the board requested the resignation of CEO J. David Barnes after the bank's first quarterly loss ever. Directors at Control Data, in the hopes of turning around that ailing computer business, are currently taking an active role in the hiring of top executives. Even at Texas Air, CEO Frank Lorenzo's power has waned since noted financier Carl R. Pohlad has joined the board.

As a result of such changes, management is being held more accountable for its actions. For some CEOs, the scrutiny may get unpleasant; for others, the change is welcome. Several CEOs have implemented compensation plans that they hope will make boards more responsive to shareholder needs. Sara Lee pays directors 30 percent of their annual fee in stock. Sanford Weil, CEO of Commercial Credit Group, believes that directors will think as shareholders if they are shareholders. Toward this end, each director is given $50,000 of the company's stock each year as pay. Either way, the shareholders are better off.

Source: Michael Galen, "A Seat on the Board Is Getting Hotter," *Business Week,* July 3, 1989, pp. 72–73; Judith H. Dobrzynski, "Taking Charge," *Business Week,* July 3, 1989, pp. 66–71; Stratford P. Sherman, "Pushing Corporate Boards to Be Better," *Fortune,* July 18, 1989, pp. 58–67.

Certain decisions appear to be better made by groups, while others appear better suited to individual decision making. Nonprogrammed decisions appear to be better suited to group decision making. Such decisions usually call for pooled talent in arriving at a solution; also, the decisions are so important that they are usually made by top managers and to a somewhat lesser extent by middle managers. Some corporations are even taking strong measures to get their boards of directors more involved in managing and decision making, as the Close-Up points out.

Tjosvold and R. H. G. Field, "Effects of Social Context on Consensus and Majority Vote Decision Making," *Academy of Management Journal,* September 1983, pp. 500–506; Fredrick C. Miner, Jr., "Group versus Individual Decision Making: An Investigation of Performance Measures, Decision Strategies, and Process Losses/Gains," *Organizational Behavior and Human Decision Processes,* Winter 1984, pp. 112–24.

Probable quality of decision

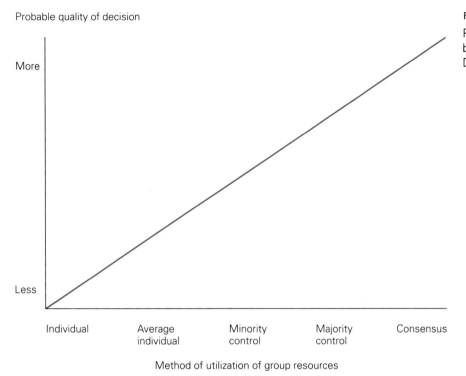

FIGURE 17–2

Probable Relationship
between Quality of Group
Decision and Method Utilized

More

Less

Individual   Average   Minority   Majority   Consensus
             individual control   control

Method of utilization of group resources

In terms of the decision-making process itself, the following points concerning group processes for nonprogrammed decisions can be made:

1. In *establishing objectives,* groups are probably superior to individuals because of the greater amount of knowledge available to groups.

2. In *identifying alternatives,* the individual efforts of group members ensure a broad search in various functional areas of the organization.

3. In *evaluating alternatives,* the collective judgment of the group, with its wider range of viewpoints, seems superior to that of the individual decision maker.

4. In *choosing an alternative,* group interaction and the achievement of consensus usually result in the acceptance of more risk than would be accepted by an individual decision maker. Also, the group decision is more likely to be accepted as a result of the participation of those affected by its consequences.

5. *Implementing a decision,* whether or not it was made by a group, is usually accomplished by individual managers. Thus, individuals bear the responsibility for implementation of the group's decision.

Figure 17–2 summarizes the research findings on group decision making. It shows the probable relationship between the quality of a decision and the method utilized to reach the decision. It indicates that as we move from individual to consensus decision making, the quality of the decision improves. Also, each successive method involves a higher level of mutual influence by group members. Thus, for a complex problem requiring pooled knowledge, the quality of the decision is likely to be higher as the group moves toward consensus.

Creativity in Group Decision Making

Because groups are better suited than individuals to making nonprogrammed decisions, an atmosphere fostering group creativity should be developed. In this respect, group decision making may be similar to brainstorming. Discussion must be free flowing and spontaneous, all group members must participate, and the evaluation of individual ideas must be suspended in the beginning to encourage participation. However, a decision must be reached, and this is where group decision making differs from brainstorming.

Techniques for Stimulating Creativity

Group decision making probably is preferable to individual decision making in many instances. However, we have all heard the statement "A camel is a racehorse designed by a committee." While the necessity and the benefits of group decision making are recognized, it also can present numerous problems, some of which have already been noted. Practicing managers need specific techniques that enable them to increase the benefits from group decision making while reducing the problems associated with it.

Increasing the creative capability of a group is especially necessary when individuals from diverse sectors of the organization must pool their judgments to create a satisfactory course of action for the organization. Three techniques have been extremely useful, when properly utilized, in increasing the group's creative capability in generating ideas, understanding problems, and reaching better decisions. The three techniques are known as brainstorming, the Delphi technique, and the nominal group technique.

BRAINSTORMING

Technique that promotes creativity by encouraging idea generation through noncritical discussion.

Brainstorming.   In many situations, groups are expected to produce creative or imaginative solutions to organizational problems. In such instances, **brainstorming** often enhances the creative output of the group. The technique of brainstorming includes a strict series of rules. The purpose of the rules is to promote the generation of ideas while at the same time removing members' inhibitions that usually stymie face-to-face groups. The basic rules are:

> No idea is too ridiculous. Group members are encouraged to state any extreme or outlandish idea.
>
> Each idea presented belongs to the group, not to the person stating it. In this way, group members utilize and build on the ideas of others.
>
> No idea can be criticized. The purpose of the session is to generate, not evaluate, ideas.

Brainstorming is widely used in advertising and some other fields, where it is apparently effective. In other situations, it has been less successful because there is no evaluation or ranking of the ideas generated. Thus, the group never really concludes the problem-solving process.

Delphi technique.   This technique involves the solicitation and comparison of anonymous judgments on the topic of interest through a set of sequential questionnaires interspersed with summarized information and feedback of opinions from earlier responses.[21]

The **Delphi process** retains the advantage of having several judges while removing the biasing effects that might occur during face-to-face interaction. The basic approach has been to collect anonymous judgments by mail questionnaire. For example, the members independently generate their ideas to answer the first questionnaire and return it. The staff members summarize the responses as the group consensus and feed this summary back, along with a second questionnaire for reassessment. Based on this feedback, the respondents independently evaluate their earlier responses. The underlying belief is that the consensus estimate results in a better decision after several rounds of anonymous group judgment. However, while continuing the procedure for several rounds is possible, studies have shown essentially no significant change after the second round of estimation.

Nominal group technique (NGT).   NGT has gained increasing recognition in health, social service, education, industry, and government organizations.[22] The term **nominal group technique** was adopted by earlier researchers to refer to processes that bring people together but do not allow them to communicate verbally. Thus, the collection of people is a group "nominally," or "in name only."

Basically, NGT is a structured group meeting in which 7 to 10 individuals sit around a table but do not speak to one another. Each person writes ideas on a pad of paper. After five minutes, a structured sharing of ideas takes place. Each person presents one idea. A person designated as recorder writes the ideas on a flip chart in full view of the entire group. This continues until all participants indicate that they have no further ideas to share. There is still no discussion.

The output of the first phase is a list of ideas (usually between 18 and 25). The next phase involves structured discussion in which each idea receives attention before a vote is taken. This is achieved by asking for clarification or stating the degree of support for each idea listed on the flip chart. The last stage involves independent voting in which each participant, in private, selects priorities by ranking or voting. The group decision is the mathematically pooled outcome of the individual votes.

Both the Delphi technique and NGT are relatively new, but each has had an excellent success record. Basic differences between them are:

1. Delphi participants are typically anonymous to one another, while NGT participants become acquainted.
2. NGT participants meet face-to-face around a table, while Delphi participants are physically distant and never meet.
3. In the Delphi process, all communication between participants is by way of written questionnaires and feedback from the monitoring staff. In NGT, participants communicate directly.[23]

DELPHI PROCESS
Technique that promotes creativity by using anonymous judgment of ideas to reach a consensus decision.

NOMINAL GROUP TECHNIQUE
Technique that promotes creativity by bringing people together in a very structured meeting that allows little verbal communication. Group decision is the mathematically pooled outcome of individual votes.

---

[21]Norman Dalkey, *The Delphi Method: An Experimental Study of Group Opinion* (Santa Monica, Calif.: Rand Corporation, 1969). This is the classic groundbreaking work on the Delphi method.

[22]See Andre L. Delbecq, Andrew H. Van de Ven, and David H. Gustafson, *Group Techniques for Program Planning* (Glenview, Ill.: Scott, Foresman, 1975), for a work devoted entirely to techniques for group decision making.

[23]Ibid., p. 18.

Practical considerations, of course, often influence which technique is used. For example, such factors as the number of available working hours, costs, and the physical proximity of participants influence selection of a technique.

Rather than to make readers experts in the Delphi process or NGT, the purpose of this section has been to indicate the frequency and importance of group decision making in every organization. The three techniques discussed are practical devices for improving the effectiveness of group decisions.

Decision making is a responsibility shared by all managers, regardless of functional area or management level. Every day, they are required to make decisions that shape the future of their organizations as well as their own futures. Some of these decisions may have a strong impact on the organization's success, while others are important but less crucial. However, all of the decisions have some effect (positive or negative, large or small) on the organization. The quality of these decisions is the yardstick of managerial effectiveness.

SUMMARY OF KEY POINTS

— Decision making is a fundamental process in organizations. Managers make decisions on the basis of the information (communication) they receive through the organizational structure and the behavior of individuals and groups within it.

— Decision making distinguishes managers from nonmanagers. The quality of the decisions that managers make determines their effectiveness as managers.

— Decisions may be classified as programmed or nonprogrammed, depending on the problem. Most programmed decisions should be made at the first level in the organization, while nonprogrammed decisions should be made mostly by top management.

— Decision making should not be thought of as an end but as a means to achieve organizational goals and objectives. Decisions are organizational responses to problems.

— Decision making should be viewed as a multiphased process in which the actual choice is only one phase.

The preceding phases are establishing goals, identifying problems, developing alternatives, evaluating alternatives, and implementing the decision.

— The decision-making process is influenced by numerous environmental and behavioral factors. Because of different values, perceptions, and personalities, different decision makers may not select identical alternatives in the same situation.

— A great deal of nonprogrammed decision making is carried on in group situations. Much evidence exists to support the claim that in most instances group decisions are superior to individual decisions. Three relatively new techniques (brainstorming, the Delphi technique, and the nominal group technique) improve the effectiveness of group decisions. The management of collective decision making must be a vital concern for future managers.

DISCUSSION AND REVIEW QUESTIONS

1. Biographies of successful executives often stress that these individuals were decision makers. In your opinion, why is so much attention paid to this ability? Does everyone have the ability to make decisions?

2. Are you a decision maker? In a short essay, describe whether or not you believe you are a decision maker and the reasons for your choice.

3. Describe in detail a situation in which you were involved in a group decision. Was the decision different from what you would have decided on your own? Now that you have had time to reflect on it, was the group decision superior to your decision? Why or why not?

4. In terms satisfactory to you, define the term *decision*.

5. Describe two situations you faced that called for programmed decisions on your part and two that called for nonprogrammed decisions. What were some of the differences between them? Did this influence your decision-making approach? How?

6. Think of a major decision you made recently. It may have involved your personal life, a major purchase, and so on. Do you believe any behavioral influences affected your decision? Discuss them.

7. What is your attitude toward risk? Has that attitude ever influenced a decision you made? What are the implications of your attitude toward risk?

8. Have you ever been a member of a committee or a task force charged with making a decision? Describe the satisfactions, dissatisfactions, and problems in this experience.

ADDITIONAL REFERENCES

Adizes, I., and E. Turban. "An Innovative Approach to Group Decision Making." *Personnel*, 1985, pp. 45–49.

Agor, W. "How Top Executives Use Their Intuition to Make Important Decisions." *Business Horizons*, 1986, pp. 62–66.

Baird, I. S., and H. Thomas. "Toward a Contingency Model of Strategic Risk Taking." *Academy of Management Review*, 1985, pp. 230–43.

Cornell, A. H. *The Decision Makers Handbook*. Englewood Cliffs, N.J.: Prentice Hall, 1989.

Duhaime, I. M., and C. R. Schwenk. "Conjectures on Cognitive Simplification in Acquisition and Divestment Decision Making." *Academy of Management Review*, 1985, pp. 287–95.

Ford, J. "The Effects of Casual Attributions on Decision Makers' Responses to Performance Downturns." *Academy of Management Review*, 1985, pp. 770–86.

Frederickson, J. W. "Effects of Decision Motive on Organizational Performance Level and Strategic Decision Processes." *Academy of Management Journal*, 1985, pp. 821–43.

Gladstein, D. L., and N. P. Reilly. "Group Decision Making under Threat: The Tycoon Game." *Academy of Management Journal*, 1985, pp. 613–27.

Hart, S.; M. Boroush; G. Enk; and W. Norwick. "Managing Complexity through Consensus Mapping: Technology for the Structuring of Group Decisions." *Academy of Management Review*, 1985, pp. 587–600.

Keyes, R. *Chancing It: Why We Take Risks*. Boston: Little, Brown, 1988.

Kindler, H. S. "Decisions, Decisions: Which Approach to Take?" *Personnel*, 1985, pp. 47–51.

Kogan, N., and M. A. Wallach. *Risk Taking: A Study in Cognition and Personality*. New York: Holt, Rinehart & Winston, 1964.

Linneman, R. E., and H. E. Klein. "Using Scenarios in Strategic Decision Making." *Business Horizons*, 1985, pp. 64–74.

Nutt, Paul C. *Making Tough Decisions*. San Francisco: Jossey-Bass, 1989.

Rowe, A. J., and R. O. Mason. *Managing with Style: A Guide to Understanding, Assessing, and Improving Decision Making*. San Francisco: Jossey-Bass, 1987.

Schweiger, D. M.; W. R. Sandburg; and J. W. Ragan. "Group Approaches for Improving Strategic Decision Making: A Comparative Analysis of Dialectical Inquiry." *Academy of Management Journal*, 1986, pp. 149–58.

Schwenk, C. R. "Devil's Advocacy in Managerial Decision Making." *Journal of Management Studies*, 1984, pp. 153–68.

_____. "The Use of Participant Recollection in the Modeling of Organizational Decision Processes." *Academy of Management Review*, 1985, pp. 496–503.

Simon, H. A. *Models of Man*. New York: John Wiley & Sons, 1957.

_____. *Sciences of the Artificial*. Cambridge, Mass.: MIT Press, 1969.

Singh, J. V. "Performance, Slack, and Risk Taking in Organizational Decision Making." *Academy of Management Journal*, 1986, pp. 562–85.

Wanos, J. P., and M. A. Youtz. "Selection Diversity and the Quality of Group Decisions." *Academy of Management Journal*, 1986, pp. 1149–58.

THE FACULTY DECISION

Tom Madden slipped into his seat at the meeting of the faculty of the College of Business Administration of Longley University. He was 10 minutes late, having come completely across campus from another meeting that had lasted 1 ¼ hours. "Boy!" he thought, "if all of these meetings and committee assignments keep up, I won't have time to do anything else."

"The next item of importance," the dean was saying, "is consideration of the feasibility report prepared by the assistant dean, Dr. Jackson, for the establishment of our Latin American M.B.A. program."

"What's that?" Madden whispered to his friend Jim Lyon, who was sitting next to him?

"Ah, Professor Madden," winked Lyon as he passed the 86-page report to him, "evidently, you've not bothered to read this impressive document. Otherwise, you'd know."

"Heck, Jim, I've been out of town for two weeks on a research project, and I've just come from another meeting."

"Well, Tom," chuckled Lyon, "the report was circulated only three days ago to, as the dean put it, 'ensure that we have faculty input into where the college is going.' Actually, Tom, I was hoping you had read it because then you could have told me what was in it."

"Dr. Jackson," said the dean, "why don't you present a summary of your excellent report on what I believe is an outstanding opportunity for our college, the establishment of an M.B.A. program in Latin America."

"Hey, Jim," said Madden, "they've got to be kidding. We're not doing what we should be doing with the M.B.A. we've got here on campus. Why on earth are we thinking about starting another one 3,000 miles away?"

Lyon shrugged, "Some friend of the dean or Jackson from down there must have asked them, I guess."

While the summary was being given, Madden thumbed through the report. He noted that the college was planning to offer the same program that it offered in the United States. "Certainly," he thought, "their students' needs are different from ours." He also noted that faculty were going to be sent from the United States on one- to three-year appointments. "You would think that whenever possible they would seek local instructors who were familiar with the needs of local industry," Madden thought. He concluded in his mind, "Actually, why are we even getting involved in this thing in the first place? We don't have the resources."

When Jackson finished the summary, the dean asked, "Are there any questions?"

"I wonder how many people have had the time to read this report in three days and think about it," Madden thought to himself.

"Has anybody thought through this entire concept?" Madden spoke up. "I mean . . ."

"Absolutely, Professor, Madden," the dean answered. "Dr. Jackson and I have spent a great deal of time on this project."

"Well, I was just thinking that . . ."

"Now, Professor Madden, surely you don't question the efforts of Dr. Jackson and myself. Had you been here when this meeting started, you would know all about our efforts. Besides, it's getting late, and we've got another agenda item to consider today, the safety and security of final examinations prior to their being given."

"No further questions," Madden said.

"Wonderful," said the dean. "Then I will report to the president that the faculty of the College of Business Administration unanimously approves the Latin American

M.B.A. program. I might add, by the way, that the president is extremely pleased with our method of shared decision making. We have made it work in this college, while other colleges are having trouble arriving at mutually agreed-upon decisions.

"This is a great day for our college. Today we have become a multinational university. We can all be proud."

After the meeting, as Madden headed for the parking lot, he thought, "What a way to make an important decision. I guess I shouldn't complain though, I didn't even read the report. I'd better check my calendar to see what committee meetings I've got the rest of the week. If I've got any more, I'll . . ."

Questions for Consideration

1. Analyze this case, and outline the factors that influenced—either positively or negatively—the faculty's decision in this case.

2. Does this case indicate that shared decision making cannot be worthwhile and effective? How could it be made more effective in the College of Business Administration?

3. Do you believe that shared decision making may be more worthwhile and effective in some organizations than in others? Discuss.

EXPERIENTIAL EXERCISE

LOST ON THE MOON: A GROUP DECISION EXERCISE

Objective

To come as close as possible to the "best solution" as determined by experts of the National Aeronautics and Space Administration (NASA).

Related Topics

Motivation, individual differences, and group development are important topics related to this exercise.

Starting the Exercise

After reading the following scenario, you will, first individually and then as a member of a team, rank the importance of items available for carrying out your mission.

The Scenario

Your spaceship has just crash-landed on the moon. You were scheduled to rendez-vous with a mother ship 200 miles away on the lighted surface of the moon, but the rough landing has ruined your ship and destroyed all of the equipment aboard, except for the 15 items listed below.

Your crew's survival depends on reaching the mother ship, so you must choose the most critical items available for the 200-mile trip. Your task is to rank the 15 items in terms of their importance for survival. Place number 1 by the most important item, number 2 by the second most important, and so on through number 15, the least important.

Work Sheet Items	1 NASA's Ranks	2 Your Ranks	3 Error Points	4 Group Ranks	5 Error Points
Box of matches	_____	_____	_____	_____	_____
Food concentrate	_____	_____	_____	_____	_____
Fifty feet of nylon rope	_____	_____	_____	_____	_____
Parachute silk	_____	_____	_____	_____	_____
Solar-powered portable heating unit	_____	_____	_____	_____	_____
Two .45-caliber pistols	_____	_____	_____	_____	_____
One case of dehydrated Pet milk	_____	_____	_____	_____	_____
Two 100-pound tanks of oxygen	_____	_____	_____	_____	_____
Stellar map (of the moon's constellation)	_____	_____	_____	_____	_____
Self-inflating life raft	_____	_____	_____	_____	_____
Magnetic compass	_____	_____	_____	_____	_____
Five gallons of water	_____	_____	_____	_____	_____
Signal flares	_____	_____	_____	_____	_____
First-aid kit containing injection needles	_____	_____	_____	_____	_____
Solar-powered FM receiver-transmitter	_____	_____	_____	_____	_____
Total error points	Individual _____		Group _____		

Completing the Exercise

Phase I: 15 minutes. Read the scenario. Then, in column 2 (Your Ranks) of the work sheet, assign priorities to the 15 items listed. Use a pencil since you may wish to change your rankings. Somewhere on the sheet, you may wish to note your logic for each ranking.

Phase II: 25 minutes. Your instructor will assign you to a team. The task of each team is to arrive at a consensus on the rankings. Share your individual solutions and reach a consensus — the ranking for each of the 15 items that best satisfies all of the team members. Thus, by the end of phase II, all members of the team should have the same set of rankings in column 4 (Group Ranks). Do not change your individual rankings in column 2.

Phase III: 10 minutes. Your instructor will provide you with the "best solution" to the problem — that is, the set of rankings determined by the NASA experts, along with their reasoning. Each person should note this set of rankings in column 1 (NASA's Ranks). (Note: While it is fun to debate the experts' rankings and their reasoning, remember that the objective of the game is to learn more about decision making, not how to survive on the moon!)

Phase IV (evaluation): 15 minutes. Now, see how well you did, individually and as a team. First, find your individual score by taking, for each item, the absolute difference between your ranks (column 2) and NASA's ranks (column 1) and writing it in the first error points column (column 3). (Thus, if you ranked "Box of matches" 3 and NASA ranked it 8, you would put a 5 in column 3, across from "Box of matches." Then, add the error points in column 3 and write the total at the bottom in the space for individual total error points.

Next, score your group performance in the same way, this time taking the absolute difference between group ranks (column 4) and NASA's ranks (column 1) and writing them in the second error points column (column 5). Add the group error points and write the total in the space provided. (Note that all members of the team have the same group error points.)

Finally, prepare three pieces of information to be submitted when your instructor calls on your team:

1. Average individual total error points (the average of all group members' individual totals). One team member should add these figures and divide by the number of team members to get the average.
2. Group total error points, as shown on each group member's work sheet.
3. Number of team members who had fewer individual total error points than the group total error points.

Using this information, your instructor will evaluate the results of the exercise and discuss group versus individual performance. Together, you will then explore the implication of this exercise for the group decision-making process.

18

Socialization and Career Processes

LEARNING OBJECTIVES

After completing Chapter 18, you should be able to:

DEFINE
organizational socialization and careers.

DESCRIBE
the way in which socialization stages correspond with career stages.

DISCUSS
the different experiences and activities that correspond to each career stage.

COMPARE
alternative socialization practices for each socialization stage.

IDENTIFY
the characteristics of effective socialization practices.

AN ORGANIZATIONAL
ISSUE FOR DEBATE   LOYALTY-BUILDING THROUGH SOCIALIZATION*

ARGUMENT FOR

In recent years, organizations have found it more and more difficult to obtain loyalty and commitment from their managers. For obvious reasons, organizations value loyal and committed employees: they work harder and achieve greater success than disloyal and uncommitted workers. But organizations cannot count on loyalty; new employees must be socialized so that they become loyal.

Socialization processes that encourage and reward loyalty take many forms and involve specific organizational practices. In one particularly effective form, that involves four key elements, the organization:

1. Induces individuals to choose to be loyal, by offering rewards.
2. Influences employees to remain loyal by enticement, not force.
3. Draws the individual away from his or her own values and goals toward the organization's values and goals.
4. Creates the appearance that the individual exercises free choice when hiring on and remaining in the job.

The organization implements this form of socialization by hiring only those individuals apparently inclined to accept the organization's values and goals. Once hired, the individual is given opportunities to work in high-status, challenging, responsible, enriched jobs. For satisfactory performance, the employee is highly rewarded through monetary compensation, plush working conditions, and job perks. Through this process, the organization engenders a high level of loyalty. Individuals, in fact, feel obligated to be loyal to such benevolent organizations.

The purpose of the status system and the enriched jobs is to constantly reinforce the value of loyalty. People in lower levels of the status hierarchy must reaffirm their commitment as a condition for advancement. Enriched jobs, with their associated responsibilities, are so demanding and time-consuming that individuals seldom can see beyond them. The reward system is the payoff for their hard work. As a consequence of these practices, individuals become loyal employees. In return for all the benefits of employment, they are willing to suspend their judgments and accept those of the organization.

ARGUMENT AGAINST

Critics of socialization that secures loyalty and commitment through inducement and enticement aptly note that it is a form of "organizational seduction." Manipulating individuals to suspend their own values and goals raises not only organizational issues but ethical issues as well.

The ethical issues concern whether individuals really exercise free will or whether the abundance of opportunities and rewards inexorably draws them into behaviors that they would otherwise not choose. Would individuals react favorably if the organization explained the purposes of its practices? Critics believe employees would feel manipulated if told that the price of status and rewards is their own seduction.

The organizational issues relate to long-range effects. One effect is to promote to top management those individuals who demonstrate the greatest loyalty and commitment. They may not, however, be the most creative, the best decision makers, the most effective problem solvers. Not only will such managers fail to perform at high levels but they are likely to expect undue loyalty and commitment from their subordinates. Consequently, they impose a confining, if not closed, mentality on those below them. As another effect, those who are insufficiently loyal and do not make it up the ladder either psychologically withdraw from or quit the organization. Anger and bitterness follow unfulfilled expectations, and unfulfilled expectations are inevitable because there is less room at the top of the status hierarchy than there are candidates.

Perhaps the greatest cost of organizational seduction is the loss of dissent. Loyalty and dissenting opinion are uneasy companions. In fact, managers often view dissent as disloyalty and violation of the "team player" idea. Insistence on agreement fosters an ever narrowing range of alternatives and perspectives to be considered. Under such circumstances, organizational effectiveness must decline.

*Source: Based on Roy J. Lewicki, "Organizational Seduction: Building Commitment to Organizations," *Organizational Dynamics*, Autumn 1981, pp. 5–21; Richard Pascale, "The Paradox of 'Corporate Culture': Reconciling Ourselves to Socialization," *California Management Review*, Winter 1985, pp. 26–41; Charles K. Goman, "Earning Employee Loyalty: New Values Demand New Approaches," *Management World*, March–April 1989, pp. 40, 42, 44.

Organizational socialization and individual career development are important processes. Through socialization, the organization attempts to achieve high levels of individual performance, although group and organizational performance are also enhanced by effective socialization efforts. Through career processes, individuals seek to enhance their own productivity and satisfaction. Organizational socialization "is the process by which an individual comes to appreciate the values, abilities, expected behaviors, and social knowledge essential for assuming an organizational role and for participating as an organization member."[1] According to one expert, the essential aim of socialization is foster "cooperation, integrity, and communication."[2] Other experts would argue that other aims are important, that cooperation can in fact preserve the status quo and thwart innovation. Thus, differences of opinion exist as to the purposes of socialization in a particular organization. In general, the purpose of socialization is to integrate individual and organizational interests, whatever they might be.

The Organizational Issue for Debate that opens this chapter raises an interesting question regarding socialization: To what extent are socialization efforts intended to reshape the individual's values to coincide with organizational values? Also, if organizations do indeed obtain employee loyalty through seductive practices, important ethical issues must be confronted.

[1] Meryl R. Louis, "Surprise and Sense Making: What Newcomers Experience in Entering Unfamiliar Organizational Settings," *Administrative Science Quarterly*, June 1980, pp. 229–30. This generally accepted definition of socialization in organizational settings reflects the view of Edgar H. Schein, "Organizational Socialization and the Profession of Management," *Industrial Management Review*, January 1968, pp. 1–16.

[2] Richard Pascale, "The Paradox of 'Corporate Culture': Reconciling Ourselves to Socialization," *California Management Review*, Winter 1985, p. 37.

From the perspective of the individual, the socialization process is related to career development. That is, the individual looks to the organization for opportunities to achieve the satisfying work experiences that make up a satisfying career. As ordinarily understood, a career consists of a sequential combination of work and nonwork roles held by an individual over time.[3] The socialization process attempts to focus an individual's perception of satisfying work activities on those that lead to effective performance. Whether and how the socialization process brings about effective performance is a complex issue involving interrelationships and interactions among characteristics of the organization, the individual, and the socialization process itself.[4]

Because the two processes are interrelated, we will discuss them together. We begin with the career process and discuss contemporary ideas regarding the concept of career, the meaning of career effectiveness, career stages, and career paths. Next, we take up organizational socialization and discuss the process and stages of socialization and the criteria for evaluating the effectiveness of organizational socialization.

ORGANIZATIONAL CAREERS

Definition of Career

CAREER

Sequence of job-related experiences and activities that create certain attitudes and behaviors in the individual.

The popular meaning of **career** is reflected in the idea of moving upward in one's chosen line of work. Upward movement implies larger salaries, more responsibility, and greater status, prestige, and power. Although we restrict our attention here to careers of those in organizations (lines of work involving gainful employment), this does not deny the existence of careers in other contexts. The concept of career can certainly be related to homemakers, mothers, fathers, volunteer workers, civic leaders, and the like. These people also advance in the sense that their knowledge and skills grow with time, experience, and training.

The definition of career used in this discussion is: "The career is the individually perceived sequence of attitudes and behaviors associated with work-related experiences and activities over the span of the person's life."[5] This definition emphasizes that career consists of both attitudes and behaviors and is an ongoing sequence of work-related activities. However, even though the concept of career is clearly work related, a person's nonwork life and roles play a significant part in it. For example, a midcareer manager who is 50 years old can have quite different attitudes about the greater responsibilities involved in job advancement than a manager nearing retirement. A bachelor's reaction to a promotion involving relocation is likely to be different from that of a father of school-age children.

---

[3]William L. Mihal, Patricia A. Sorce, and Thomas E. Comte, "A Process Model of Career Decision Making," *Academy of Management Review,* January 1984, p. 95.

[4]Gareth R. Jones, "Socialization Tactics, Self-Efficacy, and Newcomers' Adjustments to Organizations," *Academy of Management Journal,* June 1986, pp. 262–79.

[5]Douglas T. Hall, ed., *Career Development in Organizations* (San Francisco: Jossey-Bass, 1986).

From the standpoint of the individual, a career is a series of choices from among different opportunities presented. From the organization's standpoint, however, careers are processes by which the organization renews itself.[6] Although great diversity can be found in the career development practices of organizations, recent studies have begun to identify some of the more important ones. For example, practices differ depending on whether the organization gets its supply of individuals from internal or external sources and whether it assigns tasks to employees on the basis of individual or group-related contributions. Military organizations promote from within (internal supply) on the basis of contributions to the general group. By contrast, entertainment firms rely on midcareer transfers for important upper-level positions (external supply) and emphasize individual achievement in these appointments. The career development practices of these two organization types reflect differences in these two basic characteristics.[7]

Although careers have typically been thought of in terms of upward mobility, recent ideas have enlarged the concept. For example, an individual can remain in the same job, acquiring and developing skills without moving upward in an organizational or professional hierarchy. Moving among various jobs in different fields and organizations is also possible.[8] Thus, the concept of career must be broad enough to include not only traditional work experiences but also emerging work styles and lifestyles. Contemporary career development practices recognize the diversity of individual choices and career alternatives.[9]

Career Choices

How do people enter particular occupations and professions? Is it by chance or by choice? Although the matching of individuals and careers is vitally important for individuals, organizations, and society, career guidance and counseling is far from a precise science. The most obvious complication is the inherent tendency of individuals to change their interests, motivations, and abilities. But equally obvious in this day and age is the fact of changing career demands. Technology has brought irrevocable change, for example, to the demands on those seeking careers in office work, factories, medicine, banking, and government service. Thus, an individual may choose a career and prepare for it but subsequently discover that technology has rendered that preparation obsolete and irrelevant.

A reasonable way to understand career choice is that individuals tend toward careers that are consonant with their own personal orientations. This

[6]Hugh Gunz, "The Dual Meaning of Managerial Careers: Organizational and Individual Levels of Analysis," *Journal of Management Studies,* May 1989, p. 226.

[7]Jeffrey A. Sonnenfeld and Maury A. Peiperl, "Staffing Policy as a Strategic Response: A Typology of Career Systems," *Academy of Management Review,* October 1988, pp. 588–600.

[8]Meryl R. Louis, "Career Transitions: Varieties and Commonalities," *Academy of Management Review,* July 1980, p. 330.

[9]Kathryn M. Bartol, "Vocational Behavior and Career Development, 1980: A Review," *Journal of Vocational Behavior,* October 1981, pp. 123–62; Edwin L. Herr, "Comprehensive Career Guidance: A Look to the Future," *Vocational Guidance Quarterly,* June 1982, pp. 371–76.

TABLE 18—1

Holland's Six Personality
Types and Compatible
Occupations

Type	Characteristics	Occupations
Realistic	Aggressive behavior; prefers activities requiring skill, strength, and coordination	Forestry, farming, architecture
Investigative	Cognitive behavior; prefers thinking, organizing, and understanding activities	Biology, mathematics, oceanography
Social	Interpersonal behavior; prefers feeling and emotional activities	Clinical psychology, foreign service, social work
Conventional	Structured behavior; prefers to subordinate personal needs to others' needs	Accounting, finance
Enterprising	Predictable behavior; prefers power and status acquisition activities	Management, law, public relations
Artistic	Self-expressive behavior; prefers artistic, self-expressive, and individualistic activities	Art, music, education

line of thinking underlies an important theory of career choices that John Holland developed.[10] According to Holland, individuals can be classified according to six personality types that coincide with six occupational types. If people do tend to gravitate toward occupational types that coincide with their personality types and if Holland's personality and occupational types are valid, these individuals can make informed career choices. Holland's personality types and compatible occupations are shown in Table 18–1.

Holland and others have devised paper-and-pencil tests to identify an individual's primary orientation. Many counseling centers in high schools and universities use the tests as one basis for advising students on educational and career tracks. The idea is rather straightforward: individuals whose career choices match their personality types will likely persist in the required educational preparation and will prosper in the subsequent career.

Holland's theory and the counseling practices based on it are not valid in all instances. But their validity is sufficiently widespread to command considerable attention. The theory and practices are being subjected to continued study of their applicability for both initial and subsequent career choices. The importance of career choice decisions as a factor in career effectiveness cannot be overvalued.[11]

The ultimate responsibility for career choice rests with the individual making those choices. The selection of a particular life endeavor involves complex trade-offs among different, often conflicting values, such as family, security, and money values. Individuals place different importance on these values at different points in their lives and careers; moreover, the opportunities to satisfy them change with time. Although relatively sophisticated methods

[10]John L. Holland, *Making Vocational Choices: A Theory of Careers* (Englewood Cliffs, N.J.: Prentice Hall, 1973). Discussion of Holland's theory is based on Douglas T. Hall, *Careers in Organizations* (Santa Monica, Calif.: Goodyear Publishing, 1976), pp. 13–15. For an extensive review of the literature, see Manuel London, "Toward a Theory of Career Motivation," *Academy of Management Review,* October 1983, pp. 620–30.

[11]Mihal et al., "A Process Model," pp. 95–103; London, "Toward a Theory."

ORGANIZATIONS:
CLOSE-UP

CAREER COUNSELING BY MAIL

Individuals seeking career counseling can obtain a self-assessment test to complete in the privacy of their homes. The multiple-choice test is available for $34.95 from National Computer Systems, Inc., P.O. Box 1416, Minnetonka, Minnesota 55440. The test measures different interests, work values, personal traits, and verbal and numerical abilities. It takes about three hours to complete, and the responses must be returned to the vendor. Then the computer matches the individual's answers to thousands of other people who report that they are happy and satisfied with their chosen profession. Within a few days, a report is sent out that interprets the test taker's responses and suggests from 10 to 15 careers that match those responses.

Such tests, convenient and relatively inexpensive, can be instructive and can identify areas of interest that might have gone unrecognized. However, many experts would argue that they should not substitute for professional career counseling. Other experts point out that these kinds of self-analysis can be instructive and can suggest avenues of opportunity that could be explored, without major commitment in time and money.

Source: John A. Byrne, "This Test May Tell You to Switch Careers," *Business Week*, September 21, 1987, p. 125.

can be applied to making career choices, the actual choices remain largely subjective and personal.[12] In some instances, the choice of career may even be made on the basis of "mail-order" information, as reflected in the Close-Up on career counseling by mail.

CAREER EFFECTIVENESS

In organizational settings, **career effectiveness** is judged not only by the individual but also by the organization itself. But what is meant by career effectiveness? Under what circumstances will individuals state that they have had "successful" or "satisfying" careers? Will the organization share the individuals' views about their careers? Although numerous characteristics of career effectiveness could be listed, four are often cited: performance, attitudes, adaptability, and identity.

CAREER EFFECTIVENESS
Extent to which the sequence of career attitudes and behaviors satisfies the individual.

Career Performance

Salary and position are the more popular indicators of career performance. Specifically, the more rapidly one's salary increases and one advances up the hierarchy, the higher the level of career performance. The higher one advances,

[12]John R. Canada, Edward H. Frazelle, Robert H. Koger, and Earl MacCormac, "How to Make a Career Choice: The Use of the Analytical Hierarchy Process," *Industrial Management*, September–October 1985, pp. 16–22.

the greater is the responsibility in terms of employees supervised, budget allocated, and revenue generated. The organization is, of course, vitally interested in career performance, since it bears a direct relation to organizational effectiveness. That is, the rate of salary and position advancement reflects, in most instances, the extent to which the individual has contributed to organizational performance.

Two points should be made. First, to the extent that the organization's performance evaluation and reward processes do not fully recognize performance, individuals may not realize this indicator of career effectiveness. Thus, individuals may not receive those salary and promotion rewards associated with career effectiveness, because the organization either does not or cannot provide them. Many employees discover that organizations often state that performance is rewarded, when in fact they reward other, nonperformance outcomes.[13] Second, the organization may have performance expectations the individual is unwilling or unable to meet. For example, the organization may accurately assess the individual's potential as being greater than present performance; yet, because the individual has other, nonjob interests (e.g., family, community, religious), performance does not match potential. In such instances, the individual may be satisfied with career performance, yet the organization is disappointed. This mismatch occurs as a consequence of the individual's attitudes toward the career.

Career Attitudes

The term *career attitudes* refers to the way individuals perceive and evaluate their careers: individuals with positive career attitudes are those who have positive perceptions and evaluations of their careers. Positive attitudes have important implications for the organization because individuals with positive attitudes are more likely to be committed to the organization and to be involved in their jobs. The manner in which individuals come to have positive career attitudes is a complex psychological and sociological process; a full development of that process is beyond the scope of this discussion. However, positive career attitudes are likely to coincide with career demands and opportunities that are consistent with an individual's interests, values, needs, and abilities.

Specific career attitudes such as career commitment and job involvement are associated with behaviors that concern organizations. For example, one study of career commitment among bank tellers found that high career commitment is related to low turnover.[14] The study distinguishes between career commitment and job involvement, with commitment referring to attitudes about a career in banking where the teller job is seen as a first step in that career, and involvement referring to attitudes specific to the teller job. Individuals can have positive attitudes about a career in banking but be little involved in the job, although the two should be positively associated for most individuals.

---

[13]Roy J. Lewicki, "Organizational Seduction: Building Commitment to Organizations," *Organizational Dynamics*, Autumn 1981, p. 9.

[14]Gary Blau, "Testing the Generalizability of a Career Commitment Measure and Its Impact on Employee Turnover," *Academy of Management Proceedings*, 1989, pp. 53–57.

Important to management is the recognition that career-committed individuals who leave the bank usually go to another bank in a higher position, while job-involved individuals who leave the bank usually go to jobs with lower stress and demands.

Career Adaptability

Few professions are stagnant and unchanging. On the contrary, the condition of change and development more accurately describes contemporary professions. Changes occur in the profession itself, requiring new knowledge and skills to practice it. For example, medicine and engineering have advanced and will continue to advance in the utilization of new information and technology. Other professions likewise have changed markedly. Individuals unable to adapt to these changes and to adopt them in the practice of their careers run the risk of early obsolescence and the loss of their jobs. The effects of job loss on individuals have taken on considerable importance since economic pressures of the 1980s caused organizations to reduce their managerial and professional staff.[15]

Career adaptability implies the application of the latest knowledge, skills, and technology in the work of a career. Obviously, organizations benefit from the adaptiveness of employees. An expression of the mutual benefits derived from career adaptability is the dollars expended by organizations for employee training and development.

Career Identity

Career identity comprises two important components: (1) the extent to which individuals have clear and consistent awareness of their interests, values, and expectations for the future; (2) the extent to which individuals view their lives as consistent through time and themselves as extensions of their past. The idea expressed in this concept is "What do I want to be and what do I have to do to become what I want to be?"[16] Individuals who have satisfactory resolutions to this question are likely to have effective careers and to make positive contributions to the organizations that employ them.

Effective careers in organizations, then, are likely to occur for individuals with high levels of performance, positive attitudes, adaptiveness, and identity resolution. Moreover, effective careers are without doubt linked to organizational performance.

Figure 18–1 suggests possible relationships between the characteristics of career effectiveness and the criteria of organizational effectiveness. The degree to which these relationships are generally valid cannot be stated with certainty, yet some suggestions are warranted. Career performance would seem to be related to organizational production and efficiency. In most organizations, the performance evaluation process places primary emphasis on these two criteria,

[15]Janina C. Latack and Janelle B. Dozier, "After the Ax Falls: Job Loss as a Career Transition," *Academy of Management Review*, April 1986, pp. 375–92.

[16]Erik H. Erikson, "The Concept of Identity in Race Relations: Notes and Queries," *Daedalus*, 1966, p. 148, as cited in Hall, *Careers in Organizations*, p. 95.

FIGURE 18—1

Suggested Relationships
between Characteristics of
Career Effectiveness and
Criteria of Organizational
Effectiveness

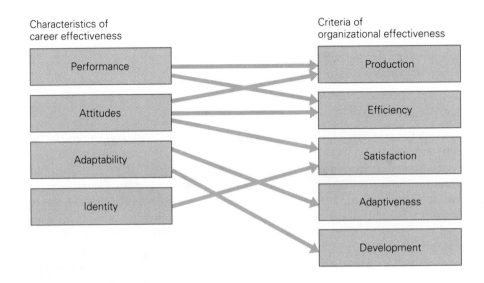

and career performance is judged accordingly. Positive career attitudes would imply commitment to production and efficiency and, perhaps by definition, satisfaction. Individuals with positive career attitudes working in organizations that emphasize employee growth and development would no doubt be effective; thus, connective arrows could also be drawn from attitudes to adaptiveness and development. Career adaptability is directly related to organizational adaptiveness and development, particularly for occupations and organizations subject to rapid change. Finally, career identity is directly related to satisfaction; it may be related to other criteria, but a level of identity resolution that excludes production and efficiency activities is possible. The importance of career effectiveness as a source of organizational effectiveness supports the allocation of resources to career programs.[17]

CAREER STAGES

CAREER STAGES

Distinctly different yet related
stages in progression of career.

Employees typically move through distinct **career stages** during the course of their careers.[18] Although numerous descriptive labels have been proposed to identify these stages, we will use a four-stage model: establishment, advancement, maintenance, and withdrawal.[19] The *establishment* stage occurs at the onset of the career. The *advancement* stage is a period of moving from job to

[17]Mary Ann Von Glinow, Michael J. Driver, Kenneth Brousseau, and J. Bruce Pine, "The Design of a Career-Oriented Human Resource System," *Academy of Management Review,* January 1983, pp. 23–32; Carol L. Parker, "Facilitating Career Development in Small Business," *Vocational Guidance Quarterly,* September 1982, pp. 86–89.

[18]Nigel Nicholson, "A Theory of Work Role Transitions," *Administrative Science Quarterly,* June 1984, pp. 172–91.

[19]Lloyd Baird and Kathy Kram, "Career Dynamics: Managing the Superior/Subordinate Relationship," *Organizational Dynamics,* Spring 1983, p. 47.

job, both inside and outside the organization. *Maintenance* occurs when the individual has reached the limits of advancement and concentrates on the job he or she is doing. Finally, at some point prior to actual retirement, the individual goes through the *withdrawal* stage. The duration of the stages varies, but individuals generally go through each one.

Needs and expectations change as individuals move through each career stage. These needs and expectations are reflected in our *career anchors,* the self-images we develop with respect to our careers.[20] Career anchors change with time and place as we move through life and careers.

A study of American Telephone & Telegraph Company (AT&T) managers found they expressed considerable concern for security needs during the establishment phase.[21] During establishment, individuals require and seek support from others, particularly their managers. It is important for managers to recognize this need and to respond by assuming the role of mentor.[22] In the advancement stage, the AT&T managers expressed considerably less concern for security need satisfaction and more concern for achievement, esteem, and autonomy. Promotions and advancement to jobs with responsibility and opportunity to exercise independent judgment are characteristics of this stage. (However, those specific factors that explain why some individuals advance, while others do not, remain obscure.[23])

The maintenance stage is marked by efforts to stabilize the gains of the past. In some respects, this phase is a plateau—no new gains are made—yet it can be a period of creativity since the individual has satisfied many of the psychological and financial needs associated with earlier phases. Although each individual and career differ, esteem is assumed to be the most important need in the maintenance stage. Many people experience what is termed the midcareer crisis during the maintenance phase. Such individuals, not achieving satisfaction from their work, may consequently experience physiological and psychological discomfort. They may suffer poor health and a heightened sense of anxiety. They no longer desire to advance and therefore underperform. They then lose support of their managers, which further intensifies their health and job problems.[24]

The maintenance phase is followed by the retirement phase. The individual has, in effect, completed one career and may move on to another one.[25] During this phase, the individual may have opportunities to experience self-actualization through activities that were impossible to pursue while

---

[20]Edgar H. Schein, "Individuals and Careers," in *Handbook of Organizational Behavior,* ed. Jay W. Lorsch (Englewood Cliffs, N.J.: Prentice Hall, 1987), p. 155.

[21]Douglas T. Hall and Khalil Nougaim, "An Examination of Maslow's Need Hierarchy in an Organizational Setting," *Organizational Behavior and Human Performance,* 1968, pp. 12–35.

[22]David M. Hunt and Carol Michael, "Mentorship: A Career Training and Development Tool," *Academy of Management Review,* July 1983, pp. 475–85.

[23]John F. Veiga, "Mobility Influences during Managerial Career Stages," *Academy of Management Journal,* March 1983, pp. 64–85.

[24]Janet P. Near, "Work and Nonwork Correlates of the Career Plateau," *Academy of Management Proceedings,* 1983, pp. 380–84.

[25]James B. Shaw, "The Process of Retiring: Organizational Entry in Reverse," *Academy of Management Review,* January 1981, pp. 41–47.

TABLE 18—2

Characteristics of General Career Stages

	Stage			→
	Establishment	Advancement	Maintenance	Withdrawal
Age	18–24	25–39	40–54	55–65
Primary work-related activities	Obtaining job-related skills and knowledge	Becoming an independent contributor	Developing the skills of others	Sharing work experiences with others
Primary psychological demands	Being dependent on others for rewards	Being dependent on self for rewards	Being dependent on others for need satisfaction	Letting go of work identity
Primary need satisfaction	Security	Achievement autonomy	Esteem	Self-neutralization

working. Painting, gardening, volunteer service, and quiet reflection are some of the many positive avenues available to retirees.

The importance of these career phases as reflecting different career anchors cannot be overestimated. One study of scientists, engineers, accountants, and professors, for example, found that high performers go through each phase, they do not skip over them. Moreover, individuals in the study who had grown older without advancing to the appropriate phases were less valued than those who did advance. The interrelationships among career phases and life stages reflect milestones in individuals' lives and serve as bases for judgments of career effectiveness.[26]

Some important characteristics of career stages are summarized in Table 18–2. This figure depicts careers in the context of organizations. It also reflects the passage of an individual along a traditional career path.

Career Paths

CAREER PATH

Sequence of jobs and/or positions associated with advancement in a specific career.

Effective advancement through career stages involves moving along career paths. From the perspective of the organization, **career paths** are important inputs into human resource planning: an organization's future personnel needs depend on the projected passage of individuals through the ranks. From the perspective of the individual, a career path is the sequence of jobs necessary to achieve personal and career goals. To integrate completely the needs of both the organization and the individual in the design of career paths is virtually impossible, but systematic career planning has the potential for closing the gap.

In the traditional sense, career paths emphasize upward mobility in a single occupation or functional area, as reflected in Figure 18–2. When recruiting personnel, the organization's representative will speak of engineers', accountants', or marketers' career paths. In these contexts, the recruiter will describe the different jobs typical individuals will hold as they work progressively

---

[26]Paul H. Thompson, Robin Z. Baker, and Norman Smallwood, "Improving Professional Development by Applying the Four-Stage Career Model," *Organizational Dynamics,* Autumn 1986, pp. 49–62.

FIGURE 18–2

Career Path, General Management

Level of
management

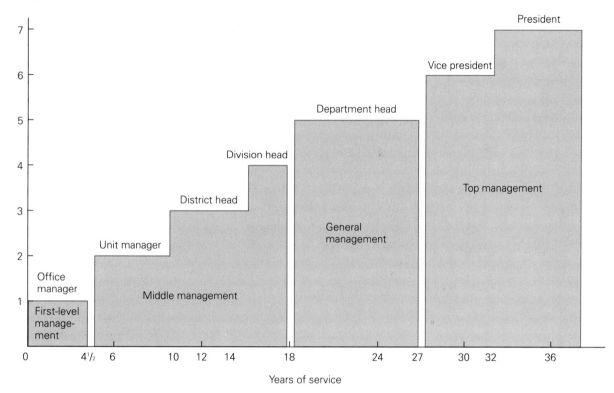

Source: Based on John M. Ivancevich and William F. Glueck, *Foundations of Personnel/Human Resource Management,* 4th ed. (Homewood, Ill.: Richard D. Irwin, 1989), p. 630.

upward in an organization. Each job, or rung, is reached when the employee has accumulated the necessary experience and ability and has demonstrated readiness for promotion. Implicit in such career paths is the attitude that not moving up after an elapsed time signals failure.

The career path concept involves the idea of moving upward in the organization along one "path," usually the managerial, or line, path. Employees in staff positions often are prevented from moving upward unless they give up their specialty and move into a line position. Organizations are beginning to recognize the importance of multiple paths as well as career planning.

Career Planning

Career pathing is the sequencing of specific jobs associated with the opportunities available in an organization. Career planning involves matching an individual's career aspirations with those opportunities. The two processes are intertwined. Planning a career involves identification of the means to achieve desired ends; and in the context of career plans, career paths are the means to achieve aspirations. Although still a relatively new practice, many organizations are turning to career planning as a proactive rather than reactive way to handle problems associated with ineffective managerial careers.

Successful career planning places equal responsibility on the individual and the organization. Individuals must identify their aspirations and abilities and, through counseling, recognize the training and development required for a particular career path. The organization must identify its needs and opportunities and, through human resource planning, provide career information and training to its employees. Companies such as Weyerhaeuser, Nabisco, Gulf Oil, Exxon, and Eaton use career development programs to identify a broad pool of talent available for promotion and transfer opportunities. Career counseling is often restricted to managerial and professional staff, but IBM, GE, TRW, and Gulf Oil provide career counseling for blue-collar as well as managerial personnel.

Matching individual and organizational needs and opportunities can be achieved in a variety of ways. The most widely used practices are informal counseling by the personnel staff and career counseling by supervisors. These two approaches are often quite informal. Less common, somewhat more formal methods involve workshops, seminars, and self-assessment centers.

Informal counseling.   The organization's personnel department often provides counseling services for employees who wish to assess their abilities and interests. Counseling may properly move into personal concerns that are important factors in determining career effectiveness. In this context, the organization views career counseling as a service to employees, but not a primary one.

Career counseling by supervisors is usually included in performance appraisals. The question of where the employee is going in the organization quite naturally arises in this setting. In fact, the inclusion of career information in performance appraisals predates the current interest in career planning. Effective performance evaluation includes letting employees know not only how well they have done but also what the future holds. Thus, supervisors must be able to counsel employees in terms of organizational needs and opportunities not only within the specific department but throughout the organization.

Formal counseling.   Since supervisors usually have limited information about the total organization, more formal, systematic counseling approaches are often necessary. Workshops, assessment centers, and career development centers are increasingly used. Such formal practices typically are designed to serve specific employee groups. To date, management trainees and "high-potential" or "fast-track" management candidates are two groups who have received most of the attention. However, women and minority employees increasingly are the targets of such programs. The adoption of career development programs for women and minority employees indicates an organization's commitment to affirmative action.

As an example of formal planning, Syntex Corporation's formal career planning system is described in the Close-Up. Whatever counseling approach

SYNTEX CORPORATION'S CAREER DEVELOPMENT CENTER

Syntex Corporation's career development center resulted from the realization that Syntex managers, too caught up in their own jobs, were unable to counsel subordinates. The center's staff first identifies the individual's strengths and weaknesses in eight skill areas Syntex believes are related to effective management: (1) problem analysis; (2) communication; (3) objective setting; (4) decision making and handling conflict; (5) selecting, training, and motivating employees; (6) controlling employees; (7) interpersonal competence; and (8) use of time. On the basis of scores in the eight areas and assisted by the center's staff, each manager sets realistic career and personal goals that reflect strengths and weaknesses in the eight areas.

The highlight of each manager's career planning effort is a weeklong seminar designed to encourage realistic self-appraisal. Usually attended by 24 managers, the seminar places each participant into simulated management situations that require applications of the eight skill areas. Afterward, each participant reviews his or her own career plan, including career goals, timetables, and required personal development. Following the seminar, the managers meet with their immediate supervisors to set up their career development plans.

is used, the crucial element of its success will be the extent to which both individual and organizational needs are satisfied.

Career planning is an increasingly widespread practice in organizations. Individuals who wish to make formal career plans are well advised to seek out organizations committed to career planning. From the organization's perspective, however, who is most likely to benefit from career planning? This question has been raised recently because not all individuals appear to benefit from the process. Career planning is most effective for people who have relatively high growth and achievement needs, the skill to carry out their career plans, and a past history of career successes.[27] Organizations should try to identify those people most likely to take advantage of career planning programs.

Individuals need not, however, rely on organizationally sponsored programs. Only lack of initiative prevents any of us from using our own resources to take control of our own careers.

ORGANIZATIONAL CAREERS IN PERSPECTIVE

The achievement of career effectiveness is a complex process. At minimum, it involves the following complexities:

---

[27]John D. Krumboltz, Richard T. Kinnier, Stephanie S. Rude, Dale S. Scherba, and Daniel A. Hamel, "Teaching a Rational Approach to Career Decision Making: Who Benefits Most?" *Journal of Vocational Behavior,* August 1986, pp. 1–6.

1. Career effectiveness involves four criteria (performance, attitudes, adaptability, and identity) that interrelate in various ways for different individuals. For example, achieving high levels of performance may either lead to or result from positive career attitudes. Individual differences in perception and personality account for differences in career effectiveness criteria.

2. The relative importance of career effectiveness criteria varies both among individuals and among organizations. Some individuals/organizations may value performance at the expense of adaptability while other individual/ organizations may value adaptability over performance. Thus, career effectiveness requires individual and organizational agreement on the importance of criteria.

3. The organization provides opportunities in the form of career paths and career planning for the realization of career effectiveness. The passage of individuals along career paths coincides with the passage of career stages. Thus, the coincidence of career paths and career stages reinforces the interrelationship and interdependence of the individual and the organization. One important link between the individual and the organization is the socialization process.

SOCIALIZATION: A LINKAGE BETWEEN CAREER EFFECTIVENESS AND ORGANIZATIONAL EFFECTIVENESS

SOCIALIZATION

Activities undertaken by organization to integrate organizational and individual purposes.

The **socialization** process continues throughout an individual's career. As the needs of the organization change, for example, its employees must adapt to those new needs; that is, they must be socialized. But although socialization is ever present, it has greater importance at some times than at others. For example, socialization is most important when an individual first takes a job in an organization or takes a different job in the same organization. Individuals are also more aware of the socialization process when they change jobs or change organizations,[28] although it occurs throughout the career stages and at every step along career paths.

Socialization Stages

The parallels between careers and socialization efforts imply the existence of socialization stages corresponding to career stages. Socialization stages coincide generally with the stages of a career. Although researchers have proposed various descriptions of the stages,[29] three sufficiently describe the process: (1) anticipatory socialization, (2) accommodation, and (3) role management.[30]

---

[28]Daniel C. Feldman and Jeanne M. Brett, "Coping with New Jobs: A Comparative Study of New Hires and Job Changers," *Academy of Management Journal,* June 1983, pp. 258–72.

[29]John P. Wanous, Arnon E. Reichers, and S. D. Malik, "Organizational Socialization and Group Development: Toward an Integrative Perspective," *Academy of Management Review,* October 1984, pp. 670–83, reviews the widely accepted models of socialization.

[30]These stages are identified by Daniel C. Feldman, "A Contingency Theory of Socialization," *Administrative Science Quarterly,* September 1976, pp. 434–35. The following discussion is based

Each stage involves specific activities that, if undertaken properly, increase the individual's chances of having an effective career. Moreover, these stages occur continuously and often simultaneously.

Anticipatory socialization.   The first stage involves all activities the individual undertakes prior to entering the organization or taking a different job in the same organization. The primary purpose of these activities is to acquire information about the new organization and/or new job. This **anticipatory stage of socialization** corresponds to the prework career stage, and the information-gathering activities include formal schooling, actual work experience, and recruiting efforts of organizations attempting to attract new employees.

ANTICIPATORY STAGE OF SOCIALIZATION
Socialization activities that occur prior to an individual becoming a member of an organization.

Prior to entering a new job or organization, people are vitally interested in two kinds of information. First, they want to know as much as they can about what working for the organization is really like. Second, they want to know whether they are suited for the jobs available in the organization. Individuals put considerable effort into seeking out this information when they are faced with the decision to take a job, whether it be their first or one that comes by way of transfer or promotion. At these times, the information is specific to the job or the organization. But we also form impressions about jobs and organizations in less formal ways. For example, friends and relatives talk of their experiences, and parents impart both positive and negative information to their offspring regarding the world of work. Thus, we continually receive information about this or that job or organization. We are, however, more receptive to it when faced with the need to make a decision.

It is desirable, of course, that the information transmitted and received during the anticipatory stage accurately and clearly depict the organization and the job. Yet, individuals differ greatly in the way they decode and receive information. If the fit between individual and organization is to be optimal, two conditions are necessary. The first condition is *realism*. That is, both the individual and the organization must portray themselves realistically. The second condition is *congruence,* which is present when the individual's skills, talents, and abilities are fully utilized by the job. Either overutilization or underutilization results in incongruence and, consequently, poor performance.[31]

The need for realism and congruence during the anticipatory socialization stage places special emphasis on the organization's recruitment efforts. Through recruitment, the organization attracts the kinds and types of people on whom it depends for future performance. All too often, however, the recruitment process is undertaken from the perspective of "getting warm bodies" or "filling slots." As a result, the organization is portrayed unrealistically: the recruits are simply not told the whole story, only the good parts. The predictable result is the creation of unrealistic expectations. Individuals are

heavily on this work, as well as Daniel C. Feldman, "A Practical Program for Employee Socialization," *Organizational Dynamics,* Autumn 1976, pp. 64–80; Daniel C. Feldman, "The Multiple Socialization of Organization Members," *Academy of Management Review,* June 1981, pp. 309–18.

[31]Feldman, "A Practical Program," pp. 65–66.

led to believe that certain things will happen to them; when expectations are not met, the natural outcome is lowered satisfaction and production.

One way to avoid unrealistic expectations in new recruits is to provide accurate information during the recruiting process. This practice reflects the idea that people should know both the bad and the good things to expect from their jobs and their organizations. In a **realistic job preview (RJP),** recruits are told not only the benefits they may expect but also the drawbacks. Studies have shown that the recruitment rate is the same for those who receive RJPs as for those who do not. More important, those who receive RJPs are more likely to remain on the job and to be satisfied with it than are those selected in the usual manner.[32] The practice of "telling it like it is" is used by a number of organizations, including the Prudential Insurance Company, Texas Instruments, and the U.S. Military Academy.[33] The retail industry has also found realistic job previews to be an important tactic for reducing attrition costs, as described in the Close-Up on "Realistic Expectations."

REALISTIC JOB
PREVIEW (RJP)
Means for providing accurate, realistic, pertinent information to prospective employees.

Accommodation.   The second stage of socialization occurs after the individual takes the job and becomes a member of the organization. During this stage, the employee sees the organization and the job for what they actually are. Through a variety of activities, he or she attempts to become an active participant in the organization and a competent performer on the job. This breaking-in period is ordinarily stressful because of anxiety created by the uncertainties inherent in any new and different situation. Apparently, the closer the individual was to realism and congruence during the anticipatory stage, the greater the likelihood that some of the stress will be lessened. Nevertheless, the demands on the individual do indeed create stress.

The **accommodation stage of socialization** comprises four major activities. All individuals must, to some degree, (1) establish new interpersonal relationships with both co-workers and supervisors, (2) learn the tasks required to perform the job, (3) clarify their role in the organization and in the formal and informal groups relevant to that role, and (4) evaluate the progress they are making toward satisfying the demands of the job and the role. Readers who have been through the accommodation stage will recognize these four activities and will recall more or less favorable reactions to them.

ACCOMMODATION STAGE OF
SOCIALIZATION
Socialization activities that occur after individual becomes a member of an organization.

If all goes well in this stage, the individual will feel a sense of acceptance by co-workers and supervisors and will experience competence in performing the tasks for the job. The breaking-in period, if successful, also results in role definition and congruence of evaluation. These four outcomes of the accommodation stage (acceptance, competence, role definition, and congruence of evaluation) are experienced by all new employees to a greater or lesser extent. However, the relative value of each of these outcomes varies from person to

[32]John P. Wanous, *Organizational Entry* (Reading, Mass.: Addison-Wesley Publishing, 1980); Paula Popovich and John P. Wanous, "The Realistic Job Preview as a Persuasive Communication," *Academy of Management Review,* October 1982, pp. 570–78.

[33]James A. Breaugh, "Realistic Job Previews: A Critical Appraisal and Future Research Directions," *Academy of Management Review,* October 1983, pp. 612–19.

REALISTIC EXPECTATIONS IN THE RETAIL INDUSTRY

Spokespersons for the retail industry lament the problems associated with high attrition rates among executive trainees hired right out of universities and colleges. Entry-level executive jobs in the industry require long hours, a frantic pace, and physical work that discouraged many trainees; 40 percent quit the industry during their first five years. Faced with the costs of this turnover, the industry has begun to realize that its recruiters should accurately describe the nitty-gritty of retailing so as to prepare trainees for the reality of their jobs.

Major retailers such as Allied Stores Corporation have implemented programs to present balanced information. They invite college professors to their stores to meet their former students and to hear how and what they are doing. They also go to campuses to hold information forums for students and faculty. The purpose of these sessions is to present both sides of the story, that retailing is hard work and the early years are filled with long hours of frustrating and not-so-glamorous work but that rewards do come eventually. The effort is designed to provide newly recruited executive trainees with accurate expectations of their futures.

Source: Marion L. Salzman, "In Search of Tomorrow's Excellent Managers," *Management Review*, April 1985, p. 43.

person.[34] Acceptance by the group, for example, may be a less valued outcome for an individual whose social needs are satisfied off the job. Regardless of differences due to individual preferences, each employee experiences the accommodation stage of socialization and will ordinarily move on to the third stage.

Role management.   The third stage of socialization, role management, coincides with the third stage of careers, stable work. In contrast to the accommodation stage, which requires the individual to adjust to demands and expectations of the immediate work group, the **role management stage of socialization** takes on a broader set of issues and problems.

Specifically, the third stage involves conflict between the individual's work and home lives. For example, the individual must allocate time and energy between the job and his or her role in the family. Since the amount of time and energy are fixed and the demands of work and family seemingly insatiable, conflict is inevitable. Employees unable to resolve these conflicts are often forced to leave the organization or to perform at an ineffective level. In any case, neither individual nor organization is well served by unresolved conflict between work and family. Organizations that recognize the conflicts between work and family assist employees in various ways. The Close-Up describes one organization's way of helping.

ROLE MANAGEMENT STAGE
OF SOCIALIZATION
Socialization activities that occur during individual's stable career period.

---

[34]Gareth R. Jones, "Psychological Orientation and the Process of Organizational Socialization: An Interactionist Perspective," *Academy of Management Review*, July 1983, pp. 464–74.

ORGANIZATIONS:
CLOSE-UP

HELPING EMPLOYEES MANAGE WORK-FAMILY CONFLICT

Employees of a leading manufacturing organization, one usually cited in lists of well-managed organizations, often expressed concerns for how their careers affected their family life. They cited the demands of their jobs that infringed on their family time: sales representatives calling them at home, a company policy that they spend 100 days each year in the field with the reps, the need for an office, and generally round-the-clock responsibilities. Although the firm's human resource training unit had prepared and presented seminars on various aspects of career management, the issues of work and family were not openly discussed.

In response to considerable interest in the topic, the human resources unit presented a two-day seminar on career and family life planning. Participants prepared for the seminar by discussing the issue with their spouses and families. The seminars focused on what the organization could do to ease the tensions between work and family. Suggestions included eliminating Sunday travel and entering family events on work calendars. But more important than these initial changes was the development of the attitude that work and family issues are now "discussable," that they are legitimate concerns the firm has an interest in resolving.

Source: Douglas T. Hall and Judith Richter, "Balancing Work Life and Home Life: What Can Organizations Do to Help?" *Academy of Management Executive*, August 1988, p. 221.

The second source of conflict during the role management stage is between the individual's work group and other work groups in the organization. This conflict can be greater for some employees than for others. For example, as individuals move up in the organization's hierarchy, they are required to interact with various types of groups both inside and outside the organization. Each group can and often does place different demands on the individual; to the extent that these demands are beyond the ability of the employee to meet, stress will result. Tolerance for the level of stress induced by these conflicting and irreconcilable demands varies among individuals, but the existence of unmanaged stress generally works to the disadvantage of both employee and organization.

Outcomes of Socialization

If an employee moves through each stage of the socialization process in a positive manner, then the groundwork is laid for an effective career. Note that it is the groundwork, or beginnings, that result from socialization. Socialization processes contribute to some but not all aspects of one's reaction to a job and the organization.

For example, general satisfaction, the degree to which individuals are satisfied and happy in their work, is related to high congruence, role definition, resolution of conflicting demands of work groups, and resolution of work-family conflicts. Congruence is an activity of the anticipatory stage, role definition occurs during the accommodation stage, and conflict resolution activities are the primary characteristics of the role management stage. Thus, each stage of the socialization process contributes to general satisfaction. However, socialization activities are unrelated to two very important variables: internal work motivation and job involvement. An individual may have either positive or negative experiences with an organization's socialization processes and, at the same time, positive or negative work motivation and job involvement. The most likely explanation for this finding is that motivation and involvement result from the nature of the work itself. Our discussion of job design in Chapter 14 noted how important job-related factors such as task identity, task significance, job freedom, and feedback are to employees' sense of job satisfaction. Thus, while organizational socialization processes can contribute to building a solid foundation for effective careers, they cannot guarantee them. It is possible, however, to incorporate motivating factors into the socialization process, and organizations committed to providing maximum career opportunities will do so.

CHARACTERISTICS OF EFFECTIVE SOCIALIZATION AND CAREER PROCESSES

Socialization processes vary in form and content from organization to organization. Even within the same organization, different individuals experience different socialization processes. For example, the accommodation stage for a college-trained management recruit is quite different from that of a member of the lowest-paid occupation in the organization. John Van Maanen has pointed out that socialization processes are not only extremely important in shaping the individuals who enter an organization, they are also remarkably different from situation to situation.[35] This variation reflects either the lack of attention by management to such an important process or the uniqueness of the process as related to organizations and individuals. Either explanation permits the suggestion that, while uniqueness is apparent, some general principles can be implemented in the socialization process.[36]

Effective Anticipatory Socialization

The organization's primary activities during the first stage of socialization are recruitment and selection and placement programs. If these programs are effective, then new recruits in an organization should experience the feeling of realism and congruence. In turn, accurate expectations about the job result from realism and congruence.

Recruitment programs are directed toward prospective employees, those not now in the organization. It is desirable to give these prospective employees information not only about the job but also about aspects of the organization

[35]John Van Maanen, "People Processing: Strategies for Organizational Socialization," *Organizational Dynamics,* Summer 1978, pp. 18–36.

[36]The following discussion reflects the research findings of Feldman, "A Practical Program."

that will affect the individual. Recruiters nearly always find it easier to stress job-related information to the exclusion of organization-related information. Job-related information is usually specific and objective, whereas organization-related information is usually general and subjective. Nevertheless, the recruiter should, to the extent possible, convey factual information about such matters as pay and promotion policies and practices, objective characteristics of the work group the recruit is likely to work with, and other information that reflects the recruit's concerns.

Selection and placement practices, in the context of anticipatory socialization, are important conveyers of information to employees already in the organization. Of prime importance is the manner in which individuals view career paths in the organizations. As noted earlier, the stereotypical career path involves advancement up the managerial hierarchy. Yet this concept does not take into account individuals' differences in attitude toward such moves. Greater flexibility in career paths would require the organization to consider lateral and downward transfers.[37]

Lateral transfers involve moves from one department to another at the same organizational level. A manager who has plateaued in production could be transferred to a similar level in sales, engineering, or some other area. The move would require the manager to quickly learn the technical demands of the new position, and there would be a period of reduced performance as this learning occurred. Once qualified, however, the manager would bring the perspectives of both areas to bear on decisions.

Downward transfers are associated in our society with failure; an effective manager simply does not consider a move downward to be a respectable option.[38] Yet, in many instances, downward transfers are not only respectable but entirely acceptable alternatives, particularly in the presence of one or more of the following conditions:

The manager values the quality of life afforded by a specific geographic area and may desire a downward transfer if this is required in order to stay in or move to that area.

The manager views the downward transfer as a way to establish a base for future promotions.

The manager is faced with the alternatives of dismissal or a downward move.

The manager desires to pursue autonomy and self-actualization in noncareer activities—such as religious, civic, or political activities—and for that reason may welcome the reduced responsibility (and demands) of a lower-level position.

The use of *fallback positions* is a relatively new way to reduce the risk of lateral and downward transfers. The practice involves identifying in advance a position to which the transferred manager can return if the new position does not work out. By identifying the fallback position in advance, the organization

[37]Douglas T. Hall and Francine S. Hall, "What's New in Career Management," *Organizational Dynamics,* Summer 1976, pp. 21–27.

[38]Douglas T. Hall and Lynn A. Isabella, "Downward Movement and Career Development," *Organizational Dynamics,* Summer 1985, pp. 5–23.

informs everyone who is affected that some risk is involved but that the organization is willing to accept some of the responsibility for it and that returning to the fallback job will not be viewed as failure. Companies such as Heublein, Procter & Gamble, Continental Can, and Lehman Brothers have used fallback positions to remove some of the risk of lateral and upward moves. The practice appears to have considerable promise for protecting the careers of highly specialized technicians and professionals who make their first move into general management positions.

Realistic career pathing, an alternative to traditional career pathing, bases career progression on real-world experiences and individualized preferences. Such paths have several characteristics:[39]

1. They include lateral and downward as well as upward possibilities, not tied to "normal" rates of progress.
2. They are tentative and responsive to changes in organizational needs.
3. They are flexible enough to take into account the qualities of individuals.
4. Each job along the path is specified in terms of acquirable skills, knowledge, and other specific attributes—not merely educational credentials, age, or work experience.

Realistic career paths, rather than traditional ones, are necessary for effective anticipatory socialization. In the absence of such information, the employee can only guess at what is available. Moreover, the development of flexible career patterns has considerable importance in the contemporary era of change. Rigid career paths work against the efforts of organizations to adapt to new environments, technologies, and competitors.[40]

Effective Accommodation Socialization

Effective accommodation socialization comprises five different activities: (1) designing orientation programs, (2) structuring training programs, (3) providing performance evaluation information, (4) assigning challenging work, and (5) assigning demanding bosses.

Orientation programs seldom receive the attention they deserve. The first few days on the new job can have very strong negative or positive impacts on the new employee. Taking a new job involves not only new job tasks but also new interpersonal relationships. The new person comes into an ongoing social system with a unique set of values, ideals, frictions, conflicts, friendships, coalitions, and all the other characteristics of work groups. Left alone, the new employee must cope with the new environment in ignorance; given some help and guidance, he or she can cope more effectively.[41]

The organization should design orientation programs that enable the new employee to meet the rest of the employees as soon as possible. Moreover,

---

[39]James W. Walker, "Let's Get Realistic about Career Paths," *Human Resource Management,* Fall 1976, pp. 2–7.

[40]Karen N. Gaertner, "Managers' Careers and Organizational Change," *Academy of Management Executive,* November 1988, pp. 311–18.

[41]Cynthia D. Fisher, "The Role of Social Support in Organizational Socialization," *Academy of Management Proceedings,* 1983.

specific individuals should be assigned the task of orientation. These individuals should be selected for their social skills and be given time off from their own work to spend with the new people. Although the degree to which the orientation program is formalized will vary, the program should not be left to chance in any case.

Training programs are invaluable in the breaking-in stage. Without question, training programs are necessary to instruct new employees in proper techniques and to develop required skills. Moreover, effective training programs provide frequent feedback on progress in acquiring the necessary skills. Less obvious is the need to integrate the formal training with the orientation program. More and more organizations are recognizing the importance of training as a principal means for forming employee perceptions and expectations. In some instances, training has become synonymous with socialization; as such, it plays a major role in how individuals make sense of and adapt to their new jobs and organizations.[42]

Most jobs involve not only the use of technical skills but also the use of social skills. Most of us must work with other people to get our work done, and the people we have to work with have unique personalities that must be understood. For example, in order to perform their duties effectively, nurses must learn about the personalities and preferences of physicians with whom they work. It takes nurses considerably longer to learn about physicians than it takes to learn the technical skills of their jobs. Thus, to the extent possible, training programs should include the social as well as the technical information required to perform specific jobs.[43]

Training occurs in both formal and informal settings. In some instances, the preferred training for the next job is the job before it. The Close-Up describes such an instance.

Performance evaluation, in the context of socialization, provides important feedback about how well the individual is getting along in the organization. Inaccurate or ambiguous information regarding this important factor can only lead to performance problems. Therefore, performance evaluation sessions must take place in face-to-face meetings between the employee and manager, and performance criteria need to be as objective as possible in the context of the job. Management by objectives and behaviorally anchored rating scales are particularly applicable in these settings.

Feedback on performance is an important managerial responsibility. Yet, many managers are inadequately trained to meet this responsibility; they simply do not know how to evaluate the performance of their subordinates. Deficient evaluations are especially damaging to new managers. They have not been in the organization long enough to be socialized by their peers and other employees. They are not as yet sure of what they are expected to believe, what values to hold, or what behaviors are expected of them. They naturally look to their own managers to guide them through this early phase. When their

---

[42]Daniel C. Feldman, "Socialization, Resocialization, and Training: Reframing the Research Agenda," in *Training and Development in Organizations,* ed. Irwin L. Goldstein and associates (San Francisco: Jossey-Bass, 1989), pp. 376–416.

[43]B. Kaye, "Career Development Puts Training in Its Place," *Personnel Journal,* February 1983, pp. 132–37.

FIRST A CLERK, THEN A TRADER

Many jobs enable individuals to "learn by doing." This approach to job preparation works very well in environments that permit some degree of error and for individuals who can perform challenging and unfamiliar tasks, accept criticism, correct mistakes, and work long hours. But in the high-stakes, high-risk environment of the stock trading firm, learning by doing could be disastrous. Successful job performance in a trading firm requires nearly instantaneous decisions in which there is little room for error. In fact, for a trading firm to issue a trader badge to new job recruits would be foolish, no matter how bright, energetic, and enthusiastic they are. Instead of learning by doing, new employees learn by observing.

To learn by observing requires employees to perform rather menial tasks. They spend the day adding, subtracting, transmitting phone messages, folding, sorting, tallying, and taking lunch orders. In short, they perform the duties typically assigned to a clerk, experiences that bear little resemblance to the usual professional training program. Individuals enter the profession, however, understanding that they must demonstrate full knowledge of the technical and professional requirements of trading *before* they enter the trading floor and begin trading, not while they are trading. The clerking experience that may test the individual's humility is also the stepping-stone to an important profession.

Source: Anonymous, "I Diligently Remain, a Clerk," *Business Today,* Winter 1987, p. 30.

managers fail to evaluate their performance accurately, they remain ignorant and confused as to whether they are meeting the organization's expectations.

Challenging work is a principal feature of effective socialization programs for new employees. Their first jobs often demand far less than they are able to deliver. Consequently, they are unable to demonstrate their full capabilities and, in a sense, are being stifled. This is especially damaging if the recruiter was overly enthusiastic in "selling" the organization when they were recruited.

Some individuals are able to create challenging jobs even when their assignments are fairly routine. They do this by thinking of ways to do their jobs differently and better; they may also be able to persuade their managers to give them more leeway and more to do. Unfortunately, many recent college graduates are unable to create challenge. Their previous experiences in school typically were experiences in which challenges had been given to them by their teachers—had been created for them, not by them.

Job enrichment is an established practice for motivating employees with strong growth and achievement needs. If the nature of the job is not intrinsically challenging, the newly hired individual's manager can enrich the assignment. The usual ways to enrich a job include giving the new employee more authority and responsibility, permitting the new employee to interact directly with customers and clients, and enabling the new employee to implement his or her own ideas (rather than merely recommending them to the boss).

Demanding bosses increase the retention rate of new employees. In this context, "demanding" should not be interpreted as "autocratic." Rather, the type of boss most likely to get new hires off in the right direction has high but achievable expectations for their performance. Such a boss instills the understanding that high performance is expected and rewarded and, equally important, that the boss is always ready to assist through coaching and counseling.

The practice of assigning demanding bosses may or may not be formalized. However, every employee will probably come under the influence of some other employee. Such influence often takes the form of a mentoring relationship, with the experienced employee taking the mentor role. Mentoring can be assumed by any employee, manager or peer.[44] The outcomes of mentoring relationships include some that are negative from the perspective of the organization (e.g., the mentor may pass on ways to reduce performance without getting caught). Thus, it makes sense for the organization to take the importance of mentoring seriously and to establish formal procedures for assigning individuals to challenging managers.

Interest in mentoring as a factor in individual career development and organizational effectiveness has stimulated numerous studies.[45] Generally conclusive evidence links mentoring to career development, organization effectiveness, and career satisfaction.[46] Organizations having relatively large numbers of employees in the maintenance phase of their careers have a pool of individuals from which to assign mentors. Not only is the role of mentor consistent with the maintenance phase, we have seen that the need for mentoring is also consistent with the establishment career stage.

Specific mentoring activities distinguish between career-related and person-related behaviors. Career-related activities include coaching and challenging protégés while also publicizing their accomplishments and protecting them from political wars. Person-related activities include friendship and counseling while serving as a role model for the protégé. The mentor is the protégé's sponsor and teacher. As such, mentoring roles are difficult and require considerable interpersonal skill and organizational savvy to perform well.

For the protégé, the potential payoff from an effective mentoring relationship can be substantial. One study of chief executive officers (CEOs) found that nearly two thirds had a mentor at some point in their career and that those who had mentors received higher salaries than those who had not.[47] Other studies of executive leadership confirm the importance of learning from mentors and from bosses. Effective managers nearly always identify mentors and former bosses as important factors in their success.[48] Although we think

---

[44]Kathy E. Kram and Lynn A. Isabella, "Mentoring Alternatives: The Role of Peer Relationships in Career Development," *Academy of Management Journal,* March 1985, pp. 110–32.

[45]Kathy E. Kram, *Mentoring at Work* (Glenview, Ill.: Scott, Foresman, 1985).

[46]Belle Rose Ragins and Dean B. McFarlin, "Mentor Roles: An Investigation of Cross-Gender Mentoring Relationships," *Academy of Management Proceedings,* 1989, p. 58.

[47]Kram and Isabella, "Mentoring Alternatives."

[48]Morgan W. McCall, Jr., Michael M. Lombardo, and Ann M. Morrison, *The Lessons of Experience: How Successful Executives Develop on the Job* (Lexington, Mass.: D. C. Heath, 1988).

ORGANIZATIONS:
CLOSE-UP

MENTORING FOR INTERNATIONAL ASSIGNEES

What happens to employees who return home after overseas assignments? Have the organizations that sent them forgotten about them while they were away? Will they return to the career path that they were on prior to leaving, or will they have to begin again? A study of the problems associated with repatriation suggests a number of negative possibilities for individuals who accept an overseas assignment. Organizations need to be sensitive to their concerns.

To overcome these problems, the study's author suggests the use of mentors. Specifically, a mentorship program can be developed that pairs the expatriate with a member of senior management in the home office. The mentor is responsible for monitoring the career path and taking care of the interests of the expatriate while he or she is abroad. Japanese organizations use this practice to allay the fears of employees assigned to Japanese organizations throughout the world. If one-on-one pairing is not possible, then the organization should create a unit to provide mentoring in the way of career counseling prior to departure, continuing career guidance while abroad, and repatriation career counseling undertaken at least six months prior to return to the home office.

Source: Rosalie L. Tung, "Career Issues in International Assignments," *Academy of Management Executive*, August 1988, pp. 241–44.

of mentoring as important to new employees, the practice has wider implications, as noted in the Close-Up on mentoring for international assignees.

Socialization programs and practices that are intended to retain and develop new employees can be used separately or in combination. A manager would be well advised to establish policies most likely to retain those recent hires who have the highest potential to perform effectively. That likelihood is improved if the policies include realistic orientation and training programs, accurate performance evaluation feedback, and challenging initial assignments supervised by supportive, performance-oriented managers and mentors. Another Close-Up describes the socialization activities of a major banking firm.

Effective Role Management Socialization

Organizations that deal effectively with conflicts associated with the role management stage recognize the impact of such conflicts on job satisfaction and turnover. Even though motivation and high performance may not be associated with socialization activities, satisfaction and turnover are; and organizations can ill afford to lose capable employees.

Retention of employees beset by off-job conflicts is enhanced in organizations that provide professional counseling services and that schedule and adjust work assignments for those with particularly difficult conflicts at work and home. Of course, these practices do not guarantee that the employee will be able to resolve or even cope with the conflict. The important point is that the

ORGANIZATIONS:
CLOSE-UP

SOCIALIZATION PRACTICES AT MORGAN GUARANTY BANK

Morgan Guaranty Bank pays a great deal of attention to the socialization of its new recruits. It expends considerable resources to instill in them the Morgan "collegial" style. This style emphasizes teamwork and cooperation as the way to get work done in the organization. The bank competes for the very best and most talented individuals and then puts them through an intensive one-year training program that tests not only their intellectual ability and stamina but also their ability to work in collaboration with others. Developing this sense of togetherness is an explicit objective of the training program.

Once the employee is on the job, the bank frequently rotates the jobs of individuals to encourage the building of interpersonal networks throughout the bank. When performance is evaluated, all managers with whom an individual interacts will have a say in the outcome. The veteran Morgan employee has learned to avoid political infighting and to succeed through teamwork. The socialization process is directed toward this end.

Source: Richard Pascale, "The Paradox of 'Corporate Culture': Reconciling Ourselves to Socialization," *California Management Review,* Winter 1985, p. 27.

organization show good faith and make a sincere effort to adapt to the problems of its employees. Table 18–3 summarizes what managers can do to encourage effective socialization.

SOCIALIZATION AS AN INTEGRATION STRATEGY

Our discussion has emphasized the interrelationships of socialization processes and career effectiveness. It is also possible to view socialization as a form of organizational integration, a strategy for achieving congruence of organizational and individual goals. Thus, socialization is an important and powerful process for transmitting the organizational culture.[49] The socialization strategies are practices and policies that have appeared in a number of places throughout this text. In this section, we will not only summarize our discussion of career and socialization processes but also cast some important organization behavior concepts and theories in a different framework.

Organizational integration is achieved primarily by aligning and integrating the goals of individuals with the objectives of organizations. The greater the congruity between individual goals and organization objectives, the greater is the integration. The socialization process achieves organization integration by, in effect, undoing the individual's previously held goals and creating new ones closer to those valued by the organization. In its most extreme form, this

---

[49]J. E. Hebden, "Adopting an Organization's Culture: The Socialization of Graduate Trainees," *Organizational Dynamics,* Summer 1986, pp. 46–72.

Socialization Stage	Practices
Anticipatory socialization	1. Recruitment using realistic job previews. 2. Selection and placement using realistic career paths.
Accommodation socialization	1. Tailor-made and individualized orientation programs. 2. Social as well as technical skills training. 3. Supportive and accurate feedback. 4. Challenging work assignments. 5. Demanding but fair supervisors.
Role management socialization	1. Provision of professional counseling. 2. Adaptive and flexible work assignments. 3. Sincere, person-oriented managers.

TABLE 18—3

Checklist of Effective
Socialization Practices

"undoing" process involves debasement techniques such as those experienced by Marine Corps recruits, military academy plebes, and sorority and fraternity pledges. However, as the Organizational Issue for Debate notes, integration of organizational and individual interests can involve ethical issues. These ethical issues are most evident when the two parties do not share the same information or hold the same legitimate power.

Rensis Likert advocates the use of leader and peer socialization. In presenting his ideas on leadership theory, Likert stresses the importance of the leader who maintains high performance standards and group-centered leadership techniques. The leader sets high standards for his or her own behavior and performance and, through group-centered leadership, encourages the group to follow that example. If successful, the leader will have created a group norm of high performance that will be apparent to a new employee assigned to the group.

The 9,9 theory of leadership (discussed in Chapter 11) involves the development of mutual understanding of objectives through discussions between the group's leader and members. The understanding, when reached, would represent a balanced but high concern for both people and production concerns. The group would then act to achieve the objectives of the group and represent the legitimacy of the objectives to new group members.

The common thread running throughout leadership theories is the active role played by the leader and the group members in integrating goals and objectives. Effective socialization, particularly during the accommodation and role management stages, requires joint and supportive efforts of leaders and peers alike.

SUMMARY OF KEY POINTS

— Socialization and career development processes occur in all organizations; through them, the interests of individuals and organizations are identified and confronted. Socialization emphasizes the interests of the organization, while career development emphasizes the interests of the individual. The preferred outcome is integration of organizational and individual interests.

— Although the popular meaning of career development can include any occupation, vocation, or life work, career development is restricted to organizational careers in the present discussion. We are focusing on the careers of individuals who choose to spend their working lives in organizations. In this context, career refers to a sequence of individually perceived attitudes and behaviors associated with organizationally relevant, work-related experiences.

— The dynamics of career choices are only vaguely understood. In one of the more influential theories of career choice, individuals choose careers that are compatible with their personality types. Moreover, according to the theory, definite relationships exist between certain personality types and occupational characteristics.

— The concept of career in organizations must be broad enough to include emerging patterns of work and nonwork life. Some of these patterns include the willingness of individuals to trade career experiences for family and personal experiences, the concern for quality of life in all its facets, and the existence of multiple careers in the same household.

— Effective careers include the characteristics of performance, attitudes, adaptability, and identity. These characteristics of individual career effectiveness can be related to criteria of organizational effectiveness to the extent that individual and organizational effectiveness criteria are congruent.

— Most individuals move through their careers in generally predictable patterns. Each career stage involves specific activity, psychological, and behavioral demands. Moreover the relative importance of specific needs changes as the individual progresses through each stage. For example, the needs of the initial hire differ greatly from those of the veteran employee.

Organizational career development practices must take these differences into account.

— Organizational socialization processes coincide with the stages of careers: anticipatory socialization occurs with the prework career stage, accommodation occurs with the establishment and advancement career stages, and role management occurs with the maintenance stage. The parallels between socialization and career development stages enable management to implement practices that maximize the chances for achieving the mutual needs of the individual and the organization.

— The success of organizational socialization depends on how well the socialization activities meet the needs of the individual and the organization at each career stage. Usual organizational practices such as recruitment, selection and placement, promotion, and transfer can be important parts of an effective socialization process if management thinks of them in terms of meeting individual as well as organizational needs.

— Organizational socialization can be viewed as a means for achieving organizational integration. A major managerial task is to achieve effective integration of the diversity that arises out of the need to create and staff specialized jobs and departments. Diversity creates the need for integration, and socialization can be one way of melding the interests of individuals and organizations.

DISCUSSION AND REVIEW QUESTIONS

1. In what socialization activities of organizations do you participate? What evidence exists that management has taken an active part in designing these activities so that they advance the purposes of the organization?

2. Describe the ways in which socialization and career processes are interrelated.

3. What are your career plans at the moment? What appeals to you about the career that you have chosen? If you have not selected a career, what do you now think you are looking for in a career?

4. Rank the relative importance of the four characteristics of effective careers from the perspective of the individual, then from the perspective of the organization. Explain your rankings.

5. Interview someone you know who has had considerable experience in a career. Ask the individual to describe the role of management activities that the organization provides.

6. Which of the three socialization stages is most important for developing high-performing employees? Explain your answer.

7. What has been your experience with job interviews and previews? Did they accurately describe the job as you subsequently experienced it? Could what you experienced have been described in a realistic job preview? Explain.

8. Why are leaders and peers considered the most important actors in socialization processes?

9. Think of your own work experience. Have managers or peers been more important in socializing you into an organization?

10. If socialization increases employee satisfaction but not production or efficiency, how can an organization justify expensive orientation programs?

ADDITIONAL REFERENCES

Arthur, M. B.; D. T. Hall; and B. S. Lawrence, eds. *Handbook of Career Theory.* New York: Cambridge University Press, 1989.

Clawson, J. G. "Is Mentoring Necessary?" *Training and Development Journal,* 1985, pp. 36–39.

Derr, C. B. *Managing the New Careerists.* San Francisco: Jossey-Bass, 1986.

Elsass, P. M., and D. A. Ralston. "Individual Response to the Stress of Career Plateauing." *Journal of Management,* 1989, pp. 35–47.

Feldman, D. C., and B. A. Weitz. "Career Plateaus Reconsidered." *Journal of Management,* 1988, pp. 69–80.

Gunz, H. *Careers and Corporate Culture.* New York: Basil Blackwell, 1989.

Hall, D. T. "Project Work as an Antidote to Career Plateauing in a Declining Engineering Organization." *Human Resource Management,* 1985, pp. 271–92.

Highman, E. L. *The Organization Woman: Building a Career.* New York: Human Sciences Press, 1985.

Kram, K. E. *Mentoring at Work: Developmental Relationships in Organizational Life.* Glenview, Ill.: Scott, Foresman, 1985.

Latack, J. C. "Career Transitions within Organizations: An Exploratory Study of Work, Nonwork and Coping Strategies." *Organizational Behavior and Human Performance,* 1984, pp. 296–322.

London, M., and E. M. Mone, eds. *Career Growth and Human Resource Strategies.* Westport, Conn.: Quorum Books, 1988.

Newman, L. "Career Management: Start with Goals." *Personnel Journal,* 1989, pp. 91–92.

Nicholson, N., and M. K. West. *Managerial Job Change: Men and Women in Transition.* New York: Cambridge University Press, 1989.

Noe, R. A. "Women and Mentoring: A Review and Research Agenda." *Academy of Management Review,* 1988, pp. 65–78.

Pringle, J. K., and U. O'C. Gold. "How Useful Is Career Planning for Today's Managers?" *Journal of Management Development,* 1989, pp. 21–26.

Ragins, B. R. "Barriers to Mentoring: The Female Manager's Dilemma." *Human Relations,* 1989, pp. 1–22.

Walsh, B. W., and S. H. Osipow, eds. *Career Decision-Making.* Hillsdale, N.J.: Erlbaum & Associates, 1988.

REFUSING A PROMOTION

Ron Riddell, a 36-year-old project manager for the Dowling Products Corporation, has established a reputation as a conscientious, prompt, and creative manager. At present, he is working on a new cleansing product that can be used to clean sink tops. The cleanser is expected to generate gross sales of $3 million the first year it is on the market.

Riddell has a permanent team of eight men and three women and a temporary team of two women and two men assigned to him only for the important cleansing product. The team plans, organizes, and controls the various project phases from development to pilot market testing. The team must work closely with engineers, chemists, production managers, sales directors, and marketing research specialists before a quality product can be finally marketed.

In the past eight years, Riddell has directed four projects that have been considered outstanding market successes and one that has been considered a "superloser" financially. His supervisor is Norma Collins, a Ph.D. chemical engineer. Collins has direct responsibility for seven projects, three of which are considerably smaller than Riddell's and three of which have about the same potential and size as Riddell's.

Collins has recently been selected to be the overseas divisional coordinator of research and development. She and three top executives have met for the past two weeks and have decided to offer her present position to Riddell. They believe that the new job for Riddell will mean more prestige and authority and certainly an increase in salary.

Collins has been given the task of offering the position to Riddell. This is the discussion that occurred in Collins's office:

Collins: Ron, how is the cleansing project going?

Riddell: As good as could be expected. I sometimes think that Joe Rambo is trying to slow down our progress. He's a bear to get along with.

Collins: Well, everyone has been a little concerned because of the main competitor's progress on their cleansing product. I'm sure we can put everything together and effectively compete in the market.

Riddell: I know we can.

Collins: I wanted to talk to you about a job that is becoming vacant in 30 days. The executive selection committee unanimously believes that Ron Riddell is the right person for the job.

Riddell: What job are you talking about?

Collins: My job, Ron. I have been promoted to overseas divisional coordinator of research and development. We want to begin turning over my job to you as soon as possible. If we drag our feet, the cleansing project may not be the success that we need to bolster our financial picture.

Riddell: I am flattered by this opportunity and really believe that professionally I can handle the challenge. My real concern is the personal problems I'm having.

Collins: Do you mean personal problems here at Dowling?

Riddell: No, I mean problems in my family that have led to sleepless nights, arguments with my wife, and hostility between myself and my best neighbor. My brother Mark has been arrested two times recently, once for vagrancy and once for possession of narcotics. As you know, my dad died four years ago, and my mother just can't handle the kid. So I have pitched in and am trying to straighten him out. Connie, my wife, is fed up with the time I spend here at work and my meddling into my brother's problems. She has even threatened to leave me and take the kids with her to Denver. The new job is really interesting, but I'm afraid it would be the "straw that breaks the camel's back."

Collins: I'm sorry to hear about these problems, Ron. I know that it is hard to separate outside problems and pressures from Dowling problems and pressures. If you are going to become a more important part of the management team, that separation will be mandatory. The new job is the challenge that we have trained you for and is a reward for your outstanding past performance. Please think over the job offer and let me know in three days. We need your talents, experience, and leadership.

Riddell left Collins's office with a sick feeling in his stomach. He had worked hard for years, and the goal he was striving for was within his reach. All he had to do was to say yes to Collins. He thought about the additional money, status, and authority attached to the new job. Then he thought about his wife, who had become more depressed about his working on Saturdays and Sundays; his daughter, whom he really had not talked to for six months; his mother, who had helped pay for his college education; and his brother, who always called and asked him to play golf or shoot pool only to be told, "I have to work, Steve. Sorry."

After thinking over the offer for three days, Ron walked into Collins's office.

Collins: Come on in, Ron, and relax.

Riddell: I can't relax, because I am extremely nervous. I really want the job, but my family must come first. My daughter, wife, and mother have helped me get to my present position. I just feel that taking on this new job will lead to so many problems that I must turn it down.

Collins: I sympathize with your dilemma and wish you the best of luck. I want you to understand, however, that this type of opportunity may never happen again. The company needs your talents now. Can't you get your wife and mother to understand the importance of this job in your career? I just can't believe that they would not understand.

Riddell: Norma, we all have priorities and personal backgrounds that just can't be ignored.

Collins: Ron, you are sounding like a behavioral scientist. I know that just as well as you. What I'm saying is that you have worked this long and hard and now decide not to accept the challenge. That is what puzzles me.

Questions for Consideration

1. What organizational responsibilities does Collins believe that Riddell is shirking by turning down the new job offer?
2. Why would the behavioral orientations of Riddell and Collins differ?
3. Do you consider personal needs and problems as more important than organizational needs and problems? Why?
4. Should organizations force an employee like Riddell to fit their plans for him? Why?

EXPERIENTIAL EXERCISE

Objectives

1. To examine what each of us considers important in our careers.
2. To illustrate the difficulties of career planning.

Related Topics

Career planning is related to topics such as goal setting, individual growth, and individual differences.

Starting the Exercise

Each student will complete the following steps:

1. Draw a horizontal line that depicts the past, present, and future of your career. Mark the line with an X to depict where you are now.
2. To the left of the X, on that part of the line that represents your past, identify events in your life that provided real and genuine feelings of fulfillment and satisfaction.
3. Examine these historical events and determine the specific causes of your feelings. Does a pattern emerge? Write as much as you can about each event and your reactions to it.
4. To the right of the X, on that part of the line that represents your future, identify career-related events that you expect will provide real and genuine feelings of fulfillment and satisfaction. Be as explicit as possible when describing these events. If you are only able to write such statements as "get a job" or "get a big raise," your career expectations are probably vaguely defined.
5. After you have identified future career-related events, rank them from high to low according to how much fulfillment and satisfaction you expect from each.
6. Now go back to step 3. Rank those historical events from high to low according to how much fulfillment and satisfaction each provided. Compare the two sets of events. Are they ranked consistently? Are you expecting the future to be different from the past in terms of sources of fulfillment and satisfaction? If the future, expected sources are quite different from the past, actual sources, are you being totally realistic about the future and what you want from your career?

Completing the Exercise

Each individual should answer the following questions and share answers with others in the class:

1. Which one of the six steps was most difficult to complete? Why?
2. What are the principal categories of fulfillment and satisfaction? Can all these sources be realized in a career? Which ones are most likely to go unrealized in the career of your choice?
3. Do you desire a career in management? Is your answer based on consideration of the potential sources of fulfillment and satisfaction that you value? Explain.

DEVELOPING ORGANIZATIONAL EFFECTIVENESS

19

Organizational Development
Improving Performance

LEARNING OBJECTIVES

*After completing Chapter 19,
you should be able to:*

DEFINE
the concept and practice of
organizational development.

DESCRIBE
sources of change and alternative change management
approaches.

DISCUSS
ways to obtain diagnostic
information.

COMPARE
alternative ways to use
change agents in the
context of organizational
development.

IDENTIFY
the important steps in organizational development
programs.

AN ORGANIZATIONAL
ISSUE FOR DEBATE   THE PRACTICE OF ORGANIZATIONAL DEVELOPMENT
                     IS UNETHICAL*

ARGUMENT FOR

Organizational development (OD) is a managerial technique for implementing major changes in organizations. As a practice intended to bring about change, OD involves a change agent applying powerful behavioral science principles to bring about performance improvements. The ethical issues center on the power relationships among the various participants in the change effort. At the most fundamental level, critics note, OD takes as given the existing power relationships in the organization, since the change effort is initiated by managers. As a managerial technique, OD necessarily implements managerial values regardless of the values of the change agent. OD is inherently unethical because it restricts the range of values that can legitimately be considered in bringing about the change. Even though OD may bring about performance improvements in the organization, the basic power relationships remain unchanged.

As a consequence of its inherently unethical nature, OD practice is susceptible to abuse and misuse. Opportunities for unethical behavior can be seen in several activities. For example, the purposes of a particular OD intervention can be misrepresented to the participants in order to win their participation. Managers may say that they want to implement management by objectives (MBO) to provide greater employee participation, when in fact they are attracted to MBO as a means of performance evaluation that holds individuals responsible for results rather than activities. A second dangerous OD activity involves data analysis. Change agents collect and analyze data to diagnose the nature of the problem and to evaluate the solution. The change agents' allegiance to the people who hire them—the organization's managers—inevitably leads to misuse when the data conflict with managers' preferences. Data indicative of management incompetence can be misused to imply employee incompetence. Finally, OD involves manipulation of individuals without informed consent. Subjects of OD interventions are not given a choice whether or not to participate, particularly when the focus of the change is group and organizational performance. Manipulation can, in fact, turn into coercion when the individual must choose between participating in the process or being fired.

The argument that OD is unethical proceeds from the recognition that OD inherently reflects only one possible set of values, managerial values. As a consequence, the OD activities that involve ethical choices will always be guided by those underlying values even when the choices involve misrepresentation, misuse, and manipulation.

ARGUMENT AGAINST

Those who dispute the argument that organizational development is inherently unethical point out that every act has ethical implications, but only because the action is taken by an individual. Machines are not capable of unethical behavior; people are more than capable of unethical as well as ethical behavior. OD is no more or less unethical than any other management technique.

The fact that OD implements managerial values to the exclusion of others is not unique to OD. By that argument, the practice of management is itself unethical because it reflects the value system of the larger society of which it is a part. Even the proponents of OD, however, recognize that special care must be taken to protect against the abuse of powerful techniques that OD change agents apply.

The best protection against misrepresentation, misuse, and manipulation is managers who create and foster an organizational culture that encourages ethical behavior. Such a culture would begin with top management's formal declaration that ethical behavior is the norm and that individuals, including OD practitioners, are to conduct themselves in an ethical manner in all actions, even when such conduct may be costly to the organization in economic and technical terms. Through the actions of top management, ethical behavior can become part of the everyday activities and decisions of each member of the organization.

Codes of ethics are suggested means for institutionalizing ethical behavior. Top management demonstrates its commitment to the code through its daily behavior. In addition, the organization reinforces ethical behavior through punishment and rewards. Deviants are dealt with swiftly, and adherents are rewarded consistently. The performance evaluation system can be a very important mechanism for demonstrating management's commitment to ethical behavior.

Thus, OD is not unethical. Individuals can be unethical, however, if rewarded for unethical behavior. Consequently, an important responsibility of management is to create an environment that fosters ethical conduct. In such an environment, the practice of OD can proceed in an ethical manner.

*Source: Based on Larry Greiner and Virginia Schein, *Power and Organization Development: Mobilizing Power to Implement Change* (Reading, Mass.: Addison-Wesley Publishing, 1988); Anthony T. Cobb, "Political Diagnosis: Applications in Organizational Development," *Academy of Management Review,* July 1986, pp. 482–96.

The process by which managers sense and respond to the necessity for change has been the focus of much research and practical attention in recent years. If managers were able to design perfect formal organizations and if the scientific, market, and technical environments were stable and predictable, there would be no pressure for change. But such is not the case. The statement that "we live in the midst of constant change" has become a well-worn but relevant cliché.

One well-known business writer states that contemporary business organizations "are facing a change more extensive, more far-reaching in its implications, and more fundamental in its transforming quality than anything since the modern industrial system took shape."[1] Popular literature, including best-sellers, warns that organizations' futures depend on their managers' ability to master change.[2] Others state that change is a pervasive, persistent, and permanent condition for all organizations. Effective managers must view managing change as an integral rather than peripheral responsibility.[3]

This chapter and Chapter 20 discuss the organizational approach to managing change. They explore the issues associated with managing change

---

[1]Rosabeth Moss Kanter, *The Change Masters* (New York: Simon & Schuster 1983), p. 37.

[2]Leon Martel, *Mastering Change* (New York: New American Library, 1987).

[3]Ralph H. Kilmann, "A Completely Integrated Program for Creating and Maintaining Organizational Success," *Organizational Dynamics,* Summer 1989, pp. 5–19.

ORGANIZATIONAL
DEVELOPMENT
Managerial technique that helps
managers prepare for and manage change in a changing world.

through the application of **organizational development (OD).** These two chapters should be considered a single unit of study, separated for purposes of presentation but otherwise quite interrelated and interdependent. They are written from the point of view that the important management responsibility of managing change can best be undertaken and accomplished through the application of the organizational development process and interventions. This chapter focuses on process issues; the next chapter focuses on interventions. Following an initial presentation of change management approaches and an explanation of organizational development, discussions in both chapters are guided by the steps suggested in Figure 19–1, a model for managing change through organizational development.

ALTERNATIVE CHANGE MANAGEMENT APPROACHES

A recent review of the literature identified several approaches that can be used to manage planned change.[4] Although the names applied to the different approaches vary from author to author and from proponent to proponent, the underlying theme is the same. The approaches to bringing about change range from the application of power, in any of its forms, to the application of reason. Midway between these two extremes is the approach that relies on reeducation.

The *application of power* to bring about change implies the use of coercion. In organizations, managers are generally considered to be the ones who have access to power and can use it to coerce nonmanagers to change in the direction they desire. Managers can implement power through their control over reward and sanctions; they can determine the conditions of employment, including promotion and advancement. Consequently, through access to these bases of power, managers can exert considerable influence in an organization.

As a manifestation of autocratic leadership, the application of power is generally not held in high esteem in contemporary organizations. In times past, autocratic management was a factor in the rise of labor unions, which formed as counterweights to the arbitrary use of managerial power. Except in crises situations in which the very existence of the organization is at stake, power is not a favored approach for bringing about change.

The *application of reason* to bring about change is based on the dissemination of information prior to and about the intended change. The underlying assumption is that reason alone will prevail and that the participants and parties to the change will all make the rational choice. The reason-based approach appeals to the sensibilities of those who take a utopian view of organizational worlds. But the reality of organizations requires that we recognize the existence of individual motives and needs, group norms and sanctions, and the fact that organizations exist as social as well as work units—all of which means that reason alone will not be sufficient to bring about change.

The middle-ground approach relies on *reeducation* to improve the functioning of the organization. Reeducation implies a particular set of activities that

---

[4]Louise Lovelady, "Change Strategies and the Use of OD Consultants to Facilitate Change: Part I," *Leadership and Organizational Development Journal* 5, no. 2 (1984), pp. 3–5.

FIGURE 19-1
FIGURE 19-1

Model for the Management of Organizational Development

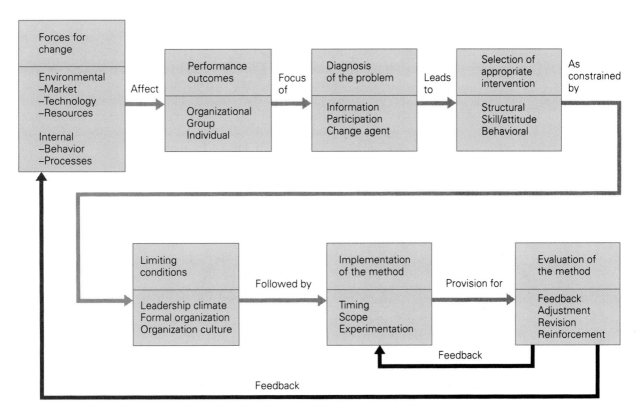

recognizes that neither power nor reason can bring about desirable change. This set of activities, the subject of much research and application, is generally understood to be the essence of organizational development.[5]

ORGANIZATIONAL DEVELOPMENT

The literature and practice of organizational development cannot be conveniently classified because of the yet unsettled nature of this aspect of organizational behavior. Various concepts and theories and their meanings and interpretations have been subject to considerable disagreement.[6] The current trend is to use the term *organizational development* to refer to "a specific set of

[5]Susan A. Mohrman, Allan M. Mohrman, Jr., and Gerald E. Ledford, Jr., "Interventions that Change Organizations," in *Large Scale Organizational Change,* ed. Allan M. Mohrman, Jr., Susan A. Mohrman, Gerald E. Ledford, Jr., Thomas G. Cummings, Edward E. Lawler III, and associates (San Francisco: Jossey-Bass, 1989), p. 146.

[6]James G. March, "Footnotes to Organizational Change," *Administrative Science Quarterly,* December 1981, pp. 563–77.

change interventions, skills, activities, tools, or techniques that are used to help people and organizations to be more effective."[7] Despite this relatively simple statement, however, little agreement exists regarding what is to be included in the specific set or from whose perspective effectiveness is judged. Since we will use the term in this and the next chapter, it is important that we clarify our meaning and interpretation.

In its most restrictive usage, OD refers to sensitivity training.[8] In this context, OD stresses the process by which people in organizations become more aware of themselves and others. Emphasis is on the psychological states of employees that inhibit their ability to communicate and interact with other members of the organization. The assumption is that organizational effectiveness can be increased if people can engage in honest and open discussion of issues.

A slightly more encompassing definition of OD states:

> Organization development is a planned, managed, systematic process to change the culture, systems and behavior of an organization, in order to improve the organization's effectiveness in solving its problems and achieving its objectives.[9]

Here, the emphasis in on OD as a planned process over time that must be justified in terms of organizational effectiveness. This definition, however, is still incomplete for our purposes.

The concept of OD must be broad enough to include not only the behavioral approach but others as well. The following definition identifies all the significant aspects of OD:

> The term "organizational development" . . . implies a normative reeducation strategy intended to affect systems of beliefs, values, and attitudes within the organization so that it can adapt better to the accelerated rate of change in technology, in our industrial environment and society in general. It also includes formal organizational restructuring which is frequently initiated, facilitated and reinforced by the normative and behavioral changes.[10]

The three subobjectives of OD are "changing attitudes or values, modifying behavior, and inducing change in structure and policy."[11] However, the OD strategy might conceivably emphasize one or another of these subobjectives. For example, if the structure of an organization is optimal in manage-

---

[7]Ellen Fagenson and W. Warner Burke, "The Current Activities and Skills of Organization Development Practitioners," *Academy of Management Proceedings,* 1989, p. 251.

[8]Wendell L. French, "The Emergence and Early History of Organization Development," *Group and Organizational Studies,* September 1982, pp. 261–78.

[9]H. M. F. Rush, "Organizational Development in Practice: A Comparison of O.D. and Non-O.D. Companies," *Organization Development: A Reconnaissance,* 1974, p. 32, as cited in Gordon L. Lippitt, Petter Longseth, and Jack Mossop, *Implementing Organizational Change* (San Francisco: Jossey-Bass, 1985), p. 27.

[10]Alexander Winn, "The Laboratory Approach to Organizational Development: A Tentative Model of Planned Change" (paper read at the annual conference of the British Psychological Association, Oxford, September 1968), cited in Robert T. Golembiewski, "Organizational Development in Public Agencies: Perspectives on Theory and Practice," *Public Administration Review,* July–August 1969, p. 367.

[11]Ibid.

ment's view, the OD process might attempt to educate personnel to adopt behaviors consistent with that structure. Such would be the case for leadership training in participative management in an organization that already has an organic structure.

Moreover, the concept of OD must include the possibility of programs aimed at providing personnel with technical skills. Effective change may not be forthcoming simply because people in the organization do not have the technical skills needed to cope with it. Management may determine that attitudes, behavior, and structure are appropriate, yet the organization cannot respond to change because key personnel do not have the skills needed to respond. The skill training programs of industry and government are important applications of OD.

The fact that the organizational development process brings about change in a social system raises the issue of change agents (discussed in a later section). A change agent is the individual or group who becomes the catalyst for change. Are change agents necessary for organizational development to take place? Once we recognize that organizational development involves substantial changes in the ways that individuals think, believe, and act, we can appreciate the necessity of someone to play the role of change agent. But who should play the role? Existing managers? New managers? Individuals hired specifically for that purpose? Depending upon the situation, either of these can be called upon to orchestrate the organizational development process.[12] The point here is that the role of the change agent, whomever it turns out to be, is necessary for organizational development to occur.

Organizational development, as the term is used in contemporary management practice, has certain distinguishing characteristics:

1. *It is planned and long-term.* OD is a data-based approach to change that involves all of the ingredients that go into managerial planning: goal setting, action planning, implementation, monitoring, and corrective action when necessary. Because of the significance of the anticipated and desired change, no quick results are expected; the entire process can take several years.

2. *It is problem oriented.* OD attempts to apply theory and research from a number of disciplines, including behavioral science, to the solution of organizational problems.

3. *It reflects a systems approach.* Both systemic and systematic, OD is a way of more clearly linking the human resources and potential of an organization to its technology, structure, and management processes.

4. *It is action oriented.* OD focuses on accomplishments and results. Unlike approaches to change that tend to describe how organizational change takes place, OD emphasizes getting things done.

5. *It involves change agents.* The process requires the facilitative role of a change agent to assist the organization in redirecting its functioning.

6. *It involves learning principles.* The basic feature of OD is the reliance on reeducation as the way to bring about change. Reeducation involves the application of fundamental learning principles.

---

[12]Manuel London, *Change Agents* (San Francisco: Jossey-Bass, 1988), pp. 41–70.

These characteristics of contemporary organizational development indicate that managers who implement OD programs are committed to making fundamental changes in organizational behavior. At the heart of the process are learning principles that enable individuals to unlearn old behaviors and learn new ones. The classic relearning sequence of unfreezing, moving, and refreezing is implemented in the OD approach to change.[13]

Learning Principles in the OD Context

To better understand how changes are brought about in individuals, it is essential to comprehend the various principles of learning discussed in Chapter 5. Managers can design a theoretically sound OD program and not achieve any of the anticipated results because they overlooked the importance of providing, for example, reinforcement or continuous feedback to employees. Such principles of learning also should be tailored to the needs of the group affected by the OD program.

Expectations and motivations. People must want to learn. Some may recognize that they need more skill in a particular job or more understanding of the problems of other units of the firm, and they are receptive to experiences that will aid them in developing new skills or new empathies. Others reject the need or play it down because they view learning as an admission that they are not completely competent in their jobs. These kinds of people face the prospect of change with different expectations and motivations. Determining the expectations and motivations of people, while not an easy task, is one that must be undertaken. Not everyone wants to participate in a change program, and it is management's responsibility to show employees why they should want to change.

Reinforcement and feedback. *Reinforcement* is an important principle of learning. It suggests that when people receive positive rewards, information, or feelings for doing something, they become more likely to do the same thing in the same or a similar situation. The other side of the coin involves the impact of punishment for a particular response; it is assumed that punishment will decrease the probability of doing the same thing at another time. The reinforcement principle, then, implies that achieving successful change is easier through the use of positive rewards. Reinforcement can also occur when the knowledge or skill acquired in a training program is reimparted through a refresher course.

A major problem associated with reinforcement is the determination of reinforcers. That is, what will serve as the appropriate reinforcer of desired behavior? Money or praise is effective for some people, while others respond more to a refresher type of training experience. Once again, situations and individuals determine what means of reinforcement will prove effective.

Employees generally desire knowledge on how they are doing, or *feedback,* especially after a change program has been implemented. Providing informa-

---

[13]Marvin R. Weisbord, *Productive Workplaces: Organizing and Managing for Dignity, Meaning, and Community* (San Francisco: Jossey-Bass, 1987), p. 94.

tion about the progress of a unit or a group lets the employees involved take corrective action. A number of studies have indicated that employees perform more effectively on a variety of tasks when they have feedback than they do when it is absent. As one might anticipate, however, individuals differ in their receptivity to feedback. In general, employees who are motivated to improve themselves or their unit react more favorably.

The timing of feedback is a factor that should be considered. Most college students want to know their course grade as soon as possible after the final examination. The same need to know exists for managers who have set their objectives for the next year; they want to know immediately whether their objectives are acceptable. Thus, immediacy is an issue. Providing feedback a long time after an action has occurred will probably not be as effective as providing feedback immediately after the action.

Management must also guard against the possibility that what a person has learned at a training site is lost when that person is transferred to the actual work site. Optimally, only a minimum amount will be lost in this necessary transfer. A possible strategy for keeping the loss to a minimum is to make the training situation similar to the actual workplace environment. Another strategy is to reward the newly learned behavior. If the colleagues and superiors of newly trained people approve new ideas or new skills, these people will be encouraged to continue to behave in the new way. If colleagues and superiors behave negatively, the newly trained people will be discouraged from persisting with attempts to use what they have learned. For this reason and others, it has been suggested that superiors be trained before subordinates. A trained and motivated superior can serve as a reinforcement and feedback source for the subordinate who has left the training confines and is now back on the job.

Numerous other principles of learning prove invaluable when managers attempt to use OD programs. Those principles noted above, however, are currently being discussed in the OD literature. The manager who fails to consider them when introducing an OD program will have a difficult time improving organizational effectiveness.

Change Agents in Organizational Development

Because managers tend to seek answers in traditional solutions, the intervention of an outsider is necessary. The intervener, or **change agent,** brings a different perspective to the situation and serves as a challenge to the status quo. The success of any change program rests heavily on the quality and workability of the relationship between the change agent and the key decision makers within the organization. Thus, the form of intervention (the type of change agent) is crucial.[14]

CHANGE AGENTS

Individual/group that brings outsiders' viewpoints and perspectives to the organizational change process. In most instances, they are used in some combination of persons from inside and outside organization.

Forms of intervention.   To intervene is to enter into an ongoing organization or among persons or between departments for the purpose of helping them improve their effectiveness. Organizations use three forms of intervention.

---

[14]Louise Lovelady, "Change Strategies and the Use of OD Consultants to Facilitate Change: Part II," *Leadership and Organizational Development Journal* 5, no. 4 (1984), pp. 2–12.

External change agents.   External change agents are temporary employees of the organization, since they are engaged only for the duration of the change process. They come from a variety of organizations, including universities, consulting firms, and training agencies. Many large organizations have individuals located at central offices who take temporary assignments with line units contemplating organizational development. At the conclusion of the change program, the change agent will return to headquarters.

The usual external change agent is a university professor or private consultant who has training and experience in the behavioral sciences. Such an individual will be contacted by the organization and be engaged for the duration after agreement is reached about the conditions of the relationship. Ordinarily, the change agent will have graduate degrees in specialties that focus on individual and group behavior in organizational settings. With this kind of training, the external change agent has the perspective to facilitate the change process.

Internal change agents.   The internal change agent works for the organization and knows something about its problems.[15] In an organization with a record of poor performance, the usual internal change agent is a recently appointed manager who took the job with the expectation that major change was necessary.

The ways that successful internal change agents undertake their OD roles has been extensively studied in recent years. For example, individuals such as Michael Blumenthal, chairman of Burroughs Corporation, who developed a substantially new management team at Burroughs, and Lee Iacocca, who brought about major change at Chrysler, have been subjects of close scrutiny by theorists and practitioners of OD.[16] The Close-Up describes some of the actions taken at Honeywell, a major data processing company.

External-internal change agents.   To exploit the resources and knowledge base of both external and internal change agents, some organizations have used a combination external-internal change team to intervene and develop programs. Using this approach, top management designates an individual or small group within the organization to serve with the external change agent as spearheads of the change effort. The internal group often comes from the personnel unit, but it can also be a group of top managers. As a general rule, an external change agent will actively solicit the visible support of top management as a way to emphasize the importance of the OD effort.[17]

Each of the three forms of intervention has advantages and disadvantages. The external change agent is often viewed as an outsider. When employees hold this belief, rapport must be established between the change agent and decision makers. The change agent's views on the problems faced by the

[15]Stephen C. Harper, "The Manager as Change Agent: 'Hell No' to the Status Quo," *Industrial Management,* May–June 1989, pp. 8–11.

[16]Noel M. Tichy and David Ulrich, "The Challenge of Revitalization," *New Management,* Winter 1985, pp. 53–59.

[17]Michael Beer and Anna Elise Walton, "Organization Change and Development," in *Organization Development: Theory, Practice, and Research,* ed. Wendell L. French, Cecil H. Bell, Jr., and Robert A. Zawacki (Homewood, Ill.: Richard D. Irwin, 1989), p. 73.

INTERNAL CHANGE AGENT AT WORK IN HONEYWELL

In 1982, James Renier took over as president of Honeywell Information Systems with a mandate to revitalize the company's computer business. The several preceding years had been hard for the company as its competition had moved ahead with new technology and market strategies. During his first six months on the job, Renier had to cut costs and find ways to increase efficiency. Simultaneously, he was developing a new business strategy and building a new management team. At the core of his efforts was an abiding commitment to the idea that people respond positively in work environments that exhibit truth, trust, and respect.

Renier's job as change agent included enlisting support for his vision of what the company's strategy and values should be. He stated publicly that he would tolerate mistakes on the business strategy but not on what he believed the organization should stand for. The underlying values of the new culture included participative decision making, emphasis on employee objectives, and having fun with the business.

Corporate strategy and values were the topics of numerous meetings and workshops with top management and others identified as leaders in the company. Renier's reeducative efforts emphasized the importance of learning and feedback.

Source: Noel M. Tichy, David L. Dotlich, and Dale G. Lake, "Revitalization: The Honeywell Information Systems Story," *Journal of Business Strategy*, Winter 1986, pp. 70–80.

---

organization often differ from the decision makers' views, and this leads to problems in establishing rapport. The differences in viewpoints often result in mistrust of the external change agent by all or some of the policymakers.

The internal change agent is often viewed as being more closely associated with one unit or group of individuals than with any other. This perceived favoritism leads to resistance to change by those not included in the "inner" circle of close friends and personnel. Knowledge of such attitudes can be crucial in preparing for and implementing change.

The combination external-internal team, while the rarest type of intervention, seems to have an excellent chance for success. The outsider's objectivity and professional knowledge are blended with the insider's knowledge of the organization and its human resources. This blending of knowledge often results in increased trust and confidence among the parties involved. The ability of the combination external-internal team to communicate and to develop a positive rapport can reduce the resistance to any forthcoming change.

Change agent–client organization relationships. The origin of the change agent is one important issue. Equally important is the way the agent relates to the client organization. The change agent, whether internal or external, can relate to the organization according to one or more approaches.

Medical approach. Perhaps the most basic of all approaches, the medical approach places the change agent in the role of adviser. The organization asks the change agent to assist in clarifying the problems, diagnosing the causes, and recommending courses of action but retains responsibility for accepting or rejecting the change agent's recommendations. The relationship is analogous to the physician-consultant arrangement; that is, the physician may seek opinions from other experts, but the choice of therapy remains with the physician.

Doctor-patient approach.   Use of this approach places the organization in the position of a "patient" who suspects that something is wrong. The change agent—the "doctor"—diagnoses and prescribes a solution that, of course, can be rejected by the patient. Yet, by virtue of the relationship, the organization will usually adopt the change agent's recommendations. The change agent engages in diagnostic and problem-identification activities jointly with the organization. The more involved the organization is in the process, the more likely management will be to accept the recommended solution.

Engineering approach.   This approach is used when the organization has performed the diagnostic work and has decided on a specific solution. For example, management desires to implement an MBO or job enrichment program, and it seeks the services of experts to aid in the implementation. An alternative form of the approach exists when the organization has defined the problem—excessive turnover, intergroup competition, or ineffective leadership behavior, for example—and requests the change agent to specify a solution. The general characteristic of the approach, however, is that management undertakes the diagnostic phase.

Process approach.   This approach is widely used by OD consultants. It involves the change agent and the organization in actual *collaboration* through which management is encouraged to see and understand organizational problems. Through joint efforts, managers and change agents try to comprehend the factors in the situation that must be changed to improve performance. The change agent avoids taking sole responsibility for either diagnosis or prescription. Rather, the change agent's emphasis is on enabling management to comprehend the problems and on teaching management how to diagnose rather than on doing the diagnosing for the organization.

The choice of an appropriate change agent approach depends on characteristics of the change agent, the organization, and the situation. One approach is not superior in all instances; rather, the appropriate approach will depend on the given circumstance.

A MODEL FOR MANAGING THE OD PROCESS

The process of managing change through organizational development can be approached systematically. The several steps involved can be linked in a logical way, as suggested in Figure 19–1. The model consists of specific steps generally acknowledged to be essential to successful change management.[18] To

---

[18]Donald L. Kirkpatrick, *How to Manage Change Effectively* (San Francisco: Jossey-Bass, 1985), pp. 101–6.

undertake an OD program, a manager considers each of them, either explicitly or implicitly. The prospects of initiating successful change can be enhanced when the managers actively support the effort and demonstrate their support by implementing systematic procedures that give substance to the OD process.[19]

The model indicates that forces for change continually act on the organization; this assumption reflects the dynamic character of the modern world. At the same time, the manager has the responsibility to sort out the information that reflects the magnitude of change forces.[20] On the basis of that information, the manager recognizes when change is needed; it is equally desirable to see when change is not needed.

Once managers recognize that something is malfunctioning, they must diagnose the problem, identify relevant alternative techniques, and select an intervention. The selected intervention must be appropriate to the problem, as constrained by limiting conditions. One example of a limiting condition that we have discussed in an earlier chapter is the prevailing character of group norms. The informal groups may support some change techniques but may sabotage others. Other limiting conditions include leadership behavior, legal requirements, and economic conditions.

Finally, the manager must implement the change and monitor the change process and change results. The feedback loops to the implementation step and to the forces for change step suggest that both the change process and the results must be monitored and evaluated. The mode of implementation may be faulty and may lead to poor results, but responsive action could correct the situation. Moreover, the feedback loop to the initial step recognizes that no change is final. A new situation is created within which problems and issues will emerge; a new setting is created that will itself become subject to change. The model suggests no "final solution." Rather, it emphasizes that the modern manager operates in a dynamic setting wherein the only certainty is change itself.

Forces for Change

The forces for change can be classified conveniently into two groups: environmental forces and internal forces. Environmental forces are beyond the control of management. Internal forces operate inside the firm and are generally within the control of management. Change also involves managers who are aware of the change and take action.

Environmental forces. Organizations seldom undertake significant change without a strong shock from their environment.[21] The external environment includes many economic, technological and social forces that can act as triggers

ENVIRONMENTAL FORCES
External forces for change, including marketplace actions, technological advancements, and social/political changes.

---

[19]J. J. Murphy, "Reappraising MBO," *Leadership and Organizational Development* 4, no. 4 (1983), pp. 22–27.

[20]Ralph H. Kilmann, "Toward a Complete Program for Corporate Transformation," in *Corporate Transformation,* ed. Ralph H. Kilmann, Teresa Joyce Covin, and associates (San Francisco: Jossey-Bass, 1989), pp. 302–29.

[21]Tichy and Ulrich, "The Challenge," p. 54.

for the change process. Students and practitioners of organizational change agree that these environmental triggers are necessary but not sufficient to initiate change.

The manager of a business firm has historically been concerned with reacting to changes in the *marketplace*. Competitors introduce new products, increase their advertising, reduce their prices, or increase their customer service. In each case, a response is required unless the manager is content to permit the erosion of profit and market share. At the same time, changes occur in customer tastes and incomes. The firm's products may no longer have customer appeal; customers may be able to purchase less expensive, higher-quality forms of the same products.

The free enterprise system generally eliminates from the economic scene those firms that do not adjust to market conditions. The isolated-from-reality manager who ignores the market signals will soon confront the more vocal (and louder) signals of discontented stockholders. By that time, however, the appropriate change may well be dissolution of the firm—the final solution. One of the positive effects of competition is to initiate and reward innovative behavior. As Wayne E. Rosing, vice president for advanced development at Sun Microsystems, Inc., stated: "Nothing motivates Sun like the fear of what a competitor might do."[22]

Suppliers of the organization's resources are another market force to be dealt with. For example, a change in the quality and quantity of human resources can dictate changes in the firm, such as the adoption of automated processes being stimulated by a decline in the supply of labor. The techniques of coal mining and tobacco farming have greatly changed during recent years due to labor shortages. Changes in the supply of materials can cause a firm to substitute one material for another: rayon stockings and synthetic rubber tires were direct outgrowths of war-induced shortages in raw materials. We need not catalog the whole range of possible changes in the resource markets that stimulate organizational change. The great potential, however, must be recognized.

The second source of environmental change forces is *technology*. The knowledge explosion has introduced new technology for nearly every business function. Computers have made possible high-speed data processing and the solution to complex production problems. New machines and new processes have revolutionized the way in which many products are manufactured and distributed.

Computer technology and automation have affected not only the technical conditions of work but the social conditions as well.[23] As new occupations have been created, others have been eliminated. Also, slowness to adopt new technology that reduces cost and improves quality will show up in the financial statements sooner or later.[24] Technological advance is a permanent fixture in the business world; as a force for change, it will continue to demand attention.

---

[22]"Sun Microsystems Turns On the Afterburners," *Business Week,* July 18, 1988, p. 115.

[23]Robert H. Hayes and Ramchandran Jaikumar, "Manufacturing's Crisis: New Technologies, Obsolete Organizations," *Harvard Business Review,* September–October 1988, pp. 77–85.

[24]Ann Majchrzak, *The Human Side of Factory Automation* (San Francisco: Jossey-Bass, 1988).

ORGANIZATIONS:
CLOSE-UP

AT&T CHANGES THE WAY IT COMPETES

Since 1983, when the firm was broken up by events following deregulation, AT&T has altered nearly every aspect of the firm's organization and strategy. These changes reflect the company's responses to the necessity to compete in markets that reward for fast adoption of new technology and adaptation to fickle customer demand.

AT&T's organization structure at the time of deregulation proved incapable of bringing about appropriate behavior. According to Chairman Robert E. Allen, who took over in 1988, AT&T's top-heavy bureaucracy created unnecessary blocks to creativity and initiative. He began efforts to flatten the organization and bring top managers closer to the customer. Lower-level managers have more authority to respond to customer issues.

The changes have not been without costs, as reflected in the 75,000 layoffs and early retirements since 1984. But staying the course is essential, according to Allen. To combat the effects of these traumatic changes, AT&T has implemented policies that give managers and employees a personal stake in the businesses they run: their salaries and advancement opportunities are tied to customer satisfaction. Allen claims to have no grand design for what AT&T will look like, but he insists that it must continue its efforts to create smaller, customer-oriented units.

Source: "Bob Allen Is Turning AT&T into a Live Wire," *Business Week*, November 6, 1989, pp. 140–141, 144, 148, 152.

The third source of environmental change forces is *social* and *political* change. Business managers must be "tuned in" to the great movements over which they have no control but that, in time, influence their firm's fate. Sophisticated mass communications and international markets create great potential for business, but they also pose great threats to managers unable to understand what is going on.[25] Finally, the relationship between government and business becomes much closer as regulations are imposed and relaxed.

These pressures for change reflect the increasing complexity and interdependence of modern living. In recent times, the banking and transportation industries have been deregulated and forced to enter into competition with other industries offering the same or similar services and products. One effect has been tremendous change in organizational strategies and structures.[26] The Close-Up describes AT&T's reaction to deregulation of the communication industry.

To cope effectively with external changes, an organization's boundary functions must be sensitive to these changes. These boundary functions must

[25]Huibert de Man, *Organizational Change in Its Context: A Theoretical and Empirical Study of the Linkages between Organizational Change Projects and Their Administrative, Strategic, and Institutional Environment* (Delft, Holland: Eburon, 1988).

[26]James L. Gibson and James H. Donnelly, "Developing Responsive Organizational Structures in Market-Oriented Bank Environments," *Journal of Retail Banking*, Fall 1985, pp. 27–42.

act as a bridge between the external environment and units of the organization. Individuals in units, such as marketing research, labor relations, personnel recruiting, purchasing, and some areas of finance, must sense changes in the external environment and convey information on these changes to managers.

Internal forces.   **Internal forces** for change, which occur within the organization, can usually be traced to process and behavioral problems. *Process* problems include breakdowns in decision making and communications. Decisions are not made, are made too late, or are of poor quality. Communications are short-circuited, redundant, or simply inadequate. Tasks are not undertaken or not completed because the person responsible did not "get the word." Because of inadequate or nonexistent communications, a customer order is not filled, a grievance is not processed, or an invoice is not filed and the supplier is not paid. Interpersonal and interdepartmental conflicts reflect breakdowns in organizational processes.

Low levels of morale and high levels of absenteeism and turnover are symptoms of *behavioral* problems that must be diagnosed. A wildcat strike or a walkout may be the most tangible sign of a problem, yet such tactics are usually employed because they arouse management to action. A certain level of employee discontent exists in most organizations, but to ignore employee complaints and suggestions is very dangerous.

The process of change includes the *recognition* phrase; at this point, management must decide to act or not to act. In many organizations, the need for change goes unrecognized until some major catastrophe occurs (e.g., employees strike or seek the recognition of a union before the management finally recognizes the need for action). But, the need for change must be recognized by some means, whether a whisper or a shout; and once that need has been recognized, the exact nature of the problem must be diagnosed. If the problem is not properly understood, the impact of change on people can be extremely negative.

Diagnosis of a Problem

Change agents facilitate the diagnostic phase by gathering, interpreting, and presenting data. Although the accuracy of data is extremely important, of equal importance is the way in which the data are interpreted and presented. This is generally accomplished in one of two ways: (1) the data are discussed with a group of top managers, who are asked to make their own diagnosis of the information; (2) the change agents may present their own diagnoses without making explicit their frameworks for analyzing the data. A difficulty with the first approach is that top management tends to see each problem separately. Each manager views his or her problem as being the most important and fails to recognize other problem areas. The second approach has inherent problems of communication. External change agents often have difficulty with the second approach because they become immersed in theory and various conceptual frameworks that are less realistic than the managers would like.

Diagnosing the symptoms of the problem necessarily precedes appropriate action. Experience and judgment are critical to this phase unless the problem is readily apparent to all observers. Ordinarily, however, managers can disagree on the nature of the problem. No formula exists for accurate diagnosis, but the following questions point the manager in the right direction:

1. What is the problem as distinct from the symptoms of the problem?
2. What must be changed to resolve the problem?
3. What outcomes (objectives) are expected from the change, and how will those outcomes be measured?

The answers to these questions can come from information ordinarily found in the organization's information system. Or it may be necessary to generate ad hoc information through the creation of committees or task forces.[27] Meetings between managers and employees provide a variety of viewpoints that can be sifted through by a smaller group. (The Close-Up describes the process of diagnosis in a Norwegian savings bank.) Interviewing key personnel is another important problem-finding method as is the attitude survey, a diagnostic approach that obtains broad-based information.

Attitude surveys can be administered to the entire work force or to a representative sample. They permit the respondents to evaluate and rate management, pay and pay-related items, working conditions, equipment, and other job-related factors. The appropriate use of such a survey requires that the questionnaire be completed anonymously so that employees can express their views freely and without threat, whether real or imagined. The objective of the survey is to pinpoint the problem or problems as perceived by the members of the organization. Subsequent discussions of the survey results, at all levels of the organization, can add further insights into the nature of the problem.

The survey is a useful diagnostic approach if the potential focus of change is the total organization. If the change focus involves smaller units or entities, the survey technique may not be a reliable source of information. For example, if the focus of change is a relatively small work group, diagnosis of the problem is better accomplished through individual interviews followed by group discussion of the interview data. In this approach, the group becomes actively involved in sharing and interpreting perception of problems. The attitude survey also can pose difficulties for organizations with relatively low levels of trust in management's sincerity to use the information in constructive ways, as noted in the Close-Up on a turnaround situation.

Identification of individual employees' problems comes about through interviews and personnel department information. Consistently low performance evaluations indicate that such problems exist, but going into greater detail is often necessary. Identifying individuals' problems is far more difficult than identifying organizational problems. Therefore, the diagnostic process must stress the use of precise and reliable information.

To summarize, the data collection process can tap information in five different ways (each useful for different purposes):[28]

1. Questionnaire data can be collected from large numbers of people.
2. Direct observations can be taken of actual workplace behavior.

---

[27]Lippitt et al., *Implementing Organizational Change,* pp. 53–74.
[28]Noel M. Tichy, *Managing Strategic Change* (New York: John Wiley & Sons, 1983), pp. 162–64.

ORGANIZATIONS:
CLOSE-UP

PROBLEM DIAGNOSIS IN A NORWEGIAN SAVINGS BANK

A group of OD consultants in Norway undertook a long-term program to develop the management skills of Norwegian bankers. These bankers had previously operated as independents, competing in relatively sheltered markets. But they now were managers in a large holding company consisting of many merger banks competing in a deregulated financial services industry.

The consultants interviewed top managers of the banks to identify the specific problems that would be encountered in developing appropriate skills to manage in the changing, competitive marketplace for banking services in Norway and Europe. The interview identified four problems that top management believed the consultants would have to overcome in the developmental effort:

1. The managers were accustomed to managing in a traditional, hierarchical organizational structure and would possibly resist efforts to move to more participative approaches.

2. The managers seemed to lack a keen awareness of their roles as managers in firms that must compete in the broader financial services market in Norway and Europe.

3. Some of the acquired banks continued to operate as relatively independent units; others had been integrated into the parent organization.

4. The bank managers had not developed the necessary proactive attitudes necessary to deal with intense competition. They continued to think in traditional reactive ways that served them well in earlier, less competitive times.

Armed with this information, the consultants were better able to design training and developmental experiences to change the attitudes and behaviors of the Norwegian banker-managers.

Source: Jan Aspund, Hakan Behrendtz, and Frank Jernberg, "The Norwegian Savings Bank Case: Implementation and Consequences of a Broadly Scoped, Long-Term, System-Driven Program for Management Development," *Journal of Applied Behavioral Science* 19, no. 3 (1983), pp. 381–94.

3. Selected individuals in key positions can be interviewed.

4. Workshops can be arranged with groups to explore different perceptions of problems.

5. Documents and records of the organization can be examined for archival and current information.

A general difficulty derives from the close relationship between diagnosis and action. One important guideline for managers of OD programs is that the form of intervention should not be separated from the diagnosis. In many OD programs, the emphasis appears to be on the implementation of a particular intervention, with little concern for whether it is appropriate. For example, Blake and Mouton concentrate on implementing the managerial grid across different companies,[29] and Seashore and Bowers designed an action program based on participative management for the Banner organization prior to

---

[29]Robert R. Blake and Jane S. Mouton, *The Managerial Grid III* (Houston: Gulf Publishing, 1985).

ALTERNATIVE TO ATTITUDE SURVEYS IN A TURNAROUND SITUATION

Organizational development was a key factor in the successful turnaround of a bank in Indiana. According to the report of the bank's experience with organizational development, the bank suffered from the "rust belt blues" and the associated declines in profitability and other measures of effectiveness. To counter the decline, the bank asked an external change agent to assist its efforts to develop a performance-oriented work environment for all bank employees.

The change agent suggested the use of an attitude survey questionnaire to identify needs and problems. However, the bank's management rejected that approach because it had conducted such surveys in the past but had never acted on the results. The survey methodology had little credibility among the bank employees, and the information obtained from it would have questionable validity. As an alternative, the change agent conducted extensive interviews with key personnel throughout the bank. These individuals were thought to reflect the various perspectives that prevailed in the bank.

Although the interview process consumed more time than an attitude survey, the resulting information was richer in detail and provided considerable insight into the problems that had to be overcome to turn the bank's performance around. The information also provided benchmarks by which to gauge the progress of the change effort.

Source: Gopal C. Pati and Robert A. Salitore, "The Resurrection of a Rust-Belt Service Organization," *Organizational Dynamics*, Summer 1989, pp. 33–49.

diagnosing specific problem areas.[30] Instead of a "canned" approach in which the diagnosis and intervention are the same for different companies, a more "tailored" approach to change is needed. That is, interventions should fit the particular problems of an organization.

Selecting Interventions

An **intervention** is a specific action that a change agent takes to facilitate the change process. Such actions are called interventions because they intervene in an ongoing system, intending to change that system. Although the term has a general meaning, it specifically refers to a formal activity in the context of organizational development.

The choice of a particular intervention depends on the nature of the problem that management has diagnosed. As we have noted, diagnosis of the problem includes specification of the outcome that management desires from the change. Management must determine which alternative will most likely produce the desired outcome, whether it be improvement in skills, attitudes, behavior, or structure.

INTERVENTIONS

Specific actions that, if undertaken, will bring about desired change in an organization.

---

[30]Stanley Seashore and David Bowers, *Changing the Structure and Functioning of an Organization: Report of a Field Experiment* (Ann Arbor: Survey Research Center, University of Michigan, 1963).

The importance of interventions is such that we devote the following chapter to a fuller explanation of some of the more important ones, including some discussed in previous chapters. These will be classified according to their major focus of change: skills, attitudes, behavior, or structure. Such a classification in no way implies a distinct division among the areas of change. On the contrary, the interrelationships among skills, attitudes, behavior, and structure must be acknowledged and anticipated. For purposes of discussion here, however, it is enough to state that the implementation of a particular intervention must follow diagnosis of the problem and be related to the cause of the diagnosed problem.

Limiting Conditions

The selection of any developmental intervention should be based on diagnosis of the problem, but the choice is tempered by certain existing conditions. Scholars identify three sources of influence on the outcome of management development programs that can be generalized to cover the entire range of organizational development efforts, whether attitudinal, behavioral, or structural. The three sources are leadership climate, formal organization, and organizational culture.

Leadership climate.   The nature of the work environment that results from the leadership style and administrative practices of superiors is termed the leadership climate. It can greatly affect an OD program. Any OD program that does not have the support and commitment of management has slim chance of success.[31] The style of leadership may itself be the subject of change; for example, the managerial grid and System 4 (discussed in Chapter 20) are direct attempts to move managers toward a certain style—open, supportive, and group centered; but participants may be unable to adopt such styles if the styles are not compatible with their own superior's style.

Formal organization.   The formal organization includes the philosophy and policies of top management, as well as legal precedent, organizational structure, and the systems of control. Each of these sources of impact, of course, may itself be the focus of a change effort. The important point is that a change in one must be compatible with all of the others.[32] It may be possible to design organizations that not only facilitate change but actually welcome change.[33]

Organizational culture.   As we have learned, organizational culture refers to the pattern of beliefs resulting from group norms, values, and informal activities.[34] The impact of traditional behavior that is sanctioned by group norms

---

[31]Noel M. Tichy, "GE's Crotonville: A Staging Ground for Corporate Revolution," *Academy of Management Executive,* May 1989, pp. 99–106.

[32]Yoram Ziera and Joyce Avedisian, "Organizational Planned Change: Assessing the Chances for Success," *Organizational Dynamics,* Spring 1989, pp. 31–45.

[33]Russell L. Ackoff, "The Circular Organization: An Update," *Academy of Management Executive,* February 1989, pp. 11–16.

[34]J. Stephen Ott, *The Organizational Culture Perspective* (Monterey, Calif.: Brooks/Cole Publishing, 1989).

but not formally acknowledged was first documented in the Hawthorne studies. If a proposed change in work methods or the installation of an automated device runs counter to the expectations and attitudes of the work group, the OD strategy must anticipate the resulting resistance.[35]

OD implementation that does not consider the constraints imposed by prevailing conditions within the present organization may, of course, amplify the problem that triggered the developmental process. If OD is implemented in this way, the potential for subsequent problems is greater than would ordinarily be expected. Taken together, the prevailing conditions constitute the climate for change, and they can be positive or negative. One important organization has undertaken efforts to overcome the barriers to change, as described in the Close-Up on Volvo.

Implementing the Intervention

Implementation of the OD intervention has two dimensions: timing and scope. *Timing* refers to the selection of the appropriate time to initiate the intervention; *scope* refers to the selection of the appropriate scale.

Timing depends on a number of factors, particularly the organization's operating cycle and the groundwork that has preceded the OD program. Certainly, it is desirable that a program of considerable magnitude not compete with day-to-day operations; thus, the change might well be implemented during a slack period. On the other hand, immediate implementation is in order for a program critical to the survival of the organization. The scope of the program depends on the strategy. The program may be implemented throughout the organization, or it may be phased into the organization level by level or department by department.

The intervention finally selected is usually not implemented on a grand scale; rather, it is implemented on a small scale in various units throughout the organization. For example, an MBO program can be implemented in one unit or at one level at a time. The objective is to experiment with the intervention — that is, to test the validity of the diagnosed solution. As management learns from each successive implementation, the total program is strengthened. Not even the most detailed planning can anticipate all the consequences of implementing a particular intervention. Thus, it is necessary to experiment and to search for new information that can bear on the program.

As the experimental attempts provide positive signals that the program is proceeding as planned, there is a reinforcement effect. The personnel are encouraged to accept the change required of them and to enlarge the scope of their own efforts. Acceptance of the change is facilitated by its positive results.

Evaluating the Program

An OD program involves an expenditure of organizational resources in exchange for some desired result. The resources take the form of money and time that have alternative uses. The result comes in the form of increased

---

[35]Gopal C. Pati and Robert A. Salitore, "The Resurrection of a Rust-Belt Service Organization," *Organizational Dynamics,* Summer 1989, pp. 33–49.

ORGANIZATIONS:
CLOSE-UP

VOLVO OVERCOMES BARRIERS TO CHANGE

Volvo Corporation attracted worldwide attention by its efforts to devise manufacturing methods that achieve efficiency and good quality of work life. After the literature of organizational development had been filled with reports of the Volvo OD programs for 20 years, two officials associated with the program reported what they believed to be some of the keys to successful organizational development. Their report includes the following seven recommendations:

1. The value system of top management must support the OD goals, and that support must be communicated throughout the organization. Moreover, these values must be congruent with larger societal values, and that congruency must be disseminated to the larger society.

2. Top management must provide the resources to support the OD program in times of hardship as well as times of prosperity. An on/off approach does not develop confidence that top management genuinely supports the program.

3. Open and honest communications among all groups and about all matters are a necessity.

4. Responsibility for implementing the required changes must reside with line managers. Staff personnel can assist the process by assuming advisory roles, but the integrity of the line units must remain intact at all times.

5. All required support systems and procedures must keep pace with the change. Not the least important are training activities and wage schemes that must keep up with changes in job responsibilities.

6. If unions are involved, they must support the effort or at least be neutral toward it.

7. Finally, interventions must be tailored to each situation. The unique characteristics of individuals, groups, and organizations preclude panaceas.

The realization of the importance of these seven points came after long years of experimentation. Successes and failures existed side by side throughout the Volvo program, and it was through both that the Volvo managers were able to distill these seven keys to overcoming barriers to change.

Source: Berth Jonsson and Alden G. Lank, "Volvo: A Report on the Workshop on Production Technology and the Quality of Working Life," *Human Resource Management*, Winter 1985, pp. 455–65.

organizational effectiveness—production, efficiency, and satisfaction in the short run; adaptiveness and development in the intermediate run; survival in the long run. Accordingly, some provision must be made to evaluate the program in terms of expenditures and results. In addition to supplying information about a specific OD program, evaluation provides a literature that can be accessed by others who are deciding whether to undertake OD. Reviews of the relative efficacy of OD interventions appear regularly in the OD literature.[36]

---

[36]Recent reviews include John M. Nicholas, "The Comparative Impact of Organization Developments on Hard Criteria Measures," *Academy of Management Review*, October 1982, pp. 531–43; Anthony P. Raia and Newton Margulies, "Organizational Development: Issues, Trends, and Prospects," in *Human Systems Development*, ed. Robert Tannenbaum, Newton Margulies, Fred

The evaluation phase has two problems to overcome: the acquisition of data that measure the desired results and the determination of the expected trend of improvement over time. Information acquisition is the easier problem to solve, although it certainly does not lend itself to naive solutions. As we have come to understand, the stimulus for change is the deterioration of performance criteria that management has traced to structural and behavioral causes. The criteria may be any number of effectiveness indicators, including profit, sales volume, absenteeism, turnover, scrappage, or costs. The major source of feedback for those variables is the organization's information system. But if the change includes the expectation that employee satisfaction must be improved, the usual sources of information are limited, if not invalid. Quite possibly, change may induce increased production at the expense of employee satisfaction. Thus, if the manager relies on the naive assumption that production and satisfaction are directly related, the change may be incorrectly judged successful when cost and profit improve.[37]

To avoid the danger of overreliance on production data, the manager can generate ad hoc information that measures employee satisfaction. The benchmark for evaluation would be available if an attitude survey was used in the diagnosis phase. Defining acceptable improvement is difficult when evaluating attitudinal data, since the matter of "how much more" positive the attitude of employees should be is quite different from the matter of "how much more" productive they should be. Nevertheless, to undertake a complete analysis of results, attitudinal measurements must be combined with production and other effectiveness measurements.

In a practical sense, the effectiveness of an OD program cannot be evaluated if objectives were not established before implementation. A program undertaken to make the organization "a better place to work" or to develop the "full potential of the employees" cannot be evaluated. If, on the other hand, measurable criteria that are valid indicators of "better places to work" and "full employee potential" are collected during the diagnostic phase and subsequently tracked as the program is implemented, bases for evaluation exist. A considerable body of literature describes methods of evaluation, and managers of OD programs should consult it for guidance in program evaluation.

Generally, evaluation should follow the procedures of evaluative research, including the following activities:

— Determining the objectives of the program.
— Describing the activities undertaken to achieve the objectives.
— Measuring the effects of the program.
— Establishing baseline points against which changes can be compared.
— Controlling extraneous factors, preferably through the use of a control group.
— Detecting unanticipated consequences.

Massarik, and associates (San Francisco: Jossey-Bass, 1985), pp. 246–72; George A. Neuman, Jack E. Edwards, and Nambury S. Raju, "Organizational Development Interventions: A Meta-Analysis of Their Effects on Satisfaction and Other Attitudes," *Personnel Psychology,* Autumn 1989, pp. 461–89.

[37]Bernard A. Rausch, "DuPont Transforms a Division's Culture," *Management Review,* March 1989, pp. 37–42.

All these activities will not always be possible. For example, managers do not always specify objectives in precise terms, and control groups are difficult to establish in some instances. Nevertheless, the difficulties of evaluation should not discourage attempts to evaluate.

ESSENTIAL STEPS FOR EFFECTIVE CHANGE MANAGEMENT

We can summarize the discussion of this chapter by presenting an abbreviated, five-stage model for managing change. This abbreviated model emphasizes management's responsibility to do the essential things that increase the probability that individual, group, and organizational effectiveness will improve as a consequence. Many consultants and practitioners have contributed to the literature of change management, and the discussion in this chapter reflects many of their contributions. The five-stage model can be considered a generally accepted statement of effective change management procedures.[38] The five essential stages of change management are:

1. *INITIATING the change*—typically undertaken by a change agent who may be internal or external to the organization and who may act alone or with a group to spearhead the program.
2. *DIAGNOSING the problem*—identifies the evidence and specific causes of problems, resulting in recognition of target(s) of change.
3. *IDENTIFYING the intervention(s)* that will cause the targets to change in the desired direction.
4. *IMPLEMENTING the intervention* at the appropriate time and scope to ensure the highest probability of successful change.
5. *EVALUATING the outcomes* to gauge the magnitude and direction of changes in the targets.

Managers who manage change in the systematic way suggested by the five stages increase the odds that the actual outcomes will be the intended outcomes. In terms of the basic relearning process that underlies the organizational development approach to change, we see that steps 1 and 2 have the effect of *unfreezing* existing but irrelevant behavior; steps 3 and 4 *move* the behavior in the desired direction; step 5 *refreezes* the desired, relevant behavior.

---

[38]Ralph H. Kilmann, "A Completely Integrated Program for Creating and Maintaining Organizational Success," *Organizational Dynamics,* Summer 1989, p. 19, provides an excellent review of the literature that supports the change model developed in this chapter.

SUMMARY OF KEY POINTS

— The need to consider organizational development arises from changes in the inter- and extraorganizational environment. Changes in input, output, technological, and scientific subenvironments may indicate the need to consider the feasibility of a long-term, systematically managed program for changing the structure, process, and behavior of the organization. Even in the absence of environmental changes, organizational processes and behavior may become dysfunctional for achieving organizational effectiveness.

— The diagnosis of present and potential problems involves the collection of information that reflects the level of organizational effectiveness. Data that measure the current state of production, efficiency, satisfaction, adaptiveness, and development must be gathered and analyzed. The purpose of diagnosis is to trace the causes of the problem. In addition to serving as the bases for problem identification, the diagnostic data also establish the basis for subsequent evaluation of the organizational development effort.

— To diagnose the problem, managers can consider these analytical questions:
1. What is the problem as distinct from its symptoms?
2. What must be changed to resolve the problem?
3. What outcomes are expected, and how will these outcomes be measured?

The managerial response to these questions should be stated in terms of criteria that reflect organizational effectiveness. Measurable outcomes such as production, efficiency, satisfaction, adaptiveness, and development must be linked to skill, attitudinal, behavioral, and structural changes necessitated by problem identification.

— Managers must evaluate the impact of limiting conditions. For example, if the organizational climate is conducive to the shared strategy, the employees would be brought into the diagnostic process and would participate with management from that point on. Through diagnosis, the problem would be associated with skill, attitudinal, behavioral, and structural causes and the appropriate method selected. If employee participation is inappropriate because the necessary preconditions do not exist, management must unilaterally define the problem and select the appropriate method. Whether the problem is related to skill, attitudinal, behavioral, or structural causes, the strategy must include provision for the learning principles of feedback, reinforcement, and transfer.

— The last step of the OD process is the evaluation procedure. The ideal situation would be to structure the procedure in the manner of an experimental design. That is, the end results should be operationally defined, and measurements should be taken, before and after, in both the organization undergoing development and in a second organization (the control group). If the scope of the program is limited to a subunit, a second subunit could serve as a control group. An evaluation not only enables management to account for its use of resources but also provides feedback. Based on this feedback, corrections can be taken in the implementation phase.

DISCUSSION AND REVIEW QUESTIONS

1. Identify the existing forces for change that are acting on the college or university you attend. Compare these forces to those acting on a firm where you work or have worked. What are the important differences in these forces? Which are more powerful, the environmental or internal forces? Which organization seems more responsive to these forces for change?

2. Under what circumstances would a manager be likely to use power to bring about change in the organization? Would the use of power bring any long-term consequences that could haunt the manager at a later date?

3. Describe and critique a personal experience with a manager's use of learning principles to assist you in doing your work.

4. What characteristics of organizational development distinguish it from casual change activities? For example, is it possible to change an organization's strategic focus without going through organizational development? Explain.

5. What are the characteristics of organizations that could rely on internal rather than external agents to bring about successful change?

6. What are the characteristics of an organization or situation for which the use of reason would be an effective approach for managing change? Are such organizations and situations relatively rare?

7. Explain the difficulties that you would encounter in attempting to obtain diagnostic information from members of two groups who believe that they are competing for scarce resources.

8. Explain why it is desirable, or even necessary, to obtain objective information in the diagnostic step. What are the characteristics of a situation for which objective information would be scarce?

9. What steps can a change agent take to identify the strength of the limiting conditions in a particular organization?

10. Explain why an OD program should be evaluated and why such an evaluation is so difficult to do.

ADDITIONAL REFERENCES

Boss, R. W. *Organizational Development in Health Care.* Reading, Mass.: Addison-Wesley Publishing, 1989.

Burke, W. W. *Organization Development: A Normative View.* Reading, Mass.: Addison-Wesley Publishing, 1989.

Clark, P., and K. Starkey. *Organization Transitions and Innovative Designs.* New York: Columbia University Press, 1988.

Cobb, A. T. "Political Diagnosis: Application in Organizational Development." *Academy of Management Review,* 1986, pp. 482–96.

Cummings, T. G., and E. F. Huse. *Organization Development and Change.* St. Paul, Minn.: West Publishing, 1989.

Davis, D. D. *Managing Technological Innovation.* San Francisco: Jossey-Bass, 1986.

Desreumaux, A. "OD Practices in France: Part I." *Leadership and Organization Development Journal,* 1985, pp. 26–32.

Dyer, W. G., and W. Dyer, Jr. "Organization Development: System Change or Culture Change?" *Personnel,* 1986, pp. 14–23.

Edmonstone, J. "The Value Problems in OD." *Leadership and Organization Development Journal,* 1985, pp. 7–10.

Foy, N. "Ambivalence, Hypocrisy, and Cynicism: Aids to Organization Change." *New Management,* 1985, pp. 49–53.

Golembiewski, R. T., and A. Kiepper. *High Performance and Human Costs: A Public Sector Model of Organization Development.* New York: Praeger Publishers, 1988.

Harrison, R. G. "OD in Central Government: Problems and Prospects." *Leadership and Organizational Development Journal,* 1985, pp. 27–31.

Howe, M. A. "Using Imagery to Facilitate Organizational Development and Change." *Group and Organizational Studies,* March 1989, pp. 70–82.

Jaeger, A. M. "Organizational Development and National Culture: Where's the Fit?" *Academy of Management Review,* 1986, pp. 178–90.

Kilman, R. H.; M. J. Saxton; R. Serpa; and associates. *Gaining Control of the Corporate Culture.* San Francisco: Jossey-Bass, 1985.

Kirkpatrick, D. L. *How to Manage Change Effectively.* San Francisco: Jossey-Bass, 1985.

Marsh, R. M., and H. Mannari. *Organizational Change in Japanese Factories.* Greenwich, Conn.: JAI Press, 1988.

Mohrman, S. A., and T. G. Cummings. *Self-Designing Organizations: Learning How to Create High Performance.* Reading, Mass.: Addison-Wesley Publishing, 1989.

Nicholas, J. M., and M. Katz. "Research Methods and Reporting Practices in Organization Development: A Review and Some Guidelines." *Academy of Management Review,* 1985, pp. 737–49.

Porras, J. I. *Stream Analysis: A Powerful Way to Diagnose and Manage Organizational Change.* Reading, Mass.: Addison-Wesley Publishing, 1987.

Von Glinow, M. A., and S. Mohrman. *Managing Complexity in High Technology Organizations.* New York: Oxford University Press, 1990.

White, L. P., and K. C. Wooten. *Professional Ethics and Practice in Organizational Development.* New York: Praeger Publishers, 1986.

Woodman, W. W., and W. A. Pasmore, eds. *Research in Organizational Change and Development.* Vol. 2. Greenwich, Conn.: JAI Press, 1988.

ORGANIZATIONAL DEVELOPMENT IN A HEALTH CARE CLINIC

A major health care clinic with more than 400 physicians and 7,000 employees undertook an organizational development program in response to problems stemming from the application of modern technology to the jobs of medical technologists. The clinic's management initiated the program when the human resources department reported the results of a job analysis of the laboratory division. The results indicated widespread dissatisfaction particularly among medical technologists in the biochemistry department, where new technology had the greatest impact.

The primary sources of dissatisfaction among the technologists were that their skills were underutilized in their work, communications within the laboratories were insufficient, work was not evenly distributed, and the medical staff did not treat them with the respect they deserved. These complaints were consistent with the general feeling that the advent of technology had simplified the work to the point that it no longer seemed to require the level of training common among medical technologists. Studies in the literature of personnel management confirmed that the absence of job challenge was a primary cause of job turnover among medical technologists.

The clinic's organizational development staff discussed the implications of the information with the manager of the laboratory division. The manager agreed that an effort should be undertaken to improve the effectiveness of the laboratory through the introduction of new technology and the enhancement of the technologists' work experiences. The challenge of the program was to develop means for increasing sources of job satisfaction among a group of employees whose job content was being changed drastically by technology. The OD experts believed that the jobs of medical technologists could be redesigned to include greater autonomy, control, feedback, and meaningfulness, these being the classic job enrichment principles.

The OD staff and the laboratory decided to focus on the jobs of two groups of medical technologists: biochemistry and microbiology. Technologists in the biochemistry labs had experienced the greatest job changes due to technology; technologists in the microbiology lab had experienced the least change. The OD program began with meetings attended by the OD staff and laboratory staff. The purpose of these meetings was to explain the purposes of the intervention, to test the level of commitment of the laboratory management and medical personnel to the process, and to recruit volunteers to assist in the analysis of the diagnostic data. After a series of meetings that the OD staff deemed to be successful, a questionnaire was administered to all technologists in the two groups.

The questionnaire enabled respondents to express their confidential opinions regarding various aspects of their jobs. The items on the questionnaire measured the extent to which respondents believed their jobs contained variety, significance, identity, autonomy, and feedback. The OD staff believed that these five job characteristics are the sources of job satisfaction. The questionnaire items also enabled respondents to express their satisfaction with different aspects of their jobs, such as pay, job security, social relations, supervision, and growth opportunities. In addition to the questionnaire, the OD staff also conducted personal interviews with a random sample of one third of all the technologists in each group. This initial data collection process took about two months.

During the next four months, the volunteer groups met weekly to discuss and analyze the data and to make recommendations for change in the laboratories. Some of the more significant changes that the volunteer groups recommended included

Source: Based on William Pasmore, Jeffrey Petee, and Richard Bastian, "Sociotechnical Systems in Health Care: A Field Experiment," *Journal of Applied Behavioral Science* 22, no. 3 (1986), pp. 329–39.

(1) the creation of dual career paths to permit advancement other than moving into administrative positions, (2) the development of opportunities for job rotation, (3) the redesign of the physical environment to improve working conditions, and (4) the provision of ways for lab managers to identify and clarify goals more precisely.

Two years later, the OD staff evaluated the results of the OD program. The staff again administered the questionnaire and found that scores on the items measuring job characteristics and satisfaction declined generally for both groups. The OD staff followed up the questionnaire with personal interviews that confirmed the impression that the technologists were disappointed with the results of the intervention. The interviewed individuals expressed many negative attitudes about the OD intervention, particularly the way in which management responded to the recommended changes. The most favorable comments were expressed by individuals who had served on the volunteer groups.

The OD staff believed that the disappointing results of the program could be traced to several possible causes. They first considered whether an intervention based on job redesign theory was applicable in a health care organization. After all, this theory was developed in industrial settings, not health care organizations. A second possible cause might be the manner in which the OD staff implemented the program. Perhaps the program depended too much on the OD staff's interest and direction and less on the real commitment of lab management. A third possible explanation might be found in cultural factors that characterize most health care organizations. Such factors include the reluctance of medical personnel to share decision-making power with technologists and the unwillingness of physicians to delegate authority to nonphysicians. The existence of these cultural barriers to collaboration would seem to limit the potential of interventions based on job redesign theory.

As the staff reviewed the results of their work, they were anxious to find some answers to their questions. A repetition of the mistakes certainly would not improve the climate for change in the clinic.

Questions for Consideration

1. Describe the extent to which the OD staff implemented the distinguishing characteristics of organizational development.
2. What was the level of intervention? Evaluate whether the depth of intervention was appropriate for the nature of the problem.
3. Why did the intervention not achieve more positive results?

ALTERNATIVE WAYS TO INITIATE CHANGE

Objective

To evaluate alternative ways to initiate training in the face of possible resistance from both the employees and their supervisors.

Related Topics

Individual, group, and leadership theories are relevant, along with ideas and concepts from organizational change and development.

Starting the Exercise

The instructor will divide the class into groups of five to seven. The groups should read the scenario below and decide which of the five alternatives the manager should implement. Although other alternatives are possible, evaluate only those indicated. Each group will prepare and present an oral report justifying its choice.

Scenario

A manager faces a problem involving mistakes employees are making. The mistakes occur in nearly every department of the plant in which this particular operation is performed. The manager believes that a training program is necessary to help employees perform better and reduce the errors. He believes that supervisors who report to him will defend existing procedures because the introduction of a training program could imply criticism of the way they have been operating. The manager also thinks that the supervisors fear resistance by employees afraid of not doing well in the training program. Given these facts and considerations, the manager believes that he has five alternative ways to initiate the needed change:

1. To the agenda of the weekly meeting with the supervisors, add a recommendation that training be undertaken.
2. Talk to the supervisors individually and get their ideas about what to do before bringing up the issue in the weekly meeting.
3. Ask the corporate training staff to come to the plant, assess the training needs, and develop a program to address those needs.
4. Tell the supervisors that the training is necessary, in the interests of the company, and that they are expected to support it with enthusiasm.
5. Appoint of team of supervisors to study the matter thoroughly and to bring a recommendation to the weekly meeting.

Completing the Exercise

Phase I: 30 minutes.   Each group of five–seven students should read the scenario, evaluate the five alternatives, and prepare an oral report defending its choice.

Phase II: 30 minutes.   As a class, discuss the choices made by the groups, as well as their reasons for picking a particular alternative.

Source: Based on Leslie W. Rue and Lloyd L. Byars, *Management,* 5th ed. (Homewood, Ill.: Richard D. Irwin, 1989), p. 526.

20

Organizational Development Interventions

AN ORGANIZATIONAL
ISSUE FOR DEBATE   TEAMS AND TEAMWORK IN THE WORKPLACE*

ARGUMENT FOR

The management literature, both popular and technical, contains many reports of firms adopting team management concepts. The basic argument for teams and teamwork is that they have higher levels of performance than do individuals acting alone. Teams of workers do more work of higher quality at a faster pace than do individuals working alone on assigned tasks. A wealth of common knowledge supports the idea that teams are preferable to individuals. Stories from both sports and business worlds reinforce our belief in the superiority of teamwork. For example, the great Green Bay Packers teams under Coach Lombardi achieved success through his ability to create the sense of teamship. Numerous applications of team management are reported in business.

One of the early success stories documented the application of team management in the Volvo truck and auto assembly plants. Other reports tell of the successes of General Motors, General Foods, Sherwin-Williams, and the Shenandoah Life Insurance Company. Each of these applications involves the creation of relatively autonomous work teams that complete entire segments of work. For example, Volvo assigns the task of assembling major units of automobiles to a work team. The team members can exchange jobs, determine the pace of work, and even stop the assembly process if it identifies quality defects. Autoworkers at certain General Motors plants also work in teams, which are patterned after the Volvo model.

Due to support from national organizations, team management has spread more rapidly in Japan and Sweden than in the United States. For example, the Japanese Union of Scientists and Engineers not only supports the concept but actually helps companies install it. In Sweden, the Employers' Federation acts as consultant for firms introducing team management. No such organizational or national support exists in the United States, even though some management experts believe that team management and its companion, participative management, are absolute necessities if the United States is to regain its competitiveness in the world markets.

The supportive arguments for work teams rest on not only improved production and quality but also increased job satisfaction. The nature of work teams and teamwork enables individuals to perform several different tasks, see and identify with the outcomes of those tasks, and experience relative autonomy while doing their work. Each of these qualities allows individual team members to feel a sense of satisfaction and pride in their work. They become part of something that satisfies the natural inclination to be productive while doing important work. Working with others in the spirit of teamwork is a powerful motivator, and team management harnesses that motivation.

ARGUMENT AGAINST

Despite many reported successes for team management, cogent arguments can be advanced in favor of management approaches that emphasize individual achievement. In fact, critics of team management point out that teams develop a sense of togetherness and cohesion that can thwart individual initiative. The important innovations and new developments in organizations and societies come from the efforts of individuals, not teams and groups. In team management, team members share the benefits of the contributions of individuals in the same manner that they share in the failures of individuals.

Another argument against the use of teams involves the necessity to have high-quality employees to make teams effective. Autonomous work teams require employees who are technically skilled in their occupational specialty and who also possess above-average interpersonal skills. They must be able to get along with other group members, and not all individuals are equally endowed with that characteristic. In fact, some critics argue that the great majority of individuals in the work force actually prefer repetitive tasks that they do independent of others.

Labor unions also must be taken into account when considering the applicability of work teams. Labor unions have invested much time and resources in bargaining for specific job classifications. Each job classification defines a particular set of activities and outcomes that separate it from other jobs. The more job classifications that exist, the greater the total number of different jobs and, accordingly, the greater the demand for individual workers. In fact, some union members believe that team management is just another form of management speedup.

One of the effects of team management is the elimination of job classifications. Since the team members are cross-trained to do all of the jobs required of the team, the question arises as to how many distinct job classifications really exist within the team. These issues, difficult and costly to resolve, may outweigh any gain to be derived from additional production, quality, and satisfaction.

Source: Andrew J. DuBrin, *Contemporary Applied Management* (Homewood, Ill.: Richard D. Irwin, 1989), pp. 175–76, 190–92; "The Payoff from Teamwork," *Business Week,* July 10, 1989, pp. 56–62; Paul S. Goodman, Rukmine Devadas, and Terri L. Griffin Hughson, "Groups and Productivity: Analyzing the Effectiveness of Self-Managing Teams," in *Productivity in Organizations,* ed. John P. Campbell, Richard J. Campbell, and associates (San Francisco: Jossey-Bass, 1988), pp. 295–327.

Effective organizational development (OD) requires the active involvement of managers. They must designate objectives, select interventions to achieve those objectives, and implement the interventions. Managers can state objectives in terms of improved production, efficiency, satisfaction, adaptiveness, and development, separately or in some combination. Managers can implement one or more organization development interventions, depending upon the objectives. This chapter focuses on the issues and problems associated with alternative OD interventions.

Each type of intervention has strengths and weaknesses, advantages and disadvantages, advocates and detractors. The Organizational Issue for Debate describes the controversy surrounding one change intervention: team management, including the concept of employee involvement. As noted in the debate, some of its more ardent proponents believe that team management is an essential management practice for firms seeking to attain or regain competitiveness. However, if the individuals who are to change as a result of the intervention do not believe or support the idea behind the intervention, then who is to say that they are incorrect? In discussing the actual implementation of organizational development interventions, we will want to take note of the roles played by those who are to be changed.

Organizational development is a complex process; it is also a people-oriented process. Consequently, controversy is bound to pervade its practice.

DEPTH OF INTENDED CHANGE

Depth of intended change refers to the scope and intensity of the organization development efforts.[1] Figure 20–1, which likens the organization to an iceberg, illustrates the concept. It draws attention to two important components: the *formal* and *informal* aspects of organizations. The formal components of an organization compare to the part of an iceberg that is above water; the informal components lie below the surface, unseen but there nevertheless. As indicated in Figure 20–1, the formal components are observable, rational, and oriented to structural factors. The informal components are, on the other hand, affective, oriented to process and behavioral factors, and not observable to all people.

Generally speaking, the greater the scope and intensity of the problem, the more likely it is to be found in the informal components. Thus, depth of intended change refers to how far management must go into the organization iceberg to solve the problem. At one extreme lie problems with the *structure* of the organization. Managers can solve such problems by changing job definitions, departmentalization bases, spans of control, and delegated authority. At the other extreme lie problems with the *behavior* of groups and individuals. These problems are related to personal views, value orientations, feelings, and sentiments, as well as activities, sentiments, and roles within and among groups. While these behaviors can certainly be affected by changes in structure, they ordinarily are deep-seated, and management must confront them more directly. The greater the depth of intervention, the greater is the risk of failure and the higher the cost of change.[2]

TARGETS OF INTERVENTIONS

The relationship between source of problem and degree of intended change is illustrated in Table 20–1, which shows eight levels, or targets, of an OD program. As the target moves from left to right and, consequently, deeper into the organization, the OD program becomes more person and group centered. It will rely more upon sociopsychological and less upon technical-economic knowledge. Levels I through IV involve formal components, including structure, policies, and practices of the organization. Levels V through VIII involve informal components, including the behavior of groups and individuals. For each of these levels, one or more OD interventions can be possible solutions. Only after the problem and its level are diagnosed should the intervention be selected.

---

[1]The relationship between organizational depth and intended change is more popularly termed depth of intervention. We have chosen to call it degree of intended change to highlight the issues associated with change rather than those related to intervention. See Roger Harrison, "Choosing the Depth of Organizational Intervention," *Journal of Applied Behavioral Science,* April–May 1970, pp. 181–202, for the original discussion of the concept; more recently, Wendell L. French and Cecil H. Bell, Jr., *Organizational Development: Behavioral Science Interventions for Organizational Improvement* (Englewood Cliffs, N.J.: Prentice Hall, 1984).

[2]Noel M. Tichy, "GE's Crotonville: A Staging Ground for Corporate Revolution," *Academy of Management Executive,* May 1989, p. 102.

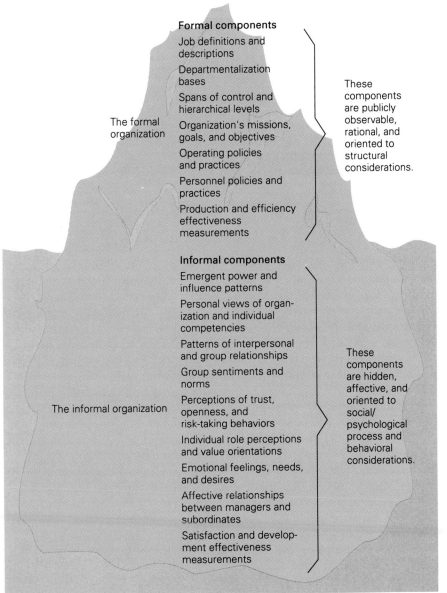

FIGURE 20–1

The Organizational Iceberg

Formal components

Job definitions and descriptions

Departmentalization bases

Spans of control and hierarchical levels

Organization's missions, goals, and objectives

Operating policies and practices

Personnel policies and practices

Production and efficiency effectiveness measurements

The formal organization

These components are publicly observable, rational, and oriented to structural considerations.

Informal components

Emergent power and influence patterns

Personal views of organization and individual competencies

Patterns of interpersonal and group relationships

Group sentiments and norms

Perceptions of trust, openness, and risk-taking behaviors

Individual role perceptions and value orientations

Emotional feelings, needs, and desires

Affective relationships between managers and subordinates

Satisfaction and development effectiveness measurements

The informal organization

These components are hidden, affective, and oriented to social/psychological process and behavioral considerations.

In keeping with current usage, we will discuss OD interventions according to a three-way classification based on depth of intended change and target of change:[3]

1. **Technostructural interventions** are ordinarily restricted in depth to levels I through IV and thus target the formal components of the organization for change. Within this group of interventions, however, the depth of change

TECHNOSTRUCTURAL INTERVENTIONS

Class of interventions intended to change jobs, job relationships, and other formal elements of organizational structure.

[3]John M. Nicholas and Marsha Katz, "Research Methods and Reporting Practices in Organization Development: A Review and Some Guidelines," *Academy of Management Review*, October 1985, pp. 737–49.

TABLE 20—1

Model of Organizational Development Targets

STRUCTURAL TARGETS ◀						▶ BEHAVIORAL TARGETS	
Level I	*Level II*	*Level III*	*Level IV*	*Level V*	*Level VI*	*Level VII*	*Level VIII*
Organizational structure	Operating policies and practices	Personnel policies and practices	Job perfor-mance appraisal and improvement	Intergroup behavior	Intragroup behavior	Individual behavior	Individual-group behavior

Depth of intended

LOW ——————————————————————▶ change ——————————————————————————▶ HIGH

Source: Adapted from Richard J. Selfridge and Stanley L. Sokolik, "A Comprehensive View of Organizational Development," *MSU Business Topics,* Winter 1975, p. 49.

HUMAN PROCESS INTERVENTIONS

Class of interventions intended to change individual and group behaviors found in informal parts of the organization.

MULTIFACETED INTERVENTIONS

Combinations of technostructural and human process interven-tions, required for most signifi-cant organizational change ef-forts.

can vary from changing jobs to changing the entire organizational structure. For example, interventions such as job enlargement, job enrichment, and job redesign focus on changing job range and depth, as we noted in Chapter 14.[4] Management by objectives (MBO) as an OD intervention increases the delegated authority of a job. Other interventions such as sociotechnical systems design and System 4 organization focus on whole groups of jobs and work units, and the results may change the very bases of the organization's structure. The fact that these interventions are at a relatively shallow depth and involve seemingly insensitive issues accounts for their popularity.

2. **Human process interventions** focus on levels V through VIII and target the informal components of the organization for change. Individual and group characteristics such as role expectations, group norms and sanctions, interactions, sentiments, and attitudes are the targets of this family of interventions.[5] The theory and practice of organizational development origi-nated in these interventions; they reflect OD's preoccupation with individual and group dynamics. Some of the typical interventions include third-party interventions, team building, survey feedback, sensitivity training, structured laboratory training, leadership development, and grid theory.

3. Having a grouping called **multifaceted interventions** acknowledges that interventions are often undertaken in combination.[6] For example, attitude survey feedback and MBO can be used in a single OD program. The increasing use of multifaceted interventions indicates a growing awareness of the inter-relationships between the formal and informal components of an organization. Combining two or more types of interventions offers a greater chance of im-proving performance than does the use of any one intervention.[7] Thus, we will usually find OD programs with technostructural and human process targets.

---

[4]George A. Neuman, Jack E. Edwards, and Nambury S. Raju, "Organizational Development Interventions: A Meta-Analysis of their Effects on Satisfaction and Other Attitudes," *Personnel Psychology,* Autumn 1989, pp. 461–89.

[5]Ibid.

[6]David A. Nadler and Michael L. Tushman, "Organizational Frame Bending: Principles for Managing Reorientation," *Academy of Management Executive,* August 1989, p. 201.

[7]Neuman et al., "Organizational Development Interventions."

TECHNOSTRUCTURAL INTERVENTIONS

Structural development in the context of organizational development refers to managerial action that attempts to improve effectiveness through a change in the formal structure of task and authority relationships. The organizational structure provides the bases for relatively stable human and social relationships. With time, these relationships can become irrelevant for organizational effectiveness. For example, jobs that people do may become obsolete and thus irrelevant; but changing the jobs also changes the relationships. Members of the organization may resist efforts to disrupt these relationships.

Structural changes affect some aspect of the formal task and authority definitions. As we have seen, the design of an organization involves the definition and specification of job range and depth, the grouping of jobs in departments, the determination of the size of groups reporting to a single manager, and the delegation of authority. This section discusses four methods designed to change all or some aspect of the organization structure: job redesign, management by objectives, sociotechnical system design, and System 4. These methods are appropriate for consideration when the problem is diagnosed as being in levels I through IV.

Job Redesign

Job redesign as an OD intervention reflects theories that production, efficiency, satisfaction, and adaptiveness increase as jobs are designed to include high levels of autonomy, feedback, and variety. When such jobs are performed by individuals with high growth need strength, organizational effectiveness should increase.[8] As a type of OD intervention, job redesign can be undertaken separately or as part of a larger organizational redesign effort. We discussed applications of job redesign in the context of organizational design in Chapter 13. Here we will describe one application in the context of organizational development.

Citibank responded to deteriorating customer service and profit margins in its international banking group by implementing an organizational development program.[9] The program began with diagnosis activities such as interviews with key personnel, flowcharting work processes, observations, and examination of documents such as policy manuals and organization charts. At the end of the diagnostic phase, job design was identified as one of the elements that contributed to the problem. Simply stated, the jobs of the group emphasized the completion of transactions and not the provision of customer service. Individuals doing the jobs had neither the motivation nor the incentive for doing anything other than completing their assigned jobs. As designed, the job contained little in the way of motivators.

After the change agents identified jobs as the focus of the OD effort, they adopted job redesign theory to guide their subsequent efforts. All supervisors and managers in the unit undertook training in the theory and practice of job

JOB REDESIGN
OD intervention to improve performance by redesigning individuals' jobs, usually along lines suggested by job characteristics model of job design.

---

[8]J. Richard Hackman and Edward E. Lawler III, "Employee Reactions to Job Characteristics," *Journal of Applied Psychology,* June 1971, pp. 259–86.

[9]Donald L. Kirkpatrick, *How to Manage Change Effectively* (San Francisco: Jossey-Bass, 1985), pp. 195–208.

redesign so they could actively participate in the actual redesign process. As part of the training, the change agents created a kind of laboratory for experiments with alternative job designs. The laboratory provided a risk-free environment in which failures would not show up on the bottom line. It also became the testing ground for what subsequently became the final design.

The final version of the job redesigns gave each employee responsibility for all transactions required to service a group of customer accounts. To perform all these transactions correctly, the employees required retraining. Ingeniously, the change agents decided to have the employees train each other. Each of them had been expert in one of the transactions prior to the changeover; with support from management, they could train each other. The redesigned jobs were fully operational six years after implementation of the diagnostic step, attesting to the long-run nature of significant OD programs.

Management by Objectives

Management by objectives (MBO) encourages individuals to participate in the establishment of job-related objectives for themselves and their units.[10] The process can also include the participation of managers and nonmanagers in the determination of their specific objectives. Successful use of MBO depends on the ability of participants to define their objectives in terms of their contribution to the total organization and to accomplish those objectives.

The application of MBO involves the following three steps:[11]

1. Superiors and subordinates meet and discuss objectives that, if met, would contribute to overall goals.
2. Superiors and subordinates jointly establish attainable objectives for the subordinates.
3. Superiors and subordinates meet at a predetermined later date to evaluate the subordinates' progress toward the objectives.

The exact procedures employed in implementing MBO vary from organization to organization and from unit to unit.[12] However, the basic elements—objective setting, participation of subordinates in objective setting, and feedback and evaluation—are usually part of any MBO program. The intended consequences of MBO include increased production, efficiency, and satisfaction in the short run and development in the long run. MBO is highly developed and widely used in business, health care, and governmental organizations. Here, we will describe a MBO project undertaken at a college of business at a major state university.[13]

---

[10]Peter Drucker, *The Practice of Management* (New York: Harper & Row, 1954); George Odiorne, *Management by Objectives* (Marshfield, Mass.: Pitman Publishing, 1965); W. J. Reddin, *Effective Management by Objectives* (New York: McGraw-Hill, 1970).

[11]Jack N. Kondrasuk, Keith Flagler, Dennis Morrow, and Paul Thompson, "The Effects of Management by Objectives on Organizational Results," *Group and Organizational Studies,* December 1984, pp. 531–39.

[12]Jan P. Muczyk and Bernard C. Reimann, "MBO as a Complement to Effective Leadership," *Academy of Management Executive,* May 1989, pp. 131–38.

[13]David E. Terpstra, Philip D. Olson, and Brad Lockeman, "The Effects of MBO on Levels of Performance and Satisfaction among University Faculty," *Group and Organizational Studies,* September 1982, pp. 353–66.

The project began on the arrival of a new dean, who found the business college beset by many problems. Among the more difficult problems were the perception of low faculty performance in research and service, fragmented curriculum, inadequate financial support, and lagging faculty morale and satisfaction. The impetus for implementing MBO was the new dean's attitude that the situation called for a system of broad-based, participatory goal setting that would move the college toward more effective performance and resolution of its perceived problems. Throughout the project, the new dean performed activities ordinarily expected of change agents in organizational development.

The process began with the formation of a faculty committee to draft a mission statement for the entire college. This committee identified the issues and the potential broad solutions to these issues. The diagnostic data consisted of faculty input and the dean's active participation. The statement of the college mission reflected the opinions of all the parties who would eventually have to implement it.

Subsequently, the mission statement became the focus of discussions between the dean and the department chairpersons. Each of the three departments (accounting, business, and economics) formulated broad goals for teaching, research, service, and other activities related to academic departments in major universities. The departmental goals reflected the individual needs and capabilities of each department, but they also had to relate and contribute to the overall college mission.

The departmental goal statements then became the bases for writing a statement of objectives for the faculty. These statements required faculty members to identify which of the departmental goals they would contribute to by their activities. The statements of individual objectives, or "contracts," were reached after discussion between the faculty and their chairpersons. Goal setting was participatory in that individuals had the opportunity to establish their own contracts; however, the contracts were constrained by the college and departmental goals.

Implementation of the MBO program in the college of business had many OD features. It was implemented through the efforts of an external change agent (the new dean), it involved efforts to diagnose problems through widespread participation, and it reflected a commitment to solve the problems through an appropriate intervention, MBO.

Compare the implementation of MBO in a health care company.[14] Boehringer Mannheim Corporation, an Indianapolis-based company, implemented MBO in the mid-1980s to stress the importance of tying the activities of professional employees to profits. The company engaged an external consultant to hold training sessions for all technical and professional units' managers, including the chief executive officer (CEO). The consultant also met with each participant in confidential sessions to grapple with the intellectual task of defining objectives for jobs with mostly intangible outcomes.

Consistent with MBO practice in other settings, supervisors reviewed progress toward objectives every four months. Performance appraisal systems

---

[14]Albert W. Schrader, "MBO Makes Dollar Sense," *Personnel Journal*, July 1989, pp. 32–37.

formally recognized each individual's progress, and rewards went to those who demonstrated progress. The program took two years to permeate the entire organization, as it was phased in on a unit by unit basis.

One important feature of this MBO application was the idea of "stretch" objectives. Although individuals are responsible for meeting the basic requirements of their assigned jobs, they and their supervisors also identify and set objectives in areas that are particularly critical for the organization's continued success. Achievement of these stretch objectives requires individuals to exercise initiative and often to work in concert with other members of the organization.

Boehringer Mannheim's MBO-based program was systematically planned, involved managerial personnel at all levels in the diagnostic and implementation stages, and identified MBO as the appropriate intervention after the problems had been identified. This company's effort to improve performance shares many of the same features as the business school's effort.

Sociotechnical System Design

This intervention attempts to integrate an organization's social and technical systems after a mismatch between the two has been diagnosed as the cause of problems.[15] Many of these efforts can be seen in modern manufacturing, as industry after industry tries to adapt to innovative manufacturing methods that require different relationships among individuals performing these methods. Typical applications of this approach are usually undertaken in conjunction with the construction of new plants or offices. The complexity of sociotechnical design theory and practice makes it easier to implement where no previous system has existed. But building new plants and offices is not always possible; most organizations have to make do with what they have. In the insurance industry, for example, the usual approach was to design jobs and organizations (the social system) according to the various functions involved in processing an insurance application. Each job and group of jobs reflected one step in the total process. This social system was appropriate when typewriters and calculators (the technical system) were state of the art. But advanced computer technology has made it possible for one individual to handle the entire process, each and every step of the application. Thus, in this and other industries, tension between the social system and the technical system increases with each new technological development.[16]

The term *sociotechnical system* refers to a set of ideas that emphasize the interrelatedness of the social and technical systems and of the total organization to its total environment.[17] Thus, **sociotechnical interventions** reflect the contingency approach that we have noted in discussions of other organiza-

SOCIOTECHNICAL
INTERVENTIONS

Efforts to integrate social organization and technological requirements; often seen in manufacturing organizations.

---

[15]Eric Trist, "The Evolution of Sociotechnical Systems," in *Perspectives on Organization Design and Behavior,* ed. Andrew H. Van de Ven and William F. Joyce (New York: Wiley Interscience, 1981).

[16]Beverly H. Burns, "Technocratic Organization and Control," *Organization Studies* 10, no. 1 (1989), pp. 1–22.

[17]Lee W. Frederiksen, Anne W. Riley, and John B. Myers, "Matching Technology and Organizational Structure: A Case Study in White Collar Productivity Improvement," *Journal of Organizational and Behavior Management,* Fall–Winter 1984, pp. 59–80.

tional behavior topics. The fundamental concept is that the building blocks of organizations are work groups. The best way to capture the effects of advanced technical systems is through the development of relatively independent and autonomous work groups. The small work groups must be able to deal with all obvious operating problems through the application of the new technology. Just as important, they must also be able to work in the context of group rather than individual jobs. OD programs making use of the sociotechnical approach focus on development of this ability.

One such OD program was undertaken in Shenandoah Life Insurance Company.[18] The company realized the necessity for change as computer technology moved into third-generation on-line systems and, at the same time, marketplace forces placed greater emphasis on product development and responsiveness to customer demands. The organization clearly saw its production, efficiency, and adaptiveness declining. An outside change agent, engaged to assist in the diagnosis of specific problems, administered an attitude survey and found that employee satisfaction was also deteriorating.

The OD program that management developed comprised three phases. The first phase consisted of a two-day work session for the president and seven vice presidents. The meeting resulted in consensus on the causes of problems and the likely solutions to those problems. Following this meeting of high-level officials, the rest of the organization's management attended similar workshops and arrived at the same general conclusions. The OD literature identifies this top-down approach as one of the important conditions for ensuring the acceptance of the effort throughout the organization.

The second phase of the program was the introduction of an experimentally self-managed work team. This team was to be the vehicle for testing sociotechnical system concepts such as the use of self-direction and autonomy to arrive at the appropriate distribution of tasks among the group members. To reinforce development of the skills and abilities required to function in such a social setting, a variety of supportive activities were undertaken. For example, the company instituted a "pay for learning" system that rewarded individuals for learning additional skills required to complete the group's assigned task. A second support activity made managers at the level above the group available as advisers. The third support activity was the development of intensive training exercises in group-oriented communications, decision making, and the dynamics of role assumption and expectations.

The third phase of the program was the broadening of the autonomous group concept throughout the organization. The experience of the experimental group was largely supportive of the concept and provided valuable documentation of what could be expected as the program was implemented on an organization-wide basis.

The change agents undertook evaluation activities during the implementation phase and at the conclusion of a major 24-month milestone. The evaluation data included comparisons of all those effectiveness criteria that were deteriorating prior to the change. Apparently, the program had a positive effect on the criteria. Such positive results have been experienced in other

---

[18]Ibid.

applications of the sociotechnical system approach, no doubt accounting for its increasing popularity as an OD intervention.

Another application of sociotechnical change took place in a British confectionary company. The intervention involved the creation of autonomous work teams in a newly constructed factory. Each work group consisted of 8 to 10 people responsible for allocating jobs, reaching production and quality targets, solving production problems, recording production data, performing all tasks from obtaining raw materials to delivering the final product, and selecting and training new employees. Because the groups were self-managing, no formal title of supervisor was used.

To maintain the sense of equality and autonomy, management made many small but important changes in the way traditional factory work is done. For example, the factory had only one designated eating area for all employees, no time clocks were installed, and employees were paid monthly through direct credit deposits to their bank accounts. Only three levels of management separated the entry-level employee from top management. The autonomous work teams expressed higher levels of job satisfaction than their counterparts in traditional plants, and the company experienced increased productivity as a result of the reduced number of indirect workers required to support the teams.[19]

System 4 Organization

SYSTEM 4 ORGANIZATION
Likert's theory of an organic organization, defined by autonomy, democracy, and supportiveness of groups.

System 4 organization is an important application of the organic organizational design. As an OD intervention, System 4 change would be undertaken in instances of a mismatch between the organizational structure and the demands of the environment, technological type, or strategic thrusts. It would also be undertaken by any management that believes System 4 organization to be ideal for achieving high levels of performance. Accordingly, any deviation from the ideal System 4 represents reduced levels of performance.

Rensis Likert and his colleagues contributed much to our understanding of how managers can change their organizations to be more like organic structures and less like mechanistic structures.[20] According to Likert, the best source of information about an organizational structure is the organization's employees. Their perceptions of the structure, rather than what appears on the organization chart, account for job performance. Thus, a System 4 type of OD intervention begins with the administration of a questionnaire to each employee. The employees indicate their perceptions of the extent to which the characteristics of a System 4 organization are present in their own organization. The aggregate responses serve as bases for discussions at all levels of the organization to add credibility to the questionnaire. More important, the discussions of the questionnaire results focus attention on the extent to which the organization must change to become more System 4–like. Subsequent

---

[19]Toby D. Wall, Nigel J. Kemp, Paul R. Jackson, and Chris W. Clegg, "Outcomes of Autonomous Workgroups: A Long-Term Field Experiment," *Academy of Management Journal,* June 1986, pp. 280–304.

[20]Rensis Likert, *The Human Organization* (New York: McGraw-Hill, 1967).

training programs can emphasize the concepts of System 4 and the application of those concepts to the present organization.

Recent reports of organizational change in firms such as Bank of America, Southwestern Bell, and Honeywell indicate increasing acceptance of the System 4 concepts:[21] use of (1) supportive, group-oriented leadership and (2) equalization of authority to set goals, implement control, and make decisions should ordinarily result in higher performance. These results derive from positive changes in employee attitudes brought about by the changes in organizational structure.[22]

Various OD programs utilizing System 4 concepts have been reported in the literature.[23] In one program, the target of the development effort was a business firm's sales unit, specifically 16 sales managers: a national sales manager, 2 divisional managers, and 13 regional managers. The short-run objectives of the program were (1) to integrate the 16 managers into an effective team following the appointment of a new national sales manager, a divisional manager, and three regional managers; (2) to facilitate development and acceptance of new roles for the regional managers who, with the introduction of a new product line, would have to spend 90 percent of their time (rather than the present 40 percent), in managerial work; and (3) to confront and resolve certain communication and interpersonal problems remaining as a result of the personnel changes. The main difficulty was the regional managers' perception that the new national head was so aggressive that he would dominate the divisional managers.

The long-run goals of the program were (1) to make actual and preferred behaviors more congruent (the managers feared that mistrust and secrecy would be required to succeed in the organization, although they preferred trusting and open relationships); and (2) to move the organization more toward the System 4 end of the continuum.

To get at these objectives, the sales managers, in training, experimented with the kinds of behaviors appropriate for a System 4 organization. Learning exercises that emphasized interpersonal and intergroup relations were important, since these are the key relationships involved in building integrated work groups. The training sessions culminated in a confrontation between regional and divisional managers and between the division and the national sales manager. These confrontations encouraged the managers to share and to test the value of openness and problem solving in the organization. As an organic

---

[21]Jeffrey Pfeffer et al., "Managing Organizational Change," *Academy of Management Executive,* February 1987, pp. 31–55.

[22]Heinz Weihrich and André-Sean Rigny, "Toward System-4 through Transactional Analysis," *Journal of Systems Management,* July 1980, pp. 30–36.

[23]An important example is reported in Alfred J. Marrow, David G. Bowers, and Stanley E. Seashore, *Management by Participation* (New York: Harper & Row, 1967). This report documents the effort of the Harwood Company management to transform the Weldon Company, which it purchased in 1961, into a System 4 organization. A follow-up study of the Harwood experience is reported in Stanley E. Seashore and David G. Bowers, "Durability of Organizational Change," *American Psychologist,* March 1970, pp. 227–33. Also see W. F. Dowling, "At General Motors: System 4 Builds Performance and Profits," *Organizational Dynamics,* Winter 1975, pp. 23–28.

type of organization, System 4 should be expected to encourage such communication patterns.[24]

The real test of openness and problem solving, however, comes in the context of the everyday work of the organization—that is, whether the behavior learned in the training sessions is transferred back to the workplace. To obtain some indication of the lasting effects of the training session and to gauge progress toward the development of a System 4 organization, the managers completed the organizational profile questionnaire prior to the training session and again four months later. That no control group was available limits the analysis, and the results must be validated by other means, such as observation of actual workplace behavior. Given these limitations, the differences between the before and after measures indicated that movement had been made toward the System 4 organization and that this movement had been facilitated by the training methodology. Thus, the behavior learned in the training sessions appears to have been made a part of the organization structure.

HUMAN PROCESS INTERVENTIONS

Levels V through VIII (see Table 20–1) require interventions that delve deeply into group and individual behavior processes. Intergroup, intragroup, individual-group, and individual behaviors are often confounded by emotional and perceptual processes that interfere with effective organizational functioning. These development targets have received the greatest amount of attention from OD experts; consequently, a considerable number of methods have been devised for attacking them. Instead of cataloging all these methods, we will discuss in detail: the managerial grid, sensitivity training, team building, and process consultation. These are the more readily used methods because they tend to span at least two and potentially three levels of targets.

The Managerial Grid

MANAGERIAL GRID

Theory of leadership based on particular optimal style of leadership that includes balance of concern for production and for people.

The **managerial grid** program is based on a particular style of leadership behavior.[25] Blake and Mouton, developers of the program, identify two dimensions: concern for production and concern for people. A balanced concern for production and people, the most effective leadership style according to Blake and Mouton, is termed 9,9. The program requires the development of not only this style but also group behavior that supports and sustains it. The entire program consists of six sequential phases spread over a three- to five-year period. The first two phases provide the foundation for the latter four phases.

1. Laboratory-seminar training. This is typically a one-week conference designed to introduce managers to the grid philosophy and objectives. Line

---

[24]John A. Courtright, Gail T. Fairhurst, and L. Edna Rogers, "Interaction Patterns in Organic and Mechanistic Organizations," *Academy of Management Journal,* December 1989, pp. 773–802.

[25]Robert R. Blake and Jane S. Mouton, *The Managerial Grid III* (Houston: Gulf Publishing, 1985).

managers of the company who have already been through this initial grid training phase conduct these seminars, in which 12 to 48 managers are assigned to problem-solving groups. The seminar begins by determining and reviewing each participant's style of behavior concerning production and people. It continues with 50 hours of problem solving, focusing on situations involving interpersonal behavior and its influences on task performance. Each group regularly assesses its problem-solving performance. This immediate, face-to-face feedback sets the stage for phase 2.

2. Intragroup development.   After phase 1, superiors and immediate subordinates explore their managerial styles and operating practices as a group. The climate of openness and candor established in phase 1 is supposed to carry over into the second phase. Taken together, the first two phases are designed to provide conditions that will enable managers to learn managerial grid concepts as an organizing framework for thinking about management practices; to build improved relationships between groups, among colleagues at the same level, and between superiors and subordinates; and to make managers more critical of outworn practices and precedents while extending their problem-solving capacities in interdependent situations. Such words as *involvement* and *commitment* become real in day-to-day tasks.

3. Intergroup development.   This phase involves group-to-group working relationships and focuses on building 9,9 group roles and norms beyond the single work group. Situations are established in which tensions that typically exist between groups are identified and discussed by group members. This phase attempts to move the groups from the usual "we win–you lose" patterns to a joint problem-solving activity. This procedure also helps to link managers who are at the same management level but belong to different work units.

4. Organizational goal setting.   The immediate objective of the fourth phase is to set up a model of an effective organization for the future. The development of such a blueprint involves acquiring convictions about ideal management practices by testing existing ones and setting practical, attainable objectives within a time frame. By focusing on the total organization, planned goals at each level can be linked.

5. Goal attainment.   Phase V uses some of the same group and educational procedures as phase 1 but with the total organization as the major concern. Once the special task groups define the problem areas, other groups are set up throughout the organization. These groups are given a written "task paragraph" that describes the problem and the goal. Group members are given packets of information on the issue under discussion. The group members study the packets and then take a test on their content. Once the group understands the information and reaches agreement, it begins to take corrective steps.

6. Stabilization.   In this final phase, changes brought about in prior phases are stabilized. After the first five phases, a period of time, perhaps as long as a year, is needed to identify weaknesses and take corrective actions in the goals set and the plans implemented. This phase also enables management to evaluate the total program.

An analysis of the implementation of the grid training program in an oil refinery and chemical plant of a major oil company identified several sources of disappointment,[26] including the following: First, realizing the full benefits of grid training requires the active support of top management, which was lacking in this application. We have stressed this requirement for success in applications of other OD interventions, so its negative effect here is not surprising. Second, successful grid training requires the completion of all six phases, which did not happen in this case. Apparently, applications of grid training often stop short of full implementation by omitting phases two through six. Managers evidently expect the seminar to be enough and do not realize the importance of the following phases, particularly the provision for follow-up evaluation and revision. Third, the total organization was not involved. All employees must be included in the effort in order to assure that the behaviors learned in grid training become the norms of the entire organization, not just the privileged few who undertook the training.

Team Building

The managerial grid approach develops a group process to support and sustain a particular leadership style. Developing group behavior around 9,9 or any other leadership style, however, is not necessary. Rather, group processes can develop to perform more effectively through **team building.**[27] Whereas the managerial grid is a comprehensive technique, the focus of team building is the work group.

TEAM BUILDING
Traditional intervention focusing on work group; has been given renewed interest as organizations rediscover power of team effort.

The purpose of team building is to enable work groups to work more effectively, to improve their performance.[28] The work group may be an existing or relatively new command or task group. The specific aims of the intervention include setting goals and priorities, analyzing the ways the group does its work, examining the group's norms and processes for communicating and decision making, and examining the interpersonal relationships within the group. As each of these activities takes place, the group recognizes explicitly the contributions, both positive and negative, of each group member.[29]

The process begins with *diagnostic* meetings. Often lasting an entire day, the meetings enable all group members to share their perceptions of problems with each other. If the group is large enough, subgroups engage in discussion and report their ideas to the total group. The purpose of these sessions is to

---

[26]Robert T. Keller, "A Longitudinal Assessment of a Managerial Grid Seminar Training Program," *Group and Organizational Studies,* September 1978, pp. 343–55.

[27]S. Jay Liebowitz and Kenneth P. de Meuse, "The Application of Team Building," *Human Relations,* January 1982, pp. 1–18.

[28]Richard W. Woodman and John J. Sherwood, "Effects of Team Development Intervention: A Field Experiment," *Journal of Applied Behavioral Science,* April–May–June 1980, pp. 211–17; R. Wayne Boss, "Organizational Development in the Health-Care Field: A Confrontational Team Building Design," *Journal of Health and Human Resources Administration,* Summer 1983, pp. 72–91.

[29]Richard L. Hughes, William E. Rosenbach, and William H. Clover, "Team Development in an Intact, Ongoing Work Group," *Group and Organizational Studies,* June 1983, pp. 161–81.

obtain and make public the views of all members. Diagnosis, in this context, implies the value of open confrontation of issues and problems previously talked about in relative secrecy. The Industrial Polymers Division of Du Pont successfully implemented team development beginning with the diagnostic step.[30]

The nature of the problems, their priority, and a *plan of action* must be agreed upon. The plan should call on each group member, individually or in a subgroup, to undertake a specific action to alleviate one or more of the problems. If, for example, an executive committee agrees that one of its problems is lack of understanding and commitment to a set of goals, a subgroup can be appointed to recommend goals to the total group at a subsequent meeting. Other group members can work on other problems. For instance, if problems are identified in the relationships among members, a subgroup initiates a process for examining the roles of each member. TRW Ramsey's approach to team building identified specific measurable objectives in areas of performance evaluation, objective setting, feedback and reinforcement, and team problem solving to direct its team-building effort.[31]

Team-building interventions do not always require a complex process of diagnostic and action meetings.[32] For example, the chief executive of a large manufacturing firm recognized that conflict within his executive group was creating tension between the functional departments. He also recognized that his practice of dealing on a one-to-one basis with the executive group members, each of whom headed a functional department, contributed to the tension and conflict: Rather than viewing themselves as team members having a stake in the organization, the functional heads viewed each other as competitors. The chief executive's practice of dealing with them individually confirmed their beliefs that they managed relatively independent units.

To counteract the situation, the chief executive adopted the simple expedient of requiring the top group to meet twice weekly. One meeting focuses on operating problems, the other on personnel problems. The ground rule for these meetings is that the group must reach consensus on decisions. After one year of such meetings, company-oriented decisions were being made, and the climate of interunit competition was replaced by cooperation.

Team building is also effective during the formation of new groups. Problems often exist when new organizational units, project teams, or task forces are created. To perform effectively, such groups typically must overcome certain characteristics. For example:

1. Confusion exists as to roles and relationships.
2. Members have a fairly clear understanding of short-term goals.
3. Group members have technical competencies that put them on the team.
4. Members often pay more attention to the tasks of the team than to relationships among the team members.

---

[30]Bernard A. Rausch, "Du Pont Transforms a Division's Culture," *Management Review,* March 1989, pp. 37–42.

[31]Donald J. Schilling and Thomas F. Bremer, "Implementing Productivity Strategies: A Program Case Study at TRW Ramsey," *National Productivity Review,* Autumn 1985, pp. 370–84.

[32]Carl E. Larson and Frank M. J. LaFasto, *Teamwork* (Newbury Park, Calif.: Sage, 1989).

As a result of these characteristics, the new group will initially focus on task problems and ignore relationship issues. By the time relationship problems begin to surface, the group is unable to deal with them, and performance begins to deteriorate.

To combat these tendencies, the new group should schedule team-building meetings during the first weeks of its life. The meetings should take place away from the work site; one- or two-day meetings often suffice. While the format of such meetings varies, they enable the group to work through its timetable and the roles of members in reaching the group's objectives. An important purpose of the meeting is to establish understanding about each member's contribution to the team and the reward for that contribution.

Although reports of team building indicate mixed results, the evidence suggests that group processes do improve through team-building efforts.[33] This record of success accounts for the increasing use of team building as an OD method.[34] In fact, one widely read business publication states that developing self-managing teams is the wave of the future in American organizations.[35] In addition to its widespread popularity in the United States, surveys of organization development practice indicate that team building has wide acceptance in European countries as well.[36]

Sensitivity Training

SENSITIVITY TRAINING
Intervention that focuses on group members' emotions as important factors in task performance; one of oldest if not the oldest of OD interventions.

This highly publicized and widely used development method focuses on individual and individual-group problems.[37] Sensitivity, in this context, means sensitivity to self and self-other relationships. **Sensitivity training** assumes that the causes of poor task performance are the emotional problems of people who must collectively achieve the goal. Removing these problems eliminates a major impediment to task performance. Sensitivity training stresses the process rather than the content of training and focuses on emotional rather than conceptual training.[38] Thus, this form of training differs significantly from traditional forms of training that stress the acquisition of a predetermined set of concepts with immediate application to the workplace.

Sensitivity training processes include communications workshops, Outward-Bound trips, and T-groups (the most common form). The T-group usually meets at some place away from the job. Under the direction of a trainer, the group engages in a dialogue with no agenda and no focus. The objective is to provide an environment that produces its own learning

[33]Kenneth P. de Meuse and S. Jay Liebowitz, "An Empirical Analysis of Team-Building Research," *Group and Organizational Studies,* September 1981, pp. 357–78.

[34]William J. Heisler, "Patterns of OD in Practice," in *Organization Development,* ed. Daniel Robey and Steven Altman (New York: MacMillan, 1982), pp. 23–29.

[35]"The Payoff from Teamwork," *Business Week,* July 10, 1989, pp. 56–60.

[36]A. Desreumaux, "OD Practices in France: Part I," *Leadership and Organization Development Journal* 6. no. 4 (1985), p. 29; A. Desreumaux, "OD Practices in France: Part II," *Leadership and Organization Development Journal* 7, no. 1 (1986), pp. 10–14.

[37]Kenneth N. Wexley and Gary P. Latham, *Developing and Training Human Resources in Organizations* (Glenview, Ill.: Scott, Foresman, 1981), p. 184.

[38]Robert E. Kaplan, "Is Openness Passe?" *Human Relations,* March 1986, pp. 229–43.

experiences.[39] By engaging in the dialogue, group members are encouraged to learn about themselves as they deal with others. They explore their needs and their attitudes as revealed through their behavior toward others in the group and through the behavior of others toward them. The T-group may be highly unstructured. As one who participated in sensitivity training points out, "It [sensitivity training] says 'Open your eyes. Look at yourself. See how you look to others. Then decide what changes, if any, you want to make and in which direction you want to go.' "

Sensitivity training develops interpersonal competence. A recent assessment of collegiate business schools notes that most management education curricula give too little attention to interpersonal competence, despite its apparent importance for management performance.[40] Some universities, Stanford for example, have retained some form of sensitivity training as part of the curriculum since the early 1960s, despite many difficulties encountered along the way.[41] Other universities, such as the University of Chicago, have recently developed courses that provide students with some sensitivity training types of experiences.[42] These activities acknowledge the importance of interpersonal competence and of sensitivity training as an important intervention for developing it. In this era of multinational commerce and trade, the development of sensitivity to interpersonal and cultural differences takes on renewed importance. Experts in training for international assignments indicate that sensitivity training can be a valuable experience for an individual preparing to take a managerial position in a foreign organization.[43]

Understandably, sensitivity training is controversial.[44] Implementing it requires that individuals expose themselves to considerable risk: they are encouraged by the trainer to experiment with behaviors that can cause breakdowns in psychological coping responses. Concerns about dangers have led to a number of variations on the basic sensitivity approach. These variations tend to delve less deeply into the non-work-related feelings and sentiments of the participants and instead focus only on task-relevant behavior. Such variants have not been fully evaluated in terms of organizational effectiveness, nor is there widespread understanding of *how* sensitivity training brings changes about. Nevertheless, the place of sensitivity training types of methods in organizational development is firmly established.

---

[39]Elliot Aronson, "Communication in Sensitivity Training Groups," in *Organization Development,* ed. Wendell L. French, Cecil H. Bell, Jr., and Robert A. Zawacki (Plano, Tex.: Business Publications, 1983), pp. 249–53.

[40]Lyman W. Porter and L. E. McKibbin, *Management Education and Development: Drift or Thrust into the 21st Century?* (New York: McGraw-Hill, 1988).

[41]David L. Bradford and Jerry I. Porras, "Developing Interpersonal Competence: The Stanford T-Group Program," *Academy of Management OD Newsletter,* Winter 1990, pp. 7–9.

[42]"Chicago's B-School Goes Touchy-Feely," *Business Week,* November 27, 1989, p. 140.

[43]Simcha Ronen, "Training the International Assignee," in *Training and Development in Organizations,* ed. Irwin L. Goldstein and associates (San Francisco: Jossey-Bass, 1989), pp. 439–40.

[44]Gary L. Cooper, "How Psychologically Dangerous Are T-Groups and Encounter Groups?" *Human Relations,* April 1975, pp. 249–60; Carl A. Bramlette and Jeffrey H. Tucker, "Encounter Groups: Positive Change or Deterioration: More Data and a Partial Replication," *Human Relations,* April 1981, pp. 303–14.

Process Consultation

Behavioral interactions within work groups are the focus of the traditional OD intervention called **process consultation**.[45] The intervention enables individuals to understand these interactions and to learn to change them to improve individual and group processes. Targeted are group processes such as communications, roles and role expectations, leadership, followership, problem solving, intergroup cooperation, and competition.

Although the exact procedure varies, process consultation requires the intervention of an outside change agent who acts as group facilitator. The change agent, often called a process consultant, meets with intact work groups identified by diagnostic activities as having difficulty with internal group processes. A common reason for intervention is conflict among group members or between groups. For example, the quality control and production line groups are unable to cooperate because each misunderstands the other's intentions and they have no way of resolving the suspicions that have arisen; or those who have been around for awhile view the newly appointed executive team with hostility and think the team is out to get them. In other applications, the change agent will deal with groups torn by internal strife due to interpersonal differences.

The change agent helps the group members understand what in the situation causes them to believe and act as they do. Rather than imposing solutions, the consultant encourages individuals to arrive at their own interpretations and prescriptions. Thus, the emphasis on "process" consultation. The intervention should end when the group members have developed the means and capacity to deal with similar circumstances in the future. As a human process technique, process consultation embodies elements of other interventions such as sensitivity training and team building.

MULTIFACETED INTERVENTIONS

The success of OD efforts depends in part on matching intervention and intended depth of intervention. Thus, a manager should be wary of the claims of proponents for all-purpose interventions. Each method—whether System 4, MBO, or sensitivity training—has a primary focus, or target, for change. Managers who expect changes in targets not affected by the intervention will be disappointed. If the required change involves several targets, or depths of intervention, then the OD program must include more than one intervention.

A recently reported multifaceted intervention combined team building and MBO.[46] The project was conducted in a silver mining company as part of a

---

[45]Edgar H. Schein, *Process Consultation: Its Role in Organization Development* (Reading, Mass.; Addison-Wesley Publishing, 1969), is the classic source. This discussion is based on Christian F. Paul and Albert C. Gross, "Increasing Productivity and Morale in a Municipality: Effects of Organization Development," *Journal of Applied Behavioral Science* 17, no. 1 (1981), pp. 59–78.

[46]Paul F. Buller and Cecil H. Bell, Jr., "Effects of Team Building and Goal Setting on Productivity: A Field Experiment," *Academy of Management Journal*, June 1986, pp. 305–28.

larger OD program directed at improving productivity and safety in the mine. Team-building exercises in intact work group meetings focused on issues such as how to do the job better and more safely. As the teams identified issues that went beyond their ability to solve, participation in the team meetings was gradually broadened to include top management. The miners and their supervisors participated fully in goal setting. The process, which proceeded as described in our discussion of MBO, involved establishing specific, difficult, and attainable goals. Each individual miner set objectives for tons and grade of ore produced per shift for three-month periods. Supervisors provided weekly feedback on progress toward the stated goals.

Combining team building and MBO enabled the mining company to deal with production and efficiency as well as satisfaction criteria of effectiveness. In fact, multifaceted interventions invariably combine technostructural and human process interventions, recognizing the complex nature of significant organizational change and its interdependence with organizational behavior.

An even more complex multifaceted program occurred in a research and development unit of a large corporation.[47] The impetus of the OD program was the unit's inability to compete for government contracts that called for developmental research. Although the unit had been successful in winning research contracts in prior years, the funding agencies had shifted priority toward projects with shorter-run payoffs, and the organization was not as successful at winning such contracts. Hampered by its inability to adapt, the unit was unable to make the major strategic shift that was necessary.

The unit's management identified organizational development as the appropriate way to manage the change. The immediate problem was to identify the specific causes of the organization's lack of adaptiveness. Under the direction of change agents, numerous diagnostic activities were undertaken, including the System 4 questionnaire, special-purpose questionnaires, and interview and problem identification sessions. The participants analyzed the questionnaire and other data and identified interpersonal and group relationships as the sources of problems. They then voted on whether to continue the OD program, based on the proviso that it would improve these relationships.

Over the next four years, the employees were targets of numerous interventions. The change agents used managerial grid training, sensitivity training, survey feedback, process consultation, and team building. This battery of human process interventions was implemented throughout the organization, which considered the intervention to be successful. Unlike the multifaceted intervention in the silver mining company, this intervention consisted exclusively of human process targets, with the exception of the System 4 questionnaire.

The idea that organizational development involves multilevels and multifunctions coincides with the conclusions of systems theory: all parts of an organization are connected to all other parts, and change in one involves change in all. Effective organizational development requires accurate diagnosis of problems, selection of appropriate targets for change, and the application of

[47]Vida Scarpello, "Who Benefits from Participation in Long-Term Human Process Interventions?" *Group and Organization Studies,* March 1983, pp. 21–44.

appropriate, usually multiple, OD methods. The valued outcome of OD is an organization whose separate parts are directed toward common purposes. Integrated, multimethod OD programs are promising means to achieve that outcome.

HOW EFFECTIVE ARE OD INTERVENTIONS?

The critical test of OD interventions is whether they lead to improvement in organizational effectiveness. Whether they do can only be determined through research, and OD has a rather long history of such research. For example, considerable research has focused on determining the effects of sensitivity training on various criteria of organizational effectiveness. (The interest in sensitivity training no doubt reflects its longevity as an OD intervention.) One important finding is that while sensitivity training induces positive changes in the participant's sensitivity to self and others,[48] such behavior may be either not possible or not permissible back in the workplace. The open, supportive, and permissive environment of the training sessions may not be found on the job, where the participant must deal with the same environment and the same people as before the training, or even at home.[49] Even so, proponents of sensitivity training would reply that the participants are better able to deal with the environment and to understand their own relationship to it. Sensitivity training may also induce negative changes in some participants' ability to perform their organizational task. Training sessions can be occasions of extreme stress and anxiety, and the capacity to deal effectively with stress varies among individuals.

The current practice of OD appears to have shifted the focus from human process interventions to technostructural and multifaceted interventions. Socio-technical interventions in particular have been the most widely used method, as reported in the literature.[50] The increasing use of technostructural interventions reflects the increasing importance of production and efficiency criteria of organizational effectiveness, the specific targets of such interventions. The priority of these criteria comes from the importance of external competitive pressures that emphasize quantity, quality, and cost improvements. Sociotechnical interventions target these variables for change, whereas human process interventions target somewhat more nebulous but nonetheless important variables such as attitudes, problem-solving skills, motivation, openness, and trust. Human process interventions have also waned in popularity because of difficulties involved in evaluating them through rigorous research designs.[51]

A recent review of the record of OD interventions in bringing about change concludes that multimethod approaches have better success than single-

---

[48]Peter B. Smith, "Controlled Studies in the Outcomes of Sensitivity Training," *Psychological Bulletin,* July 1975, pp. 597–622.

[49]Peter B. Smith, "Back-Home Environments and With-Group Relationships as Determinants of Personal Change," *Human Relations,* January 1983, pp. 53–67.

[50]Nicholas and Katz, "Research Methods and Reporting Practices."

[51]Richard W. Woodman and Sandy J. Wayne, "An Investigation of Positive-Finding Bias in Evaluation of Organization Development Interventions," *Academy of Management Journal,* December 1985, pp. 889–913.

method ones.[52] Nicholas, for example, compared the effects of sensitivity training, team building, job enrichment, and job redesign. He concluded that no one method is successful in all instances (an expected conclusion, given what was said above). He also found that significant changes occurred when several methods were combined. One such combination includes three discrete steps involving all levels of the organization: (1) all employees participate in goal setting, decision making, and job redesign; (2) employee collaboration is developed through team building; and (3) the organizational structure is reorganized to accommodate the new levels of participation and collaboration. Applying these three steps can go a long way toward meeting some of the arguments against specific OD methods.[53] In evaluating interventions, the overriding managerial concern is transfer of learning to the work environment; only if this happens can OD methods be considered effective.

GUIDELINES FOR MANAGING CHANGE THROUGH OD

What should managers do when they recognize the need to change their organization through the application of organizational development interventions? Although no absolute guarantees exist to assure success in every instance, the accumulated experience of those involved with organizational development suggests some guidelines. We share the views of one such individual, William G. Dyer, who has spent 30 years helping organizations reach their potential effectiveness. Dyer believes certain conditions must be present for the OD intervention to have some chance of bringing about the desired change:[54]

1. Management and all those involved have high and visible commitment to the effort.

2. Individuals involved have information in advance that enables them to know what will happen and why they need to do what they are to do.

3. The effort is connected to other parts of the organization, especially the evaluation and reward systems.

4. The effort is directed by line managers and assisted by a change agent if necessary.

5. The effort is based on good diagnosis and is consistent with the conditions in the organization.

6. Management remains committed to the effort throughout all of its steps, from diagnosis through implementation and evaluation.

7. Evaluation takes place and consists of more than asking people how they felt about the effort.

8. People see clearly the relationship between the effort and the organization's mission and goals.

9. The change agent, if used, is clearly competent.

---

[52]John B. Nicholas, "The Comparative Impact of Organization Development Interventions on Hard Criteria Measures," *Academy of Management Review,* October 1982, pp. 531–42.

[53]Mark Mendenhall and Gary Oddou, "The Integrative Approach to OD: McGregor Revisited," *Group and Organizational Studies,* September 1983, pp. 291–302.

[54]William G. Dyer, "Team Building: A Microcosm of the Past, Present, and Future of O.D.," *Academy of Management OD Newsletter,* Winter 1989, pp. 7–8.

These nine conditions summarize the important points we have made in this and the previous chapter. Taken together, they enable us to see that organizational development is a significant undertaking and that managers should go about it in a systematic way. The model for managing change that we introduced in Chapter 19 offers a systematic process for realizing the above nine conditions for success, which Dyer states are necessary but not sufficient for bringing about organizational effectiveness.

Of crucial consideration is the role of managers in the OD process. Although Dyer's nine steps clearly include the activities of competent change agents, they also clearly specify an active role for managers, who must support all the required activities, be involved, and even direct the effort. As we move into the 1990s, we expect to see even greater managerial commitment and involvement in OD processes.[55]

---

[55]Michael Beer and Anna Elise Walton, "Organization Change and Development," in *Annual Review of Psychology,* ed. Mark Rosenzweig and Lyman W. Porter (Palo Alto, Calif.: Annual Review, 1987), pp. 339–67.

SUMMARY OF KEY POINTS

— After diagnosing the problem and identifying targets for change, management must select the most promising development intervention. The philosophy of OD emphasizes that the correct order of analysis is problem to intervention, not intervention to problem.

— Management must tailor the OD program to the problems and personnel of the organization. Throughout, the discussions of organizational design, motivation, and leadership have stressed the contingency approach. This point of view is fundamental to the process of organizational development and change.

— Inherent in the contingency approach is the understanding that each organization must adapt in unique ways to its environment. Accordingly, conditions exist that limit the range of the development interventions and strategies available to management. A development intervention such as sensitivity training or System 4 can fail if management does not support the behavioral changes induced by the OD program.

— Analysis of the problem, identification of alternatives, and recognition of constraints lead to selection of the most promising intervention and strategy. The selection is based on the principle of maximizing expected returns to the organization.

— Although the levels for which a particular intervention is appropriate overlap considerably, each has a primary focus. One would not expect, for example, that MBO will be effective in changing behaviors at level VIII, although it may have some effect on behaviors at levels V and VI.

— The number of OD interventions is considerable and increases constantly. Only a few of the more widely used ones have been discussed. Managers considering the possibility of OD should consult a more detailed description of them. Several such descriptions appear in the citations and additional references included in this chapter.

DISCUSSION AND REVIEW QUESTIONS

1. Explain why the depth of intended change is an important issue for analysis prior to implementing a particular intervention.

2. What is your understanding of the concept of targets of intervention? Why is it important to identify the specific targets of change in an OD intervention?

3. Give your opinion regarding the use of team management in organizations. Do you personally prefer to work alone or in teams? What would probably be the opinions of others in the class? Explain your answers.

4. Explain why OD programs to bring about significant change often must use more than one form of intervention.

5. Which of the interventions discussed in the chapter would be most applicable to improving the performance of student organizations to which you belong?

6. What are the differences between MBO and System 4 organization? Are the differences simply matters of emphasis, or are there fundamental differences?

7. What cultural values underlie the application of OD interventions? Are these values universal? Would they apply equally in different regions of the United States?

8. What specific motivation theories explain the apparent success of MBO? Develop your answer fully.

9. Explain how team-building exercises apply group development theory as explained in Chapter 8.

10. Now that you have completed both chapters on OD, do you agree that it is the only suitable way to manage large-scale changes in organization behavior, structure, and process? Explain.

ADDITIONAL REFERENCES

Beer, M. "Revitalizing Organizations: Change Process and Emergent Model." *Academy of Management Executive,* 1987, pp. 51–55.

Bridges, W. "Managing Organizational Transitions." *Organizational Dynamics,* 1986, pp. 24–33.

Burke, W. W. *Organization Development: A Normative View.* Reading, Mass.: Addison-Wesley Publishing, 1987.

Dalton, D. R., and I. F. Kesner. "Organizational Performance as an Antecedent of Inside/Outside Chief Executive Succession: An Empirical Assessment." *Academy of Management Journal,* 1985, pp. 749–62.

Dyer, W. G. *Team Building: Issues and Alternatives.* 2nd ed. Reading, Mass.: Addison-Wesley Publishing, 1987.

Eden, D. "OD and Self-Fulfilling Prophecy: Boosting Productivity by Raising Expectations." *Journal of Applied Behavioral Science,* 1986, pp. 1–13.

Fitzgerald, T. H. "The OD Practitioner in the Business World: Theory versus Reality." *Organizational Dynamics,* 1987, pp. 20–32.

Gardner, D. G.; R. B. Dunham; L. L. Cummings; and J. L. Pierce. "Employees Focus of Attention and Reactions to Organizational Change." *Journal of Applied Behavioral Science,* 1986, pp. 351–70.

Hackman, J. R., ed. *Groups that Work (and Those that Don't).* San Francisco: Jossey-Bass, 1989.

Hardie, K. R., and R. G. Harrison. *Organization Development: An Annotated Bibliography for the Practitioner.* Greensboro, N.C.: Center for Creative Leadership, 1987.

Jaeger, A. M. "Organization Development and National Culture: Where's the Fit?" *Academy of Management Review,* 1986, pp. 178–90.

Johnson, C. R. "An Outline for Team Building." *Training,* 1986, pp. 48–58.

Kilmann, R.; J. Covin; and associates. *Corporate Transformation.* San Francisco: Jossey-Bass, 1988.

Levy, A. "Second-Order Planned Change: Definitions and Conceptualization." *Organizational Dynamics,* 1986, pp. 4–20.

Reddy, W. B., and K. Jamison. *Team Building: Blueprints for Productivity and Satisfaction.* Alexandria, Va.: NTL Institute, 1988.

Seashore, S. E.; E. E. Lawler III; P. H. Mirvis; and C. Cammann. *Assessing Organizational Change: A Guide to Methods, Measures, and Practices.* New York: John Wiley & Sons, 1983.

Ucko, S. J., and E. H. Kazemek. "Creating Effective Workteams." *Healthcare and Financial Management,* 1986, pp. 80–82.

Varney, G. H. *Building Productive Teams.* San Francisco: Jossey-Bass, 1989.

Wall, T. D.; N. J. Kemp; P. R. Jackson; and C. W. Clegg. "Outcomes of Autonomous Workgroups: A Long-Term Field Experiment." *Academy of Management Journal,* 1986, pp. 305–28.

Walton, R. E. *Innovating to Compete: Lessons for Diffusing and Managing Change in the Workplace.* San Francisco: Jossey-Bass, 1987.

Weisbord, M. R. *Productive Workplaces.* San Francisco: Jossey-Bass, 1987.

MANAGING CHANGE AT FMC CORPORATION

FMC Corporation is a major international producer of machinery and chemicals for industry, agriculture, and government. From the company's headquarters in Chicago, top management directs 28,000 employees in 118 factories and mines in 29 states and 15 other nations. During the 1980s, FMC faced increasingly stiff domestic and international competition. Top management realized that the firm's survival depended on implementing modern manufacturing technology and information systems. They also recognized the importance of developing an organizational culture that encouraged innovation and risk-taking.

FMC's management information system (MIS) became the focus of attention when an organization-wide attitude survey indicated considerable dissatisfaction with MIS services. MIS consisted of some 800 professionals throughout the organization. For some time, managers of MIS units had been aware of their inability to fully meet the demands for increasingly complex information technology applications. The attitude survey results documented the extent of dissatisfaction with MIS services and made it evident that corrective action was necessary. MIS management's immediate response to the problem was to announce that "user satisfaction" was the primary goal for all MIS units throughout FMC. Consequently, MIS's entire energies focused on that goal; in a short time, user satisfaction began to increase.

MIS managers throughout FMC achieved the goal by becoming increasingly task directed. They planned project activities and schedules without consulting the people who were to do the work. To meet the planned deadlines, overtime became the rule rather than the exception. Managers viewed employees' reluctance to work overtime as disloyalty to the unit. Centralization of authority created delays, as decisions had to move up and down the hierarchy. Meeting the goal of user satisfaction while maintaining employee satisfaction became increasingly difficult.

Two years after implementing the program to improve user satisfaction, employees' dissatisfaction surfaced in a meeting of MIS managers and employees. The meeting was one of the scheduled quarterly meetings referred to as "town hall" meetings in the MIS units. Top management used this particular meeting to report the improved results in achieving user satisfaction and to congratulate employees on their accomplishment. One employee chose this same meeting to voice concern for the costs of the accomplishment in deteriorating employee satisfaction, as evidenced by management's apparent lack of concern for employees' needs. The discussion that followed indicated that performance levels were, in fact, beginning to slip and that employee turnover was increasing.

The discussion of problems during the town hall meeting stimulated MIS management to appoint an employee task force to design and administer an attitude survey specifically for MIS. Survey results revealed that employee dissatisfaction and turnover were making it more and more difficult, if not impossible, to meet the ever growing demands for high-level information technology applications in FMC. If the problem was not resolved, line units in FMC would begin to turn to external vendors for MIS services. After discussions with a consultant in organizational development, the MIS director decided to focus on the survey results at the annual planning meeting he held with the 11 managers who reported directly to him.

In previous years, the planning meetings had established goals and performance measures for the upcoming year. But this year, the director and the consultant believed that employee concerns must be addressed. They were certain that

Source: Edmund J. Metz, "Managing Change toward a Leading-Edge Information Culture," *Organizational Dynamics*, Autumn 1986, pp. 28–40.

solutions could be found if the 11 managers focused on new ways to manage people. Specifically, the director wanted managers to define MIS's mission and philosophy to include beliefs about service to customers, the worth of the individual, and operational cost effectiveness and performance. The result of four days of intensive and often heated discussions, the group-prepared statement of MIS's mission and philosophy, embodied values that gave purpose and direction to efforts to adopt and implement it throughout the company.

To implement the mission and philosophy, significant changes were required in performance review, career development, policy and procedures, and managerial behavior. To guide the change effort, the director formed a steering committee of managers and supervisors. The steering committee then broke into four task groups to tackle each of the four areas. Because of the prevailing management styles in MIS, these task groups were unskilled in teamwork and team skills. The consultant facilitated training in team building; soon thereafter, the four groups were under way.

The task groups completed their work and made 78 recommendations for changing the performance review processes, career development practices, administrative policies and procedures, and daily management behavior. Among the more significant changes implemented were the training of managers in performance evaluation, training in team building, decentralization of authority, and active participation of employees in decision making. All of these changes were consistent with MIS's statement of mission and philosophy.

Four years after the initial attitude survey, many of the significant changes were in place. A follow-up attitude survey confirmed that employee satisfaction had increased and that turnover had decreased. MIS managers also pointed to renewed commitment to meet user needs as evidence that progress had been made in improving MIS's performance.

Questions for Consideration

1. Was the second FMC change effort successful? If so, what did it do right? If not, what did it do wrong?

2. Which roles did the attitude surveys play in the change effort?

3. What depth of intervention was necessary to change FMC's MIS function in order to improve its performance? What was the alternative to change? Did management have a choice in the matter?

EXPERIENTIAL EXERCISE

Objectives

To understand how different interventions can be applied to bring about change.

Related Topics

Individual, group, and leadership theories are relevant, along with ideas and concepts from organizational change and development.

Starting the Exercise

The instructor will divide the class into groups of five to seven students. Each group is to prepare a short consultant's report concerning the Southeast Par Telephone staffing situation described in the scenario below. Specifically, the president wants the consultants to determine the organization's problems and develop a solution that has the fewest negative side effects. The report should diagnose the problem, identify the key performance factor that measures the extent of the problem, determine the depth of intended change and targets of intervention, suggest the specific intervention that should be implemented, and advise the scope and timing of the intervention.

The exercise is more informative if one group serves as evaluator of the presentations. This group would be the panel reviewing the analyses of the other groups.

Scenario

For the past three years, Southeast Par Telephone Company has had very little success in recruiting young, qualified management trainees for positions in the accounting, operations, traffic, and maintenance departments. The company has a reputation of paying and treating employees well, but it is also considered to be an organization with limited advancement opportunities.

Management is puzzled about the company's inability to bring in qualified people for well-paying trainee positions. The company is searching for young men and women between 21 and 35 years old, with college degrees (preferably some graduate education), who are willing to work different shifts during the two-year training cycle. The unemployment rate in the city is 5.1 percent, below the national average, and the company is located 8 miles west of the city.

Procedures and Techniques for Studying Organizations: Behavior, Structure, Processes

SOURCES OF KNOWLEDGE ABOUT ORGANIZATIONS

The vast majority of the research reports and writing on organizations is contained in technical publications known as journals. Some of these journals, such as the *Academy of Management Review,* are devoted entirely to topics of management and organization, while such journals as *Organizational Behavior and Human Decision Processes* are devoted largely to the results of laboratory studies. Such journals as *Harvard Business Review* and *Business Management* are general business journals, while *American Sociological Review* and *Journal of Applied Psychology* are general behavioral science journals. These general business and behavioral science journals often contain articles of interest to students of management.

Table A–1 presents a selective list of journals. These sources provide information, data, and discussion about what is occurring within and among organizations. This knowledge base provides managers with available research information that could prove useful in their own organizations or situations.[1]

History

The oldest approach to the study of organizations is through the history of organizations, societies, and institutions. Organizations are as old as human history. Throughout time, people have joined with others to accomplish their goals, first in families, later in tribes and other more sophisticated political units. Ancient peoples constructed pyramids, temples, and ships; they created systems of government, farming, commerce, and warfare. For example, Greek historians tell us that it took 100,000 men to build the great pyramid of Khufu in Egypt. The project took over 20 years to complete. It was almost as high as the Washington Monument and had a base that would cover eight football fields. Remember, these people had no construction equipment or computers. One thing they did have, though, was *organization.* While these "joint efforts" did not have formal names such as XYZ Corporation, the idea of "getting organized" was quite widespread throughout early civilizations. The literature of the times refers to such managerial concepts as planning, staff assistance, division of labor, control, and leadership.[2]

The administration of the vast Roman Empire required the application of organization and management concepts. In fact, it has been said that "the real secret of the greatness of the Romans was their genius for organization."[3] This is because the Romans used certain principles of organization to coordinate the diverse activities of the empire.

If judged by age alone, the Roman Catholic Church would have to be considered the most effective organization of all time. While its success is the result of many factors, one of these factors is certainly the effectiveness of its organization and management. For example, a hierarchy of authority, a

[1]David W. Stewart, *Secondary Research: Information Sources and Methods* (Beverly Hills, Calif.: Sage Publications, 1984).

[2]C. S. George, Jr., *The History of Management Thought* (Englewood Cliffs, N.J.: Prentice Hall, 1968).

[3]J. D. Mooney, *The Principles of Management* (New York: Harper & Row, 1939).

TABLE A–1
Selected Sources of Writing and Research about Organizations

1. *Academy of Management Executive*
2. *Academy of Management Journal*
3. *Academy of Management Review*
4. *Administrative Science Quarterly*
5. *Advanced Management Journal*
6. *American Sociological Review*
7. *Business Horizons*
8. *Business Management*
9. *California Management Review*
10. *Fortune*
11. *Harvard Business Review*
12. *Health Psychology*
13. *Hospital and Health Services Administration*
14. *Human Organization*
15. *Industrial and Labor Relations Review*
16. *Industrial Management Review*
17. *Journal of Applied Behavioral Science*
18. *Journal of Applied Psychology*
19. *Journal of Business*
20. *Journal of Human Stress*
21. *Journal of Management Studies*
22. *Management International Review*
23. *Management Review*
24. *Management Science*
25. *New Management*
26. *Organizational Behavior and Human Decision Processes*
27. *Organizational Dynamics*
28. *Personnel*
29. *Personnel Administrator*
30. *Personnel Journal*
31. *Personnel Psychology*
32. *Public Administration Review*
33. *Public Personnel Review*
34. *Training and Development Journal*

territorial organization, specialization of activities by function, and use of the staff principle were integral parts of early church organization.

Finally, and not surprising, some important concepts and practices in modern organizations can be traced to military organizations. Like the church, military organizations were faced with problems of managing large, geographically dispersed groups and adopted the concept of staff as an advisory function for line personnel early on.

Knowledge of the history of organizations in earlier societies can be useful for the future manager. In fact, many of the early concepts and practices are being utilized successfully today. However, one may ask whether heavy reliance on the past is a good guide to the present and future.[4] We shall see that time and organizational setting have much to do with what works in management.

Experience

Some of the earliest books on management and organizations were written by successful practitioners. Most of these individuals were business executives, and their writings focused on how it was for them during their time with one or more companies. They usually put forward certain general principles or practices that had worked well for them. Although using the writings and experiences of practitioners sounds "practical," it has drawbacks. Successful managers are susceptible to the same perceptual phenomena as each of us. Their accounts are therefore based on their own preconceptions and biases. No matter how objective the approach, experiential accounts may not be entirely complete or accurate. They may also be superficial, since they are often after-the-fact reflections of situations in which, when the events were occurring, the managers had little time to think about how or why an action was

---

[4]Robert S. Goodman and Evonne Jonas Kruger, "Data Dredging or Legitimate Research Method: Historiography and Its Potential for Management Research," *Academy of Management Review,* April 1988, pp. 315–25.

taken. As a result, suggestions in such accounts are often oversimplified. Finally, as with history, what worked yesterday may not work today or tomorrow.[5]

Science

A major interest in this book is the behavioral sciences that have produced theory, research, and generalizations concerning the behavior, structure, and processes of organizations. The interest of behavioral scientists in the problems of organizations is relatively new, becoming popular in the early 1950s. At that time, an organization known as the Foundation for Research on Human Behavior was established with the objectives of promoting and supporting behavioral science research in business, government, and other organizations.

Many advocates of the scientific approach believe that practicing managers and teachers have accepted prevalent practices and principles without the benefit of scientific validation. They believe that scientific procedures should be used to validate practice whenever possible. Because of their work, many of the earlier practices and principles have been discounted or modified, and others have been validated.

BEHAVIORAL SCIENCES RESEARCH AND METHODS

Research

Present research in the behavioral sciences varies greatly with respect to the scope and methods used. One common thread among the various disciplines is the study of human behavior through the use of scientific procedures. Thus, it is necessary to examine the nature of science as it is applied to human behavior.

Some critics believe that a science of human behavior is unattainable and that the scientific procedures used to gain knowledge in the physical sciences cannot be adapted to the study of humans, especially humans in organizations. While this is not the appropriate place to become involved in these arguments, we believe that the scientific approach can be applied to management and organizational studies.[6] Furthermore, as we have already pointed out, means other than scientific procedures have provided important knowledge concerning people in organizations.

The manager of the future will draw from the behavioral sciences just as the physician draws from the biological sciences. The manager must know what to expect from the behavioral sciences, their strengths and weaknesses, just as

---

[5]W. H. Gruber and J. S. Niles, "Research and Experience in Management," *Business Horizons,* Fall 1973, pp. 15–24.

[6]A similar debate has taken place for years over the issue of whether management is a science. For relevant discussions, interested readers should consult R. E. Gribbons and S. D. Hunt, "Is Management a Science?" *Academy of Management Review,* January 1978, pp. 139–43; O. Behling, "The Case for the Natural Science Model for Research in Organizational Behavior and Organization Theory," *Academy of Management Review,* October 1980, pp. 483–90.

TABLE A–2

Characteristics of the
Scientific Approach

1. *Procedures are public.* A scientific report contains a complete description of what was done, to enable other researchers in the field to follow each step of the investigation as if they were actually present.
2. *Definitions are precise.* The procedures used, the variables measured, and how they were measured must be clearly stated. For example, if examining motivation among employees in a given plant, researchers must define what is meant by motivation and how it was measured (for example, number of units produced, number of absences).
3. *Data collection is objective.* Objectivity is a key feature of the scientific approach. Bias in collecting and interpreting data has no place in science.
4. *Findings must be replicable.* This enables another interested researcher to test the results of a study by attempting to reproduce them.
5. *The approach is systematic and cumulative.* This relates to one of the underlying purposes of science, to develop a unified body of knowledge.
6. *The purposes are explanation, understanding, and prediction.* All scientists want to know "why" and "how." If they determine "why" and "how" and are able to provide proof, they can then predict the particular conditions under which specific events (human behavior in the case of behavioral sciences) will occur. Prediction is the ultimate objective of behavioral science, as it is of all science.

Source: Bernard Berelson and Gary A. Steiner, *Human Behavior: An Inventory of Scientific Findings* (New York: Harcourt Brace Jovanovich, 1964), pp. 16–18.

the physician must know what to expect from bacteriology and how it can serve as a diagnostic tool. However, the manager, like the physician, is a practitioner who must make decisions in the present, whether or not science has all the answers. Neither can wait until it finds them before acting.[7]

The Scientific Approach

Most current philosophers of science define science by what they consider to be its one universal and unique feature: *method.* The greatest advantage of the scientific approach is its characteristic of *self-correction,* which no other method of attaining knowledge has.[8] The approach is an objective, systematic, and controlled process with built-in checks all along the way to knowledge. These checks control and verify the scientist's activities and conclusions to enable the attainment of knowledge independent of the scientist's own biases and preconceptions.

Most scientists agree that rather than a single scientific method, scientists can and do use several methods. Thus, it probably makes more sense to say that there is a scientific *approach.* Table A–2 summarizes the major characteristic of this approach. While only an "ideal" science would exhibit all of them, they are nevertheless the hallmarks of the scientific approach. They exhibit the basic nature—objective, systematic, controlled—of the scientific approach, which enables others to have confidence in research results. What is important is the overall fundamental idea that the scientific approach is a controlled rational process.

[7]Edward E. Lawler III, A. M. Mohrman, S. A. Mohrman, G. E. Ledford, Jr., and T. G. Cummings, *Doing Research that Is Useful for Theory and Practice* (San Francisco: Jossey-Bass, 1985).
[8]F. N. Kerlinger, *Foundations of Behavioral Research* (New York: Holt, Rinehart & Winston, 1973).

Methods of Inquiry

How do behavioral scientists gain knowledge about the functioning of organizations? Just as physical scientists have certain tools and methods for obtaining information, so too do behavioral scientists. These are usually referred to as *research designs*. In broad terms, three basic designs are used by behavioral scientists: the case study, the field study, and the experiment.

Case study.   A case study attempts to examine numerous characteristics of one or more people, usually over an extended time period. For years, anthropologists have studied the customs and behavior of various groups by actually living among them. Some organizational researchers have done the same thing. They have actually worked and socialized with the groups of employees that they were studying.[9] The reports on such investigations are usually in the form of a case study. For example, a sociologist might report the key factors and incidents that led to a strike by a group of blue-collar workers.

The chief limitations of the case study approach for gaining knowledge about the functioning of organizations are:

1. Rarely can two cases be meaningfully compared in essential characteristics. In other words, in another firm of another size, the same factors might not have resulted in a strike.
2. Rarely can case studies be repeated or their findings verified.
3. The significance of the findings is left to the subjective interpretation of the researcher. Like the practitioner, the researcher attempts to describe reality, but it is reality as perceived by one person (or a very small group). The researcher's training, biases, and preconceptions can inadvertently distort the report. A psychologist may give an entirely different view of a group of blue-collar workers than would be given by a sociologist.
4. Since the results of a case study are based on a sample of one, the ability to generalize from them may be limited.[10]

Despite these limitations, the case study is widely used as a method of studying organizations. It is extremely valuable in answering exploratory questions.

Field study.   Attempting to add more reality and rigor to the study of organizations, behavioral scientists have developed several systematic field research techniques, such as personal interviews, observation, archival data, and questionnaire surveys. They use these methods, individually or in combination, to investigate current practices or events. With these methods, unlike some other methods, the researcher does not rely entirely on what the subjects say. He or she may personally interview other people in the organization—fellow workers, subordinates, and superiors—to gain a more

[9]Robert K. Yin, *Case Study Research: Design and Methods* (Beverly Hills, Calif.: Sage Publications, 1984).

[10]Kathleen M. Eisenhardt, "Building Theories from Case Study Research," *Academy of Management Review,* October 1989, pp. 532–50.

balanced view before drawing conclusions.[11] In addition, archival data, records, charts, and statistics on file may be used to analyze a problem or hypothesis.

A very popular field study technique involves the use of expertly prepared questionnaires. Not only are such questionnaires less subject to unintentional distortion than personal interviews, but they also enable the researcher to greatly increase the number of individuals participating. Figure A–1 presents part of a questionnaire used in organizations to evaluate ratee perceptions of a performance appraisal interview program. The questionnaire enables the collection of data on particular characteristics that are of interest (for example, equity, accuracy, and clarity). The seven-point scales measure ratee perceptions of the degree to which the performance appraisal interviews possess a given characteristic.

In most cases, surveys are limited to a description of the current state of the situation. However, if researchers are aware of factors that may account for survey findings, they can make conjectural statements (known as hypotheses) about the relationship between two or more factors and relate the survey data to those factors. Thus, instead of just describing ratee perceptions of performance evaluation, the researchers could make finer distinctions (for example, distinctions regarding job tenure, salary level, or education) among groups of ratees. Comparisons and statistical tests could then be applied to determine differences, similarities, or relationships. Finally, *longitudinal* studies involving observations made over time are used to describe changes that have taken place. Thus, in the situation described here, we can become aware of changes in overall ratee perceptions of appraisal interviews over time as well as those relating to individual managers.[12]

Despite advantages over many of the other methods of gaining knowledge about organizations, field studies are not without problems. Here again, researchers have training, interests, and expectations that they bring with them.[13] Thus, a researcher may inadvertently ignore a vital technological factor while concentrating on only behavioral factors in a study of employee morale. Also, the fact that a researcher is present may influence how the individual responds. This weakness of field studies has long been recognized and is noted in some of the earliest field research in organizations.

Experiment.   The experiment is potentially the most rigorous of scientific techniques. For an investigation to be considered an experiment, it must contain two elements: manipulation of some variable (independent variable)

---

[11]G. R. Salancik, "Field Simulations for Organizational Behavior Research," *Administrative Science Quarterly,* December 1979, pp. 638–49.

[12]The design of surveys and the development and administration of questionnaires are better left to trained individuals if valid results are to be obtained. Interested readers might consult S. Sudman and N. M. Bradburn, *Asking Questions: A Practical Guide to Questionnaire Design* (San Francisco: Jossey-Bass, 1982).

[13]For an excellent article on the relationship between what researchers want to see and what they do see, consult G. Nettler, "Wanting and Knowing," *American Behavioral Scientist,* July 1973, pp. 5–26.

FIGURE A—1

Scale for Assessing GANAT
Appraisal Interviews

Part A: Appraisal Interview

The following items deal with the formal appraisal interview used in conjunction with the GANAT project program. Please circle the number that best describes your opinion of the most recent interview session.

	Very False						Very True
1. The appraisal interview covered my entire job.	1	2	3	4	5	6	7
2. The discussion of my performance during the appraisal interview was covered equitably.	1	2	3	4	5	6	7
3. The appraisal interview was accurately conducted.	1	2	3	4	5	6	7
4. I didn't have to ask for any clarification.	1	2	3	4	5	6	7
5. The interview was fair in every respect.	1	2	3	4	5	6	7
6. The interview really raised my anxiety level.	1	2	3	4	5	6	7
7. The interview's purpose was simply not clear to me.	1	2	3	4	5	6	7
8. The appraisal interview really made me think about working smarter on the job.	1	2	3	4	5	6	7
9. The appraisal interview was encouraging to me personally.	1	2	3	4	5	6	7
10. I dreaded the actual interview itself.	1	2	3	4	5	6	7
11. The boss was totally aboveboard in all phases of the interview.	1	2	3	4	5	6	7
12. The interview gave me some direction and purpose.	1	2	3	4	5	6	7
13. The interview really pinpointed areas for improvement.	1	2	3	4	5	6	7
14. The interview was disorganized and frustrating.	1	2	3	4	5	6	7
15. I disliked the interview because the intent was not clear.	1	2	3	4	5	6	7
16. The appraisal interviewer (boss) was not well trained.	1	2	3	4	5	6	7
17. The interview has been my guide for correcting weaknesses.	1	2	3	4	5	6	7
18. I understood the meaning of each performance area better after the interview.	1	2	3	4	5	6	7
19. The interview time was too rushed.	1	2	3	4	5	6	7
20. I received no advanced notice about the interview.	1	2	3	4	5	6	7
21. During the interview, my performance was fairly analyzed.	1	2	3	4	5	6	7
22. I was often upset because the interview data were not accurate.	1	2	3	4	5	6	7
23. My record, as it was introduced in the interview, contained no errors.	1	2	3	4	5	6	7

Source: This interview appraisal form was developed by John M. Ivancevich and sponsored by research funds provided by the GANAT Company.

and observation or measurement of the results (dependent variable) while maintaining all other factors unchanged. Thus, in an organization, a behavioral scientist could change one organizational factor and observe the results while attempting to keep everything else unchanged[14] in one of two general types of experiments.

In a *laboratory experiment,* the researcher creates the environment. For example, a management researcher may work with a small voluntary group in a classroom. The group may be students or managers. If a student sample is used, it is important to determine (1) if the population of interest is similar to the student sample and (2) if research results can be generalized from a student sample to organizational employees.[15] Samples in a laboratory experiment may be asked to communicate, perform tasks, or make decisions under different sets of conditions designated by the researcher. The laboratory setting permits the researcher to closely control the conditions under which observations are made. The intention is to isolate the relevant variables and to measure the response of dependent variables when the independent variable is manipulated. Laboratory experiments are useful when the conditions required to test a hypothesis are not practically or readily obtainable in natural situations and when the situation to be studied can be replicated under laboratory conditions. For such situations, many schools of business have behavioral science laboratories where such experimentation is done.

In a *field experiment,* the investigator attempts to manipulate and control variables in the natural setting rather than in a laboratory. Early experiments in organizations included manipulating physical working conditions such as rest periods, refreshments, and lighting. Today, behavioral scientists attempt to manipulate a host of additional factors.[16] For example, a training program might be introduced for one group of managers but not for another. Comparisons of performance, attitudes, and so on could be obtained later, either at one point or at several different points (a longitudinal study), to determine what effect (if any) the training program had on the managers' performances and attitudes.

The experimental design is especially appealing to many researchers because it is the prototype of the scientific approach. It is the ideal toward which every science strives. However, while its potential is still great, it has not yet produced a great breadth of knowledge about the functioning of organizations. Laboratory experiments suffer the risk of artificiality: the results of such experiments often do not extend to real organizations. Teams of business administration or psychology students working on decision problems may provide a great deal of information for researchers. Unfortunately, extreme

---

[14]For a volume devoted entirely to experiments in organizations, see W. M. Evan, ed., *Organizational Experiments: Laboratory and Field Research* (New York: Harper & Row, 1971).

[15]M. E. Gordon, L. A. Slade, and N. S. Schmitt, "The Science of the Sophomore Revisited: From Conjecture to Empiricism," *Academy of Management Review,* January 1986, pp. 191–207.

[16]See an account of the classic Hawthorne studies in F. J. Roethlisberger and W. J. Dickson, *Management and the Worker* (Boston: Harvard Business School, 1939). The original purpose of the studies, which were conducted at the Chicago Hawthorne Plant of Western Electric, was to investigate the relationship between productivity and physical working conditions.

caution must be used in determining whether this knowledge can be extended to a group of managers or nonmanagers making decisions under severe time constraints.[17]

Field experiments also have drawbacks. First, researchers cannot control every possible influencing factor (even if they knew them all), as they can in a laboratory. Also, here again, the presence of a researcher may make people behave differently, especially if they are aware that they are participating in an experiment. Experimentation in the behavioral sciences and, more specifically, in organizations is a complex matter.[18]

In a *true experiment,* the researcher has complete control over the experiment: the who, what, when, where, and how. A *quasi experiment,* however, is one in which the researcher lacks the degree of control over conditions that is possible in a true experiment. In the vast majority of organizational studies, complete control is impossible. Thus, quasi experiments are typically the rule when organizational behavior is studied via an experiment.

Finally, with each method of inquiry utilized by behavioral scientists, some *measurement* is usually necessary. Knowledge, to be meaningful, must often be compared with or related to something else. As a result, research questions (hypotheses) are usually stated to show how differences in magnitude of some variable are related to differences in the magnitude of some other variable.

The variables studied are measured by research instruments. Those instruments may be psychological tests, such as personality or intelligence tests; questionnaires designed to obtain attitudes or other information, such as the questionnaire shown in Figure A-1; or, in some cases, electronic devices to measure eye movement or blood pressure.

That a research instrument be both *reliable* and *valid* is very important. Reliability is the consistency of the measure. In other words, repeated measures with the same instrument should produce the same results or scores. Validity is concerned with whether the research instrument actually measures what it is supposed to be measuring.[19] A research instrument may be reliable but not valid. For example, a test designed to measure intelligence could yield consistent scores over a large number of people but not be measuring intelligence.

RESEARCH DESIGNS

Experiments to study organizational behavior utilize a number of designs. To illustrate some of the available designs, we use the example of a training program being offered to a group of first-line supervisors. Suppose that the task of the researcher is to design an experiment that permits the assessment of

---

[17]Karl E. Weick, "Laboratory Experimentation with Organizations: A Reappraisal," *Academy of Management Review,* January 1977, pp. 123–27.

[18]J. P. Campbell, "Labs, Fields, and Straw Issues," in *Generalizing from Laboratory to Field Settings,* ed. Edwin A. Locke (Lexington, Mass.: Lexington Books, 1986), pp. 269–74.

[19]James L. Price and Charles W. Mueller, *Handbook of Organizational Measurement* (Marshfield, Mass.: Pitman Publishing, 1986).

the degree to which the program influenced the performance of the supervisors. We use the following symbols in our discussion:[20]

S = The subjects, the supervisors participating in the experiment.

O = The observation and measurement devices used by the researcher (that is, ratings of supervisors' performance by superiors).

X = The experimental treatment, the manipulated variable (that is, the training program).

R = The randomization process.

One-Shot Design

If we assume that all supervisors go through the training program, the researchers will have difficulty evaluating it. This is because the researchers cannot compare the group with another group that did not undergo the training program. This design, called a *one-shot* design, is diagramed as:

$$X \ O$$

The letter X stands for the experimental treatment (that is, the training program), the letter O for the observation of performance on the job. The measure of performance could be in the form of an average score based on ratings of superiors. However, the researchers can in no way determine whether performance was influenced at all by the training program. This experimental design is rarely used because of its weaknesses.

One-Group Pretest-Posttest Design

The previous design can be improved upon by first gathering performance data on the supervisors, instituting the training program, and then remeasuring their performance. This is diagramed as:

$$O_1 \ X \ O_2$$

Thus, a pretest is given in time period 1, the program is administered, and a posttest is administered in time period 2. If $O_2 > O_1$, the differences can be attributed to the training program.

Numerous factors can confound the results obtained with this design. For example, if new equipment has been installed between O_1 and O_2, this could explain the differences in the performance scores. Thus, a *history* factor may have influenced the results. The most recurrent factors that could also influence results are listed along with their definitions in Table A–3.[21] Examination of the table indicates that results achieved in this design may be confounded by *maturation* (the supervisors may learn to do a better job between O_1 and O_2, which would increase their performance regardless of training), *testing* (the measure of performance in O_1 may make the supervisors aware that they are being evaluated, which may make them work harder and increase their

---

[20]R. H. Helmstader, *Research Concepts in Human Behavior* (New York: Appleton-Century-Crofts, 1970); D. W. Emery, *Business Research Methods* (Homewood, Ill.: Richard D. Irwin, 1980).

[21]Ibid.

TABLE A—3

Recurring Sources of Error in
Experimental Studies

Factor	Definition
1. History	Events other than the experimental treatment (X) that occurred between pretest and posttest.
2. Maturation	Changes in the subject group with the passage of time that are not associated with the experimental treatment (X).
3. Testing	Changes in the performance of the subjects because measurement of their performance makes them aware that they are part of an experiment (that is, measures often alter what is being measured).
4. Instrumentation	Changes in the measures of participants' performance that are the result of changes in the measurement instruments or the conditions under which the measuring is done (for example, wear on machinery, boredom, fatigue on the part of the observers).
5. Selection	When participants are assigned to experimental and control groups on any basis other than random assignment. Any selection method other than random assignment will result in systematic biases that will result in differences between groups that are unrelated to the effects of the experimental treatment (X).
6. Mortality	If some participants drop out of the experiment before it is completed, the experimental and control groups may not be comparable.
7. Interaction effects	Any of the above factors may interact with the experimental treatment, resulting in confounding effects on the results. For example, the types of individuals withdrawing from a study (mortality) may differ for the experimental group and the control group.

performance), and *instrumentation* (if the performance observations are made at different times of the day, the results could be influenced by fatigue). Each of these factors offers explanations for changes in performance other than the training program. Obviously, this design can be improved.

Static-Group Comparison Design

In this design, half of the supervisors would be allowed to enroll for the training. Once the enrollment reached 50 percent of the supervisors, the training program would begin. After some period of time, the group of supervisors who enrolled in the program would be compared with those who did not enroll. This design is diagrammed as:

$$X \ O$$
$$O$$

The addition of a *control group* (comparison group) has eliminated many of the error factors associated with the first two designs. However, since the supervisors were not randomly assigned to each group, the supervisors who enrolled may very possibly be the more highly motivated or more intelligent supervisors. Thus, *selection* is a major problem with this design. Because the subjects were not randomly assigned to the experimental group (undergoing training) and the control group (no training), differences may exist between the two groups that are not related to the training.

The three designs discussed thus far (one-shot, one-group pretest-posttest, static-group comparisons) have been described as "pseudo-experimental" or "quasi-experimental" designs. When true experimentation cannot be achieved, these designs (especially the last two) are preferred over no research at all or over relying on personal opinion. The next three designs can be considered true experimental designs because the researcher has complete control over the situation, determining precisely who will participate in the experiment and which subjects will or will not receive the experimental treatment.

Pretest-Posttest Control Group Design

This design, one of the simplest forms of true experimentation used in the study of human behavior, is diagramed as:

$$R \ O_1 \ X \ O_2$$
$$R \ O_1 \quad O_2$$

It is similar to the one-group pretest-posttest design except that a control group has been added and the participants have been randomly assigned to both groups, as indicated by R. Which group is to receive the training (experimental group) and which will not (control group) is also randomly determined. The two groups may be said to be equivalent at the time of the initial observations and at the time the final observations are made; they are different only in that one group has received training while the other has not. In other words, if the change from O_1 to O_2 is greater in the experimental group than in the control group, we can attribute the difference to the training program rather than selection, testing, maturation, and so forth.

The major weakness of the pretest-posttest control group design is one of *interaction* (selection and treatment), where individuals are aware that they are participating in an experiment. In other words, being observed the first time makes all of the participants work more diligently, both those who are in the training group and those who are in the control group. Hence, the participants in the training program are more receptive to training because of the pretest. This problem of interaction can be overcome by using a posttest-only control group design.

Posttest-Only Control Group Design

In this design, the participants are randomly assigned to two groups, the training is administered to one group, and the scores on the posttests are compared (performance evaluated). It is diagramed as:

$$R \ X \ O$$
$$R \quad O$$

This eliminates the problem of the previous design by not administering a pretest. However, the dependent variable (performance) is an ultimate rather than a relative measure of achievement. Also, the researcher does not have a group that was pretested and posttested without receiving the experimental treatment (training program). Such a group can provide valuable information on the effects of history, maturation, instrumentation, and so on. However, where a pretest is difficult to obtain or where its use is likely to make the participants aware that an experiment is being carried on, this approach may be much preferred to the pretest-posttest control group design.

Solomon Four-Group Design

This design, which combines the previous two designs, is the most desirable of all the designs examined here. It is diagramed as:

Group 1   R O_1 X O_2
Group 2   R O_1 O_2
Group 3   R   X O_2
Group 4   R O_2

Where gain or change in behavior is the desired dependent variable, this design should be used. While it does not control any more sources of invalid results, it permits the estimation of the extent of the effects of some of the sources of error. In our example, supervisors are randomly assigned to four groups, two of which will receive the training, one with a pretest and one without. Therefore, the researcher can examine, among other things, the effects of history (group 1 to group 2), testing (group 2 to group 4), and testing-treatment interaction (group 2 to group 3). Clearly, this design is the most complex, because it utilizes more participants, and is more costly. The added value of the extra information will have to be compared to the additional costs.[22]

QUALITATIVE RESEARCH

Instead of using experimental designs and concentrating on measurement issues, some researchers also use qualitative research procedures. The notion of applying qualitative research methods to studying behavior within organizations has been addressed in leading research outlets.[23] The term *qualitative methods* describes an array of interpretative techniques that attempt to describe and clarify the meaning of naturally occurring phenomena. It is, by design, rather open-ended and interpretative. The researcher's interpretation and description are the significant data collection acts in a qualitative study. In essence, qualitative data are defined as those (1) whose meanings are subjective, (2) that are rarely quantifiable, and (3) that are difficult to use in making quantitative comparisons.

The quantitative approach to organizational behavior research is exemplified by precise definitions, control groups, objective data collection, use of the scientific method, and replicable findings. These characteristics, presented in Table A–2, stress the importance of reliability, validity, and accurate measurement. On the other hand, qualitative research is more concerned with the meaning of what is observed. Since organizations are so complex, a range of quantitative and qualitative techniques can be used side by side to learn about individual, group, and organizational behavior.[24]

---

[22]Kerlinger, *Foundations,* pp. 300–376; Emory, *Business Research,* pp. 330–65.

[23]John Van Maanen, ed., *Qualitative Methodology* (Beverly Hills, Calif.: Sage Publications, 1983).

[24]R. L. Daft, "Learning the Craft of Organizational Research," *Academy of Management Review,* October 1983, pp. 539–46.

Qualitative methodology uses the experience and intuition of the researcher to describe the organizational processes and structures being studied. The data collected by a qualitative researcher require him or her to become very close to the situation or problem being studied. For example, a qualitative method used by anthropologists is the *ethnographic method*:[25] the researcher typically studies a phenomenon for long periods of time as a *participant-observer,* becoming part of the situation in order to feel what it is like for the people in that situation. The researcher becomes totally immersed in other people's realities.[26]

Participant observation is usually supplemented by various quantitative data collection tools such as structured interviews and self-report questionnaires. A variety of techniques are used so that the researcher can cross-check the results obtained from observation and recorded in field notes.

In training researchers in the ethnographic method, a common practice is to place them in unfamiliar settings. A researcher may sit with and listen to workers on a production line, ride around in a police car to observe police officers, or do cleanup work in a surgical operating room. The training is designed to improve the researcher's ability to record, categorize, and code what is being observed.

An example of qualitative research involvement is presented in John Van Maanen's participant-observer study of a big-city police department. He went through police academy training and then accompanied police officers on their daily rounds; he functioned with police officers in daily encounters. Thus, he was able to provide vivid descriptions of police work.[27]

Other qualitative techniques include content analysis (e.g., the researcher's interpretation of field notes), informal interviewing, archival data surveys and historical analysis, and the use of unobtrusive measures (e.g., data whose collection is not influenced by a researcher's presence). An example of the last would be the wear and tear on a couch in a cardiologist's office. As reported in the discussion of the Type A behavior pattern in Chapter 7, the wear and tear was on the edges of the couch, which suggested anxiety and hyperactive behavior. Qualitative research appears to rely more on multiple sources of data than on any one source. The current research literature suggests the following characteristics associated with qualitative research:[28]

1. *Analytical induction.* Qualitative research begins with the close-up, first-hand inspection of organizational life.

2. *Proximity.* Researchers desire to witness firsthand what is being studied. If the application of rewards is being studied, the researcher would want to observe episodes of reward distribution.

3. *Ordinary behavior.* The topics of research interest should be ordinary, normal, routine behaviors.

---

[25]A. F. C. Wallace, "Paradigmatic Processes in Cultural Change," *American Anthropologist,* 1972, pp. 467–78.

[26]Catherine Marshall and Gretchen B. Rossman, *Designing Qualitative Research* (Newbury Park, Calif.: Sage, 1989), pp. 79–83.

[27]John Van Maanen, J. M. Dobbs, Jr., and R. R. Faulkner, *Varieties of Qualitative Research* (Beverly Hills, Calif.: Sage Publications, 1982).

[28]Van Maanen, *Qualitative Methodology,* pp. 255–56.

4. *Descriptive emphasis.* Qualitative research seeks descriptions for what is occurring in any given place and time. The aim is to disclose and reveal, not merely to order data and to predict.

5. *Shrinking variance.* Qualitative research is geared toward the explanation of similarity and coherence. There is a greater emphasis on commonality and on things shared in organizational settings than on things not shared.

6. *Consumer enlightenment.* The consumer of qualitative research could be a manager. A major objective is to enlighten without causing confusion. Providing coherent and logically persuasive commentary accomplishes this.

Researchers and managers do not have to choose either quantitative or qualitative research data and interpretation. Convincing and relevant arguments exist for using more than one method of research when studying organizational behavior. Quantitative and qualitative research methods and procedures have much to offer practicing managers. Blending and integrating quantitative and qualitative research are what researchers and managers must do in the years ahead to better understand, cope with, and modify organizational behavior.

Comprehensive Cases

Dick Spencer

Hovey and Beard Company

Provident National Bank
Trust Division

CASE METHOD: HOW TO ANALYZE THE CASES

The "real world" cases in the book place the student in an organization as a manager, leader, or nonmanager who must make decisions. A *case* is "a story of organizational issues which actually have been faced by people, together with facts, opinions, and prejudices on which decisions must be made. A key feature of a case is that decisions that require action must be made."[1]

With the *case method,* the process of arriving at an answer is more important than the answer itself. By working through cases, students develop an understanding of the process of reaching decisions and can support and communicate these decisions to others. Instead of sitting back and reacting to the comments made by an instructor, students make decisions, typically with incomplete information and in a limited time period—the usual situation faced by most managers.

No ideal solutions exist for any of the cases in this book. Searching for the perfect answer is futile. Instead, students should learn to think through the issues, problems, facts, and other information presented in the cases. *Critical* thinking is required to make better decisions; *thorough* thinking is needed so that the decisions reached can be intelligently communicated in classroom discussions. Such discussions about the cases should clearly illustrate the thinking processes used by students.

The preparation for classroom discussion of the cases in this book could follow a set pattern. We suggest that you:

1. *Read* the case rather quickly to get a feel for what is involved.
2. *Reread* the case and sort out the assumptions, hunches, and facts. Since all of the cases are incomplete, students should make plausible assumptions about the situation. List those assumptions and be able to support their plausibility. The assumptions enable you to "fill in the blanks" in the case. In organizations, decisions are generally made with incomplete information and some uncertainty.
3. *Identify* the major *problems* and subproblems that must be considered in the case.
4. *List* the problems in the order of their importance or priority. That is, show which problems must be solved first.
5. *Develop* a list of alternative courses of action that minimize or eliminate the problems. If possible, have at least two fully developed alternatives that are feasible solutions.
6. In developing alternative courses of action, *outline* the constraints (e.g., resources, historical precedent, competition, skill limitations, attitudes) that limit success.
7. *Select* the best course of action for the problems identified in step 3. Show how the course of action would work, and be able to discuss why it would be the most successful alternative for solving the problems.

---

[1]Kenneth L. Bernhardt and Thomas C. Kinnear, *Cases in Marketing Management* (Plano, Tex.: Business Publications, 1978), p. 3.

DICK SPENCER

After the usual banter when old friends meet for cocktails, the conversation between a couple of university professors and Dick Spencer, a former student who was now a successful businessman, turned to Spencer's life as a vice president of a large manufacturing firm.

"I've made a lot of mistakes, most of which I could live with, but this one series of incidents was so frustrating that I could have cried at the time," Dick said in response to a question. "I really have to laugh at how ridiculous it is now; but at the time, I blew my cork."

Spencer was plant manager of Modrow Company, a Canadian branch of the Tri-American Corporation. Tri-American was a major producer of primary aluminum, with integrated operations ranging from the mining of bauxite through the processing to fabrication of aluminum into a variety of products. The company also made and sold refractories and industrial chemicals. The parent company had wholly owned subsidiaries in five U.S. locations and affiliates in 15 countries.

Tri-American mined bauxite in Jamaica and shipped the raw material by commercial vessels to two plants in Louisiana, where it was processed into alumina. The alumina was then shipped to reduction plants in three locations for conversion into primary aluminum. Most of the primary aluminum was then moved to the company's fabricating plants for further processing. Fabricated aluminum items included sheet, flat, coil, and corrugated products; siding; and roofing.

Tri-American employed approximately 22,000 employees in the total organization. The company was governed by a board of directors, which included the chairman, the vice chairman, the president, and 12 vice presidents. However, each of the subsidiaries and branches functioned as an independent unit. The board set general policy, which was then interpreted and applied by the various plant managers. In a sense, the various plants competed with one another as though they were independent companies. This decentralization in organizational structure increased the freedom and authority of the plant managers but increased the pressure for profitability.

The Modrow branch was located in a border town in Canada. The total work force in Modrow was 1,000. This Canadian subsidiary was primarily a fabricating unit. Its main products were foil and building products such as roofing and siding. Aluminum products were gaining in importance in architectural plans, and increased sales were predicted for this branch. Its location and its stable work force were the most important advantages it possessed.

In anticipation of estimated increases in sales, Modrow completed a modernization and expansion project. At the same time, its research and art departments combined talents in developing a series of 12 new patterns of siding that were being introduced to the market. Modernization and pattern

Source: This case was developed and prepared by Dr. Margaret Fenn, Graduate School of Business Administration, University of Washington. Reprinted by permission.

development had been costly undertakings, but the expected return on investment made the project feasible. However, the plant manager, who was a Tri-American vice president, had instituted a campaign to cut expenses wherever possible. In his introductory notice of the campaign, he emphasized that cost reduction would be the personal aim of every employee at Modrow.

Salesman

The plant manager of Modrow, Dick Spencer, was an American who had been transferred to this Canadian branch two years previously, after the start of the modernization plan. Spencer has been with the Tri-American Company for 14 years, and his progress within the organization was considered spectacular by those who knew him well. Spencer had received a master's degree in business administration from a well-known university at the age of 22. Upon graduation, he had accepted a job as a salesman for Tri-American. During his first year as a salesman, he succeeded in landing a single, large contract that put him near the top of the sales volume leaders. In discussing his phenomenal increase in sales volume, several of his fellow salesmen concluded that his looks, charm, and ability on the golf course had contributed as much to his success as his knowledge of the business or his ability to sell the products.

During the second year of his sales career, Spencer continued to set a fast pace. Although his record set difficult goals for the other salesmen, he was considered a "regular guy" by them, and both he and they seemed to enjoy the few occasions when they socialized. However, by the end of the second year of constant traveling and selling, Spencer began to experience some doubt about his future.

His constant involvement in business matters disrupted his marital life, and his wife divorced him during his second year with Tri-American. Spencer resented her action at first, but he gradually seemed to recognize that his career at present depended on his freedom to travel unencumbered. During that second year, he ranged far and wide in his sales territory and successfully closed several large contracts. None of them was as large as his first year's major sale, but in total volume he was again one of the top salesmen for the year. Spencer's name became well known in the corporate headquarters, and he was spoken of as "the boy to watch."

Spencer had met the president of Tri-American at a company conference during his first year as a salesman. After three days of golfing and socializing, they developed a relaxed camaraderie that was considered unusual by those who observed the developing friendship. Although their contacts were infrequent after the conference, their easy relationship seemed to blossom the few times that they did meet. Spencer's friends kidded him about his ability to make use of his new friendship to promote himself in the company, but Spencer brushed aside their gibes and insisted that he'd make it on his own abilities, not on someone's coattail.

By the time he was 25, Spencer began to suspect that he did not want to look forward to a life as a salesman for the rest of his career. He talked about his unrest with his friends, and they suggested that he groom himself for sales manager. "You won't make the kind of money you're making from commissions," he was told, "but you will have a foot in the door from an administrative standpoint, and you won't have to travel quite as much as you do now." Spencer took their suggestions lightly and continued to sell the product, but he was aware that he felt dissatisfied and he did not seem to get the satisfaction out of his job that he had once enjoyed.

By the end of his third year with the company, Spencer was convinced that he wanted a change in direction. As usual, he and the president spent quite a bit of time on the golf course during the annual company sales conference. After their match one day, the president kidded Spencer about his game. The conversation drifted back to business, and the president, who seemed to be in a jovial mood, started to kid Spencer about his sales ability. In a joking way, he implied that anyone could sell products as good as Tri-American's, but that it took real "guts and know-how" to make the products. The conversation drifted to other things, but this remark stuck with Spencer.

Some time later, Spencer approached the president formally with a request for a transfer out of the sales division. The president was surprised and hesitant about this change in career direction for Spencer. He recognized Spencer's superior sales ability, but he was unsure that Spencer was willing or able to assume responsibilities in any other division of the organization. Spencer sensed the hesitancy but continued to push his request. He later remarked that the initial hesitancy of the president seemed to have convinced him that he needed an opportunity to prove himself in a field other than sales.

Troubleshooter

Spencer was finally transferred back to the home office of the organization and indoctrinated into production and administrative roles in the company as a special assistant to the senior vice president of production. As a special assistant, Spencer was assigned several troubleshooting jobs. He acquitted himself well in this role, but in the process he succeeded in gaining a reputation as a ruthless headhunter among the branches where he had performed a series of amputations. His reputation as an amiable, genial, easygoing guy from the sales department was the antithesis of the reputation of a cold, calculated headhunter that he earned in his troubleshooting role. The vice president, who was Spencer's boss, was aware of the reputation that Spencer had earned but was pleased with the results that were obtained. The faltering departments that Spencer had worked in seemed to bloom with new life and energy after Spencer's recommended amputations. As a result, the vice president began to sing Spencer's praises, and the president began to accept Spencer in his new role in the company.

Overseas Manager

About three years after Spencer's switch from sales, he was given an assignment as assistant plant manager of an English branch of the company. Spencer, who had remarried, moved his wife and family to London, and they attempted to adapt to their new routine. The plant manager was English, as were most of the other employees. Spencer and his family were accepted, with reservations, into the community life as well as into the plant life. The difference between British and American philosophy and performance within the plant was marked for Spencer, who was imbued with modern managerial concepts and methods. Spencer's directives from headquarters were to update and upgrade performance in this branch. However, his power and authority were less than those of his superior, so he constantly found himself in the position of having to soft-pedal or withhold suggestions that he would have liked to make or innovations that he would have liked to introduce. After a frustrating year and a half, Spencer was suddenly made plant manager of an old British company that had just been purchased by Tri-American. He left his first English assignment with mixed feelings and moved from London to Birmingham.

As the new plant manager, Spencer operated much as he had in his troubleshooting job for the first couple of years of his change from sales to administration. Training and reeducation programs were instituted for all of the supervisors and managers who survived the initial purge. Methods were studied and simplified or redesigned whenever possible, and new attention was directed toward production that better met the needs of the sales organization. A strong controller helped to straighten out the profit picture through stringent cost control; by the end of the third year, the company showed a small profit for the first time in many years. Because he felt that this battle was won, Spencer requested a transfer back to the United States. This request was partially granted when nine months later he was awarded a junior vice president title and was made manager of a subsidiary Canadian plant, Modrow.

Modrow Manager

Prior to Spencer's appointment as plant manager at Modrow, extensive plans for plant expansion and improvement had been approved and started. Although Spencer had not been in on the original discussions and plans, he inherited all of the problems that accompany large-scale changes in any organization. Construction was slower than had been planned originally; equipment arrived before the building was finished; employees were upset about the extent of change expected in their work routines with the installation of additional machinery; and in general, morale was at a low ebb.

Various versions of Spencer's former activities had preceded him, and on his arrival he was viewed with dubious eyes. The first few months after his arrival were spent in a frenzy of catching up. This entailed attending constant conferences and meetings, reading volumes of past reports, becoming acquainted with the civic leaders of the area, and handling a plethora of dispatches to and from the home office. Costs continued to climb unabated.

By the end of Spencer's first year at Modrow, the building program had been completed, although behind schedule, the new equipment had been installed, and some revamping of cost procedures had been incorporated. The financial picture at this time showed a substantial loss, but since it had been budgeted as a loss, this was not surprising. The managers of the various divisions had worked closely with their supervisors and accountants in planning the budget for the following year, and Spencer began to emphasize his personal interest in cost reduction.

As he worked through his first year as plant manager, Spencer developed the habit of strolling around the organization. He was apt to leave his office and appear wherever there was activity concerned with Modrow—on the plant floor, in the design offices, at the desk of a purchasing agent or accountant, or in the plant cafeteria rather than the executive dining room. During his strolls, he looked, listened, and became acquainted. If he observed activities that he wanted to talk about or heard remarks that gave him clues to future action, he did not reveal this at the time. Rather, he had a nod, a wave, or a smile for the people near him but a mental note to talk to his supervisors, managers, and floor leaders in the future. At first, his presence disturbed those who noted him coming and going; but after several exposures to him without any noticeable effect, the workers came to accept his presence and continue their usual activities. The supervisors, managers, and floor leaders, however, felt less comfortable when they saw him in the area.

Their feelings were aptly expressed by the manager of the siding department one day when he was talking to one of his floor bosses: "I wish to hell he'd stay up in the front office where he belongs. Whoever heard of a plant manager who had time to wander around the plant all the time? Why doesn't he tend to his paperwork and let us tend to our business?"

"Don't let him get you down," joked the other man. "Nothing ever comes of his visits. Maybe he's just lonesome and looking for a friend. You know how these Americans are."

"Well, you may feel that nothing ever comes of his visits, but I don't. I've been called into his office three separate times within the last two months. The heat must really be on from the head office. You know these conferences we have every month where he reviews our financial progress, our building progress, our design progress, and so forth? Well, we're not really progressing as fast as we should be. If you ask me, we're in for continuing trouble."

In recalling his first year at Modrow, Spencer said that he had constantly felt pressured and badgered. He had always sensed that the Canadians he worked with resented his presence since he was brought in over the heads of the operating staff. At the same time that he had felt this subtle resistance from his Canadian work force, he had believed that the president and his friends in the home office were constantly on the alert, waiting for him to prove himself or fall flat on his face. Because of the constant pressures and demands of the work, he had literally dumped his family into a new community and had withdrawn into the plant. In the process, he had built up a wall of resistance toward the demands of his wife and children, who in turn had felt that he was abandoning them.

During the course of the conversation with his university friends, Spencer began to recall a series of incidents that had probably resulted from the conflicting pressures. When describing some of these incidents, he continued to emphasize the fact that his attempt to be relaxed and casual had backfired. Laughingly, Spencer said, "As you know, both human relations and accounting were my weakest subjects during the master's program, and yet they are the two fields I felt I needed most at Modrow at this time." He described some of the cost procedures that he would have liked to incorporate. However, without the support and knowledge furnished by his former controller, he had busied himself with details that were unnecessary. One day, as he described it, he had overheard a conversation between two of the accounting staff members with whom he had been working very closely. One of them commented to the other, "For a guy who's a vice president, he sure spends a lot of time breathing down our necks. Why doesn't he simply tell us the kind of systems he would like to try, and let us do the experimenting and work out the budget?" Without commenting on the conversation he had overheard, Spencer then described himself as attempting to spend less time and be less directive in the accounting department.

Another incident he described that apparently had had real meaning for him was one in which he had called a staff conference with his top-level managers. They had been going "hammer and tongs" for better than an hour in his private office and in the process of the heated conversation had loosened ties, taken off coats, and really rolled up their sleeves. Spencer himself had slipped out of his shoes. In the midst of this, his secretary had reminded him of an appointment with public officials. Spencer had rapidly finished up his conference with his managers, straightened his tie, donned his coat, and wandered out into the main office in his stocking feet.

Spencer fully described several occasions when he had disappointed, frustrated, or confused his wife and family by forgetting birthdays, appointments, dinner engagements, and so on. He seemed to be describing a pattern of behavior that had resulted from continuing pressure and frustration. He was setting the scene to describe his baffling and humiliating position in the siding department. In looking back and recalling his activities during this first year, Spencer commented on the fact that his frequent wanderings throughout the plant had resulted in a nodding acquaintance with the workers but had probably also resulted in floor leaders and supervisors spending more time in getting ready for his visits and in reading meaning into them afterward than in attending to their specific duties. His attempts to know in detail the accounting procedures being used had required long hours of concentration and detailed conversations with the accounting staff that had been time consuming and very frustrating for him, as well as for them. His lack of attention to his family life had resulted in continued pressure from both wife and family.

The Siding Department Incident

Siding was the product that had been budgeted as a large profit item of Modrow. Aluminum siding was gaining in popularity among both architects and builders because of its possibilities in both decorative and practical uses. Panel sheets of siding were shipped in standard sizes on order; large sheets of the coated siding were cut to specifications in the trim department, packed, and shipped. The trim shop was located near the loading platforms, and Spencer often cut through the trim shop on his wanderings through the plant. On one of his frequent trips through the area, he suddenly became aware of the fact that several workers responsible for the disposal function were spending countless hours at high-speed saws cutting scraps into specified lengths to fit into scrap barrels. The narrow bands of scrap that resulted from the trim process varied in length from 7 to 27 feet and had to be reduced in size to fit into the disposal barrels. Spencer, in his concentration on cost reduction, picked up one of the thin strips, bent it several times, and fitted it into the barrel. He tried this with another piece, and it bent very easily. After assuring himself that bending was possible, he walked over to a worker at the saw and asked why he was using the saw when material could easily be bent and fitted into the barrels, resulting in a saving of time and equipment. The worker's response was, "We've never done it that way, sir. We've always cut it."

Following his plan of not commenting or discussing matters on the floor but distressed by the reply, Spencer returned to his office and asked the manager of the siding department if he could speak to the boss of the scrap division. The manager said, "Of course. I'll send him up to you in just a minute."

After a short time, the floor boss, very agitated at being called to the plant manager's office, appeared. Spencer began questioning him about the scrap disposal process and received the standard answer: "We've always done it that way." Spencer then proceeded to review cost-cutting objectives. He talked about the pliability of the strips of scrap. He called for a few pieces of scrap to demonstrate the ease with which it could be bent and ended what he thought was a satisfactory conversation by requesting the floor boss to order heavy-duty gloves for his workers and use the bending process for a trial period of two weeks to check the cost saving possible.

The floor boss listened throughout most of this hour's conference, offered several reasons why it wouldn't work, raised some questions about the record-keeping process for cost purposes, and finally left the office with the forced agreement to try the suggested new method of bending, rather than cutting, for disposal. Although Spencer was immersed in many other problems, his request was forcibly brought home to him one day as he cut through the scrap area. The workers were using power saws to cut scraps. He called the manager of the siding department and questioned him about the process. The manager explained that each floor leader was responsible for his own processes; since Spencer had already talked to that man, perhaps he had better talk to him again. When the floor leader arrived, Spencer began to question him. He received a series of excuses and some explanations of the kinds of problems that they were meeting by attempting to bend the scrap material. "I don't care what the problems are," Spencer nearly shouted. "When I request a cost-reduction program instituted, I want to see it carried through."

Spencer was furious. When the floor boss left, he phoned the maintenance department and ordered the removal of the power saws from the scrap area immediately. A short time later, the boss of the scrap department knocked on Spencer's door to report his astonishment at having maintenance men step into his area and physically remove the saws. Spencer reminded the man of his unavailing request for a trial at cost reduction and ended the conversation by saying that the power saws were gone and would not be returned and that they had damned well better learn to get along without them. After a stormy exit by the floor boss, Spencer congratulated himself on having solved a problem and turned his attention to other matters.

A few days later, Spencer had cut through the trim department and literally stopped to stare. As he described it, he had been completely nonplussed to discover gloved workmen using hand shears to cut each piece of scrap.

HOVEY AND BEARD COMPANY

Part 1

The Hovey and Beard Company manufactured wooden toys of various kinds: wooden animals, pull toys, and the like. One part of the process involved spraying paint on the partially assembled toys.

The toys were cut, sanded, and partially assembled in the wood room. Then they were dipped into shellac, following which they were painted. The toys were predominantly two-colored; a few were made in more than two colors. Each color required an additional trip through the paint room.

For years, production of these toys had been entirely handwork. However, to meet tremendously increased demand, the painting operation had recently been reengineered so that the eight workers who did the painting sat in a line by an endless chain of hooks. These hooks were in continuous motion, past the line of workers and into a long horizontal oven. Each worker sat at a separate painting booth so designed to carry away fumes and to backstop excess paint. Each worker would take a toy from the tray, position it in a jig inside the painting cubicle, spray on the color according to a pattern, then release the toy and hang it on the hook passing by. The rate at which the hooks moved had been calculated by the engineers so that each worker, when fully trained, would be able to hang a painted toy on each hook before it passed beyond her reach. (All of the workers were women.)

The employees working in the paint room were on a group bonus plan. Since the operation was new to them, they were receiving a learning bonus that decreased by regular amounts each month. The learning bonus was scheduled to vanish in six months, by which time it was expected that they would be on their own—that is, able to meet the standard and to earn a group bonus when they exceeded it.

Part 2

By the second month of the training period, trouble developed. The employees learned more slowly than had been anticipated, and it began to look as though their production would stabilize far below projected figures. Many of the hooks were going by empty. The workers complained that the hooks were going by too fast and that the time study man had set the rates too high. A few people quit and had to be replaced with new workers, which further aggravated the learning problem. The team spirit that the management had expected to develop automatically through the group bonus was not in evidence except as an expression of what the engineers called "resistance." One worker, whom the group regarded as its leader (and the management regarded as the ringleader), was outspoken in making the various complaints of the group to the supervisor: the job was a messy one, the hooks moved too fast,

Source: From W. F. Whyte, *Money and Motivation* (New York: Harper & Row, 1955), pp. 90–94. Used with permission.

the incentive pay was not being correctly calculated, and it was too hot working so close to the drying oven.

Part 3

A consultant brought into this picture worked entirely with and through the supervisor. After many conversations with the consultant, the supervisor felt that the first step should be to get the workers together for a general discussion of the working conditions. He took this step with some hesitation, but he took it on his own volition.

The first meeting, held immediately after the shift was over at 4 o'clock in the afternoon, was attended by all eight workers. They voiced the same complaints again: the hooks went by too fast; the job was too dirty; the room was hot and poorly ventilated. For some reason, it was this last item that they complained of most. The supervisor promised to discuss the problem of ventilation and temperature with the engineers, and he scheduled a second meeting to report back to the employees. In the next few days, the supervisor had several talks with the engineers. They and the superintendent felt that this was really a trumped-up complaint and that the expense of any effective corrective measure would be prohibitively high.

The supervisor came to the second meeting with some apprehension. The workers, however, did not seem to be much put out, perhaps because they had a proposal of their own to make. They felt that if several large fans were set up to circulate the air around their feet, they would be much more comfortable. After some discussion, the supervisor agreed that the idea might be tried out. The supervisor and the consultant discussed the question of the fans with the superintendent, and three large, propeller-type fans were purchased.

Part 4

The fans were brought in. The workers were jubilant. For several days, the fans were moved about in various positions until they were placed to the satisfaction of the group. The employees seemed completely satisfied with the results, and relations between them and the supervisor improved visibly.

The supervisor, after this encouraging episode, decided that further meetings might also be profitable. He asked the workers whether they would like to meet and discuss other aspects of the work situation. They were eager to do this. The meeting was held, and the discussion quickly centered on the speed of the hooks. The employees maintained that the time study man had set them at an unreasonably fast speed and that they would never be able to reach the goal of filling enough of them to make a bonus.

The turning point of the discussion came when the group's leader frankly explained that the point wasn't that they couldn't work fast enough to keep up with the hooks but that they couldn't work at that pace all day long. The supervisor explored the point. The workers were unanimous in their opinion that they could keep up with the belt for short periods if they wanted to. But they didn't want to because if they showed they could do this for short periods, they would be expected to do it all day long. The meeting ended with an unprecedented request: "Let us adjust the speed of the belt faster or slower depending on how we feel." The supervisor agreed to discuss this with the superintendent and the engineers.

The reaction of the engineers to the suggestion was negative. However, after several meetings, it was granted that there was some latitude within which variations in the speed of the hooks would not affect the finished product. After considerable argument with the engineers, it was agreed to try out the workers' ideas.

With misgivings, the supervisor had a control with a dial marked "low, medium, fast" installed at the booth of the group leader; she could now adjust the speed of the belt anywhere between the lower and upper limits that the engineers had set.

Part 5

The workers were delighted, and they spent many lunch hours deciding how the speed of the belt should be varied from hour to hour throughout the day. Within a week, the pattern had settled down to one in which the first half hour of the shift was run on what the employees called a medium speed (a dial setting slightly above the point marked "medium"). The next 2½ hours were run at high speed; the half hour before lunch and the half hour after lunch were run at low speed. The rest of the afternoon was run at high speed with the exception of the last 45 minutes of the shift, which was run at medium.

In view of the workers' reports of satisfaction and ease in their work, it is interesting to note that the constant speed at which the engineers had originally set the belt was slightly below medium on the dial of the control that had been given the employees. The average speed at which they were running the belt was on the high side of the dial. Few, if any, empty hooks entered the oven, and inspection showed no increase of rejects from the paint room.

Production increased, and within three weeks (some two months before the scheduled ending of the learning bonus) the workers were operating at 30 to 50 percent above the level that had been expected under the original arrangement. Naturally, their earnings were correspondingly higher than anticipated. They were collecting their base pay, a considerable piece-rate bonus, and the learning bonus, which, it will be remembered, had been set to decrease with time and not as a function of current productivity. They were earning more now than many skilled workers in other parts of the plant.

Part 6

Management was besieged by demands that this inequity be taken care of. With growing irritation between superintendent and supervisor, engineers and supervisor, superintendent and engineers, the situation came to a head when the superintendent revoked the learning bonus and returned the painting operation to its original status: the hooks moved again at their constant, time-studied designated speed; production dropped again; and within a month, all but two of the eight original workers had quit. The supervisor himself stayed on for several months but, feeling aggrieved, then left for another job.

PROVIDENT NATIONAL BANK TRUST DIVISION

The December 31, 1986, issue of *Trust Division Newsletter,* the monthly news-letter for employees of Provident National Bank Trust Division, contained the following message from Tom Stewart, executive vice president and Trust Division manager:

> As 1986 draws to a close, I would like to thank all of you for the Trust Division's most outstanding year. Our results in 1986 and our future are, in a very important sense, dependent upon those who have preceded us. This year we will celebrate the holiday season without the leadership of Dick Boylan, Ted Mygatt, John Karnick and others who had so much influence over Provident's Trust Division. Their wisdom and guidance will be sorely missed. However, with such a talented and dedicated group of employees, I am confident that, with continued effort, team-work, and a focus on results, we will achieve even more in 1987 as we continue to execute our strategic plan.

With that message, Tom Stewart captured the spirit and significance of a year that marked the end of one era and the beginning of a new one in the life of the Trust Division. Every one of the 400 Trust Division employees will remember 1986 as the year of leadership change, reorganization, and the strategic plan. The Trust Division's record of accomplishments impressed the financial services industry as innovative and groundbreaking. As Tom Stewart noted in his message, the strategic plan was a key to augmenting that record.

As 1986 came to a close, the Trust Division Fact Sheet noted that it was then the fifth largest trust department in the country in terms of assets managed by the holding company, PNC Financial Corporation. The division managed more than $30 billion in assets and generated revenues in excess of $70 million, establishing it as the largest trust operation in Philadelphia. It was the first to advise a mutual fund, one of the first to automatically sweep cash balances in trust accounts and package the service into a cash management account, one of the few banks to sell its investment research nationally and internationally, and the only one to deliver it electronically. Through the offices of direct and indirect subsidiaries, it manages the assets of mutual funds, acts as transfer agent for mutual funds, provides clearing and subcustodial services for money market funds, and manages the assets of employee benefit plans. PNC Financial Corporation's report to the stock-holders for the first nine months of 1986 noted that trust income was 21 percent higher than during the same period of 1985. This record of growth, innovation, and profitability was accomplished through the leadership of J. Richard Boylan, who headed the division from 1973 until his death on March 30, 1986.

Source: Adapted from "Provident National Bank Trust Division (A)" and "Provident National Bank Trust Division (B)," copyright © James L. Gibson and Bank Marketing Association. This case study is intended to provide a focus for discussion and to illustrate neither correct nor incorrect management policies, strategies, and tactics.

The Boylan Strategy

J. Richard "Dick" Boylan joined Provident in 1954, after a four-year stint with a securities firm. His first assignment at Provident was in the Investment Advisory Department, from which he moved rapidly through the ranks: assistant trust department officer (1956), assistant vice president (1963), senior vice president (1968), and vice chairman of the bank (1981). Throughout his career, Dick Boylan attracted attention by redefining what was thought possible in the trust business: where others saw obstacles, he saw possibilities. He was inventive and creative, capable of inspiring incredible loyalty and effort from those around him. However much of his success was due to personal traits, he was also a skilled strategist who had a plan for the development of the Trust Division.

Provident's trust strategy evolved from top management's decision to develop Provident's investment capabilities. When the bank looked at its trust business in the early 1960s, it found itself in fourth place in the Philadelphia market in terms of trust assets. Market surveys indicated that consumers did not differentiate among trust companies in terms of investment ability. The choice of a trust company was based on relationships and price. Provident decided that its best course of action was to spend heavily on people to improve its investment capabilities. By causing consumers to become more conscious of the investment performance of different banks, Provident hoped to differentiate its product in the regional market.

In 1972, Dick Boylan learned that he had cancer. He shared this information only with his immediate family and continued his unrelenting pace at Provident. By 1984, the issue of executive succession had become critical due to the recurrence of Boylan's illness. In that year, Thomas S. Stewart was named deputy division manager of Provident's Trust Division. From this position, Tom Stewart was expected to prepare for eventual succession to division manager.

The Stewart Strategy

Tom Stewart's career at Provident began in 1964, when he joined Provident National Bank as a management trainee. In 1965, he took a position in the Trust Division as personal trust portfolio manager, which he held until 1971. He managed employee benefit and endowment portfolios from 1971 to 1975, at which time he was named manager of the Personal Trust Investment Department. He managed this department until 1978, when he was elevated to manager of the Personal Services Group. Three years later, in 1981, Stewart was named director of economic and investment research, where he remained until his appointment as deputy division manager. In the course of Stewart's career, he has been associated with the two principal components of the Trust Division—investment and personal trust—as well as with numerous task groups to convert ideas into products and services. Thus, it came as no surprise to anyone when Tom Stewart was elected executive vice president and named manager of the Trust Division effective July 1, 1986.

Stewart expressed his philosophy of what the trust business could become in articles published in the journal *Estates and Trusts*. He argues that trust departments should be leading the banking industry's efforts to implement relationship banking. Trust departments, he believes, have always been relationship oriented, by the very nature of their traditional activities. But despite being the resident practitioners of relationship banking, trust personnel must, according to Stewart, make fundamental changes if they are to compete in the financial services market.

The first required change is to develop customer- and market-driven attitudes to displace product-driven attitudes. Too many trust departments express the attitude: "Here is our investment style, take it or leave it." That attitude must be replaced with one that begins with consultation with the customer to determine the customer's financial requirements as well as the customer's beliefs about money and wealth. This initial consultation provides the groundwork for continuing consultation as the customer moves through the financial life cycle. At each stage of the cycle, the consultative relationship will identify financial needs appropriate to that point in the cycle and plans for the next stage.

The consultative relationship with customers takes on greater significance in the contemporary financial market because the traditional trust customers, large wealthy families with established trusts for future generations, no longer exist in large numbers. To survive, trust departments must continue to serve families and individuals with established wealth, but they must begin to focus on those who are in the wealth accumulation phase of their financial life cycles.

Provident's Trust Division managers and employees generally understand Tom Stewart's ideas. They expected that when he assumed the job of division manager he would begin to implement the changes necessary to make his ideas the guiding principles of Provident's Trust Division.

Initiating the Strategic and Organizational Changes

When 1985 rolled around, Tom Stewart had been in his new job for less than a year. It was already generally understood that he would be the next division manager. Despite his experience in the two most important line units in the division, Tom recognized that he had to tap the ideas of the entire management cadre to maintain the momentum of the Boylan years. During the first six months of 1985, he conducted a series of one-on-one meetings with all the group and major department managers. Exhibit 1 shows the organization chart at that time. These meetings stimulated discussions about where the division was headed in the coming years and what was to be expected of each group and department. These discussions were held against the backdrop of excellent performance in all areas of trust activities.

On August 20, 1985, Stewart reviewed the division's six-month performance for all officers of the Trust Division. According to Stewart, revenues for the first six months of 1985 were up 13 percent, while expenses were down slightly by .2 percent. Assets managed by the division were $25.9 billion, compared to $23.7 billion at the end of 1984. Moreover, all but one of the common trust funds exceeded the Dow Jones Industrial Average. Generally, all the performance news was good news. Little surprise then that the advice that Stewart got from some quarters was "don't fix what isn't broken."

EXHIBIT 1

Provident National Bank Trust Division: Organization Chart

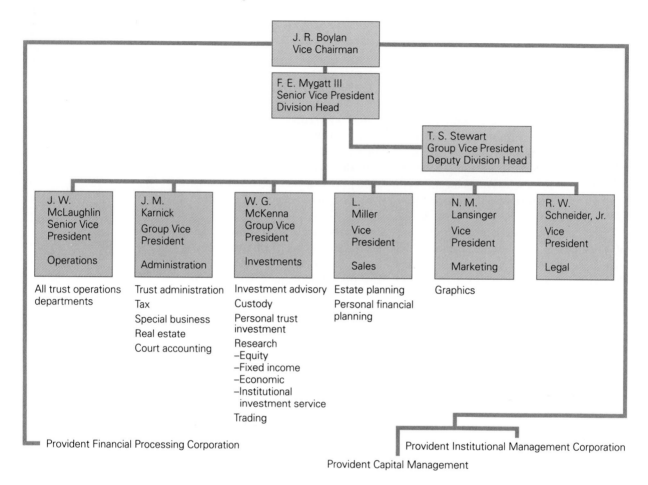

Forces for change.   The impetus for considering long-run, strategic issues was reinforced by the actions of senior officers of PNC Financial Corporation, who had undertaken a comprehensive review of the holding company's strategic plan. In a September 20, 1985, memo to the 11 group managers of the division, Stewart stated:

> The growing complexity of the financial services environment requires that we pay more attention to the strategic issues which define the character of our business. We must ask the key strategic questions: What are the nature and direction of the organization? What is its basic purpose? And we must develop answers to these questions. Only then, after we know where we're headed, can we determine how to get there. Our meeting next Wednesday is designed to deal with strategic issues. It is not intended to result in a series of action plans. I am hopeful that a statement of mission can be developed and that we will leave the meeting with a better sense of direction. Then we can begin to determine our key objectives and what will be required in terms of resources and effort to achieve those goals.

The *Trust Division Newsletter* reported the meeting of the group managers. The item noted that Tom Stewart had led a full day's discussion of the mission and direction of the division. It also reported that Tom Whitford would serve as coordinator of the planning process. Whitford had joined the Trust Division on September 3, 1985, as vice president in a position of planning and product development. Tom had been with Provident's Community Banking Division for two years, in product management and related activities. Prior to joining Provident, he had worked for Booz Allen & Hamilton as a planning consultant. With these announcements, the strategic planning process was initiated.

The first meeting of the strategic planning group resulted in several important conclusions. One of the most important conclusions was that the Trust Division's future driving force will be market needs. The market needs driving force focuses attention on taking advantage of market opportunities by providing product and services to meet current and emerging customer needs. The planning group believed that this driving force differed significantly from the existing products-offered driving force, although not so different from the driving force of some of the division's nontraditional trust businesses.

The transition from product-driven to market-driven strategy would be most important in the personal trust business, due to increasingly complex and competitive financial services and significant changes in customer needs. In particular, the redirection of the driving force would require greater efforts on market research to determine customer needs and then on developing, delivering, and servicing products to meet those needs.

Tom Stewart indicated to the planning group that the next several months would be spent in determining the current and future implications of market needs as a driving force on market scope, product scope, organizational structure, system and productions requirements, sales/distribution, and re-source requirements/allocations. To determine these implications, Stewart directed the group to focus on what the financial services industry will be like in the 1990s. Defining and clarifying a vision for the 1990s will enable Provident Trust to develop a clear mission statement that will be more than an extrapolation of current product and service demand. Through the application of creativity and innovation, Stewart believed that the Trust Division could develop its own strategic direction that would be specific enough to guide current activities, yet flexible enough to permit adjustment to changing market needs.

Tom Whitford would meet with each member of the planning group to discuss his/her "vision for the 90s." Since the planning group consisted of group managers and major department managers, the focus of these discussions would be the contributions of existing organizational units to the achievement of the eight objectives. After these one-on-one meetings, Whitford would consolidate the information in a working draft, after which the planning group would reconvene to review the document and the preliminary tactics. A target date for the completion of these initial planning tasks was November 21, 1985.

The November 21 meeting introduced some themes that were to carry through the remainder of the planning process. The group reaffirmed the importance and implications of the market-needs driving force. It also acknowledged the importance of management development and human resources planning as necessary ingredients of strategic change. Details and issues began to surface regarding the division's market and product scope, environmental analysis, and key strategic issues. Tom Stewart reported that a consulting firm had been engaged to assist the division as it moved forward with its strategic planning.

Activities of the consultants. Two consultants from a Boston-based firm spent several days in December 1985 and January 1986 interviewing key management personnel in the division, including members of the strategic planning group. The consultants, who had been retained after considerable discussion with Tom Stewart and Tom Whitford, proposed a process that emphasized the importance of shared values and wide participation in the process. With these two points in mind, the consultants proposed the following activities and timetable for obtaining a strategic plan by April 30, 1986.

The strategic planning team. The first activity, to be completed in January 1986, was the appointment of a strategic planning team. The team would include key managers or representatives from the functional groups of the division. The team would be the forum in which the elements of the strategic plan would be deliberated during the next four months. The team that Tom Stewart headed contained the membership of the original planning group that had been meeting since September plus two other individuals representing key departments in the division—trust administration and investment research. The strategic planning team consisted of 14 individuals, including Tom Stewart. Tom Whitford continued in the role of internal coordinator.

The task forces. The second major activity was the appointment of task forces to develop general strategies around a limited number of key strategic issues. Discussions among the consultants and the planning team narrowed the key issues to seven:

1. The emerging affluent market.
2. The wealth accumulator market.
3. The wealth maintainer market.
4. The institutional market.
5. Human resources.
6. Technology.
7. Competition.

These seven issues reflected the general concerns that had been the focus of much discussion in the preceding months.

The first four issues referred to market segments that have distinctly different demographic profiles, sources of wealth, attitudes toward investments, and attitudes toward credit. Consequently, they have different needs for financial services and are appropriate bases for product differentiation. These four segments emerged from discussions within the strategic planning team on the issue of which markets Provident should target for strategic resource allocation during the next four to five years. If Provident was to be a market-driven organization, then it must identify which markets would drive it.

The emerging affluent market is 20- to 45-year-old, married college graduates with household incomes of $50,000 to $75,000 from employment sources. They are in the white-collar, fast-track professions but would like to start their own businesses. They are looking for means to build their asset base but are not all that sophisticated in making investment decisions.

The wealth accumulator market is individuals aged 45 to 65, with household incomes of more than $75,000. Their accumulated wealth derives from business, investment, and inheritance sources. They are members of professional occupations such as physicians, corporate executives, attorneys, and entertainers but also entrepreneurs.

The wealth maintainer market members are aged 55 and older, with liquid assets in excess of $75,000 and income from inheritance and employment-related income and benefit plans. They tend to have the same educational, career, and demographic characteristics as wealth accumulators, except their sources of income are relatively secure.

The institutional market segment consists of bank trust units, regional brokers, insurance companies, pension funds, investment advisory institutions, international banks and brokers, investment counselors, and mutual fund managers. This particular market segment had been the focus of much of Provident's innovative products under Boylan's leadership.

The human resources and technology task forces reflected the strategic planning team's understanding of the importance of assessing strategic issues for human and technological resources. They were charged with responsibility for identifying the contributions of people and technology to the achievement of market-driven strategic objectives.

Finally, the task force on competition was to add to the existing information and assumptions regarding the strategic direction of the financial services industry. Although separate entities, the three task forces were expected to initiate and to respond to interactions with the four market segment task forces.

Diagnosing issues and assessing opportunities. Each of the task forces contained 10 to 15 members, including at least one member from the strategic planning team. The seven task forces met throughout the months of January and February 1986 with the expectation that each would prepare and present its report at a mid-March meeting. These reports were presented March 18 and 19. Each of the market segment reports contained detailed description and analysis of (1) the segment's characteristics, (2) its product and service needs, (3) Provident's current ability to serve the segment, and (4) key competitors. With this information as background, the reports identified strategic issues associated with the segment, strategies for targeting and serving the segment, and specific product and delivery proposals.

The human resources and technology reports emphasized the importance of developing these resources to be compatible with whatever strategic thrusts the division adopted. The competition task force made its report; since its findings were incorporated in the market segment reports, it was disbanded after the March meeting.

Inappropriate organizational structure.   The March meeting was pivotal because a number of issues crystallized during the discussion of the reports. One issue that attracted considerable discussion was that the current organizational structure does not always correspond to the needs of the market segments it is attempting to address. As one participant stated: "To be truly market driven, the organizational structure should be molded to fit the marketing strategy, and not the reverse. This implies the possibility of organizational changes that, in some cases, might be fairly major." Another participant echoed the same idea when discussing the division's markets and marketing: "Market segments, unfortunately, do not always correspond with the organizational structure. The organizational structure must eventually be altered to correspond to the needs of markets and market segments."

Inappropriate organizational culture.   Along similar lines, the idea of the appropriate attitude of managers in market-driven organizations began to take form, as noted by one individual: "Provident trust managers must practice thinking first of markets and customers, and second of products and services. Put another way, products and services can only be thought of within the context of market and customer needs. This is the essence of being market driven and is the basis of the inside → out approach to strategy formulation."

The theme of being market driven carried through the human resources task force report, which recommended that Provident's culture become more heavily influenced by incentives, targets, performance, and MBO-type systems. The key values in the culture should be risk-taking, cross-selling, accountability, technological literacy, and a marketing and customer focus. As stated by the chairperson of the task force: "Provident Bank must be prepared for major change within the Trust Division over the next five years—change involving people, organizational structure, systems and procedures, and culture. Since change is always a difficult, painful, and disruptive process, Provident's management must be prepared to orchestrate such change in the most positive and constructive manner possible." The human resources task force played an important and instrumental role by articulating the importance of "people issues" in the development and implementation of strategy.

Anticipating implementation issues.   Implementation plans were important, not only from a planning and accountability perspective but also from an organizational perspective because the intensive nature of necessary intergroup communication and coordination became apparent. For example, the implementation plan for the wealth maintainer market segment identified individuals from the marketing, sales, trust administration, trust investment, institutional investment services, and operations departments who would be responsible for completing specific tasks related to the strategic plan.

It also became clear that effective implementation of the market-driven strategy would involve extensive and intensive interdivisional cooperation and coordination. Some of the activities could not be completed by the Trust

EXHIBIT 2

Provident National Bank Trust Division, Reorganized

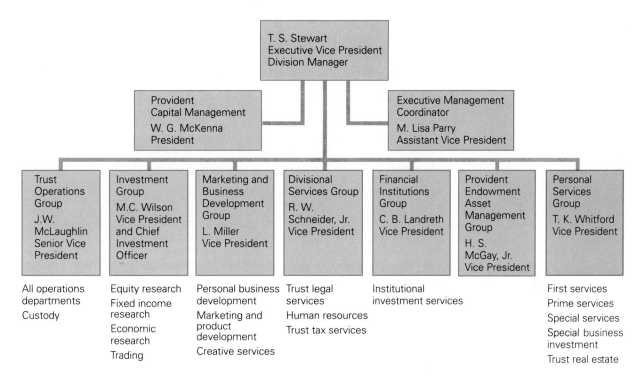

Division alone; Provident's Commercial and Retail Divisions were key actors in many activities. For example, serving the emerging and accumulator market segments will require that some products developed in the Trust Division be distributed in retail, commercial, and private banking departments.

Announcing the Change

The Trust Division strategic plan was formally unveiled on May 15, 1986. Ted Mygatt, Robert Chappel, and Tom Stewart presented the plan to some 200 officers of the Trust Division and guests from the PNC affiliates as well as other bank divisions. That presentation was followed by a June 18 letter from Stewart to all employees of the Trust Division, announcing the reorganization of the division. The reorganized division is depicted in Exhibit 2.

The new organizational structure derives directly from the strategic plan and is designed to enable the division to serve customers more effectively and efficiently. In the June 18 letter to the employees, Stewart stated that the changes in the organizational structure are intended "to facilitate communications—with our customers and among ourselves—and to enable us to execute our strategic plan." Top management had earlier decided to transfer Provident Financial Processing Corporation and Provident Institutional Management Corporation to the bank's Operations/Mutual Funds Division.

The June 18 letter explained the groups in the new organization as follows:

Trust Operations Group: In addition to the operations departments now in the Operations Group, we are adding the Custody Department. Our custodial services activities have grown quite rapidly during the last few years, especially our involvement with investment counseling organizations. By becoming an integral part of the Operations Group, our Custody Department can develop new, more efficient ways to provide custodial services to institutions and individuals.

Investment Group: Skip Wilson will continue to have overall responsibility for the Economic and Investment Research Group; in addition, he will become our chief investment officer. Rapid changes in the nature of the securities markets make it essential that investment research and securities trading activities be effectively coordinated. As a result, the Trading Department will become part of the Investment Group.

Marketing and Business Development Group: By combining our marketing, product development, personal financial planning, and personal sales efforts into one group, our new business development activities will become more focused and more effective. We are merging the Personal Financial Planning Department into the Estate Planning Department, and the new entity will be known as the Personal Business Development Department. Nan Lansinger will manage the Marketing and Product Development Department, and the Graphics Department will continue to report to Nan.

Divisional Services Group: This newly formed group will combine three departments that provide important services to the entire Trust Division. In addition to the Trust Legal Department, the Trust Tax Department will also report to Bob Schneider. We are forming a Trust Human Resources Department, which will support the division in its training and development, recruiting, and salary administration activities and which will act as a primary coordination point for our communications with the bank's Personnel Division.

Financial Institutions Group: The Institutional Investment Service becomes the foundation for this new group, which will sell a variety of investment and other services to financial organizations in this country and abroad.

Endowment Asset Management Group: In order to concentrate our efforts on serving the charitable market locally and nationally, we are creating a special group to address these customers. With an excellent base of Philadelphia area customers, this group will be staffed by several members of the Investment Advisory Department.

Personal Services Group (PSG): The most significant changes that will occur involve the transition from being organized functionally in our account management activities to being organized according to our customer segments. Replacing the Trust & Estate Administration, Personal Trust Investment, and Investment Advisory Departments, three new departments, Special Services, Prime Services, and First Services are being formed. Each department will consist of portfolio managers and trust administrators whose efforts will be directed to serving their customers as effectively as possible. Persons in the Trust & Estate Administration, Personal Trust Investment, and Investment Advisory Departments will, for the most part, be assigned to one of the new departments.

Existing account assignments will not be altered immediately. Over time, however, I anticipate that some changes in account assignments will occur as we work increasingly to segment our customer base and to provide high-quality but differentiated levels of service. New accounts will be assigned to the appropriate department beginning July 1.

To the extent possible, personnel in each department will have offices and work spaces that are located together. This will require a substantial number of physical moves, which will occur in the months ahead.

Recognizing the need to retain a mechanism through which the investment managers and trust administrators can communicate effectively about their functional specialties, Bob Warth and the managers of the investment management units will oversee portfolio management issues, while Lou Sozio and the trust administration unit managers will be responsible for trust administration matters.

By combining the Special Business and Real Estate Investment Departments into PSG, we expect to improve operating efficiencies in both departments. In addition, this group will develop more effective ways to serve business owners through close coordination with our Commercial Division.

Provident Capital Management: Bill McKenna has been named as president of Provident Capital Management. PCM will continue to operate as an independent subsidiary providing investment and administrative services to the employee benefit market.

Executive Management Coordinator: The purpose of this newly created position is to assist the division manager in a wide range of activities.

Stewart and the strategic planning team recognized that the most significant changes were to occur in the Personal Services Group. They anticipated that portfolio size would be the basis for assigning accounts to each of the three new departments. Initially, they thought that portfolios in excess of $2 million would be assigned to Special Services; portfolios greater than $500,000 but less than $2 million would be assigned to Prime Services; and portfolios greater than $100,000 but less than $500,000 would be assigned to First Services. The departmental managers would work together to settle important issues related to levels of service to be delivered in each of the three departments. The team also anticipated that important issues would arise related to interfaces among these three departments and Trust Division groups and bank divisions.

Making the Changes Work in the Personal Services Group

The strategic and reorganization plans had implications for every group in the Trust Division. The individuals and departments that focus on the financial needs of individuals played crucial roles. The Personal Services Group was formed from personnel previously assigned to the Administration and Investments Groups. Trust administrators had been in the Administration Group; trust portfolio managers had been in the Investments Group. The strategic planning process had identified the need to bring together in one organizational group all the tasks whether administrative or investment, associated with delivering personal trust services. The decision to relocate individuals in the new organizational unit and to establish processes, procedures, and performance expectations for the new unit set in motion a series of required implementation steps. The outcomes of these steps could be the critical factors in the strategic plan's success.

Tom Stewart appointed Tom Whitford as manager of the Personal Services Group. Stewart believed that the key to implementing the strategic plan in the Personal Services Group was the integration of "marketing thinking" into the account management area. Accordingly, he clearly communicated his expectation that while Whitford would be responsible for the account management and support services, Ludlow Miller, vice president for marketing and business development, would be responsible for sales and marketing in the Personal Services Group. Stewart expected that Whitford and Miller would work in tandem to develop the Personal Services Group's capability to achieve its mission and objectives.

The team of Tom Whitford, Ludlow Miller, and the three personal trust department managers undertook the difficult process of implementing the strategic plan and reorganization. They expressed considerable concern that the effects of the reorganization would not fall too heavily on employees and clients. As they viewed their tasks, four changes with severe implications for both groups were readily apparent:

1. Personnel had to be reassigned to each of the three new departments and be integrated in their new jobs and units.
2. Existing accounts had to be reassigned to the appropriate department and, within the department, to the appropriate individual(s).
3. Levels and types of service to be delivered in each of the three departments had to be determined.
4. Performance expectations for personnel assigned to each of the three departments had to be devised and made known to individuals.

Reassignment and integration of personnel.   The reassigned employees numbered approximately 75. They were split more or less evenly between the administration and investment groups prior to reorganization. Previously, they had been located on different floors and were physically separated by functional responsibility. The reorganization plan called for individual administrators and portfolio managers to be assigned to one of the three departments.

Prior to reorganization, individuals were assigned responsibility for accounts largely on the basis of experience and maturity as administrators and portfolio managers. Consequently, the assignment of significant accounts to an individual was an important indicator of the individual's performance. The task that confronted Whitford and the three department managers was to deal with the attitude that assignment to the Special Services Department would be far more desirable than assignment to either of the other two departments. There also existed considerable uncertainty and anxiety that is quite normal and to be expected whenever an organization undertakes major change that dislocates key personnel.

One idea considered was the creation of an intern program. The program would enable members of the First Services Department to serve on a rotating basis as interns to administrators or portfolio managers in the other two departments. The interns would serve for three to six months and devote 20 percent of their time as backups to experienced senior trust officers. The program would enable interns to receive additional experience and exposure in dealing with large-client relationships and other administrative and portfolio matters. For example, the interns would assist with the preparation of account/relationship plans, development of investment programs, and other projects. The underlying purpose would be to enhance the depth and breadth of experiences of First Services personnel while maintaining their primary responsibility to their own accounts and departmental activities.

In addition to the difficulty posed by the perceived higher status of the Special Services Department, Whitford and his colleagues had to consider the compatibility of individuals who would work in tandem inside each market segment department. Prior to reorganization, each trust administrator would be assigned to accounts with any number of investment officers. Thus, an administrator would have to develop working relationships with as many as 20 different individuals. Teamwork was quite difficult under these circumstances. The reorganization plan recognized that the existing assignment procedure was cumbersome.

The initial plan was to assign an administrator and an investment manager to each account to work as a team. Thus, each account would be serviced by two individuals working together. Not all accounts would be assigned to two individuals, because the strategic plan anticipated that levels of service would have to take into account the size of the portfolio. Thus, many accounts in the First Services Department would be assigned only to an administrator, since the funds would be invested in the Trust Division's common trust funds (CTFs).

The 75 individuals assigned to the Personal Services Group were spread rather evenly throughout the three departments, with the Prime Services Department being somewhat larger. Robert Warth, an experienced investment manager continued as manager of the Special Services Department, Lou Sozio, an experienced trust administration manager, continued as manager of the Prime Services Department, and Karen Minyard, an experienced trust administrator, continued as manager of the First Services Department.

Reassignment of accounts.   The reassignment of accounts was no less troublesome than the reassignment of personnel. The reassignment of accounts to appropriate departments was to be based on size of account, as well as other factors that differentiated trust accounts. For example, some accounts required sensitivity to family relationships, while others were generally stand-alone accounts. Some accounts were highly complex in terms of portfolio composition, tax implications, longevity of the trust, and continuing trusts for successive generations, while others were simple agreements to invest portfolios in CTFs. Some accounts had significant implications for other banking and trust business, while others were relatively simple revocable accounts. Taken together, all these factors form three rather discrete clusters of accounts with different needs for service.

As long as the reassignment of accounts coincided with the reassignment of personnel, no major problems were encountered. But when an individual who administered accounts large enough to be assigned to the Special Services Department was assigned to one of the other two departments, he or she would have to give up the large account. And that created the problem, because the reassignment disrupted the close personal and professional relationship that develops between trust administrators, portfolio managers, and the family or individual whose assets are entrusted to them. Not only did administrators and portfolio managers object to being removed from the relationship but the client may, and sometimes did, object to the reassignment.

The close personal relationship between trust administrators, portfolio managers, and clients is a core professional value. Thus, administrators and portfolio managers were reluctant to relinquish their accounts, and many made persuasive arguments for retaining them even when doing so violated the spirit of the reorganization. Whitford noted that it was important to maintain the appropriate balance between the reorganization objectives and the customer service objectives.

The account reassignment process involved developing a notification procedure for informing the client of the new status of the account. The procedure involved letters and phone calls from both the previous and new administrators and portfolio managers. The process also involved developing ways to transfer the accounts so as to maintain continuity of the trust agreements, relationships, and investment philosophies. Although the process would appear to be a rather straightforward transfer of information from one individual to another, it was complicated by the diversity of trust agreements and relationships that typified the unique requirements of trust clients and beneficiaries.

Determination of service levels.   The strategic decision to create three departments in the Personal Services Group reflected the assumption that each department would meet the needs of a particular market segment through differentiated service levels. The existing personnel had sufficient experience to make first approximations of each segment's needs and to deliver those services profitably. These first approximations became topics of considerable discussion among Whitford, Miller, and the three market segment managers. As noted above, the accounts assigned to the three departments differed along several dimensions, notably but not exclusively the size of investable assets. The other important dimensions also had implications for service provided and fees to be charged.

The implementation team recognized that existing clients would have service expectations based on their historical relationships with Provident. These expectations would have to be honored regardless of profitability, or lack thereof. New business in the departments, however, would have to meet certain criteria related to the appropriate service level. In a general sense, the service levels would differ along the familiar high-tech/high-touch dimension. The First Services Department's service would emphasize the delivery of high-tech service wherever appropriate. The Special Services Department would deliver high-touch service. The Prime Services Department would provide a balance of tech and touch. However, these distinctions were to be general guidelines only and were in no way to reflect quality of service to be delivered in the three units.

The initial discussions focused on the components of service traditionally provided in trust departments. These components include the form and content of contacts and meetings with customers, responses to customer inquiries and questions, distribution of account and check schedules, payment of customers' bills, coordination of customers' needs with other units and divisions of Provident, appropriate investment vehicles, distribution of written materials, and nature of administration services. As the discussion of the optimum service levels developed, it was to be informed by market research, which would identify with greater specificity the characteristics and service needs of the three market segments.

Performance standards.   From the beginning of the strategic planning process, planners recognized that the plan and reorganization required the development of performance standards for personnel throughout the division. The strategic redirection and reorganization required new work behaviors, which required new standards to define appropriate levels of performance. The strategic planning task force advocated management by objectives as the approach offering the best chance of reducing ambiguity in these standards. Each group and department manager had to lead the way in the development of these standards.

The three PSG market segment managers had to develop performance standards for themselves and for their immediate subordinates. The standards were to be consistent with the service level definitions and strategic initiatives of the PSG. After the performance standards were defined for the managers of the units, the process would move on to define standards for the investment and administrative personnel in each unit. The standards were to reflect the different missions of the three departments.

How to do it all.   As Miller, Whitford, and the PSG department managers reviewed the many tasks before them, they were impressed with what they had accomplished to date. But they also realized that easy tasks tend to be done first. In particular, they were concerned with the interrelationships among each of the tasks. They expressed a need to develop a fairly detailed plan for implementing the tasks. The plan would have to take into account the specific requirements of each task as well as the interrelationships among the other tasks and groups within the division.

ABC Analysis   The analysis of antecedents, behavior, and consequences when investigating work- or job-related issues.

Ability   A trait, biological or learned, that permits a person to do something mental or physical.

Accommodation Stage of Socialization   Socialization activities undertaken or experienced after an individual takes a job or enters an organization.

Adaptiveness   A criterion of effectiveness that refers to the ability of the organization to respond to change that is induced by either internal or external stimuli. An equivalent term is *flexibility,* although adaptiveness connotes an intermediate time frame, whereas flexibility is ordinarily used in a short-run sense.

Affect   The emotional segment of an attitude.

Alcoholism   A disease characterized by repeated excessive drinking that interferes with an individual's health and work behavior.

Anticipatory Stage of Socialization   Socialization activities undertaken or experienced prior to taking a job or entering an organization.

Assembly-Line Technology   A form of manufacturing in which component parts are brought together and combined into a single unit of output. It is used to produce relatively standard products that have a mass market.

Assessment Centers   An evaluation technique that uses situational exercises to identify promotable, trainable, and high-potential employees.

Attitudes   Mental states of readiness for need arousal.

Attribution Leadership Theory   A theory of the relationship between individual perception and interpersonal behavior. The theory suggests that understanding of and the ability to predict how people will react to events are enhanced by knowing what their causal explanation for those events is.

Authority   Formal power a person holds because of his or her position in the organizational hierarchy. The recognition of authority is necessary for organizational effectiveness and is a cost of organizational membership.

Banking Time Off   A reward practice of allowing employees to build up time-off credits for such things as good performance or attendance. The employees would then receive the time off in addition to regular vacation time granted by the organization because of seniority.

Baseline   The period of time before a change is introduced.

Behavior   Anything that a person does, such as talking, walking, thinking, or daydreaming. The action that results from an attitude.

Behavior Modification   An approach to motivation that uses the principles of operant conditioning, achieving individual learning by reinforcement. This term can be used interchangeably with the term *organizational behavior modification.*

Behavioral Self-Management (BSM)   A process whereby a person is faced with immediate response alternatives involving different consequences. The person selects or modifies his or her behavior by managing cognitive processes, causes, or consequences.

Behaviorally Anchored Rating Scales (BARS)   Rating scales developed by raters and/or ratees that use critical behavioral incidents as interval anchors on each scale. Approximately 6 to 10 scales with behavioral incidents are used to derive the evaluation.

Boundary-Spanning Role   The role of an individual who must relate to two different systems, usually an organization and some part of its environment.

Brainstorming   The generation of ideas in a group through noncritical discussion.

Bureaucratic Theory   The theory developed by Max Weber that defines the characteristics of an organization that maximize the stability and controllability of its members. The ideal bureaucracy is an organization that contains all of these characteristics to a high degree.

Cafeteria-Style Fringe Benefits   The employee is allowed to develop and allocate a personally attractive fringe benefit package. The employee is informed of what the total fringe benefits allowed will be and then distributes the benefits according to his or her preferences.

Career   The sequence of work-related experiences and activities over the span of a person's life, that create certain attitudes and behaviors in the individual.

Career Effectiveness   The extent to which the sequence of career attitudes and behaviors satisfies the individual.

Career Paths   Sequence of jobs and/or positions associated with a specific career.

Career Stages   Distinctly different yet related stages in the progression of a career.

Case Study An examination of numerous characteristics of a person, group, or organization, usually over an extended time period.

Central Tendency Error. The tendency to rate all ratees around an average score.

Centralization A dimension of organizational structure that refers to the extent to which authority to make decisions is retained in top management.

Charismatic Leadership The ability to influence followers that is based on a supernatural gift and powers that are attractive. Followers enjoy being with the charismatic leader because they feel inspired, correct, and important.

Classical Design Theory A design theory that emphasizes the design of preplanned structure for doing work and minimizes the importance of the social system. Evolved from scientific management, classical organization, and bureaucratic theory.

Classical Organization Theory A body of literature that developed from the writings of managers who proposed principles of organization intended to serve as guidelines for other managers.

Coercive Power Influence over others based on fear; the opposite of reward power. A subordinate perceives that failure to comply with the wishes of a superior would lead to punishment or some other negative outcomes.

Cognition This is basically what individuals know about themselves and their environment. Cognition implies a conscious process of acquiring knowledge. The perception, opinion, or belief segment of an argument.

Cognitive Dissonance A mental state of anxiety that occurs when there is a conflict among an individual's various cognitions (for example, attitudes and beliefs) after a decision has been made.

Cohesiveness The strength of group members' desires to remain in the group, and their commitment to the group.

Command Group The group of subordinates who report to one particular manager. The command group is specified by the formal organization chart.

Commitment A sense of identification, involvement, and loyalty expressed by an employee toward the company.

Communication The transmission of information and understanding through the use of common symbols, verbal and/or nonverbal.

Complexity A dimension of organizational structure that refers to the number of different jobs, units, and authority levels within an organization.

Confrontation Conflict Resolution A strategy that focuses on the conflict and attempts to resolve it through such procedures as the rotation of key group personnel, the establishment of superordinate goals, improving communications, and similar approaches.

Conscious Goals The main goals that a person is striving for and is aware of when directing behavior.

Consideration Acts of the leader that show supportive concern for the followers in a group.

Content Theories of Motivation Theories that focus on the factors within a person that energize, direct, sustain, and stop behavior.

Contingency Approach to Management This approach to management states that there is no one best way to manage in every situation but that managers must find different ways that fit different situations.

Contingency Design Theory An approach to organization design that states that the effective structure depends on factors in the situation, including technology, environmental uncertainty, and strategic choice.

Continuous Reinforcement A schedule that is designed to reinforce behavior every time the behavior exhibited is correct.

Counterpower Leaders exert power on subordinates, and subordinates exert power on leaders. Power is a two-way flow.

Criterion In performance evaluation, the dependent or predicted measure for appraising the effectiveness of an individual employee.

Critical Incidents An observable human activity that permits inferences and predictions to be made about the person performing the work.

Decentralization Basically, pushing the decision-making point to the lowest managerial level possible. It involves the delegation of decision-making authority.

Decision A means to achieve some result or to solve some problem. The outcome of a process that is influenced by many forces.

Decision Acceptance An important criterion in the Vroom-Yetton model that refers to the degree of subordinate commitment to the decision.

Decision Quality An important criterion in the Vroom-Yetton model that refers to the objective aspects of a decision that influence subordinates' performance, aside from any direct impact on motivation.

Decoding The mental process that the receiver of a message goes through to decipher the message.

Defensive Behavior Defense mechanisms evoked when an employee is blocked in attempts to satisfy needs to achieve goals. They include withdrawal, aggression, substitution, compensation, repression, and rationalization.

Delegated Strategies   Organizational change strategies that allow active participation by subordinates.

Delegation of Authority   The process by which authority is distributed downward in an organization.

Delphi Technique   A technique used to improve group decision making that involves the solicitation and comparison of anonymous judgments on the topic of interest through a set of sequential questionnaires interspersed with summarized information and feedback of opinions from earlier responses.

Departmentalization   The process in which an organization is structurally divided. Some of the more publicized divisions are by function, territory, product, customer, and project.

Depth   The degree of influence or discretion that an individual possesses to choose how a job will be performed.

Depth of Intended Change   In the context of organizational development, the scope and magnitude of intended change effort. A key issue in managing change.

Descriptive Essays   A performance evaluation method wherein the rater provides a description in his or her own words of the ratee's strengths and weaknesses.

Development   A criterion of effectiveness that refers to the organization's ability to increase its responsiveness to current and future environmental demands. Equivalent or similar terms include institutionalization, stability, and integration.

Diagonal Communication   Communication that cuts across functions and levels in an organization; important when members cannot communicate through other channels.

Differentiation   An important concept in the Lawrence and Lorsch research that refers to the process by which subunits in an organization develop particular attributes in response to the requirements imposed by their particular subenvironments. The greater the differences among the subunits' attributes, the greater is the differentiation.

Discipline   The use of some form of sanction or punishment when employees deviate from the rules.

Division of Labor   The process of dividing work into relatively specialized jobs to achieve advantages of specialization.

Dominant Competitive Strategy   A concept defined in the Lawrence and Lorsch research to refer to the subenvironment that is crucial to the organization's success. The dominant strategy may be production, marketing, or product development, depending on the industry.

Downward Communication   Communication that flows from individuals in higher levels of the organization's hierarchy to those in lower levels.

Drive   When a person is aroused because he or she is deprived or stimulated.

Dysfunctional Conflict   Any confrontation or interaction between groups that hinders the achievement of organizational goals.

Effectiveness   In the context of organizational behavior, effectiveness refers to the optimal relationship among five components: production, efficiency, satisfaction, adaptiveness, and development.

Efficiency   A short-run criterion of effectiveness that refers to the organization's ability to produce outputs with minimum use of inputs. The measures of efficiency are always in ratio terms, such as benefit-cost, cost-output, and cost-time.

Emblems   Gestures much like sign language that quickly convey an understood word or phrase.

Encoding   The conversion of an idea into an understandable message by a communicator.

Environmental Certainty   A concept in the Lawrence and Lorsch research that refers to three characteristics of a subenvironment that determine the subunit's requisite differentiation. The three characteristics are the rate of change, the certainty of information, and the time span of feedback or results.

Environmental Diversity   A concept in the Lawrence and Lorsch research that refers to the differences among the three subenvironments in terms of certainty.

Environmental Forces   Forces for change beyond the control of the manager. These external forces include marketplace actions, technological advancements, and social and political changes.

Equity Theory of Motivation   A theory that examines discrepancies within a person after the person has compared his or her input/outcome ratio to that of a reference person.

Employee Stock Ownership Plan (ESOP)   Employees share in the ownership of the company under employee stock ownership plans.

ERG Theory of Motivation   A theory developed and tested by Alderfer that categorizes needs as existence, relatedness, and growth.

Eustress   A term made popular by Dr. Hans Selye to describe good or stimulating stress.

Expectancy   The perceived likelihood that a particular act will be followed by a particular outcome.

Expectancy Theory of Motivation   A theory in which the employee is faced with a set of first-level outcomes and selects an outcome based on how this choice is related to second-level outcomes. The preferences of the individual are based on the strength (valence) of desire to achieve a second-level state and the perception of the relationship between first- and second-level outcomes.

Experiment An investigation containing two elements: manipulation of some variable (independent variable) and observation of the results (dependent variable).

Expert Power Capacity to influence related to some expertise, special skill, or knowledge. Expert power is a function of the judgment of the less powerful person that the other person has more ability or knowledge.

Extinction In a learning situation, the decline in the response rate because of nonreinforcement.

Extrinsic Rewards Rewards external to the job, such as pay, promotion, or fringe benefits.

Field Experiment An experiment in which the investigator attempts to manipulate and control variables in the natural setting rather than in a laboratory.

Fixed Interval Reinforcement A situation in which a reinforcer is applied only after a certain period of time has elapsed since the last reinforcer was applied.

Flexible Manufacturing Technology (FMT) Modern manufacturing methods that combine computer and robot to achieve high levels of production as well as high levels of flexibility.

Formal Group A group formed by management to accomplish the goals of the organization.

Formalization A dimension of organizational structure that refers to the extent to which rules, procedures, and other guides to action are written and enforced.

Friendship Group An informal group that is established in the workplace because of some common characteristic of its members and that may extend the interaction of its members to include activities outside the workplace.

Functional Conflict A confrontation between groups that enhances and benefits the organization's performance.

Functional Job Analysis (FJA) A method of job analysis that focuses on the worker's specific job activities, methods, machines, and output. Widely used to analyze and classify jobs.

Functions The inherent tasks of specific organization types. The functions of a business organization include production, marketing, and finance.

Gainsharing An innovative reward strategy wherein employees share in the financial rewards of achieving set objectives.

General Adaptation Syndrome (GAS) A description of the three phases of the defense reaction that a person establishes when stressed. These phases are called alarm, resistance, and exhaustion.

Goal A specific target that an individual is trying to achieve; a goal is the target (object) of an action.

Goal Approach to Effectiveness A perspective on effectiveness that emphasizes the central role of goal achievement as the criterion for assessing effectiveness.

Goal Commitment The amount of effort that is actually used to achieve a goal.

Goal Difficulty The degree of proficiency or the level of goal performance that is being sought.

Goal Orientation The focus of attention and decision making among the members of a subunit.

Goal Participation The amount of person's involvement in setting task and personal development goals.

Goal Setting The process of establishing goals. In many cases, goal setting involves a superior and subordinate working together to set the subordinate's goals for a specified period of time.

Goal Specificity The degree of quantitative precision (clarity) of the goal.

Graicunas' Model The proposition that an arithmetic increase in the number of subordinates results in a geometric increase in the number of potential relationships under the jurisdiction of the superior. Graicunas set this up in a mathematical model:

$$C = N\left(\frac{2^N}{2} + N - 1\right)$$

Grapevine An informal communication network that exists in organizations and short-circuits the formal channels.

Graphic Rating Scales The oldest and most widely used performance evaluation method, wherein the rater evaluates an employee's qualities and characteristics on a written form.

Grid Training A leadership development method proposed by Blake and Mouton that emphasizes the balance between production orientation and person orientation.

Group Two or more employees who interact with one another in such a manner that the behavior and/or performance of one member is influenced by the behavior and/or performance of other members.

Groupthink The deterioration of the mental efficiency, reality testing, and moral judgment of the individual members of a group in the interest of group solidarity.

Halo Error A positive or negative aura around a ratee that influences a rater's evaluation.

Hardiness A personality trait that appears to buffer an individual's response to stress. The hardy person assumes that he or she is in control, is highly committed to lively activities, and treats change as a challenge.

Hawthorne Studies A series of studies undertaken at the Chicago Hawthorne Plant of Western Electric from

1924 to 1933. The studies made major contributions to the knowledge of the importance of the social system of an organization. They provided the impetus for the human relations approach to organizations.

Herzberg's Two-Factor Theory of Motivation The view that job satisfaction results from the presence of intrinsic motivators and that job dissatisfaction stems from not having extrinsic factors.

History A source of error in experimental results that consists of events other than the experimental treatment that occur between pre- and post-test measurement.

Horizontal Communication Communication that flows across functions in an organization; necessary for coordinating and integrating diverse organizational functions.

Horizontal Differentiation The different units existing at the same level in an organization. The greater the horizontal differentiation, the more complex is the organization.

Human Process Interventions A class of interventions with the intended effects of changing individual and group behaviors found in the informal parts of the organization.

Humanistic Personality Theories Theories that place emphasis on the growth and self-actualization of people.

Illustrators Gestures that give a picture of what is being said (e.g., extended hands to illustrate the size of an object).

Incentive Plan Criteria To be effective in motivating employees, incentives should (1) be related to specific behavioral patterns (e.g., better performance), (2) be received immediately after the behavior is displayed, and (3) reward the employee for consistently displaying the desired behavior.

Individual Differences Individuals are similar, but they are also unique. The study of individual differences such as attitudes, perceptions, and abilities helps a manager explain differences in performance levels.

Influence A transaction in which a person or a group acts in such a way as to change the behavior of another person or group. Influence is the demonstrated use of power.

Informal Group A group formed by individuals and developed around common interests and friendships rather than around a deliberate design.

Information Flow Requirements The amount of information that must be processed by an organization, group, or individual to perform effectively.

Initiating Structure Leadership acts that imply the structuring of job tasks and responsibilities for followers.

Instrumentality In the expectancy theory of motivation, the relationship between first- and second-level outcomes.

Instrumentation A source of error in experimental results, caused by changes in the measurement instruments or the conditions under which the measuring of participants' performance is done (e.g., wear on machinery, fatigue on the part of observers).

Integration A concept in the Lawrence and Lorsch research that refers to the process of achieving unity of effort among the organization's various subsystems. The techniques for achieving integration range from rules and procedures to plans, to mutual adjustment.

Interaction Any interpersonal contact in which one individual acts and one or more other individuals respond to the action.

Interaction Effects The confounding of results that arises when any of the sources of errors in experimental results interact with the experimental treatment. For example, results may be confounded when the types of individuals withdrawing from any experiment (mortality) may differ for the experimental group and the control group.

Interest Group A group that forms because of some special topic of interest. Generally, when the interest declines or a goal has been achieved, the group disbands.

Intergroup Conflict Conflict between groups, which can be functional or dysfunctional.

Intermittent Reinforcement A schedule that results in reinforcing behavior only after some responses and not after each response.

Internal Forces Forces for change that occur within the organization and that can usually be traced to *process* and *behavioral* causes.

Interpersonal Communication Communication that flows from individual to individual in face-to-face and group settings.

Interpersonal Orientation A concept that refers to whether a person is more concerned with achieving good social relations than with achieving a task.

Interpersonal Rewards Extrinsic rewards such as receiving recognition or being able to interact socially on the job.

Interpersonal Style The way in which an individual prefers to relate to others.

Interrole Conflict A type of conflict that results from facing multiple roles. It occurs because individuals simultaneously perform many roles, some of which have conflicting expectations.

Intervention The process by which either outsiders or insiders assume the role of a change agent in the OD program.

Intrapersonal Conflict The conflict that a person faces internally, as when an individual experiences personal frustration, anxiety, and stress.

Intrarole Conflict A type of conflict that occurs when different individuals define a role according to different sets of expectations, making it impossible for the person occupying the role to satisfy all of the expectations. This type of conflict is more likely to occur when a given role has a complex role set.

Intrinsic Rewards Rewards that are part of the job itself. The responsibility, challenge, and feedback characteristics of the job are intrinsic rewards.

Job Analysis The process of defining and studying a job in terms of behavior and specifying education and training needed to perform the job.

Job Content The specific activities required in a job.

Job Context The physical environment and other working conditions, along with other factors considered to be extrinsic to a job.

Job Definition The determination of task requirements of each job in the organization. The first subproblem of the organizing decision.

Job Depth The amount of control that an individual has to alter or influence the job and the surrounding environment.

Job Description A summary statement of what an employee actually does on the job.

Job Descriptive Index A popular and widely used 72-item scale that measures five job satisfaction dimensions.

Job Enlargement An administrative action that involves increasing the range of a job by increasing the number of tasks. Supposedly, this action results in better performance and a more satisfied work force.

Job Enrichment An approach, developed by Herzberg, that involves increasing the individual's discretion to select activities and outcomes. It seeks to improve task efficiency and human satisfaction by means of building into people's jobs greater scope for personal achievement and recognition, more challenging and responsible work, and more opportunity for individual advancement and growth.

Job Evaluation The assignment of dollar values to a job.

Job Order Technology A form of production in which products are tailor-made to customer specifications.

Job Range The number of operations that a job occupant performs to complete a task.

Job Redesign Redesigning the jobs of individuals, usually along the lines suggested by the job characteristics model of job design, in order to improve performance. May be used as an intervention in organizational development.

Job Relationships The interpersonal relationships required or made possible on a job.

Job Requirements Factors such as education, experience, degrees, licenses, and other personal characteristics required to perform a job.

Job Rotation A form of training that involves moving an employee from one workstation to another. In addition to achieving the training objective, this procedure is also designed to reduce boredom.

Job Satisfaction The attitude that workers have about their jobs. It results from their perception of the jobs.

Laboratory Experiment Experiments for which the environment in which the subject works is created by the researcher. The laboratory setting permits the researcher to control closely the experimental conditions.

Leader–Member Relations A factor in the Fiedler contingency model that refers to the degree of confidence, trust, and respect that the leader obtains from the followers.

Leadership An attempt to use noncoercive types of influence to motivate individuals to accomplish some goal.

Learned Needs Theory A theory which proposes that a person with a strong need will be motivated to use appropriate behaviors to satisfy the need. A person's needs are learned from the culture of a society.

Learning The process by which a relatively enduring change in behavior occurs as a result of practice.

Learning Transfer An important learning principle that emphasizes the carryover of learning into the workplace.

Legitimate Power Capacity to influence derived from the position of a manager in the organizational hierarchy. Subordinates believe that they "ought" to comply.

Life Change Events Major life changes that create stress for an individual. The work of Holmes and Rahe indicates that an excessive number of life change events in one period of time can produce major health problems in a subsequent period.

Linking-Pin Function An element of System 4 organization that views the major role of managers to be to represent the groups they manage to higher-level groups in the organization.

Locus of Control A personality characteristic that describes people who see the control of their lives as coming from inside themselves as *internalizers*. People who believe that their lives are controlled by external factors are *externalizers*.

Machiavellianism   A term used to describe political maneuvers in an organization. Used to designate a person as a manipulator and power abuser.

Management   The process of getting work done through people.

Management by Objectives (MBO)   A process in which superior and subordinate jointly set goals for a specified time period and then meet again to evaluate the subordinate's performance toward previously established goals.

Managerial Grid   Theory of leadership based on particular optimal style of leadership that includes balance of concern for production and for people. Basic leadership and group development activities are undertaken in managerial grid interventions to bring about desired leadership and individual group behaviors.

Matrix Organization   An organizational design that superimposes a product- or project-based design on an existing function-based design.

Maturation   In experimental studies a source of error that results from changes in the subject group with the passage of time that are not associated with the experimental treatment.

Mechanistic Model of Organizational Design   The type of organizational design that emphasizes the importance of production and efficiency. It is highly formalized, centralized, and complex.

Merit Rating   A formal rating system that is applied to hourly paid employees.

Minnesota Multiphasic Personality Inventory (MMPI)   A widely used inventory for assessing personality.

Mission   The ultimate, primary purposes of an organization. An organization's mission is what society expects from the organization in exchange for its continuing survival.

Modeling   A method of administering rewards that relies on observational learning. An employee learns the behaviors that are desirable by observing how others are rewarded. Proponents assume that behaviors will be imitated if the observer views a distinct link between performance and rewards.

Mortality   A source of error in experimental studies that occurs when participants drop out of the experiment before it is completed, resulting in the experimental and control groups not being comparable.

Motion Study   The process of analyzing a task to determine the preferred motions to be used in its completion.

Motivation   A concept that describes the forces acting on or within an employee that initiate and direct behavior.

Motivator-Hygiene Theory   The Herzberg approach that identifies conditions of the job that operate primarily to dissatisfy employees when they are not present (hygiene factors—salary, job security, work conditions, and so on). Other job conditions lead to high levels of motivation and job satisfaction. However, the absence of these conditions does not prove highly dissatisfying. The conditions include achievement, growth, and advancement opportunities.

Multifaceted Interventions   Combinations of techno-structural and human process interventions, required for most significant organizational change efforts.

Multinational Corporations (MNCs)   Firms that do business in more than one country.

Multiple Risk Factor Intervention Trial (MRFIT) Study   A large study of 3,110 adults used as a clinical trial to alter behaviors associated with traditional coronary heart disease factors.

Multiple Roles   Roles individuals play simultaneously because they occupy many different positions in a variety of institutions and organizations.

Myers-Briggs Type Indicator (MBTI)   A scale that assesses personality or cognitive style. The respondent's answers are scored and interpreted to classify him or her as extroverted or introverted, sensory or intuitive, thinking or feeling, and perceiving or judging. Sixteen different personality types are possible.

Need for Power (n Pow)   A person's desire to have an impact on others. The impact can occur from such behaviors as strong action, producing emotion, or concern for reputation.

Need Hierarchy Model   Maslow assumed that the needs of a person depend on what he or she already has. This in a sense means that a satisfied need is not a motivator. Human needs organized in a hierarchy of importance, are classified as physiological, safety, belongingness, esteem, and self-actualization.

Needs   Deficiencies that an individual experiences at a particular point in time.

Negative Reinforcement   Reinforcement that strengthens a response because the response removes some painful or unpleasant stimulus or enables the organism to avoid it.

Noise   Interference in the flow of a message from a sender to a receiver.

Nominal Group Technique (NGT)   A technique to improve group decision making that brings people together in a very structured meeting that does not allow for much verbal communication. The group decision is the mathematically pooled outcome of individual votes.

Nonprogrammed Decisions   Decisions required for unique and complex management problems.

Nonverbal Communication   Messages sent with body posture, facial expressions, and head and eye movements.

Norms   Generally agreed-upon standards of individual and group behavior that have developed as a result of member interaction over time.

Objectives   More specific and concrete than goals, objectives enable managers to gauge the short-run progress of the organization toward its goals.

Operants   Behaviors amenable to control by altering the consequences (rewards and punishments) that follow them.

Optimal Balance   The most desirable relationship among the criteria of effectiveness. Optimal, rather than maximum, balance must be achieved in any case of more than one criterion.

Organic Model of Organization   The organizational design that emphasizes the importance of adaptability and development. It is relatively informal, decentralized, and simple.

Organizational Behavior   The study of human behavior, attitudes, and performance within an organizational setting; drawing on theory, methods, and principles from such disciplines as psychology, sociology, and cultural anthropology to learn about *individual* perceptions, values, learning capacities, and actions while working in *groups* and within the total *organization;* analyzing the external environment's effect on the organization and its human resources, missions, objectives, and strategies.

Organizational Behavior Modification (OBM)   An operant approach to organizational behavior. This term is used interchangeably with the term *behavior modification.*

Organizational Climate   A set of properties of the work environment, perceived directly or indirectly by the employees, that is assumed to be a major force in influencing employee behavior.

Organizational Culture   The pervasive system of values, beliefs, and norms that exists in any organization. The organizational culture can encourage or discourage effectiveness, depending on the nature of the values, beliefs, and norms.

Organizational Design   A specific organizational structure, that results from managers' decisions and actions. Also, the process by which managers choose among alternative frameworks of jobs and departments.

Organizational Development (OD)   The process of preparing for and managing change in organizational settings.

Organizational Politics   The activities related to acquiring, developing, and using power and other resources to obtain one's preferred outcome when there is uncertainty or disagreement about choices.

Organizational Processes   The activities that breathe life into the organizational structure. Among the common organizational processes are communication, decision making, socialization, and career development.

Organizational Profile   A diagram that shows the responses of the members of an organization to the questionnaires that Likert devised to measure certain organizational characteristics.

Organizational Structure   The formal pattern of how people and jobs are grouped in an organization. The organizational structure is often illustrated by an organization chart.

Organizations   Institutions that enable society to pursue goals that could not be achieved by individuals acting alone.

Participative Management   A concept of managing that encourages employees' participation in decision making and matters that affect their jobs.

Path-Goal Leadership Model   A theory that suggests that a leader needs to influence the followers' perception of work goals, self-development goals, and paths to goal attainment. The foundation for the model is the expectancy motivation theory.

Perceived Job Content   The characteristics of a job that define its general nature as perceived by the person who does the job.

Perception   The process by which an individual gives meaning to the environment. It involves organizing and interpreting various stimuli into a psychological experience.

Performance   The desired results of behavior.

Performance Evaluation   The systematic, formal evaluation of an employee's job performance and potential for future development.

Personality   A stable set of characteristics and tendencies that determine commonalities and differences in the behavior of people.

Personality Test   A test used to measure the emotional, motivational, interpersonal, and attitude characteristics that make up a person's personality.

Personal-Behavioral Leadership Theories   Theories based primarily on the personal and behavioral characteristics of leaders. The focus is on *what* leaders do and/or *how* they behave in carrying out the leadership function.

Person-Role Conflict   A type of conflict that occurs when the requirements of a position violate the basic values, attitudes, and needs of the individual occupying the position.

Political Behavior   Behavior outside the normal power system designed to benefit an individual or a subunit.

Pooled Interdependence Interdependence that requires no interaction between groups because each group, in effect, performs separately.

Position Analysis Questionnaire (PAQ) A method of job analysis that takes into account human characteristics as well as task, and technological factors of job and job classes.

Position Power A factor in the Fiedler contingency model that refers to the power inherent in the leadership position.

Positive Reinforcement Action that increases the likelihood of a particular behavior.

Power The ability to get things done in the way that one wants them to be done.

Power Illusion The notion that a person with little power actually has significant power. The Miligram experiments indicated that the participants were obedient to commands given by an individual who seemed to have power (wore a white coat, was addressed as "doctor," and acted quite stern).

Process In systems theory, the technical and administrative activities brought to bear on inputs to transform them into outputs.

Processes Those activities that breathe life into the organization structure. Common processes are communication, performance evaluation, decision making, socialization, and career development.

Process Interventions Interventions that target groups for change. The specific intervention varies from situation to situation, but the underlying theme is to identify and act on the sources of intergroup, and intragroup problems.

Process Motivation Theories Theories that describe and analyze how behavior is energized, directed, sustained, and stopped.

Process Technology An advanced form of manufacturing in which a homogeneous input is converted into a relatively standardized output having a mass market.

Production A criterion of effectiveness that refers to the organization's ability to provide the outputs that the environment demands of it.

Programmed Decisions Situations in which specific procedures have been developed for repetitive and routine problems.

Progressive Discipline Managerial use of a sequence of penalties for rule violations, each penalty being more severe than the previous one.

Proxemics The use of space when interpersonally communicating with others.

Psychodynamic Theories Freudian approach which discusses the id, superego, and ego. Special emphasis is placed on unconscious determinants of behavior.

Punishment An uncomfortable consequence for a particular behavior response or the removal of a desirable reinforcer because of a particular behavior response. Managers can punish by application or by removal.

Qualitative Overload A situation in which a person feels that he or she lacks the ability or skill to do a job or that the performance standards have been set too high.

Quantitative Overload A situation in which a person feels that he or she has too many things to do or insufficient time to complete a job.

Range The number of tasks a person is expected to perform while doing a job. The more tasks required, the greater the job range.

Ranking Method The ranking of ratees on the basis of relevant performance.

Realistic Job Previews (RJP) A procedure used at the point of employee recruitment that provides the prospective employee with accurate and realistic information about the job.

Recency of Events Error The tendency of recent events to bias ratings.

Reciprocal Causation The argument that follower behavior causes leader behavior and that leader behavior causes follower behavior.

Reciprocal Interdependence Interdependence that requires the output of each group in an organization to serve as input to other groups in the organization.

Recognition Management acknowledgment of work well done.

Referent Power Power based on a subordinate's identification with a superior. The more powerful individual is admired because of certain traits, and the subordinate is influenced because of this admiration.

Reinforcer Any object or event that increases or sustains the response given by a person.

Relationships Interpersonal relationships required or made possible on a job.

Response A person's behavioral activity that has resulted from a stimulus.

Reward Power An influence over others based on their hope of reward; the opposite of coercive power. A subordinate perceives that compliance with the wishes of a superior leads to positive rewards, either monetary or psychological.

Role An organized set of behaviors expected of an individual in a specific position.

Role Ambiguity A person's lack of understanding about the rights, privileges, and obligations of a job.

Role Conflict Stessor that arises when a person receives incompatible messages regarding appropriate role behavior.

Role Management Stage of Socialization Socialization activities undertaken or experienced during the stable career/work stage.

Role Set Individuals' expectations for the behavior of a person in a particular role. The more expectations, the more complex is the role set.

Rumor An unverified belief that is in general circulation and that contains three components: the target, the allegation, and the source.

Satisfaction A criterion of effectiveness that refers to the organization's ability to gratify the needs of its participants. Similar terms include morale and voluntarism.

Scalar Chain The graded chain of authority that is created through the delegation process.

Scientific Management A body of literature that emerged during the period 1890–1930 and that reports the ideas and theories of engineers concerned with such problems as job definition, incentive systems, and selection and training.

Scope The scale on which an organizational change is implemented (e.g., throughout the entire organization, level by level, or department by department).

Selection A source of error in experimental studies that occurs when participants are assigned to experimental and control groups on any basis other than random assignment. Any other selection method causes systematic biases that result in differences between groups unrelated to the effects of the experimental treatment.

Self-Efficacy The belief that one can perform adequately in a situation. Self-efficacy has three dimensions: magnitude, strength, and generality.

Sensitivity Training A form of educational experience that stresses the process and emotional aspects of training.

Sequential Interdependence Interdependence that requires one group to complete its task before another group can complete its task.

Shared Approach An OD strategy that involves managers and employees in the determination of the OD program.

Shared Strategies Strategies for introducing organizational change that focus on the sharing of decision-making authority among managers and subordinates.

Situational Theories of Leadership An approach to leadership that advocates that leaders understand their own behavior, the behavior of their subordinates, and the situation before utilizing a particular leadership style. This approach requires the leader to have diagnostic skills in human behavior.

Skill-Based Pay Wages paid at a rate calculated and based on the skills employees possess and display in performing their jobs.

Skills Task-related competencies.

Socialization Refers to the processes by which members learn the cultural values, norms, beliefs, and required behavior that permit them to be effective contributors to the organization.

Socialization Processes The activities by which an individual comes to appreciate the values, abilities, expected behaviors, and social knowledge that are essential for assuming an organizational role and for participating as an organization member.

Social Learning The extension of Skinner's work initiated by noted psychologist Albert Bandura. Bandura views behavior as a function of a continuous interaction between cognitive (person), behavioral, and environmental determinants. Contrary to Skinner, Bandura believes that cognitive functioning must not be ignored in explaining and modifying behavior.

Social Support The comfort, assistance, or information that an individual receives through formal or informal contacts with individuals or groups.

Sociotechnical Interventions In change efforts an attempt to integrate social organization and technological requirements. Many of these efforts can be seen in modern manufacturing, as industry after industry must adapt to innovative manufacturing methods that require different relationships among individuals performing these methods.

Span of Control The number of subordinates reporting to a specific superior. The span is a factor that affects the shape and height of an organizational structure.

Status In an organizational setting, status relates to positions in the formal or informal structure. Status is designated in the formal organization; in informal groups, it is determined by the group.

Status Consensus The agreement of group members about the relative status of members of the group.

Stereotype A set of beliefs that one has about a group of other individuals.

Stimulus A cue that encourages some type of response.

Strategic Contingency An event or activity that is extremely important for accomplishing organizational goals. Among the strategic contingencies of subunits are the ability to cope with uncertainty, centrality, and substitutability.

Stress An adaptive response, mediated by individual differences and/or psychological processes, resulting from any environmental action, situation, or event that places excessive psychological and/or physical demands on a person.

Stressor An external event or situation that is potentially harmful to a person.

Strictness or Leniency Rater Errors Rater errors that occur when a harsh rater gives ratings that are lower than the average ratings usually given or a lenient rater gives ratings higher than the average ratings usually given.

Structure The established patterns of interacting in an organization and of coordinating the technology and human assets of the organization.

Structure (in Group Context) The standards of conduct that are applied by the group, the communication sys- tem, and the reward and sanction mechanisms of the group.

Substitutability Extent to which other subunits can perform the job or task of a subunit.

Substitutes for Leadership Task, organizational, and subordinate characteristics that can substitute for leader behaviors. A leader will have little or no effect if certain situations, skills, or tasks exist.

Superordinate Goals Goals that cannot be achieved without the cooperation of the conflicting groups.

Survey A survey usually attempts to measure one or more characteristics in many people, usually at one point in time. Basically, surveys are used to investigate current problems and events.

System 4 Organization Likert's universalistic theory of organization design, defined in overlapping groups, linking-pin management, and the principle of supportiveness.

Systems Theory An approach to the analysis of organizational behavior that emphasizes the necessity for maintaining the basic elements of input-process-output and for adapting to the larger environment that sustains the organization.

Task Group A group of individuals who are working as a unit to complete a project or job task.

Task Structure A factor in the Fiedler contingency model that refers to how structured a job is with regard to requirements, problem-solving alternatives, and feedback on how correctly the job has been accomplished.

Team Building A traditional intervention focusing on work groups; has been given renewed interest as organizations rediscover the power of team effort.

Technology An important concept that can have many definitions in specific instances but that generally refers to

actions, physical and mental, that an individual performs upon some object, person, or problem to change it in some way.

Technostructural Interventions A class of interventions with the intended effects of changing jobs, job relationships, and other formal elements of organizational structure.

Testing A source of error in experimental studies that occurs when the performance of the subject changes because previous measurement of performance made the subject aware of the experiment.

Thematic Apperception Test (TAT) A projective test that uses a person's analysis of pictures to evaluate such individual differences as need for achievement, need for power, and need for affiliation.

Time Delay Error The error made by a rater who fails to record an observation at the time it occurs. By delaying the documentation, there is a chance of forgetting or being inaccurate at the time the observation is actually recorded.

Time Orientation A concept that refers to the time horizon of decisions. Employees may have relatively short- or long-term orientations, depending on the nature of their tasks.

Time Study The process of determining the appropriate elapsed time for the completion of a task.

Timing The point in time that has been selected to initiate an organizational change method.

Tolerance of Ambiguity The tendency to perceive ambiguous situations or events as desirable. In contrast, intolerance of ambiguity is the tendency to perceive ambiguous situations or events as sources of threat.

Trait Personality Theories Theories based on the premise that predispositions direct the behavior of an individual in a consistent pattern.

Trait Theory of Leadership Theory that attempts to identify specific characteristics (physical, mental, personality) associated with leadership success. Relies on research that relates various traits to certain success criteria.

Transactional Leadership A leader who identifies what followers want or prefer and helps them achieve the level of performance that results in rewards that satisfy them.

Transformational Leadership The ability to inspire and motivate followers to achieve results that are greater than originally planned and are for internal rewards.

Type A Behavior Pattern (TABP) Pattern of behavior associated with research conducted on coronary heart disease. The Type A person is an aggressive driver who is ambitious, competitive, task-oriented, and always on the move. Rosenman and Friedman, two medical researchers, suggest that Type A's have more heart attacks than do Type B's.

Type A Managers Managers who are aloof and cold toward others and are often autocratic leaders. Consequently, they are ineffective interpersonal communicators.

Type B Behavior Pattern Pattern of behavior in which person is relaxed, patient, steady, and even-tempered. The opposite of the Type A.

Type B Managers Managers who seek good relationships with subordinates but are unable to express their feelings. Consequently, they are usually ineffective interpersonal communicators.

Type C Managers Managers more interested in their own opinions than in those of others. Consequently, they are usually ineffective interpersonal communicators.

Type D Managers Managers who feel free to express their feelings to others and to have others express their feelings; the most effective interpersonal communicators.

Unilateral Strategies Strategies for introducing organizational change that do not allow for participation by subordinates.

Universal Design Theory A point of view that states there is "one best way" to design an organization.

Upward Communication Upward communication flows from individuals at lower levels of the organizational structure to those at higher levels. Among the most common upward communication flows are suggestion boxes, group meetings, and appeal or grievance procedures.

Valence The strength of a person's preference for a particular outcome.

Values The guidelines and beliefs that a person uses when confronted with a situation in which a choice must be made.

Vertical Differentiation The number of authority levels in an organization. The more authority levels an organization has, the more complex is the organization.

Vroom–Yetton Leadership Model A leadership model that specifies which leadership decision-making procedures are most effective in each of several different situations. Two of the proposed leadership styles are autocratic (AI and AII); two are consultative (CI and CII); and one is oriented toward joint decisions (decisions made by the leader and the group, GII).

Weighted Checklist A rating system consisting of statements that describe the various types and levels of behavior for a particular job. Each statement is weighted according to its importance.

Whistle-Blowing Game The process in which an employee, because of personal opinions, values, or ethical standards, concludes that an organization needs to change its behavior or practices and informs an outsider, bypassing the organization's authority system.

Woodward Research A groundbreaking research project that documented the association between technology and organizational structure and stimulated a wide range of subsequent studies that contributed to the contingency design point of view.

Work Module An important characteristic of job redesign strategies that involves the creation of whole tasks so that the individual senses the completion of an entire job.

Realistic job previews, 614–15
Reciprocal causation and Japanese
    management techniques, 414
Reciprocal interdependence, 303
Recognition, motivating effect, 201
Recruitment programs, information
    necessary to, 613, 617–18
Referent cognitions theory, 156
Referent power
    defined, 332
    personal nature of, 332–33
Regulators in body language, 545
Reinforcement
    contingencies, 131
    continuous, 136
    importance of in organizational
        development, 642
    intermittent, 136
    negative, 135
    positive, 134–35
    self-reinforcement, 144
    strategies, 142
Reinforcement theory, 134–45
    research, 142–43
Reinforcer, 130
Relaxation for stress reduction, 252–53
Reliable performers, negotiating with,
    316
Renewal Factor, 22
Requisite Task Attribute Index, 481
Research
    content analysis in, 707
    ethnographic method, 707
    historical analysis in, 707
    methods, 696–702
    qualitative approach, 706–8
Research and development function in
    organizational design, 450
Research design
    one-group pretest-posttest, 703–4
    one-shot, 703
    posttest-only control group, 705
    pretest-posttest control group, 705
    solomon four-group, 706
    static-group comparison, 704
    types, 698–706
Resource allocation
    based on compliance, 336–37
    based on performance, 336–37
    intergroup conflict over, 303
    as a power source, 336
Resources
    expanding, 311
    slack, 522
Response
    conditioned versus unconditioned,
        131
    defined, 130
    learned, 131

Reward power
    versus coercive power, 331
    defined, 331
    relationship to legitimate power,
        331
Reward systems; *see also* Fringe benefits
    and Motivation *and* Salaries
    aspects of, 12
    as conflict sources, 304
    equity in, 205
    favorable comparisons, 205
    goals, 196
    importance of, 12
    incentive plans; *see also* Incentive pay
        plans
    individual differences in, 179
    and job performance, 77
    for management, 199
    merit ratings in, 205
    model, 196–97
    money in, 178, 198–201
    and motivation, 179
    necessary elements, 198
    objectives, 196
    perceived favoritism in, 181
    and performance appraisal, 178
    quality-based, 426
    relevance of, 206
    role of, 198
    satisfaction from, 197
    types, 13, 207–11
Risk in the decision-making process,
    581, 583
Robot management, 58
Role ambiguity
    defined, 229
    detection, 248–49
    and social support, 242
    and stress, 229–31
Role conflict
    in boundary-spanning roles, 524
    defined, 228, 284
    and group membership, 275
    minimizing, 285
    results of, 285–86
    sources, 283–84
    types, 284–85
Roles
    boundary-spanning, 523–25
    defined, 282
    within groups, 282
    multiple, 282, 285
    organizationally defined, 284
    perception of, 283–84
Role set
    complex, 285
    defined, 282
Rotter Internal-External Scale, 94
Rumor box, 539

Rumors
    components of, 548
    defined, 548
    internal versus external, 548
    management-planted, 317, 538
    negative aspects, 538–39
    types of, 548

S

Salaries; *see also* All-salaried teams *and*
    Reward systems
    meetings addressing, 180
    as a motivator, 198
Satisfaction-progression process in needs
    satisfaction, 105
Scalar chain principle, 504–5
Scientific management
    basic assumptions, 475–76
    goal-setting in, 156
    personnel testing component, 370
Scientific method
    characteristics, 697
    applied to organizational behavior, 8
    role of, 8
Selective listening, 553–54
Self-actualization
    characteristics, 96
    defined, 81
    needs defined, 102–3
    and needs hierarchy, 96–97
    pitfalls in, 97
Self-appraisal
    in performance evaluation, 186–87
    pitfalls, 187
Self-contained units
    advantages, 522
    use of, 521–22
Self-control
    defined, 145
    in social learning theory, 132
Self-directed team concept, 508
Self-efficacy
    defined, 132
    dimensions, 132
    importance of feedback in, 133–34
Self-image, change in over time, 607
Self-management
    defined, 145
    effectiveness of, 146
Self-managing teams, future trends,
    682
Self-motivation, goal setting, 165
Self-regulation, three-stage model, 146,
    147
Self-reinforcement, 144
Sensitivity training
    defined, 682
    negative aspects, 683, 686